INTERNATIONAL ECONOMICS

The Irwin Series in Economics
Consulting Editor   Lloyd G. Reynolds   *Yale University*

International economics

Charles P. Kindleberger
Massachusetts Institute of Technology

Peter H. Lindert
University of California at Davis

1978

 Sixth edition

RICHARD D. IRWIN, INC.   Homewood, Illinois   60430
Irwin-Dorsey Limited   Georgetown, Ontario   L7G 4B3

ISBN 0-256-02028-0
Library of Congress Catalog Card No. 77–83563

Printed in the United States of America

5 6 7 8 9 0 MP 5 4 3 2 1 0

Preface

Major changes in the international economy call for changes in the study of international economics. Such developments as the OPEC victory over the oil-importing countries, other fresh attempts at forming international cartels, the increased flexibility of exchange rates since 1971, and new complexities in the relationship of trade policy to international investment flows need to find their way into the textbooks. Ours is the delicate task of suggesting what new kinds of analysis these events require, while at the same time showing how they are often easier to understand when one uses analytical tools already at hand.

We have attempted to fit new events and new improvements in theory together in this thoroughgoing revision. The wave of cartels has earned a chapter of its own (Chapter 10). Experience with fluctuating exchange rates has yielded a rich empirical record and a mixed verdict, as we note in Parts Three and Four. Chapter 12 on the political economy of trade barriers unifies a slowly growing theory of why we have the trade barriers we do with a new literature testing such theories against the experience of the United States, Canada, and other countries. Refinements in the link between trade and income distribution, led by Ronald W. Jones' development of simple general-equilibrium models, have been carefully combined with the growing empirical literature on the same subject, much of it spawned by attempts to unlock the older Leontiev paradox, in Chapter 5. And some of the more durable advances resulting from the resurgence of the monetary approach to international payments adjustment have been worked into an extensive revision of Chapter 17.

The present edition should serve at least as wide a range of students as past editions. The level of difficulty can be tuned fairly finely by adjusting the amount of appendix material used. The style of the text chapters is designed to suit both readers with broad interests in international relations and readers seeking more specialized tools of analysis. The appendixes are aimed mainly at the latter group. Those seeking review exercises to firm up their command of the analytical tools can use the Questions for Review at the ends of the building-block chapters.

Thanks are again due to the hosts of students, colleagues, and teachers at other campuses who volunteered suggestions for improving on previous editions. Our thanks also to Lloyd G. Reynolds of Yale University for editorial assistance.

CHARLES P. KINDLEBERGER
December 1977   PETER H. LINDERT

Contents

Prices affect the income distribution. The Stopler-Samuelson theorem.
The factor-price equalization theorem. A more general view of trade and
factor rewards: *Factor specialization. Factor mobility. Consumption
patterns*. Who are the exporting and the import-competing factors? The
Leontiev paradox. The paradox retained: A closer look at trade and factor
proportions. U.S. labor's stake in foreign trade.

part II
Trade policy

A preview of conclusions. The effect of a tariff on consumers. The effect
on producers. The effective rate of protection. The tariff as government
revenue. The net national loss from the tariff. Past measurements of the
national loss. Toward better measures. The tariff again, with production
and indifference curves.

The nationally optimal tariff. Retaliation. The troubled world of second
best: *A rule of thumb. A tariff to promote domestic production. The
infant-industry argument. The infant-government argument.* Noneconomic arguments.

The import quota: *Reasons for quotas. Quota versus tariff. Ways of allocating import licenses.* Export barriers. Differences in tax rates and tax
systems. State trading. Trade among socialist countries. East-west trade.
Dumping. Retaliation against dumping. Adjustment assistance.

The theory of customs unions. The real world. The dynamic effects of
customs union. Beyond customs union. Some lesser problems of customs
unions and free-trade areas. EEC's special regime for agriculture. Regional integration among developing countries.

The rise of OPEC. Monopoly as a model for cartels. The theoretical limits
to cartel power. Prospects for OPEC. Cartels for other primary products.

The issue of primary-product instability. Commodity price stabilization.

ISI: Import substituting industrialization. Barriers to exports from developing countries.

What explains our trade barriers? The goals of policymakers. Biases in lobbying power. Recent evidence of trade lobbying bias. Reinterpreting the history of trade barriers. The political role of the analysis of trade.

part III
Foreign exchange and the payments adjustment process

Functions of the foreign exchange market: *International clearing. Hedging. Speculation.* The forward market. The spot exchange rate. Types of official intervention. The Eurodollar market.

Definition. Economic transactions. Balance-of-payments accounting. Balances within the total: *The merchandise balance. The current account balance. The liquidity balance. The overall balance (official settlements balance).* Banker's deficits. The international investment position. Nations and currencies.

A preview of policy issues. The specter of unstable exchange markets. Linking the foreign exchange market to export and import markets. Does devaluation improve the trade balance? *It isn't obvious. Four important cases. The pattern. The general formula, and the Marshall-Lerner condition.* Elasticity, pessimism, and optimism. Devaluation and relative prices: *Devaluation and the terms of trade. In the background: Nontraded goods and money.*

Setting prices aside. Trade depends on income. Equilibrium income in an open economy. The foreign trade multiplier. Foreign income repercussions. Devaluation and national income. Devaluation and income distribution.

From the balance of payments to the money supply. From the money supply to the balance of payments: *Hume's price-specie-flow mechanism. Modern variations.* Exchange rates and the money supply. Purchasing power parity. Money, prices, and exchange rates in the long run.

part IV
Adjustment policies

The options for one country. Financing temporary disequilibriums. Reserve-center financing. Exchange controls. Who should adjust?

The *IS-LM-FE* model: *Assumptions. The* FE *curve. The* IS *curve. The* LM *curve.* Two policies and two targets. The assignment problem. Perfect capital mobility. Qualifications.

Flexible exchange rates in the *IS-LM-FE* model. Monetary policy with flexible exchange rates. Fiscal policy with flexible exchange rates. Is national income more stable with fixed or with flexible exchange rates? *Export demand shocks. International capital-flow shocks. Internal shocks.*

The issue of price "discipline." The risk argument. Destabilizing speculation. International currency experience: *The gold standard era, 1870–1914. Interwar instability. The Bretton Woods era, 1944–1971. Floating rates after 1971.* The limited case for flexible exchange rates.

The issues. International money. National money. Optimum currency area. Europe of the nine as an optimum currency area. The costs and benefits of a single money. Compromise solutions. Regional compromise. Symmetry. Seigniorage.

part V
Factor movements

Labor migration. The international labor market. Patterns of labor movement. The European labor market. Does emigration benefit the sending country? Does immigration benefit the receiving country? Technical assistance. Freedom of movement and social interaction.

Forms of long-term capital. New bond issues. Foreign and domestic investment. The institutional pattern of lending. Capital movements and welfare. The feasibility of controlling capital movements. Tied loans. The project basis for loans. Debt service ratio.

Direct investment as capital movement. Monopolistic competition. Bilateral monopoly: Direct investment in resource industries in developing countries. Direct investment and welfare. The international corporation. Direct investment and the balance of payments: *In the home country. The impact on the balance of payments of the host country.*

Instinctive reactions. Foreign enterprise and exports. Foreign control. Market failure. Restricting nonessentials. Mitigating the effects of foreign investment. Joint ventures. Selectivity. Limiting takeovers. Excluding foreigners from the local capital market. Taking the package apart. Disinvestment and disappearing investment. The Burke-Hartke bill. Government guarantees and insurance. A forum for resolving conflicts over direct investment.

1

The study of
international economics

The subject matter of this book will always require a separate body of analysis, distinct from the rest of economics. The mere existence of sovereign nations introduces complications requiring that we make changes in our ordinary tools of economic analysis before we can apply them to international economics. These complications are what makes the study of international economics fascinating and sometimes difficult. Future events are certain to keep reminding us of the problems that are special to international economics. To see why, let us look at four events of the 1970s that have shaped the approach and subject matter of this book.

FOUR EVENTS

Floating the dollar

In a dramatic televised speech on August 15, 1971, President Nixon stunned both the nation and the world by announcing a new economic policy. On the domestic front he unveiled a freeze on wages and most prices, plus some tax changes, designed to check inflation overnight without adding to unemployment. On the international front he ended one era and began another with a few terse sentences announcing that the value of the U.S. dollar must be changed in terms of other nations'

1

currencies and gold. He soon had his way on the international currency issue. Soon the exchange rates between the dollar and other currencies were drifting toward higher values for other currencies and lower values for the dollar. Suddenly international travelers, long accustomed to fixed exchange rates between dollars and other currencies, found that their dollars exchanged for fewer German marks, Japanese yen, and other currencies. The change also affected firms and individuals trading goods between countries. U.S. firms such as Boeing found it easier to sell their aircraft and other products abroad now that foreigners felt that they could afford more dollars and more U.S. goods priced in dollars. Foreign firms used to selling large amounts of goods to the United States felt a new kind of pressure. Volkswagen found that the same dollar prices for VWs in North America brought it fewer West German marks with which to pay West German workers and shareholders. It soon had to raise its car prices in dollars, losing some business to its U.S. and Canadian competitors.

The change brought a different kind of crisis headline to the newspapers. Before August 15, 1971, the system of keeping fixed rates of exchange between national currencies had been cracking, with increasingly frequent "balance-of-payments crises." Now the headlines began to shift, dropping the usual references to the balance of payments and replacing them with news of rising marks, falling dollars, and wavering pounds. Officials felt at least as much sense of crisis as before, and hurriedly arranged meetings to deal with the new system. Meeting at the Smithsonian Institution in Washington on December 18, 1971, the governments and central banks of major countries announced an agreement to make the dollar worth less in gold and a few major currencies, and to try to hold fixed the new exchange rates between certain European currencies and the dollar. Yet the float more or less continued, with further changes in the ability of each currency to buy others, despite the Smithsonian agreement and a second round of unsuccessful attempts to make rates more fixed in early 1973. By July 1973 the U.S. dollar had sunk in its ability to buy other currencies by about 26 percent relative to the exchange rates of three years earlier. The Swiss franc, West German mark, and Japanese yen had risen by about 40 percent in dollar value. The Canadian dollar had risen over the U.S. dollar by about 12 percent for a year, but had returned to its old U.S. dollar value by mid-1973. There was an early rise and then a prolonged fall in the dollar values of the British pound sterling, Italian lira, and French franc.

Whether the new system of fluctuating exchange rates was better or worse than the system it replaced is a very complex issue that will be pursued in Parts III and IV of this book. Yet it is clear that this issue is unique to the international sphere in economics. Exchange rates do not change between Kansas and Missouri, or between Alberta and British Columbia. The usual tools that economics applies to domestic issues have to be modified and extended if we are to make sense of what changes in exchange rates mean to ordinary people.

U.S. protectionism and the near miss of 1970–1973

In the early 1970s the Congress of the United States generated heated debate over another kind of policy move that is unique to the international side of economics: it debated bills proposing to clamp down on the import of foreign goods into the United States. The pressure to do so had been building for some time, as one U.S. manufacturing industry after another felt the competition of rising imports. The United States was importing larger and larger shares of its clothing, steel, automobiles, motorcycles, radios, TV sets, ships, and other products. A CBS documentary at the start of the 70s, entitled "Made in Japan," scared viewers by arguing that more and more of them would lose their jobs to foreign competition that was unpatriotically backed by U.S.-based multinational firms ("You can be sure if it's Westinghouse—it's made in Japan"). Even the Stars and Stripes were being imported from the Far East. The U.S. trade surplus dwindled, and in 1971 and 1972, for the first time since World War II, the United States imported a greater value of goods and services than it exported.

The rising fear of losing jobs and profits to import competition caused many congressmen to switch to favoring import restrictions, such as higher tariffs (import duties) and tougher quotas (quantitative limits on imports). A protectionist (import-cutting) bill was passed by the U.S. House of Representatives and by a Senate committee late in 1970, but it narrowly missed passage when a few senators favoring continued liberal policies toward imports were able to stall until the year-end adjournment of Congress. Had a vote been forced, the Senate might have passed the protectionist bill, putting pressure on an election-minded president to follow suit.

The pressure continued through 1973, largely because the largest organized labor group, the AFL–CIO, was vehemently determined to push for protection against imports. From late 1971 through mid-1973, Congress debated the historic Burke-Hartke Bill, which would have slashed imports into the United States and put new limits on the ability of U.S. firms to set up manufacturing subsidiaries abroad, in order to defend U.S. jobs. The bill ultimately failed to pass and even yielded to a moderately trade-liberalizing law at the very end of 1974. Yet the protectionist sentiment remains, calmed only marginally by a few presidential decisions to restrict imports on such goods as beef, sugar, and footwear. The issue of whether or not to try defending U.S. jobs by cutting imports also remains.

The issue of protection against imports requires a specifically international analysis. Within nations, such protection is illegal except in subtle and slight forms. California is not allowed to put up, say, a 50 percent tax on all goods and services imported into that state from the rest of the United States. The argument that doing so would protect the jobs of Californians against "unfair" Eastern competition would receive the retort that protecting California jobs in this way would destroy jobs in the companies elsewhere that counted on being able to sell to California. The interests of the rest of the nation cannot be ignored, and are explicitly defended against intranational trade barriers by the U.S. Constitution. Yet foreign interests can be more easily ignored, and any analysis of the likely effects of protectionist laws must explicitly distinguish between effects within the nation and effects of foreigners. Such analysis is offered in Parts I and II of this book.

The victory of OPEC

A chain of events in late 1973 revolutionized the world oil economy. In a few months' time, the 13 members of the Organization of Petroleum Exporting Countries (OPEC) effectively quadrupled the dollar price of crude oil, from $2.59 to $11.65 a barrel.[1] Oil-exporting countries became rich, though still "underdeveloped" in some cases, almost overnight. The industrial oil-consuming countries sank into their deepest depression since the 1930s. The "economic miracles" of superfast growth in oil-hungry Japan and Brazil came to a halt.

OPEC had already been building its collective strength earlier in the 1970s, after having little apparent power for the first decade after its formation in 1960. First in 1971 and again in 1972 OPEC had demanded and won both higher official oil prices and a greater share of oil profits and ownership at the expense of the major international oil companies. The rise in OPEC's power was greatly accelerated when the Arab-Israeli "Yom Kippur War" broke out in early October 1973. The war stiffened the resolve of the Arab oil-exporting countries, whose representatives were then in Vienna arguing over oil prices with the major private international oil companies. The Arab negotiat-

---

[1] OPEC was created by a treaty among five countries—Iran, Iraq, Kuwait, Saudi Arabia, and Venezuela—in Baghdad in September 1960. Since then the following countries have joined: Qatar, January 1961; Indonesia, June 1962; Libya, June 1962; Abu Dhabi, November 1967; Algeria, July 1969; Nigeria, July 1971; Ecuador, 1973; Gabon, associate member by 1973, full member in 1975.

ing team became excited at the early news of Arab military successes and began passing around newspaper photographs of huge U.S. shipments of arms to Israel. The team's new firmness matched that of the oil companies, and negotiations ceased. Then, at a historic meeting in Kuwait on October 16, six key Persian Gulf oil countries decided that henceforth oil prices would be set by each country without consulting the major oil companies.

Meanwhile, oil buyers were beginning to panic. The Arab boycott against selling oil to the United States or other countries suspected of being pro-Israeli added to already existing fears that oil would become very scarce. The fears soon fulfilled themselves. Iran tested the market by auctioning off crude oil in early December 1973. Several smaller oil companies bid $16–18 a barrel for oil that cost less than a dollar a barrel to produce and that had earlier sold for $5 or less. There were also reports that Libyan and Nigerian crude oil was fetching as much as $20 a barrel. With such solid evidence of buyer panic, OPEC imposed a price of $11.65 a barrel at its Teheran meeting of December 22–23, 1973. This price remained even after the Arab oil embargo was lifted in early 1974.

Thus unfolded the most successful artificial price hike of all time. Receiving $11.65 for each barrel, OPEC gained far more than John D. Rockefeller's Standard Oil Company or any other monopoly or cartel ever had. This judgment would stand even if OPEC were to break up tomorrow and start slashing its prices competitively.

The strengths and weaknesses of OPEC as a cartel relate to uniquely international developments. The Arab-Israeli conflict played an unquestionably important role in making the Arab majority in OPEC insist on a hard line. The persistent U.S. foreign policy of support for Israel was also decisive in causing the Saudi government to sever its friendship with the U.S. and use oil as a political weapon. The exporting countries, being sovereign nations, were also beyond the legal reach of their main consumers. Irate U.S. consumers could not threaten Venezuela or Saudi Arabia with government antitrust actions the way they could threaten domestic oil interests. On the other hand, the fact that no one government reigns over the oil exporters has made it more difficult for them to force one another to hold back production to keep oil prices up. Any country wanting to go its own way could reject the demands of the other OPEC members and sell as much oil as it wished, compromising the power of the cartel over buyers.

Thus any analysis of OPEC, like the analysis of exchange rates between currencies, must recognize the distinctly international dimensions of this outstanding cartel. The well-established economic literature on how cartels work and how they break down must be modified to deal with OPEC, since that literature concentrates almost exclusively on cartels among private firms within a country. Chapter 10 faces this issue.

Regulating the multinationals

In 1974 Canada set up a Foreign Investment Review Agency to ride herd on U.S. investments in Canadian firms wholly or predominantly owned by U.S. firms. The agency soon denied several U.S. firms the legal right to expand their ownership in new or existing Canadian enterprises. As a result of this new regulation of U.S. investments in Canada, several enterprises have not been set up and several others have remained in the hands of Canadian owners who probably would have sold them to U.S. companies if they had not been prevented from doing so by the agency. All indications are that this sort of regulation of foreign investments will remain part of Canadian policy indefinitely.

The creation of the Foreign Investment Review Agency was part of a prolonged cooling trend in Canada's attitude toward incoming U.S. investors. After welcoming U.S. investment inflows for a few decades, Canada took a steadily dimmer view of them from the early 1960s on. There was widespread concern over the large shares of Canadian firms owned and controlled from below the border. Specifically, there was concern that the U.S.-controlled firms would drain money from Canada when sending profits back to U.S. parent companies, and that the same firms might become a lobbying force that would subvert the Canadian government itself.

The spirit of skepticism about multinational firms has not been confined to Canada. Japan has traditionally put high hurdles in the way of U.S. and other foreign firms trying to set up subsidiaries producing in Japan. Recently Brazil, a country that had heretofore rolled out the red carpets for foreign investors, has also leaned hard on foreign-owned firms to sacrifice profits more heavily than domestic firms during the post-OPEC austerity program. In fact, multinational investments have also faced new resistance within the United States, the main investing country. Organized labor has called for limitations on the ability of U.S. firms to invest in subsidiaries abroad, on the argument that their foreign investments will tend to destroy U.S. jobs and replace them with foreign jobs producing the same goods. In addition, would-be U.S. investors have shown some new skittishness about foreign investments, which they now view as endangered by the threat of foreign expropriation and exchange-rate fluctuations.

It is in some ways remarkable that a profit-pursuing move could have so many enemies. Yet controlling investments in one company by a firm based in another has often been a focal point for friction. Both host countries and investing countries have viewed the international investors as virtually an alien group, with partial justification. There is indeed a long history of interference by the international firms in the affairs of both the investors' home country and the host country. Yet under what conditions does the international investment bring net gains to the rest of either country? To investigate this question is to draw national boundaries and take close looks at the political and economic effects on both sides of each boundary. That is what Canada has chosen to do, and that is what this book's special analysis of international investments undertakes to do, in Part V.

ECONOMICS AND THE NATION STATE

It should be clear from these four events that international economics has to be a separate branch of economics as long as nation-states are sovereign. For every country there is a whole set of national policies. And for each country, those policies will always be designed to serve some part of the national constituency. Nation-states almost never give the interests of foreigners the same weight as domestic interests. In most cases national politics is simply indifferent to the interests of foreigners. That is why the protectionists in the United States have seldom had to ask how their barriers to imports of, say, footwear, would affect the jobs and incomes of people making footwear in Italy or Taiwan. That is also why Canada could hammer out a policy of limiting U.S. investments in Canada without investigating the effects of doing so on U.S. firms or consumers. Although international economics does not need to confine its view to the interests of one country, it does have to analyze the different national interests separately, in order to be relevant to the national level of decision making.

DIFFERENT MONEYS

To many economists, and especially to the average person, the principal difference between domestic and international trade is that the latter involves the use of different moneys. A dollar is accepted in California and in Maine. But the Swiss franc, which is the coin of the realm in Basel, must be converted into French francs or West German deutsche marks before it can be used to buy goods in Strasbourg in France or Freiburg in West Germany, each but a few miles away.

With a little more sophistication, however, it is evident that the important fact is not the different moneys so much as the possibility of change in their relative value. When Switzerland, Belgium, and France belonged to the Latin Monetary Union and all three francs were convertible into each other on a one-for-one basis, people would be almost indifferent whether they held one franc or another, unless they were on the verge of making a purchase. For actual buying, it was necessary to have the unit acceptable to the seller; but if exchange rates were fixed, currencies were convertible, and both were expected to remain so, one currency was as good as another. This ability to be indifferent between several currencies has faded as exchange rates came to change more frequently. Between World War I and 1971 people became increasingly aware of the threat that any given exchange rate might change. After August 15, 1971, the float made this threat a day-to-day reality. People soon became accustomed to the notion that holding any currency other than the one in which they would usually buy and sell involved a certain special gamble. The currency awareness, combined with the fact that nations tended to price their goods and services and assets in their own currencies, meant that international trade was increasingly subject to a kind of day-to-day price change not experienced within countries.

With each nation's monetary authorities issuing and managing its own currency comes a separate set of financial markets for each country. Since such IOUs as bills and bonds promise to repay in the national currency, it follows that each country's financial markets have their own set of interest rates. Stock markets also proliferate in different countries, in part because shares entitle their holders to repayment in local currency.

DIFFERENT FISCAL POLICIES

For each sovereign nation there is not only a separate currency but also a separate government with its own public spending and power to tax. Differences in national tax policies are as a rule more pronounced than differences between the tax policies of states, provinces, or cities. Thus in the international arena tax differences set off massive flows of funds and goods that would not have existed without the tax discrepancies. Banks set up shop in the Bahamas, where their capital gains are less taxed and their books less scrutinized. Shipping firms register in Liberia or Panama, where registration costs almost nothing and where they are free from other nations' requirements to use higher-paid national maritime workers. Sovereignty in tax policies and government spending also leads to lobbying and bribery on an international scale. Korean agents have bribed U.S. officials to continue subsidizing the export of U.S. rice to Korea. U.S. aircraft manufacturers have bribed several foreign governments to favor their aircraft. United Brands was caught in a "Bananagate" scandal, trying to bribe

Honduran officials into lowering their country's export tax on bananas. At a more mundane level, each country's array of export subsidies and duties and import barriers is a separate fiscal policy. The contrasts among the fiscal regimes of states, provinces, and localities are usually not so sharp.

FACTOR MOBILITY

In differentiating international from domestic trade, classical economists stressed the behavior of the factors of production. Labor and capital were mobile within a country, they believed, but not internationally. Even land was mobile within a country, if we mean occupationally rather than physically. The same land, for example, could be used alternatively for growing wheat or raising dairy cattle, which gave it a restricted mobility.

The importance of this intranational mobility of the factors of production was that returns to factors tended to equality within countries but not between countries. The wages of French workers of a given training and skill were expected to be more or less equal; but this level of wages bore no necessary relation to those of comparable workers in Germany or Italy, England or Australia. If a weaver received higher wages in Lyons than in Paris, Parisian weavers would migrate to Lyons in sufficient numbers to bring down wages there and raise them in Paris, until equality had been restored. But no such forces are at work between Lyons and Milan, Dresden, Manchester, or New Bedford. The wages of weavers in these cities are independently determined and can fluctuate without affecting one another. The same equality of return within a country, but inequality internationally, was believed to be true of land and capital.

Today it is thought that this distinction of the classical economists has been made too rigidly. There is some mobility of factors internationally. Immigration has been important for the United States and is currently of great significance to the economic life of Australia, Argentina, and Israel, to name but a few examples. Emigration has been a factor in the economic life of many European countries, but perhaps outstandingly of Ireland (now Eire) and Italy. Perhaps the most interesting aspect of migration in the postwar period, however, has been the mass movement, affecting as many as 4 million workers, from the Mediterranean countries of Portugal, Spain, southern Italy, Yugoslavia, Greece, and Turkey northward across the mountains, especially to France, West Germany, and Switzerland. Although the movement slowed at the end of the 1960s as economic growth in Europe settled down to a slower pace and some countries, such as Switzerland, found themselves overwhelmed by the large proportion of foreigners, it did not reverse itself. There is even a sense in which it is now possible to think of a European market for labor.

There is also some considerable degree of immobility within countries. The example used of Paris and Lyons is particularly unapt because the French do not typically move about. Migration within the United States takes place on a broad scale under the influence of major forces such as war. The invasion of Ohio, Michigan, and Illinois by Southerners in and immediately following World War I was paralleled by a similar movement to California and Texas in World War II. But movement on this scale is not normal.

It is accurate to say that there is a difference of degree in factor mobility interregionally and internationally and that in the usual case people will migrate within their own country more readily than they will emigrate abroad. This is true in part because identity of language, customs, and tradition are more likely to exist within countries than between countries.

Capital is also more mobile within than between countries. It is not, however, completely mobile within countries; and regional differences in interest rates do exist. At the same time, it is not completely immobile between countries. We shall see in Part V what happens when capital moves from country to country.

To the extent that there are differences in factor mobility and equality of factor returns internationally as compared with interregionally, international trade will follow different laws. If there is a shift in demand from New England pure woolens to southern synthetic woolen compounds, capital and labor will move from New England to the South. If, however, there is a shift in demand from French to Italian silk, no such movement of capital and labor to Italy takes place. Some other adjustment mechanism is needed.

SEPARATE MARKETS

Apart from purposeful state interference, however, national markets are frequently separate. On occasion, this separation will exist because of interference by the state for national reasons. The British drive on the left; the French drive on the right. These traffic regulations are decreed by governments for national traffic safety. Since it is safer for the driver to sit close to the side of the car which passes the stream of traffic coming in the opposite direction, the British use right-hand-drive cars, the French left-hand. To export automobiles to foreign markets requires a variety of design changes which slow down the assembly line, raise costs, and separate markets to some extent.

But markets are also separated by language, custom, usage, habit, taste, and a host of other causes of difference. Standards differ. Some goods are designed in inches, feet, pounds, and short tons; some in metric measurements. Even within the nonmetric system, the Americans reckon oil in barrels per day, the British in short tons per year. Export and import trade must get outside the culture of the domestic market to become acquainted with different goods, described in different words, using differing measurements, and bought and sold on different terms for different currency units. Australia, New Zealand, and the United Kingdom shifted to the decimal system in money to simplify economic calculation in the age of the computer; but the British are preparing to convert to the metric system in weights and measures as they join the Common Market, to enable their producers and consumers to gain more from integration into the wider European market—in the long run after the costs of adjustment have been overcome.

THE SCHEME OF THIS BOOK

This book deals first with international trade theory and trade policy, asking in Part I how trade seems to work and in Part II what policies toward trade would bring benefits, and to whom. This essentially microeconomic material precedes the macroeconomic and financial focus of Parts III and IV. In places this involves some momentary inconvenience, as when we look at an exchange-rate link between cutting imports and cutting exports in Chapter 4, or when we note in Chapter 6 that changing a tariff affects the exchange rate and therefore welfare. Yet there are gains in logic in proceeding from micro to macro, as in the way that the demand and supply analysis of trade in individual markets sets the stage for the use of the same tools at a more aggregate level in the treatment of international finance. It is in Part III that we enter the world of currencies, examining foreign exchange markets, the balance of payments, and the basic macroeconomics of open economies. Part IV surveys the policy issue of how nations have managed their foreign payments positions and their exchange rates, and how such policies might be improved. Part V looks at the special problems raised by the partial international mobility of humans and other factors of production.

part I

The theory of international trade

90-Day   Futures 9230   .9242
80-Day   Futures 9227   .9241
hina-Taiwan   (Dollar)   .026   .02 5
olombia   (Peso)   .027   .0275
enmark   (Krone)   .1631   .1632
cuador   (Sucre)   .0385   .03 5
inland   (Markka)   2
ance   (Franc)   .2052   .2043
0-Day   Futures   .20   0
0-Day   Futures   5
80-Day   Futures   .2025   .2022

reece   (Drachma)   .0280   .0280
ong   Kong   (Dollar)   .2139   .2142
dia   (Rupee)   .1170   .1165
done   (Rupiah)   .00259   .002590
an   (Rial)   .01416   .01416
aq   (Dinar)   3.44   3.44
rael   (Pound)   .0951   .0951
aly   (Lira)   .001135   .001135
pan   (Yen)   .003818   .003818
0-Day   Futures   .00   .002
0-Day   Futures   .003861   .38
0-Day   Futures   .003887   .00

banon   (Pound)   .3229   .3231
alaysia   (Dollar)   .4079   .4076
exico   (Peso)   .0441   .0441
therlands   (Guilder)   .4089   .4078
w   Zealand   (Dollar)   .9815   5
orway   (Krone)   .18
kistan   (Rupee)   .1025   .025
ru   (Sol)   .0124
ilippines   (Peso)   .1355   .1355
rtugal   (Escudo)   .0246   .0246
Arabia   (Riyal)   .2833   .2833
pore   (Dollar)   .4109   .4110
Africa   (Rand)   1.1522   1.1522

S. Russia Resolve Key Points of Accord On Shipping Grain to U.S.S.R. This Year

Vancouverites, Lured by Lower U.S. Prices, Shop In Washington State and Vex Merchants at Home

Sugar Price Rises As Europe Enters Scramble for Crop

Stevenson Favors Proposal To Swap Surplus Oil From Alaska With Japan

2

The pure theory of international trade: Supply

THE TRADE ISSUE

With international trade, as with so many other human interactions, people have tended first to ask how it should work before getting interested in how it actually works. The systematic study of international trade emerged in the era of mercantilist economics (roughly the 16th through 18th centuries in Europe) as a crude set of hypotheses about how nations should conduct their trade. It was felt that each nation's self-interest was served by encouraging its exports and discouraging its imports. The mercantilist view began to yield, after the late 18th century, to a free-trade view, a view arguing that a nation's self-interest and the world interest would both be served best by just letting people trade as they saw fit. The main hypothesis continued to be one about how trade should be conducted.

Economists studying trade soon found that the issue of what trade policy was best could not be resolved until there was a firmer theory of what made trade flow in the directions it did. At the superficial level, the answer might seem obvious: people will trade if they find it privately profitable. But profitable for whom? For everybody? If not for everybody, then how do we know that the gains it brings to some people outweigh the losses it brings to others? If one country gains from trade, do its trading partners lose? These immediate questions show that the answer to the question of what should be cannot be divorced from the task of explaining what is. We cannot know how a nation or an economic group within a nation gains or loses from trade until we know what makes some people find trade profitable and what goods they will trade if given the chance. To put the point in terms of the recurring concern felt in the United States about trade with Japan, we cannot know who would gain or lose by cutting down our trade with Japan until we know why it is that Japan sells steel, autos, and other goods to the United States in exchange for aircraft, grain, and other goods. Only when we know why trade proves profitable and whose income is tied to trade can we know who would be affected by policies restricting it.

This chapter and the next three thus follow two related sets of issues at once. We investigate both what determines the directions and amounts of trade flows and who is affected by trade or its absence. To simplify the discussion, we shall contrast free trade with no trade at all, leaving to Part II the additional task of contrasting free trade with partial trade barriers that reduce but do not eliminate trade.

AN EARLY VIEW—RICARDO'S LAW OF COMPARATIVE ADVANTAGE

The way in which the desire to pass a welfare judgment on trade leads quickly to a search for the causes of trade was illustrated neatly by the attempt of David Ricardo to convince his fellow Englanders of the virtues of free trade in the early 19th century. His efforts to make his case for free trade yielded a simple and classic statement of how both countries are likely to gain from trade. Yet for all its persuasiveness, his demonstration of the gains from trade was valuable mainly for the questions it raised but failed to answer about the causes of trade.

The advocate of free international trade faced a formidable task as of the appearance of the several editions of Ricardo's *Principles of Political Economy and Taxation* in the early 19th century. Trade was restricted by an elaborate array of taxes and prohibitions on imports and exports. Equally elaborate was the set of mercantilist arguments that had developed as excuses for those restrictions. Taxing imports was often justified as a way of creating jobs and income for the national population. Imports were also supposed to be bad because they had to be paid for, which might cause the nation to lose specie (gold or silver) to foreigners if it imported a greater value of goods and services than it sold to foreigners. Imports were also to be feared because those same foreign goods might not be available in time of war. And lurking behind the whole set of mercantilist arguments for restricting trade, especially imports, was the belief that the world's material wealth was a fixed pie to be divided among warring nations. On this fixed-pie reasoning, whatever the foreigners gain we must lose. The very fact that foreigners want to sell goods to us means that they see gain in it, which must mean that we should avoid buying from them as much as possible.

Ricardo was not the first to challenge the mercantilist orthodoxy. In his *Wealth of Nations* (1776), Adam Smith had ridiculed the fear of trade by comparing nations to households. Since every household finds it worthwhile to produce only some of its needs and to buy others with products it can sell, the same should apply to nations:

> It is the maxim of every prudent master of a family, never to attempt to make at home what it will cost him more to make than to buy. The taylor does not attempt to make his own shoes, but buys them from the shoemaker . . . .
>
> What is prudence in the conduct of every private family, can scarce be folly in that of a great kingdom. If a foreign country can supply us with a commodity cheaper than we ourselves can make it, better buy it of them with some part of the produce of our own industry, employed in a way in which we have some advantage. (Adam Smith, *An Inquiry into the Nature and Causes of the Wealth of Nations* [Modern Library edition], pp. 424–25.)

Yet Smith's argument was incomplete in many ways. He had not faced the earlier argument that restricting imports would create jobs. He had not refuted, and in fact himself accepted, the national defense argument for restricting trade with potential enemies. His argument also assumed that each nation really had enough absolute advantages over its trading partners to enable it to export as much as it imported if trade were left unrestricted and unregulated. Yet earlier writers had already posed the obvious questions he was suppressing. What if a nation has no advantages? Would other nations be willing to trade with it? If they were, shouldn't that nation fear that by trading it would end up importing more from productive foreigners than it could entice them to buy of its exports? Wouldn't this trade deficit cause the nation to lose money to the foreigners? How could it be sure that free trade would resolve those issues in a way that would still leave it with a net gain from trade?

Ricardo strengthened the case for trade by freeing it of some of its earlier restrictive assumptions. He did so with a set of numerical examples showing that a nation could gain from foreign trade even if it had advantages over foreigners in the production of nothing, or of everything. His examples were somewhat uncharacteristic of the rest of his writings in that they showed only net effects on whole nations, ignoring the effects on the internal distribution of well-being that was usually uppermost in Ricardo's mind.

The essence of Ricardo's contribution can be grasped by looking at two examples that paraphrase his key point about the gains from trade.[1] The first example is one of **absolute advantage,** in which each country can produce more of something per unit of inputs than can the rest of the world. Suppose that the United States can produce wheat, but not cloth, more cheaply than the rest of the world, as follows:

In the United States, one unit of inputs can produce 50 bushels of wheat, or 25 yards of cloth, or any combination of wheat and cloth in between.

In the rest of the world, one unit of inputs can produce 40 bushels of wheat, or 100 yards of cloth, or any combination in between.

If there were no trade, each country would have to consume its own production. This means that the most the United States or the rest of the world could consume without trade is the set of wheat-cloth amounts shown along the solid lines in Figures 2.1 and 2.2. The

FIGURE 2.1
Absolute advantage and the gains from trade

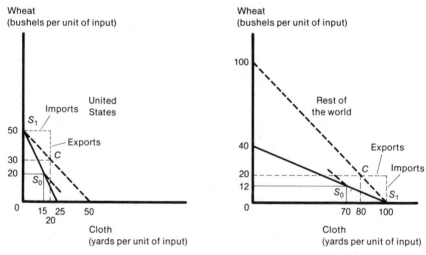

United States, for example, could supply itself with 50 bushels of wheat and no cloth (Point S_1), or with 25 yards of cloth, or with a mixture in between, such as the 20 bushels of wheat and 15 yards of

---

[1] Ricardo's own illustrations were couched in terms of the labor cost it would take England and Portugal to produce given units of wine and cloth. We have turned this upside down, looking at the amounts of two goods that two countries could produce with given resources, where resources are not necessarily confined to labor as in his examples. For the original version, see Ricardo's *On the Principles of Political Economy and Taxation,* in vol. 1 of his *Works and Correspondences,* ed. Piero Sraffa (Cambridge: Cambridge University Press, 1951), pp. 133–49.

cloth at Point S_0. Where would the self-sufficient United States choose to supply itself and consume? Smith and Ricardo could not exactly say. Nor can we, without knowing more about the tastes that lie behind the country's demand behavior. Only when the model includes both supply and demand (as in the next chapter) can we say what combination the country will choose. Let us say that the pattern of tastes is such that the United States would prefer to consume at Point S_0 rather than at any other point on the solid line. Similarly, let us suppose that the rest of the world chooses to consume 12 bushels of wheat and 70 yards of cloth at its Point S_0 on the right-hand diagram.

Without trade the prices of wheat and cloth look different in the two "countries" (the United States and the rest of the world). Assuming that both goods are competitively supplied, the relative costs of each good will dictate relative prices. A bushel of wheat will tend to cost half a yard of cloth in the United States. Or, to state the same price ratio upside down, a yard of cloth will tend to cost two bushels of wheat in the United States. If any other price ratio prevailed, somebody would make greater profits by shifting resources. For example, a price ratio of 1 bushel = 1 yard could last only temporarily without trade because people would quickly find that they could take resources out of cloth production and be able to produce two bushels of wheat for each yard of cloth they stop producing with the same inputs. For the same reason, the foreign price ratio will gravitate toward the wheat-cloth cost ratio of 2.5 (= 100/40) yards per bushel without trade.

To see the gains from trade, let us now imagine that the opportunity to trade internationally is opened up. Somebody will notice a price discrepancy: in the United States, they are selling wheat cheaply, getting only half a yard of cloth for each bushel of wheat, while each bushel of wheat trades for 2½ yards of cloth in other countries. If transport costs are low (let's say they are zero), somebody will see a chance to pay only half a yard of cloth for each bushel of wheat and will ship bushels of wheat to another country, selling each bushel for 2½ yards of cloth. This sort of trade can quickly make that somebody rich, since he will end up converting each half yard of cloth into 2½ yards of cloth. Whether the trade remains in one person's hands or spreads to others who compete and ship themselves, the direction of trade is clearly driven by the contrast in cost ratios. Because wheat is relatively cheap in the United States and cloth is relatively cheap abroad, the United States will export wheat and import cloth.

The story of the gains from trade is still quite incomplete, since we don't yet know where the pattern of production and consumption will settle in response to international trade. Nor do we know what price ratio will be the final result. In fact, this kind of example does not give enough information to determine the international price ratio, the "terms of trade" between the United States and the rest of the world. We cannot know this ratio yet for the same reason that we could not know the exact production and consumption points when there was no trade: we do not have any information about the demand side, about the pattern of tastes in the United States and the rest of the world. Lacking the demand side, Ricardo could only say how trade would bring gains if the world price ratio were such and such.

We are not completely without information about the international price ratio, however. We know that it must lie somewhere in between the no-trade cost ratios in the United States and the rest of the world—somewhere between half a yard per bushel and 2½ yards per bushel. To see why, suppose that the United States was asked to consider trading at the ratio of only one-fifth yard of cloth for each bushel of wheat. The United States would certainly not export wheat abroad in exchange for one-fifth yard of cloth when it can get half a yard of cloth for the same bushel in the United States. Indeed, at the price of one-fifth yard per bushel the United States might offer to export *cloth*. But the rest of the world would not want to give up five bushels of wheat to get each yard of cloth from the United States when it can get the same yard of cloth by giving up only two fifths of a bushel in its own economies. Thus the international price ratio must settle somewhere between the two no-trade price ratios.

Let us say that demand patterns are such as to make the international price ratio settle at the intermediate level of one bushel of wheat for one yard of cloth. If the United States engaged in trade on these terms without shifting its production mix away from Point S_0, it could experience some gains from trade. These gains are evident from the fact that the United States, by giving up some wheat and getting some cloth, would be moving out from S_0 in Figure 2.1 along the short unlabeled dashed line. Each point on that line is superior to some points below it and to the left on the solid line representing the no-trade opportunities for consumption. The chance to consume more seems to suggest gains. The same suggestion emerges from noting that the rest of the world could move out on the dashed line to the north-west from S_0, reaching points that were unattainable as consumption combinations when there was no trade.

The gains from trade are considerably magnified in Ricardo's kind of example when we allow production to respond to the opening of trade. The United States should not continue to produce 20 bushels of wheat and 15 yards of cloth at Point S_0. The United States should, in this example, stop producing cloth altogether. Why use any resources to produce cloth when the same resources could be shifted into wheat production, producing two bushels of wheat for every yard of cloth not produced, and allowing the United States to get two yards of cloth from abroad for each two bushels of wheat it exports? The United States could *specialize completely* in producing wheat at Point S_1 and trade some wheat for cloth, moving southeast to consume at points like Point C. Similarly, the rest of the world could specialize completely in the good it produces more cheaply, producing cloth alone at its Point S_1 and trading cloth for wheat to reach a point such as its Point C.

The chance to specialize and trade at the international price ratio of one yard per bushel allows both the United States and the rest of the world to gain from trade. Though we still cannot say exactly where they will choose to trade until demand conditions are introduced in the next chapter, it is clear that the dashed international price line allows each country to trade wheat for cloth and reach points that it could not reach without trade. The United States could not reach Point C if it were forced to be self-sufficient along the solid line. For each consumption combination the United States could reach without trade (solid line), there is a point on the international price line that allows the nation to consume at least as much of both goods by specializing and trading. The rest of the world also gains. The gains will equal the values of the extra consumption made possible by trade.

Thus far, we have examined an example of absolute advantage, in which each country could produce more of one good per unit of input than the other country. The United States could produce more wheat (50 bushels versus 40 bushels) per unit of input, while the rest of the world could produce more cloth (100 yards versus 25 yards). But this example fails to put to rest the fears that others had already expressed when Smith and Ricardo wrote: What if we have no absolute advantage, and the foreigners can produce more of *anything* per unit of input? Will they want to trade? And if they do, should we want to?

Ricardo showed that the gains from trade still accrue to both sides even when a country has no absolute advantage whatsoever. As long as the price ratios differ at all between countries in the absence of trade, every country will have a **comparative advantage,** an ability to find some good which it can produce at a lower relative cost disadvantage (starting from the initial opening of trade) than other goods. This good it should export in exchange for some of the others.

Ricardo demonstrated his **law of comparative advantage,** namely that every country has a comparative advantage in something and gains from trading it for other things, with a numerical example of the following sort. Suppose now that

in the United States, one unit of inputs can produce 50 bushels of wheat, or 25 yards of cloth, or combinations in between, as before; while in the rest of the world, one unit of inputs can produce 67 bushels of wheat, or 100 yards of cloth, or combinations in between.

To see that both countries gain from bartering U.S. wheat for foreign cloth in this case, it may be easiest just to glance back at the absolute-advantage case and see that the gains from trade did not depend in any way upon the fact that the United States could produce more wheat per unit of input than the rest of the world (the 50 versus 40 bushels in Figure 2.1). The gains came not from absolute advantage but from the simple fact that the cost ratios without trade (the slopes of the solid lines) were different.

To look more closely at the gains from following comparative advantage, let us examine Figure 2.2, which puts a Ricardo-like example

FIGURE 2.2
Comparative advantage and the gains from trade

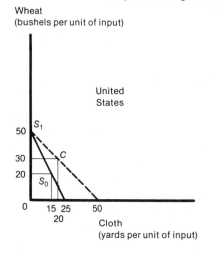

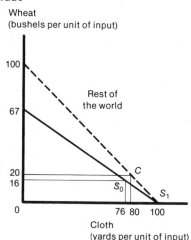

into geometric form. Here we show the pessimistic case in which the United States has somehow been hopelessly surpassed by the rest of the world in ability to produce wheat or, especially, cloth with each unit of inputs. If trade is prohibited, the United States must be self-sufficient and consume its own supplies at a point on the solid line, such as Point S_0. So must the rest of the world.

Opening trade provides a new opportunity even though the United States produces both goods in a more costly way. With trade possible, somebody will notice that a bushel of wheat can be bought in the United States for only half a yard of cloth and shipped and sold abroad for one and a half yards of cloth ($1\frac{1}{2}$ = 100/67). Wheat will start flow-ing from the United States in exchange for cloth from other countries, without regard for how many inputs it took to produce each good in each country. Soon the expansion of trade will tend to bring the two countries' price ratio into line. We know, again, that trade will be profitable to both sides only at an international price ratio somewhere between the U.S. no-trade ratio ($\frac{1}{2}$ yard per bushel) and the rest of the world's no-trade ratio ($1\frac{1}{2}$ yards per bushel). And again, as with the ab-solute-advantage case, it will pay each side to specialize completely so as to reach the highest consumption possibilities, the United States specializing in wheat and the rest of the world specializing in cloth. If the international price ratio turns out to be one yard per bushel, trade might result in each side's settling at its Point C, with the United States exporting 20 bushels of wheat in exchange for 20 yards of foreign-made cloth. The gains from trade are the extra consumption possible at points such as C but not possible without trade at points such as S_0.

Ricardo gave this kind of numerical example extra persuasiveness by showing that the gains from trading according to comparative ad-vantage were also obtained when one recognized that money is used in international transactions. So far our example has assumed that wheat is bartered directly for cloth. This is not realistic, since nations conduct their trade using foreign exchange markets where one na-tion's currency is traded for other currencies to pay for exports and imports. To follow this part of his argument in detail takes us ahead of our story, into Part III of this book. Suffice it to say here that Ricardo made the correct point that even with national money in the picture, a country will have a comparative advantage and will gain from trading. If at some rate of exchange between its national currency and others, it is unable to make its export receipts match its import bills, it can still bring the two into line by changing the relative money prices of its goods and foreign goods. This balancing of payments in a mone-tized world can be achieved either by letting the exchange rates be-tween currencies find a new equilibrium or by adjusting all money-price levels within one or both countries, as we shall note at length in Part III. Adding the fact that real-world trade is conducted in money terms does not compromise Ricardo's law of comparative advantage.

PRODUCTION POSSIBILITY CURVES WITH CONSTANT COSTS

Subsequent writers extended Ricardo's analysis in a number of di-rections. Among these extensions was a clarification of the role of

Ricardo's own assumptions about comparative costs of production. Ricardo had made the basic point that trade could follow from differences in commodity cost ratios alone, and did not depend on each absolute cost in terms of inputs. In the above example of comparative advantage, what made trade profitable was the fact that producing wheat cost more *in yards of cloth* in one country than in others, not the cost of wheat or of cloth alone in terms of inputs. We do not need to keep referring to how much wheat or cloth can be produced per unit of input, as Ricardo did when originally comparing the labor costs of wine and cloth in England and Portugal. It is simpler just to follow later writers in speaking only about the different amounts of wheat and cloth that a nation could produce with all its resources, dropping the phrase *per unit of input*. We shall do so, in order to focus on the aggregate production and consumption of nations.

To summarize what a nation as a whole could produce, it is useful to deal with **production-possibility curves,** or **transformation curves,** which show the different combinations of commodity amounts that a nation could produce if it employed its resources "fully and efficiently." The solid lines in Figures 2.1 and 2.2 above can be interpreted as production possibility curves if the axes are changed to read outputs per year (for example, billions of bushels or millions of yards per year), rather than outputs per unit of input. The production possibility curves thus continue to define the outer limits of what a nation could produce. They do not tell us exactly what a nation will produce until we add information about the price ratios producers will face.

Gottfried Haberler and others noted that the production possibility curves implied by Ricardo's kind of example embody a special assumption about **opportunity costs,** or the amounts of other goods that must be given up in order to produce more of one good, such as wheat. In an example like Figure 2.2 above, we have followed Ricardo in assuming **constant** opportunity costs. That is, it has been assumed that producing an extra bushel of wheat requires giving up half a yard of cloth in the United States, or a yard and a half in the rest of the world, no matter how much wheat is being produced. To produce another bushel of wheat cost half a yard of cloth in the United States whether we were at the point on the curve where the United States was initially producing 25 yards of cloth and no wheat, or at Point S_1, where we produced the 50th bushel of wheat by giving up the last half yard of cloth. The assumption of constant opportunity cost is betrayed by the fact that the solid lines in Figures 2.1 and 2.2 are straight lines, where the constancy of the slope shows the constancy of the assumed trade-off between extra wheat and extra cloth.

INCREASING OPPORTUNITY COSTS

Later writers developed several objections to Ricardo's simple assumption of constant opportunity costs. First, they noted empirically that many industries seemed to be characterized by rising, rather than constant, marginal costs, so that more and more of other commodities had to be given up to produce each succeeding extra unit of one commodity. Second, they thought of some good theoretical reasons for expecting rising opportunity costs in expanding one industry at the expense of others. One obvious possibility is that each individual industry, contrary to the assumption of Ricardo's trade example, may itself have diminishing returns, or rising costs. Even if every industry has constant "returns to scale," the shift from one industry to another may still involve increasing opportunity costs because of subtle effects stemming from the fact that different goods use inputs in different proportions, a point to which we return below.

Perhaps the most damaging objection to the assumption of constant opportunity costs is that it implied something that failed to fit the facts of international trade and production patterns. The constancy of opportunity costs in Figures 2.1 and 2.2 led us to conclude that each country would maximize its gain by specializing its production completely in its comparative-advantage good.[2] The real world fails to show such frequent total specialization. In Ricardo's own day, it may have been reasonable for him to assume that England grew no wine grapes and relied on foreign grapes and wines, but even with cloth imports from England the other country in his example, Portugal, made most of its own cloth. Specialization is no more common today. The United States and Canada continue to produce most of their domestic consumption of goods they partially import—textiles, cars, and TV sets, for example.

Considerations like these led economists to replace the constant-cost assumption with the assumption about opportunity costs that is likely to hold in most cases. They have tended to assume *increasing opportunity costs:* as one industry expands at the expense of others, increasing amounts of the other goods must be given up to get each extra unit of the expanding output. Figure 2.3 shows a case of increasing opportunity costs. This can be seen by following what happens to the opportunity cost of producing an extra yard of cloth as we shift more and more resources from wheat production to cloth production. When the economy is producing only 20 billion yards of cloth, the slope of the production possibility curve at Point S_1 tells us that an

---

[2] With constant costs one of the two trading countries can fail to specialize completely only in the special case in which the international terms of trade settle at the same price ratio prevailing in that country with no trade.

FIGURE 2.3
Production possibilities under increasing costs

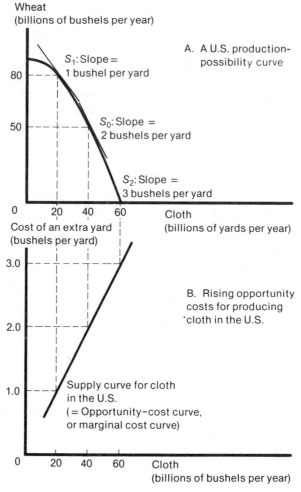

extra yard could be made each year by giving up a bushel of wheat.
When 40 billion yards are being made each year, getting the resources
to make another yard a year means giving up two bushels of wheat, as
shown at Point S_0. To push cloth production up to 60 billion yards a
year requires giving up wheat in amounts that rise to three bushels for
the last yard of cloth. These increasing costs of extra cloth can also be
interpreted as increasing costs of producing extra wheat: when one
starts from a cloth-only economy at Point S_2 and shifts increasing
amounts of resources into growing wheat, the costs of an extra bushel

mount (from one-third yard at S_2 to one-half yard at S_0, one yard at S_1, and so forth).

The increasing opportunity costs are reexpressed in a familiar form in the lower half of Figure 2.3. Here the vertical axis plots the opportunity costs of extra cloth, which were the slopes in the upper half of the figure. The resulting curve is properly called a supply curve for cloth, since the opportunity costs of producing extra cloth are just the marginal costs that a set of competitive U.S. cloth suppliers would bid into equality with the price they receive when selling the cloth. Although this reexpression adds no new information by itself, it helps set the stage for converting the entire basic model of trade into familiar supply and demand curves, a task to which we return in the next chapter.

Under conditions of increasing costs, trade has the same basic effects as when constant costs were assumed. Both sides still stand to gain from trade in the aggregate, and both tend to respond to trade opportunities by specializing more on producing their comparative-advantage products. The two changes brought by assuming increasing rather than constant costs are both changes in the direction of realism: countries tend to specialize incompletely, and marginal costs are bid into equality between countries.

The effects of opening trade with increasing costs are shown for one country in Figure 2.4. (A similar diagram and results could be shown for the rest of the world.) Without trade, the United States must consume its own production. Let us say that U.S. production possibilities and taste patterns (tastes are not shown on the diagram) are such that the economy settles at Point S_0, where the price (and marginal cost) of cloth is two bushels per yard and the economy is producing 50 billion bushels and 40 billion yards a year. Opening trade gives the United States the opportunity to exchange wheat for cloth at a new price. As with our earlier examples, let us say that the pretrade price of cloth is lower abroad than in the United States, so that the United States ends up exporting wheat in order to import the cheaper cloth. Once again, we cannot determine exactly what the new international-trade price of cloth will be or how much the United States will trade at that price until we have added the demand side of the trade model in the next chapter, but the direction of effects from trade is already clear.

Even if the United States continues to produce at S_0, it stands to gain from trading. The nation still has the option of refusing to trade and being no worse off than before at S_0. Yet it can also exchange wheat for cloth at some new international price ratio, such as the one bushel per yard price shown in Figure 2.4. At this price the United States would certainly not want to export cloth and import wheat, since it could get two bushels of wheat for each yard of cloth forgone just by shifting

FIGURE 2.4
The effects of international trade under increasing costs
Wheat
(billions of bushels per year)

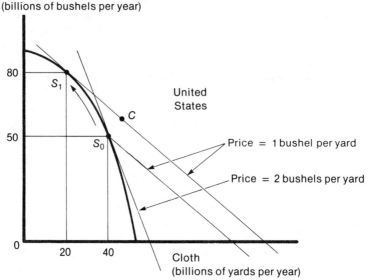

resources from cloth to wheat in U.S. production. But by exporting wheat at the international price, the United States could reach consumption points that were unattainable without trade. These are the points on the international price line extending southeast from S_0. The chances are that one of these previously unattainable points will be preferable to S_0.

Yet the United States stands to gain even more from trade by changing its output mixture. U.S. producers will soon realize that if foreigners are willing to pay one yard of cloth for each bushel of exported wheat, it is a bargain to shift more resources out of cloth production and into wheat, losing only half a yard of cloth for each extra bushel grown. They will shift more resources into wheat, causing a movement from S_0 to S_1. In this increasing-cost case, unlike the less realistic constant-cost case, they will not specialize completely, however. Under increasing-cost conditions, the more resources they shift into wheat, the higher the cost of producing extra wheat. Specialization will only be profitable up to the point where the opportunity cost of extra wheat has risen to meet the price received for wheat on world markets. This will be at Point S_1, where both the opportunity cost and the world price of wheat are one yard per bushel. The result, then, is that under increasing costs, nations are still likely to gain from trade, especially if they specialize more in their comparative-advantage export lines, but find it best to specialize only incompletely.

FACTOR PROPORTIONS

It is clear that the shapes of production-possibility curves are crucial to the explanation of how supply conditions can create a basis for trade. This observation leads immediately to three other questions:

1. What information is needed to derive the production-possibility curve of each country?
2. Why are increasing-cost curves likely to occur so frequently?
3. What makes for differences in comparative costs? That is, why do the production-possibility curves have different shapes in different countries?

A country's production-possibility curve, or transformation curve, is derived from information on total factor supplies and on the production functions that relate factor inputs to output in various industries. In Appendix A we show how the production-possibility curves are derived under several common assumptions about production functions in individual industries.

The answer to the second question emerges from the formal derivation of the transformation curves, yet we can sketch the explanation for the prevalence of increasing costs even without a rigorous demonstration. The key point is that different products use inputs in very different proportions. To stay with our wheat-cloth example for a moment, wheat uses relatively more land and less labor than cloth, whether the yarn for the cloth comes from synthetic fibers or from such natural fibers as cotton and silk. This basic fact of variation in input proportions can set up an increasing-costs transformation curve even if constant returns to scale exist in each industry. When resources are released from cloth production to be shifted into wheat production, they will be released in proportions different from those initially prevailing in wheat production. The cloth industry will release a lot of labor and not much land relative to the labor and land use pattern in wheat. To employ these factors, the wheat industry must shift toward using much more labor-intensive techniques. The effect is close to that of the law of diminishing returns (which, strictly speaking, refers to the case of adding more of one factor to fixed amounts of the others): adding so much labor to slowly changing amounts of land causes the gains in wheat production to decline as more and more resources, mainly labor, are released from cloth production. Thus successive extra bushels of wheat production require greater and greater losses in cloth production.

The basic fact of differences in. factor proportions has also been viewed as a key to the explanation of comparative-cost differences and the existence of trade by the Swedish economist Bertil Ohlin, following some insights by his teacher Eli Heckscher. The **Heckscher-Ohlin** explanation of trade patterns can be abbreviated as follows: different goods require different factor proportions, and different countries have different relative factor endowments; therefore countries will tend to have comparative advantages in producing the goods that use their more abundant factors more intensively; for this reason each country will end up exporting its abundant-factor good in exchange for imported goods that use its scarce factors more intensively. If wheat is technologically best produced with lots of land relative to labor and capital, countries that have an abundance of land will be able to produce wheat cheaply. This is why Australia, Argentina, Canada, Minnesota, and the Ukraine export wheat. On the other hand, if cloth requires much labor relative to capital and land, countries that have an abundance of labor—Hong Kong, Japan, India—will have a comparative advantage in the manufacture of cloth and will be able to export it.

As is noted in Appendix A, there may be some ambiguity about the technological factor proportions involved in producing a given commodity. Where these factor proportions are technically unalterable, we can agree that one commodity is more labor intensive than another. Oil refining is more capital intensive than cabinetmaking, and hydroelectric power generation unambiguously requires land, in the form of specialized waterpower sites. But in the production of many commodities, there is a range within which one factor can be substituted for another. Eggs can be produced by chickens roaming the range, using land, or cooped up in batteries of nests, where capital substitutes for land and labor. Thus it is impossible to say that one commodity is more capital intensive or labor intensive than another until we know more about the possibilities of factor substitution.

The factor endowments explanation of trade further rests on the assumption that each country has the same technological possibilities of producing a given good, that is, that the production functions are the same in both countries. This assumption will be modified in Chapter 4, where we explore the existence of trade based on technological differences between countries.

Again there is considerable difficulty in defining what a factor is for the purpose of using this explanation. For one thing, to define factors broadly as land, labor, and capital is to overlook the point that these factors are not homogeneous for many purposes, but divide into noncompeting groups. It is not enough to have land to raise sheep—one must have grazing land; nor can minerals be produced by land in general, but only by certain ore-bearing types. Many natural resources are so-called specific factors, limited to one or a few countries. If one defines factors narrowly and makes separate factors out of noncompeting groups or specific factors, it turns out that much trade is based on absolute advantage, the existence of a factor in one country but not in its trading partner. One can keep the explanation of comparative advantage developed by Ohlin from the insights of Eli Heckscher and overlook noncompeting groups and specific factors, or one can define factors narrowly and give up the broad Heckscher-Ohlin explanation of why prices differ before trade.

Another difficulty is that it is hard to separate goods from factors, especially when one recognizes that much of world trade is in intermediate goods, those sought not for final consumption but for use in making other goods. Lacking copper mines, it is not necessary to import copper if one can import copper ore. Britain could produce cotton cloth without growing cotton by dint of importing the fiber. But this means that the Heckscher-Ohlin account of comparative advantage should be linked not with commodities so much as with activities. Mining copper ore must be done in countries with ore deposits, but refining copper can be done anywhere in the world that the abundant capital, skilled labor, and copper ore can be combined. The fact that Japan imports iron ore from Australia and coal from the United States suggests that trade in intermediate goods has reduced the importance of specific factors as an explanation of comparative advantage.

Despite the difficulty of deciding how broadly or narrowly to define factors and whether to relate factors to commodities or economic activities, most economists regard the Heckscher-Ohlin explanation of trade as broadly true. They can sustain this conclusion, however, only after carefully qualifying it. As we shall see in Chapter 5, the pattern of trade is not always correctly guessed by analysis based on just two or three factors of production. The simple presumption that the United States is capital abundant and should export capital-intensive goods has been upset empirically by the "Leontiev paradox," which has forced economists to take a closer look at the factor-proportions argument, as explained in Chapter 5.

TRADE AND FACTOR EFFICIENCY

What about trade between two countries with the same factor proportions and different factor efficiencies (and, what we have yet to discuss, the same tastes)? Suppose we have two countries, Sweden and Austria, with the same proportions of land, labor, and capital, but with these factors of production more efficient in Sweden than in Austria. Let us assume that labor is more efficient in Sweden than in Austria not because it is combined with more capital and land but merely because it works harder in every industry. And Swedish land is richer, let us assume, than Austrian; and Swedish machinery more highly developed. Can trade take place then?

The answer is no. Austrian factors of production will receive less income than Swedish because of their reduced effectiveness in production; but this will not help trade, because all factors receive proportionately less. The production-possibilities curves of the two countries will resemble those set forth in Figure 2.5, showing the Austrians capable of producing less than the Swedes. But if tastes are the same

FIGURE 2.5
The case of identical comparative costs

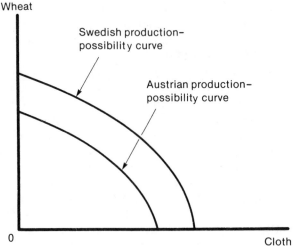

Wheat

Swedish production–
possibility curve

Austrian production–
possibility curve

0   Cloth

in the two countries, the prices of wheat in terms of cloth and of cloth in terms of wheat—to restrict ourselves to our two familiar commodities—will be the same. When the Austrian production-possibilities curve is adjusted to a common point with the Swedish, as must be done following the technique of this chapter, it will be seen that the shapes of the two curves are identical. This clinches the point that with identical tastes and identical comparative costs trade is impossible.

It follows from this that it is not the efficiency of factors as a whole which creates a basis for trade but the existence of factor differences, or of differences in factor efficiency which are not the same for all commodities and which are not offset by differences in tastes. If Austrian people were more efficient in cloth because they had a predilection for city life and were less efficient in agriculture, the basis for a difference in relative prices and for trade would exist.

The fact is, of course, that Austria and Sweden do trade to a considerable extent, even though they have similar overall capital-labor and land-labor endowment ratios. The reason is that the real world contains more commodities and factors than our simple two-by-two-by-two (two-commodity, two-factor, two-country) model. Both countries possess relative advantages in the endowments of all sorts of specific technological factors of production, such as skilled personnel with detailed expertise in different narrow industrial lines. Behind the similarity of overall factor proportions lie many contrasts in endowments of more narrowly defined, and noncompeting, factors.

DECREASING COSTS (INCREASING RETURNS TO SCALE)

Despite the apparent prevalence of increasing-cost conditions in most industries, many industries may be characterized by conditions that bring the opposite result, namely decreasing opportunity costs of expanding one industry at the expense of others. Many large-scale modern manufacturing industries, in particular, are subject to such pronounced economies of scale (increasing returns to scale) that the transformation curves linking them may show decreasing costs of shifting from one to the other even though the factor proportions may differ between industries. The international banking and financial "industry" is also subject to such pronounced economies of centralizing financial information and wealth into a few centers as to be a decreasing-cost case. Figure 2.6 shows a decreasing-cost situation. The number of ships that would have to go unbuilt in shifting resources from a shipbuilding specialization to producing more aircraft tends to decrease. At Point C the United States would have to take a large amount of resources away from shipbuilding in order to produce the first plane at very high unit cost. As further resources are shifted, the economies of scale in aircraft manufacture take over and the opportunity costs decline.

In the world of decreasing-cost industries, there are still gains from trading and countries will still find it profitable to follow their comparative advantage. What is different here from the increasing-costs case is that with decreasing-cost industries, as in Ricardo's constant-cost industries, countries are likely to specialize completely. In Figure 2.6, the United States would not settle for long at an unstable intermediate point such as Point B. Any slight disruption of this temporary equilibrium would probably cause a shift to specialization at either A or C. The reason is simply that at any price, even the one at B,

FIGURE 2.6
Trade and specialization under decreasing costs
(increasing returns to scale)

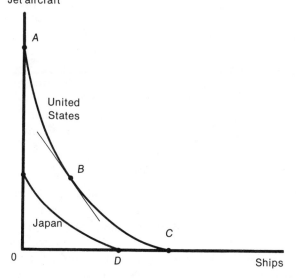

the United States can reach better consumption points from A or C. Given the existence of a Japanese comparative advantage in ship-building, the United States would be likely to end up specializing in aircraft at A, whereas Japan would be likely to specialize in shipbuilding at D. This pattern matches the real-world result in aircraft and shipbuilding, though the real world is far more complex than the model in Figure 2.6.

SUMMARY

The basis for trade, so far as supply is concerned, is found in differences in comparative costs. One country may be more efficient than another, as measured by factor inputs per unit of output, in the production of every possible commodity; but so long as it is not equally more efficient in every commodity, a basis for trade exists. It will pay the country to produce more of those goods in which it is relatively more efficient and to export them in return for goods in which its relative advantage is least.

The basic law of comparative advantage was first successfully argued by David Ricardo in the early 19th century, under the assumption of constant costs. Relaxing this assumption to allow for increasing (or decreasing) opportunity costs does not overturn comparative advantage.

International differences in comparative costs, or the shape of the production-possibility curve, stem largely from the facts that (1) different goods use the factors of production in different ratios, and (2) nations differ in their relative factor endowments. The Heckscher-Ohlin explanation of trade patterns builds on these two facts to argue that nations will tend to export the goods that use their relatively abundant factors more intensively, in exchange for the goods that use their scarce factors more intensively.

SUGGESTED READING

See suggested reading for Chapter 3 and Appendixes A and B.

QUESTIONS FOR REVIEW

1. Which of the following pretrade cost ratios was crucial to the existence of a basis for gainful trade: (a) the ratio of the input cost of U.S. wheat to the input cost of foreign wheat, (b) the ratio of the input cost of U.S. wheat to the input cost of U.S. cloth, or (c) the ratio of the cost of U.S. wheat in yards of cloth to the cost of other countries' wheat in yards of cloth?

2. To test your understanding of how the supply curve or opportunity-cost curve for one good is derived from the production-possibilities curve, sketch the U.S. supply curve for wheat that derives from Figure 2.4.

3. Explain what is wrong with the following statement: "Trade is self-eliminating. Opening up trade opportunities bids prices and costs into equality between countries. But once prices and costs are equalized, there is no longer any reason to ship goods from country to country, and trade stops."

3

The pure theory of
international trade: Demand

Knowing supply without knowing demand accomplishes little, like one blade of a scissors or one hand clapping. Chapter 2 focused on supply alone. Each of its examples of the effects of opening trade had to say something vague and unsatisfactory, such as "*Suppose* that demand conditions were such that the new price is one bushel per yard and that at this price exports and imports are," and so on. There is a temptation to be more concrete in linking trade flows to the supply side alone. Some economic literature comes close to saying that the law of comparative advantage determines what commodities will be exported or imported by each country, whereas demand conditions set the prices at which they will be traded. Yet this is not correct. In the marketplace, demand and supply *together* determine *both* the quantities of goods bought and sold *and* their relative prices. Demand and supply interact just as simultaneously in international trade as in local domestic markets.

The importance of having a complete explicit model of both prices and quantities in international trade can be quickly appreciated by remembering the importance of the international price in the examples of Chapter 2. In order to describe the gains and effects of trade, we had to know where the international price settled. In the Ricardian constant-cost example of comparative advantage, the price had to be somewhere in between the U.S. pretrade price ratio of two bushels of wheat per year of cloth and the foreign pretrade price ratio of two-thirds bushel per yard. But where in between? There may be a tendency for the lazy theorist to split the difference (1⅓ bushels per yard), but this will not do. If the world price ended up equaling the pretrade U.S. price, trade would be a matter of indifference to the United States and any gains from trade would accrue to the rest of the world, whose prices changed with trade. Conversely, if the price in the rest of the world remains unaffected by trade, only the United States will gain from being able to trade at prices different from those dictated by pretrade conditions. The important matter of how the gains from trade are divided clearly hangs on what the new price will be, and we cannot answer this question by referring to supply alone.

TRADE WITH DEMAND AND SUPPLY

The demand side of any marketplace is dictated by the tastes and incomes of the users of final products (plus the cost conditions facing the suppliers of a final product, if we are discussing the demand for an intermediate product). These tastes and incomes constrain how the quantity demand will react to changes in price.

Once we know the demand curves relating the quantity demanded to price, we can combine them with the supply curves derived from cost conditions (in Chapter 2 and Appendix A) to show the production, consumption, and price effects of international trade. The demand-and-supply-curve framework is the main geometric tool that will be used in analyzing trade policy options. Let us thus begin by examining what answers the demand-supply framework yields once the shapes of the curves are known, and turn thereafter to a look at how the relevant demand curves could be derived from underlying information about tastes and incomes.

Figure 3.1 summarizes the impact of trade on production, consumption, and prices in the United States and the rest of the world. The national supply curves, or marginal cost curves, are derived from the production-possibility curves (as in Figure 2.3 in Chapter 2), which in turn come from production technology and factor-supply conditions (as shown in Appendix A). The demand curves can be derived as shown in the next section.

If no trade is allowed, the U.S. and the rest-of-world markets for cloth clear at different prices. Cloth costs two bushels of wheat per yard in the United States at Point A, as it did in the examples of the last chapter. In the absence of any trade with the United States, the rest of the world finds its demand and supply matching at the lower price of two-thirds bushel per yard, at Point H.

Opening up trade frees people in both the United States and the rest of the world from the necessity of matching national demand with national supply. This presents a new opportunity for U.S. cloth buyers

FIGURE 3.1
The effects of trade on production, consumption, and price, shown with demand and supply curves

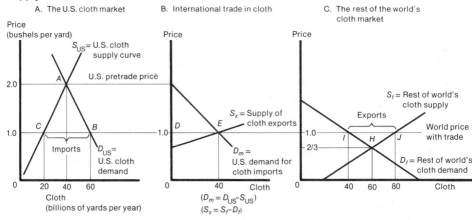

and foreign cloth sellers. U.S. buyers will soon find that they can get cheaper cloth from abroad, where cloth had been selling at only two-thirds bushel per yard. And the foreign sellers will find that they need not settle for this low price of two-thirds bushel when they can sell to the United States for more. The two groups will increasingly get together and start transacting to exchange U.S. wheat for foreign cloth at prices somewhere in between two-thirds bushel and two bushels per yard.

The final price that results in world trade can be determined now that our analysis contains the demand curves as well as the supply curves. There is only one price ratio at which *world* demand and *world* supply are in balance. To find this price one can compare the first and third diagrams of Figure 3.1. The excess of U.S. demand over U.S. supply matches the excess of foreign supply over foreign demand at only one price: the price of one bushel per yard. At this price the U.S. excess demand, or CB, equals the foreign excess supply, or IJ. At a slightly higher price, say at 1.2 bushels per yard, the U.S. excess of demand over supply would be less than 40 (billion yards a year), whereas the rest of the world's excess supply would be above 40. This imbalance would force the price to fall, back to the equilibrium value of one bushel per yard. Conversely, a price below unit would not last because world (U.S. plus foreign) supply would be below world demand.

The balancing of world demand and supply can also be seen in a single diagram showing international trade in cloth, as in the middle diagram of Figure 3.1. The two curves shown there are trade curves derived from the national demand and supply curves. The curve showing U.S. demand for cloth imported from other countries is an excess demand curve, showing the quantity of cloth demand minus cloth supply in the United States for each price level. Similarly, the supply curve of the rest of the world's cloth exports is an excess supply curve, plotting the quantity gaps between cloth supply and demand in the rest of the world. The trade demand and supply curves cross at E, yielding exactly the same international flow of cloth ($DE = CB = IJ$) and the same world price as the other diagrams. In what follows, the middle diagram of Figure 3.1 will be used when it is desirable to focus on international exchanges, and diagrams like those to the left and right will be used when it is important to focus on the effects of trade and trade restrictions on domestic producer and consumer groups. Either set of curves has the advantage of being not only familiar to anyone introduced to the demand-supply basics but also empirically measurable.

BEHIND THE DEMAND CURVES: INDIFFERENCE CURVES

In using the demand curves now introduced, it is helpful to know what behavior and what welfare meaning might lie behind them.

Very few assumptions are strictly necessary to derive the main empirically observed features of demand curves from underlying behavior. The mere fact that consumers face income constraints suffices to explain why demand curves usually slope downward, why goods tend on the whole to be substitutes for each other, and why demand rises with income on the average. The existence of demand curves is thus easily understood. The welfare meaning of demand curves remains more controversial.

Among economists it is traditional, though not necessary, to assume that demand curves are derived from the maximization of subjective utility by households subject to the constraint that their budgets stay within their incomes. The derivation involves the use of a geometric tool commonly known as the **indifference curve**, which shows the different combinations of commodity quantities that would bring the individual the same level of utility.

The indifference curve may be compared with a contour line on a map. A single curve represents a single level of satisfaction or utility, made up of varying combinations of two goods. Let us take our familiar products, wheat and cloth. The indifference curve $a-a$ in Figure 3.2A shows an example in which a consumer is indifferent to whether he has seven bushels of wheat and four yards of cloth (v), or three bushels of wheat and eight yards of cloth (w), or any other combination which may be read off the same curve.

FIGURE 3.2A
Single indifference curve

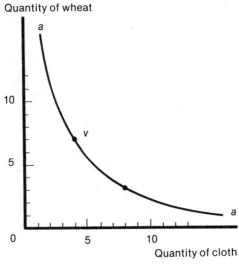

Quantity of wheat

Like contour lines, indifference curves are arranged in maps in which the parallel lines indicate progress in the indicated direction from a lower degree of satisfaction (or altitude) to a higher. In Figure 3.2B, for example, point *b* on indifference curve *III* is taken to represent a higher level of satisfaction or welfare than point *a* on indiffer-

FIGURE 3.2B
Indifference map

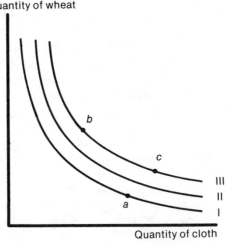

Quantity of wheat

ence curve I, even though it has more wheat and less cloth. The extra wheat is more than sufficient to compensate for the loss of cloth. Point c, where there is more of both, is clearly superior in satisfaction to point a, and the consumer is indifferent between c and b.

The higher branches of economic theory raise a difficult question about **community indifference curves.** It is agreed that the indifference map of an individual is conceptually satisfactory and could be set down if anyone could be found who was sufficiently confident of the logic and stability of his tastes to submit to questioning. If an individual believes that he is better off than he was before with five more bushels of wheat and two less yards of cloth—substantially better off—there is no one to gainsay him. But there may be objection, it is suggested, to the notion that the community is better off with an average of five bushels more and two yards less. Some members of the community lose, while others gain. Who can say that the increase in satisfaction of the one is greater than the decrease in satisfaction of the other? Or if the changes are evenly distributed, there is still a problem if there are some who vastly prefer cloth over wheat and others with opposite tastes. In this case it is impossible to say that the gain of the wheat devotees outweighs the loss of the cloth addicts. Levels of satisfaction or welfare cannot be compared from one person to another.

These are real difficulties, as we shall see later in our discussion of commercial policy. If one group in the community is better off as a result of some action but others are in a worse position, it is impossible to say how the welfare of the community as a whole has been affected. The change in income distribution where people have different tastes produces a new indifference map whose contours intersect those of the original. But indifference curves are only useful when they do not intersect. Intersecting curves imply that utility level I is sometimes superior to and sometimes inferior to utility level II, an intolerable state of affairs. Despite these difficulties, however, we continue to use indifference curves—although with caution. One basis for so doing is the simplifying assumptions that the tastes of the community can be described by the tastes of an individual, that these are consistent from one period to another, and that there is no change in income distribution. These assumptions are clearly contrary to realism. Another justification used by welfare economists has been the "compensation principle": If it is clear that the beneficiaries of a change in price have enough additional income to compensate (or bribe) the losers for their loss, and some left over, the new position represents an improvement. *If* the compensation actually takes place, there are no losers and the change is unambiguously an improvement (as long as nobody hates to see others gain). Yet losers are seldom compensated, and without the compensation, the principle that an aggregate change is good as long the gainers could (yet don't) compensate the losers is unpersuasive, unless one accepts some explicit value judgments that will be discussed when we return to the gains from trade.

The community indifference curve is thus to be used only with caution and, as we shall see, with the reminder that it is based on value judgments that could yield the same policy conclusions without its use. Yet the community indifference curve is a neat schematic device. Among other things, it provides one way of deriving demand curves and thus determining the prices and quantities that will be involved with or without trade. Let us look first at its use in portraying situations without and with trade, and then at its ability to yield demand curves.

Figure 3.3 uses community indifference curves to summarize in-

FIGURE 3.3
Indifference curves and production possibilities without trade
Wheat
(billions of bushels per year)

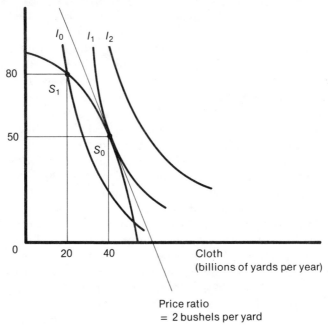

Price ratio
= 2 bushels per yard

formation about tastes, in an economy that does not trade with the rest of the world. In this illustration the United States must be self-sufficient and find the combination of domestically produced wheat and cloth that will maximize community material well-being. Of all the points at which the United States can produce, only S_0 can reach the indifference curve I_1. A point such as S_1 can only yield a lower indifference curve, such as I_0. At S_1 either consumers or producers or both will find that the prevailing price ratio allows them to be better off by moving toward S_0. If the price ratio is temporarily tangent to the production-possibility curve at S_1, consumers will find that this makes cloth look so cheap that they would rather buy more cloth than 20 billion yards and less wheat than 80 billion bushels. Their shift in demand will cause producers to follow suit and shift more resources into cloth production and out of wheat. The tendency to move along the production-possibility curve will persist until the economy produces and consumes at S_0.

As long as increasing costs exist, there will be one and only one such optimizing point. While there is only one production-possibility curve, there is an infinite number of indifference curves which can be drawn representing infinitesimally small increases in real income. If these indifference curves do not intersect, as we assume they do not, any production-possibility curve must produce one point of tangency to a family of indifference curves.

The slope of this tangent at S_0 is the price line. It is also the **marginal rate of substitution in consumption** on the indifference curve and the **marginal rate of transformation** on the production-possibility curve. When the price ratio equals the marginal rate of substitution in consumption, as it does at S_0, consumers are in equilibrium. When the price ratio equals the marginal rate of transformation in production, producers are in equilibrium. When the marginal rate of substitution in consumption equals the marginal rate of transformation in production, without external trade, producers and consumers are both in equilibrium, and markets are cleared at existing prices.

The community indifference curves also offer one way of showing how a given set of tastes interacts with what is known about production possibilities to determine the outcome of opening trade. Figure 3.4A shows how the optimization process allows a nation to reach a higher indifference curve by trading with other nations. Trade brings both the United States and the rest of the world to higher indifference curves at their Points C_1, points determined by tastes and by the requirement that both sides must agree on the same trade bargains. The United States cannot reach just any higher point by trading: there can only be one point like C_1, where the amounts of U.S. cloth imports and wheat exports are also what the rest of the world wants to trade at the same price. To see this, imagine the possibility of a price even flatter (making cloth even cheaper) than the price of one bushel per yard. The United States would be able to reach an even higher (undrawn) indifference curve at such a price, by producing above and to the left of Point S_1 and trading large volumes, in order to consume out beyond

FIGURE 3.4
Two views of the effects of trade
    A. With indifference curves and production-possibility curves

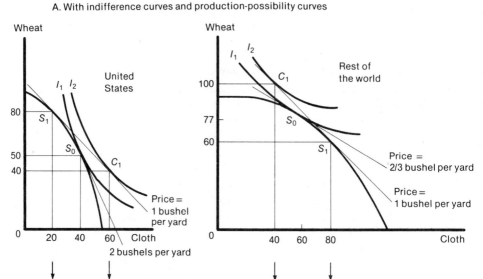

    B. With demand and supply curves again

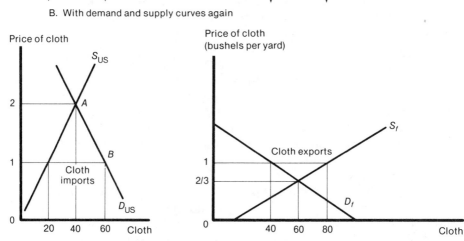

C_1. The catch, however, is that the rest of the world would not want to trade so much at a price ratio that made cloth look cheaper than one bushel per yard. This can be seen by finding the tangency of the new flat price line to the rest of the world's production-possibility and indifference curves on the right-hand side of Figure 3.4A. The result of a price ratio making cloth cheaper than one bushel per yard is closer to S_0, the no-trade point. With the rest of the world wanting so little trade at such a price, the United States would soon have to yield in the marketplace to bring into line the trade desired by both sides. The only equilibrium price would be the unitary price shown in Figure 3.4.

The community indifference curves can also be combined with the production-possibility curves to plot out demand curves for cloth or wheat. A demand curve for cloth is supposed to show how the quantity of cloth demanded responds to its price. To derive the United States demand curve for cloth, start in Figure 3.4A with a price ratio and find how much cloth the United States would be willing and able to consume at that price. At two bushels per yard, the United States is willing and able to consume 40 billion yards a year (at S_0). At one bushel per yard, the United States would consume 60 billion yards (at S_1). These demand points could be replotted in Figure 3.4B, with the prices on the vertical axis. Point S_0 above becomes Point A below; Point C_1 above becomes Point B below; and so forth. The same could be done for the rest of the world. (The demand-curve derivation is like that found in ordinary price-theory textbooks, except that the nation's income constraint takes the form of a production-possibilities surface instead of a fixed-income point.) In this way the handy demand-supply framework can be (though it need not be) derived from community indifference curves plus production-possibility curves.

The theoretical literature on international trade often uses the indifference and production-possibility curves to derive not demand and supply curves but an equivalent known as "offer curve." An offer curve is another way of showing how a nation's offers of exports for imports from the rest of the world depend on international price ratios. A nation's offer curve shows the same information as its export supply or import demand curve. While the offer curve adds nothing not already embodied in demand and supply curves, its frequent use by trade theorists makes it an important device for anyone with a special interest in the theory of international trade. Appendix B shows how an offer curve can be derived and used.

THE GAINS FROM TRADE

All of the devices we have used to show the price and quantity effects of international trade can also be used to show what both sides gain from trade. The community indifference curves in Figure 3.4A allow us to point directly at the gains from trade by comparing indifference curves. We can say that both the United States and the rest of the world gain whatever gain in utility a group gets when moving from I_1 to I_2. This is not very helpful by itself, since levels of community utility are unmeasurable. As long as we rely on the indifference curves themselves to tell us about the gains, we can only make qualitative statements about whether a country gains or loses, not quantitative statements of how much they gain or lose.[1]

Another shortcoming of using the indifference curves to show the gains from trade is that they can only claim to show an effect on aggregate national well-being. As we noted when introducing the indifference curves, this simplification hides the crucial fact that opening trade actually hurts some economic interests while bringing gains to others. Even the quickest glance at the history of trade policy discloses that freer trade is consistently opposed by groups who fear that imports will compete away their incomes and jobs. Any theory of the gains from trade must at a minimum contain a way of quantifying the stake of import-competing groups to see how their stake compares with the effects of freer trade on other groups.

The demand-supply framework allows us to look separately at the effects of freer trade on import-competing producers and on groups who consume but do not produce imports. In practice, of course, many people belong to both groups. U.S. cloth producers also consume cloth, and foreigners who produce wheat in competition with U.S. wheat exports also consume some wheat themselves. Yet people do specialize in production, and nothing is lost or incorrectly assumed away by talking as though the producer and consumer groups were separate.

Figure 3.5 shows what trade means to U.S. cloth producers and to U.S. cloth consumers separately. To understand either set of effects, one must begin by remembering how to interpret demand and supply curves as measures of (private) marginal benefits and costs. Turning first to cloth consumers, we recall that their cloth demand curve shows for any level of cloth purchases per year the maximum amount (of wheat) that somebody in the nation would be willing and able to give up to get an extra yard of cloth per year. A Point A, with 40 billion yards being bought a year, the demand curve is telling us that somebody would be willing to pay as much as two bushels of wheat to get another yard of cloth. That person would not be willing to pay any more than two bushels, and at any higher price of cloth even some of the buyers of the first 40 billion yards would decide that cloth isn't

---

[1] More concrete quantitative measures of the gains can be made on the basis of Figure 3.4A itself. One can convert the gains into units of wheat or cloth by using price ratios to put a nation's consumption into a single dimension. In Figure 3.4A this is done by extending price lines from Points S_0 and C_1 to either axis and comparing the total values in wheat or cloth. For the United States, this procedure shows that at the pretrade price ratio (two bushels per yard), the gains from trade equal 30 billion bushels of wheat a year on the vertical axis, while at the free-trade price of one bushel per yard the U.S. gains in units of wheat come to 10 billion bushels a year. The gains at the average price come to 20 billion bushels a year, the same figure we will get from demand-supply analysis in the text.

FIGURE 3.5
The welfare effects of trade on import consumers, import-competing producers, and the nation as a whole

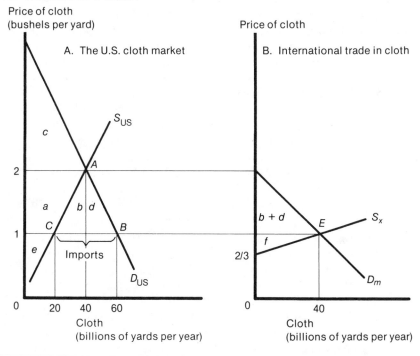

Price of cloth
(bushels per yard)   Price of cloth

A. The U.S. cloth market   B. International trade in cloth

Cloth
(billions of yards per year)

Cloth
(billions of yards per year)

| | Gains from exchanging wheat for cloth | | |
Group	Without international trade	With international trade	Net gain from International trade
U.S. cloth consumers	c	a +b +c +d	a +b +d
U.S. cloth producers	a +e	e	−a (i.e., a loss)
U.S. as a whole .... (cloth consumers plus cloth producers)	c +a +e	a +b +c +d +e	b +d

All of these areas of gain or loss are measured in bushels of wheat per year.

worth the price to them and would stop buying. In this way the demand curve revealed by people's behavior is a private marginal benefits curve, plotting marginal benefits from extra cloth on the vertical axis against the flow of cloth purchases on the horizontal axis. Therefore we can interpret the whole area under the demand curve up to the point of consumption as a measure of what it is worth to cloth consumers to be able to buy cloth at all.

The marketplace does not give cloth away for free, of course. The buyers of cloth must pay the market price, thus losing part of the gains they get from buying cloth. Yet paying the price will not take away all of their gains, except in the case of a price so high that nobody buys. At Point A, without international trade, consumers must pay 80 billion bushels of wheat each year to buy their 40 billion yards of cloth. This means that their net consumer gain from being able to buy cloth is not the whole area under the demand curve, but this minus the 80 billion bushels below the price line paid out to get the cloth. Thus consumers' net gain from buying cloth at all is only area c without international trade. This area of net gain below the demand curve but above the price line is called the **consumer surplus.** The area measures what it is worth to consumers of the product to be able to buy the cloth at a price lower than the prices some of them would be willing and able to pay.

The opening of international trade brings a net gain to cloth consumers. Common sense says that, since trade means lower prices for cloth. The concept of consumers' surplus allows us to quantify what the better price is worth to cloth consumers. At Point B consumers are enjoying all the gains from cloth purchases represented by the whole area under the demand curve out to Point B, and paying only the area under the lower price line, or 60 billion bushels of wheat a year, to get the cloth. This means that with free international trade, the consumers' surplus will equal areas $a + b + c + d$. Thus the opening of trade brought consumers of cloth a net gain of areas $a + b + d$. Remember that this is a gain spread over many people, many of them producers of wheat, but some of them producers of cloth.

Yet the effect of opening trade on cloth producers is quite different. To see why, let us first return to the supply curve and recall that it is a measure of the (private) opportunity cost of producing and selling an extra yard of cloth, as explained in Chapter 2. At Point A without trade, producers are making 40 billion yards a year, and the supply curve tells us that making an extra yard a year would require that two bushels of wheat (on the vertical axis) be given up to provide the extra resources for cloth production. What is true of an extra yard at the 40-billion-yard level of production is also true of each earlier yard: if we add up all of the supply-curve heights to get the total area under the supply curve between 0 and 40 billion, what we have is the total variable cost of all cloth production.

When selling the cloth at Point A without trade, the producers receive revenues equal to price times quantity, or 2 bushels per yard × 40 billion yards = 80 billion bushels per year. After the producers have paid the costs under the supply curve out of these revenues, they are left with the area above the supply curve and below the price line, or areas $a + e$, without trade. This net gain in producer revenue minus cost is often referred to as the **producer surplus**. It is meant to be a measure of what it is worth to producers to be able to sell cloth for wheat.[2] These producers are themselves consumers of both wheat and cloth, and their producer surplus is intended to be added to the consumer surplus in order to judge the net effects of some market change on the two groups together.

As a result of the opening of trade, cloth producers are faced with a lower price for their product. Our theory agrees with common sense that this must mean a loss of income for some people who were producing cloth when trade opened up. The reduction in the income gains from producing cloth is likely to cause some resources to be shifted out of cloth production (and into wheat production). At Point C in Figure 3.5 less cloth is being produced than at Point A. The reason is that the lower price makes it unprofitable to produce the extra yards that added a cost of more than one bushel of wheat for each yard of cloth produced. So at Point C with trade, producers of cloth end up with lower quantities produced and sold as well as with lower prices and lower marginal opportunity costs. Their producer surplus is reduced to area e alone. Allowing free international trade has cost them area a, which is a loss of producer surplus on both the 20 billion yards of cloth that are still produced and on the 20 billion yards that were produced profitably without trade but are now imported instead of being produced domestically.

It must be stressed that Figure 3.5 does not enable us to identify the "producers" who are experiencing these losses of producer surplus from the opening of international trade and the new competition from foreign cloth. If one views the supply curve as the marginal cost curve facing competitive entrepreneurs who face fixed prices for both outputs and inputs, then it is natural to talk as though whatever changes producer surplus affects just these entrepreneurs' profits and not the incomes of the workers or the suppliers of capital in the cloth industry. Taking this approach implicitly assumes that workers and suppliers of capital are completely unaffected by the fortunes of the cloth industry because they can just take their labor and capital elsewhere and earn exactly the same returns. Yet this kind of microeconomic focus is not justified, either by the real world or by the larger model that underlies the demand and supply curves. Though the present diagrams cannot show the entire model of international trade at once, they are based on a general-equilibrium model that shows how trade affects the rates of

---

[2] The producer surplus areas are, more accurately, intended to measure net gains from being producers and sellers of cloth minus some fixed costs of being sellers of cloth at all. These fixed costs are generally ignored, except in our discussion of "displacement costs" late in Chapter 8 and in a footnote to Figure 10.2 in Chapter 10.

pay of productive inputs as well as commodity prices and quantities. As we shall see in Chapter 5 and Appendix C, anything that changes the relative price of a whole sector in our examples, such as the cloth industry, must also change the whole distribution of income within the nation. If, for example, cloth is a labor-intensive industry, then opening trade will tend to bid down the wage rate on labor, since large numbers of cloth-released workers can find work in the less-labor-intensive wheat industry only by bidding down the wage rate of workers in that industry. To repeat, the issue of how trade affects the distribution of income will be taken up later. Now the key point is simply that as the price of cloth drops and the economy moves from Point A to Point C, the producer surplus being lost is a loss to workers and other input suppliers to the cloth industry, not just a loss to cloth-firm entrepreneurs. To know how the change in producer surplus is divided among these groups, one would have to consult the full model that will be completed by the end of Chapter 5 and Appendix C.

If consumers gain areas $a + b + d$ from the opening of trade and producers lose area a, what can we say about the net effect of trade on the United States, which comprises cloth consumers and cloth producers? There is no escaping the basic point that *we cannot compare the welfare effects on different groups without imposing our subjective weights to the economic stakes of each group.* Our analysis allows us to quantify the separate effects on different groups, but it does not tell us how important each group is to us. For example, we can tell from Figure 3.5 that cloth consumers gained 50 billion bushels of wheat (or its cloth equivalent at average prices), the value of the rectangle and triangle that equal areas $a + b + d$. We can also say that the cloth producers lost 30 billion bushels when losing area a. Yet how much of the consumer gain does the producer loss of 30 billion bushels offset in our minds? No theorem or observation of economic behavior can tell us. The result depends entirely on our value judgments. This basic point came up when community indifference curves were introduced, and it returns here in the demand-supply context.

Economists have tended to resolve the matter by imposing the value judgment that we shall call the "one-dollar, one-vote yardstick" here and throughout this book. The yardstick says that one shall measure any dollar of gain or loss equally, regardless of who experiences it. The yardstick implies a willingness to judge trade issues on the basis of their effects on aggregate well-being, without regard to their effects on the distribution of well-being. This does not signify indifference to the issue of distribution. It only means that one considers the distribution well-being to be a matter better handled by compensating those hurt by a change or by using some other non-trade-policy means of redistributing well-being toward those groups (for example, the poor) whose dollars of well-being seem to matter more to us. If the distribution of well-being is handled in one of these ways, trade and trade policies can be judged in terms of simple aggregate gains and losses.

You need not accept this value judgment. You may feel that the stake of, say, cloth producers matters much more to you, dollar for dollar or bushel for bushel, than the stake of cloth consumers in international trade. You might feel this way, for example, if you knew that cloth producers were, in fact, poor unskilled laborers spinning and weaving in their cottages, whereas cloth consumers were rich wheat farmers. And you might also feel that there is no politically feasible way to compensate the poor clothworkers for their income losses from the opening of trade. If so, you may wish to say that each bushel of wheat lost by a cloth producer means five or six times as much to you as each bushel given to cloth consumers, and taking this stand allows you to conclude that opening trade violates your conception of the national interest. Even in this case, however, you could still find the demand-supply analysis useful as a way of quantifying the separate stakes of groups whose interests you weigh unequally.

If the one-dollar, one-vote yardstick is accepted, it gives a clear formula for the net national gains from trade. Let us use bushels of wheat here to measure what will later become "dollars" of purchasing power over all goods and services other than the one being discussed (cloth here). It is clear that if cloth consumers gain areas $a + b + d$ and cloth producers lose area a, then the net national gain from trade must be areas $b + d$, or a triangular area worth 20 billion bushels per year $[= \frac{1}{2} \times$ (imports of $60 - 20$ billion yards) $\times (2 - 1)$ bushels per yard]. It turns out that very little information is needed to measure the net national gain. All that is needed is an estimate of the amount of trade (here represented by the amount of cloth imports) and an estimate of the change in price brought about by trade. With these data, one can measure areas $b + d$ on either side of Figure 3.5.

One can use the same tools to show that the net gains from trade to the rest of the world will equal area f in Figure 3.5B, an area measuring the difference between foreign cloth producers' gains from selling at the higher world price and foreign cloth consumers' losses from this same increase in cloth price. All that is needed to quantify this net effect on the rest of the world is the amount of trade and the effect of trade on foreign prices. The same results can be obtained either from a study of trade in cloth, as here, or from a study of trade in wheat. Since the rest of the world gains area f and the United States gains areas $b + d$, it is clear from the analysis that the world as a whole gains from trade.

In addition to showing that both sides gain in the aggregate from trade, Figure 3.5B shows how the gains are divided internationally. It turns out that the division of the gains depends only on whose prices changed more, since the gains on both sides are tied to the same quantity of trade. In our example, the United States gained more (areas $b + d$ are greater than area f) because trade cut the U.S. price of cloth by a greater percentage of its average level than it raised the foreign price as a percentage of its average level. To know how the gains from international trade are being divided, one should therefore start by investigating whose prices were more affected. The side with the less elastic trade curves (the United States in Figure 3.5B) will gain more. We return to this point when discussing the position of primary-producing countries in world trade, in Chapter 4.

THE TERMS OF TRADE

It is clear that the effects of world trade on production, consumption, and well-being depend heavily on the international price ratios that are established. For this reason economists have paid close attention to the **terms of trade,** or *the ratio of a country's export prices to its import prices.* In our simple wheat-and-cloth examples, the terms of trade for the United States are the price of wheat in yards of cloth per bushel. The terms measure the number of yards of cloth that the United States gets for each bushel of wheat that it exports to foreigners. Conversely, the terms of trade for the rest of the world equal the relative price of their export good, cloth. Our diagrams so far have actually been plotting the terms of trade for the rest of the world, in bushels per yard.

When the concept of the terms of trade is applied to more than one commodity, it must be defined as an index-number measure of the price of exports relative to the price of imports. To calculate the terms of trade from real-world data, one starts with an index of export prices (in units of currency) of the form

$$P_x = \sum_{i\text{'s}} x_i p_i,$$

where x_i is the share of each ("i^{th}") commodity in the total value of exports in a base year, and p_i is the ratio of the current price of the same commodity to its price in the base year. A similar index can be calculated for import prices: let

$$P_m = \sum_{i\text{'s}} m_i p_i,$$

where m_i is the share of each commodity in the total value of imports in a base year, and p_i is defined as above. Such export-price and import-price indices are regularly calculated by national governments and reported by the International Monetary Fund in its monthly *International Financial Statistics*. The terms of trade are then equal to the ratio of the two indices: $T = P_x/P_m$.

It is common practice to speak of a rise in a country's terms of trade as a "favorable" movement in the terms of trade. The idea is that if foreigners pay us a greater quantity of imports for each unit of exports we sell them, we are somehow getting better off. But this does not follow. Looking at the terms of trade alone never gives a good measure of either well-being or the gains from trade, and movements in the terms are correlated with the directions of changes in well-being only under certain circumstances. *If* the terms of trade rise because of changes in foreign behavior, this is indeed favorable. If foreign demand for our exports and foreign supply of our imports shift outward, we do gain more from trade and are indeed better off. But suppose that the terms of trade are being changed by changes in our own behavior. Suppose that the United States, in our examples, finds a much cheaper way of growing wheat and that the extra U.S. supply of wheat exports lowers the price of wheat and the U.S. terms of trade. It does not follow either that the United States is worse off or that the United States is gaining less from trade. The nation may be gaining from its improvements in wheat productivity and also gaining more from trading greater amounts of cheaper wheat. The terms of trade offer important information for welfare conclusions, but must be combined with information about quantities and causes.

DIFFERENT TASTES AS A BASIS FOR TRADE

With the demand side now added to the basic model of international trade, it is easy to see how differences in tastes by themselves could create a basis for mutually advantageous trade, even in a world in which there were no differences among nations in the production possibilities, that is, no differences in supply conditions. This can be shown either with community indifference curves or with demand and supply curves.

Figure 3.6 shows a case in which two countries can produce wheat or rice equally well, having the same production-possibility curves, but have different tastes in grain foods. In the absence of international trade, the preference for bread in Country A (the A indifference curves) leads to a higher price for wheat, through the interaction of demand and supply, than will prevail without trade in the rice-preferring country. The pretrade positions are represented by Points R and S, respectively. Opening trade makes it profitable for somebody to ship wheat to the bread-preferring country in exchange for rice. When

FIGURE 3.6
Trade based solely on differences in tastes

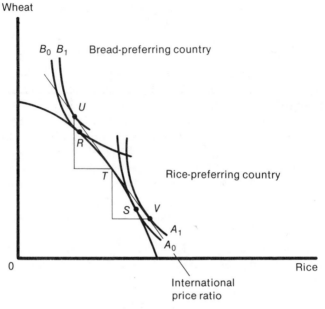

a new equilibrium price ratio is reached through international trade, producers in both countries will shift their production so as to make their marginal costs equal the same international price ratio. Since both countries are assumed to have the same production possibilities, they will both produce at the same point, T. The bread-preferring country will cater to its greater taste for wheat-based bread by importing wheat and reaching the higher indifference curve at Point U. The same trade allows the rice-preferring country to reach higher satisfaction at Point V. In this case, with tastes but not supply differing, trade leads to greater specialization in consumption but less specialization in production. The same result could be shown using demand and supply curves, by giving both countries the same supply curves for production but different demand curves.

MORE COMMODITIES, MORE COUNTRIES

The analysis of this chapter has been limited to two countries and two commodities. There are a number of economists who believe that the analysis is fundamentally altered if it is broadened to include more countries and more commodities. The majority, however, do not accept this view, believing that the two-country, two-commodity analysis is capable of extension, by means of a variety of techniques, to the more intricate and more realistic models.

Given, say, five commodities produced in each of two countries, these can be ranged in order of comparative advantage in each country. Initially one can say only that a country will export the commodity in which it has the largest advantage and import the commodity in which its disadvantage is greatest. The question of whether it will export or import the three commodities between these limits will then depend upon the balance of trade. If the demand for imports of the commodity offering a large disadvantage is very great, the country may have to export all four of the other commodities, given the nature of the foreign demand for them, to balance its accounts.

For most purposes our aggregating all countries but one into "the rest of the world" will serve well enough. Yet this may obscure certain problems rather than illuminate them. Chapter 9 deals with three or more countries in exploring the economics of trade discrimination by country through customs unions and free-trade areas.

SUMMARY

The main effects of international trade can be determined once information about tastes and the demand side has been combined with information about supply. One way of portraying the importance of tastes is to use community indifference curves. Another is to use demand curves, which can be, but need not be, derived from community indifference curves.

Both sides are likely to gain in the aggregate from opening up international trade. Community indifference curves imply this by showing that trade allows each side to reach higher level of aggregate satisfaction. Demand and supply curves reach the same result in a more measurable way, one that allows us to see the separate effects of trade on consumers and producers of the importable good in each country. These welfare effects can be measured by using the devices of consumer and producer surplus, with the warning that it is hard to associate either kind of surplus with a fixed set of people. It turns out that what consumers of the importable good gain from opening trade is clearly greater in value than what the import-competing producers lose. If one is willing to weigh each dollar of gain or loss equally, regardless of who experiences it, then the net national gains from trade equal a simple measurable function of the volume of trade created and the change in prices caused by trade.

Although both sides are likely to gain from international trade, the gains are divided between nations in a way that depends on whose price ratios change more. More is gained from trade by the country whose terms of trade (or ratio of export prices to import prices) change more. Differences in tastes can themselves be a basis for mutually advantageous trade. If a country differs from the rest of the world in taste patterns but not in production capabilities, trade will lead to some international specialization in consumption but not in production.

SUGGESTED READING

Texts

For a less rigorous but readable survey emphasizing the history of early trade theory, see Paul T. Ellsworth and J. Clark Leith, *The International Economy*, 5th ed. (New York: Macmillan, 1975). For alternative presentations using the traditional Meade geometry to portray the Heckscher-Ohlin model, see Herbert G. Grubel, *International Economics* (Homewood, Ill.: Richard D. Irwin, 1977); and Richard E. Caves and Ronald W. Jones, *World Trade and Payments* (Boston: Little Brown, 1974).

Treatises, etc.

For a survey of the development of international trade theory with an extensive bibliography, see Jagdish Bhagwati's survey in the March 1964 *Economic Journal*, reprinted with an addendum in his *Trade, Tariffs, and Growth* (Cambridge, Mass.: MIT Press, 1969).

The complete general-equilibrium model has been given all sorts of statements. A useful one in prose is Bertil Ohlin's *Interregional and International Trade* (Cambridge, Mass.: Harvard University Press, 1933; rev. ed., 1967). chaps. 5–7 and 13. The theory is presented mathematically in J. L. Mosak, *General Equilibrium Theory in International Trade* (Bloomington, Ind.: Principia Press, 1944). A linear programming solution to comparative advantage is given in Robert Dorfman, Paul A. Samuelson, and Robert M. Solow, *Linear Programming and Economic Analysis* (New York: McGraw-Hill, 1958), chap. 5 and especially pp. 117–121.

On extending the model to more than two factors of production and two commodities, see the papers by Ronald W. Jones and by Jaroslav Vanek and Trent Bertrand, in Jagdish N. Bhagwati et al., *Trade, Balance of Payments, and Growth.*

The technical literature is enormous, and cannot be cited here. In addition to works mentioned here and in Appendixes A and B, see two seminal collections: American Economic Association, *Readings in the Theory of International Trade* (Homewood, Ill.: Richard D. Irwin, 1949); and American Economic Association, *Readings in International Economics* (Homewood, Ill.: Richard D. Irwin, 1967).

Points

The present interpretation of the consumer and producer surplus concepts has been influenced by E. J. Mishan, "What is Producer Surplus?" *American Economic Review,* vol. 58, no. 5 (December 1968), pp. 1269–82; and Robert Willig, "Consumer Surplus without Apology," *American Economic Review,* vol. 66, no. 4 (September 1976), pp. 589–97.

Excerpts from classical writings are presented in William R. Allen, *International Trade Theory: Hume to Ohlin* (New York: Random House, 1965).

J. B. Condliffe, *The Commerce of Nations* (New York: Norton, 1950), gives an excellent account of the development of laissez-faire in the 19th century which makes useful supplementary reading. See especially chaps. 6–8 and 13.

The teacher who wants to illustrate the theory of comparative advantage in practice is referred to G. D. M. MacDougall's essay in American Economic Association, *Readings in International Economics;* B. Balassa, "An Empirical Demonstration of Classical Comparative Costs," *Review of Economics and Statistics,* August 1963; and Robert M. Stern, "British and American Productivity and Comparative Costs in International Trade," *Oxford Economic Papers,* October 1962. An attempt to apply the theory to reality is set out in chaps. 3–5 of C. P. Kindleberger, *Foreign Trade and the National Economy* (New Haven: Yale University Press, 1962).

QUESTIONS FOR REVIEW

1. Be sure you know how to interpret exports and imports as the flows that separate what a nation produces from what it consumes. In diagrams like those in Figure 3.4A, make sure that you can point to the exports and imports of each country.

2. Can you derive the demand and supply curves for wheat from the diagrams in Figure 3.4A?

3. What is consumer surplus? What is producer surplus? What are the terms of trade? Can you list the information you would need to measure each of these concepts from real-world data?

4

Economic growth and changes in trade

The world keeps changing. If we are to understand how the patterns and effects of trade flows change over time in a growing world economy, we need to extend the trade theory of Chapters 2 and 3 to include testable hypotheses about what happens as all the relevant curves shift over time. Economists have already provided several hypotheses about how demand and supply conditions drift over time, and how these changes affect trade and the effects of trade on welfare. These dynamic theories are the subject of this chapter.

We shall note ways in which both theories and facts about the dynamics of growth and trade can be aligned with a simple model of trade. The basic trade model involving two goods and two countries or regions can be given extra working parts that allow it to look something like both the more imaginative theories of trade dynamics introduced here and the facts that inspired those theories. We wish to stress that the resemblance between the basic trade model, suitably modified, and the facts of trade dynamics does not *prove* that the simple trade model makes either correct assumptions or correct predictions. The real world is always more complex than any simple model. The simple model is being offered as a useful parable, a likely analogy to the real world. In showing conclusions that follow rigorously within the assumptions of the simple, the theorist is posing an "as if" question: Don't the available facts suggest that the real world operates *as if* the same forces affecting trade and its welfare effects in the simple model are operating in the same way in the more complicated real world? It is in this spirit of suggesting a resemblance between a model and a more complicated world, without being able to prove rigorously that the real causes and effects of trade are those highlighted in the model, that we compare theory and fact in this chapter and throughout Part I.

SHIFTS IN DEMAND

Many observers have noted that tastes and demand patterns seem to change in systematic ways with the growth of production and trade. Let us look first at a way in which trade itself may trigger changes in tastes, and then at two ways in which economic growth affects demand patterns and therefore trade patterns.

It is possible that opening trade itself has an effect on tastes that can be captured only by explicitly modifying the model of Chapter 3. Our earlier analysis of the opening of trade between two countries that had never traded before predicates a gain from trade on the existence of fixed tastes unchanged by the fact of newly opened trade. This, of course, is highly unrealistic. Trade has many origins—the exchange of gifts between primitive tribes; the plundering of the Middle East by Europeans during the Crusades or of Europe by Scandinavian pirates; and the opening of the western hemisphere by Spanish, Portuguese, and English explorers. In most historical origins of trade, the initial exchanges involved the creation of new wants, as well as their satisfaction. Tastes change with trade, even as trade satisfies existing wants more fully.

The point has significance beyond recalling the origin of cotton, muslin, sugar, and even tariffs as Arabic words, or the introduction of tobacco, rum, and the potato from North America to Europe. Ragnar Nurkse has pointed to the **demonstration effect** under which underdeveloped countries have learned about the existence of goods in developed nations which will lighten their burdens, satisfy their physical appetites, and titillate their innate sense of self-expression or exhibitionism. When modern methods of production are introduced into some particularly primitive societies, it is necessary to introduce modern methods of consumption. With the initiation of plantation cultivation of fruit, sugar, rubber, tea, and the like, there must come a change in the diet of native laborers, and the varied native subsistence fare must be replaced by staple imported foodstuffs. With the alteration in the pattern of living, there may be a worsening in the nutritional level of the diet and increased dietary deficiencies.

When the price of exports rises with trade or that of imports falls, with all tastes and means of production unchanged, trade may be said to result in an unambiguous gain for a country as a whole, leaving aside the distribution of the gain within the country and the difficulties inherent in measuring the extent of the gain. But when the improvement in the terms of trade is accompanied by a shift in tastes in favor of imports, leading to an increase in demand for them, the case is not so clear. One can say that there is an improvement, as compared with the hypothetical case of increasing the demand for imports without satisfying it. A new want coming into existence along with trade to fill it, however, involves a departure from the classical assumptions and raises doubts as to the classical conclusion of gain. It is not easy to quantify the bargain that trade offers by selling people imports for less than they would willingly pay for them if we try to measure the gains according to the pretrade situation in which people never had or demanded those goods.

It is hard to say how important the demonstration effect is, for the simple reason that it is hard to separate this effect from the ordinary response of demand to better availability of imports, which acts just like an ordinary drop in price. Yet there is some crude qualitative evidence that the demonstration effect is stronger today than, say, before World War I. To take what may seem to be a trivial example but one that is of some importance for international trade, international exchanges increased greatly in the 19th century without bringing about any substantial homogeneity of taste in dress, diet, consumer goods, or cultural pursuits. Such is less and less true. Trade in Europe in the 19th century continued side by side with different styles of national diet and cooking: the British breakfast was distinct from the continental breakfast, and on the Continent itself Italian, French, German, and Scandinavian cooking all differed. Today in Japan, rice is increasingly abandoned in favor of wheat; and Coca-Cola is a trademark known round the world. While the demonstration effect is more significant for underdeveloped countries, even among developed countries the changes in taste which come with the introduction of new goods are significant, as the shift in American taste toward European products such as small cars demonstrates. And technological changes, of course, bring new tastes along with them. As often said, not only is necessity the mother of invention, but invention is the mother of necessity.

A second systematic pattern relating economic growth to shifts in demand and therefore to trade is **Engel's Law,** named after the 19th-century German economist Ernst Engel. Engel's Law says that if demographic variables (family size and composition) are held constant, a rise in income will lower the share of consumer expenditures spent on food. Of all the "laws" that have been tested by economists, this is the most firmly established. It shows up whether we are comparing the behavior of individual households or the behavior of several nations or the behavior of one nation over time. It means that as per capita incomes grow with economic growth, demand should shift increasingly against food producers with the lowest income elasticities of demand, especially producers of grain and other "staples." Engel's Law is a statement about how a fixed set of tastes tends to lead to lower expenditure shares on food as incomes increase. It is not, strictly speaking, an assertion that tastes, represented by the whole set of indifference curves, are shifting.

Engel's Law implies that if productivity grows at the same rate in all industries, the resulting income growth will shift demand against food and cause the price of food to drop on world markets relative to the prices of luxuries, including most manufactured goods. This may seem clear enough on the basis of common sense. It could be shown using the diagrams of Chapter 3 as well. In terms of production-possibility curves and community indifference curves, one can show that the relative price of food in international trade is likely to drop if all production-possibility curves expand with no change in shape, yet the indifference curves favor consumption points farther and farther from the food axis for any given price ratio. The same point emerges from demand-supply diagrams, where Engel's Law can be represented by equal percentage shifts to the right in all supply curves accompanied by a smaller outward shift in the food demand curves and a larger outward shift in demand for luxuries, again yielding a drop in the relative price of food. We shall look at the evidence on food price trends later in this chapter, when discussing the trade trends of primary-producing countries.

The final argument about how economic growth affects tastes and trade is an imaginative one advanced by the Swedish economist and politician Staffan Burenstam Linder. Linder's **representative-demand** hypothesis draws causal arrows from income to tastes to technology to trade as follows: a rise in per capita incomes shifts a nation's representative-demand pattern toward luxuries that the nation can now afford, as Engel's Law also implied; this new concentration of demand on affordable luxury manufactures causes producers to come up with even more impressive improvements in the technology of supplying those goods in particular; their gains in productivity actually outrun the rises in demand that caused them, leading the nation to export those very goods at lower prices. Linder's argument does not rest on any one explicit set of assumptions, but would be helped along if there were economies of scale or of learning by doing in luxury manufacturing. His view has not yet received a definitive test. Its prediction of exports and lower prices for representative-demand goods fit the rough look of the automobile market, where nations tend to export the types of autos most appropriate to the income levels in their own economies. It also prepares us for the possibility that luxury manufactures may become increasingly cheap even though income growth shifts demand toward them.

FACTOR GROWTH

Factor endowments tend to grow, contrary to the static assumption of fixed endowments that was used in Chapters 2 and 3. To show the different possible effects of factor-supply growth on trade, it is convenient to assume for the moment that tastes and technology are fixed, whereas factor endowments grow. Capital and population are the factors that grow. Land presumably does not, and may even shrink through depletion (although this statement, like so many general statements, is subject to qualification: land can expand in an economic sense through changes in technology which may make old ore deposits useful, for example, and through capital investment, as in reforestation and in new discovery, which seems to have run its course on this terrestrial globe but may not have so far as the universe is concerned). Suppose that we start with the simple case of a two-country, two-commodity, two-factor model, based on capital and labor, where capital and labor grow in the same proportion, with technology and tastes fixed.

It is intuitively evident, and can be demonstrated with the geometry of Appendix A, that with an equal expansion of the two factors and no change in technology, the production-possibility curve will be expanded by pushing out evenly in all directions. In Figure 4.1, the production-possibility curve $A-B$ will now become $A'-B'$. But what happens to trade and the terms of trade? The answer, like the answer to every question in economics at this level of generality, is, "It depends." But this answer is not enough to satisfy the teacher, and the student must go on to explain what it depends on. It depends on the nation's tastes and on the foreigners' trade curves (export supply and import demand).

In Figure 4.1, let the triangle $T-P-C$ represent trade before factor growth, with exports, $T-P$, being exchanged for imports, $C-T$, at the terms of trade, $P-C$. P is the production point, and C the consumption point. The operational trick is to find out what happens to production and consumption with growth, at the original terms of trade. If it turns out that the country wants to trade more at the old terms of trade, it is likely that it is going to have to accept a lower price for its exports and to pay more for its imports. If, on the other hand, it wants to trade less, again at the original terms of trade, the outcome is likely to be the reverse: a higher price for exports and cheaper imports.

Since the growth of the production-possibility curve has been uniform, the production point P' on the new production-possibility curve

FIGURE 4.1
Effect of neutral expansion of the production-possibility curve on trade

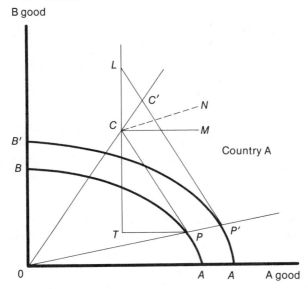

A'–B' will lie on a straight-line ray from the origin O–P, which intersects A'–B' at P'. This is the result of the underlying linear homogeneous production functions, P'–C', and the assumed unchanged terms of trade. The question now is what happens to demand. If a right angle such as L–C–M is drawn with its origin at C, increased income from increased overall output will mean that the demand for both the A-good and the B-good expand, unless one of them is an inferior good. If we rule out inferior goods, the new consumption point has to lie within the triangle L–C–M. A neutral assumption is that the income elasticity of demand for the two goods is unity, that is, that at the same price, goods A and B will be consumed in exactly the same proportions with the enlarged income as with the smaller. This possibility would put the new consumption point on a straight-line ray from the origin through C. With this assumption it is now clear what will happen: line segment P'–C' is parallel to and longer than P–C, which means that at the same terms of trade as before, the country would want to offer more of commodity A for more of commodity B.

But there is no need for demand to be homothetic, as the condition of consumption in fixed proportions with expanding income and constant price is called. If the path of consumption with increasing income but constant prices, the so-called **Engel's curve** (of which there is one curve for every possible price), through C is steeper than C–C', demand favors the import good. With the demand for the B-good income elastic, A will want to trade even more than the amounts of exports and imports implicit in the length and slope of $P'-C'$, and the market-clearing terms of trade, assuming that A faces a B offer curve of less than infinite elasticity, will deteriorate still more. Indeed, the Engel's curve can favor the export good for a bit, and A will still want to trade more of the A-good for more of the B-good because its expansion of production possibilities for the A-good exceeds its demand bias in favor of it. If a dotted line $C-N$ is drawn exactly parallel to $P-P'$ in Figure 4.1, and if the Engel's curve follows this line, A will want to trade the same amount before growth as after, and the terms of trade will remain unchanged. If the curve falls below the line, demand favors the export good more than export production possibilities have grown. But if the Engle curve cuts $P'-L$ curve anywhere above $C-N$, the terms of trade will decline, provided that the foreign trade curves are not infinitely elastic, or flat lines.

Of course, there is no need for the production-possibility curve to expand neutrally, pushing out symmetrically along its whole length. If the A-good is capital intensive, and capital grows but not labor, the production-possibility curve will evidently grow in an export-biased fashion, as in Figure 4.2A. Or the factor which is intensively used in the import industry may be the one with the only or the greater expansion, as in Figure 4.2B. Note that growth can now be more than merely **export or import biased**. In Figure 4.2A a right angle set with its origin at P marks the boundaries within which growth can be defined to be import biased, neutral, or export biased. But on the production side,

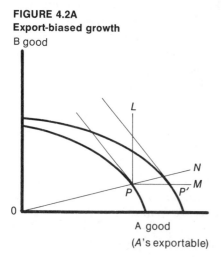

FIGURE 4.2A
Export-biased growth
B good

A good
(A's exportable)

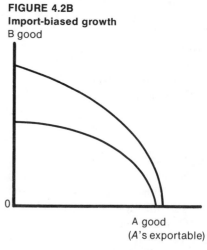

FIGURE 4.2B
Import-biased growth
B good

A good
(A's exportable)

the tangency of the old price line to the new production-possibility curve can lie outside these limits, as at P', where growth is **ultra– export biased**. This occurs when, with new production possibilities and the old trading price, the country will produce not only more of the export good but positively less of the import good. Growth now has a good chance to worsen the terms of trade (here P_A/P_B). And ultra-import-biased growth (not shown in Figure 4.2B) may well improve the terms of trade.

The pattern, then, is that the more factor growth tends to occur in factors of production associated with export lines, the greater the likelihood that this growth will bid down the country's terms of trade. Conversely, the more factor growth favors import lines, the more it will tend to bid down the relative price of *im*ports, raising the country's terms of trade. The effect on the terms of trade depends, to repeat, on the country's income elasticity of demand and on the foreign demand and supply conditions.

This theoretical framework has some applications to real-world issues. One application is its ability to shed light on the claim by less developed countries that investing their private and public resources in expanding export capacity backfires by reducing the terms of trade. This argument is believed to have particular relevance to countries exporting primary products, which are thought to face inelastic foreign demand and volatile price responses to shifts in their supply. The argument makes theoretical sense. Private individuals may overinvest in expanding the supply of land, capital, and labor to export industries, because each individual (rightly) acts as though his own investments in the export industry have no effect on its world price. Governments may also overinvest capital in the export lines if their benefit-cost calculations do not recognize an effect of this supply expansion on export prices. We shall expand on the theoretical basis for this suspicion about export promotion when examining the case of "immiserizing growth."

A second application of this portrayal of factor growth and trade is its ability to show the evolving position of the United States with regard to natural resource products. Land, as already indicated, is a complex factor of production. In a given state of the arts, land can be increased by discovery or reduced by depletion, or, simultaneously, both. But land, like every other factor, can only be defined in terms of a technological process. An innovation will expand or contract the amount of land viewed as an economic agent. Land bearing low-grade taconite ores became an economic resource only after the taconite refining process was discovered.

It is hard to know whether, in the economic history of the United

States since the Civil War, land has been an expanding, a fixed, or a contracting factor. For some purposes, such as oil production, land was enormously abundant and is now relatively scarce. In other minerals, depletion has exhausted the richest deposits. But discoveries and improvements in technology continue. Drilling for oil takes place in the continental shelf in the Gulf of Mexico, offshore in the Pacific, on the North Slope in Alaska, and is planned, or threatened, off Georges Bank in the Atlantic. Improvements in refinery techniques have just about reached the point where it will pay to extract oil from the abundant shales of the Rocky Mountain area. Land, the "fixed" factor, is seen to be subject to all sorts of changes.

By any plausible measure, the supply of land has grown more slowly than the supplies of labor and (especially) skills and nonhuman capital across the 20th century. The faster growth of capital and labor supplies has changed the nature of comparative advantage for the United States. The United States used to be an exporter of a wide variety of metals and minerals. Now it is a net importer of all but two—coal and molybdenum. Copper, zinc, lead, iron, and especially oil, which we used to export, are now on a net import basis. Figure 4.3 shows a stereotyped representation of the nature of the change. The vertical axis measures land-intensive goods; the horizontal axis, on the other hand, represents the goods embodying primarily labor and capi-

FIGURE 4.3
Schematic representation of the change in U.S. land-intensive commodities from comparative advantage to comparative disadvantage

Land - intensive mineral products

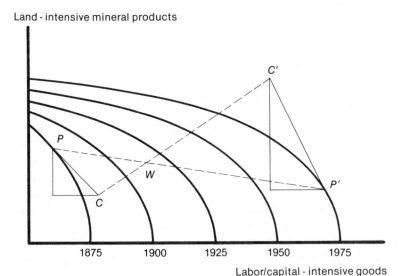

Labor/capital - intensive goods

tal. The inner production-possibility curve, marked 1875, shows a strong specialization in land-intensive production, which is in part exchanged for labor/capital-intensive goods. With the passage of time, the shape of the production-possibility curve changes. Land is fixed, and capital and labor grow. Production possibilities in the land-intensive product increase somewhat, as more capital and labor will produce more land-intensive products even with land unchanged. But the production-possibility curve grows mainly to the right. By 1920, as the figure is drawn, the production-possibility curve is fairly balanced on the scales shown. By 1950, it is skewed in favor of labor/capital-intensive products in place of its original skewness in the opposite direction.

The dotted line $P-P'$ represents the locus of points of tangency to the successive production-possibility curves, where production has taken place. $C-C'$ signifies the path of consumption. To the left of the intersection, that is, prior to about 1920 as shown on the figure, land-intensive products were exported and labor/capital-intensive products imported. After 1920 or thereabouts, when the curves intersect, the trade position was reversed. The United States exported labor/capital-intensive products and imported the products of land.

This representation is, of course, purely schematic. It departs from reality in a hundred ways—two goods, constant technology, a fixed factor, incomplete specialization, and so forth. The problems of defining land-intensive products make it impossible to pin down when the change from an export to an import basis occurred in minerals. It probably took place more nearly after World War II than after World War I. Nonetheless, the demonstration has validity in a very broad sense and helps illustrate how comparative advantages change with factor growth.

TECHNOLOGICAL PROGRESS—MAKING OLD GOODS MORE CHEAPLY

The analysis of technological change in existing goods follows much the same lines as the analysis of factor growth. Technological progress in existing industries represents reductions in input-output ratios. If there were a 10 percent rise in the amount of output produced with given amounts of factor inputs, this 10 percent rise in the productivity of all the factors of production is equivalent to a 10 percent rate of growth in all the factors, with the proviso that with the technological progress each factor ends up getting paid 10 percent more per unit of factor input. The effect of such a neutral expansion in the productivity of all factors on the terms of trade is the same as the effect of an equal expansion in all factor endowments: the country is likely to have to give up some of its potential gain from greater technological efficiency through lower terms of trade, unless it faces fixed world prices or unless its own demand patterns are biased in an offsetting way.

Biased technological progress, like biased factor growth, is more complex. If a technological change reduces unit labor units by 10 percent but reduces unit capital inputs by only 4 percent, technological progress is laborsaving. It has the same effects on prices, output, and factor rewards as a 10 percent growth in the labor supply and a 4 percent growth in the capital supply. The effects of biased technological progress on international trade cover the same range of possibilities as does unbalanced factor growth. If biased progress in the export good augments the abundant factor, this will lead to export-biased growth, in fact to ultra-export-biased growth, since two are tendencies working to expand exports. And biased technological growth in the import-competing good which augments the scarce factor will lead to ultra-import-biased growth. In between there are evidently a variety of intermediate cases, such as growth in the import sector which saves the abundant factor, or growth in the export sector which augments the scarce factor, where one cannot say much without the specific data.

THE CASE OF IMMISERIZING GROWTH

Our analysis of factor growth and technological progress in the presence of trade has shown that growth and progress can raise or lower trade, and raise or lower a nation's terms of trade (export price relative to import price), depending on a number of conditions. The same analysis warns us of a further paradoxical possibility, namely the possibility of *immiserizing growth,* an expansion of factor supply or productivity that makes the growing and trading country worse off.

The possibility of immiserizing growth, which was underlined by Jagdish N. Bhagwati, is not a reference to the neo-Malthusian vision of the ecological limitations of economic growth. Rather, it hinges on the simple fact that improvements in the ability to supply some goods already being exported tend to lower their price on world markets, perhaps badly enough to make the growth damaging. Figure 4.4 illustrates the case of immiserizing growth. It imagines that Brazil has expanded its capacity to grow coffee beans more rapidly than it has expanded its manufacturing capacity. For any given terms of trade (international price ratio), this would make Brazil desire to supply much more coffee in exchange for more manufactures. But because Brazil already has a large share of the world coffee market and because the demand for coffee in other countries is price inelastic, Brazil's expansion of coffee supply bids down the world price. And the way

Figure 4.4 shows it, this adverse effect on Brazil's terms of trade is so severe that Brazil's own improvements in supply capacity actually make it worse off, dropping it to a lower indifference curve at the consumption Point C_1. It may seem foolish for a nation to undergo an expansion that makes it worse off. Yet it must be remembered that the expansion was undertaken, both in this model and in Brazilian history, by many small competitive farmers, each of whom rightly assumed that *his own* coffee expansion had no effect on the world price. Individual rationality can add up to collective irrationality.

FIGURE 4.4
A case of immiserizing growth in a trading country

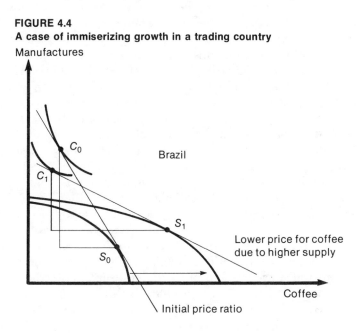

What conditions are necessary for immiserizing growth to occur? Three seem crucial: (1) the country's growth must be biased toward the export sector; (2) the foreign demand for the country's exports must be price inelastic, so that an expansion in export leads to a large drop in price; and (3) the country must already be heavily dependent on trade for the welfare meaning of the drop in the terms of trade to be great enough to offset the gains from being able to supply more. Brazil might have been in this situation with its coffee expansion before the 1930s, when it already had a large enough share of the world coffee market to face an inelastic demand for its exports, although this possibility has not been tested quantitatively. It is not likely that many other less developed countries face the same case, especially where their exports of modern manufactures are concerned, since they typically have too small a share of world-markets to face inelastic demand curves for their exports. Immiserizing is a possibility, though, and it brings an extreme result: not only does export expansion bring a lower rate of return to society than do other kinds of growth, but it even brings a negative social return.

THE TRADE POSITION OF PRIMARY-PRODUCT EXPORTERS

The case of immiserizing growth illustrates the point that simply expanding trade and following the dictates of comparative advantage can backfire under certain conditions. Such doubts about the wisdom of comparative advantage have been expanded into a whole challenge to orthodoxy by economists and politicians in countries exporting primary products (agricultural products and minerals). This challenge was sounded by Argentine economist Raúl Prebisch and others in the early 1960s. They argued in general that primary-exporting countries, particularly those that were less developed, were not gaining and would not gain from expanding their agricultural and mineral exports. Their policy recommendation was that less developed countries should concentrate more resources on expanding their modern industry and less resources on expanding output and exports in their primary sectors. One concrete policy recommendation was to restrict imports of industrial goods into less developed countries and to replace such imports with domestic industrial goods. Another was to seek a reduction in the barriers of industrial countries to imports of manufactured goods from less developed countries. These recommendations will be examined in more detail in Chapter 11.

The argument that primary-product exporters gain little or even lose from expanding their agricultural and mineral exports consists of the following more specific arguments:

1. The initial opening of trade in a less developed country brings less benefit to that country than to the industrial countries which purchase its new primary-product exports.
2. The terms of trade have worsened, and will continue to worsen, for primary-product exporters. If governments can see this downward trend more clearly than can private decision-makers, governments should discourage the investment of more resources into primary production and should favor investments in industry.
3. Expanding primary-production capacity (for example, planting more coffee trees) makes the terms of trade worse than they would otherwise be. An extreme form of this argument if the contention that "immiserizing growth" prevails. Again, the policy implication

is that government should discourage investments in primary production and should favor industry.
4. In addition, industry should be favored over primary products because industry gives side benefits in the form of the spread of modern technical knowledge and modern attitudes.

These arguments are certainly not implausible, and they deserve to be tested. It is possible to combine our basic trade model and real-world observation to test them. We shall defer comment on the fourth argument until Chapter 11. The third argument, as was suggested above in connection with "immiserizing growth," may hold for large countries like Brazil, but it is not likely to hold for many smaller less developed countries exporting primary products in a large world market. We turn here to the evidence on the first two arguments, the ones relating to the opening of trade and the subsequent trends in the terms of trade.

The gains from opening trade

When trade has been opened in previously isolated countries, most of the gains have usually accrued to persons and enterprises operating in those countries. This conclusion has very different social meanings, however, in different settings. Two Asian examples of the opening of trade seem to have given a socially benign result. When Thailand opened trade with the outside world in the 1850s, price relationships changed much more dramatically within Thailand than in the rest of the world. The price of rice, Thailand's newly booming export, rose greatly relative to that of cloth and other importables on Bangkok markets, but its relative price was not greatly affected in Singapore or Calcutta or London. Our analysis of the gains from trade suggests that most of these gains must have accrued to Thai rice farmers. Thus, the main gainers were a rural lower-income unskilled group, who responded by clearing more of the country's abundant land for cultivation.

The opening of trade had similar effects on Japan in the 1850s and 1860s. Forced to allow expanded trade with the outside world, Japan responded by exporting large amounts of silk and tea in exchange for rice and manufactures. The relative prices of silk and tea shot up within Japan, though they were apparently affected little in the rest of the world. The analysis of the gains from trade suggests that the gains went mainly to the Japanese producers of silk and tea. As in the Thai case, these tended to be rural lower-income families, whose women and children cultivated and spun the silk.

In other cases the same tendency of the gains to concentrate in the newly trading country had a very different social meaning. Often the gainers were citizens of powerful industrial countries who controlled land and mining rights in the newly trading country. The ownership and profits from Chilean nitrate exports in the late 19th century fell into the hands of British and American entrepreneurs, whose interests were furthered by British and American pressures on Chile to give these entrepreneurs, in effect, Chile's gains from trade. During the early history of the development of Mideast oil, more of the gains from exports accrued to the international oil companies than accrued to the exporting nations. And even the classic Ricardian example of comparative advantage, in which Portugal was better off exporting wine in exchange for British cloth, is less impressive as a policy argument inasmuch as Portugal was forced by British power and treaties to specialize in wine export without encouraging manufactures that would compete with imports from Britain.

TRENDS IN THE TERMS OF TRADE FOR PRIMARY-PRODUCT EXPORTERS

Raúl Prebisch and others have repeatedly argued that the prices received for primary products in international trade have been declining and unstable. These contentions have been used to underscore the unfairness of the way in which world markets distribute income, with less developed exporters of primary products allegedly playing the role of the most disadvantaged.

Many economists have now investigated this issue, and Figure 4.5 presents some of their calculations of the terms of trade over long stretches of time. Each series plotted there is a relative-price index, dividing a price index for some primary products by a price index for the manufactured goods and (in some series) services traded for the primary products internationally. An upward trend means more expensive primaries, a "favorable" trend in the terms of trade for the exporters of agricultural and mineral products. Let us first note what the series say when taken at face value. We shall then turn to possible biases in these series, and to the task of interpreting the results.

Series like those in Figure 4.5 reveal some historical fluctuations, as well as trends, in the terms of trade. The Great Depression of the 1930s stands out as an era in which exporters of agricultural and mineral products took a beating on the relative-price front. For them the depression came in this relative-price form, whereas the industrial countries, where prices were less flexible downward, took their losses mainly in the form of unemployment and lost output. The Korean War era, like the eras of the two world wars, for which data are not available

FIGURE 4.5
The terms of trade for primary-product exporters, 1871–1976

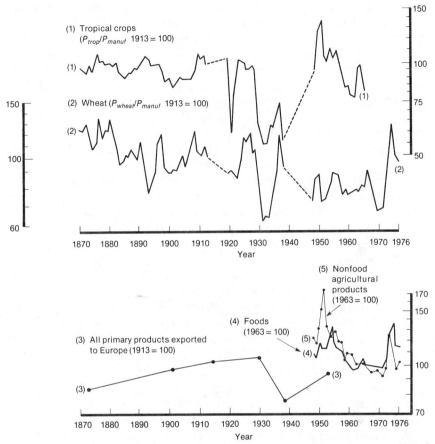

Each series plots an index of the ratio of primary-product export prices to the export prices of manufactured goods. The series are computed from prices, usually in dollars, in the United States and Europe. The figures for 1976 refer only to the first three quarters of the year. A series for the relative prices of metal ores, not plotted here, behaved like that for foods after 1948.

Sources: Series (1) and (2), 1871–1965: W. Arthur Lewis, *Aspects of Tropical Trade, 1883–1965* (Stockholm: Almqvist and Wiksell 1969), table 10. Series (3): Charles P. Kindleberger, *The Terms of Trade: A European Case Study* (New York: Wiley, 1956), p. 259. All other: International Monetary Fund, *International Financial Statistics;* and United Nations, Department of Economic and Social Affairs, *Monthly Bulletin of Statistics,* various issues.

here, was one of boom for primary producers. It was in the Korean War years that the United States had one of its greatest waves of fear about running out of raw materials. From the end of the Korean War to about 1970, most primary products suffered a moderate relative-price decline. In 1973–74, at the height of the oil crisis that brought the OPEC victory, all primary-product prices shot up relative to the prices of manufactures. This brief boom was apparently due to a mixture of bad harvests, some cartel successes (for example, in bauxite), and considerable speculation that a new era of scarce primary products had arrived. The boom was reversed, but only in part, by 1976.

The series in Figure 4.5 show only a gentle downward trend in the terms of trade for primary-product exporters in the long run. This trend differs with the primary commodities chosen. The primary with the most severe downward trend—not shown separately here, though it is part of the tropical group in Series (1)—is natural rubber, which has experienced a serious price drop over the half century from 1920 to 1970. Another product with an apparently declining relative price in world trade is wheat, exported by the United States, Canada, Argentina, and Australia. Series (2) implies that the volume of manufactures that could be bought in world trade by selling a bushel of wheat has dropped by about 25 percent over 105 years—not a severe decline, but a noticeable one. Other primary products have clearly risen in relative price. The most obvious case, of course, is that of oil and other fossil fuels, whose relative prices reached unprecedented levels in 1974. Forest products have also risen in relative price since 1900, both within the United States and in international trade. Other primary products, on the whole, showed no clear trend.

These price series probably understate the "favorable" (upward) trend in primary prices, for three reasons. First, the prices were gathered in Europe and North America, not in the primary-exporting countries. Transport costs have been persistently falling as a percentage of the value of trade. This has meant that the prices actually received by the primary-exporting countries improved relative to the prices paid by industrial countries. Similarly, the decline of transport markups also lowered the import prices of industrial goods in primary-exporting countries faster than these data, gathered in the industrial countries, reflect. Second, the underlying price figures are biased because they fail to reflect quality improvements in manufactures. Machinery exports were in some cases priced per ton of machine weight, ignoring the obvious improvements in the economic value of the machines per ton. This means that the prices of manufactures of given quality were dropping faster, and the terms of trade for primary-product exporters improving faster, than these series show. Finally, new manufactures have fallen in price to a greater extent than the series underlying Figure 4.5 can measure. When radios, for example, first went onto international markets they initially fell quite a bit in price as costs were cut in the newly emerging industry. Yet they were not introduced into the price indexes until some time after their initial entry into international trade. Thus much of their cheapening escaped measurement, again understating the declines in manufactured-good prices and also understating the improvement in the terms of trade for primary-product exporters. Although these three biases are hard to quantify, it seems likely that eliminating them from the price series would leave us with revised measures showing no real decline, and probably a gentle rise, in the terms of trade for primary-product exporters.

If the trends in the terms of trade have not really been unfavorable to primary-product exporters, except exporters of natural rubber and possibly wheat, how can we explain this result? And is it consistent with the relative poverty of many third-world primary-exporting countries? Although economists have not resolved all the problems of explaining what happened to primary-product prices, part of the explanation is at hand. It seems clear that the severe fall in natural rubber prices was due to the ability of the industrial countries to discover a whole chain of cost-cutting improvements in the making of synthetic rubber, which rapidly replaced natural rubber. It also seems clear that the failure of real wheat prices to rise, and the possibility that they fell slightly, is largely due to Engel's Law: economic growth has shifted demand toward luxuries at the expense of this staple grain. The fact that other primary products had stable or rising terms of trade has forced some rethinking of the economics of primary products. One factor tending to bid up their prices has been the natural limits on the availability of good farmland and mineral deposits. At the same time, these agricultural and mining sectors have had generally slower rates of growth in overall productivity, again making their prices rise relative to the prices of manufactures being produced with the help of rapid cost-cutting improvements. And for many primaries it was never the case that the demand for them grew only slowly with economic growth. With growing demand and relatively sluggish improvements in supply, such primary products as beef have enjoyed improving relative prices.

The same relative slowness of productivity growth in agriculture and mining that helps explain why the terms of trade have not moved greatly against primary producers also helps explain why these producers have not gained in income (except for oil exporters, of course) relative to manufacturing nations. The primary-producing sector of the world economy has had stable or slightly favorable price trends yet slightly slower growth in output per unit of input, leaving a slightly widening income gap between the manufacturing and primary sectors. The main problem has not been one of immiserizing growth in primary production. It is more likely to have been one of insufficient growth in primary production.

The evidence on the terms of trade thus leaves the clear impression that policymakers do not need to discourage primary-sector investments on the ground that these sectors face unfavorable price trends. As for the other arguments for favoring industry over agriculture and mining in developing countries, we return to these in Chapter 11.

NEW GOODS AND THE PRODUCT CYCLE

Economists have noted increasingly that trade in manufactures cannot be adequately explained by using the simple versions of the Heckscher-Ohlin trade model featuring the two factors "labor" and "capital." Their studies have increasingly underlined the empirical importance of technological progress in explaining trade patterns, especially where new goods are being introduced.

An early clue to this need for focusing on technology came from an empirical investigation by Irving Kravis into the Heckscher-Ohlin model. Kravis wanted to see whether labor-intensive exports were produced by especially low-wage labor, and found to his evident surprise that in virtually every country the exporting industries were those that paid the highest wage rates. What a country produced and exported, he decided, was what it had "available," that is, the goods its entrepreneurs and innovators developed. Availability meant an "elastic" supply. It did no good for a country to have the cheap labor to produce, say, transistors, if in fact it lacked inventors, or for an inventor to license an invention if the country lacked the innovators, entrepreneurs, skilled workers, and so on, needed to produce the product. This theory challenged the assumption of the classical doctrine that technology was the same all over the world.

A good deal of work has been done in pursuing this and other leads into the technological basis for trade in new goods. Donald B. Keesing, for example, pushed forward to rescue the Heckscher-Ohlin analysis by exploring the connection between exports and high expenditure on research and development and between exports and advanced labor skills, such as those embodied in scientists and engineers. When the top commodity groups with the highest research effort—computers, electronics, nuclear energy, space equipment, and aircraft—are separated from 14 other major industries, it appears that the former export four times as much per dollar of sales as the latter. Or the measures can be put in terms of skilled labor as a percentage of total employment. Whatever the measure, it has been found that U.S. exports have had a high technological component and that many of these exports diminish or disappear when the technological lead of the United States narrows or is lost.

Trade may thus be based on a **technological gap**, created either by a substantial endowment of the necessary knowledge of skills, or by the market for new goods, or both. But few countries long maintain a monopoly of the knowledge needed to make anything. Invention and innovation may give a country an absolute advantage for a time, but they are followed in relatively short order by imitation, which leads back to the conditions of similar production functions worldwide—the assumption underlying the Heckscher-Ohlin basis for trade.

Raymond Vernon has generalized this pattern of experience into what he calls the **product cycle**, or the cycle in the life of a new product. The product is first new, then maturing as it spreads to other industrialized countries, and finally standardized. Computers are at one end of the spectrum today, and textiles, leather goods, rubber products, and paper are at the other. Some years ago a British economist suggested that automobiles would turn out to be the textiles of tomorrow. The spread of automobile production into the developing countries of Asia and Latin America—largely with heavy protection, but with exports emerging in copious quantities from Japan—suggests that automobiles are trembling on the verge of "standardization."

The trade patterns one might expect over the life cycle of a new product are illustrated in Figure 4.6. In the early stage of development with time measured along the horizontal axis, the innovation and production begin in, say, the United States, at time t_0 (the invention may have occurred anywhere; what counts is the first commercial production). Soon, at t_1, the United States begins to export some of the new product to other industrial countries. Yet after a lag these countries develop their own ability to produce the new good, perhaps with the help subsidiaries set up abroad by U.S. producers. What makes this shift to production outside the United States possible is the as-

FIGURE 4.6
How trade balances might evolve over the "product cycle" of a new good

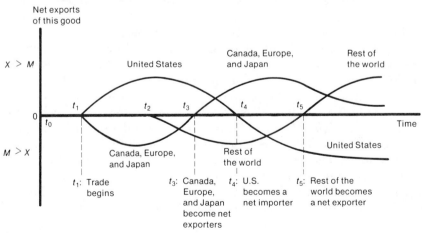

sumed fact that the initial technological advantage of the United States erodes. This is a plausible assumption for many new manufactures, for which production technology becomes more standardized and learnable. Increasing imitation by other industrial countries makes them net exporters of the product, as at time t_3 in Figure 4.6. As the technology in this product line ages and becomes increasingly standardized, the United States loses its comparative advantage and becomes a net importer of this good (at t_4). Yet it is also reasonable to expect that the rest of the world can also catch up in time with the technological knowledge of Canada, Europe, and Japan in this aging product line. At time t_5, the product cycle enters its final phase as far as trade is concerned, with the product being exported from the rest of the world (for example, from less developed countries) to the United States and the other higher-income countries. What makes the mature product settle in less developed countries is the fact that sooner or later their wage-rate advantage will outweigh the dwindling gap in knowledge and make this product line a comparative-advantage export item for less developed countries.

Note that if all goods pass through such a product life cycle, it does not follow that the technological leader, here the United States, has to have any deterioration in its trade balance for all products. As long as the leader keeps coming up with new goods to introduce into world trade, it can retain its comparative advantage in a changing set of newest goods and have enough exports to match its imports forever.

A series of studies of the product cycle in particular industries suggests that the pace of imitation is speeding up. In synthetic fibers, G. C. Hufbauer noted that comparative advantage is not based on raw materials. Countries that produce wood pulp (Canada and Sweden) and those with petroleum (in the Middle East and, for example, Venezuela) are notably not engaged in the production of fibers. In this industry, trade started with a technological breakthrough leading to a technological gap, became supported by economies of scale, ultimately spread through imitation, and became widely disseminated. In the end, comparative advantage shifted away from the innovators and settled to rest on wage costs, or factor proportions. A similar study in petrochemicals traced the product cycle in a closely related field.

A steady comparative advantage in research-intensive goods produces one structure of trade. The product cycle relates to a single good in which comparative advantage is lost and may turn into comparative disadvantage. The two can be combined into a dynamic process in which comparative advantage in new goods continues over a changing range of goods. The possibility that this explained U.S. trade was put forward as early as 1929 by John H. Williams. The notion languished as a general explanation although it survived in a number of studies of particular industries.

Erik Hoffmeyer observed the evolving character of U.S. trade in office machinery. At the earliest stage, U.S. innovators pioneered in typewriters, adding machines, and cash registers. With the increasing use of these products in the domestic market, producers began to export them. With the passage of time, however, relatively simple machines were widely produced abroad, on the one hand, and replaced by the production of more complex machinery in the United States, on the other. In time, therefore, the United States imported mechanical typewriters, adding machines, and so on, and exported electric typewriters, cash registers, and data processing machinery.

A thesis at the Massachusetts Institute of Technology on international trade in motion pictures observed that the United States pioneered in many film innovations and that after each one—the feature-length picture, talkies, color, wide-screen movies, and so on— there was a surge of exports. After a lag, based on the need to see whether the innovation would succeed and on the time required to imitate it, foreign producers followed suit. When the technology was widely known and adopted, the United States might or might not continue to export, or trade in differentiated products might move in both directions.

A recent study traces the diffusion of semiconductors within the United States and outward to Britain, France, West Germany, and Japan—and could have traced it to the lesser producers in Hong Kong and Taiwan. This study examines the product cycle in a single commodity and its major innovations. In this instance, lack of economies of scale assisted diffusion, but learning by doing and a rapidly advancing product made imitation dangerous.

NEED FOR A NEW THEORY OF TRADE IN MANUFACTURED GOODS?

Does the existence of technological change and rising real income which demands improvements in goods alter the fundamental case for trade based on factor proportions? An attempt by a conference of economists to resolve this issue failed to reach a clear-cut decision. Changing incomes, tastes, technology, factor proportions, and so on, complicate the analysis. Whether the change in degree is sufficient to constitute a change in kind is perhaps at basis a philosophic riddle depending upon definitions, rather than anything which can be handled on a yes-no level.

At this conference, Hufbauer assembled seven theories of the basic composition of trade in manufactures, ranging from the orthodox

Heckscher-Ohlin doctrine based on factor proportions down to the Linder heterodoxy which emphasized trade in goods similar to those produced at home for the home market. Between them lay theories emphasizing "human skills," "scale economies," "stages of production," "technological gap," and "product cycle" which overlapped and merged into each other and could be regarded as legitimate descendants of the Heckscher-Ohlin doctrine, rather than its antithesis. The attempt was made to test the various theories against trade data. Some support was found for each. We are left then with the rather awkward position that there is an established explanation of trade, the Heckscher-Ohlin theory, but that manufactures conform to it only after it is modified to make the underlying assumptions more realistic. The unreality of the assumptions of neoclassical theory, however, are not sufficient to justify discarding it. Students still have to learn it, and as we shall see later, there is enough truth in the basic theory, and especially in the corollaries and implications for policy, for it to serve as the basis for analysis of interferences with trade.

SUMMARY

As economics grow, there are major changes in technology, factor supplies, and possibly tastes. Tastes may be shifted by the growth of trade itself through the demonstration effect. This effect may be analyzed in trade models either as a shift in tastes toward newly imported modern goods or as a reason why elasticities of demand for modern importables soon rise to high levels, with no basic shift in tastes, after initial exposure to these goods. A second link between growth and trade via tastes is forged by Engel's Law. As incomes grow, people reduce the share of their expenditures devoted to food, causing a reduction in the relative price of foods in international trade, other things equal. A final tastes effect is sketched by Linder's representative-demand hypothesis. Linder argued that as a country's per capita income grows, its representative-demand pattern causes an expansion in the domestic production of certain luxuries. This expansion causes such reductions in the costs of these luxuries that they become the country's new comparative-advantage exports. In this way, he suggests, countries come to export their representative-demand products.

Factor-supply growth can affect trade in any of several ways. If all factors grow at the same rate, or if a growing factor is used in the same proportions in all industries, this balanced expansion of the production possibilities will only raise the volume of trade without affecting relative prices or the share of trade in production. If a country's factor growth is export biased, trade will expand relative to production and the terms of trade *may* shift against the country. In the extreme case of immiserizing growth, export-biased growth causes such a severe drop in the terms of trade as to make the country actually worse off. If factor growth is import biased, it will reduce trade and may shift the terms of trade in the country's favor. The analysis of the trade effects of biased technological progress are analogous to that of biased factor growth.

The possibility of immiserizing export-biased growth has been expanded into a whole set of arguments to the effect that developing countries should channel their resources away from the sectors exporting agricultural and mineral products into industry. Some of these arguments were tested in this chapter. It appears that the gains from the initial opening of trade accrue mainly to the primary-product exporters in the newly trading country itself. The social meaning of this result depends on whether the primary-product exporters are indigenous farmers or colonizing expatriates from richer countries. The long-run trend in the terms of trade has apparently not been adverse to the primary exporters, except in the case of natural rubber and possibly wheat. For most other primary products it is not true that their purchasing power in exchange for manufactures has declined.

Trade in manufactures evolves with economic growth in ways that can be incorporated into the basic Heckscher-Ohlin trade model only after it has been carefully modified. A better theory of trade in manufactures must recognize the role of new technology and technological diffusion among nations. The apparent trade patterns in an individual manufactured good show some conformity with Raymond Vernon's product-cycle hypothesis, which predicts that as the technology of a product becomes more standardized and static, the product migrates to lower-income countries where labor costs become a more important basis for comparative advantage than do research and development. Such links between trade and technology can be incorporated into the Heckscher-Ohlin framework emphasizing factor endowments, but only when one defines all specific technological advantages as relative endowments of knowledge and skills.

SUGGESTED READING

Staffan Linder's representative-demand hypothesis is sketched in his *Trade and Trade Policy for Development* (New York: Praeger, 1967).

The classic statement of the possibility of immiserizing growth is Jagdish N. Bhagwati, "Immiserizing Growth," reprinted in American Economic Association, *Readings in International Economics* (Homewood, Ill.: Richard D. Irwin, 1967).

The view that international trade turns increasingly unfavorable to primary-exporting less developed countries is expounded in Raúl Prebisch, secretary-general, United Nations Conference on Trade and Development,

Towards a New Trade Policy for Development (New York: UN, 1964). Prebisch's views are criticized in Harry G. Johnson, *Economic Policies toward Less Developed Countries* (New York: Praeger, 1967), appendix A, and the sources cited there.

The product-cycle view of the evolution of trade patterns is put forth and tested in Raymond Vernon, "International Investment and International Trade in the Product Cycle," *Quarterly Journal of Economics*, vol. 80, no. 2 (May 1966), pp. 190–207; Raymond Vernon (ed.), *The Technology Factor in International Trade* (New York: NBER, 1970); and Gary C. Hufbauer, *Synthetic Materials and the Theory of International Trade* (Cambridge, Mass.: Harvard University Press, 1966).

QUESTIONS FOR REVIEW

1. Could you reinterpret Linder's representative-demand hypothesis in terms of either production-possibility and indifference curves or demand and supply curves for the representative luxury goods?

2. What conditions are crucial in producing the case of immiserizing growth?

3. Why haven't most primary products fallen in relative price over the long run?

4. If every new product goes through the product cycle, will the technological initiator (for example, the United States) fall behind and develop chronic trade deficits?

5

Trade and income distribution

The issue of whether a nation should trade freely has generated, and will always generate, heated debate that cannot be understood as long as one looks only at the aggregate national effects of trade. If it seems so likely that a nation gains from opening trade, why should free-trade policies have so many opponents year in and year out? We shall return to this question repeatedly here and in Part II. The answer, we shall find, does *not* lie mainly in public ignorance about the effects of trade. An objective look at those effects finds that trade does typically hurt large groups within any country, and many of the opponents of freer trade probably perceive this point correctly. To make our analysis of trade an effective policy guide, we must be able to show just who stands to be hurt by freer trade. This is the task of the present chapter. Part II elaborates on this point and also introduces the special cases in which freer trade could also bring aggregate losses to the nation.

PRICES AFFECT THE INCOME DISTRIBUTION

The key reason why international trade is almost sure to divide society into gainers and losers from trade is that whatever changes relative commodity prices is likely to raise the rewards of some factors of production at the expense of others.

Different sectors of the economy use different proportions of the various factors of production, as we noted when discussing "factor proportions" in Chapter 2. The farm sector obviously makes heavier use of rural land than does any other major sector of production. The personal services industry, which supplies such products as haircuts, beauty services, and housecleaning, uses a greater proportion of low-skilled labor than does the rest of the economy. The computer industry demands much greater ratios of highly skilled labor (engineers, and so on) than does the rest of the economy. Furthermore, this pattern of relative concentration of certain factors into certain industries changes only very slowly over time.

As long as factor proportions vary widely, a change in relative output prices due to international trade or any other outside force will have profound effects on how the sellers of different kinds of factor services are rewarded. To see how, let us return to the example of the opening of trade in a land-abundant, labor-scarce economy, such as the United States in our wheat-and-cloth examples. If the opening of trade makes wheat more expensive and cloth cheaper within the United States, producers will feel some incentive to produce less cloth and more wheat. They will invest less capital, and use less land and labor, in making cloth (and its material inputs, such as cotton). They will invest more, and hire more, in wheat production. To simplify the discussion for the present, let us talk as though there were only two mobile factors of production, "land" (including all nonhuman wealth) and labor. Let us further assume that before trade each 100 bushels of wheat uses 30 person-hours of labor and two units of land, while each 100 yards of cloth use 50 person-hours of labor and one unit of land.

As producers respond to the better price for wheat and the worse price for cloth, their new uses of factors to make wheat will not match the ratio in which they stop employing factors to make cloth. Let us say that as the economy approaches the international price ratio of 1 bushel = 1 yard, as in our examples in Chapters 2 through 4, each extra bushel of wheat is produced by cutting back one yard of cloth production. This sets up a clear imbalance in the markets for factors. Unless something gives somewhere, each shift replacing 100 yards of cloth with 100 bushels of wheat will tend to employ 20 fewer person-hours of labor (50 minus 30) and to employ an extra unit of land. Something has to give if there are fixed supplies of land and labor. With the supply of land fixed (or at least not responsive to land's rate of reward), the purchase prices and the use rents earned by land must be bid up, to induce both industries to cut back on their land use enough to offset the shift toward what has been the more land-using sector. The opposite will happen to the rewards for laborers. At first, the shift from cloth to wheat will tend to create some labor unemployment. Over the longer run, the wage rate will tend to drop, as the unemployed settle for lower wages in order to obtain work. This drop in wage rates will cause some shifting toward more labor-using techniques in both industries to offset the shift from the labor-using cloth sector. In this way the process of accommodating the shift from cloth to wheat to the given total factor supplies brings a rise in income for owners of land and a drop in income for laborers. Trade, or any other outside force shifting relative prices, makes one group better off and the other worse off. Trade matters very much to the distribution of income simply because trade affects commodity prices.

THE STOLPER-SAMUELSON THEOREM

What our illustration has just sketched can in fact be proved rigorously under certain assumptions. The proof was first supplied by Wolfgang Stolper and Paul Samuelson in 1941. Their assumptions and results were as follows:

> *Assumptions:* A country produces two goods (for example, wheat and cloth) with two factors of production (for example, land and labor); neither good is an input into the production of the other; competition prevails; factor supplies are given; both factors are fully employed; one good (wheat) is land intensive and the other (cloth) is labor intensive with or without trade; both factors are mobile between sectors (but not between countries); and opening trade raises the relative price of wheat.

> *The Stolper-Samuelson theorem:* Under the assumptions just stated, moving from no trade to free trade unambiguously raises the returns to the factor used intensively in the rising-price industry (land) and lowers the returns to the factor used intensively in the falling-price industry (labor), regardless of which goods the sellers of the two factors prefer to consume.

Aside from establishing this point rigorously instead of with casual illustrations, Stolper and Samuelson rendered a further service by showing that the result did not depend at all on which goods were consumed by the households of landowners and laborers. This result clashed with an intuition many economists had shared. It seemed that if laborers spent a very large share of their incomes on cloth, they might possibly gain from free trade by having cheaper cloth. Not so, according to the theorem. An expanded proof by Ronald Jones in 1965 showed why. Within such a model, there is in fact a "**magnification effect**": a 10 percent rise in the relative price of one good, say wheat, brings a *greater* percentage rise in the rewards to its intensive factor, land, measured in units of cloth, and a drop in the ability of the other factor, labor, to buy even the cheapened cloth. That is, the resulting change in the ratio of factor rewards is more magnified than the change in the wheat-cloth price ratio that caused it. Therefore, the wage rate earned by workers falls in terms of either wheat or cloth.

THE FACTOR-PRICE EQUALIZATION THEOREM

The same basic two-by-two-by-two trade model (two factors, two commodities, two countries) that predicts that one factor will lose from the move from no trade to free trade also makes an even more surprising prediction about the effects of trade on factor prices and the distribution of income. Beginning with a proof by Paul Samuelson in the late 1940s, a theorem was established about the effect of trade on international differences in factor prices:

> *Assumptions:* (1) There are two factors (for example, land and labor), two commodities (wheat and cloth), and two countries (the United States and the rest of the world); (2) competition prevails in all markets; (3) each factor supply is fixed, and there is no factor migration between countries; (4) each factor is fully employed in each country with or without trade; (5) there are no transportation or information costs; (6) governments do not impose any tariffs or other barriers to free trade; (7) the production functions relating factor inputs to commodity outputs are the same between countries for any one industry; (8) the production functions are linearly homogeneous (if all factors are used 10 percent more, output will be raised by exactly 10 percent) and (9) not subject to "factor intensity reversals" (if wheat is land intensive at one factor-price ratio, it remains so at any factor-price ratio); and (10) both countries produce both goods with or without trade.
>
> *The factor-price equalization theorem:* Under the long list of assumptions above, free trade will equalize not only commodity prices, but also factor prices, so that all laborers will earn the same wage rate and all units of land will earn the same rental return in both countries, regardless of the factor supplies or the demand patterns in the two countries.

This is a remarkable result. It implies that laborers will end up earning the same wage rate in all countries even if labor migration between countries is not allowed. Trade makes this possible, within the assumptions of the model, because the factors that cannot migrate between countries end up being implicitly shipped between countries in commodity form. Trade makes the United States export wheat and import cloth. Since wheat is land intensive and cloth is labor intensive, trade is in effect sending a land-rich commodity to the rest of the world in exchange for labor-rich cloth. It is as though each factor were migrating toward the country in which it was scarcer before trade.

Even the most casual glance at the real world shows that the predictions of the factor-price equalization theorem are not borne out. One of the most dramatic facts of economic development is that the same factor of production, for example, the same labor skill, does not earn the same pay in all countries. The international pay gaps for comparable work are wide and perhaps widening. Barbers do not earn the same pay in Mexico or India as in the United States or Canada. Nor do domestic servants. It seems clear that the assumptions made in proving the theorem must be the cause of the discrepancy between model prediction and fact. It is hard to say just which assumptions are most "at fault." A true believer in free trade might be tempted to argue that factor prices have not been equalized between countries because we do not have free trade. Yet even in the freer-trade era of the 19th century, English unskilled workers earned noticeably more than did their Irish or Indian counterparts despite fairly free trade and unprohibitive transportation costs. It must be that the whole set of assumptions contains many crucial departures from reality. Yet the factor-price theorem remains an important exercise in the use of rigorous models of trade, and some of its main proofs are presented in Appendix C.

A MORE GENERAL VIEW OF TRADE AND FACTOR REWARDS

The Stolper-Samuelson and factor-price equalization theorems prove little by themselves, resting as they do on oversimplified assumptions. Yet manipulating clearly oversimplified models is often a useful way of thinking of nonobvious results that may hold in the real world even if they are hard to prove rigorously. So it is with the theory of trade and factor rewards. Economists have gradually extended this analysis by relaxing some of the assumptions while retaining others, in order to get a feel for what results would remain valid in the much more complicated real world. Certain real-world patterns are suggested, though not proved, by current theorizing on the income-distribution effects of trade.

Factor specialization

One clear pattern seems to be that the more a factor is specialized, or concentrated, into the production of exports, the more it stands to gain from trade. Conversely, the more a factor is concentrated into the production of the importable good, the more it stands to lose from trade. This pattern was an unambiguous result in the simple wheat-cloth example: trade clearly helped landowners and hurt labor. It is also suggested by all of the theoretical extensions of the model. It is also suggested by common sense.

To measure the specialization of a factor into export or importable sectors in the multifactor, multicommodity real world, one needs detailed information. The kind of measure of export specialization versus import specialization one wants is something like the factor-content ratio

$$S_{i,x/m} = \frac{\theta_{ix}}{\theta_{im}} ,$$

where $S_{i,x/m}$ is the measure of specialization of factor i in exports more than imports, θ_{ix} is the share of factor i incomes in the total value of exports, and θ_{im} is the share of factor i incomes in the import-competing production that could replace the total value of imports. To calculate such a ratio, one needs to go beyond the shares of the factor's incomes in value added within the export and import-competing sectors themselves. One needs to use elaborate input-output information to find out what shares of export and import-competing production consist of payments for factor i in the industries *supplying* the export and import-competing industries as well as in these industries themselves. For example, in calculating the share of returns to farmland in the value of Canadian exports, one must take account of the contribution of farmland to the value of exported whiskey and wool sweaters as well as the more obvious contribution of farmland to wheat exports.

With the help of such empirical measures, our simple theory can suggest that the factors likely to gain more from freer trade are those more associated with exportable-good production than with import-competing production. We shall return to this predicted tendency when we discuss the Leontiev paradox and the stake of labor and other factors in U.S. foreign trade later in this chapter.

Factor mobility

Closely related to the likely importance of factor specialization is that of factor mobility. A factor which can be used in only one sector is an extreme case of specialization. And if trade lowers the relative price of this sector's product by letting in competing imports, the factor that cannot migrate away from this sector will lose heavily and persistently from the new import competition (since this factor's $S_{i,x/m}$ will always be zero, or at least well below unity).

Factors are less mobile in the short run than in the long run. If new competition from imports suddenly lowers the price of cloth and other textile products, inducing firms to suffer capital losses and lay off textile workers, one should expect the textile workers to suffer large short-run losses, as though they were committed to either work in the textile industry or remain completely unemployed. Yet over the longer run they will seek and find jobs in other industries, becoming part of a larger mobile pool of labor of various skills. In terms of our specialization measure, the shift from initial immobility to eventual mobility and exodus from the import-injured sector means that $S_{i,x/m}$ rises from zero toward (but probably not to) unity.

The tendency toward increasing mobility over time in response to a price shift means that factors can be affected one way in the short run and the opposite way in the long run, as recently noted by Michael Mussa. In our wheat and cloth examples, this could well happen to wheat-farm workers and to cloth-industry landowners. When the opening of trade first brings a boom to the wheat sector, the attempt to expand wheat production will raise the demand for farm labor and cause wage rates to rise in farm areas, when wage rates are measured in terms of cloth and possibly even in terms of wheat. But once labor mobility sets in, the influx of new laborers from the declining cloth sector will bid wage rates back down in the wheat sector. The fact that wheat is less labor intensive than cloth means that even in the wheat sector wage rates will end up lower (as shown in the Stolper-Samuelson theorem). The owners of land in the cloth industry, such as cotton-growing land or sheep pasture for wool, will also experience a reversal of effects. At first they will lose out, as the lower price for cloth and the loss of sales to imports cause the value of their land to sink. But over the years they can shift part of their land to wheat cultivation. As more and more land shifts to wheat, landowners will end up experiencing net gains from the opening of trade simply because wheat is land intensive. Such reversals of the effects of trade may apply to many factors in the multifactor real world.

Consumption patterns

In the simple two-factor models, it was possible for Stolper and Samuelson to show that there was one gaining factor and one losing factor, regardless of what goods each factor preferred to consume. Yet it is very wrong to conclude that the consumption patterns of different groups play no part in the effects of trade on their economic well-being. Even within the simple two-factor, two-commodity model, how U.S. workers chose to spend their incomes still affected *how much* they lost. The more they concentrated their purchases on cloth, the less the percentage of their income loss (though they still lost from trade). And when we move to the multifactor world, we can readily see that for a whole range of "intermediate" factors, those that are neither the most export specialized nor the most import specialized, their stake in the export and import industries as consumers must help determine whether they are gainers or losers from trade.

To see the ambiguity of the position of the intermediate factors used extensively in all sectors, let us consider a classic political fight over the issue of free trade. In the early 19th century Britain, then the "workshop of the world," exported capital-intensive manufactures and imported land-intensive grain. Yet this trade was greatly restrained by the Corn Laws, which taxed grain imports and held up the relative domestic price of grain to the advantage of landlords and the irritation of capitalists, for whom the Corn Laws just meant the lower ability of foreigners exporting grain to buy their products and the higher wages they had to pay their factory workers to offset the higher cost of food.

What position should labor groups have taken in this debate? They lacked the right to vote, for the most part, but still had some influence through mass demonstrations and petitions.

Labor groups were in fact quite ambivalent about this debate over the Corn Laws before these were repealed in 1846. They had little reason to embrace the laws, which made bread more expensive. On the other hand, they showed only a lukewarm response to the plea of the capitalist-oriented Anti-Corn-Law League that they support its fight for free trade. Today, over a century later, even the most sophisticated trade models would have to agree that the labor groups had reason to be uncertain about their stake in free trade (apart from their antipathy to any firm alliance with the factory owners they were fighting against over wages and working conditions in the factories). To be sure, free trade would make food cheaper for workers' families—yet it would also make manufactures relatively more expensive, as export demand competed increasingly against British consumers for cloth and other manufactures. Which of these two cost-of-living effects was more important to workers depended on the shares of their household expenditures devoted to food (especially grains) and to exportable manufactures. The effect of free trade on wage rates was also unclear. If free trade meant more exports of manufactures and declining home production of grain, this meant more demand for labor in manufacturing areas but less demand for labor in farm areas, with no clear net effect. As the "intermediate" factor, less specialized by sector than land or capital, laborers would have been rightly ambivalent on the issue of free trade even if they had thought in terms of today's trade models.

Trade theorists are still grappling with the issue of how to weigh the importance of imports and exports in a factor's consumption against the subtle and complicated effects of trade on the factor's income. The more factors of production one allows into the model, the murkier the result. Yet three patterns stand out. First, consumption patterns do matter, in the direction suggested by intuition. The more a factor group's purchases tend to be for importable goods (whether imported or produced domestically at prices affected by imports), the more it stands to gain from freer trade. Second, for the most specialized factors the magnification still seems strong enough to outweigh the subtle effects of trade on their consumption costs. If we ranked, say, 17 different factors of production according to their trade specializations (that is, according to their $S_{i,x/m}$'s), the factor most specialized in exports will gain from trade and the 17th factor, that most specialized in the import-competing sector, will lose from trade, regardless of what goods these factors consume. Third, factors in a "neutral" position will gain from trade on balance. The term *neutral* here refers to a factor group, such as semiskilled typists, whose commitment to export and import industries is exactly balanced (roughly speaking, the group's $S_{i,x/m}$ equals 1) and whose consumption shares devoted to exportables and importables are exactly the same. This group will tend to gain from trade because the aggregate national gains from trade tend to bid up the demand for this exactly neutral factor enough to give it better ability to buy the balanced bundle of goods it prefers. A corollary of this result, shown by Roy Ruffin and Ronald W. Jones under certain assumptions, is that there are probably some factor groups whose incomes are just slightly more tied to import-competing industries than is their consumption who will still be net gainers from free trade, especially in the long run, when they are mobile between sectors.

WHO ARE THE EXPORTING AND THE IMPORT-COMPETING FACTORS?

The analysis of the effects of trade on factor groups' incomes and purchasing power makes it clear that we need measures of export orientation versus import orientation, such as the measure $S_{i,x/m}$ suggested above. With such indicators we can take an important step toward sorting out the groups who are likely to gain and lose from specific proposals to liberalize or restrict foreign trade. Knowing who these groups are, national policymakers can better anticipate their views on trade and can plan ahead for ways to compensate the groups likely to be injured, if society wishes to compensate them. Knowing the patterns of export orientation and import orientation also helps interest groups know their own stakes in the trade issue.

Economists have devoted a great deal of energy to identifying the export-oriented and import-competing groups, especially for the United States. As it happens, the rich empirical economic literature was not inspired primarily by the policy issue of how trade effects the income distribution. Rather, its authors shed light on this distributional issue while pursuing a theoretical question: Is the Heckscher-Ohlin trade model (sketched in Chapter 2) correct in predicting that countries will tend to export the goods that use their relatively abundant factors more intensively? More specifically, they asked whether or not the United States really exported capital-intensive goods in exchange for labor-intensive goods. Let us first follow the empirical debate over this theoretical issue on its own terms and then turn to what it showed about the policy issue of gainers and losers from trade.

THE LEONTIEV PARADOX

The debate was touched off by an ingenious empirical study by Wassily Leontiev, published in 1953. Leontiev computed the ratios of capital stock to number of workers in the U.S. export industries and import-competing industries in 1947. As the main pioneer in input-output analysis, he had the advantage of knowing just how to multiply the input-output matrix of the U.S. economy by vectors of factor inputs, export values, and import values to derive the desired estimates of capital-labor ratios in exports and import-competing production. He intended his results to be a direct test of the Heckscher-Ohlin prediction that the United States would export its abundant factor, as embodied in commodities, while importing its scarce factor in commodity form. Which factors were abundant and which scarce for the United States? Everybody assumed that the United States was above all capital abundant and labor scarce relative to the rest of the world, and what Leontiev had available were estimates of the capital stock and persons employed in each industry. So the test was set: if the Heckscher-Ohlin model was right, the U.S. export bundle should embody a higher capital-labor ratio, when all the contributions of input industries were sorted out, than the capital-labor ratio embodied in the U.S. production that competed with imports.

Leontiev's results posed a stunning paradox: the United States was exporting labor-intensive goods to the rest of the world in exchange for capital-intensive imports! His key numerical result is shown in the second set of rows in Table 5.1. There it is clear that the capital-labor ratio in export industries was actually only about 77 percent as high as in the industries that competed against U.S. imports in 1947, whereas

TABLE 5.1
Capital and labor requirements in U.S. exports and import-competing replacements

Year for input-output structure (I–O) and trade pattern	Factor requirements per million dollars of product	Exports	Competitive imports	Ratio of exports to imports
(1) 1899 I–O and trade structure (Whitney)	Capital stock	$2,621,200	$2,589,700	
	Labor (person-years)	1,122.5	1,240.2	
	Capital/labor ratio	$2,335.1	$2,088.3	1.118
(2) 1947 I–O and trade structure (Leontiev)	Capital stock	$2,550,780	$3,091,339	
	Labor (person-years)	182	170	
	Capital/labor ratio	$14,010	$18,180	0.771
(3) 1958 I–O and 1962 trade structure (Baldwin)	Capital stock	$1,876,000	$2,132,000	
	Labor (person-years)	131	119	
	Capital/labor ratio	$14,200	$18,000	0.789

Sources: (1) William G. Whitney, "The Structure of the American Economy in the Late Nineteenth Century," unpublished Ph.D. dissertation, Harvard University, 1968, calculated from table V–3; (2) Wassily W. Leontiev, "Factor Proportions and the Structure of American Trade: Further Theoretical and Empirical Analysis," *Review of Economics and Statistics,* vol. 38, no. 4 (November 1956), pp. 392, 397; (3) Robert E. Baldwin, "Determinants of the Commodity Structure of U.S. Trade," *American Economic Review,* vol. 61, no. 1 (March 1971), table 1 on p. 134.

the Heckscher-Ohlin model would have predicted a ratio above 100 percent if the United States were truly capital abundant. Leontiev himself wrestled with this oddity in several ways. He cross-checked his results against several possible corrections for measurement error or faulty test design, but the paradox remained. He suggested that perhaps the United States was really labor abundant relative to the rest of the world in the sense that, as he conjectured, U.S. workers were so much more efficient than foreign workers that they contributed three times as much labor per person-year as did foreign workers. This might be due, he thought, to superior U.S. entrepreneurship and organization of industry, which somehow coaxed much more efficiency out of U.S. workers. While we shall find that the idea of differentiating between kinds of labor by efficiency is a good clue to follow, Leontiev's tentative conjecture about U.S. entrepreneurship and organizational superiority has persuaded nobody, and his paradox posed a clear challenge to the presumption that the Heckscher-Ohlin theory fit the facts.

THE PARADOX RETAINED: A CLOSER LOOK AT TRADE AND FACTOR PROPORTIONS

Leontiev's paradoxical result set off a flurry of activity among trade economists, with some plunging back into a complex reappraisal of theory and others gathering new data and performing new tests. For some time, the main result was to reinforce the paradox. Using the 1958 U.S. input-output table instead of the 1947 table used by Leontiev made little difference, as suggested by the bottom set of results in Table 5.1. A rough calculation for 1899 gave historical dimension to the paradox by showing that the paradox does not seem to have existed for the United States at the turn of the century, when the U.S. relative capital abundance was presumably less pronounced.

Tests on data from other countries turned up as many fresh contradictions to the usual beliefs as they did confirmations. A study of Canada's foreign trade in the 1950s, most of which was with the more capital-abundant United States, showed that Canada exported more capital-intensive goods than it imported. Japan also exported capital-intensive goods and imported labor-intensive goods in the 1950s, a pattern that seems puzzling, given Japan's heavy dependence on trade with the United States. The results for India in the 1950s seemed fine on one front and paradoxical on another. In its trade with all of the rest of the world, India exported labor-intensive products and imported capital-intensive products. Yet in its bilateral trade with the United States, India exported capital-intensive products to the United States in exchange for labor-intensive products. It began to look as though either the United States was the ultimate labor-abundant and capital-scarce country or the whole trade model was hopelessly wrong.

One proffered explanation that did not pan out tried to use differences in tastes to unlock the paradox. Taking up on a point made in Chapter 3, some economists conjectured that perhaps the United States simply had such an extraordinary taste for capital-intensive products relative to the rest of the world that it ended up importing these products even though it was capital abundant. Yet what is known about national consumption patterns and relative prices rejects the notion that tastes are so different between countries as to override the differences in factor endowments.

Further investigations both retained and resolved the paradox. The paradox has been retained in the sense that as long as one calculates simple capital-labor ratios, the United States will continue to look like an exporter of labor-intensive goods. The paradox now seems to have been resolved in that trade economists, prodded by the Leontiev results, have come up with a list of important factors that seem to account for these results and at the same time have done a lot to improve on the original simple interpretations of the Heckscher-Ohlin model. In approximately ascending order of importance, from least to most, these are the four main sources of the paradox:

1. Factor-intensity reversals.
2. Tariffs and other government barriers to trade.
3. Differences in skills and human capital.
4. Differences in natural resource endowments.

Factor-intensity reversals. The key results of the Heckscher-Ohlin trade model assume, among other things, that if a good is more capital-intensive than another good at one ratio of factor prices, it will be more capital intensive at all factor-price ratios. Suppose, on the other hand, that this is not the case. Suppose that in the United States, Good A is more labor-intensive than Good B with capital cheap and labor expensive, while in the rest of the world, where capital is more expensive and labor cheaper, Good A is more capital intensive than Good B. This could happen if it is much harder to substitute one factor for the other in producing Good A than in producing Good B. This is a case of factor-intensity reversal, which is illustrated at greater length in Appendix C. In this case it could turn out that the United States exports Good A, which is labor-intensive in the United States, while importing Good B, which is labor-intensive abroad.

Such reversals may make a contribution toward unraveling world trade patterns. A study by Michael Hodd has shown that in their bilateral trade both the United States and Britain export the goods that are capital-intensive in their own countries. This looks like a factor-intensity reversal case, though it does not explain why the U.S. total trade pattern is characterized by exports of labor-intensive goods.

Trade barriers. It is also possible that the United States does not import many relatively labor-intensive goods because government policy does not allow it. Studies have indeed shown that labor-intensive U.S. imports are more restricted with high import barriers than are less labor-intensive imports. Especially protected are the unskilled and semiskilled labor groups, a point to which we return later in this chapter. If there were free trade, the United States would tend to import more labor-intensive products than it now does. The studies that have established the tendency to protect less skilled U.S. labor have not yet put this finding into a form allowing us to quantify the contribution of protection to the Leontiev paradox, but this is one source of the paradox.

Skills and human capital. A major part of the paradox seems to have been due to the fact that the skill content of labor differs greatly across countries as well as across individuals. An hour of labor worked by an unskilled worker is not the same thing as an hour worked by an engineer, a computer systems analyst, or a physician. Several authors followed up this point by investigating the relationship between skills and the U.S. trade position. They found that whether an industry was a U.S. export industry was strongly tied to any of three measures of its technological sophistication and skill requirements: average pay per employee, the share of employees in the high-skill occupational groups, and research and development (R&D) expenditures as a share of the value added in the industry. This result is consistent with the product-cycle hypothesis of Chapter 4, which argued that the United States would persistently find its comparative advantage in the newest-technology products (as long as the United States remained in the technological forefront). When the Leontiev calculations were repeated using measures of *human* capital per worker, rather than nonhuman man-made capital per worker, U.S. exports were indeed more (human) capital-intensive than U.S. import-competing production. Perhaps human skills are the factor of production in which the United States is relatively most abundant.

Natural resources. Most of the mysteries posed by the capital-labor calculations could not be fully resolved until careful attention was paid to the heterogeneity of natural resource endowments and their relationship to capital and labor. Nations differ greatly in the types and amounts of the natural resources with which they are endowed. The Arabian peninsula is full of oil and little else. Japan has only a little farmland and practically no minerals or forests. The United States has abundant farmland and coal and moderate and declining reserves of timber and most minerals. Canada is well endowed with all natural resources except those specific to the tropics. Britain has coal and offshore oil and gas, but little else.

To judge the contribution of natural resources to trade patterns, one should begin by valuing the rents earned by farmland, the value of mineral reserves depleted, and forest stumpage charges in each industrial sector. These resource-rent contributions should then be filtered through the input-output system to find out the natural resource content of exports and import-competing production. Natural resource rents are hard to quantify in practice, however. Economists have therefore tried to judge the role of natural resources in trade by simply identifying some sectors as resource intensive and separating them from other sectors.

The available evidence on the role of natural resources in trade does help to explain the more peculiar capital-labor results. One reason that Leontiev found such capital intensity in U.S. import-competing industries is that the United States is a heavy importer of minerals and forest products. These products are intensive users not only of natural resources but of nonhuman capital as well. On the export side, the United States is exporting farm products that happen to be relatively intensive users of both labor and land. To this extent the Leontiev paradox appears to have been a mirage: the United States imports natural resource products that happen to have high capital-labor ratios while exporting others that happen to have low capital-labor ratios. To quantify the factor contents of U.S. exports and import-competing industries it is essential to value the contributions of natural resources on both sides.

The role of natural resources seems to help explain some of the puzzling capital-labor results for other countries as well. Canada seemed to be exporting capital-intensive products to the United States largely because it was exporting minerals, again with high capital-labor ratios. Japan seemed to be exporting more capital-intensive products than it imported largely because it was importing rice, which is produced in a labor-intensive manner in Japan. And the seeming tendency of India to export capital-intensive goods to the United States in exchange for labor-intensive goods may have been due largely to its imports of U.S. food grains with the help of the Food for Peace program and U.S. Public Law 480.

The wave of empirical tests set off by Leontiev has been very instructive. It underlines an important point that we noted when we looked at the patterns of trade in manufactures in Chapter 4: to explain why trade flows in the directions it does, one cannot rely solely on the simple two-factor view of the world. The Heckscher-Ohlin emphasis on the importance of relative factor endowments may still be correct, but the tendency to lump the factors of production into "capital" and "labor," or labor and land, can be very misleading.

At a minimum, a correct anatomy of the factor content of U.S. exports and of U.S. imports competing with domestic production must distinguish the factor contributions of farmland, minerals, skilled labor, unskilled labor, and nonhuman capital. Figure 5.1 does so, giving a rough picture of how the total value of exports and the total value of competitive imports are probably divided among these factors.

FIGURE 5.1
A schematic view of the factor content of U.S. exports and competing imports

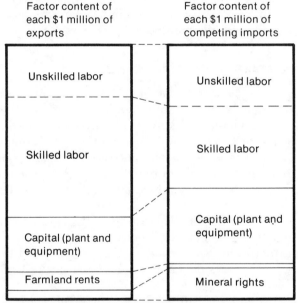

Note: Vertical distances are meant to give rough impressions of factor-content proportions in U.S. exports and the set of outputs that would replace the U.S. imports which compete with domestic products. The estimates must be rough since we lack correct calculations of the rents earned by farmland, mineral depletion, and plant and equipment. The proportions here are meant to represent postwar U.S. conditions. The share of mineral-depletion content in competitive imports would be higher after the start of 1974 than before, due to oil price jumps.

Labor incomes account for a greater share of the value of exports than of the value of imports that compete with domestic production. This labor-intensiveness of exports is due in part to the fact that there are more jobs associated with exports than with an equal value of imports, as is shown in Table 5.1 for the postwar period. At the same time it is due in part to the greater average skill and pay levels on the export side. If an arbitrary division were made between the pay of skilled labor and that of unskilled labor, it would turn out that exports embodied more skilled labor, but slightly less unskilled labor, than did imports, using the factor contents of import-competing U.S. industries to decompose the value of imports. Figure 5.1 also suggests a way of resolving the Leontiev paradox in summary form. Yes, the capital/labor ratio is lower on the export side, but this is because capital never was the most abundant factor in the United States relative to the rest of the world. Rather, the U.S. is most abundantly endowed with skilled labor and farmland. With this revision in our view of which factors are abundant, we can perhaps accept a more complicated variant of the Heckscher-Ohlin hypothesis emphasizing factor proportions as the main determinants of trade patterns.

U.S. LABOR'S STAKE IN FOREIGN TRADE

The estimates of the factor content of U.S. exports and imports have yielded a great deal of insight into the question of which groups are likely to gain, and which are likely to lose, from expanded trade. The patterns revealed in Table 5.1 and Figure 5.1 help to show, in particular, the likely effects on U.S. jobs and wages of either new trade barriers or the elimination of old trade barriers. Understanding these effects is crucial to an understanding of the political debate over U.S. trade barriers.

To see how the results aimed at testing the Heckscher-Ohlin model can be put to policy use, let us first look at what they say about the job effects of putting up higher barriers to U.S. imports, and then look at the apparent job impacts of removing the barriers the United States now has.

Between 1970 and 1973 the U.S. Congress came close to passing two bills that would have greatly restricted imports into the United States. The more important of these was the Burke-Hartke Bill, mentioned in Chapter 1. The Burke-Hartke bill was backed by the AFL–CIO as a bill that would protect American jobs. The bill's proposal regarding imports was to put up such restrictive quantitative quotas on legal imports that imports might have fallen by about a third. To the charge that the bill would raise the cost of imports to consumers, its backers replied that this was not too great a price to pay for the extra U.S. jobs that would be saved by shutting out some of the import competition. The job effects must be quantified, in view of the high likelihood that this same argument will come up again and again in future debates over trade policy.

To appraise the net effects of trade restrictions or freer trade on the number of jobs available at given wage rates, it is necessary to proceed in two steps: (1) to recognize and quantify the extent to which cutting imports would cut the value of exports as well; and (2) to multiply the changes in import value and export value by the ratios of jobs per dollar that seem to characterize the export and import-competing industries.

The first crucial step in judging the impact of new trade barriers is to recognize that *cutting the value of imports is likely to cut the value of exports by the same amount.* This is not obvious, yet there are four reasons for expecting this result:

(1) *Exports use importable inputs.* Barriers that make importable goods more costly in the domestic market raise the cost of producing for export. Examples would be the tendency of the U.S. import quotas on oil (1959–73) to raise the cost of U.S. chemicals sold on world markets, and the tendency of U.S. restrictions on steel imports to raise the prices of U.S. autos. To this extent, import barriers tend to price U.S. exportable-good industries out of some export business.

(2) *Foreigners who lose our business cannot buy so much from us.* If higher import barriers deny sales and income to foreign exporters, foreign national incomes may sag. This is especially likely if our country is a large part of world trade and we cut imports severely. The impoverishment of foreigners will cut the value of the exports they buy from us.

(3) *Foreign governments may retaliate.* All national governments are subject to pressure from individual industry groups wanting protection against import competition. If the United States were to impose severe restrictions on imports, it would become harder for foreign governments to resist raising their own import barriers, especially those on U.S. exports. The retaliation would be likely to cut U.S. export values further.

By themselves, these first three arguments have an uncertain quantitative importance. It is not clear, though very possible, that they imply export value cuts equal to the import value cuts. But whatever slack they leave between the import and export value cuts is likely to be taken up by the fourth argument:

(4) *Cutting imports will bring the same net cut in export value through an exchange-rate adjustment.* Here it is necessary to step ahead of our survey of international trade to pick up a basic point of international finance from Part III. Our trade models have ignored just how it is that export goods and import goods are exchanged between countries. They are not bartered, but are bought and sold in exchange for national currencies, and persons wanting to sway currencies after trading goods do so in a foreign exchange market. Demand and supply for any national currency on international markets must retain a rough

balance. If the exchange rates between the U.S. dollar and other currencies are flexible and are determined by demand and supply in the marketplace, then the supply of dollars (to buy foreign goods, services, and assets) will roughly match the demand for dollars (to buy U.S. goods, services, and assets) even in the very short run. If officials try to keep the exchange rates fixed, demand and supply for the dollar will be balanced only over the long run. But they will be balanced.

Putting up import barriers will cut the value of dollars that are being supplied in order to demand foreign currencies, to import foreign goods. With the United States not demanding so much foreign currency as before, the value of the dollar will tend to rise, and the value of foreign currencies will tend to fall, in foreign exchange markets. In the process, foreigners will have to reappraise their purchases of dollars to get U.S. goods and services and assets. Now that each dollar costs foreign buyers more, any given dollar price of a U.S. export looks more expensive to foreign buyers. They will therefore tend to cut their purchases of our exports. To what extent? Roughly until the value of the dollars they demand to buy our exports has dropped by the same amount as the dollars we are willing to give up to buy imports (which are subject to the new extra import barriers). In other words, the workings of the foreign exchange market are likely to make our export values drop by as much as our import values drop, through the effects of exchange-rate changes on foreign ability to buy our exports. The conclusion, then, is that cutting imports is likely to bring roughly a dollar-for-dollar cut in export value.

If imports and exports decline by the same dollar value per year in response to the new import barriers, what, then, do we know about the net job effect? We can see that on the one hand jobs are being protected or created in import-competing industries that are now shielded from import competition, yet on the other hand it seems clear that jobs may be lost in export lines. To see which job effect is likely to prevail, let us now return to the evidence on the job content of exports and imports.

The literature that grappled with the Leontiev paradox compared the factor contents of a given amount of exports, say $1 billion of exports, with those of the same value of imports. It therefore asked the kind of question we now need to ask to judge the stake of laborers in U.S. foreign trade: Are there as many jobs tied to an extra billion dollars of exports as there are to the domestic industries that would replace a billion dollars of imports?

Table 5.2 gives some of the estimates of export and import-competing job content. These figures and others like them make it clear that since World War II there have been more jobs tied to a billion dollars of exports than to a billion dollars of import-competing

TABLE 5.2
The number of U.S. jobs tied to a billion dollars of exports and a billion dollars of import-replacing production

Year for estimate	Source	Jobs per $1 billion of exports	Jobs per $1 billion of import replacement
(1) 1899	Whitney	1,122,500	1,240,200
(2) 1947	Leontiev	182,000	170,000
(3) 1958/1962	Baldwin	131,000	119,000
(4) 1971	Brimmer	66,000	65,000
(5) 1970/1971	Krause	111,000	88,600

Note: The first four sets of estimates measure average jobs per dollar of trade value. Krause's estimates measure the more relevant ratio of changes in jobs to changes in exports or imports.
    Sources: (1) through (3): Table 5.1; (4) Andrew F. Brimmer, "Imports and Economic Welfare in the United States," remarks before the Foreign Policy Association, New York, February 16, 1972, pp. 11–17; (5) Lawrence B. Krause, "How Much of Current Unemployment Did We Import?" *Brookings Papers in Economic Activity*, 1971, no. 1, pp. 421–25.

production. This is the main policy message that can be gleaned from the literature on the Leontiev paradox. To that message we can add another point: it is also true that the average wage rate for workers in export industries tends to be higher than in import-competing industries. So the estimates imply that more wages (jobs times average rate of pay) are tied to exports than to imports. It must be stressed that these job-effect estimates are very rough, as their authors point out. Yet it does seem that all the studies that have confronted the comparison do find exports more job-intensive and wage-intensive. It is hard, then, to argue that a balanced cut in exports and imports, which a comprehensive import-cutting bill like the Burke-Hartke Bill would produce, will bring a net gain in U.S. jobs. The evidence is clearly leaning toward the opposite conclusion that jobs and wages would be cut by such import cuts.

If a sweeping cut in imports would end up costing jobs rather than adding jobs, why would labor groups favor such import cuts? To arrive at an answer, it helps to note which labor groups have favored a major increase in import protection. The major backer of the Burke-Hartke Bill, and still a major lobbyist for protection against imports, is the AFL–CIO. It so happens that this organization has its membership concentrated in industries that are more affected by the import competition than is the economy as a whole. That is, AFL–CIO membership is heavily concentrated in the most import-threatened industries, the only exception being the heavily AFL–CIO tobacco industry, which is an export industry for the United States. It is thus quite practical for the AFL–CIO to lobby for protectionist bills that would create and defend AFL–CIO jobs and wages, even if the same bills would cost many jobs and wages outside this labor group. To understand who is pushing for protection, at any rate, it is important to know whose incomes are most tied to competing against imports.

The analysis so far has argued that a large and balanced raising of *new* U.S. import barriers would bring a net loss in jobs and wages. It does not follow that the *existing* import barriers have the same job effect. On the contrary, a study by Robert E. Baldwin for the U.S. Labor Department has shown that the barriers against U.S. imports have been made most restrictive on goods that have higher than average job content, especially in the unskilled job categories. The U.S. political process has thus far been somewhat selective in giving protection against imports, favoring industries that make fairly heavy use of lower-skilled workers, such as cotton textiles and footwear. Thus it turns out that eliminating the *existing* U.S. import barriers would bring a very slight net job loss—even though raising new barriers against all imports would also cost U.S. jobs. Raising new barriers to imports could result in a net gain in U.S. jobs and wages only if the import barriers were confined to those industries with especially high job content per dollar of output value.

The same sort of analysis can be applied to other countries. Some sketchy evidence suggests that in Canada's case, manufactured exports make relatively heavy use of unskilled labor and that mineral exports make heavy use of natural resources and capital (often owned by Canadian subsidiaries of U.S. firms), while one main group competing with imports is skilled labor. If so, then a general restriction of imports into Canada should have the effect of helping skilled labor and hurting unskilled labor and mineral-owning firms. In Canada's case, this result would be moderated by the fact that whatever affects labor incomes may affect international migration as well. Thus if protection started to worsen the absolute income position of Canadian unskilled labor, this would tend to retard the inflow of unskilled immigrants into Canada. Similarly, restricting Canada's foreign trade might tend to retard somewhat the emigration of skilled laborers seeking better incomes in the United States. These predictions for Canada, however, are based on thinner evidence than the conclusions about the better-documented job content of U.S. foreign trade.

SUMMARY

To know who gains and loses from trade or restrictions on trade, it is essential that one see how relative output prices affect factor incomes. In a simple two-factor, two-commodity model, the Stolper-Samuelson theorem has shown that opening trade and raising the relative price of the exportable good bring clear income gains to the factor of production used intensively in the exportable industry, and also bring clear income losses to the factor used intensively in the import-competing industry. Within the same model, adding a few extra assumptions, the factor-price equalization theorem has shown that free trade gives each factor of production the same material reward in each country.

To apply the theory of how trade and product prices affect the distribution of income among factors, it is necessary to go beyond the simple two-factor, two-product model. More general analyses have yielded fewer clear mathematical proofs, but some useful principles. One is that the shares of their incomes that the members of a factor group spend on exportables and importables matter to their stake in foreign trade. Another is that the factors most extremely specialized in exportable and importable production will still clearly gain and lose, respectively, from expanded trade.

Economists have devoted considerable energy to finding out who the exporting and import-competing factors of production are. Their efforts centered on the Leontiev paradox, which showed that the United States was exporting less capital-intensive and more labor-intensive goods than it was producing in competition with imports. The paradox led to a more careful and elaborate view of the factor content of foreign trade, especially for the United States.

It turns out that U.S. export industries involve more jobs than do U.S. import-competing industries. Since a general cut in U.S. imports is likely to bring an equal cut in the value of U.S. exports, it appears that cutting imports would bring a net loss of U.S. jobs and wages, contrary to the frequent argument for shutting out imports to save jobs. On the other hand, eliminating existing U.S. import barriers might also bring a slight job and wage loss, since existing barriers happen to be concentrated in the most labor intensive of the import-competing industries.

SUGGESTED READING

The Stolper-Samuelson theorem was presented in Wolfgang F. Stolper and Paul A. Samuelson, "Protection and Real Wages," *Review of Economic Studies, November 1941*, reprinted in Jagdish N. Bhagwati (ed.), *International Trade: Selected Readings* (Baltimore: Penguin, 1969).

The differences between factors' short-run and long-run fortunes from expanded trade were noted by Michael Mussa, "Tariffs and the Distribution of Income," *Journal of Political Economy,* vol. 82, no. 6 (November/December 1974), pp. 1191–1204.

The original Leontiev presentation of his paradoxical input-output results is his "Domestic Production and Foreign Trade: The American Position Reexamined," *Proceedings* of the American Philosophical Society, September 1953, reprinted in the Bhagwati volume cited above. The best survey of the Leontiev-paradox literature is given in the article by Baldwin cited in Table 5.1.

part II

Trade policy

-Day Futures	.9230	.9242
-Day Futures	.9227	.9241
na-Taiwan (Dollar)	.026	5
ombia (Peso)	.0275	.0275
mark (Krone)	.1631	.1632
ador (Sucre)	.0385	.0385
land (Markka)		
nce (Franc)	.2052	.2043
-Day Futures	.2048	.2040
-Day Futures	.2039	.2035
-Day Futures	.2025	.2022
ece (Drachma)	.0280	.0280
(Dollar)	.215	.2142
(Rupee)		.1165
nesia (Rupiah)	.00259	.2590
(Rial)	.01416	.1416
(Dinar)	3.44	3.44
(Pound)	.0951	.0951
(Lira)	.0011	.001135
an (Yen)	.003834	.003818
-Day Futures	.003845	.003827
-Day Futures	.003861	.003839
-Day Futures	.003887	.003862
on (Pound)	.3229	.3231
(Dolar)	.4079	.4076
Peso)	.0441	
herland (Guilder)		.4078
Zealand (Dollar)	.9815	25
way (rone)	.1820	
stan (upee)		.1025
u (Sol)	.0124	
ppines (Peso)		1355
ugal (Escudo)	.0246	.0246
l Arabia (Riyal)	.2833	.2833
apore (Dollar)	.4109	.4110
h Africa (Rand)	1.1522	1.1522

As Global Commerce Rebounds, Measures To Limit It Spread

Britons Curb Imports of TV Sets; U.S. Trims Quotas Of Foreign Beef, Sugar

Oil Buyers Beginning to Cut Purchases From OPEC States Raising Prices 10%

Europe's steelmakers want an anti-Japan cartel

Senate Votes Long-Stalled Bill on Trade

Asian Rubber Nations Move Toward Pact To Stabilize the Product's Volatile Price

6

The basic analysis
of a tariff

Something there is that doesn't love a wall, with economists as with others. A majority of economists have consistently favored letting nations trade freely with few tariffs or other barriers to trade. Indeed, economists have tended to be even more critical of trade barriers than have other groups in society, even though economists have taken great care to list the exceptional cases in which they feel trade barriers can be justified. Such consistent agreement is rare within the economics profession.

The presumption in favor of free trade is based primarily on a body of economic analysis demonstrating that there are usually net gains from freer trade both for nations and for the world. We caught an initial glimpse of this analysis in Chapter 3 above, which showed that free trade brings greater well-being than no trade. The main task of this chapter and the following chapters of Part II is to compare free-trade policies with a much wider range of trade barriers, barriers that do not necessarily shut out all international trade. It is mainly on this more detailed analysis of trade policies that economists have based their view that free trade is generally preferable to partial restrictions on trade, with a list of exceptions. Once this analysis is understood, it is easier to understand what divides the majority of economists from groups calling for restrictions on trade.

A PREVIEW OF CONCLUSIONS

The economic analysis of what is lost or gained by putting up barriers to international trade starts with a close look at the effects of the classic kind of trade barrier, a tariff on an imported good. This chapter and the next spell out who is likely to gain and who is likely to lose from a tariff, and the conditions under which a nation or the world could end up better off from a tariff. Later chapters take up other kinds of barriers to trade.

Our exploration of the pros and cons of a tariff will be detailed enough to warrant listing its main conclusions here at the outset. This chapter and the next will find that:

1. A tariff almost always lowers world well-being.
2. A tariff usually lowers the well-being of each nation, including the nation imposing the tariff.
3. As a general rule, whatever a tariff can do for the nation, something else can do better.
4. Exceptions to the case for free trade.
   (a) The "national optimal" tariff: When a nation can affect the prices at which it trades with foreigners, it can gain from its own tariff.
   (b) "Second-best" arguments for a tariff: When other incurable defects exist in the economy, imposing a tariff *may* be better than doing nothing.
5. A tariff absolutely *helps* groups tied closely to the production of import substitutes, even when the tariff is bad for the nation as a whole.

THE EFFECT OF A TARIFF ON CONSUMERS

Intuition would suggest that buyers of a good that is imported from abroad would be hurt by a tariff. The very fact that some of the good is imported means that consumers have found buying the foreign product to be a better bargain than confining their purchases to the domestic product. If the government charges a tariff on imports of this product, consumers will end up paying higher prices, buying less of the product, or both. The tariff, by taxing their imports, should make them worse off.

The demand and supply analysis of a tariff agrees with our intuition. It goes beyond intuition, though, by allowing us to quantify in dollars just how much a tariff costs consumers.

Figure 6.1 gives the basic demand-supply diagram of a tariff, here a tariff on bicycles. If there were no tariff, bicycles would be imported freely at the world price of $200. Competition between foreign bikes

FIGURE 6.1
The effect of a tariff on consumers

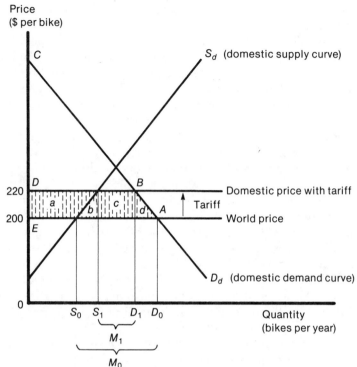

Shaded area = Cost of the tariff to consumers.

and comparable domestic bikes would make the domestic bikes also settle at a price of \$200. At this price consumers would buy S_0 bikes a year from domestic suppliers and would import M_0 bikes a year, buying $D_0 = S_0 + M_0$ bikes in all.

We can quantify what consumers gain from being able to buy bikes, and how much a tariff would cut their gains, if we understand the meaning of their demand curve. The demand curve can be interpreted in either of two ways, as we noted in Chapter 3. It tells us how much would be demanded at each price. It also tells us, for each quantity bought each year, the highest price that some consumer would be willing to pay to get another bike. The demand curve in Figure 6.1 tells us that at the free-trade price of \$200, somebody in our country is just willing to pay that \$200 for the last bike bought at Point A. It also says that at Point B somebody was willing to pay \$220 for a bike that made total purchases come to D_1 a year. Similarly, if no bikes were being bought for some reason, there is apparently somebody willing to pay a high price, such as $1,000, to get the first bike, up at Point C. This view of the demand curve allows us to add up dollar measures of how much consumers are gaining from being able to buy bikes at all. The very first bike each year brings $800 in net gains to somebody who would have paid up to $1,000 to get it (Point C) but who gets it at the world price of only $200. Similarly, as we go down the demand curve from Point C toward Point A, we find that the vertical gap between the demand curve and the world price of $200 shows us that somebody is getting another bargain by paying less for the bike than the maximum amount that person would have been willing to pay for a bike. So summing up the entire area between the demand curve and the $200 price line tells us the amount of "consumer surplus" from buying bikes, the amount by which what consumers would have been willing to pay as individuals exceeds what they end up paying. This "consumer surplus" area, triangle ACE, is an approximation to what being able to buy bikes is worth to consumers.

A tariff of $20, or 10 percent, raises the price of bicycles and cuts the gains that are represented by the consumer surplus. By raising the price to $220, the tariff in Figure 6.1 forces some consumers to give up an extra $20 per bike to get the same D_1 bikes they would rather have bought at $200, while it makes other consumers decide that a bike is not worth $220 to them, so that total demand drops back from D_0 to D_1. The net loss to consumers from the tariff is the total shaded area, or areas $a + b + c + d$. This is the amount that consumers lose by having their consumer surplus from bicycle purchases cut from triangle ACE to triangle BCD.

The cost of a tariff to consumers can be measured, and it can turn out to be large. It can be large partly because the tariff makes consumers pay more on the domestic product as well as on imports. When the tariff is first imposed, individual consumers will try to avoid paying the extra $20 by buying more domestic bikes. But the domestic supply cannot be increased without bidding up marginal costs above $200 (if it could, then domestic suppliers could have outcompeted foreign suppliers even with no tariff). So the sales by domestic suppliers expand only up to S_1, at which level of output their marginal costs and their price also equal $220, making the consumers pay more on all bikes, not just on foreign bikes. To measure the shaded area of consumer loss, one needs to know the prices of bikes with and without the tariff and the amounts that consumers would buy with and without the tariff (D_0 and D_1). Knowing these, one can compute the areas of the rectangle $a + b + c$ and the triangle area d. Even if one does not know the exact slope of the demand curve, one could approximate the amount of consumer loss: it would be slightly underestimated by multiplying the tariff gap ($20) by the amount imported with the tariff (M_1), or slightly overestimated by multiplying the tariff gap by the amount imported without the tariff (M_0).

THE EFFECT ON PRODUCERS

A tariff brings gains for domestic producers who face import competition, by taxing only the foreign product. The more it costs consumers to buy the foreign product, the more they will turn to domestic suppliers, who get the benefit of extra sales and higher prices thanks to the tariff.

FIGURE 6.2
The effect of a tariff on producers

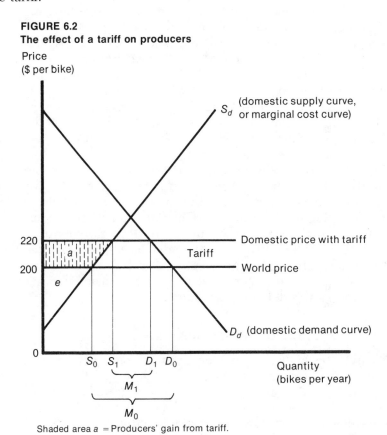

Shaded area *a* = Producers' gain from tariff.

The producer gains from the tariff can be quantified with the help of Figure 6.2, which portrays from a producer's point of view the same bicycle market as is shown in Figure 6.1. As we have seen, the tariff drives up the price of domestic bikes from $200 to $220. Domestic firms respond by raising their output and sales as long as that is profitable. They will expand from S_0 to S_1. It is at output S_1 that their costs of producing each extra bike, shown by the supply curve, rise as high as the tariff-ridden market price of \$220. It is not profitable for them to raise their output any higher, because doing so would raise their marginal costs above \$220, the price they receive when selling bikes in competition with foreign firms in the domestic market.

The profits that producers make are the difference between their total revenues and their total costs. In Figure 6.2, these profits, or more accurately "economic rents," take the form of a triangular area between the price line and the marginal cost curve. To see why, focus first on how total revenues for producers are represented in Figure 6.2. Total revenues equal price times quantity sold, or \$200 times S_0 without the tariff and \$220 times S_1 with it. The tariff has clearly raised the total sales revenues of the domestic producers. But not all of the revenues are profits. The part of total revenues lying below the supply curve, or marginal cost curve, represents the variable costs of producing bicycles. Only the part lying above the marginal cost curve and within the total-revenue area represents profits above costs. Thus the tariff raises profits in the domestic bicycle industry only by the amount of area a, from area e to areas $a + e$.

What domestic producers gain from the tariff is smaller than what the tariff costs consumers. The reason is straightforward: producers gain on the price markup on only the domestic output, while consumers are forced to pay the same price markup on both domestic output and imports. Figures 6.1 and 6.2 bring this out clearly for the bicycle example. The tariff brought bicycle producers only area a in gains, but cost consumers this same area a plus areas $b + c + d$. As far as the effects on bicycle consumers and bicycle producers alone are concerned, the tariff is definitely a net loss.

THE EFFECTIVE RATE OF PROTECTION

Clearly, the higher the percentage tariff on a good is, the more protection the tariff gives to the domestic firms producing in that industry. Yet to understand just who is being protected by a tariff or by a set of tariffs, one needs to take a closer look at the industrial structure.

A tariff on the product of an individual industry protects more than just the firms producing that product domestically. It also helps protect the incomes of workers and others whose inputs are counted in the "value added" in that industry. Beyond these groups, the firms in the industry and their workers, the tariff also protects the incomes of other industries selling material inputs to that industry. Thus our tariff on bicycles may help not only bicycle firms but also bicycle workers and firms selling steel shapes, rubber, and other material inputs to the bicycle industry. This slightly complicates the task of measuring how much the bicycle tariff helps bicycle firms.

Firms in a given industry are also affected by tariffs on their inputs as well as tariffs on the products they sell. The firms selling bicycles, for example, would be hurt by tariffs on steel or rubber. This again complicates the task of measuring the effect of whole sets of tariffs, the whole tariff structure, on an individual industry's firms.

To take account of these points, postwar economists have developed the concept of the *effective rate of protection* of an individual industry, which is defined as the percentage by which the entire set of a nation's trade barriers raises the industry's value added per unit of output. The effective rate of protection for the industry can be quite different from the percentage tariff paid by consumers on its output. This difference is brought out clearly by Figure 6.3, which shows the effective rate of protection of a 10 percent tariff on bicycle imports and a 5 percent tariff on imports of steel, rubber, and all other material inputs into the bicycle industry. The 10 percent tariff on bicycles by itself would raise their price, and the value added by the bicycle industry, by $20 per bike, as before. The 5 percent tariffs on bicycle inputs would cost the bicycle industry $7 per bike by raising the domestic prices of inputs. The two sets of tariffs together would

FIGURE 6.3
Illustrative calculation of an effective rate of protection

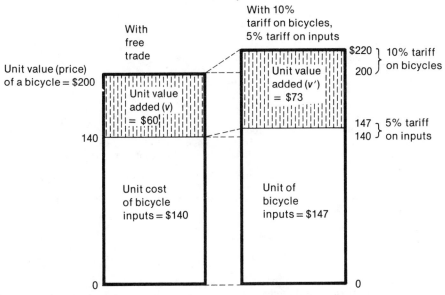

Effective rate of protection for bicycle industry $= \dfrac{v'-v}{v} = \dfrac{\$73 - \$60}{\$60} = 21.7\%$

raise the industry's unit value added by only $13 per bike. But this extra $13 represents a protection of value added (incomes) in the bicycle industry of 21.7 percent of value added, not just 10 percent or less as one might have thought from a casual look at the nominal tariff rates themselves.

The example in Figure 6.3 illustrates two of the basic points brought out by the concept of effective rate of protection: a given industry's incomes, or value added, will be affected by trade barriers on its inputs as well as trade barriers on its output, and the effective rate of protection will be greater than the nominal rate when the industry's output is protected by a higher duty than its inputs.[1] Thus, to get an accurate picture of just who is being protected by either a single tariff or a whole tariff structure, one needs to watch the input-output relationships in the economy.

Empirical estimates of effective rates of protection have turned up several interesting patterns. First, they show that the effective rates of protection on most industries tend to be well above the nominal rates. This is because there tends to be an "escalation" of the tariff structure over the stages of production: by and large, nominal rates tend to be higher on the more finished products than on intermediate products,

---

[1] The formula for the effective rate of protection in terms of the nominal tariff rates on the output and inputs is:

$$e_j = \frac{t_j - \sum_i a_{ij} t_i}{1 - \sum_i a_{ij}},$$

where e_j is the effective rate of protection for industry j, t_j, is the nominal tariff on the output of industry j, the t_i's are the tariffs on the inputs into industry j, and the a_{ij}'s are the shares of the costs of the various inputs in the value of the output of industry j, with free trade. This formula has been implicitly used in Figure 6.3, where $t_j = 0.10$, the one and only input tariff $t_i = 0.05$, and $a_{ij} = 0.70$, so that $e_j = 0.217$.

To see how this formula emerges from the definition of the effective rate, let us look at the ways in which tariffs affect value added. Without tariffs, if units are measured so that the free-trade price of the jth product is 1, then the unit value added, or v, equals $1 - \sum_i a_{ij}$. With tariffs, unit value added, v' equals (price of output) − (unit costs of inputs), or $(1 + t_j) - \sum_i a_{ij}(1 + t_i)$, assuming that all the goods are traded at fixed world prices and that the physical input-output ratios behind the a_{ij}'s do not change. From these relationships if follows that

$$e_j = \frac{v' - v}{v} = \frac{1 + t_j - \sum_i a_{ij} - \sum_i a_{ij} t_i - 1 + \sum_i a_{ij}}{1 - \sum_i a_{ij}} = \frac{t_j - \sum_i a_{ij} t_i}{1 - \sum_i a_{ij}}.$$

This formula confirms that the effective rate is greater than the nominal rate ($e_j > t_j$) whenever the nominal tariff on the product is greater than the average tariff on inputs, as stated in the text.

both in developing and in more developed countries. This means that producers of final goods tend to receive higher effective rates of protection than do sellers of intermediate goods, as illustrated by bicycles and bicycle inputs here. There are exceptions, however. Studies have found cases in Pakistan for example, in which the complicated national structure of trade barriers gave negative effective protection to several industries, cutting their unit value added more with barriers on the importation of inputs than the protection afforded the industries on their output. The same is suspected about some industries in 19th-century Europe: it is believed that the metal-using engineering industries in Italy and Russia, and the coal-using ferrous metals industries in France, may have suffered negative effective protection due to high tariffs on their key inputs.

Although it serves to underline these basic points about the incidence of protection across industries, the effective rate of protection is in some respects less helpful to a welfare evaluation of trade barriers than the demand-supply framework used in the previous sections. It does not really quantify how much any group gains or loses from a tariff or set of tariffs because it measures only impacts on value added *per unit of output,* while avoiding the important issue of how much output itself would change in response to the tariff or tariffs. It also lumps profits and other incomes within the industry together into the value-added aggregate, without showing us separately what share of the effect on unit value added goes to the managers and owners who make the decisions about how much to expand or contract the industry's output in response to tariffs. For these reasons the effective rate of protection does not directly quantify who gains or loses how much from a tariff. Measuring the gains and losses is better approached through the demand-supply framework itself, supplemented where necessary with information on how individual industries are affected by tariffs in other sectors.

THE TARIFF AS GOVERNMENT REVENUE

The effects of a tariff on the well-being of consumers and producers do not exhaust its effects on the importing nation. As long as the tariff is not so high as to prohibit all imports, it also brings revenue to the government. This revenue equals the unit amount of the tariff times the volume of imports with the tariff, or area c back in Figure 6.1.

The tariff is a definite gain for the nation, since it is revenue collected by the government. This gain could take any of several forms. It could become extra government spending on socially worthwhile projects. It could be matched by an equal cut in some other tax, such as the income tax. Or it could just become extra income for greedy government officials. Although what form the tariff takes can certainly matter, the central point is that it represents revenue that accrues to somebody within the country, and thus counts as an element of gain to be weighed in with the consumer losses and producer gains from the tariff.

THE NET NATIONAL LOSS FROM THE TARIFF

By combining the effects of the tariff on consumers, producers, and the government, we can determine the net effect of the tariff on the importing nation as a whole. To do so, we need to impose a further value judgment. We need to state explicitly how much we care about each dollar of effect on each group. That is unavoidable. Indeed, anybody who expresses an opinion on whether a tariff is good or bad necessarily does so on the basis of his or her own value judgments about how important each group is.

The basic analysis starts out by using a *one-dollar, one-vote* yardstick: *Every dollar of gain or loss is just as important as every other dollar of gain or loss, regardless of who the gainers or losers are.* Let us use this welfare yardstick here. Later we discuss what difference it would make if we chose to weigh one group's dollar stakes more heavily than those of other groups.

If the one-dollar, one-vote yardstick is applied, then a tariff like the one graphed in Figures 6.1 and 6.2 brings a clear net loss to the importing nation, as well as to the world as a whole. This can be seen by studying Figure 6.4, which returns to the bicycle example used above. We have seen that the dollar value of the consumer losses exceeded the dollar value of the producer gains from the tariff. We have also seen that the government collected some tariff revenue, an element of national gain. The left-hand side of Figure 6.4 makes it clear that the dollar value of what the consumers lose exceeds even the sum of the producer gains and the government tariff revenues:

The same net national loss can be shown in another way. The right-hand side of Figure 6.4 shows the market for imports of bicycles. Our demand curve for imports of bicycles is a curve showing the amount by which our demand for bicycles exceeds our domestic supply of bicycles at each price. It is thus a curve derived by subtracting our domestic supply curve from our domestic demand curve for bicycles at each price (horizontally), since imports = demand minus domestic supply. This allows us to show the net national loss, or area $(b + d)$, on the right-hand side of Figure 6.4 as well as on the left. Since area b and area d have the same tariff height and relate, respectively, to the net shift from imports to domestic supply and the total decline in demand, area $(b + d)$ is a triangle with the tariff as its

FIGURE 6.4
The net national loss from a tariff, in two equivalent diagrams

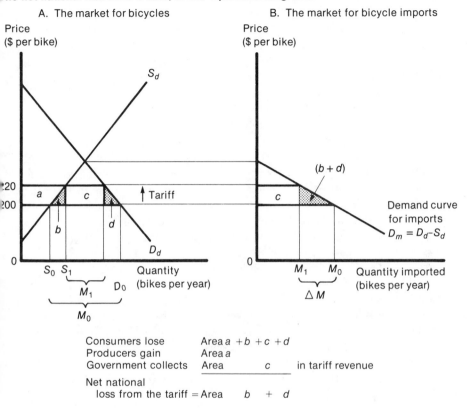

A. The market for bicycles

B. The market for bicycle imports

Consumers lose	Area $a + b + c + d$
Producers gain	Area a
Government collects	Area c in tariff revenue
Net national loss from the tariff = Area	$b + d$

height and the total cut in imports as its base, as shown on the right-hand side.

The net national loss from the tariff shown in Figure 6.4 is not hard to estimate empirically. The key information one needs consists only of the height of the tariff itself and the estimated volume by which the tariff reduces imports, or M. The usual way of arriving at this information is to find out the percentage price markup the tariff represents, the initial dollar value of imports, and the percentage elasticity, or responsiveness, of import quantities to price changes. It is handy, and perhaps surprising, that the net national loss from the tariff can be estimated just using information on imports, as on the right-hand side of Figure 6.4, without even knowing the domestic demand and supply curves.

What logic lies behind the geometric finding that the net national loss equals areas $b + d$? With a little reflection, it is not hard to see that these areas represent gains from international trade and specialization that are lost because of the tariff. **Area d,** sometimes called the "**consumption effect**" of the tariff, shows the loss to consumers in the importing nation that corresponds to their being forced to cut their total consumption of bicycles. They would have been willing to pay prices up to $220 to get the extra foreign bicycles lost in area d, yet the tariff prevents their being able to get them for less than $220 even though the extra bicycles would have cost the nation only $200 a bike in payments to foreign sellers. What the consumers lose in area d, nobody else gains. Area d is a "deadweight" loss, an element of overall inefficiency caused by the tariff.

Area b is a welfare loss tied to the fact that some consumer demand is shifted from imports to more expensive domestic production. The tariff is raising domestic production by $S_0 S_1$ at the expense of imports. The domestic supply curve, or the marginal cost curve, is assumed to be upward-sloping, so that each extra bicycle costs more and more to produce, rising from a resource cost of $200 up to a cost of $220. Yet society is paying more for the bicycles than the $200 price at which the bicycles are available abroad. This extra cost of shifting to more expensive home production, sometimes called the "**production effect**" of the tariff, is represented by area b. Like area d, it is a deadweight loss. It is part of what consumers pay, but neither the government nor producers gain it. It is the amount by which the cost of drawing domestic resources away from other uses exceeds the savings from not paying foreigners to sell us the extra $S_0 S_1$. Thus the gains from trade lost by the tariff come in two forms: the consumption effect of area d plus the production effect of area b.

The basic analysis of a tariff identifies areas b and d as the net national loss from a tariff only if certain assumptions are granted. The clearest key assumption is that the one-dollar, one-vote yardstick is an appropriate common measure of different groups' interests. It was by using this yardstick that the analysis above was able to imply that consumers' losing areas a and c was exactly offset, dollar for dollar, by producers' gaining area a and the government's collecting area c. That is what produced $(b + d)$ as the net loss for the nation. Suppose that you personally reject this yardstick. Suppose, for example, that you think that each dollar of gain for the bicycle producers is somehow more important to you than each dollar of consumer loss, perhaps because you see the bicycle consumers as a group society has pampered too much. If that is your view, you will not want to accept areas b and d as the net national loss from the tariff. The same basic analysis of the tariff is still useful to you, however. You can stipulate by how much you weigh each dollar of effect on bicycle producers and government more heavily than each dollar for consumers, and apply your own differential weights to each group's dollar stake to see whether the net effect of the tariff is still negative.

Other assumptions have been made which also affect one's view of the tariff. Here are some of the most important ones:

1. It has been assumed that the importing nation is a "price taker," a country that is unable to affect the world price by its own actions.

2. The analysis so far has ignored the balance of payments between countries, by not taking any note of the fact that the tariff will cut the amount being paid to foreigners. This drop in expenditures on imports will either affect the exchange rate or shift the balance of payments toward surplus. These balance-of-payments effects have implications not spelled out here.

3. The analysis has been implicitly assuming that we live in a "first-best" world in which the gains and losses for individual decision-makers are also society's gains and losses without the tariff. Only the tariff itself is allowed to enter here as a factor that makes social costs and benefits different from private ones.

We return to these assumptions later in this and the next chapter, asking in each case what difference it would make if the assumption were thrown out in ways that make the analysis more realistic.

PAST MEASUREMENTS OF THE NATIONAL LOSS

Since the late 1950s several economists have made empirical estimates of the net national welfare losses from tariffs and other trade barriers. Their estimates often take account of refinements that will be introduced only later in this chapter and in Chapter 7. Yet basically their procedure has been simply to estimate the sizes of areas $b + d$ in Figure 6.4 for several internationally traded commodities. They have used information on the extent of imports and the height of the tariff or other price-raising import barrier, and an estimate of the price elasticity of import demand for each product. Table 6.1 summarizes the findings of several of these studies.

The early attempts to quantify the costs of tariffs centered on the cases of the United States and Australia. The correct way of measuring the deadweight loss was spelled out in 1960 by Harry G. Johnson, who went on to argue that the value of the loss from tariffs had to be a positive but trivial share of a nation's gross national product. Johnson noted that for any commodity

$$\frac{\text{Net national loss from the tariff}}{\text{GNP}} = (\tfrac{1}{2}) \times (\% \text{ of tariff})$$

$$\times \% \text{ change in import quantity} \times \frac{\text{Import value}}{\text{GNP}}.$$

TABLE 6.1
The results of some past estimates of the welfare effects of trade barriers

Country, year	Estimated effect of trade barriers	Nature of the estimate
(1) Hypothetical	Small shares of GNP	Hypothetical gains from removing all tariffs (that is, losses from the tariffs) (H. G. Johnson)
(2) Chile, 1950s	Less than 2.5% of GNP	Chile's losses from all its import barriers, very rough guesswork (Harberger)
(3) Germany, 1956–57	0.18% of GNP	Germany's gains from cutting tariffs on finished industrial products in half (Wemelsfelder)
(4) United States, 1960	Less than 0.11% of GNP	U.S. gains from removing all 1960 U.S. tariffs, ignoring "terms of trade" effects (see Chapter 7) (Stern)
(5) United States, 1960	Less than 0.11% of GNP	U.S. *losses* from removing all 1960 tariffs, the losses resulting from "terms of trade" effects (see Chapter 7) (Basevi)
(6) Industrial countries, 1967	Various net gains, all way below 1% of GNP	Gains to various industrial countries from the Kennedy Round tariff cuts (Balassa and Kreinin)
(7) Developing countries, 1960s	From 9.5% of GNP (Brazil) down to −0.4% of GNP (Malaya)	Gains from removing trade barriers in six developing countries (Balassa)
(8) United States, 1971	About 1% of GNP	U.S. gains from removing all barriers on trade, ignoring "terms of trade" effects (Magee)

Sources: (1) Harry G. Johnson, "The Cost of Protection and the Scientific Tariff," *Journal of Political Economy*, vol. 68, no. 4 (August 1960), pp. 327–45; (2) Arnold C. Harberger, "Using the Resources at Hand More Effectively," *American Economic Review*, vol. 49, no. 2 (May 1959), pp. 134–46; (3) J. Wemelsfelder, "The Short-Run Effect of Lowering Import Duties in Germany," *Economic Journal*, (March 1960), pp. 94–104; (4) Robert M. Stern, "The U.S. Tariff and the Efficiency of the U.S. Economy," *American Economic Review*, vol. 54, no. 2 (May 1964), p. 465; (5) Giorgio Basevi, "The Restrictive Effect of the U.S. Tariff and Its Welfare Value," *American Economic Review*, vol. 58, no. 4 (September 1968), pp. 840–52; (6) Bela Balassa and Mordechai Kreinin, "Trade Liberalization under the "Kennedy Round': The Static Effects," *Review of Economics and Statistics*, vol. 49, no. 2 (May 1967), pp. 125–37; (7) Bela Balassa, *The Structure of Protection in Developing Countries* (1971), p. 82; (8) Stephen P. Magee, "The Welfare Effects of Restrictions on U.S. Trade," Brookings Papers in Economic Activity, 3 (1972), pp. 645–707.

By studying these fractions, one can see why this kind of measure of the net loss from a tariff might easily look like a small fraction of GNP. Suppose, for example, that a nation's import tariffs were all 10 percent tariffs, and that they caused a 20 percent reduction in import quantities. Suppose that total imports of all commodities were 10 percent of

GNP—above the 5 percent share prevailing for the United States, but below the share of imports in GNP in many other countries. In this realistic case, the net national loss from all tariffs on imports equals ½ × 0.10 × 0.20 × 0.10, or only 0.1 percent of GNP! Johnson thus argued that the net national loss from tariffs is not likely to be great, at least for a large country not totally dependent on foreign trade, such as the United States.

Other empirical studies soon seemed to confirm Johnson's hunch. As suggested in Table 6.1, studies of the United States and other industrial countries came up with estimated losses from trade barriers that were 1 percent or less of GNP, with the trade barriers actually bringing net gains in some cases. Only when a less developed country's trade barriers were being studied were the estimated losses a large share of GNP, as in Brazil's loss of 9.5 percent of GNP from trade barriers in the early 1960s. The authors of these studies concluded that trade barriers did impose net costs, but that these costs were "small" as a share of GNP. If they are right, then there is certainly reason to wonder how much political energy a nation should expend over the issue of tariffs and other trade barriers.

TOWARD BETTER MEASURES

There are many reasons why one should not accept the standard measures of areas *b* plus *d* as the true measures of what tariffs do to a country's well-being. It is possible to identify several biases in the usual measures. Although these biases are easier to state than to quantify, knowing about them allows one to decide whether a standard measure is likely to be too low or too high. As it turns out, most of the biases suggest that the usual measures underestimate the costs of trade barriers.

1. *What is "small"?* The authors who concluded that the net losses were small reached that conclusion by comparing the net losses to gross national product. GNP is a very large denominator, one likely to make many numerators look "small." For example, the 1 percent of U.S. GNP estimated by Magee for 1971 (he did not call it small) was up to $10 billion per year. That may be only 1 percent of GNP, but it is also a lot of hamburger.

2. *The net national loss is smaller than the consumer loss.* If one is to understand why debates over trade barriers have generated as much heat as they have in the past, one must not lose sight of the fact that trade barriers cost some groups a lot more than their net cost to the whole nation. Figure 6.4 brought this point out clearly for the case of an import tariff. There consumers lost a lot—areas *a*, *b*, *c*, and *d*—even

though the net national loss was only a smaller area ($b + d$). Most trade barriers have opposite effects on the material well-being of different groups, so that the net effect for all of these groups can look deceivingly small. In other words, trade barriers can redistribute income within a country even more than they impose a net cost on the whole country.

3. *There is an administrative cost to any trade barrier.* The basic analysis of a tariff is incomplete if it fails to recognize that a trade barrier ties up resources that society could have used in some other way. To enforce an import tariff, a country must employ customs officials at its borders. Part of the revenue of the tariff, represented by area c in Figure 6.4, is thus a payment for administering the tariff itself. But the people administering the tariff could have been usefully employed elsewhere. To this extent, part of what is being transferred from consumers to the government does represent a social waste of resources. This means that part of area c should be added to areas b plus d in calculating the net national loss from the tariff, even though most studies of the costs of trade barriers do not do so.

4. *Protection could slow technological progress.* The usual estimates of the cost of a tariff implicitly assume that the tariff has no effect on the tendency of domestic producers to seek and find new ways of cutting costs and shifting their marginal cost curves downward. That assumption may be incorrect. Many economists suspect that whatever protects producers' economic rents and profit margins dulls their incentive to look for technological improvements that allow them to produce at lower cost. This suspicion has been countered by the opposite view, associated with the work of Joseph Schumpeter and John Kenneth Galbraith, that fatter profit margins can accelerate technological improvements by giving large firms greater resources and security for spending on research and development. The issue has not been resolved empirically. If later work proves the suspicion of many economists to be correct, then a tariff could cost the nation more than has been estimated, by retarding the advance of productive knowledge.

5. *The effect of tariffs on import quantities may have been underestimated.* The measure of the net cost of a tariff depends critically on the estimate of the amount of imports it discourages. But estimates of the effect of tariffs and prices on import quantities are often biased downward. There are several reasons for this chronic underestimation of the responsiveness of imports to changes in prices: (1) the usual statistical estimates of import-price elasticity are usually short-run elasticity estimates, which run lower than long-run elasticities; (2) the usual estimates are based on highly aggregated commodity classes, a

procedure which underestimates how sensitive imports can be when the tariffs affecting their prices apply only to certain specific, and highly substitutable, commodities within these broad classes; (3) the usual estimates are often based on incorrect measures, especially for the prices of imports and their domestic substitutes, another procedure which has been shown to cause underestimation of the price (and tariff) elasticity of imports; and finally (4) the usual estimates are beset by problems of "simultaneity bias," which again tend to cause underestimation of how much tariffs and price matter to import quantities. The underlying explanation of why these problems arise is too technical to be covered here. They all mean that the effect of tariffs on imports has usually been underestimated, causing past studies to underestimate the size of the net national losses from tariffs.

So far all of the steps suggested for improving our measures of the net national cost of a tariff would have the effect of making the true cost larger than the usual estimates, such as those in Table 6.1, would suggest. Not all of the possible refinements would tend to magnify the cost of the tariff, however. Here are two that might reduce it.

6. *A tariff affects the exchange rate in a way that can cut the welfare cost of the tariff.* As we noted above, the basic analysis of a tariff usually ignores any discussion of how the tariff affects the exchange rate between our currency and foreign currencies. This omission stems from the subtlety of how this relates to the welfare cost of the tariff, and from the convenience of keeping discussions of exchange rates completely separate from discussions of trade politics. Nonetheless, it is worth noting that an exchange-rate effect is linked to the cost of the tariff.

Imposing a tariff cuts the quantity of imports. It also cuts the total value spent on imports, since the tariff's effect on the price paid to foreigners is either zero (as assumed in this chapter) or negative. This means that the tariff cuts the value of the foreign exchange that this country buys for the purpose of buying imported goods. As we shall see in detail in Part III, this tends to cut the price of foreign currency in terms of our own currency. That is, it tends to make each of our dollars buy more foreign currency. But this change in exchange rates will affect the quantities and dollar prices of our exports and imports. If foreigners must pay more units of their currencies to get each dollar for buying our exports, then they will tend to buy less of our exports and the dollar price of our exportable goods may even decline somewhat. Similarly, residents of our country will begin to find foreign goods costing fewer dollars than they cost originally, now that each dollar buys more units of foreign currency. So the tariff may end up raising the dollar price of imports by less than the amount of the tariff itself. If, for example, a 10 percent tariff causes the dollar to buy 3 percent more of each foreign currency, the domestic dollar price of importable goods will rise only about 7 percent.

These exchange-rate repercussions of the tariff tend to cut the national loss from the tariff to a degree that can be roughly quantified. The results of a recent article on these exchange-rate effects by Giorgio Basevi make it clear that the national cost of a tariff would tend to be reduced by the proportion of the exchange-rate change in the tariff change. For example, if the 10 percent tariff did cut the dollar price of foreign currencies by 3 percent, then the national loss from the tariff would equal 70 percent of the usual measure of national loss (areas b and d). The smaller the share of total imports taken up by goods being subjected to a new tariff, the less the exchange rate will change in response, and the more safely one could ignore this refinement relating to exchange rates.

7. *Tariff changes bring displacement costs.* The net cost of a tariff is also modified by recognizing the unrealism of another assumption implicitly made by the usual basic analysis. So far we have been assuming that the domestic supply curve was also the marginal cost curve of domestic production for the nation as well as for the private bicycle firms facing those marginal costs. This assumption was based on the further assumption that any labor or other inputs used in the domestic bicycle industry were just barely enticed away from other uses that were nearly as productive as was their use in the bicycle industry—and paid nearly as well. Thus, it was implicitly assumed that bicycle workers earning $4 an hour could also have found work elsewhere that paid them nearly $4 an hour. For this reason the cost of bicycle labor and other inputs paid by the bicycle firms was assumed to equal the social cost of not using those inputs in other industries.

It often does not work that way. If the bicycle industry, or any other industry, were to lay off workers and other inputs, those workers would not simply move to some other productive employment with virtually the same marginal product. People's next best alternatives are well below their best ones, especially if they have become committed to their current employments by gearing their choices of residence and their personal skills to those employments. It is well known that displaced workers sustain prolonged income losses while trying to find new jobs. These displacement costs must be considered when toting up the net effects of tariff changes.

How displacement costs affect the national loss from a tariff depends on whether the tariff is being imposed or removed. Removing an existing tariff would clearly displace workers in import-competing industries, such as the bicycle industry in the current example. The bicycle workers would lose income for some time before finding new jobs. Similarly, managers and shareholders in the bicycle industry would experience capital losses due to the keener competition from imports. The losses suffered by those in the bicycle industry are real losses to society. Even if the taxpayers, through government agencies, paid people in the bicycle industry full compensation for their private income and capital losses, society would still be losing something in displacement costs: in this case the loss would show up as a burden to taxpayers. Clearly, the amount of these displacement costs should be subtracted from the national gains achieved by removing existing tariffs. Recent studies have shown that in some cases the estimated displacement costs have been great enough to cancel out the gains from tariff removal and that in other cases they have offset only part of the gains from freer trade.

The national losses that would result from imposing a new tariff, on the other hand, would not be reduced by allowing for displacement costs. If there were a new tariff on bicycles, obviously bicycle workers would not be laid off by the tariff. On the contrary, the bicycle industry would expand its output and employment in response to the new protection. If there were displacement costs to consider, they would take a subtler form and would appear in other industries. The only displacement costs to consider would be those arising from the indirect tendency of the new tariff to cause other sectors to contract. One such sector would be the whole export sector. The new tariffs on imports could make exports contract in several ways. They raise the value of our currency and thus could make foreigners buy less of our exports, as mentioned above. They could provoke foreign governments into retaliating with new tariffs against our exports. For these and other reasons, new import tariffs can cause losses of jobs and incomes in exportable-good sectors. Reckoning the displacement costs would raise the estimated national losses from imposing new tariffs.

Economists have recently been grappling with the task of quantifying how such refinements as the seven items discussed above would change our estimates of the national losses from tariffs and other trade barriers. Some of these desirable refinements have been easier to quantify than others. So far, the last two, those that could reduce the net estimated loss from a tariff, have been quantified fairly satisfactorily. It has been harder to put dollar values on some of the others. This complicates the task of deciding how bad a tariff is. But it does not render the task hopeless, since rough but reasonable adjustments can be made. And even without being able to attach dollar numbers to each of the seven points listed, an advocate of freer trade can still use the orthodox measures of national losses from the tariff but note that important points escaping easy quantification (for example, points 1–5 above) tend to reinforce the case against the tariff.

THE TARIFF AGAIN, WITH PRODUCTION AND
INDIFFERENCE CURVES

Throughout Part II we shall be using the demand-supply framework to bring out basic points about the pros and cons of trade barriers. This section will show that the results already established with the use of the demand-supply framework are consistent with the use of the production and indifference curves discussed in Part I.

Figure 6.5 shows how the effects of a tariff are portrayed using a nation's production and indifference curves. The free-trade position is

FIGURE 6.5
The effects of a tariff, portrayed with production and indifference curves

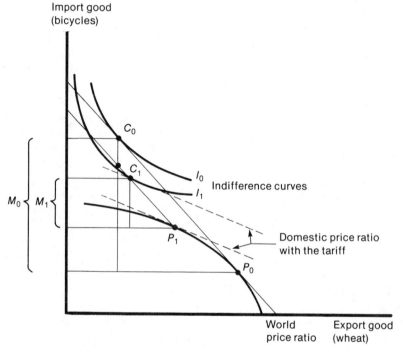

represented by Points P_0 and C_0. The nation is producing more wheat and fewer bicycles at P_0 than it is consuming at C_0. By consuming at C_0, it is achieving a higher level of utility (I_0) than it could achieve if it had to consume only what it produced, along the production curve. This higher level of well-being is made possible by trading at the world price ratio, at which the country exports some wheat in exchange for its M_0 imports of bicycles.

Imposing a tariff on bicycles makes the domestic price of bicycles higher in terms of wheat than the world price. In terms of Figure 6.5, this means that the domestic price ratio is represented by a flatter line (it takes more wheat to buy a bicycle) than the world price line. The tariff makes both domestic producers and domestic consumers respond to the new price ratio, just as in the demand-supply framework above. Domestic producers shift resources out of the wheat industry into the now-protected bicycle industry until the marginal costs of producing each are brought into line with the tariff-ridden price ratio at Point P_1. Meanwhile consumers also adjust, by setting their consumption at a point (C_1) where the marginal utilities of the two goods are in the same ratio as the domestic prices. In the process trade has shrunk, from imports of M_0 to imports of M_1.

The tariff has clearly lowered welfare, in Figure 6.5 as in the figures above. At Point C_1 the nation is enjoying only the level of utility represented by the indifference curve I_1, which is inferior to the I_0 enjoyed with free trade. The tariff cuts welfare in two ways, both analogous to welfare effects introduced earlier in this chapter. The fact that domestic production is shifted from wheat toward bicycles costs the nation something, since in moving from P_0 to P_1 the nation incurs production costs on bicycles exceeding what these bicycles cost on the world market. This "production effect," like its counterpart in Figure 6.4 above, is part of what the nation loses. It is a welfare loss represented by the fact that when producing at P_1, the nation is constrained to find its best consumption point somewhere on the world price line running northwest from P_1. The nation further loses by having the tariff distort its consumption pattern. The tariff makes consumers find a consumption point where the indifference curve is tangent to the domestic price ratio, even though this fails to correspond to the nation's trading opportunities at the world price ratio. This "consumption effect" on welfare is represented by the fact that private consumer decisions will leave us at Point C_1 instead of the nationally better range of points just to the northwest of C_1.

The national loss from the tariff thus equals the sum of a "production effect" and a "consumption effect" on national well-being, just as the national loss from the tariff equaled the sum of the same two effects (areas b and d again) in the earlier sections of this chapter.

SUMMARY

Under the assumptions of this chapter, a tariff on imports clearly lowers national well-being. It costs consumers more than it benefits producers and the government, which collects the tariff revenue. The tariff thus redistributes income from consumers of the imported product toward others in society.

The usual empirical measures of this net national loss show it to be positive but "small." These empirical measures need to be refined in a number of ways, however, and most of the necessary refinements have the effect of making the net losses from the tariff look greater.

The effects of tariffs on producer interests are further clarified by the concept of the effective rate of protection, which measures the percentage effect of the entire tariff structure on the value added per unit of output in each industry. This concept incorporates the point that one industry's tariff affects a number of industries, and that incomes in any one industry are affected by the tariffs of many industries.

SUGGESTED READING

For an alternative textbook statement of the welfare effects of a tariff, from an explicitly free-trade viewpoint, see Leland B. Yeager and David Tuerck, *Foreign Trade and U.S. Policy: The Case for Free International Trade* (New York: Praeger, 1976).

The concept of the effective rate of protection is clearly introduced for the nonspecialist by Herbert Grubel in his article in *International Trade and Finance: Readings*, ed. Robert E. Baldwin and J. David Richardson (Boston: Little, Brown, 1974), chap. 5.

A handy survey of the literature on the gains and losses from tariffs and other trade barriers is Robert M. Stern, "Tariffs and Other Measures of Trade Control: A Survey of Recent Developments," *Journal of Economic Literature*, vol. 11, no. 3 (September 1971), pp. 857–88.

For a somewhat technical treatment of the statistical problems that often cause underestimation of import elasticities and the welfare costs of tariffs, see Edward Leamer and Robert M. Stern, *Quantitative International Economics* (1970), chaps. 2 and 8.

The official U.S. tariff schedules are given in U.S. International Trade Commission, *Tariff Schedules of the United States Annotated* (Washington, D.C.: Government Printing Office, 1976). Those for Canada are cited and summarized in James R. Melvin and Bruce W. Wilkinson, *Effective Protection in the Canadian Economy*, Economic Council of Canada, Special Study no. 9 (Ottawa: Queen's Printer, 1968).

QUESTION FOR REVIEW

You have been asked to quantify the welfare effects of the U.S. sugar duty. The hard part of the work is already done: Somebody has estimated how many pounds of sugar would be produced, consumed and imported by the U.S. if there were no sugar duty. You are given the following information:

	Situation with import tariff	Estimated situation without tariff
World price (delivered in New York)	$0.10 per pound	$0.10 per pound
Tariff (duty)	$0.02 per pound	0
Domestic price	$0.12 per pound	$0.10 per pound
U.S. consumption (billions of per year)	20	22
U.S. production (billions of per year)	8	6
U.S. imports (billions of per year)	12	16

Calculate the following measures:

a. The U.S. consumers' gain from removing the tariff.
b. The U.S. producers' losses from removing the tariff.
c. The U.S. government tariff revenue loss.
d. The net effect on U.S. national wellbeing.

Answers: (a) U.S. consumers gain $420 million per year, (b) U.S. producers lose $140 million per year, (c) the U.S. government loses $240 million per year, and (d) the U.S. as a whole gains $40 million a year.

7

Arguments for and against
a tariff

The basic analysis of a tariff seemed to prove that free trade was better than any tariff, by showing that the tariff brought net losses to the nation as a whole. The empirical attempts to measure the net welfare effects of trade barriers also showed national losses in most cases. Yet the assumptions underlying the basic analysis and the usual empirical measurements are not always valid. We began to see how the true welfare effects might deviate from the usual measures of those effects when we discussed how the standard estimates of tariff losses might be improved. The arguments for and against a tariff are subtler and more varied than those presented in Chapter 6. Both critics and defenders of tariffs need to know just where the limits to the case for free trade lie.

This chapter explores those limits, identifying the conditions under which a tariff can be better than doing nothing, or better than any other policy. We shall establish some of the policy conclusions previewed at the start of Chapter 6: there are valid "optimal tariff" and "second-best" arguments for a tariff, yet some other policy is usually better than the tariff in the second-best cases. It turns out that the valid arguments for a tariff are quite different from the usual defenses of a tariff.

THE NATIONALLY OPTIMAL TARIFF

One of the underpinnings of the conclusion that we are hurt as a nation by our own tariff is the assumption that we cannot affect the world price of the imported good. The basic analysis in Chapter 6 assumed this when it implied that the tariff on bicycle imports did not affect the world price of bicycles, which stood fixed at $200, tariff or no tariff. In other words, the basic analysis assumed that we are competitive *price takers* in the world markets for the goods we import.

This assumption is often valid. Trade between nations is frequently very competitive, often even for commodities for which trade within a nation is dominated by a few sellers. Moreover, individual nations usually control smaller shares of world markets for individual commodities as importers than they do as exporters, since nations tend to specialize more as exporters than as importers. Thus in most cases an importing nation cannot force foreign suppliers to sell for less by trying to strike a tougher bargain. If Canada tried to demand a lower import price for bicycles by taxing foreign sales of bicycles to Canada, the foreign suppliers might simply decide to avoid sales to Canada altogether and sell elsewhere at the same world price. Similarly, Britain could not expect to force foreign sellers of rice to supply it more cheaply: any attempt to do so would simply prove that Britain was a price taker on the world market by causing rice exporters to avoid Britain altogether with little effect on the world rice price.

Yet in some cases a nation has a large enough share of the world market for one of its imports to be able to affect the world price unilaterally. A nation can have this **monopsony power** even in cases where no individual firm within the nation has it. For example, the United States looms large enough in the world market for automobiles to be able to force foreign exporters like Volkswagen to sell autos to the United States at a lower price (or to move their plants to the United States) by putting a tariff on foreign autos. The United States probably also has the same monopsony power to some extent in the world market for TV sets, radios, motorcycles, and many other goods.

A nation with such power over foreign selling prices can exploit this advantage with a tariff on imports, even though no competitive individual within the nation could do so. Suppose that the United States were to impose a small tariff on bicycles. Imposing the tariff markup would make the price paid by U.S. consumers exceed the price paid to foreign suppliers, as in Chapter 6. Now, however, the markup is likely to lower the foreign price as well as raise the domestic price a bit. As long as they can produce and sell to the United States smaller amounts at a lower marginal cost, foreign suppliers are likely to prefer to cut their price to the United States a bit in order to limit the drop in their sales to the United States. This is what makes it possible for the United States to gain as a nation from its own tariff. On all the bicycles that continue to be imported, the United States succeeds in paying a lower price to foreigners, even though the tariff-including price to U.S. consumers is slightly higher. To be sure, there is still a deadweight loss in economic efficiency for the United States and the world on the imports prevented by the tariff. In discouraging some imports that would have been worth more to buyers than the price being paid to cover the foreign seller's costs, the tariff still has its costs. But as long as the tariff is small, those costs are outweighed for the United States by the gains from continuing most of the previous imports at a lower price. So there is some positive level of the tariff, perhaps a low level, at which the United States as a nation is better off than with free trade.

This same point can be made more fully using the illustration given in Figure 7.1, which shows the same diagram of the market for bicycle imports as in Figure 6.4B, except that now the foreign supply curve slopes upward instead of being flat at a fixed world price. Suppose again that the United States imposes a very small tariff, say a $2 tariff, on bicycles, driving up the domestic price to $201 and lowering the foreign price to $199. Figure 7.1A shows that the United States loses a bit on the 0.02 bicycles that consumers decide not to buy each year now that they must pay the extra dollar. This loss is very small, however. It is easily outweighed by the gain reaped by the United States at the expense of foreign suppliers on the remaining 0.98 million bicycles imported each year. By getting the foreigners to sell those bicycles at a dollar less, the United States has made them pay for part of the tariff. This national gain ($1 × 0.98 million bikes a year) easily outweighs the small triangle of deadweight loss on discouraged imports.

If a tiny tariff works for the nation with power over prices, higher tariffs work even better—but only up to a point. To see the limits to a nation's market power, we can start by noting that *a prohibitive tariff cannot be optimal.* Suppose that the United States were to put a tariff on bicycle imports that was so high as to make all imports unprofitable, as would a tariff of over $112 a bike in Figure 7.1, driving the price received by foreign suppliers below $144. So stiff a tariff would not be successful in getting the foreigners to supply the United States at low prices, since they would decide not to sell bicycles to the United States at all. Lacking any revenues earned partly at the expense of foreign suppliers, the United States would find itself saddled with nothing but the loss of all gains from trade in bicycles. The optimal tariff must be somewhere in between no tariff and a prohibitively high one.

The optimal tariff can be derived in the same way as the optimal price markdown for any monopsonist, any buyer with market power. Appendix D derives the formula for the optimum tariff rate from static analysis. It turns out that the optimum tariff rate, as a fraction of the price paid to foreigners, equals the reciprocal of the elasticity of the foreign supply of imports to us. It makes sense that the lower the foreign-supply elasticity, the higher our optimum tariff rate: the more

FIGURE 7.1
National gains from a tariff that affects foreigners' selling price

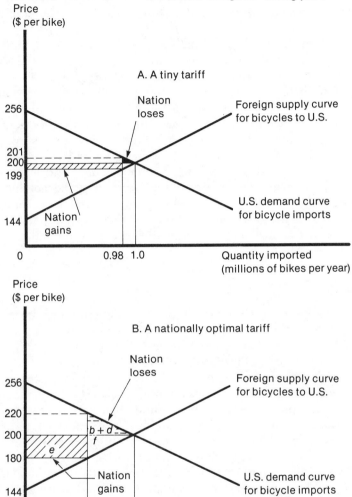

inelastically foreigners keep to supplying a nearly fixed amount to us, the more we can get away with exploiting them. Conversely, if their supply is infinitely elastic, facing us with a fixed world price as in Chapter 6, then we cannot get them to accept lower prices. If their supply elasticity is infinite, our own tariffs only hurt us as in Chapter 6, and the optimal tariff is zero.

Figure 7.1B shows such an optimal tariff. The nation gains the markdown on foreign bicycle imports, represented by area e, which considerably exceeds what the nation loses as a net consumer of bicycles in area $b + d$.

Note, however, that the nationally optimal tariff is still unambiguously bad for the world as a whole. What the nation gains is less than what foreigners lose from our tariff. Figure 7.1B brings this out clearly. The United States gained area e only at the expense of foreign suppliers, dollar for dollar, leaving no net effect on the world from this redistribution of income through price. But foreign suppliers suffered more than that: they also lost area f in additional producer surplus on the imports discouraged by the tariff. So for the world as a whole, the tariff still looks as bad as it did in Chapter 6. The world loses areas $b + d$ and f, which are the gains from trade caused by the fact that U.S. consumers value foreign bicycles more highly below the level of imports of 1.0 million a year than it would cost foreign suppliers to make and sell them. The tariff may be nationally optimal, but it still means a net loss to the world.

RETALIATION

The optimal tariff argument assumes that the foreigners do not retaliate, either by taxing their exports to us or by taxing their imports from us. This assumption may not be valid. They may respond to our import tariffs with import tariffs of their own. If the United States were to try to raise its tariff on bicycles, cars, and other manufactures from Europe and Japan, those countries might raise their tariffs on manufactures and farm products from the United States. If they did, their actions would damage us, perhaps enough to make our own tariff bad for us as well as for the world. If one country's higher tariffs touch off a general tariff war, it is likely, though not certain, that all countries will end up worse off, as trade and the gains from trade dwindle. That is essentially what happened in the retaliatory tariff war between France and Italy in the late 1880s. The mutual raising of tariff barriers in the early 1930s was also damaging to all major economies. Knowing this, free-trade advocates stress that a seemingly optimal tariff can backfire even for a selfish nation.

THE TROUBLED WORLD OF SECOND BEST

To discover where the boundaries to the free-trade argument lie, it is necessary to go beyond another simplifying assumption made in the basic analysis of a tariff. So far we have been assuming that any demand or supply curve could do double duty, representing both private and social benefits or costs. Our demand curve was supposed to represent not only the marginal benefits of an extra bicycle to the private buyer but also the net benefits of another bicycle to society as a whole. Our supply curve was supposed to represent not only the marginal cost to private producers of producing another bicycle at home but also the marginal cost to society as a whole. That is, we assumed that there were no "distortions," no gaps between the private and social benefits or costs or any activity, in the absence of the tariff. In this Garden of Eden the tariff was the original sin, introducing a distortion between the marginal cost of a bicycle to consumers (the tariff-including domestic price) and the marginal cost to society of buying another bicycle abroad (the world price).

It is often not realistic to assume that the distortions in our domestic economy are either zero or happen to cancel each other out. Distortions are widespread, and pose some of the most intriguing policy problems of economics. They include the wide range of effects that economists have also called "externalities" or "spillover effects": net effects on parties other than those agreeing to buy and sell in a marketplace. Pollution is a classic example: the buyers and sellers of paper products do not reckon the damage done by the paper mills' river pollution into the price of paper unless special action is taken, nor do the buyers and sellers of petroleum fuels reckon the social cost of pollution from consuming those fuels into the prices of the fuels. Such distortions between the interests of private parties and the net interests of society as a whole occur in many other spheres as well, for a host of reasons. We live in a "second-best" world, one riddled with gaps between private and social benefits or costs. As long as these gaps exist, private actions will not lead to a social optimum.

In a second-best world, a tariff can be justified by the existence of a domestic distortion. The easiest way to see how this can be true is to consider an example to which we shall return more than once. Suppose that jobs in a certain import-competing domestic sector will generate greater returns for society than are perceived by the people who are deciding whether or not to take those jobs. This can happen if the sector is a modern one in which jobs bring gains in knowledge and skills, and changes in attitudes, benefiting persons other than the workers and employers in that sector. Or it can happen if defects in labor markets make the wage rate in the sector exceed the value of the alternative uses of workers' time, such as leisure or jobs in other sectors. Or perhaps the short-run costs of moving to jobs in this high-paying sector seem higher to the workers outside this industry than they do to society as a whole. For any of these reasons, the social cost of attracting workers into this sector may be a lot lower than the wage rate the firms in the sector would pay their workers. If so, there is a case for policy devices to attract workers to the sector.

Such a gap between the private and social costs of creating jobs in a sector can make a tariff beneficial on balance. Tariff protection can encourage firms in this sector to expand output and hire more labor. The social side benefits of creating the extra jobs can outweigh the losses caused by the fact that consumers and domestic firms are paying more to get extra units at home than they would cost to buy abroad if there were no tariff. The fact that such side benefits can exist complicates the task of judging whether a tariff is good or bad for the nation as a whole. Realizing this, some scholars have stressed that trade policy has to be agnostic in a second-best world. Once you realize that domestic distortions are common, there is little you can say in the abstract about the net gain or loss from a tariff. Each case must be judged on its own merits.

A rule of thumb

In the world of second best we are not cast totally adrift. It is often possible to gather information on a case-by-case basis to quantify the various benefits and costs of an individual tariff, given what is known about relevant distortions in the home economy. Furthermore, there are some general rules of thumb that are valuable even when one lacks detailed information about the situation of each industry. Here is one rule of thumb that serves well for policymaking in a distortion-riddled economy:

> The **specificity rule:** It is more efficient to use those policy tools that are closest to the locus of the distortions separating private and social benefits or costs.

The specificity rule applies to all sorts of policy issues. Let us illustrate it first by using some examples removed from international trade. Suppose that the most serious distortion to be attacked is crime, which creates fear among third parties as well as direct harm to victims. Since crime is caused by people, we might consider combating crime by reducing the whole population through compulsory sterilization laws or taxes on children. But those are obviously very inefficient ways of attacking crime, since less social friction would be generated if we fought crime more directly through greater law enforcement and programs to reduce unemployment, a major contributor to crime. A less extreme example of the specificity rule brings us back to the paper mills polluting rivers. To attack this problem, we could tax all production of paper products or subsidize the installation of a particular waste treatment device where the mills' pipes meet the river. But the specificity rule cautions us to make sure that we are as close as possible to the source of the problem. Taxing all paper products is likely to be too broad an instrument, since it simply discourages the consumption and production of all paper without regard to the extent of pollution associated with the way in which any kind of paper is being produced. The paper manufacturers would get the signal that society wants them to make less paper, but not the signal to look for less polluting ways of making paper. On the other hand, subsidizing the installation of a waste treatment device may be too narrow an instrument. Nothing assures us that the waste treatment approach is the cheapest way to reduce pollution. Perhaps a change in the internal production processes of the paper mills could cut down on the load of waste needing any pipeline treatment more cheaply than the cost of the waste treatment equipment. The problem arose from the failure to provide the paper manufacturers with incentives for cutting pollution, not from their failure to adopt a particular method. The specificity rule thus directs us to look at incentive policies geared to the act of pollution itself: such policies as taxes or quantitative limits on the amount of pollution discharged (effluent charges and environmental quality standards).

The specificity rule tends to cut against the tariff. Although a tariff can be better than doing nothing in a second-best world, the rule shows us that some other policy instrument is usually more efficient than the tariff in dealing with a domestic distortion. To see how, let us begin with the domestic target at which a tariff is most often aimed.

A tariff to promote domestic production

Debates over trade policy often come up with reasons for giving special encouragement to the domestic production of a commodity that is currently being imported. These reasons are varied. In fact, most of the popular second-best arguments for tariff protection can be viewed as variations on the theme of favoring a particular import-competing industry. The infant-industry argument is one variant. A tariff to create jobs at the expense of imports is another. Most of the "noneconomic" arguments for a tariff, such as the national defense and national pride arguments, are also of this type. Each argument stresses that there are social benefits to domestic production in this particular import-competing industry that cannot be captured, and therefore are not sufficiently pursued, by the domestic industry unless it is given tariff protection. We shall take up these arguments below. First, let us examine the general pros and cons of a tariff to promote domestic production, setting aside for the moment the reasons for thinking that there are social side benefits to domestic production.

A nation might want to encourage domestic production of bicycles, either because it thought the experience of producing this manufactured good generated modern skills and attitudes or simply because it took pride in producing its own modern bikes. It could foster this objective by putting a $20 tariff on imported bicycles, as shown in the diagram of the national bicycle market in Figure 7.2A. The tariff brings the nation the same elements of net loss that it did back in Chapter 6 (and Figure 6.4A): the nation loses area b by producing at greater expense what could be bought for less abroad, and it loses area d by discouraging purchases that would have brought more enjoyment to consumers than the world price of a bicycle. But now something is added: the lower part of the diagram portrays the social side benefits from home production, benefits not captured by the domestic bicycle producers. By raising the domestic price of bicycles, the tariff has encouraged more production of bicycles. This increase in domestic production, from S_0 to S_1, has brought area g in extra gains to the nation.

The tariff in Figure 7.2A could be good or bad for the nation, all things considered. The net outcome depends on whether area g is larger or smaller than the areas b and d. To find out, one would have to develop empirical estimates reflecting the realities of the bicycle industry. One would want to estimate the dollar value of the annual side benefits to society, and also the slope of the domestic supply curve. The net national gain $(g - b - d)$ might turn out to be positive or negative. All that one can say in the abstract is that the tariff might prove to be better or worse than doing nothing.

We should use our institutional imagination, however, and look for other policy tools. The specificity rule prods us to do so. The locus of the problem was domestic production, not imports as such. What society wants to encourage is more domestic production of this good, not less consumption or less imports of it. Why not encourage the domestic production directly by rewarding people on the basis of the amount of this beneficial good they produce?

Society could directly subsidize the domestic production of bicycles, by having the government pay bicycle firms a fixed amount, or by lowering their taxes by a fixed amount, for each bicycle produced and sold. Doing this would probably encourage them to produce more bicycles. Any increase in production that a given tariff could coax out of domestic firms could also be yielded by a production subsidy. Figure 7.2B shows such a subsidy, namely a $20 subsidy per bicycle. This subsidy is just as good for bicycle firms as the extra $20 in selling price that the tariff made possible. Either tool gets them to raise their annual production from S_0 up to S_1, giving society the same side benefits.

FIGURE 7.2
Two ways to promote import-competing production

A. With a tariff:

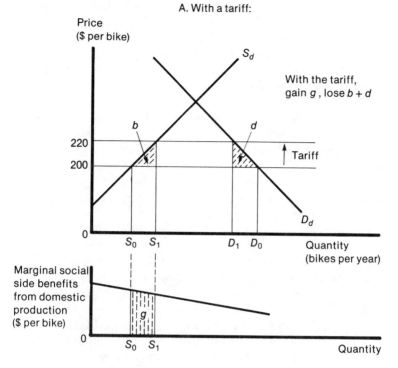

Price
($ per bike)

S_d

With the tariff,
gain g, lose $b + d$

b d

220

200   ↑ Tariff

D_d

0   S_0 S_1 D_1 D_0 Quantity
(bikes per year)

Marginal social
side benefits
from domestic
production
($ per bike)

g

0   S_0 S_1 Quantity

B. With a subsidy on domestic production:

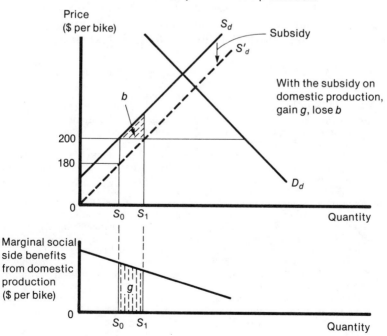

Price
($ per bike)

S_d Subsidy

S'_d

With the subsidy on
domestic production,
gain g, lose b

b

200

180

D_d

0   S_0 S_1 Quantity

Marginal social
side benefits
from domestic
production
($ per bike)

g

0   S_0 S_1 Quantity

The $20 production subsidy in Figure 7.2B is definitely better than the $20 tariff in Figure 7.2A. Both generate the same social side benefits, and both cause domestic firms to produce $(S_1 - S_0)$ extra bicycles each year at a higher direct cost than the price at which the nation could buy foreign bicycles (in both cases this extra cost is area b). Yet the subsidy does not discourage the total consumption of bicycles by raising the price above $200. It only enables domestic firms to capture part of the same total consumption from foreign competition at the same world price of $200. Consumers do not lose the additional area d. This is a clear net advantage of the $20 production subsidy over the $20 tariff. What made the production subsidy better was its conformity to the specificity rule: since the locus of the problem was domestic production, it was less costly to attack it in a way that did not also affect the price at which consumers bought from foreigners.[1]

If our concern is with expanding jobs, rather than output, in the import-competing industry, the same results hold with a slight modification. A production subsidy would still be preferable to the tariff, since it still achieves any given expansion in both bicycle production and bicycle jobs at lower social cost. We could come up with even better alternatives, however. If the locus of the problem is really the number of jobs in the bicycle industry, it would be more efficient to use a policy tool that not only encouraged production but encouraged firms to come up with ways of creating more jobs per dollar of bicycle output. A subsidy tied to the number of workers employed might be better than a subsidy tied to output. (Alternatively, if the object is to create jobs and cure unemployment throughout the entire domestic economy, then it is logical to look first to economy-wide

---

[1] Although this conclusion is broadly valid, it should be noted that a special assumption was needed to make the net advantage of the production subsidy exactly equal area d. It has been assumed here that no other distortions between private and social incentives result when the government comes up with the revenues to cover the production subsidies to the bicycle firms. That is, it has been assumed that there is no net social loss from having the government either raise additional taxes or cancel some spending to pay this subsidy to bicycle producers.

This assumption is strictly valid if the tax revenues going into the subsidy come from a head tax, a tax on people's existence, which should only redistribute income and not affect production and consumption incentives. Yet head taxes are rare, and the more realistic case of financing the production subsidy by, say, raising income taxes or cutting other government spending programs is somewhat murkier. If the income tax already exists, raising it further might or might not affect people's incentives to earn income through effort. Or if the government spending reallocated to the production subsidy had previously been providing some other public goods worth more than their marginal cost, there is again an extra loss that can attend the production subsidy. These possible source-of-subsidy distortions would have to be considered in policymaking. Yet it seems reasonable to presume that they are less important than the distorting of consumption represented by area d.

We return to this issue of how alternative policy tools are to be financed when discussing the infant-government argument below.

expansionary policies, such as fiscal policy or monetary policy, and again not to the tariff.)

The infant-industry argument

The analysis of the use of a tariff to promote domestic production helps us judge the merits of many of the most popular and time-honored arguments for protection. Of all the protectionist arguments, the one that has always enjoyed the most prestige among both economists and policymakers is the infant-industry argument, which asserts that in less developed countries a temporary tariff is justified because it cuts down on imports of modern manufactures while the infant domestic industry learns how to produce at low enough costs to compete without the help of a tariff. The argument stresses that industries learn by doing, and that their cost curves will fall if they can gain experience. Tariff protection gives them this chance by keeping manufacturing competition from more advanced countries at bay while they incur the high initial costs of getting started. The infant-industry argument differs from the optimal tariff argument in that it claims that in the long run the tariff protection will be good for the world as well as the nation. It differs from most other tariff arguments in being explicitly dynamic, arguing that the protection is needed only for a while.

The infant-industry argument has been popular with developing countries at least since Alexander Hamilton used it in his *Report on Manufactures* in 1791. Friedrich List reapplied it to the cause of shielding nascent German manufacturing industries against British competition in the early 19th century. It has also been echoed by several postwar economists, who have modified it slightly to refer to whole sectors of the economy and not just to individual industries. It is an argument that will continue to deserve attention since there will always be infant industries. The development of new products with new technologies will continue to contribute a growing share of world production and trade, and nations will have to consider time and again what to do about the development of new industries in which other countries have a current comparative advantage.

To the extent that the infant-industry argument is an argument for encouraging current domestic production, the above analysis applies. If the infant home industry will bring side benefits by causing the labor force and other industries to develop new skills, subsidizing production can achieve this more cheaply than can taxing imports. If the extra foreseen benefits take the form of future cost reductions for the *same* industry, through learning by doing, then there is another alternative more appropriate than either the tariff or the production subsidy. If an industry's current high costs are outweighed by the later cost cutting that experience will allow, then the industry can borrow against its own future profits and make it through the initial period in which costs are higher than the prices being charged on imports. Our bicycle industry, for example, could survive its youth by borrowing and then repaying the loan out of the profits it will make as a healthy competitor later on. Or, if defects in lending markets prevent that, the government could advance loans to new industries—still not using the tariff.

If the need for help is truly temporary, there is another argument against using the tariff to protect the infant. Tariffs are not easily removed once they are written into law, and there is the danger that an "infant" that never becomes efficient will use part of its tariff-bred profits to sway policymakers to make a bad tariff immortal. A production subsidy, by contrast, has the advantage of being subject to more frequent public review as part of the government's ordinary budget review process. It can be removed in cases where the earlier help to an infant industry has proved to be a mistake.

More sophisticated versions of the infant-industry argument give more complicated defenses, yet each of these is better viewed as a defense of some policy other than protection against imports. Consider, for example, the correct point that workers trained in modern manufacturing skills in a firm struggling to compete against imports may leave that firm and take their skills to a competing firm. This threat is likely to make new firms underinvest in training their workers. A tariff to protect this modern firm is not quite on target, though, since the tariff will not keep workers from taking their new skills from firm to firm in the same protected industry. More appropriate is a subsidy on training itself, compensating the firm giving the training for benefits that would otherwise accrue largely to others. Again, the specificity rule cuts against the tariff: although protecting an infant industry and its skill creation with a tariff on imports may be better than doing nothing, some other method can get at the problem more efficiently than the tariff.

This line of reasoning can be applied to the case of computer manufacture and computer services as an infant industry. Should the governments of Canada and Japan protect their computer industries against competition from IBM and other U.S. firms? If so, how? There is abundant evidence that the benefits of an expanding computer sector spill over to many industries and are not fully appropriated by computer firms. These side benefits in the form of new productive knowledge are generated both by the industry that produces computers and by the industries that use computer services. The gains and losses from any one policy can be quantified only with a detailed investigation of the alternatives for developing these industries in Canada and Japan. Yet the above analysis makes three things clear: there is a case for some sort of government encouragement; a tariff may or may not help; and other forms of help are clearly better than the tariff. The tariff is likely to be especially inferior to direct subsidies to production, training, and research in a technologically complex industry like computers, where many of the gains in knowledge occur in the consuming industries. If the encouragement is to be extended to the total use of computer services as well as to the domestic production of computers, it will not help to retard the use of computers with a tariff. This point seems reflected in the approach of Japan's Ministry of International Trade and Industry. MITI has indeed protected the Japanese computer industry against imports, but it has leaned increasingly on other forms of assistance—loans, patents, tax breaks, and so forth.

The infant-government argument

Import tariffs can still be justified by another second-best argument relating to conditions in less developed countries. In a newly emerging nation, the tariff as a source of revenue may be beneficial and even better than any alternative policy, both for the new nation and for the world as a whole.

For a newly independent nation with low living standards, the most serious "domestic distortions" may relate to the government's inability to provide an adequate supply of public goods. Poor nations would receive large social benefits if they expanded such basic public services as the control of infectious diseases, water control for agriculture, primary schooling, and national defense. Yet the administrative resources of many poor nations are not great enough to capture these social gains (others, of course, have the necessary administrative resources and use them inefficiently).

In such nations the import tariff becomes a crucial source, not of industrial protection but of public revenue. With severe limits on the supply of literate civil servants and soldiers, such nations will find tariffs efficient: revenue can be raised more cheaply by just guarding the borders with a few customs officials who tax imports and exports than with more elaborate and costly kinds of taxes. Production, consumption, income, and property cannot be effectively taxed or subsidized when they cannot be measured and monitored. It is largely for this reason that many lower-income countries get between one quarter and three fifths of their government revenue from customs duties, a higher dependence on customs than is found in such equally trade-oriented high-income countries as Canada. Although the practice of infant governments may diverge from the principle, the principle remains that in an infant-government setting the tariff can bring greater social gains than alternative policies, gains that may even make the world as a whole benefit from tariffs in low-income countries.

NONECONOMIC ARGUMENTS

The other leading arguments for tariff protection relate to the national pursuit of "noneconomic" goals. Although aggressive economists may insist that nothing lies outside their field, these arguments do relate to points that are not usually thought of as part of standard economic analysis. The potential range of such arguments is limitless, but the view that man does not live by imported bread alone usually focuses on three other goals: national pride, income distribution, and national defense.

Nations desire symbols as much as individuals do, and knowing that some good is produced within our own country can be as legitimate an object of *national pride* as having cleaned up a previous urban blight or winning Olympic medals. And as long as the pride can only be generated by something collective and nationwide, and not purchased by individuals in the marketplace, there is a case for policy intervention. The above analysis in fact still applies to a country seeking to derive national pride from home production. If the pride is generated by domestic production itself, then the appropriate policy tool seems to be the domestic production subsidy (setting aside the infant-government cases). Only if the pride comes from not importing as such is the tariff the best policy approach.

A second "noneconomic" objective to which trade policy might be addressed is the *distribution of income* within the nation. Often one of the most sensitive issues in national politics is either "What does it do to the poor?" or the effect of some policy on different regions or ethnic groups. A tariff might be defended on the ground that it restores equity by favoring some wrongly disadvantaged group, even though it may reduce the overall size of the pie to be distributed among groups. It is certainly important to know the effects of trade policy on the distribution of income within a country, a subject already treated in Chapter 5 and one to which we return several times later in Part II. It is fair to ask, though, whether the specificity rule should not be reapplied here. If the issue is inequity in how income is distributed within our country, why should trade policy be the means of redressing the inequity? If, for example, greater income equality is the objective, it could well be less costly to equalize incomes directly through taxes and transfer payments than to try to equalize them indirectly by manipulating the tariff structure. Still, if political constraints were somehow so binding that the income distribution could be adjusted only through tariff policy, then it is conceivable that tariffs could be justified on this ground.

The *national defense* argument for protection has a richer history and several interesting twists to its analysis. English mercantilists in the 17th century used the national defense argument to justify tariffs on the use of foreign ships and shipping services: if we force ourselves to buy English ships and shipping, we will foster the growth of a shipbuilding industry and a merchant marine that will be vital in time of war. Even Adam Smith departed from his otherwise scathing attacks on trade barriers to sanction the restrictive Navigation Acts where shipping and other dimensions of national defense were involved. The national defense argument says that a tariff would help the nation accumulate more crucial materials for future economic or military warfare, in the form of either stockpiles or emergency capacity to produce.

The importance of having strategic reserves on hand for emergencies is clear. Yet a little reflection shows that none of the popular variants of the national defense argument succeeds in making a good case for a tariff. A peacetime tariff does not stockpile goods for use in war. Instead it merely makes us buy more home-produced goods instead of foreign goods. The national defense argument presumes that this creates more productive capacity by encouraging the domestic industry. Yet the industry will only install as much capacity as seems adequate to meet the peacetime needs, not any extra emergency capacity. If that is to be created, it is best subsidized directly.

The possibilities of storage and depletion also argue against the use of a tariff to create defense capability. If the crucial goods can be stored, the cheapest way to prepare for the emergency is to buy them up from foreigners at the low world price during peace. Thus the English mercantilists might have given more thought to the option of stockpiling cheap and efficient Dutch-made ships to use when war later broke out between the English and the Dutch, while concentrating England's own resources on its comparative-advantage products. And if the crucial goods are depletable mineral resources, such as oil, the case for the tariff is even weaker. Restricting imports of oil when there is no foreign embargo causes us to use up our own reserves faster, cutting the amount we can draw upon when an embargo or blockade is imposed. To believe that restricting imports would increase our untapped reserves, we would have to accept two doubtful propositions: (1) protecting domestic oil producers makes them discover extra reserves faster than it makes them sell extra oil for peacetime consumption; and (2) there is no more direct way to encourage further oil exploration within the country. Yet the national defense argument was used repeatedly by oil interests to defend the U.S. restrictions on oil imports between 1959 and 1972.

The closest the national defense argument comes to justifying a tariff is when it is not really a national defense argument but instead an optimal tariff or cartel-fighting argument. If the United States could force the members of the OPEC oil cartel or some other potentially hostile foreign suppliers to sell at a lower price by imposing a tariff, then the tariff is in the U.S. national interest. The tariff would in this case succeed in making the crucial good cheaper to the nation during peace, and might also succeed in damaging the unity of a foreign cartel. But this optimal tariff or cartel-busting argument is not the one made when tariffs are defended in terms of "national defense" in public debate.

SUMMARY

There are valid arguments for a tariff, though they are quite different from those usually given. One way or another, all valid defenses of a tariff lean on the existence of relevant "distortions," or gaps between private and social costs or benefits.

When a nation as a whole can affect the price at which foreigners supply imports, a positive tariff can be nationally optimal. This national monopsony power is equivalent to a distortion, since there is a gap between the marginal cost at which society as a whole can buy imports and the price any individual would pay if acting alone without the tariff. The nationally optimal tariff rate equals the reciprocal of the foreign-supply elasticity. If the foreign supply curve is infinitely elastic, and if the world price is fixed for the nation, the optimal tariff rate is zero. The less elastic the foreign supply, the higher the optimal tariff rate. The tariff is only optimal, however, if foreign governments do not retaliate with tariffs on our exports. And with or without retaliation, the nationally optimal tariff is still bad for the world as a whole.

When there are distortions in the domestic economy, then imposing a tariff may be better than doing nothing. Whether or not it is better depends on detailed empirical information. Yet when imposing the tariff is better than doing nothing, something else is still often better than the tariff. The specificity rule argues for using the policy tool that is closest to the locus of the distorting gap between private and social incentives. This rule of thumb cuts against the tariff, which is usually only indirectly related to the source of the domestic distortion. Thus many of the main arguments for a tariff, such as the infant-industry argument or the national defense argument, fall short of showing that the tariff is better than other policy tools. The case for a tariff is most secure in the infant-government setting, in which the country is so poor and its government so underdeveloped that the tariff is a vital source of government revenue to finance basic public investments and services.

SUGGESTED READING

An elementary but good textbook treatment is found in Leland B. Yeager and David Tuerck, *Foreign Trade and U.S. Policy: The Case for Free International Trade* (New York: Praeger, 1976). Less elementary but also helpful is Caves and Jones, *World Trade and Payments*, chap. 13.

The theory of trade policy in the presence of distortions can be followed in Jagdish N. Bhagwati, *Trade, Tariffs, and Growth* (Cambridge, Mass.: MIT Press, 1969); and Harry G. Johnson, "Optional Trade Policy in the Presence of Domestic Distortions," in *Trade, Growth, and the Balance of Payments*, ed. Robert E. Baldwin (Chicago: Rand McNally, 1965). The theory is succinctly applied to the case of the infant-industry argument by Robert E. Baldwin, "The Case against Infant-Industry Tariff Protection," *Journal of Political Economy*, May/June 1969.

A handy survey of the recent evolution of thinking on trade policy is Robert M. Stern, "Tariffs and Other Measures of Trade Control: A Survey of Recent Developments," *Journal of Economic Literature*, September 1971.

QUESTION FOR REVIEW

As in the question at the end of Chapter 6, you have been asked to quantify the welfare effects of removing an import duty, and somebody has already estimated the effects of U.S. production, consumption, and imports. This time the facts are different. The import duty in question is the 5 percent tariff on motorcycles, and you are given the following information:

	Current situation, with 5 percent tariff	Estimated situation, without tariff
World price of motorcycles (landed in San Francisco)	$2,000 per cycle	$2,050 per cycle
Tariff at 5 percent:	$ 100 per cycle	0
U.S. domestic price in	$2,100 per cycle	$2,050 per cycle
Number of cycles bought in U.S. per year	100,000	105,000
Number of cycles made in U.S. per year	40,000	35,000
Number of cycles imported by U.S. per year	60,000	70,000

Calculate (*a*) the U.S. consumer gain from removing the duty, (*b*) the U.S. producer loss from removing the duty, (*c*) the U.S. government tariff revenue loss, and (*d*) the net welfare effect on the United States as a whole.

Why does the net affect on the nation as a whole differ from the result in the question at the end of Chapter 6?

Answers: (*a*) U.S. consumers gain $5,125,000 (*b*) U.S. producers lose $1,875,000, (*c*) U.S. government loses $6,000,000 in tariff revenue, and (*d*) the United States as a whole *loses* $2,750,000 each year from removing the tariff. The U.S. national loss stemmed from the fact that the U.S. tariff removal raised the world price paid on imported motorcycles. In the Chapter 6 question, it was assumed that removing the duty had no effect on the world price (of sugar).

8

Other national policies affecting trade

There must be 50 ways to restrict foreign trade without using a tariff. Modern governments have discovered many of them. At times the United States has molded its sanitary standards so that Argentine beef could not meet them. Colombia has used "mixing requirements" forcing steel importers to buy so many tons of more expensive domestic steel for each ton imported. Many governments put up a host of other nontariff barriers to trade: state monopolies on foreign trade, buy-at-home rules for government purchases, administrative red tape to harass foreign sellers, complicated exchange controls, and so forth. Many of these barriers relate to legitimate regulatory functions which happen to interfere with trade, while others are transparent manipulations of rules for the primary purpose of discriminating against foreign trade.

In the postwar era, the importance of nontariff barriers to trade has been on the rise. In the late 1940s and early 1950s these barriers had an especially restrictive effect since many countries used them to keep tight control over their international payments while recovering from either World War II or longer-term underdevelopment. Since the 1950s nontariff barriers have been reduced only a little, while multilateral negotiations have succeeded in cutting tariffs significantly. By the time the Kennedy Round of tariff cuts was consummated in 1967, nontariff barriers had emerged as the main remaining impediment to the gains from freer trade. As one writer put it, "The lowering of tariffs has, in effect, been like draining a swamp. The lower water level has revealed all the snags and stumps of non-tariff barriers that still have to be cleared away."

This chapter surveys some of these nontariff barriers affecting trade. Most of them take the form of policies restricting imports. These will be compared with the import tariff. Others restrict exports or trade in general. One, adjustment assistance, does not restrict trade at all but instead softens the harmful effects of freer trade on import-competing workers and firms.

THE IMPORT QUOTA

The most prevalent nontariff trade barrier is the import quota, a limit on the total quantity of imports allowed into a country each year. One way or another, the government gives out a limited number of licenses to import legally, and prohibits imports without a license. As long as the quantity of imports licensed is less than the quantity that people would want to import without the quota, the quota has the effect not only of cutting the quantity imported but also of driving the domestic price of the good up above the world price at which the license-holders buy the good abroad. In this respect, it is similar to the import tariff.

Reasons for quotas

There are several reasons why governments have often chosen to use quotas rather than tariffs as a way of limiting imports. The first is as insurance against further increases in import spending when foreign competition is becoming increasingly severe. In the wake of World War II many countries found their competitive position weak and deteriorating at official exchange rates, and their governments tried stringent measures to improve the balance of payments. For a government official trying to enforce an improvement in the balance of payments, the quota helps by assuring that the quantity of imports is strictly limited. If increasing foreign competitiveness lowers the world price of imports, that will simply hasten the reduction in the total amount spent on imports. A tariff, by contrast, allows later foreign price cuts to raise import quantities and values if our demand for imports is elastic, thus complicating the planning of the balance of payments.

Quotas are also chosen in part because they give government officials greater administrative flexibility and power. International trade agreements such as the Kennedy Round have limited the power of governments to raise tariff rates. If import-competing industries mount greater protectionist pressures, the government cannot legally comply with higher tariffs except where certain escape clauses permit. But it is freer to impose more restrictive import quotas. Government officials also find that import quotas give them power and flexibility in dealing with domestic firms. As we shall discuss below, they usually have discretionary authority over who gets the import licenses under a quota system, and can use this power to advantage. For their part, protectionist interests also see in a quota system an opportunity to lobby for special license privileges, whereas a tariff is a source of government revenue to which they do not have any easy access.

These are some common reasons why government officials and protectionist industries often prefer quotas. Note that these are not arguments showing that quotas are in the interest of the nation as a whole.

Quota versus tariff

When we analyze the welfare effects of an import quota, we find that the quota is no better, and that in some cases it is worse, than a tariff for the nation as a whole. To compare the two, let us compare an import quota with an equivalent tariff, that is, a tariff just high enough to make the quantity of imports equal to the amount allowed by the quota if the quota is used.

The effects of a quota on bicycles are portrayed in Figure 8.1. It is assumed here that the domestic bicycle industry is competitive and not monopolized with or without the quota, and that the quota is limited enough to be less than what people would want to import at the world price. Domestic buyers as a group face a supply curve that equals the domestic supply curve plus the fixed quota, at all prices above the world price. Their inability to buy as much as they want at the world price drives up the domestic price of bicycles, in this case to $220.

The welfare effects of the quota are equivalent to those of a tariff under competitive conditions. The quota in Figure 8.1 has induced domestic producers to raise their production from S_0 to S_1, costing the nation area b by having bicycles produced at home at marginal costs rising up to $220 when they could have been bought abroad for $200 each without the quota. At the same time, consumers lose area d without its being a gain to anyone else. The price markup on the allowed imports, or the parallelogram c, is an internal redistribution from consumers to whoever commands the licenses. So the net national loss is again areas b and d. This is the same set of results that we got with a $20 tariff (back in Figure 6.4), the tariff that let in the same amount of imports as the quota.

The import quota looks best, or least bad, under these competitive conditions, which make it no better or worse than the equivalent tariff.

FIGURE 8.1
The effects of an import quota under competitive conditions

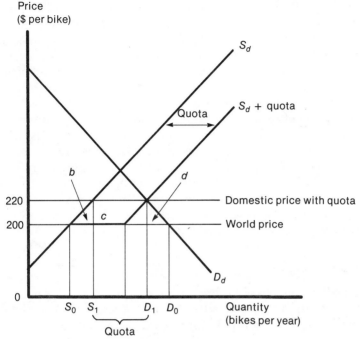

Price
($ per bike)

S_d

S_d + quota

Quota

b

d

220 ———————————————————— Domestic price with quota

c

200 ———————————————————— World price

D_d

0

S_0 S_1 D_1 D_0 Quantity
                                          (bikes per year)

Quota

The quota looks worse than the tariff under either of two sets of conditions: (1) if the quota creates monopoly powers; or (2) if the licenses to import are allocated inefficiently. Let us look at these two kinds of situations in order.

The import quota turns out to cost the nation more than the equivalent tariff if the quota creates a domestic monopoly. It may do so. A dominant domestic firm, such as Schwinn in U.S. bicycles, cannot get much monopoly power from a nonprohibitive tariff, because it faces an elastic competing supply at the world price plus the tariff. With a quota, however, the domestic firm knows that no matter how high it raises its price, competing imports cannot exceed the quota. So a quota gives the dominant domestic firm a better chance of facing an inelastic demand curve, and thus a better chance to reap monopoly profits with higher prices. So with the monopoly-creating quota we get even higher prices, lower output, and greater national losses than from a tariff that would have given us the same amount of imports. Appendix E shows this result geometrically, and shows how to quantify the extra losses from a monopoly-creating import quota.

The quota can also harm the nation more than a tariff by giving monopoly power to foreign exporters. This odd result has occurred in the case of the "voluntary export restraint" quotas which the United States has forced on Asian and other foreign suppliers of U.S. imports since the early 1960s. First in textiles, and later in steel and other products, the U.S. government found itself wanting a quota or its equivalent in order to ease protectionist lobbying pressures. Yet the U.S. government wanted to avoid the embarrassment of imposing im-port quotas itself while still professing to be leading the world march toward free trade. It thus intimidated foreign suppliers into allocating a limited quota of exports to the U.S. market among themselves. The result was a quota on U.S. imports—but the foreign suppliers, who had previously competed among themselves, were forced to collude like a group monopoly and apparently responded by charging their few U.S. buyers the full U.S. price instead of delivering at a competitive world price. The result: the same U.S. losses as with an equivalent tariff plus the failure to keep the price markup within the United States. Appendix E also shows this result geometrically.

Ways of allocating import licenses

The welfare effects of an import quota further depend on how the government allocates the legal rights to import. Whoever gets these rights without paying for them captures the gains represented by area c in Figure 8.1 at the expense of consumers. Here are the main ways of allocating import licenses:

1. Competitive auctions.
2. Fixed favoritism.
3. Resource-using application procedures.

Of these methods, competitive auctions are potentially the least costly and the fairest, while the third method is probably the most costly.

The government can auction off import licenses on a competitive basis, either publicly or under the table. The public auction might work as follows. Every three months the government announces that licenses to import so many tons of steel or so many bicycles or what-ever will be auctioned off at a certain time and place. Such a public announcement is likely to evoke a large enough number of bidders for the bidding to be competitive, especially if bid-rigging is a punished crime. The auction is likely to yield a price for the import licenses that approximately equals the difference between the foreign price of the imports and the highest home price at which all the licensed imports can be sold. Returning to Figure 8.1, we can see that such an auction would tend to yield a price of $20 per imported-bicycle license, since that is the price markup at which all competitive license-holders can resell imported bicycles in the home market. In this case of a public auction, the quota system does not cost the nation any more than an equivalent tariff. The proceeds of the quota, or area c in Figure 8.1, amount to a redistribution of income within the country, with bicycle consumers implicitly paying for the proceeds in the higher home price of bicycles and the proceeds being distributable by the government either as a cut in some other kind of tax or as spending on public goods worth this amount to society. The public auction revenues are essentially just tariff revenues under another name. The public auction, although the least costly way to allocate import licenses, is not used in the real world.

Some use is made of a variant on the competitive auction. Government officials can be corrupt and do a thriving business of auctioning import licenses under the table to whoever pays them the highest bribes. This variant entails some obvious social costs. Blatant and persistent corruption of this sort can make talented persons choose to become corruption-harvesting officials instead of productive economic agents. Public awareness of such corruption also raises social tensions by advertising injustice in high places.

Import licenses adding up to the legal quota can also be allocated on the basis of fixed favoritism, with the government simply assigning fixed shares to firms without competition or applications or negotiations. One common way of fixing license shares is to give established firms the same shares they had of total imports before the quotas were imposed. This is how the U.S. government ran its oil import quotas between 1959 and 1973. Licenses to import, worth a few billion dollars a year in price markup, were simply given free of charge to oil companies on the basis of the amount of foreign oil they had imported before 1959. This device served the political purpose of compensating the oil companies dependent on imports for their cutbacks in allowed import volumes so that they would not lobby against the import quotas designed to help oil companies selling U.S. oil in competition with imported oil. This resulted, of course, in a redistribution of income toward oil companies away from the rest of the United States, which could have benefited from the proceeds of a public auctioning of import licenses instead of this fixed distribution of free licenses.

The final way of allocating import licenses is by resource-using application procedures. Instead of holding an auction, the government can insist that people compete for licenses in a nonprice way. One common, but messy, alternative is to give import licenses on a first-come, first-served basis each month or each quarter. This ties up many people's time in standing in line, time which they could have put to some productive use. Another common device for rationing imports of industrial input goods is to give them to firms on the basis of how much productive capacity they have waiting for the imported inputs. This also tends to foster resource waste, by getting firms to overinvest in idle capacity in the hope of being granted more import licenses. Any application procedure forcing firms or individuals to demonstrate the merit of their claim to import licenses will also cause them to use time and money lobbying with government officials, a cost that is augmented by the cost of hiring extra government officials to process applications. Anne Krueger has estimated that import-rationing procedures have cost the economies of Turkey and India large shares of their gross national product (7.3 percent for India in 1964, 15 percent for Turkey in 1968). As a rough rule of thumb, she suggests that this resource cost will approximate the amount of potential economic rents being fought for, or something like area c in Figure 8.1. This will tend to be the result since firms will tie up more resources in expediting their applications for import licenses up to the point where these resource costs match the expected economic rents from the licenses, or area c. Note that this is quite different from the result of the public auction. The auction caused area c to be redistributed within society, from consumers of the importable good through the government to the beneficiaries of the government's auction revenues. The application procedures tend to convert area c into a loss to all of society by tying up resources in red tape and expensive rent-seeking. Thus the public auction emerges as the least costly way of administering an import quota system.

EXPORT BARRIERS

Nations can restrict their foreign trade by erecting barriers to exports as well as imports. It is intuitively clear that the analysis of export barriers should be a mirror image of the analysis of import barriers, and so it turns out.

Figure 8.2 shows the effects of an export duty on wheat from Canada under the assumption that Canada's policies cannot affect the world price of wheat. This diagram and its results are analogous to the case of a tariff on bicycle imports in Figure 6.4 in Chapter 6. The export duty of $1 a bushel causes exporters to get a lower return on wheat exports, and they respond by shifting some of their wheat back to the domestic market. This bids the domestic price of wheat back down to $5 a bushel from the world price of $6 a bushel. At the new equilibrium, wheat farmers will have shifted resources to some extent out of wheat growing and into other pursuits, while domestic consumers will have raised their consumption of wheat somewhat.

The welfare effects of the export duty are clear and quantifiable. Wheat farmers in the Prairie Provinces lose heavily by receiving only

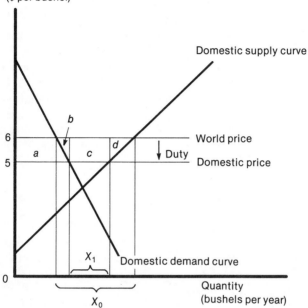

FIGURE 8.2
The effects of an export duty

Price
($ per bushel)

Domestic supply curve

6 — b

World price

a   c   d   ↓ Duty

5 — Domestic price

X₁

Domestic demand curve

0

X₀

Quantity
(bushels per year)

$5 a bushel instead of $6 a bushel. Their losses of net income add up to areas $a + b + c + d$. Consumers of wheat, concentrated in urban areas, gain area a through the reduction in wheat prices. The government collects and somehow redistributes area c in export duty revenues on the X_1 of exports that continue despite the duty. The nation as a whole loses areas b and d, the areas lost by exporters but gained by nobody.

If the exporting nation possesses some monopoly power in the world market, it could use the export duty to exploit this power to national advantage. Just as there was an optimal import tariff for the nation with monopsony power in Chapter 7, so there is a nationally optimal export duty, one that increases with the increase in the number of foreigners who are dependent on exports from the exporting nation. It is the hope of exploiting national monopoly power and getting the foreigner to pay more that prompts many export duties. Rice exports have been taxed in Thailand and Burma in part because these countries have some limited ability to get other Southeast Asian nations to pay them a higher price for rice given the duty (and in part simply to raise government revenues, albeit partly at the expense of rice-growing farmers). Furthermore, as we shall see in Chapter 10, the most important example of an export duty is the duty levied simultaneously by several nations joined in an international cartel. Here again, the main objective is the pursuit of monopoly profits by restricting exports. Canada may possess some small amount of this national monopoly power over world prices on wheat and minerals.

The issue of export barriers takes a somewhat different form for the United States. The U.S. Constitution prohibits the taxing of exports. The issue of export restriction has thus centered on export quotas, or quantitative controls. Not surprisingly, nonfarm groups have favored such quotas in years of bad harvests to restrain the inflation of food prices, whereas farm groups have fought for freedom to export as much as they want. This is what one would have predicted from the basic analysis of an export quota, which simply modifies Figure 8.2 to show a quota instead of an export duty.

DIFFERENCES IN TAX RATES AND TAX SYSTEMS

International trade is affected by taxes other than those levied on trade itself. Almost any form of taxation can distort international comparative advantage when the tax is applied differently in different countries. The most extreme cases of trade responses to tax differences are those in which firms themselves migrate in search of lighter taxes, a topic to which we return when discussing multinational firms in Part III. To avoid higher taxes in the United States and other major countries, many banks and shipping lines will set up shop in the West Indies or Panama or some other tax haven and export their services from there. Several dot-on-the-map nations gain considerable revenues by acting as competitive suppliers in the cheap-government market.

More generally, any turnover tax on production or consumption can affect international trade, either by its mere existence or by international differences in its rate. For example, a stiff excise tax on the consumption of coffee in consuming nations damages trade with coffee-exporting countries, even if the consuming nations grow and tax some coffee of their own. When turnover tax rates differ between countries, consumers may take advantage of the difference. There will be instances in which the consumer can escape the payment of any excise tax at all: he has left one tax sovereignty, and in transit by ship or airplane, or pausing in the customs-free portion of an international airport, he has not yet entered another. When he does, he will typically have a tourist's exemption from customs duty which enables him to escape taxes in both countries. But this loophole is not likely to be very large. Where the tourist exemption is large, the quantities of articles subject to excise tax—liquor, tobacco, and so on—which may be imported by tourists are typically limited. We refer rather to the distortion induced by differences in excise rates between countries, much like the distortion along state lines in the United States, with different states imposing different taxes on gasoline, cigarettes, and alcoholic beverages.

Where rates are low and the excise tax is levied at the retail level, the distortions in trade introduced by differences in rates are relatively unimportant. They are limited to the border and to what the individual consumer finds it worthwhile to transport. Where the excise tax applies at a higher stage of production or distribution, however, say on the gasoline refiner or the coffee roaster, it is necessary to apply excise duties along with tariffs at the border. Thus far no problem. But, as will be seen in Chapter 9, when two countries form a customs union, the fact of differences in excise taxes above the retail level does pose a choice: either submit to the tax-induced and distorted trade, with consumers individually buying in the low-tax country, or maintain customs inspectors at the border for the sole purpose of collecting domestic excise taxes. To escape the dilemma there has arisen strong pressure to harmonize excise taxes. Such **harmonization** generally takes the form of equalization and evidently has revenue, equity, and allocational effects in those countries where rates are changed.

If one looks just at the tax side, there is an important gain in simplicity from harmonization. But it is by no means clear that this gain is a net one. To do the job completely it may be necessary to harmonize benefits as well. Assume two countries with two different tax systems: one has public schools financed by a tax on alcoholic beverages and cigarettes; the other private schools without the taxes. To harmonize the tax system without doing something about the benefits will evidently be awkward, giving rise to budget and allocation problems in one country or both.

The difficulties posed by differences in rates become enhanced when we consider different systems. Assume two countries of roughly the same size, government revenue, and allocation of public benefits. If these assumptions cannot be granted, there is evident distortion. But if one country taxes goods and services and the other country taxes incomes of factors, even with equal-size revenue and the same allocation of expenditure, there is almost certain to be distortion. There must be some distortion of effort in the income-taxing country and of consumption in the nation taxing goods and services. It is virtually unthinkable that these distortions would be offsetting. Hence comparative advantage would be altered.

So much is highly academic. The more lively issues involve the administration of turnover taxes, the question of turnover taxes versus the value-added tax, and social security taxes. The first two issues pose problems of **border adjustment,** as one jurisdiction responds to the need for fitting internationally traded goods to the fiscal requirements of another.

When a trading country taxes goods through a levy on sales, or turnover, it must decide whether to apply the tax on the **origin** or the **destination** principle. In autarky, they come to the same thing. With foreign trade, however, the question is how to handle the taxes on exports and imports. Under the origin principle, there is no need to tax exports, since these are already taxed at the factory (let us say), nor to tax imports, since these are presumably taxed when produced abroad. Under the destination principle, however, a turnover tax is applied to imports at some level, and the turnover taxes already collected on goods produced for export must be refunded.

The level of taxation under the destination principle is awkward, since it should depend on how many stages of production the goods go through, paying taxes at each stage as they turn over. Most countries apply a so-called cascaded tax, which assumes a certain number of vertical stages. If the turnover tax were at 4 percent, for example, and if it were assumed that the average number of stages of production before foreign shipment was three, then the cascaded tax would be fixed at 12 percent, which would be applied to imports and remitted for exports. Where a good was produced by a vertically integrated company which paid only one tax on final product, the cascaded turnover tax remitted on exports would be larger than the tax actually paid, equivalent to a subsidy. And the same tax levied on imports produced by a vertically integrated firm abroad would be an added penalty to trade. A turnover tax based on the destination principle is thus clearly a distortion.

The turnover tax is disliked by public finance experts because it provides an incentive to vertical integration which may not be economically desirable. To meet this objection, French experts devised the administratively tricky but analytically elegant device of a **value-added tax.** Each stage of production pays a tax only on the value added by the stage, or rather, pays a tax on the total value sold but claims a rebate for taxes paid on components or materials bought from earlier stages. There is thus no incentive to integrate vertically and no need for a cascaded tax. The rate of tax for border-tax adjustment is the same as the tax actually paid.

Assume that country A applies the VAT on the origin principle, and that country B has a VAT of the same level but uses the principle of destination. A's goods going to B are taxed as exports by A and as imports by B. B's goods shipped to A are not taxed by A, and the taxes already paid by producers in B are refunded to the last processor. Goods going the first way are subjected to double taxation; those going the other way are not taxed at all, net, and there may be some distortion between early and late stages of production and the exporting stage.

When the problem first presented itself in the European Coal and Steel Community (ECSC), formed in 1950, it was thought to be serious. A distinguished committee of economists was appointed under the chairmanship of Jan Tinbergen of the Netherlands to examine it and make recommendations. The French, in particular, thought that the Germans should adopt their system as a matter of harmonization. But the economists observed that so long as the bilateral payments between the two countries were appropriately balanced in the long run, it made no difference. Any tax distortion in favor of France, which taxed on the destination principle, and against Germany, which used origin, was balanced out by a somewhat higher exchange rate. The balance-of-payments, terms-of-trade, production, consumption, and other effects of the taxes could be offset by equal and opposite influences on the side of the exchange rate. Like other distortions between social and private marginal values, the tax system had already been absorbed into the general-equilibrium system. The experts recommended that the problem be ignored.

This recommendation is no longer universally supported by economists, on the ground that exchange-rate changes are much more general than even the very general VAT. Depreciation which will correct the distortion in the current account between two countries will produce new distortions in capital items between them, and in all payments and receipts with third countries. The Common Market countries chose not to settle the problem by ignoring the tax difference and adjusting the exchange rate.

Harmonization of excise taxes without harmonization of the total fiscal system (including benefits) produces new distortions. To take just revenue, it reduces the revenue of the government whose tax system had relied most on excise taxes and increases the revenue of the one that had used such taxes least. Pressure to harmonize any one aspect of the economy seems to lead to new pressures to harmonize further. The end is the merging of fiscal sovereignties, which in the European Economic Community still lies some distance ahead.

STATE TRADING

Governments are themselves buyers and sellers and have the power to shun or foster international trade in ways not available to private firms. Among capitalist countries this power has been applied mainly in the direction of autarky. Governments are free to do as they like in their purchases for their own use. Here there are no international rules nor any international standard of conduct. All governments tend to buy at home. The tendency was accentuated during the 1930s depression, when "Buy British," "Buy French," and "Buy American" campaigns were urged on the public to expand employment. In the United States, the Buy American criterion for government purchases, which was laboriously reduced from 25 percent as a normal rate in the 1930s to 10 percent in the 1950s, was raised to 50 percent in the balance-of-payments weakness of the 1960s.

Governments pay no tariffs, so that perhaps some nominal preference for domestic supplies, such as 10 percent, is understandable. Buy-local campaigns, like putting up a tariff during a depression, are clearly a beggar-thy-neighbor policy. And to jam up the rate to 50 percent, as the United States did in the early 1960s, is clearly to set up a double standard—no balance-of-payments tariffs or quotas for the private sector, because of international commitments, and near autarky for the government. For the United States to buy dairy products in Wisconsin for its troops in West Germany, next door to Denmark, is evidently uneconomical—wasteful of real resources and causing the Department of Defense budget to run out faster than it otherwise would, thereby raising appropriations and the need for tax revenues.

Governments tend to buy at home under most normal circumstances. Larger governments are unwilling, for example, to buy arms from any country that is not a certain ally. And considerations of prestige require that U.S. government officials ride in U.S. limousines rather than Daimler-Benzes and fly on U.S. airlines. Many of these considerations are not even articulated. But the economic rule remains the presumptively correct one: one should buy in the cheapest market and sell in the dearest, whether household, firm, or government sector.

TRADE AMONG SOCIALIST COUNTRIES

The question of how states should trade becomes even more important among socialist countries, where the state itself is usually the sole exporter and importer. With each government intervening between a controlled domestic economy and the rest of the world, how should trading states go about deciding what goods to buy and sell, and at what prices? Initially, after World War I, when the Soviet Union was the only "socialist" country in the world, it chose to use foreign trade as a device to achieve autarky. Not without reason, it feared dependence on imported supplies and pushed its traditional exports—wheat, timber, furs, manganese, and so on, largely primary materials—to buy the machinery which would make the country independent of foreign supplies. Its success in certain commodities, such as steel, was impressive, and in all but a few primary commodities, such as rubber and wool, and in most basic manufactures, the Soviet Union did well. It was especially successful in heavy industry.

When after World War II there were other socialist countries, in China and Eastern Europe, the notion of using foreign trade to get rid of foreign trade made less sense. The Soviet Union, for one, was planning for the **socialist division of labor**, a concept which has never become clear. Other socialist countries, such as China and Romania, thought it useful to follow the Soviet path and build their own heavy industry. Even if socialist countries were to agree on the principle of a division of labor, putting it into practice would not be easy, given a series of national plans, independent prices, and inconvertible currencies.

Soviet planning, with its emphasis on materials balances, is regarded as biased against balanced foreign trade. Plan fulfillment as a prime administrative target means holding back on exports and speeding up imports to make good the gaps in the plan. But foreign trade in independent plans in seven countries becomes even more difficult to regulate. The trade organization of the Soviet bloc, COMECON, or CMEA, has been searching for a fundamental way to organize the foreign trade of its members, without great success. Meanwhile, trade continues on an ad hoc basis, and even that gives rise to serious problems of deciding what countries export and import what commodities and at what price, and of balancing the national value of exports against the value of imports on a multilateral basis. In particular, there is no effective way of deciding whether, say, Hungary should sell shoes to Romania or whether Czechoslovakia should sell it shoe machinery so that the Romanians could ultimately produce shoes for their own market.

Since the Soviet Union traded at world prices in the interwar period, one solution for the pricing problem in principle was to value trade among the bloc countries at world prices. This has proved difficult in practice. For bulky commodities, it is not clear what the world price of a commodity is in Eastern Europe, until a decision is made as to whether the Eastern bloc would export or import that commodity to the West. The price in North America or Western Europe is clearly inappropriate because of transport costs, but the question of whether transport costs should be added or subtracted cannot be decided until it is clear which way the trade would go. For differentiated products, moreover, the question of quality can be decided only on an arbitrary basis: Is the Moskvich more like the Renault, the Volkswagen, or the Cortina? Studies of the prices actually used in Eastern trade suggest that the Eastern countries frequently trade with each other at higher prices than those at which they trade with the West. Various explanations have been used to account for this phenomenon, including trade discrimination, a "customs union effect" which has produced an island of bloc prices higher than those in the outside world, and rather arbitrary adjustment of prices after trade to help balance exports and imports.

A related problem for socialist governments is that of deciding what goods to trade. Part of the difficulty lies in the lack of an efficient price system within each country. Real prices used in consumption and production differ widely because of heavy turnover taxes, which are added to imports and subtracted from exports to make it possible to trade abroad at arbitrary exchange rates. But even after prices are adjusted for taxation, they fail to reflect economic values. If capital is not regarded as a factor of production, capital-intensive goods tend to be relatively cheap, over-produced, and exported, which is inefficient for the system as a whole. Planning techniques without prices, or with only implicit shadow prices, became too complex, even with computers, when seven systems have to be meshed, subject to the constraint that excess demand in one commodity in one country is matched by an excess supply in another, and that the value of all exports equals the value of all imports for each country, on a multilateral basis. These issues are solved in the West with prices and money. The Soviet bloc tries to operate without explicit prices reflecting scarcity values, and with a monetary system which is unsatisfactory so that its countries are unwilling to hold ruble balances. Thus far the bloc is making slow work of it. COMECON has organized trade in ways variously described as "absolute advantage" or "empiricism," and has resolved conflicts at the "highest political level," all the time seeking and failing to find an objective, scientific basis for international socialist specialization.

The suggestion has been put forward by a Hungarian economist that trade in the Eastern bloc needs convertible currencies and international corporations to make effective price comparisons so as to see where comparative advantage and disadvantage lie. Along with effective goods prices and international money in which to compare them, the bloc needs at least a notional set of factor prices (sometimes called "shadow prices") to calculate the desirability of investing capital to take advantage of foreign trade opportunities. Without such pricing, the bloc remains condemned in its internal trade to traditional, empirical, ad hoc, or arbitrary trade, on which it is impossible to be sure of gains.

In the long run, however, socialist countries are likely to trade among themselves at price ratios that move in somewhat parallel fashion with price ratios in the world market, for the simple reason that each socialist nation has some leeway to avoid socialist trade in favor of trade with capitalist countries. A dramatic illustration came with the oil crisis of 1973–74. The quadrupling of oil prices presented the

Soviet Union and Romania with the choice of selling oil to desperate Western countries at the new high world price or of selling to their equally desperate COMECON partners at a lower agreed price based on Western prices over the previous five years. Both countries shifted toward selling to the West as discreetly as possible, and forced through a revision of the COMECON pact that speeded up price adjustments in socialist trade, so that they were soon able to more than double the oil price they received from their bloc partners.

EAST-WEST TRADE

Trade between the private enterprise economies of the West and the state trading organizations of the Soviet bloc poses a variety of difficult institutional and organizational problems. But it has not been possible for the United States to tackle many of these because of its restrictions on trading with the East. The U.S. position has eased somewhat since the passage of the rigid Battle Act of 1951 at the height of the Korean War. After long, unsuccessful efforts at détente on the part of President Johnson, President Nixon, the business community, and some limited portions of Congress (interrupted when the Vietnam War intensified), the visits of President Nixon to Communist China and the Soviet Union in 1972 started a movement toward resolution. But the problems abound. They include concern for political independence, one-sided economic advantages, the Eastern need for credit, the problem of what the East should sell to the West, and the problem of making two different systems function in tandem.

Fear of dependence on, say, Soviet trade on political grounds finds support in the Soviet Union's sudden cutting of purchases of Icelandic fish in 1948 and of sales of oil to Israel in 1956. But in its turn the United States abruptly reduced the Cuban sugar quota in 1960. There is risk of great dependence on any supplier or outlet, and Western governments may have to exert pressure, when they do, more overtly and publicly. The fact that socialist trade organizations are governmental may enable them to squeeze a customer or a supplier more gradually. But the difference between East and West is probably small, since the trading organization in Eastern countries is different from the Politburo.

Who gains from East-West trade? Our basic analysis of the gains from trade is potentially applicable here, even though this trade is between capitalist and socialist countries. Since any trade bargains are entered voluntarily on both sides, it is likely that both sides gain. Which side gains more depends on how close the trading prices are to the prices that would prevail in West or East without East-West trade. If, for example, expanding East-West trade has no effect on Western prices, it seems safe to guess that only a small share of the gains accrue to the Western traders. The distribution of the gains is difficult to judge, however, since we do not know the true scarcities, the "shadow prices," of individual goods and services in the socialist countries in the absence of expanded trade. The closer one comes to measuring these socialist shadow prices, the closer one comes to an estimate of how the gains from greater trade would be distributed between East and West.

There is reason to suspect that a state-run socialist economy might have certain advantages in the private Western marketplace. It has been suspected that the Soviet Union may have cashed in big on its monopoly of information about Soviet crop conditions when it bought unprecedented amounts of U.S. grain in 1972. The fear is that the Soviets, knowing that their own harvest would be very poor, could quietly buy large amounts of grain at low prices from individual Western grain dealers who lacked knowledge of the impending Soviet crop, and thus make a killing at the expense of Western suppliers. (Conversely, if the Soviets knew that their crops were going to be better than Western dealers expected, they could make futures contracts to resell Western grain at the mistakenly high futures prices.) This exploitation of a Soviet monopoly on information is a legitimate object of Western fear, and there is a case for having Western governments insist on better access to hard information about the Soviet economy as a price for letting Soviet state agencies deal directly with private Western parties.

It should be noted, however, that the experience of the 1972 grain deal did not really demonstrate the Soviet exploitation of a monopoly on an economic secret. The Soviet purchases in fact unfolded over several months, and the U.S. Department of Agriculture and major grain dealers knew the extent of the aggregate purchases the Soviets intended to make when negotiating most of the contracts. What allowed the Soviets a continuing bargain on U.S. grain was the failure of the U.S. Department of Agriculture to shut off its obsolete subsidies on the export of "surplus" grain. Because the department failed to change its surplus-disposal policies when a surplus no longer existed, U.S. taxpayers went on paying subsidies so that the Soviets could buy U.S. grain more cheaply than could U.S. residents. Yet even though the Soviet bargain buys on grain in 1972 related to U.S. government subsidies and not to Soviet secrets, the fear of dealing with a Soviet government that has better information is still justified.

The analysis of East-West trade is further complicated by the interdependence of utilities. Many observers on both sides feel that anything benefiting the other side, the Enemy, is harmful to their own side. For such observers there is a case for restricting trade between the blocs even if such trade brings direct economic gains to their own side.

East-West trade has also been plagued by the difficulty of finding sufficient goods and services for the socialist countries to sell, or sufficient credit for them to borrow, at the officially quoted terms of trade. To obviate the possibility that Western nations would overextend credit to the East or compete too avidly for sales by loose credit terms, a Berne convention signed in the 1930s set a five-year limit on credits. Recent competition has broken this barrier, and the Organization for Economic Cooperation and Development (OECD) is seeking to provide at least exchanges of information in the West so that the separate lenders can make a judgment as to the extent to which safe limits of credit extension are being approached. The Soviet Union has some uncertain amount of gold (and an excellent record on repaying the few commercial credits it has received in the past). Communist China earns a substantial amount of sterling from trade with Hong Kong. Most Communist countries are jealous of their credit standing. But there is some limit on the amount of credit which can safely be extended, a limit dependent upon Eastern success in selling in Western markets. Thus far East-West trade has been limited less by Western regulations, especially those of the United States, than by the lack of goods for the East to sell.

There is much that can be done to improve East-West trade: limiting the provision of the Battle Act to narrowly military items; extending most-favored-nation treatment to the Eastern countries in the matter of tariffs, especially in the United States; and understanding, in matters like the blockade of Cuba, that bygones are bygones after ten years or so, and that blockades may well be counterproductive. The prospect for a lively expansion of trade between East and West to a meaningful level is dim, although percentage gains from low numbers are readily achieved. Despite the difficulties, the pursuit of expansion is probably worthwhile for peace, and possibly for the sake of the trade itself.

DUMPING

The next dimension of government policy bearing on trade is an area in which import duties are applied for a special reason, and with a peculiar range of possible results.

Dumping is international price discrimination in which an exporting firm sells at a lower price in a foreign market than it charges in other (usually its home-country) markets. **Predatory dumping** occurs when the firm discriminates in favor of some foreign buyers temporarily with the purpose of eliminating some competitors and of later raising its price after the competition is dead. **Persistent dumping,** as its name implies, goes on indefinitely.

The issue of dumping has heated up most in times of international economic upheaval. In the stormy 1920s and 1930s, dumping was frequently alleged and probably frequently practiced both in manufacturing and in primary-product trade. The issue has returned to public notice in the international turbulence of the 1970s. In the early 1970s, as part of a larger campaign for relief against foreign competition, the U.S. government charged firms in several countries with dumping their products in the U.S. market. One major case was that brought against SONY of Japan in 1970. Investigations showed that SONY was selling TV sets made in Japan for $180 while charging Japanese consumers $333 for the same model. Japanese consumer groups joined U.S. TV manufacturers in protest against SONY. In 1975 the U.S. Treasury opened the largest dumping investigation to date by charging foreign auto firms in eight countries with dumping in the U.S. market. The threat issued to the alleged dumpers was that if they did not raise their export prices up to the prices charged in their home markets, the U.S. would impose a tariff on U.S. imports of their products. It may have been partly in response to this threat that both SONY and Volkswagen announced plans to shift their supply for the U.S. market to new plants built in the United States.

To understand whether dumping is good or bad and whether or not retaliation against it is in order, it is first necessary to understand what makes some firms charge foreign buyers less. A firm will maximize profits by charging a lower price to foreign buyers if it has greater monopoly power in its home market than abroad and if buyers in the home country cannot buy the good abroad and import it cheaply. When these conditions hold, the firm is able to exploit home-country buyers more heavily.

Figure 8.3 shows such a case of profitable price discrimination, under the diagram-simplifying assumption that the firm faces a constant marginal cost of production. The illustration is that of SONY's treatment of the U.S. and Japanese TV markets back in 1970. What makes the dumping profitable is that the firm faces a less elastic, (steeper) demand curve in its home market than in the more competitive foreign market. Sensing this, the firm will charge prices so as to maximize profits. In any one market, profits are maximized by equating marginal cost and marginal revenue. In the U.S. market the profit-maximizing price is $180, which makes U.S. consumers buy X_1 sets a year, at which marginal revenue just equals marginal cost. In the Japanese home market, where consumers have fewer substitutes for SONY sets, the profit-maximizing price is $333, which causes consumers to buy S_1 sets a year, again equating marginal costs and revenues.

FIGURE 8.3
Dumping

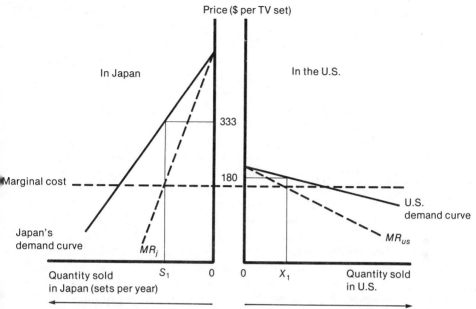

The discriminating monopolist (SONY) maximizes profits by equating marginal revenue in each market with marginal cost.

This price discrimination is more profitable for the firm than charging the same price in both markets, which would yield lower marginal revenues in Japan than in the United States. As long as transport costs and import duties make it uneconomical for Japanese consumers to import Japanese-made TV sets all the way from the United States, the firm continues to make greater profits by charging a higher price in the Japanese market.

RETALIATION AGAINST DUMPING

Under pressure from import-competing firms, the governments of importing countries have often levied antidumping tariffs when given evidence that the foreign supplier is dumping. This tariff retaliation against dumping has taken two different forms. The United States, following its Anti-Dumping Act of 1921, charges the full price difference as a tariff as long as the dumping continues, thereby equating the U.S. and home-market retail prices on the dumper's product. The International Anti-Dumping Code, signed as part of the Kennedy Round of trade liberalization in 1967, urges importing countries to levy a fixed duty high enough to offset "injury" to import-competing firms, even if this tariff is lower than the one that would equalize prices.

Who gains and who loses from an antidumping tariff is a question with a subtle answer. The free trader's first instinct is that the importing country, the "dumpee," should not retaliate against persistent dumping but only against predatory dumping. After all, if the foreign firm wants to go on selling to us at a cheaper price year in and year out, why not relax and enjoy it? Won't the gains to our consumers outweigh the losses to our import-competing producers (such as Zenith, in the case of SONY TV exports to the United States)?

This free-trade prescription is only partly correct where dumping is involved. Consider first the case in which the law calls for forcing the dumping firm to equalize its prices (f.o.b. its factory), as under U.S. law. This is indeed harmful for the importing country, which might as well enjoy bargain imports, as the free-trade position says. But it is helpful for the more exploited buyers back in the higher-priced home market. If the firm is forced to equalize its prices, it will find it in its interest to cut its previously higher prices somewhat. In the TV example, this gives a price break to Japanese consumers. And since the distortion of price above marginal cost was greater in their market than in the lower-priced export market, forcing the firm to equalize prices and shift its sales back toward the home market probably brings gains to the world as a whole even if it deprives the importing country (the United States) of a bargain. The analysis of the fixed antidumping duty which falls short of forcing the firm to equalize prices is also complex. A fixed duty, which shifts the U.S. demand curve down to the southwest in Figure 8.3, can have the effect of getting the dumping firm to charge a lower price to the U.S. market (exclusive of the tariff itself). This might even bring gains to the importing country itself, along the lines of the nationally optimal tariff in Chapter 7. There is thus some basis for tariffs that retaliate against dumping. This is especially true when failure to follow a consistent set of antidumping rules could arouse protectionist sentiments enough to get stiffer import barriers enacted. Dumping is thus an issue on which an advocate of free trade may wish to concede a case for retaliatory tariffs, since it is one in which the market distortion is indeed specific to international trade.

ADJUSTMENT ASSISTANCE

The last policy relating to trade is not so much a policy affecting trade as a way of responding to trade competition. It is the policy, now being increasingly practiced, of compensating those whose jobs and investments are displaced by import competition.

As we noted in Chapter 6, greater import competition entails displacement costs, whether or not this extra competition is the result of tariff reductions. These displacement costs are real and measurable, even though the usual analysis often leaves the impression that anybody whose job or investment is displaced by import competition simply finds another opportunity that is just as rewarding. In some cases, as noted, these costs can outweigh the efficiency benefits of freer trade, making a particular tariff reduction inadvisable.

Where the displacement costs are significant yet not high enough to justify maintaining higher tariff levels, society can consider the option of compensating those hurt by the keener import competition. As long as the freer trade policy brings net gains to the nation, the gainers can compensate the injured while still retaining net gains from the free trade. The United States and other countries have recently adopted this policy of **adjustment assistance,** or government financial aid to relocate and retrain workers (and firms) for reemployment in sectors less threatened by import competition. The U.S. adjustment assistance program, launched by President Kennedy's Trade Expansion Act of 1962, failed to fulfill its expectations in the 1960s because the standards for eligibility for assistance were so stringent that nobody received any aid. Labor groups complained that the displaced workers had been betrayed. In the early 1970s a series of reforms relaxed the eligibility rules and made the terms of aid more generous.

Adjustment assistance is likely to remain one of the main policy prescriptions of advocates of free trade, for a pragmatic political reason. A true believer in the free marketplace might ask why society should give special aid to those whose incomes are lowered by competition from imports. Why, one might ask, don't we give equally generous aid to those whose incomes are lowered by technological change, or government rerouting of highways, or bad weather? If we care about people who suffer income losses, why not cushion the fall of all incomes, regardless of the cause? What is so special about people hurt by import competition? These are valid questions. Some countries, most notably Sweden, indeed apply their income-maintenance and manpower retraining programs across the board, without singling out those injured by trade changes. Yet in countries where such a broad approach is not politically feasible, there is a special case for tying adjustment assistance to import injury. Where foreign trade is involved, there is an extra danger that uncompensated injured parties will join lobbying alliances that produce more sweeping protectionist legislation. It is to forestall such a protectionist alliance, if simple concern for those displaced by import competition is not sufficient, that advocates of continued free trade are politically well advised to endorse adjustment assistance for the import-injured even if it is not forthcoming for people who lose income in other ways.

SUMMARY

Nontariff policies affecting international trade have emerged as the more important kind of trade distortion as tariffs have been gradually lowered in the postwar era. Government officials have many reasons for turning to import quotas and other nontariff barriers. Whatever these reasons, the basic analysis of the main nontariff barrier to trade, an import quota, indicates that at its best it is no worse than a tariff. It is more costly than the tariff if it creates monopoly power or if resources are used up in the private pursuit of licenses to import legally.

Barriers to exports are symmetrical with import barriers. An export duty hurts exporting producers more than it helps consumers or gives revenue to the government, leaving a net cost to the nation, if the nation faces a fixed world price for its exports. If the nation has some monopoly power over world prices, it can reap net gains from an export duty, just as the nation with some monopsony power can levy an optimal import duty.

Differences in tax rates and tax systems also affect international trade in complicated ways. Differences in turnover tax rates affect trade even when they apply to home and foreign goods alike. Even across-the-board turnover taxes, such as the value-added tax, distort trade incentives when one country applies the origin principle and its trading partners apply the destination principle, and these distortions are hard to offset neatly, even with adjustments in overall exchange rates.

Trade involving government agencies follows no easy rules. Western governments have generally been required by law to shun importing and to buy from domestic producers, even at higher cost. The gains from trade involving socialist countries can be measured in principle by knowing how scarce different goods would be in those countries without expanded trade, but in practice the necessary data for such measurements are lacking. Western countries have some institutional reasons to fear that a large socialist government, such as that of the Soviet Union, will have an inordinate trading advantage by having a monopoly on information about the state of its own economy. Recent experience fails either to confirm or to refute these fears, however.

Dumping, or international price discrimination in favor of foreign buyers, occurs when firms have greater monopoly power in one national market, usually their home country, than in others. Temporary and predatory dumping needs to be countered with a tariff in the importing country. Persistent dumping poses a different policy puzzle for the importing country. The usual free-trade prescription is simply to relax and enjoy the cheap imports in the knowledge that they bring more gains to consumers than losses of income to import-competing producers. There are arguments in favor of retaliating against persistent dumping with a tariff, however. A tariff designed to force the dumper to equalize prices will bring net gains to the world, though not to the importing country. A lower fixed antidumping tariff could benefit the importing nation by causing the dumper to deliver at a lower price.

The fact that increased international trade competition displaces import-competing firms and workers can be an argument for adjustment assistance, or income support while they relocate or retrain. Adjustment assistance is preferable to preventing import competition with trade barriers if the displacement costs of the free trade are less than the efficiency gains.

SUGGESTED READING

A wealth of empirical information for the United States on nontariff barriers, dumping, adjustment assistance, and trade with socialist countries can be found in the Williams report, *United States International Economic Policy in an Interdependent World*, papers submitted to the U.S. Commission on International Trade and Investment Policy, 1971. Robert E. Baldwin's concise survey of nontariff barriers in vol. 1 of the Williams report is given in more detail in his *Nontariff Distortions of International Trade* (Washington, D.C.: Brookings Institution, 1970).

The analysis of resource-using application procedures in the pursuit of import quota licenses is given in Anne O. Krueger, "The Political Economy of a Rent-Seeking Society," *American Economic Review*, June 1974.

There is an extensive literature on tax harmonization. See, for example, H. C. Johnson, P. Wonnacott, and H. Shibata, *Harmonization of National Economic Policies under Free Trade* (Toronto: University of Toronto Press, 1969).

U.S. perspectives on East-West trade are usefully surveyed in U.S. Congress, Joint Economic Committee, *Soviet Economic Prospects for the Seventies* (Washington, D.C.: Government Printing Office, 1973), part 6. I. Vajda, in *International Economic Relations*, ed. Paul A. Samuelson (New York: St. Martin's Press, 1969), is the source of the suggestion that COMECON needs a convertible currency and international corporations. A detailed account of the historic 1972 U.S.-Soviet grain deal can be found in J. Albright, "Some Deal: How Amerika Got Burned and the Russians Got Bread," *New York Times*, November 25, 1973 Section 6, pp. 36ff.

Adjustment assistance and displacement costs are analyzed in Robert E. Baldwin and John H. Mutti, "Policy Issues in Adjustment Assistance: The United States," in *Prospects for Partnership: Industrialization and Trade Policies in the 1970s*, ed. Helen Hughes (Baltimore: Johns Hopkins Press, 1973).

Empirical studies on a host of nontariff trade barriers are found in the National Bureau of Economic Research series on *Foreign Trade Regimes and Economic Development*, ed. Jagdish Bhagwati and Anne O. Krueger (New York: Columbia University Press, 1973–76), which includes country volumes on Turkey, Ghana, Israel, Egypt, the Philippines, India, South Korea, Chile, Colombia, and Brazil.

9

Economic integration

We will start our analysis of economic integration (which will not be completed until we consider monetary unification in Part V) with a discussion of customs unions and free-trade areas—the elimination of trade barriers between two or more countries while maintaining them against the rest of the world. The difference between a customs union and a free-trade area is that in a customs union it is necessary to agree on a common tariff nomenclature or schedule and identical tariff rates, whereas the countries in a free-trade area maintain their own tariffs against outsiders while scrapping duties among themselves.

THE THEORY OF CUSTOMS UNIONS

Our interest is in the theory of customs unions and in the paradox that not every step toward freer trade is desirable in welfare terms even when free trade is a welfare optimum. This is an example of the **theory of the second best,** which we discussed more generally in Chapter 7. One example has been suggested in connection with the effective rate of the tariff: a tariff increase on the raw material may reduce the effective rate of the tariff on the finished good and add to welfare rather than reduce it. In the same way, as we shall see, reducing trade barriers between two partners may worsen rather than improve welfare.

The welfare effects of eliminating trade barriers between partners can be illustrated in Figure 9.1. D–D and S–S are the demand and supply curves of a "home" country which imports M–M of a product

FIGURE 9.1
Trade creation and trade diversion
Price of imports

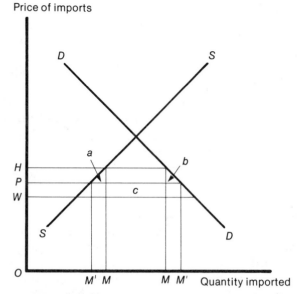

with a tariff *WH*. The world price *OW* is assumed to represent an infinitely elastic supply schedule, which eliminates adverse terms of trade effects on the rest of the world after the formation of the customs union. In short, the world price is fixed no matter what happens. The partner's supply is also assumed to be infinitely elastic at the price *OP*. Before customs union the prospective partner, facing the same tariff as the rest of the world, is out of the market, since its pretariff price is higher than that in the outside world. After the union, with no tariffs against partner and the tariff *WH* still applying to imports from the rest of the world, all imports come from the partner and none from the rest of the world.

Forming the customs union affects trade and welfare in two opposing ways. First, it brings **trade creation** by raising total imports from *MM* to *M'M'*. The world welfare gain associated with this trade creation equals the triangles *a* and *b*, as in Chapter 6. Second, it diverts *MM* of imports from the low-cost foreign supplier to the high-cost partner. This **trade diversion** brings a deadweight loss of *c*, measured by the increased cost of getting *MM* produced in the partner country.

In this one-commodity case, trade creation and the gains from the customs union are evidently greater, the greater the elasticities of demand and supply in the home country (or the flatter the demand and supply curves in the figure), the wider the cost differences between the home country and the partner, and the smaller these differences between the partner and the world. On the other hand, the trade diversion loss is greater, the less elastic the demand and supply curves in the home country, and the smaller the cost differences between the home country and the partner and the wider the cost differences between the partner and the world.

In this simple case of fixed world and partner prices, it happens that the net welfare effect for the home country—area a plus area b minus area c—is also the net static welfare effect for the world. The welfare results are more complicated when the present simplifying assumptions are relaxed, but the rule remains that *the world's gains are tied to trade creation and its losses to trade diversion.*

THE REAL WORLD

Trade creation and trade diversion are not purely hypothetical concepts. In U.S. history the foremost example is the customs union between the plantation agriculture of the South and the nascent manufacturing of the North. These were not separate countries, but they were different regions in terms of factor proportions, factor prices, and comparative advantage. Before World War I, in fact, trade between the North and the South was conducted much like international trade and unlike internal trade. Little capital moved south, and little labor moved north. With factor immobility, factor prices failed to equalize, and it paid to employ different factor proportions. The South had a labor- and land-intensive agriculture; the North, a capital-intensive manufacturing industry.

The inclusion of the agricultural South in the customs area of the North, which is what a common customs meant, required the South to buy in a protected market while it was selling in a free market. The price of its imports increased, and its terms of trade were reduced. This economic exploitation of the South by the North is- generally regarded as a factor contributing to the Civil War.

A further example can be given from the history of Germany, in which the Zollverein, or customs union, actually preceded political union by many years. The Zollverein was formed in 1834; Bismarck united Germany under the leadership of Prussia in 1870. In 1879 the first increase took place in the tariff on grain. This was combined with a tariff on steel; but Germany was in the business of exporting steel, so that the tariff was useful only in widening its scope for dumping. The tariff on rye, on the other hand, raised the cost of living of the worker in western Germany well above what it would have been had Germany bought its grain on the world market. Customs union thus involved the exploitation of the working classes by the Prussian Junkers, who were both soldiers and managers of estates which grew rye. After World War II unsophisticated observers thought that West Germany would be harmed by being cut off from its traditional source of food in the east. As it turned out, however, West Germany gained by being able to obtain its food abroad at low world prices, rather than from protected high-cost farms in the east.

The net welfare impact of trade creation and trade diversion effects of the European Economic Community (EEC, or Common Market) is difficult to weigh. The gains in trade in manufactures within the union have been substantial, and there has been some relative loss in the trade of the United States. In 1958, 50 percent of manufactured products of the EEC countries were bought from other members, whereas in 1968, ten years later, the percentage was 60. Most of the diversion was from the other countries of Europe that had originally declined to join. Lawrence Krause estimates that U.S. manufactures exported to the Community fell $275 million as a result of the customs union, but that 40 percent of this was made up as a result of faster growth in the Community resulting from the union. Such gains and losses in trade must be distinguished from welfare gains and losses, however, because they do not take into account the alternative uses of the resources absorbed in the one case or released in the other.

Trade diversion is much more substantial in agriculture and was substantially increased as Britain became a full member of the EEC. France has long been protectionist in farming and continues to be so. Germany and Britain, which used to protect and subsidize agriculture while importing what they needed additionally from the cheapest sources overseas, now import from high-cost France and divert some purchases of tropical products away from Latin America and the independent African states, generally to former French colonies in Africa.

The trade diversion effect may not be serious for the world because of the narrowness of the difference in cost between the excluded outside seller and the favored inside one. It is still painful to the outside seller. This is why the Norwegians (until they decided against it), British, and Danes were so anxious to join the EEC, and why the neutrals (Austria, Sweden, and Switzerland) and the underdeveloped countries (Greece and Turkey) were so concerned to find a basis of association. Trade diversion also adversely affected the United States, which, however, was able to mitigate the economic hurt of discrimination in industrial products by establishing facilities to manufacture inside the Common Market boundaries. The United States was in any event prepared to pay the economic price of European integration to obtain the political benefits of strengthening the Free World. But the other outsiders—Japan (where cost differences in manufactures were substantial), the Commonwealth, and the producers of tropical products which were discriminated against by the preferential position in the Common Market given to former colonies—were adversely affected. The U.S. Trade Expansion Act of 1962 attempted to reduce the damage by providing for mutual lowering of tariffs. If the tariff, WH in Figure 9.1, is reduced below WP, the home country will buy nothing in the partner country, which, in its turn, will buy for the first time in the world market. The greater the number of countries that join the customs union, and the lower the common external tariff, the less will be the extent of trade diversion and the more nearly will the customs union approach the free-trade ideal.

THE DYNAMIC EFFECTS OF CUSTOMS UNION

Trade creation and trade diversion are static effects of customs union or trade integration. There is some doubt as to their importance. A number of scholars have sought to measure the effects of tariff reductions, both total and partial, and the impact on national income usually turns out to be exiguous, to use a fancy word, or very small. Imports, say, are 20 percent of national income. The elimination of a 10 percent tariff may expand trade to 22 or 24 percent of income. But the change is not a clear gain for national income, as diagrams such as Figure 9.1 remind us. The protective effect and the consumption effect are represented, not by the total change in trade, which includes resources, but by the increment in trade times the change in price made possible by the new arrangements—in the case of trade creation, the higher price for exports and the lower price for imports. Even if this is substantial, we end up with a small measure of the static gain.

Not all the gains are static, however. Dynamic gains include economies of scale, the stimulus of competition, and the stimulus to investment. Economies of scale were touched upon in Chapter 2. As specialization takes place, costs may fall for a number of reasons: through learning to make the product more effectively by repetition, through spreading a number of capital items of a lumpy character more thinly per unit of output, and so on. These matters are discussed more thoroughly in courses in intermediate theory. Economies of scale are the great hope of customs unions among less developed countries, and they are much debated. They may occur in customs union among manufacturing countries through product specialization which enables manufacturers in two countries to concentrate on particular sizes or models of a product rather than make a full line (this is even sometimes the result of a business agreement). Many Europeans assert that the advantage of the United States is that it has a large internal market which enables its manufacturers to achieve economies of scale. The opponents point to the efficiency of many small companies and to the sluggishness of some large ones, and note that such countries as Sweden and Switzerland have efficient manufacturing where the market extends beyond the national boundaries. The importance of economies of scale cannot be demonstrated. This gives us students of international economics much to argue about.

The competitive effect has been touched on in Chapter 6. Tibor Scitovsky believes that this has been the most important impact of the EEC. As suggested in the earlier discussion, high tariffs foster monopoly in which one or two large companies preside over a larger aggregation of small, inefficient producers. The big companies like the quiet life and prefer high prices to substantial volume, which they could achieve to drive out the little firms if they choose. With lower tariffs, the big companies are forced to compete and the little ones to merge, combine, become efficient, or go under. This effect has been observed particularly in France. It may be a function of lower tariffs within the EEC, or their anticipation.

Finally among the dynamic effects, the change in relative prices and the prod to competition stimulate domestic investment, to take advantage of export opportunities or to meet new import competition. One important aspect of the change in domestic investment is the pull of market-oriented industry to the frontier nearer markets in the trading partner. This is hard on such regions as southern Italy, southwest France, or southeast Germany, which lie far from the markets in the union partners. New investment to take advantage of opportunities is accompanied by disinvestment in industries adversely affected by trade creation, that is, the import-competing industries which are no longer able to make a go of it. The investment stimulus of new industries is likely to be greater than the disinvestment discouragement in old industries, unless substantial excess capacity is available. On this score, customs union may be said to be inflationary.

The possibility that investment will decline in the remote and backward portions of a newly integrated area has led to special measures to assist them. Thus the EEC established a European Investment Bank to undertake new ventures in the adversely affected portions of the Six (the original members of the EEC) This constituted explicit acknowledgment that in the absence of policy certain parts of the integrated area would suffer.

In addition to the dynamic stimulus to domestic investment, however, there is the possibility of inducing investment from abroad. This is of two kinds. There may be rearrangement of existing foreign capacity in the community to take advantage of the new conditions. This effect is identical to the pull to the border in the market-oriented industries, with this difference, that domestic firms are not likely to cross the border and that foreign firms, without roots in the particular country, may be drawn across. Or the trade-diverting effect of the customs union may induce foreigners who have served the various national markets by exports, and now are discriminated against, to substitute tariff factories for trade. U.S. firms undertook massive investment in Europe after about 1955 for a variety of reasons or excuses, and the EEC may have been one or the other. To a considerable extent, in the judgment of more than one writer, the effect of the EEC was not so much that it provided the marginal conditions under which a close calculation revealed that it was better now to invest in Europe than to provide that market from the United States, but rather that it called the attention of manufacturers who had neglected to notice investment opportunities in Europe to the fact that here was a growing, vigorous market from which outsiders might be expelled and which it was useful to join.

BEYOND CUSTOMS UNION

Ascending (so to speak) from a free-trade area and customs union are common market, economic union, and complete economic integration. In the usual definitions, a **common market** goes beyond the customs union for goods by removing all restrictions on the movement of the factors of production, labor, and capital. **Economic union** goes farther and provides for harmonization of national economic policies. **Economic integration** is still more intimate and requires some common policies in the macroeconomic field, especially monetary and fiscal policies.

We cannot explore this institutional framework fully until we get to Parts IV and V, but there is merit in analyzing a number of definitions of economic integration which have been put forth by economists.

In his *International Economic Integration*, Jan Tinbergen suggests that economic integration is free trade. Removal of tariffs, however, is insufficient to provide for free movement of all goods. It is necessary first to get rid of the border guards, who are still required so long as excise taxes are not harmonized in the trading countries.

Bela Balassa's definition of integration goes beyond Tinbergen's to encompass the absence of all government discrimination against movements of goods or factors. This evidently includes harmonization of excise taxes and freedom for migration and may involve, for the movement of capital, parallel or identical policies in the regulation of capital markets, interest rates, foreign exchange, and the like. It may require comparable programs in such things as agriculture and wages. Is even this enough?

The absence of government discrimination is perhaps not the ultimate definition of economic integration. Suppose that Iceland and New Zealand were to adopt regulations granting each other's nationals not most-favored-nation treatment, but **national treatment,** that is, treatment identical with each country's own nationals over a wide area. There might be customs union, harmonization of tax policy, and even parallel policies in other fields. Would this result in economic integration? Evidently not.

The reason an Iceland–New Zealand customs union of this sort would not result in economic integration is that whether or not governments discriminate between the two countries, Nature does. By putting them in separate hemispheres, both East-West and North-South, Nature has reduced the economic contacts between Iceland and New Zealand to what one may presume, without being burdened by the facts, is virtually zero. So it is not government discrimination alone that counts.

This brings us to a definition of economic integration which makes it a standard of measurement, but one which, like absolute zero in low-temperature physics, is never reached. Economic integration is factor-price equalization. This can be produced by trade, without factor movements, by factor movement without trade, or by some combination of the two. But any interference with trade, whether by tariffs or transport costs, prevents goods prices, and therefore factor prices, from being equalized. And discrimination can be carried on by governments or by the public.

Take first transport costs. The reason that an Iceland–New Zealand customs union would fail to produce economic integration is that distance would prevent an equalization of goods prices. In addition to distance, moreover, two such widely different countries are almost certain to be completely specialized, thus eliminating another of the significant assumptions of the factor-price equalization theorem. Both points make clear why the EEC was a much more serious step in the direction of integration than was the European Free Trade Association (EFTA) among Britain, the three Scandinavian countries, Austria, Switzerland, and Portugal. The Six—France, Belgium, the Netherlands, West Germany, and Italy—share common frontiers, across which transfer costs, after the removal of tariffs, are zero. The countries of the EFTA are spread out in an enormous circle around the EEC, with long distances between many of them, whether physical, as between Portugal and Sweden, or economic, as between Austria and Switzerland, where the economically important areas are divided by mile after mile of Alps. The issue is of prime importance also in the Latin-American Free Trade Area (LAFTA), where countries which are contiguous are not necessarily close economically. Argentina and

Chile, with a long common border, find it cheaper to ship steel around the south coast of South America by sea than to lug it up over the passes of the Andes. In economic terms, therefore, Buenos Aires is not much nearer Valparaiso than is the Sparrows Point plant of the Bethlehem Steel Company in Baltimore.

Next is the possibility of private discrimination, even when governmental discrimination has been eliminated. When Benelux (the economic union among Belgium, the Netherlands, and Luxembourg which preceded the EEC and was absorbed into it) finally lifted the barriers to the movement of capital and labor between its member countries, nothing happened. The Dutch preferred to keep their capital in Holland, and the Belgian workers preferred to live and work in Belgium, both despite the possibility of higher monetary rewards from the newly permitted migration. Thus private discrimination prevents economic integration.

Under the factor-price equalization definition, economic integration is likely never to be fully achieved. The definition is useful, however, as a standard. The content of integration then becomes one price, as in the law of one price. In one market there is one price, and if there are transactions and one price, there is, in effect, one market. By this definition the labor market in the United States is not integrated, since wages are not the same everywhere, and the market for blacks and whites is still not integrated, despite governmental prohibition of discrimination, because blacks earn less than whites even when they have entry to the same jobs. The test of whether customs union works toward integration is whether it narrows factor-price differences.

One quibble with this definition of economic integration may be worth raising: Suppose that factor-price equalization is achieved not through direct dealings in goods, factors, and policies between two countries, but through third markets and factors in third countries. If these third-party dealings produce factor-price equalization, have they produced integration? Goods prices in countries A and B can be equalized through their separate trade with C, without any trade between A and B. This is hardly integration between A and B in the ordinary sense of the word. It happens that wages within the Common Market have been narrowed by the readiness of outside labor—from Portugal, Spain, southern Italy (inside the market to be sure), Greece, and Turkey—to move from one country to another among the Six in search of higher pay. Interest rates can be brought into line by lending to and borrowing from the external Euro-currency market (about which more below) without direct capital movements among the participating countries. American international corporations (again, more later) act to foster factor-price equalization by moving from high- to low-cost locations, or by contracting in the former and expanding in the latter.

The outside factors may be less rooted in any one country of the Six and hence more ready to move. Local forces do nothing, outside forces do it all. Is this economic integration?

SOME LESSER PROBLEMS OF CUSTOMS UNIONS AND FREE-TRADE AREAS

The development of a single tariff schedule in a customs union is a difficult task. First, there is the problem of arriving at a common tariff nomenclature. There is no unique way to classify goods. Most countries have their own systems, and when two or more systems are joined, the task is to develop a new one which is agreeable to all. Like all classification systems in a world of change, moreover, there are different rewards and penalties for retaining an old system and for altering it frequently in light of new conditions. The one gives comparability in time; the other best suits current problems. The experts of the EEC spent several years working out a common tariff nomenclature even before it was time to set the rates.

Rates come next. GATT (General Agreement on Tariffs and Trade) rules, which authorize customs unions, state that the common tariff must be no higher than the average tariffs of the countries which go to make it up. There are problems both in measuring the height of a tariff and in choosing a suitable average of more than one. The simplest system of measuring the height of a tariff is to average separate ad valorem tariff rates. This is misleading, as there should be a weighted average. What weights? To weigh by actual trade is likely to give a biased result, since the higher the tariff, the more it keeps out trade and the lower its impact. A prohibitive tariff would get no weight, which is absurd. The correct system of weighting is no way of knowing these without an enormous amount of information on elasticities. A proxy for free-trade weights is domestic consumption; here goods which enjoy a prohibitive tariff (a strong protective effect) enter the index.

The Belgian, French, and Italian tariffs were reduced in the EEC averaging, and the Dutch and West German tariffs were raised. Observe that this means more trade creation for the first group and more trade diversion for the second. The discussion of trade creation and trade diversion earlier in this chapter assumed a constant and uniform rate of tariff. But if any country raises its tariff, trade diversion is evidently accentuated, and for those that lower theirs, the reverse occurs.

Once given the common tariff, what happens to the financial proceeds? They evidently must be divided among the members. How? A simple system is to have each country keep the proceeds it collects, but this is more practical than equitable. Should the Netherlands keep the duties on goods for West Germany which enter at Rotterdam on their way up the Rhine, or should Italy keep the duties for goods transshipped across the Alps from the Mediterranean? But to trace goods to the country of consumption and assign it the duties requires more organization than is desirable. In the Zollverein, Prussia bought the adherence of a large number of the smaller, poorer German states by offering to share customs proceeds on a per capita basis. This was expensive for Prussia, with more trade per capita, but it accomplished the political objective of winning adherence. The Rome Treaty of 1957 turned the question over to be resolved by a commission.

In a free-trade area, there is no problem about dividing customs receipts: to each his own. But differences among tariff schedules give rise to a problem because of the possibility of arbitrage, that is, entering the goods into the free-trade area in the country with the lowest duty and then reshipping them to another country with a higher duty. This problem may not be serious when the countries are far apart, as are Portugal and Norway, or Switzerland and the United Kingdom, in EFTA: the saving in tariffs is likely to be less than the added transport costs. But the problem is sufficiently significant to require control. This is provided by certificates of origin. Goods going from one member of a free-trade area to another are accompanied by a certificate of origin, issued to attest that the goods originated in the member country and not in a third country. The process of issuing such certificates and verifying the facts is tiresome, but inescapable.

EEC'S SPECIAL REGIME FOR AGRICULTURE

The Rome Treaty of 1957, which created the EEC after the partial "functional integration" in iron and steel and coal of the European Coal and Steel Community, proposed a special regime for agriculture. This sector is a problem in virtually every country and was supported by subsidies and restrictions on trade in particular ways in each member country. No country except the Netherlands was willing to let its farmers compete in world markets. But most countries were unwilling to apply simple tariffs because of uncertainty as to the shape of the foreign excess supply curves and, therefore, as to what the protective and redistribution effects of the tariff might be.

The negotiations on agriculture proved to be difficult politically. There was initially the question of the system and then that of details under the system. The system adopted was one of a sliding tariff of the sort that Britain used at one time under the Corn Laws. First a domestic support price for separate commodities in the Common Market is determined. The sliding tariff is the difference between this support price and the world price. If domestic supplies are short and the price tends to rise above the support price, the world price plus tariff (equal to the support price) will bring it down. If, on the other hand, the crop is heavy, the domestic price will sag and the tariff will become prohibitive. The student should have no trouble figuring out the partial-equilibrium diagrams. The tariffs on agriculture, incidentally, are paid into a special fund designed to modernize EEC agriculture.

The system was one thing. Agreement on support prices proved much more difficult. West Germany, where the Christian Democratic party depended on farmer support, wanted a high price for wheat. France, where agricultural efficiency was rising rapidly, was afraid that a high price would keep too many people on the land and produce a larger surplus than West Germany could absorb. These negotiations were complicated by U.S. insistence in the Kennedy Round negotiations that provision be made for quota minimums representing amounts of wheat, cotton, soybeans, and so on, that the Common Market would continue to import despite the sliding tariff.

The British application to join the Common Market was made the first time, and subsequently, on political grounds, but Britain's very different agricultural system posed serious problems. The British started with world prices of foodstuffs and added subsidies for farmers. To move to the EEC system required a large increase in the price of foodstuffs, and the difference between the world price and the new high prices would in effect be paid to modernize French, West German, and Italian farms, since the British were already efficient.

The British swallowed their irritation at moving from a good to a poor system of agricultural subsidy and entered the Common Market despite limited success in modifying the terms of the agricultural agreement. Perhaps they hoped to modify them when they became a full member. Membership, however, did imply, along with trade diversion for the Commonwealth (the most importantly affected country being New Zealand), a sharp rise in the cost of living in Britain, which might create new problems.

REGIONAL INTEGRATION AMONG DEVELOPING COUNTRIES

The most successful case of economic integration thus far is the European Economic Community. Regional integration is a device often recommended for the less developed countries, however. Some have come to fruition, such as the Central American Common Market (CACM), or are struggling to make the grade, such as LAFTA. Others have broken up already, such as the West Indian Federation or the arrangements on the East Coast of Africa among Kenya, Uganda, and Tanganyika. Some have been in the talking stage for years—the Arab League. Others are now being talked about for the first time, among the Maghreb countries of Tunisia, Algeria, and Morocco, and the Asian countries of the Philippines, Malaya, and Thailand. That with the most current momentum is the Andes pact formed as a subgroup of LAFTA in August 1966 among Chile, Colombia, Ecuador, Peru, and Venezuela. Bolivia joined later, and Venezuela refused to accept the final treaty.

The purpose of regional integration in all cases is to industrialize. National markets are thought to be too narrow; a regional market may be able to support modern industry. There is much less interest in trade creation through destroying inefficient producing units existing in the member countries than in trade diversion—shifting purchases from the rest of the world to member countries, and more constructively, the achievement of economies of scale. If the countries are going to industrialize anyway, it is best to do so with minimum inefficiency.

But the difficulties are great. On the economic side, the lagging country becomes frightened that by giving its partners free access to its market, it will never be able to start any industry. Thus Bolivia refuses to join LAFTA on the ground that this would impede its development rather than assist it. It regards LAFTA as a device to speed up the development of Mexico, Argentina, and Brazil—now leading in industry in the area—at the expense of the slower countries. In the Andes pact it is recognized that unless Bolivia and Ecuador gain in the sense of catching up to some degree with Chile, Colombia, and Peru, the arrangement will not have succeeded.

Various devices are being developed to meet this objection. The lagging country may be given special treatment. This may consist of investment assistance, as in Europe, or in reducing the obligations of the less developed countries to the others. In the EEC, the association agreement covering Greece and Turkey provided for access to the markets of the Six, but the reciprocal reduction of their duties was delayed for five years. Similar asymmetric treatment of the laggards is promised in LAFTA.

One device for which support is still strong is industrial planning. This would assign certain industries to certain countries in the union and would forbid them to others. The Central American Common Market tried this with little success: inevitably each country was pleased with the monopoly it was granted but sought to chisel on those granted the other countries. Industrial planning with assigned industries broke down even before the collapse of the CACM over the "soccer war" between Honduras and El Salvador.

The fact is that despite their geographic proximity, the less developed countries are not economically unified. They are typically more competitive than complementary, and their competitive interests make it hard for them to form a community. Forming a single area with good communication, as they do, the EEC members for the most part have an economic advantage over the outside world in the markets of the community. In the developing countries, many of them with only exterior lines of communication (as noted for Argentina and Chile), there is no natural unity, and the artificial unity of political resolve is difficult to sustain. The fact that benefits for one member are costs for the others is divisive.

If the political difficulties can be overcome, however, there can be little doubt that industrialization in a few large units is better than industrialization at the same levels of protection in five times that number of small units. The question may be raised, however, whether economic integration into the world market may not be more efficient, because it is trade-creating, than regional integration of a trade-diverting sort would be.

SUMMARY

The welfare effects of discrimination are shown by analysis of customs union. As an example of the theory of the second best, not every step toward freer trade increases welfare. In addition to trade creation, there is trade diversion, the expansion of high-cost production at the expense of low-cost production. The analysis is presented in partial and general equilibrium.

Beyond customs union (and free-trade areas), there are common markets, economic union, and economic integration. Economic integration is defined as factor-price equalization, achieved through joined goods markets, joined factor markets, or a combination of the two. It is noted that third-country markets and factors can serve to equalize factor prices between two countries that are not in a strict sense integrated.

Attention is called to problems of the height of tariffs, to the division of the proceeds of customs unions, to special regimes for agriculture, and to the difficulties faced by regional integration of developing countries, including their attempts to solve them by industrial planning.

SUGGESTED READING

Texts

See Bela Balassa (ed.), *Changing Patterns of Foreign Trade and Payments* (New York: Norton, 1964) (paperback), part 2.

Treatises

On a theoretical level, see Bela Balassa, *The Theory of Economic Integration* (Homewood, Ill.: Richard D. Irwin, 1961); Richard G. Lipsey, *The Theory of Customs Union: A General Equilibrium Analysis* (London: Weidenfeld & Nicholson, 1970). See also Lipsey's survey article in American Economic Association, *Readings in International Economics*, with its citations of the vast literature.

The student is left to find his way around in the rest of the abundant literature. He might start, however, with Lawrence B. Krause's *European Economic Integration and the United States* (Washington, D.C.: Brookings Institution, 1968); and J. Gruenwald, M. S. Wionczek, and Martin Carnoy, *Latin American Economic Integration and U.S. Policy* (Washington, D.C.: Brookings Institution, 1972).

Points

The works of Viner, Scitovsky, and Tinbergen cited in the text are:

Jacob Viner, *The Customs Union Issue* (New York: Carnegie Endowment for International Peace, 1953).

Tibor Scitovsky, *Economic Theory and Western European Integration* (London: Unwin University Books; reprinted with a new introduction, 1962) (paperback).

Jan Tinbergen, *International Economic Integration* (Amsterdam: Elsevier, 1965).

Useful material on the integration of Europe and of the developing countries can be found in the Williams Commission, *Papers Submitted to the Commission on International Trade and Investment Policy*, vol. 2.

10

International cartels

Trade can be restricted multilaterally, by governments and companies from different countries acting in concert. History records many attempts at international **cartels,** or agreements to restrict selling competition. Major international companies cartelized trade in tobacco and railway services in the 1880s. The 1920s and 1930s saw repeated unsuccessful attempts at primary-product cartels. A predecessor of the Organization of Petroleum Exporting Countries (OPEC) was the short-lived Achnacarry Agreement of 1928, in which three top international oil firms, plus the otherwise anticartel government of the Soviet Union, agreed to avoid profit-shaving competition in export markets. The postwar period has seen cartellike international agreements not only in oil but in such primary products as sugar, coffee, and European farm products. Western European countries have also organized steel cartels, both in the period between World Wars I and II and in the 1970s.

No other cartel has yet approached the resounding success of OPEC. Before OPEC, the average life expectancy of cartels had been so short that the economic analysis of cartels tended to stress the inevitability of their collapse. The usual analysis has correctly pointed to pressures that tend to make cartel power erode, as some cartel members defect and turn competitive and as some buyers find ways of avoiding purchases from the cartel. One of the central tasks of international economics is to reconcile this presumption that cartels inevitably fail with OPEC's continuing success.

THE RISE OF OPEC

The victory of OPEC in 1973 climaxed a more gradual convergence of forces that tipped the balance of power in favor of oil-exporting countries. The most important forces were: the changing world demand-supply situation for oil, the rising determination of oil-rich Arab nations to use oil as a weapon against Israel, and a set of changes in the oil position of the United States.

World demand for crude oil had grown rapidly by 1973. World energy consumption had been growing a bit faster than 5 percent a year between 1950 and 1972. Oil's share of world energy consumption rose from 29 percent to 46 percent over the same period, so that oil use itself grew at about 7.5 percent a year, a rate well above the growth rate of world output of all products.

FIGURE 10.1
Selected price series for light Arabian crude oil, compared with U.S. export prices for goods and services, 1950–1976

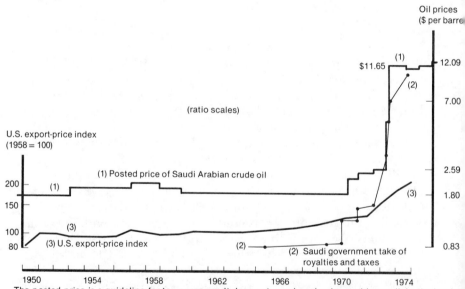

The posted price is a guideline for tax purposes. It does not equal, and only roughly parallels, the harder-to-document true prices being received by OPEC governments or paid by oil importers.

It has been estimated that as of January 1974 the true prices were related as follows: the Saudi government took $7.01 a barrel, this take being calculated by applying tax and royalty percentages to the posted price; production costs were 10 cents a barrel at the Saudi oil fields; oil company profits before U.S. taxes were 50 cents a barrel; transportation markups between the Persian Gulf and the U.S. Gulf Coast were $1.48, and the sum of these costs was the U.S. Gulf Coast delivered price of $9.09 (Raymond Vernon [ed.], *The Oil Crisis* [New York: Norton, 1976], p. 290).

Sources: Series (1)—Morris Adelman, *The World Petroleum Market* (Baltimore: Johns Hopkins Press 1972), table V–A–1; Vernon, *Oil Crisis*, p. 26; and recent press releases. Series (2)—Vernon, *Oil Crisis*, p. 26; and recent press releases. Series (3)—*Economic Report of the President*, recent years, appendixes.

The *world* supply of crude oil grew at least as fast as world demand. World "proved" reserves represented about 34 years' oil consumption as of the end of 1972. This ratio of reserves to annual consumption had been maintained, with some fluctuations, ever since the mid-1950s despite the rapid growth of oil consumption. Postwar oil price trends also failed to show any tendency for world oil supply to lag behind demand. Between 1950 and 1970, the ratio of the price of crude oil to U.S. export or wholesale prices either remained steady or dropped slightly, depending on the specific price series one chooses. And one certainly cannot explain the OPEC price jumps of the 1970s in terms of shifts in competitive world supply and demand. Throughout the early 1970s the production cost of a barrel of Persian Gulf crude was still only about 10 cents (plus that part of the oil companies' 50-cent profit representing average fixed costs), while the Persian Gulf nations raised their take from $1.62 to $7.01 a barrel (Figure 10.1). The 1973–74 oil price jumps were man-made, and not the result of exhaustion of the earth's available oil reserves.

Yet world demand was growing far faster than *non-OPEC* supplies. Postwar oil discoveries have been very unevenly distributed among countries. The invisible hand of Allah has given OPEC most of the world's oil. The share of OPEC countries in world crude oil production rose from about 20 percent in 1938 to over 40 percent when OPEC was founded in 1960, and to over 50 percent by 1972. Furthermore, OPEC's share of proved reserves—roughly, its share of future production—is over two thirds. Ample oil reserves are still being discovered the world over, but they happen to be concentrated increasingly in the Middle East, forcing importing nations into greater dependence on OPEC nations.

Meanwhile, the steady deepening of Arab-Israeli hostilities began to affect the oil-rich Arab countries. In the early 1970s, Saudi Arabia informed the United States that the spread of Arab radicalism would pose an increasing threat to both governments if the United States did not pressure Israel to withdraw from the territories "occupied" by Israel after the Six-Day War, in 1967. The defection of Saudi Arabia from traditional ties to the United States was a crucial step toward the oil price showdown.

And by the early 1970s, the United States was for the first time becoming vulnerable to pressure from oil-exporting countries. In the United States, as elsewhere, the demand for oil had consistently grown faster than either total energy consumption or gross national product. This rapid growth pushed a new generation of "independent" U.S. oil companies to seek new foreign sources of crude oil. Oil-exporting countries found that they could now circumvent the eight international "majors"[1] which had held sway over oil production, prices, and exploration in the OPEC countries.

The rising U.S. oil demand increasingly spilled over into imports, aided by several developments in the late 1960s and 1970s. The rise of U.S. concern over environmental quality not only accelerated the demand for oil, which polluted less than coal, but also held back the expansion of domestic energy supply. Nuclear power plants, oil and gas leasing, oil pumping in the Santa Barbara Channel, and the Alaska pipeline were all held up by (reasonable) objections that they would cause environmental damage. U.S. discoveries of oil and gas reserves were tapering off. Thus the United States, which had been largely immune to oil threats in earlier Middle East crises, found itself importing a third of its oil consumption, part of it from Arab countries, by 1973.

These were the main reasons why the OPEC countries were able to observe a scramble among buyers to pay higher prices for oil in 1973. The stage was set for their victory, described briefly in Chapter 1.

MONOPOLY AS A MODEL FOR CARTELS

If a group of nations or firms were to form a cartel, as OPEC did, what is the greatest amount of gain they could reap at the expense of their buyers and world efficiency? Clearly, if all of the cartel members could agree on just maximizing their collective gain, they would behave as though they were a perfectly unified profit-maximizing monopolist. They would find the price level which would maximize the gap between their total export sales revenues and their total costs of producing exports. When cutting output back to the level of demand yielded by their optimal price, they would take care to shut down the most costly production units (for example, oil wells) and keep in operation only those with the lowest operating costs.

Figure 10.2 portrays a monopoly or cartel that has managed to extract maximum profits from its buyers. To understand what price and output yields that highest level of profits, and what limits those profits, one must first understand that the optimal price lies above the price that perfect competition would yield, yet below the price that would discourage all sales.

If perfect competition reigned in the world oil market, the marginal cost curve in Figure 10.2 would also be the supply curve for oil exports. Competitive equilibrium would be at Point C, where the margi-

---

[1] Exxon, Mobil, Gulf, Texaco, Standard of California, all U.S.-based; British Petroleum, based in the United Kingdom before British Petroleum's merger with Standard of Ohio in the early 1970s; Royal Dutch/Shell, based in the United Kingdom and the Netherlands; and Compagnie Française des Petroles, based in France.

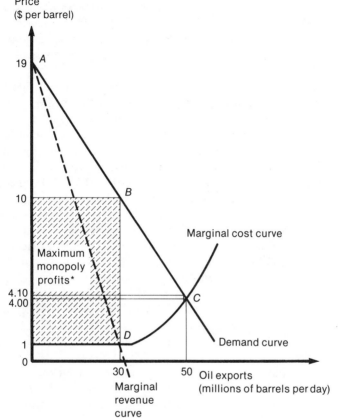

FIGURE 10.2
A cartel as a profit-maximizing monopoly

*Including some fixed costs.

nal cost of raising oil exports has risen to meet $4, the amount that extra oil is worth to buyers (as shown by the demand curve). Point C is not the optimal point for the set of producers. If they were to agree to raise prices a tiny bit, say to $4.10 a barrel, they would surely gain. Demand would be cut only very slightly, costing sellers little business. At the same time, they would get a costless ten-cent markup on all of the nearly 50 million barrels that they would continue to sell. The markup on the 50 million barrels would easily outweigh the profits lost on the small amount of lost sales, making a slight positive price increase and export reduction better than competitive pricing.

Yet the negative slope of the demand curve for the cartel's product limits how high its members could push their common price. This point is clear enough if we just consider the extreme case of a prohibitive price markup. If the cartel were foolish enough to push the price to $19 a barrel in Figure 10.2, it would lose all of its export business, as shown at Point A. The handsome markup to $19 could be worthless, since nobody would be paying it to the cartel. Thus the cartel's best price must be well below the prohibitive price, and the more elastic the demand curve for the cartel's product, the lower the best price for the cartel must be.

The cartel members could find their most profitable price through trial and error, trying out several prices in between the competitive and prohibitive limits to see what price seemed to maximize profits. The basic model of monopoly shows that the highest possible profits are those corresponding to the level of sales at which the marginal revenue curve intersects the marginal cost curve. These maximum profits would be reaped at Point B in Figure 10.2, with a price set at $10 a barrel, yielding 30 million barrels of export sales a day and monopoly profits of ($10 − $1) × 30 million barrels = $270 million a day. If the cartel had not been formed, competition would have limited the profits of its members to the area below the $4 price line and above the marginal cost curve (minus some fixed costs not shown in the diagram). (If an exact number were put on this competitive-profit area as drawn in Figure 10.1, it would come to a little over $120 million a day, well below the cartel's maximum of $270 million a day.) Given the demand curve and the marginal cost curve, the profits reshaped by pushing price and quantity to Point B is the best the cartel can do.

The cartel that is optimal for its members is not optimal for the world, of course. The extra profits for the cartel above the $4 price line are just a redistribution of income from buying countries to the cartel, with no net gain for the world. Furthermore, the cartel causes net world losses by curtailing oil exports that would have been worth more to buyers around the world than those exports would have cost the cartel members themselves. The world net loss from the cartel is represented in Figure 10.1 by the area BCD (which would equal a little over $90 million a day as drawn in Figure 10.1). This area shows that what the cartel is costing the world as a whole is the gaps between what buyers would have willingly paid for the extra 20 million barrels a day, as shown by the height of the demand curve, and the height of the marginal cost curve between 30 million barrels and 50 million barrels.

THE THEORETICAL LIMITS TO CARTEL POWER

The theory of cartel policy can identify several constraints on cartel success, and by international politics pose some additional practical constraints. Let us look first at the limits to cartel market power in the extreme case in which the cartel members succeed in behaving just like the unified monopoly in Figure 10.2. We then note some additional theoretical reasons for expecting cartel success to fade away with time. In the following section we deal with some practical complications arising in the case of OPEC.

The basic theory of monopoly stresses that the elasticity of demand limits the power of any monopoly. More specifically, the formula for the optimal monopoly markup is

$$t^* = \frac{\text{Optimal price minus marginal cost}}{\text{Price}} = \frac{1}{|d_c|} ,$$

where d_c is the elasticity of demand for the cartel's sales (here, the elasticity of export demand, if the cartel members do not charge the same high price within their own countries). This formula applies equally to pure private domestic monopolies and to international cartels behaving like monopolies. It shows that the more (less) elastic the demand for the cartel's sales over the relevant range of prices, the lower (higher) is the optimal monopoly markup. In the extreme case in which the cartel faces an infinite elasticity of demand at a given world price, the optimal markup is zero, and the cartel might as well be dissolved.

The elasticity of demand facing the cartel (d_c) depends on three other parameters: the elasticity of world demand for the product (d), the elasticity of competing noncartel supply of the product (s_0), and the cartel's share of the world market (c). The importance of each factor is easy to see. A highly elastic world demand for the product (a highly negative d) means that buyers find it easy to find other ways of spending their money if the price of the product rises much, so that the cartel has very limited power to raise profits by raising prices. A cartel's chances for continued high profits also depend on the elasticity of supply from other countries (s_0) in the obvious direction: the harder it is for other countries to step up their competing output and sales when the cartel posts its high prices, the better are cartel's chances of success. That is, a low s_0 enhances cartel power in the world market. Finally, the higher the cartel's current share of world sales (c), the better the cartel's prospects.

The dependence of the cartel's success on these three factors can be summarized in a single convenient formula. As shown in the middle of Appendix D, the demand elasticity facing the cartel is related by definition to the other three parameters:

$$d_c = \frac{d - s_0(1 - c)}{c} ,$$

and the optimal cartel markup rate, as a fraction of price, is:

$$t^* = \frac{c}{\left| d - s_0(1 - c) \right|} \cdot$$

To see how the formula works, consider two examples. The first is a case in which cartel members control half of world exports when their cartel is set up ($c = \frac{1}{2}$), and face a world elasticity of export demand of only minus two ($d = -2$) and an equal positive elasticity of competing supply ($s_0 = 2$). In this case, the formula implies that the optimal cartel markup can be as high as one sixth of price, so that marginal costs are only five sixths of price. Alternatively, consider a cartel that commands only a quarter of world export sales ($c = \frac{1}{4}$), and faces a world demand for exports of the product of minus six and a supply elasticity from other countries of eight ($d = -6, s_0 = 8$). Then the formula implies that the optimal markup is only $\frac{1}{48}$, or just above 2 percent of price. Even this small markup could bring handsome gains to selling countries if costs were already a high share of revenue without the cartel, but buying countries would not experience a large percentage price increase.

Yet even when perfect solidarity makes a cartel able to act like the maximal monopoly, theory points out that the forces summarized in the formula above work increasingly against the cartel over time. When the cartel is first set up, it may well enjoy low elasticities and a high market share. Yet its very success in raising price is likely to set three countervailing trends in motion. First, the higher price will make buying countries look for new ways to avoid importing the cartel's product. They search for new domestic supplies of the product and will seek substitutes for it. The price would make private parties search for new supplies even if there were no government policy of fostering reductions in imports of the newly cartelized product. If the search has any success at all, the imports of the buying countries will drop increasingly for any given cartel price, making these countries' long-run demand curve for imports of the product more elastic than their short-run demand curve. The elasticity d will become more negative with time.

Second, the initial cartel success will accelerate the search for exportable supplies in noncartel countries. If the cartel product is an agricultural crop, such as sugar or coffee, the cartel's price hike will cause farmers in other countries to shift increasing amounts of land, labor, and funds from other crops into sugar or coffee. If the cartel product is a depletable mineral resource, such as oil or copper, noncartel countries will respond to the higher price by redoubling their explorations in search of new reserves, as countries the world over have done in the wake of OPEC's victory. Again, if the noncartel countries have any luck at all, their competing supply will become increasingly elastic with time, and s_0 will rise.

Finally, the cartel's world market share (c) will almost surely fall after the cartel's initial price hike. To raise its price without piling up ever-rising unsold inventories, the cartel must cut its output and sales. Since nonmembers will be straining to raise their output and sales, the cartel's share of the market must drop even if all of its members cooperate solidly. Thus c will fall while the absolute values of the key elasticities d and s_0 rise, undercutting the cartel's optimal markup and its profits on three fronts at once.

Theory and experience add another reason for gradual cartel erosion: cartel members may defect by behaving competitively. The cartel will, if it can, prevent this by having some overseeing government pass laws forbidding competition. Yet defection cannot be thus prevented when there is no overseeing government, as with cartels among sovereign nations, or when the government will not condone cartel-enforcing laws on behalf of the private firms in the cartel. Without government checks on competition, cartel members with small individual market shares will indeed feel strong incentive to behave competitively. To see why, suppose that you were a small member of the successful oil export cartel shown back in Figure 10.1 and that when the cartel was set up, your exports were only 1 percent of the cartel total. Yet, let us say, you have enough oil reserves to go on pumping and selling 3 percent of the total cartel exports for as long in the future as you need to plan. Raising your output above the 1 percent share might cost you only, say, a dollar a barrel at the margin. Yet buyers are willing to pay ten dollars for each barrel you sell, since the larger cartel members are faithfully holding down their output. Why not attract the extra buyers to you by shaving your price just a little bit below $10, say to $9.70? Why not do so in grand style, until you are competitively selling the 3 percent of the cartel's market that you can afford to sell without depleting your reserves too fast? If the other cartel members have any economic or military clubs over you or could finance the overthrow of your government, you should do your competing clandestinely, by disguising your export volumes and prices somehow. But if they wield no such clubs, you can compete openly, while justifying your behavior as necessary to develop your nation's economy. You can do so in the knowledge that you are still so small a share of the cartel that your individual actions will not cause the cartel price to drop much, if at all. Theory says that if a large share of cartel output consists of the outputs of individually small members, their incentive to act competitively undermines the whole cartel. The individually large members can keep the cartel effective to some extent by drastically cutting their own outputs to offset the extra sales from competitors. Their aggregate size determines how long they can hold out.

The usual theory of cartels thus points to several reasons for believing that cartel profit margins and profits will erode with time, if no new members with large individual shares of the world market join the existing cartel. Yet the theory does *not* say that cartels are unprofitable or harmless. On the contrary, it underscores the profitability of cartel formation to cartel members. Even a cartel that eventually erodes can bring vast fortunes to its members. What the theory does do is offer a listing of four key indicators to watch when judging the prospects for an existing or potential cartel: the demand elasticity for the product, the competing-supply elasticity, the members' initial market share, and the share of the cartel held by defection-prone small members.

PROSPECTS FOR OPEC

A careful interpretation of theory can be combined with a careful reading of recent experience to form a rough judgment of the prospects for continued OPEC success at the expense of oil-importing countries. This judgment rests on a rough reading of the four key indicators of cartel longevity just mentioned, and must of course be qualified by noting that the actual outcome will depend heavily on wars in the Middle East and other events that are difficult to predict.

The elasticity of import demand on the part of oil-importing countries has thus far been quite low. The first couple of years after the OPEC victory of 1973–74 showed only limited success for importing countries' attempts to cut their dependence on oil and on energy use in general. They have managed, with the help of the 1974–75 recession, to hold their oil and energy use to very small increases, but have not actually reduced their consumption overall. This, of course, meant a considerable reduction in the rate of growth in oil use below its previous postwar average of 7.5 percent per year, but that is not a very dramatic drop in total demand in response to a quadrupling of the relative price of oil.

The elasticity of competing supplies of oil has also been limited thus far, despite an acceleration of expenditures on exploration. This low short-run elasticity of supply, plus the limits on the demand reduction achieved by importing countries, has meant that OPEC has not had to cut its exports drastically to make its historic price jump stick. OPEC production and exports only dropped by something like 9 percent from early 1973 to 1974–75. They would have grown by about 8 percent if the 1970–73 rate of increase had been maintained, suggesting that something like a 17 percent decrease in purchases was achieved by the importing countries in response to the much larger percentage price increase. Accordingly, OPEC's share of the world market dropped little. What we have seen about elasticities and market shares in the short run suggests the pessimistic prospect that even large discoveries of non-OPEC oil would not free oil-importing countries from large OPEC price markups for a long time to come.

One of the main hopes held out by observers in importing countries was that some OPEC members would defect and behave competitively, forcing the others to lower their prices as well. There has indeed been evidence of such competitive behavior by OPEC countries. Iraq, Indonesia, and Nigeria have all raised their oil output since the showdown in late 1973. This in itself is not concrete evidence of price-cutting, but rumors about such cuts on the part of these three countries and Algeria have persisted (perhaps fanned eagerly by the governments of importing countries).

It is hard to predict just which OPEC countries will behave competitively in the future. One would presume that the incentive to cut prices a bit to achieve large increases in export volume would be higher in countries that are populous and poor, thereby needing large development investments in the near future; in countries that are small oil exporters, as predicted in the theory summarized above; and in non-Arab countries, which would not feel the desire to use export cuts as a weapon in the struggle against Israel. The pattern of OPEC members' behavior only roughly fits these presumptions so far.

Yet even if all OPEC members that fit *any* of these descriptions— poor, populous, having a small share of OPEC exports, or non-Arab—were to defect and cut prices competitively to just below the OPEC level, the countries still adhering faithfully to the cartel could by themselves keep world prices well above their own marginal costs. Even if Venezuela and Iran joined the defectors in pursuit of short-run revenues for national development, that would still leave the non-populous rich Arab major exporters, Libya and the Arabian peninsula from Kuwait south. These countries alone controlled 67 percent of OPEC's total "proved" oil reserves, or 46 percent of the world's proved reserves, as of 1972. Thus what we know of world oil, combined with the theory of cartels, suggests that even the thus shrunken version of OPEC would be sufficient to maintain high profit margins for its members at the expense of importing countries for a long time to come, barring unforeseeable increases in world elasticities of demand or competing supply.

CARTELS FOR OTHER PRIMARY PRODUCTS

The success of OPEC has inspired countries exporting primary products other than oil to rejuvenate the previously unsuccessful idea of forming international cartels for their primary-product export staples. In the wake of the OPEC victory even speculators in buying countries seemed to expect new cartels for primaries. Between late 1973 and the spring of 1974 the world prices on all sorts of primary products jumped faster than did the worldwide inflation of industrial product prices. For most of these primary products the bubble burst within months, and prices were soon as low as before 1973 despite general inflation. Yet in the meantime hard talks about forming cartels went on around the world, with some results.

Cartel gains have been posted in two other minerals besides oil. One is phosphate rock, in rapidly growing demand for use in fertilizers and detergents; the other is bauxite. Led by Morocco (which controls one third of world exports) and Tunisia, the main phosphate exporters converted a low price elasticity of demand into a 400 percent price rise between mid-1972 and the end of 1974. In March 1974 the International Bauxite Association (IBA) was formed (Australia, Guinea, Guyana, Jamaica, Sierra Leone, Surinam, and Yugoslavia). Although some defections are to be expected, IBA, led by Jamaica, has managed to raise its tax and royalty rates on bauxite almost fivefold.

It appears unlikely that other minerals will repeat the success of OPEC, IBA, and the phosphate group though a uranium cartel has also enjoyed temporary success. The closest candidate would be nickel, of which Canada alone controls almost half of the world's exports. Deposits of most other metals tend to be more evenly spread around the globe. And in two other cases of relatively concentrated deposits—gold (South Africa, the Soviet Union) and copper (Chile, Peru, Zambia, Zaire)—political differences and the availability of substitutes stand in the way of effective cartel power. The cartelization of metals is further undermined by the ease of turning to more intensive recycling of scrap in the importing countries in response to any cartel price rise.

Among crops, the food grains sector has the best economic basis for international cartelization. Canada, the United States, and Australia together account for a large share of world food grains exports, and world demand is notoriously inelastic. Such a three-country grain cartel could be effective despite the elasticity with which some other countries could become competing suppliers. The main constraint on grain cartelization, however, is political: extracting monopoly rents on food grains in a partially starving world wins few friends.

Cartelization would seem to provide poor prospects for other agricultural crops. Some crops have the advantage of being concentrated into a small number of countries that already have regional ties: natural rubber, dominated by Malaysia, Indonesia, Thailand, and Sri Lanka; tea, by India and Sri Lanka; coffee, by Brazil and Colombia; and bananas, by Central American countries and Ecuador. Yet some of these crops, especially bananas, face a highly elastic world demand, and all of them face a very high elasticity of competing supply, since land in many countries can be shifted from other crops into newly cartelized crops. Agricultural crops are not very likely candidates for long-lived international cartels.

SUMMARY

The most successful exercise of cartel power in history, the victory of OPEC in late 1973, resulted from several simultaneous developments. World demand for oil had grown rapidly; world supply growth was concentrated in OPEC countries; and the Arab-Israeli conflict broke out anew in a context of new U.S. dependence on oil imports.

If international cartels are able to act like unified monopolists, they can reap large gains at the expense of buying countries and world efficiency. Their ability to do so is proportional to the inelasticity of world demand for their exports. This dependence of buying countries on a cartel's exports can in turn be linked to four factors: the elasticity of world demand for the cartel's product, the elasticity of competing supply, the cartel's share of the world market, and the share of cartel sales consisting of sales by small cartel members, who are likely to feel a strong incentive to behave competitively despite their cartel membership. A formula given above links the optimal cartel price markup over marginal cost to the first three of these four factors.

The experience of OPEC and other attempts at primary-product cartels can be interpreted with the help of the monopoly model of cartel success and failure. Oil clearly faces lower elasticities of demand and competing supply than do most other exported primary products. Even if many members of OPEC were to defect and behave as open competitors in world oil markets, the cartel would retain great powers at the expense of buying countries as long as the nonpopulous rich Arab oil exporters (Libya and the Arabian peninsula) continued to run a cartel on the monopoly model. OPEC's success has been emulated by countries exporting phosphate rock and bauxite, but very few other primary products entering world trade are likely to be cartelized with lasting success.

SUGGESTED READING

The best narrative of the events leading to the 1973–74 OPEC victory, and of the roles played by several countries and the major oil companies, is to be found in Raymond Vernon (ed.), *The Oil Crisis* (New York: Norton, 1976). For two opposing views of the proximate causes of the oil crisis, see Jahangir Amuzegar, "The Oil Story: Facts, Fiction, and Fair Play," *Foreign Affairs*, vol. 51, no. 4 (July 1973), pp. 676–89; and Morris Adelman, "Politics, Economics, and World Oil," *American Economic Review*, vol. 64, no. 2 (May 1974), pp. 58–67.

The standard theory of cartels along the lines of the group monopoly model is surveyed in Frederick M. Scherer, *Industrial Market Structure and Economic Performance* (Chicago: Rand McNally, 1971), pp. 158–91 and 208–12; and George J. Stigler, "A Theory of Oligopoly," *Journal of Political Economy*, February 1964, reprinted as chap. 5 of his *The Organization of Industry* (Homewood, Ill.: Richard D. Irwin, 1968). For an application of the standard theory to the international cartelization of copper, bauxite, coffee, and bananas, see Carl Van Duyne, "Commodity Cartels and the Theory of Derived Demand," *Kyklos*, 28 (1975), 3, pp. 597–611.

The success of the International Bauxite Association in raising taxes and prices on bauxite exports is usefully reviewed in C. Fred Bergsten, "A New OPEC in Bauxite," *Challenge*, vol. 19, no. 3 (July/August 1976), pp. 12–20.

11

Trade policy and
developing countries

The less developed countries of the world have repeatedly charged that their per capita income levels remain lower largely because world trade is conducted on terms unfavorable to them. In particular, these countries believe that the expansion of world trade is unfavorable to their growth; that the markets in which they sell primary products are unstable, with adverse repercussions on sustained development efforts; that the terms of trade are evolving systematically against them; and that they are discriminated against in trade in manufactures. Acting on these beliefs, developing countries have sought to restrict and control their primary-product exports and their imports of manufactures. They have experimented with cartels like those discussed in Chapter 10, with commodity stabilization schemes, with pressuring the developed countries to lower their import barriers on manufactures from developing countries, and with the strategy of import-substituting industrialization. Although trade still accounts for a large share of their national economies, the developing countries have higher trade barriers on the average than do the Western industrialized countries.

Should the trade policy choices facing developing countries be analyzed with the same tools used for judging trade barriers in developed countries? Are the problems of developing countries different in ways that require a different kind of analysis? Is government control of foreign trade more justified in a less developed setting? These are the issues surveyed in this chapter.

THE ISSUE OF PRIMARY-PRODUCT INSTABILITY

There are two main aspects of the widespread concern over prices and export earnings in world markets for primary products. One aspect is concern with the price trend; the other is concern with short-run instability. We saw in Chapter 4 that the evidence on long-run price trends is mixed. Some products, notably natural rubber and wheat, have indeed experienced a secular decline in their ability to buy manufactured goods. In these instances a case might be made for government restrictions on supply expansion if it could be shown that the government would be better able to foresee the downward price trend than would private growers. Many other products, such as forest products, most metals, and beef, have either held their own or experienced improving terms of trade across the 20th century.

The empirical evidence on export instability is as mixed as the evidence on long-run price trends. Surveying data for the early postwar era, Alistair I. MacBean, Joseph D. Coppock, and others found the alleged instability in some cases but not in others. It seemed in general that the export prices, quantities, and revenues of less developed countries were slightly more unstable than those of developed countries. This was a fragile conclusion, however, and the slight contrast seemed to disappear when the comparison was made between primary-product exporters and others instead of between less developed countries and others. The contrasts are blurred by the fact that only some primary products have shown true instability in, say, price, and by the fact that the instability of this subgroup (rubber, jute, copra, cocoa, tin) has existed only in certain countries. Furthermore, MacBean found little evidence that export instability, where it existed, had harmful effects on investment or growth.

Even if the actual instability of primary-product exports contrasts only slightly with that of exports of manufactures, it is still important to ask what causes the instability that does beset primary-product exports and just how a primary-exporting country should react to this instability.

The causes of instability in primary-product prices and quantities can be summarized as resulting from the interaction of unpredictable demand and supply shocks, on the one hand, with the inelasticity of demand and supply curves, on the other. The supply of agricultural crops, for example, depends on the weather. A crop failure due to drought or frost can send the price soaring while export quantities drop. Conversely, a good harvest can send export quantities soaring but world prices plummeting. Moreover, planting can take place in response to a favorable set of price signals, only to have the harvest arrive when market conditions have changed for the worse later on. There are strong "cobweb" instabilities set up by lagged supply responses in such long-gestation tree crops as coffee, cocoa, and rubber. The prices of such crops may rise today, but planting cannot affect their supply for five years or more. This may mean five years of high prices and high planting followed by a large expansion of supply and dropping prices. (This cobweb excessive response is also found in modern long-gestation products, such as tanker shipbuilding and the production of engineers and scientists.)

In minerals, the instability tends to arise from cyclical swings in demand and from speculation, both of which run demand up and down against a relatively inelastic supply. The resulting price fluctuations are especially pronounced for metals that are used by the less stable capital-goods sector of the industrial economies, such as copper, tin, and bauxite for aluminum.

In deciding what to do about the degree of instability in export markets, a country must first decide what kinds of instability it cares to reduce. Is it important to stabilize export prices, or export quantities, or export values (prices times quantities)? The best answer is probably "none of the above." Nations and individuals care most directly about the level and instability of some measure of their material welfare, which is related to their net incomes above all costs. The closest counterpart to this concept in a nation's exports is its net gains from trade. An exporting nation cares most about the level and variance of its net gains from exporting, which correspond to the area between the world price line and its own export supply curve (the marginal cost of exports). This more basic measure of well-being is not easily linked to stability of export prices, or export quantities, or export values. The welfare implications of trying to stabilize one of these more easily measured export magnitudes are subtle and controversial.

Countries exporting primary products have adopted a wide variety of arrangements for controlling these exports, arrangements sometimes aimed at export quantities and sometimes at export prices. Export quotas have been applied at different times in the past, notably to coffee and cocoa. The objective of the export quotas has been not to stabilize exports but to raise export prices. The use of export quotas has thus been equivalent to an attempt to reap national monopoly gains on exports, as with the international cartel arrangements surveyed in Chapter 10, though in principle export quotas could be combined with variable taxes on exports if a country wished to stabilize both its export quantities and the export prices received by its own producers.

COMMODITY PRICE STABILIZATION

The most commonly discussed scheme for export stabilization is the one that concentrates on stabilizing the export price around its apparent trend. Price stabilization was practiced by the International Wheat

Agreement among wheat-exporting and wheat-importing nations before the 1970s, and has also been practiced by the International Tin Agreement throughout the postwar period. Let us survey first the way in which such schemes are supposed to stabilize prices and then examine how stabilizing prices would affect the well-being of selling and buying countries.

Officially stabilizing the prices of a commodity requires that some overseeing body, formed by one or more governments, stand ready to buy and sell the commodity in large amounts. In one way or another a *buffer stock* of the commodity must be maintained. When the price rises up to the ceiling that the officials consider the highest acceptable price, they must be ready to sell as much of the commodity as necessary to match the current excess demand at that high price. Only in this way can the officials keep the price from going higher. When market conditions threaten to push the price of the commodity lower than the level wanted by the officials, they must be prepared to buy the commodity in amounts sufficient to absorb the excess supply. Maintaining the funds and the commodity stocks necessary to stabilize in this way obviously entails certain costs. The commodity must be stored at an expense for space, labor, insurance, and so forth. Both the commodity and money must stand at readiness at a cost in interest forgone. If the overseeing body is international, there is the further problem of negotiating which governments will bear which shares of the total costs of the buffer stock scheme.

The essential problem in stabilizing price with a buffer stock is that of correctly guessing what the long-run trend price will be, and mustering sufficient resources to keep the price near that trend. If the contracting parties fail to foresee just how steep the upward trend in the commodity's price will be, they are likely to run out of stocks sooner or later. Once they have run out, the price will rise further than it would have if they had let it rise gently earlier by selling out of their stocks at a slow rate. If they have failed to foresee downward trends in the price, they will find themselves stuck with increasing stocks of a good whose market value will fall faster than they had anticipated. As soon as the contracting parties give up and sell off their stocks to cut official losses, the price will drop faster than if they had let it sag more gently by buying stocks at a slower rate. In either case of trend misjudgment, the final result is that the buffer stock authorities have made the price a bit less stable—and have lost some money themselves by guessing wrong. Given the limits on the amounts the officials want to devote to the task of stabilizing prices, it would be better, both for smoothing the price trend and for avoiding financial losses, if they guessed correctly and spread their purchases or sales evenly over the periods in which market pressures pushed the price away from trend.

This is not easy to do in practice, of course. The managers of the international tin buffer stocks have run out of tin stocks during the postwar price peaks and have had to stop buying up tin during some of the troughs. Still, the price of tin probably varied less because of their actions than it would have otherwise.

If the authorities were really successful in keeping the price right on its long-run trend in the face of fluctuations in private demand and supply, who would benefit from their actions? Would selling countries benefit more than buying countries? Would the world experience any net gain or loss? It turns out that the world is likely to experience a net gain from price stabilization, though the division of this gain between selling and buying countries is an elusive matter that is pursued at greater length in Appendix F.

To see the likely net gain to the world, let us assume that the authorities can maintain a buffer stock of tin at low cost and can correctly guess that the long-run trend in the price of tin is the same as that for other goods in general, so that there is no net trend in the real price of tin. In all years with extraordinarily high demand for tin relative to its supply, the officials sell off tin from their stocks. In years of relatively flagging demand, they buy up tin. If they have correctly guessed the trends, as we assume, they can keep the same average stock indefinitely by selling off the same amount in high-demand years as they buy up in low-demand years. By successfully stabilizing prices, the officials are bringing the world the same net gains that any merchant or arbitrageur brings by improving the connections between buyers who value a good highly and sellers who can produce it at low cost. What the officials are doing is transporting tin across time in a way that evens out prices between times. They are, in effect, taking tin from the time periods in which private parties give it a low value and selling it in the time periods in which it is assigned a high value. The gaps between the peak-period net demand curves and the trough-period net supply curves (minus the costs of maintaining the buffer stock) are a measure of what the world as a whole gains by having the officials buy cheap and sell dear so as to stabilize prices. This net gain exists even if one ignores any special arguments about the subjective gains obtained from being able to plan on stable prices.

Whether selling countries (or buying countries) gain from price stabilization is less obvious than one would presume from the fact that price-stabilizing schemes have usually been justified as beneficial to the interests of sellers. To see why the sellers may not be the ones to gain, consider the case of tin, where price fluctuations usually come from the demand side of the world market and where supply is a bit upward-sloping. If there were no price stabilization, the tin price on the markets in London and New York would be higher in some years than in others. As one would have presumed, it is indeed the case that stabilizing the price tends to stabilize the year-to-year export gains reaped by the exporting countries (Bolivia, Malaysia, Thailand). But this stability has a cost. By stabilizing the price to exporters, the international officials have kept the producers from taking advantage of the higher prices in peak-demand periods by making larger sales at those times. The international officials have in effect helped out the buying countries by keeping them from having to buy their peak-period volumes at higher prices. The net effect on the overall gains for the exporting countries can end up negative, even though the scheme does stabilize their gains across periods.

The complexity of the effects of price stabilization on the two sides of the world market is shown in Appendix F. The general pattern is that (a) in markets where most instability is due to *demand-side* fluctuations (for example, the metals), stabilizing price tends to make importing countries bear a greater share of the overall risk, though it may bring them long-run average gains at the expense of exporters; and that (b) in markets dominated by *supply-side* instability (for example, coffee), stabilizing price tends to make exporting countries bear a greater share of the overall risk, though it may bring them long-run gains at the expense of importers.

The fact that the net world gains from price stabilization are clearer than are the gains to either side of the world market might be construed as an argument in favor of a truly worldwide solution to the problem of international commodity markets, one reached and administered jointly by both exporting and importing countries. This is correct in principle, and there have been repeated attempts to negotiate a grain world commodity agreement. The negotiating problems are acute, however. It is impossible for an international conference to discuss stabilization of a relative or absolute (dollar) price around its trend without raising enormous and practically insoluble problems of what the market trend really is, what commodities to include in the agreement, who should bear the cost of administering any buffer stocks, and above all, whether or not the agreement should aim at redistributing income across the globe by deliberately raising some prices relative to others. Commodity price stabilization schemes are likely to be worked out by groups of sellers or buyers in one market at a time as long as no one group of countries has the power to impose a sweeping program on other countries.

No discussion of the effects of official price stabilization should overlook the real possibility that whatever the officials could do would be done anyway in decentralized commodity markets. Recall that our stabilizers succeeded by buying cheap and selling dear. They made a net profit by correctly guessing the long-run trends in prices. Yet if there is no reason to believe that officials have better knowledge of price trends than do private market experts, then it may be that the easiest way to keep maximum price stability in the face of unpredictable random shocks is to let private speculators try to maximize their profits. As we shall see in discussing foreign exchange markets in Part III, several observers have indeed argued that profitable private speculation is on balance a stabilizer of price. Nevertheless, there is at least a basis for arguing that official price stabilization is more likely to bring world gains in those specific cases where it can be presumed that officials can judge price trends more accurately than private speculators.

ISI: IMPORT-SUBSTITUTING INDUSTRIALIZATION

It is natural to view industrialization as a force contributing to overall economic improvement. Most high-income countries are industrial countries, the obvious main exceptions being the rich oil-exporting countries. To develop, officials from many countries have argued, they must cut their reliance on exporting primary products and must adopt government policies allowing industry to grow at the expense of the agricultural and mining sectors. Can this emphasis on industrialization be justified, and if so should it be carried out by restricting imports of manufactures?

There is ample historical precedent for the strategy of promoting industrialization by restricting imports of manufactures. Russia did so quite explicitly before World War I. The United States also protected its manufactures heavily at times, though it did so as much to generate customs revenue and appease industrial interests as to use industrialization as a path to overall growth. Protection was also high for manufactures in Spain and Portugal. These early experiences revealed no obvious correlation between import-substitution and the national growth rate. Some protectionist nations and some free traders grew rapidly, whereas other nations in each group grew slowly.

The Great Depression caused many more countries to turn toward ISI. Across the 1930s world price ratios turned severely against most primary-product-exporting countries. Although this decline in the terms of trade did not prove that primary exporters were suffering more than industrial countries, it was common to suspect that this was so. Several primary-exporting countries, among them Argentina and Australia, launched industrialization at the expense of industrial imports in the 1930s.

The ISI strategy gained additional prestige among newly independent nations in the 1950s and 1960s. The new legitimacy of central planning made import-substitution very convenient. Even without detailed industry studies, planners could find industrialization targets just by looking over the lists of manufactures imported by their own countries. Whatever manufactures were being imported in volumes large enough to occupy one or more large factories made good candidates for protected domestic production. The very fact that the goods were being imported showed that a ready market existed for those products. During the postwar period this approach soon prevailed in most developing countries, whose barriers against manufactured imports came to match those of the most protectionist prewar industrializers.

In the late 1960s and early 1970s, doubts about the wisdom of ISI were raised increasingly. Several studies questioned both the belief that economic development required promoting industry over agriculture and the belief that cutting imports was the way to industrialize. Yet this retreat from ISI has not proceeded as far in actual policy as it has in the thinking of Western economists, and ISI is still the prevailing trade policy among developing nations.

The more recent doubts about the ISI strategy have arisen mainly from detailed empirical studies of protected industries in Argentina, Brazil, Mexico, India, Malaya, Pakistan, the Philippines, Taiwan, and Turkey between the late 1950s and the early 1970s. The conclusions about ISI were resoundingly negative.

Aggregate data showed net national welfare losses ranging up to 9.5 percent of national product. The only country not viewed as losing from its trade barriers was Malaya, which got "optimal tariff" benefits by turning the terms of trade in its favor at the expense of the rest of the world. In general, the countries with the greater losses were those with the higher trade barriers. In most cases, the measures omitted some of the extra resource waste arising from complicated bureaucratic controls over trade.

The microlevel data also revealed a baffling variability in the degree of effective protection received by different industries (on the effective rate of protection, see Chapter 6). Some industries received negative protection because their inputs were more protected than their outputs, as in the case of some Indian auto assembly firms damaged by the extreme protection given their metal and chemical suppliers. Other industries received effective rates of protection of 300 percent or more, most frequently in Argentina, Brazil, India, and Pakistan. The pattern bore no discernible relationship to the likely distribution of favorable "externalities" across industries. Nor were the most protected industries the newest: the protection rate was often highest for some long-established industries, suggesting that the "infant-industry" argument cannot explain or justify the observed pattern of industrial protection. The same gaps between principle and practice were evident in the protection patterns of Italy and Russia before World War I: as noted in Chapter 6, both countries handicapped their new and skill-generating engineering industries by overprotecting their more established domestic suppliers of ferrous metals.

A further drawback of the ISI strategy is its tendency to retard the growth of some modern industrial (as well as most primary) sectors through an exchange-rate feedback. By reducing some imports, protection raises the international value of a nation's currency as foreigners find it less available now that they are selling less to the protectionist nation. Driving the value of the nation's currency above its free-trade equilibrium exchange rate makes the nation's exports appear more expensive to foreign buyers, who respond by cutting their purchases of the exports. At the same time, relatively unprotected import-competing industries also suffer new foreign competition once the overvaluation of the currency has made it easier to buy abroad. To the extent that the export and import-competing lines disadvantaged by the currency overvaluation are produced by modern industries, the argument that ISI brings side benefits from general modernization is partly self-checking.

If the case for ISI is ever to enjoy a renaissance among economists, it would have to be on the basis of new evidence that industrialization at the expense of imports brings very large side benefits overlooked by the orthodox measures of the effects of protection, aide benefits that cannot be better captured in other ways. Measures would have to emerge which could quantify the gains from national pride in domestic modern industry and from the creation of new transferable skills and attitudes. Yet even on the issue of these general side benefits, the trend among economists has been toward skepticism. The process of urbanization and industrialization, once credited with side benefits of modernization, is now viewed by migration studies as a generator of socially dangerous urban unemployment. The expansion of urban industry creates a small number of very high-paying jobs. Migrants are apt to be drawn into the cities by the chance to obtain such jobs, even if searching for them brings an uncertain period of unemployment. This extra unemployment is viewed as a social cost, though its empirical importance remains the subject of unresolved debate.

Another social side effect of ISI is its impact on the degree of income inequality within developing nations. Recent studies by the OECD and the World Bank have charged that ISI worsens the relative income position of agriculturists and the poor. It does seem clear that it harms the relative position of agriculture. Its effect on the rich-poor gap is less certain. On the one hand, the highest import barriers are often those on luxury imports, inconveniencing the rich by raising the cost of high living. On the other, luxury industries, such as automobiles, tend to be heavy users of capital and skills, and lighter users of common labor. Protecting these industries, while giving high salaries and power to government bureaucrats administering the import protection, gives new rewards to already affluent groups. At best, ISI redistributes income among the rich in developing countries. At worst, it favors the industrial rich over the poor. Again, the alleged side benefits of industrialization remain in doubt.

BARRIERS TO EXPORTS FROM DEVELOPING COUNTRIES

If import-substitution has its own costs, shouldn't developing countries redirect their resources toward expanding exports in line with their comparative advantage? This is, of course, what orthodox economic analysis has prescribed since Adam Smith and David Ricardo. How much growth potential this comparative-advantage strategy offers developing countries depends on how competitive their exports can be in world markets.

Ever since the early 1960s developing countries have charged that they cannot gain much from the comparative-advantage strategy because their exports face higher barriers in developing countries than do the exports from other developing countries. Starting with the meeting of UNCTAD (the United Nations Conference on Trade and Development) in Geneva in 1964, the developing countries demanded that these barriers not only be removed, but be removed preferentially. That is, the developing countries demanded that discrimination against the manufactures they tended to export be converted into discrimination in favor of exports from their countries, so that they would face lower import barriers than were faced by more developed countries exporting the same products. The developing countries limited their demand to their manufactures because they believed that it would be impossible to get the main industrial countries to agree to free importation of all products.

The United States rejected this demand at Geneva. It was strongly opposed to any sort of discrimination or preference by country on manufactures. Its main argument against preferences was that granting them would open the door to all sorts of trade discrimination by country of origin, the kind of discrimination that the General Agreement on Tariffs and Trade (GATT) was supposed to hold to a minimum. The United States also foresaw complicated government surveillance over the national origins of values added to the products arriving from developing nations, and complicated international negotiations over what was a "fair" pattern of discrimination in favor of the manufactures of developing nations.

The subsequent negotiations did prove complicated. At the New Delhi meeting of UNCTAD, the developed countries gave in to the political pressure for preferences. Led by Australia, they agreed to preferences on the manufactures of developing nations. The United States insisted, however, that the new system be one of **generalized preferences,** with an abandonment of the special "reverse" preferences given to French manufactures in the Communauté in Africa and to British manufactures in the Commonwealth. The principle of generalized preferences was accepted, but the new preferences for the manufactures of developing countries did not go far. Generalized preferences were granted within strict import-quota limits, beyond which the old higher tariffs applied. These quota limits were so stringent that most students of the subject regard the new help for the manufactures of developing countries as more shadow than substance.

Meanwhile, the more developed countries have imposed many new import barriers that have harmed the export sectors of both the developing nations and Japan. Taiwan's success in exporting TV sets to such countries as Britain and Italy has been checked by the stiff barriers imposed on TV imports by these countries in the mid-1970s in the name of improving the balance of payments. The United States and Canada have separately forced several Asian nations to hold down their exports of clothing. Most ominous for the future of manufacturing exports from developing countries is the rough treatment received by Japan, the very model of a rising exporter of manufactures. The more Japan has succeeded in penetrating new export markets for its textiles, steel, TV sets, and autos, the more it is forced to cut back on such exports to the United States and the EEC countries because of the lobbying power of import-competing industries in those countries. The new protection has also extended to primary products, with the United States raising its sugar tariff and tightening its beef import quotas.

The developing nations would thus be fully justified in charging that the more developed nations have not practiced the policies of free trade and comparative advantage that the latter have urged on them. Furthermore, the departures of practice from preaching have been greatest on manufactures exported from developing countries. It is likely that in future international negotiations along the lines of UNCTAD and the North-South dialogue over a new international order, one of the most sensitive issues should and will be the hard-to-justify barriers that have been placed on manufactures from developing countries.

SUMMARY

Several kinds of trade policy have been proposed specifically for newly developing nations. Those developing nations that export primary products have discussed and formed commodity price stabilization schemes as well as the price-raising cartels discussed in Chapter 10. Individual developing nations have adopted the strategy of import-substituting industrialization (ISI). There has also been rising pressure on the more developed countries to lower their import barriers on manufactures from developing countries.

The case for stabilizing primary-product prices is more complicated than it might at first appear. The evidence does not really establish that past price or export earnings fluctuations have been damaging to primary exporters, or that these fluctuations have been much more severe for primary exporters than for other countries. The welfare economics of price stabilization is also tricky. It is easy to argue that the world as a whole gains from truly successful price stabilization that somehow manages to keep price at its long-run equilibrium trend. But how these world gains are distributed between buying and selling countries is a complicated matter, depending mainly on whether the source of the instability is on the demand side or the supply side of the world market.

The prevailing trade policy of developing nations continues to be import-substituting industrialization. Standard analysis, like that in Chapters 6 through 8, would say that ISI brings net costs to these nations themselves, by lowering their gains from trade and by creating additional resource waste when complicated import-licensing or exchange-control schemes are set up. Recent detailed empirical studies of industrial protection have reinforced these doubts about ISI. If the strategy is to be justified, it must be on the grounds that industrialization brings side benefits beyond the private gains of industrialists and their employees, benefits that somehow could not be reaped by relying on manufacturing exports. Yet even on this front recent evidence has created some doubts. The urbanization associated with industrialization has been suspected of increasing social frictions and social unrest. And the effect of the industrialization on income inequality is not likely to be favorable, even though ISI has concentrated on restricting imports of the luxury goods consumed by the rich. Protecting these capital-intensive sectors has raised the incomes of the higher-income groups owning property and possessing skills, and has disadvantaged lower-income groups by propping up the international value of the nations' currencies, making it harder for them to sell labor-intensive products in international competition.

Developing nations have rightly complained about import barriers against their new manufactures on the part of the more developed countries. Such barriers have indeed been higher than the barriers on manufactures traded between developed countries, and have risen since the late 1960s. If developing countries are to remain sangiune about the wisdom of relying on new manufacturing exports, they will need to see a new willingness of developed countries to shift their own resources out of these sectors, perhaps with the help of the sort of adjustment assistance discussed in Chapter 8, instead of erecting new barriers against imports.

SUGGESTED READING

For a thorough treatment of developed-country policy toward developing countries, see Harry G. Johnson, *Economic Policies toward Less Developed Countries* (Washington, D.C.: Brookings Institution, 1967).

On the theory and practice of commodity agreements, see the Massell article cited in Appendix F; three earlier studies on export instability—J. W. F. Rowe, *Primary Commodities in International Trade* (Cambridge: Cambridge University Press, 1965); Alistair I. MacBean, *Export Instability and Economic Development* (London: Allen and Unwin, 1966); and J. D. Coppock, *International Economic Instability* (New York: McGraw-Hill, 1962); and the description of the International Coffee Agreement given in T. Geer, *An Oligopoly: The World Coffee Economy and Stabilization Schemes* (New York: Dunellen, 1971).

Detailed studies of industrial protection and the ISI strategy are found and cited in Ian Little, T. Scitovsky, and M. Scott, *Industry and Trade in Some Developing Countries* (London: Oxford University Press for OECD, 1970); the NBER volumes cited in Chapter 8; Bela Balassa et al., *The Structure of Protection in Developing Countries* (Baltimore: Johns Hopkins Press, 1971); and Anne O. Krueger, *The Benefits and Costs of Import Substitution in India: A Microeconomic Study* (Minneapolis: University of Minnesota Press, 1975).

12

The political economy of
trade barriers

WHAT EXPLAINS OUR TRADE BARRIERS?

Chapters 6 through 9 have laid out some principles for judging whether or not trade barriers are in the best interests of the nation or the world. The "one-dollar, one-vote" welfare yardstick was applied, so that the net national and world effects of a tariff or other trade barrier were calculated by simply adding up the dollar values of the effects on individual groups, weighing all dollars of gain or loss the same, regardless of who experienced these dollar gains or losses. It turned out that on this yardstick trade barriers could be justified under certain specific conditions. For example, the infant-government revenue argument for tariffs and export duties was valid when the young nation had no other way of raising revenues for needed public goods and services. There was also the nationally optimal tariff, which was better than any other policy tool for exploiting national monopsony power over world prices (at the expense of the world as a whole). Trade barriers were also shown to be better than doing nothing in a host of "second-best" situations, though some other policy was usually more appropriate than the trade barrier in such cases.

Yet the range of cases of trade barriers that are better than doing nothing is still quite limited, according to the usual analysis, and fewer still are the cases in which a trade barrier is the best of all possible policies. Even the most casual look at actual trade barriers shows them to be more widespread and more complicated than the usual analysis could justify. The evidence that real-world trade barriers are excessive has been cited several times. Chapter 6 quantified the net national losses from national import and export barriers (in Table 6.1). Chapters 8 and 11 added evidence that much of the industrial protection in developing countries involves both excessively high rates of protection and extra waste through resource-using procedures for awarding import and foreign exchange licenses. Chapter 9 added that the case for regional trade integration, as in the formation and expansion of the European Common Market, is uncertain from the national welfare standpoint and especially from the world welfare standpoint. It is abundantly clear that actual trade policies differ greatly from the prescriptions of the basic analysis of trade policy, usually in the direction of greater restriction of trade.

One possible explanation for this departure of practice from economic prescription is that the policymakers do not correctly perceive the effects of trade barriers. Such ignorance can explain a small part of the discrepancy. It is indeed likely that in many settings firms and workers in export industries have been unaware of the likelihood that higher import barriers would cost them income by making export sales more difficult (through the input-cost, foreign-income, retaliation, and exchange-rate feedbacks discussed in connection with U.S. labor's stake in foreign trade in Chapter 5). Consumers and buying industries may also at times have been unaware of the effect of import barriers on their costs. Yet detailed studies of past debates over trade legislation have shown a remarkable degree of sophistication on the part of representatives of all affected groups. If pointing out their stakes were enough to make all groups defend their dollars with equal vigor, then many of the trade barriers we observe today would have been defeated or repealed. The explanation for our trade barriers must go beyond misinformation on the part of affected groups. It must be that actual trade policy is based on different values than the one-dollar, one-vote welfare values applied in the previous chapters.

THE GOALS OF POLICYMAKERS

Political scientists and, more recently, economists have devoted considerable energy to forming and testing models of just what it is that policymakers are trying to maximize. Their focus has been mainly on the behavior of elected officials and candidates for elected office, though there is also a growing literature on explaining the behavior of appointed officials. This focus on policymakers and not on public opinion itself is very appropriate for a study of trade policy, since one of the outstanding facts about commercial policy is that it is not formed by direct public referendum. Voters are not given the chance to go to the polls and vote for and against, say, "Proposition P: 'The import duty on motorcycles shall be raised from 5 percent to 10 percent ad valorem: _____Yes   _____No.' " Trade policy is left to elected legislators and heads of state, or to appointed officials who are given discretion to interpret rules handed down by elected officials. Just how officials decide on such trade matters makes a fascinating subject for political inquiry. In fact, part of the original theorizing about bargaining among elected officials was inspired by the example of tariff legislation.

The usual assumption is that elected officials act as though they were trying to maximize their probability of getting reelected, much as nonincumbent candidates act as though they were trying to maximize their election chances. Taken literally, this theoretical assumption may evoke the cynical image of incumbents who will stop at nothing to get reelected and who care only about the glory, salary, and power that come with retaining office. Yet the reelection-maximizing assumption need not imply this. The incumbents may in fact be motivated primarily by their own loftier vision of the "national interest" and how they would serve it with some key steps if reelected. Yet all officeholders are faced with a much wider range of issues than the ones that inspired them to seek office. On most issues their objective is to take the stance that will best make others foster their reelection (or make others support them on the issues about which the officeholders care most). For most issues, the objective is to maximize votes, and the dollars that buy votes through advertising, for the next election.

The goal of the appointed official can differ from that of the elected official or the candidate for elected office, though it will not do so by much in a government bureaucracy run by elected officials. Studies of bureaucracy and of regulation of the economy by appointed officials identify several goals for appointed officials. One tendency is to try to maximize the importance of one's own office by seeking to expand subordinate staff and by insisting that the problems for which one is responsible are indeed complex and "ongoing." Beyond this, appointed officials seem to show a pattern of being responsive to their elected superiors and to the groups that mount the greatest pressure on their superiors. The groups exerting the greatest pressures will influence appointed officials both by the threat of securing their demotion by elected superiors and by direct persistent prodding, persuasion, and harassment. In what follows, then, we concentrate our attention on the behavior of elected officials as the prime locus of policymaking.

BIASES IN LOBBYING POWER

It is evident that the goals of elected officials differ from the maximization of the national interest as it is traditionally defined in the analysis of trade. Yet it differs from the usual analysis in a different direction from what one might infer from the one-man, one-vote rule of electoral democracy. Both theory and some evidence presented below agree that the maximization of reelection chances does not make officials maximize the number of voters who stand to gain from the official's trade positions. If that were true, free trade would be a much more prevalent policy. Most tariffs benefit a small number of import-competing firms and workers while harming a *larger* number of consumers of the product. To be sure, protectionist forces could get together and design trade-restricting proposals that would cover enough industries to benefit a majority of voters by inflicting greater harm on a minority, but most trade restrictions seem not to have been born through such carefully designed tyrannies of the majority.

Rather the reelection-maximizing goal seems to push policy away from both the democratic "one-man, one-vote" pattern and the "one-dollar, one-vote" yardstick of economic analysis. Any incumbent knows that to get reelected he needs to approach each individual issue asking, "How can I maximize the votes and the campaign backing of those people for whom *this* is the issue that is key to their election sentiments?" He understands that many people who are affected by his actions on, say, a trade bill will not make up their minds on reelecting him on the basis of this trade bill. He can retain many of their votes by opposing their interest on this peripheral issue as long as he appeals to them on some other fronts. As far as the trade bill goes, he can take the side of those people whose votes ride most on this issue, even if they are fewer in voter numbers—and have a smaller dollar stake in this issue—than their opposition.

Thus one bias in the influence or lobbying power felt by elected officials is a bias toward helping voters whose *individual* stakes in the issue are large as a share of their total income or their total emotional concern. Their votes are likely to ride on this issue. This bias, stemming from the fact that people vote for candidates but not directly for policies, tends to bias trade legislation in favor of producer groups, since in most industries the producer interest is concentrated into a smaller number of firms and of workers than is the consumer interest, which is diffused across a larger number of retailing firms and ultimate consumers. This bias favors *import-competing* producer groups as a rule. Most trade debates focus on curtailing imports, and the indirect harm done by import restrictions to export producers is often spread over (and maybe only dimly perceived by) many different export industries. In a debate over import restrictions, many a legislator will see that more votes are at stake in the import-threatened industries among his constituents than among his import-serving consumer constituents and his exporter constituents.

This same bias toward more concentrated producer groups is reinforced by a bias in the contributions of personal effort and financial contributions to lobbying efforts. The *costs of getting organized* are usually greater for large and diffused groups than for smaller concentrated groups. As anybody knows who has tried to gather support among many people with individually small stakes in an issue, there can be acute problems both in reaching them and in getting them to commit effort to the common cause. People who feel that their stake is small or that their individual efforts make only a small difference are likely to behave like classic "free riders," reasoning that the common lobbying effort will either succeed or fail without them, and besides they are busy, and so forth. Their frequent decision not to commit time or money to the lobbying effort causes their collective stake in the issue to be undervalued in the policy struggle. By contrast, more concentrated groups find it easier to get together and contribute to a common lobbying effort. Each member, being a sizable part of the group's total membership and resources, knows that his participation does indeed make a difference to the group's success in securing government favors, just as a large member of a cartel like OPEC knows that his participation in the agreement to hold back output does matter to the cartel's price. Thus more concentrated groups raise more dollars and person-hours of lobbying resources per dollar of their stake in an issue than do more diffused groups.

Perceiving these biases, officials often see it as in their interest to favor small groups, even many such groups with smaller dollar stakes, in policy conflicts in order to maximize their chances for reelection and reappointment. This causes officials to favor import protection in many cases where the import barriers harm more people than they help and bring a net dollar loss to the nation. This bias of the political system toward protectionism is likely to be stronger, of course, the more diffused and the less organized export producers are, since export producers have a stake in freer trade.

RECENT EVIDENCE OF TRADE LOBBYING BIAS

This theory of interest-group influence on trade policy finds support in the pattern of trade barriers and in the rules laid down for multilateral trade negotiations among countries.

The quickest way to see the lobbying bias in favor of concentrated groups is to recall the prevalence of "escalation" in the tariff structure. As we noted in Chapter 6, tariffs and other import barriers tend to be higher on finished goods sold to consumers than on intermediate manufactured goods sold to industry, though there are exceptions. This tendency seems to be the result of the poorer political organization of diffused consumer interests. Faced with the high costs of getting a lobbying effort organized, costs that are only partly surmounted by consumer groups like those headed by Ralph Nader, consumers tend to lose to protectionists in consumer-goods industries, such as beef, sugar, and textiles, despite the consumers' larger dollar stake and larger numbers. When it comes to intermediate goods, the story can be quite different. The buyers of intermediate goods are themselves firms and can organize lobbying efforts through trade organizations as easily as can their suppliers. The outcome of a struggle over higher tariffs on intermediate goods is thus less likely to favor protection.

Some recent detailed studies of protection patterns in Canada and the United States have also found evidence of bias in favor of well-organized import-competing groups. Studying the tariff structure of Canada in 1963, Richard E. Caves found better support for the present interest-group-bias model than for two other models of what made tariffs higher in some industries than in others. He found that one could probably reject the simple democracy model which predicted that tariffs would be high only where high tariffs benefited a majority of voters. Also partially discredited was one version of the national interest model, which predicted that Canada would give more protection to those industries with infant-industry growth potential or those with a higher share of value added in gross value of output. Yet Caves's tests showed higher protection for industries having concentrated producer interests and diffused buyer interests, as predicted by the interest-group-bias model.

Two recent studies of protectionist patterns in the United States have both supported and elaborated on the interest-group-bias model. Studying U.S. House and Senate votes on a trade bill in 1973 and 1974, Robert E. Baldwin found that the protectionist position was taken by congressmen whose districts or states had a concentration of import-competing industries. Interestingly, the concentration of export industries in a congressional district or state seemed to have no significant effect on congressmen's and senators' votes, again suggesting that export groups are less well organized to defend their stake in freer trade than import-threatened groups are organized to lobby for protection. Jonathon Pincus' study of the pattern of U.S. tariffs on manufactures in 1824 brought the interest-group-bias model into sharper focus by carefully distinguishing and testing the role of different kinds of producer concentration. Pincus found that higher protection was granted to those manufacturing industries that were dominated by a few large firms, or were concentrated into a few producing counties within each state, or were characterized by a wide dispersion of sales across states. Manufacturers in such industries would find it easier to get in touch with one another, whereas their buyers would not. On the other hand, Pincus found that higher protection went to industries that were spread across several states, securing them a broader base of support in Congress. The pattern, in other words, seemed to be that more generous protection was granted to industries that were concentrated in ways that eased the task of group organization, yet were spread across enough congressional districts and states to have several elected supporters.

Another kind of confirmation of the bias in favor of producers' interest groups comes from the rules of multilateral trade negotiations among countries. In negotiations such as the Kennedy Round of tariff reductions consummated in 1967, there are explicit guidelines as to what constitutes a fair balance of concessions by all contracting nations. A "concession" was any agreement to cut one's own import duties, thereby letting in more imports. Each country's import-liberalizing concessions were to be balanced in their estimated effect on import values by roughly equal expansions of the country's exports made possible by foreign tariff cuts. This insistence that each country be compensated for its import increases with export increases seems odd from the perspective of Chapters 6 through 8. After all, cutting its own import tariffs should bring a country net *gains* even if other countries do not lower their tariffs. The concession-balancing rule can only be interpreted as further evidence of the power of producer groups over consumer groups. The negotiators viewed their own import tariff cuts as "concessions" simply because they had to answer politically to import-competing producer groups but not to consumer groups.

REINTERPRETING THE HISTORY OF TRADE BARRIERS

The dependence of trade policy on the organizational strength of different groups makes it possible to explain some of the broader movements of trade policy in terms of several forces that make protectionists better organized relative to free traders in some periods than in others. Let us do so, using Figures 12.1 and 12.2 to outline some of the past swings in trade policy. These figures convey a rough idea of the ebb and flow of import barriers by graphing average rates of import duty since the start of the 19th century in the United States and Britain, and since the 1867 Confederation in the case of Canada. The data fail to reflect the fact that duties differed greatly across industries, with many goods entering duty-free and many others being subject to prohibitive duties. They also fail to capture the considerable importance of nontariff barriers since the 1930s, and thus overstate the postwar drift toward freer trade. The figures plotted in Figure 12.2 also overstate British protectionism by including revenue-raising duties levied on major imports for which there was no domestic industry to protect, notably tea and tobacco. Yet these data and other historical evidence

FIGURE 12.1
Average import duties, United States, 1792–1974

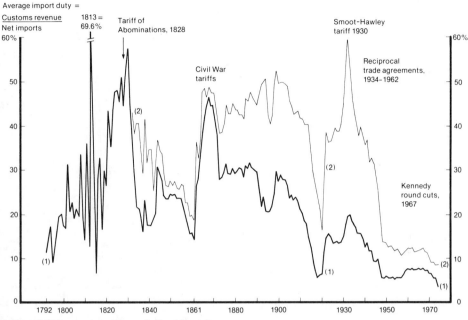

(1) = Duties as a percentage of all net imports.
(2) = Duties as a percentage of dutiable imports only.

do help to reveal several patterns in past trade policy, patterns that are likely to recur in the future. These patterns take the form of forces that make for protectionism or for free trade.

1. *When export interests have been organized, policy has tended toward freer trade.* John Stuart Mill once observed, "A good cause seldom triumphs unless someone's interest is bound up in it." This formula fits the history of the free-trade cause, if one takes care to amend it to read "someone's well-organized interest." We have already noted that export groups have often been poorly organized in debates over import barriers, leading to victory for protectionists. This same point can be underlined by noting the freer-trade tendencies of two of the historical settings in which exporters were relatively well organized. One such setting was the United States between about 1830 and the outbreak of the Civil War in 1861. In this setting, U.S. economic growth was strongly tied to the rise of cotton exports from the South. The growing strength of this export interest was enhanced by the voice given to cotton exporters in Congress. The economic stake in freer trade of cotton exports for manufactured and other imports was partly concentrated in a slave-owning elite which the congressional

FIGURE 12.2
Average import duties, United Kingdom, 1796–1972, and Canada, 1868–1972 (selected years)*

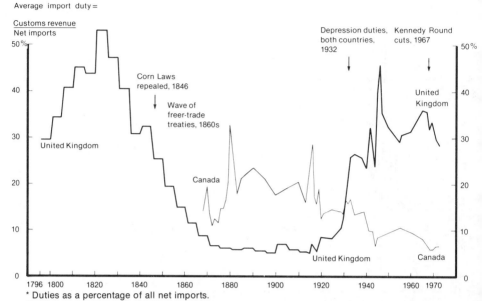

Average import duty =

$\dfrac{\text{Customs revenue}}{\text{Net imports}}$

* Duties as a percentage of all net imports.

Sources and notes for Figure 12.1 and Figure 12.2: United States: U.S. Bureau of the Census, *Historical Statistics of the United States: Colonial Times to 1970* (Washington, D.C.: Government Printing Office, 1976), series U193, U211, U212, and Y353; and idem, *Statistical Abstract of the United States, 1975* (Washington, D.C.: Government Printing Office, 1975), table 1370.

United Kingdom: Albert H. Imlah, *Economic Elements of the Pax Britannica* (Cambridge, Mass.: Harvard University Press, 1958), pp. 121 and 160; Brian Mitchell and Phyllis Deane, *Abstract of British Historical Statistics* (Cambridge: Cambridge University Press, 1965), pp. 284, 394, and 395; Brian Mitchell and H. G. Jones, *Second Abstract of British Historical Statistics* (Cambridge: Cambridge University Press, 1971), pp. 130 and 159; and Great Britain, Central Statistical Office, *Statistical Abstract of the United Kingdom, 1974* (London: HMSO, 1974), pp. 263 and 328.

Canada: M. C. Urquhart and Kenneth A. H. Buckley, *Historical Statistics of Canada* (Toronto: Macmillan, 1965), pp. 173, 197, and 198; Canada, Statistics Canada, *Canada Year Book* (Ottawa; Information Canada, various years).

For the United Kingdom and Canada, some of the ratios compare fiscal-year customs revenues with calendar-year imports.

structure endowed with heavy representation, thanks to the slave-owners' diffusion across several states and the constitutional provision allocating House seats according to a population count that multiplied the slave population by three fifths, thus giving extra House votes, in effect, to slaveowners. Slaveowners used this convenient congressional strength to argue eloquently for freer international trade, somehow not finding any conflict between the case for free trade and the case for slavery. Their group will did not always prevail, as the steep occasional tariff increases before 1830 testify. Yet the slaveowners won some rate reductions, especially in the 1830s. It is partly for this reason that lower average rates of import duty were recorded from the 1830s to 1861, as shown in Figure 12.1.

The Civil War broke up the organizational strength of the Southern export interest. Southerners, of course, continued to be cotton exporters interested in having cheaper access to imported manufactures. They also continued to be heavily represented in Congress. Yet the Civil War defeat left Southern representatives discredited in Northern eyes and placed a large number of Midwesterners firmly in the Republican camp, where they backed candidates whose protectionism harmed their economic interest, thus passing up most opportunities to ally with Southerners against protectionist industrialists on the trade issue. The result was a maintenance of the high Civil War duties on dutiable imports of manufactures for half a century.

The other case of strong exporter organization to be mentioned here was the triumph of free-trade policies in Britain in the middle of the 19th century. As Great Britain increasingly became the "workshop of the world" across the late 18th and early 19th centuries, its industrialists chafed more and more at restrictions on trade. They correctly perceived that many of their number could export more profitably abroad if they were freed from the higher costs imposed by import duties on food and other goods. The heavy duties on grain imports under the Corn Laws and heavy duties on noncolonial sugar and other tropical goods raised the money wages these industrialists had to pay their workers to be offering any given level of real wages. Those duties also raised the industrialists' cost of living directly (more expensive sugar, for example), and they probably lowered the ability of Britain's trading partners to afford to buy Britain's exports of manufactures.

By itself this rising collective stake in freer trade might not have sufficed to carry the day for the manufacturers of exportables. However, their interests were also served by two other gathering forces. One was the rising intellectual appeal of the laissez-faire attack on all sorts of government restrictions on economic intercourse. Another was the organization provided by the fact that the name rising manufacturing interests also shared other political goals. One such goal was electoral reform: the rising industries capable of expanding exports shared a political disadvantage because the outmoded set of parliamentary districts severely underrepresented the populations of new industrial areas. The common cause of electoral reform, which slowly had its way, brought together groups that shared a trade policy cause championed by the Anti-Corn-Law League. By 1846 this organization, plus the spread of the liassez-faire ideology and an Irish potato famine that dramatized the cost of duties on food imports, won the repeal of the Corn Law duties on food grain imports. The momentum continued for the rest of the century, with Britain taking the initiative in a wave of bilateral trade-liberalizing treaties across the 1860s.

2. *Policy tends more toward free trade in countries whose imports are noncompetitive or are inputs into important industries.* If a country's imports compete with little or no established domestic industry, it will be easy for the political system to develop a consensus that imports are to be viewed mainly as something that individuals should be able to buy as cheaply as possible. Protectionism persuades few when there is nothing to protect. Similarly, a good that is a key input into industries that are much larger than the import-competing industry will tend to be imported with little or no duty, though there are certainly exceptions.

One kind of evidence for this pattern of lower protection on inputs is the tendency of most tariff structures toward "escalation," already noted in Chapter 6 and earlier in this chapter. The existence of an industrial buying interest for an imported input acts to offset the ability of the import-competing industry to win higher trade barriers. An even clearer illustration of this pattern was given by the varied responses of five West European countries to a common disturbance, the arrival of cheap American grain in the 1870s. Thanks to rapid drops in transport costs by rail and ship and to the settlement of Canada's Prairie Provinces and the Midwestern United States, grain prices in Europe fell considerably faster than did other prices across the decade, and stayed low thereafter. The American grain invasion evoked a free-trade response in Britain and Denmark but a return toward protectionism in France, Germany, and Italy. The farm sector in Britain had by this time already shrunk to a such low share of the population and of private wealth that its cries for new duties on grain imports were easily drowned out by the insistence of industrialists, and the acquiescence of labor, in favor of letting the grain keep coming in duty-free. Farmers were given no choice but to switch to grain-using products, such as dairy and meat products, or to leave agriculture altogether. Danish farmers also accepted the free-trade prescription despite their greater political power, apparently because the cheaper grain poured in at a juncture in the history of Danish agriculture when they were already deciding to switch to specialization in grain-using dairy (exportable) products. The large continental vested interests in grain reacted differently. The powerful landed Junkers in the German Empire, who had earlier insisted that Prussian policy allow relatively free trade of their grain exports for imported goods, now were thrown into the import-competing position. They responded by forming a protectionist alliance, the "compact of iron and rye," with certain industrial groups that were also feeling import competition. The Junkers had the collective size to prevail politically and lacked the economic ability to take the grain-importing, dairy-producing alternative route. A similar reversion to previous protectionist habits was made by the highly organized agricultural syndicates of France and the large grain-growing interest in Italy. Again, the degree of import competition seems to have been crucial in determining the national responses to a common import-supply shock.

3. *Depression and sudden jumps in competing imports tend to breed protectionism.* This pattern has appeared repeatedly. It was evident in the United States after the end of the War of 1812 (and of the Napoleonic Wars in Europe), when both a series of general commercial and industrial depressions and a sudden return of cheap British manufactures after the war caused panic in manufacturing industries. Figures 12.1 and 12.2 also register the switch toward protectionism in North America and Britain in the great slump at the start of the 1930s,[1] a move followed in almost all other countries as well. The same protectionist reaction to depression has been evident in milder form in the post-OPEC recession of 1974–75, especially in those countries, such as Italy, Britain, and Brazil, where the trade balance has dipped seriously.

The link between protectionism and the combination of depression and an import surge can also be observed upside down in the early postwar experience of the United States and Canada. Both countries emerged from World War II with unprecedented prosperity and a chronic ability to compete so well at prevailing exchange rates that the world rightly spoke of a "dollar shortage." Like the free-trade British industrialists in the middle of the 19th century, both countries could afford the complacent view that adjustments to new import competition would be relatively painless and were warranted by the advantages of freer trade for their healthy and highly competitive export groups. Figures 12.1 and 12.2 show the U.S. and Canadian trend toward lower duties across the 1940s and 1950s, a trend contrasting with the maintenance of higher duties by Britain, whose trade deficits remained a chronic postwar adjustment problem.

It is not difficult to explain the link between depressions and import surges. When unemployment is high and new imports are disruptive to jobs and to the solvency of firms, the natural reaction is to jump for protection in defense of domestic jobs and income. This natural reaction in fact has a reasonable economic basis: when unemployment is

---

[1] Figure 12.2 tends to understate the rise in protectionism imposed by Canada's tariff hikes in 1931 and 1932. These hikes were sufficiently prohibitive on many goods so as to halt imports, and therefore tariff revenues, on high-duty items, leaving only the lower-duty items to affect the average rates of duty shown in Figure 12.2. The importance of this same point is hinted at in Figure 12.1, which shows that the U.S. Smoot-Hawley tariffs dramatically raised rates on dutiable imports while having a more modest-looking effect on tariff rates for all imports.

high and imports threaten jobs directly, one can argue that the displacement costs noted in Chapter 8 are likely to be high. This does not mean, of course, that protection is the most appropriate way of defending those threatened jobs and incomes, but it does mean that protection can look better at such times than the other *quick* politically feasible alternative, which is doing nothing. Any macroeconomic policies that promote the goal of full employment throughout the economy are likely to have the favorable side effect of weakening the case for saddling the nation with higher trade barriers.

THE POLITICAL ROLE OF THE ANALYSIS OF TRADE

Both facts and currently developing theories of political behavior make it abundantly clear how far trade policy is likely to depart from the one-dollar, one-vote prescriptions of the usual economic analysis of trade policy. The realities of the political marketplace tend to yield higher barriers to international trade than can be justified by an appeal to the maximization of aggregate economic well-being, even after some generous allowance has been made for second-best arguments for trade barriers.

This does not mean that the usual economic analysis is naive or irrelevant. Economists looking at trade policy are quite aware of the biases in political lobbying power discussed in this chapter. Their continued use of the economic analysis of trade policy should be interpreted not as naiveté, but as an informed way of offering insights to people with different values while soft-selling a particular set of values at the same time. As we noted in Chapter 6, the basic analysis of trade policy can be used by any group with any set of values attached to the interests of different producer and consumer groups. If one rejects the one-dollar, one-vote yardstick that produced the conclusions about "net national" gains and losses, one can still find the measures of the effects on different groups very useful, to be combined with one's own defense of the interests of particular groups.

At the same time, the conclusions about net national and world welfare effects can be interpreted as the trade economist's way of suggesting that these values are an appropriate set of subjective weights to apply to trade policy debates. By choosing a set of weights that assign equal value to any dollar stake in trade, regardless of who gets that dollar of gain or loss, the economist's usual analysis is in effect challenging people who reject the usual analysis to (1) reveal their own values, (2) explain why the dollar stakes of some groups should be given more weight in policy decisions than those of other groups, and (3) explain why their desire to favor the well-being of some groups over others cannot be better served in some other way. If it achieves this, the economic analysis of trade policy has made a major contribution to public decision making.

SUGGESTED READING

Two general discussions of the theory of political behavior and lobbying biases are to be found in Anthony Downs, *An Economic Theory of Democracy* (New York: Harper and Row, 1957); and Mancur Olson, *The Logic of Collective Action: Public Goods and the Theory of Groups* (Cambridge, Mass.: Harvard University Press, 1965). Downs deals at some length with tariff policy examples. Similar theorizing with applications to Canada can be found in two provocative works by Albert Breton: "The Economics of Nationalism," *Journal of Political Economy*, vol. 72, no. 4 (August 1964), pp. 376–86; and *The Economic Theory of Representative Government* (Chicago: Aldine, 1974).

The three recent empirical studies of North American trade policy patterns cited above are: Richard E. Caves, "Economic Models of Political Choice: Canada's Tariff Structure," *Canadian Journal of Economics*, vol. 4, no. 2 (May 1976), pp. 278–300; Robert E. Baldwin, *The Political Economy of Postwar U.S. Trade Policy*, New York University, Graduate School of Business Administration, Bulletin, 1977; and Jonathon Pincus, "Pressure Groups and the Pattern of Tariffs," *Journal of Political Economy*, vol. 83, no. 4 (July/August 1975), pp. 757–77.

The history of U.S. tariff policy revolves around Frank Taussig's classic *The Tariff History of the United States*, 8th ed. (New York: Putnam, 1931). Canadian commercial policy is surveyed in O. J. McDiarmid, *Commercial Policy in the Canadian Economy* (Cambridge, Mass.: Harvard University Press, 1946); and J. H. Dales, *The Protective Tariff in Canada's Development* (Toronto: University of Toronto Press, 1966). European patterns in the rise of free trade and the subsequent turn toward protectionism later in the 19th century are interpreted in C. P. Kindleberger, "The Rise of Free Trade in Western Europe, 1820–1875," *Journal of Economic History*, vol. 35, no. 1 (March 1975), pp. 20–55; and Kindleberger, "Group Behavior and International Trade," *Journal of Political Economy*, vol. 59, no. 4 (February 1951), pp. 30–47.

part III

Foreign exchange and the payments adjustment process

90-Day Futures	.9230	.9242
30-Day Futures	.9227	.9241
China-Taiwan (Dollar)		
Colombia (Peso)	.0275	.0275
Denmark (Krone)	.1631	.1632
Ecuador (Sucre)	.0385	.0385
Finland (Markka)		
France (Franc)	.2052	.2043
30-Day Futures		
90-Day Futures		
30-Day Futures	.2025	.2022
Greece (Drachma)		
Hong Kong (Dollar)	.2139	.2142
India (Rupee)	.1170	.1165
Indonesia (Rupiah)		
30-Day Futures		
30-Day Futures		
30-Day Futures		
Lebanon (Pound)	.3229	.3231
Malaysia (Dollar)	.4079	.4076
Mexico (Peso)	.0441	.0441
Netherlands (Guilder)		.4078
New Zealand (Dollar)	.9815	
Norway (Krone)		.1823
(Rupee)	.1025	.1025
(Sol)		.0124
Philippines (Peso)	.1355	
(Escudo)	.0246	
Saudi Arabia (Riyal)	.2833	.283
Singapore (Dollar)		.4110
South Africa (Rand)	1.	1.1522

British Pound Falls, *Germany Exporters There Reap Windfall Profits* — Their Effective Prices Rise Abroad, Limiting Market At Least for Time Being

U.S. Payments Skidded Into Red In Third Quarter — Current-Account Deficit Is Widest in 2 Years; Trade, Grants Abroad Are Cited

13

The foreign exchange market

Much of the study of international finance is like a trip to another planet. It is a strange land, far removed from the economics of an ordinary household. It is populated by strange creatures—hedgers, arbitrageurs, the Gnomes of Zurich, the Snake in the Tunnel, the gliding band, and the crawling peg. It is an area in which it is unsafe to rely on ordinary household intuition. In fact, it is an area in which you cannot apply ordinary micro- or macroeconomic theory without major modifications.

Yet the student of international finance is helped by the presence of two familiar forces: profit maximization and competition. The familiar assumption that individuals act as though they are out to maximize the real value of their net incomes ("profits") appears to be at least as valid in international financial behavior as in other realms of economics. To be sure, people act as though they are maximizing a subtle concept of profit, one that takes account of a wide variety of economic and political risks. Yet the parties engaged in international finance do seem to react to changing conditions in the way that a profit-maximizer would.

It also happens that competition prevails in most international financial markets, despite a folklore full of tales about how groups of wealthy speculators manage to corner those markets. There is competition in the markets for foreign exchange and in the international lending markets. Thus for these markets, one can repair to variants on the familiar demand and supply analysis of competitive markets. Here again, it is important to make one disclaimer: it is definitely not the case that all markets in the international arena are competitive.

Monopoly and oligopoly are very evident in most of the direct investment activity we shall discuss in Chapters 25 and 26 in Part V, as well as in the cartels already discussed in Chapter 10. Ordinary demand and supply curves would not do justice to the facts in these areas. Yet in the financial markets that play a large role in the material of Parts III and IV, competitive conditions do hold, even more so than in most markets usually thought of as competitive.

What gives international finance its esoteric twist is the existence of national moneys. This makes a big difference. In ordinary microeconomics one usually discusses how the price of one good in terms of other goods matters and what determines it. Macroeconomics discusses how the money supply relates to goods and bonds and work. Yet there are as many money supplies and monetary policies as there are sovereign nations. There are also the same number of separate interest-rate structures and government fiscal policies, as already stressed in Chapter 1. It is the existence of these national currencies and financial structures that poses a special challenge to both students and business executives.

FUNCTIONS OF THE FOREIGN EXCHANGE MARKET

International clearing

The bridge over which one travels to get from one national currency to another is the foreign exchange market. Unlike traveling on an ordinary bridge, on this bridge one must exchange with somebody else who is coming across the other way. For anybody wanting to sell dollars to get British sterling, there must be somebody else wanting to cross over from the pound sterling into the dollar at the same exchange rate, or the price of one currency in units of the other. The foreign exchange market performs an international clearing function by bringing together the parties wanting exchange currencies and giving them the chance to clear their balances in individual currencies by agreeing on a market rate of exchange. The clearing process that transfers purchasing power through the foreign exchange market is the international analogue of the domestic bank clearing that takes place informally between banks of the same community, in city clearinghouses, within a Federal Reserve district, and in the Interdistrict Settlement Fund.

The foreign exchange market takes place between banks and brokers in financial centers around the world. During the hours of business common to different time zones, they rapidly exchange shorthand messages expressing their bids for different currencies. To make a profit on foreign exchange maneuvers, a trader or broker has to make quick decisions correctly. Foreign exchange traders lead an exciting and hectic life, and the pressure shortens many careers.

The fastest possible communications are used. Before the transatlantic cable was laid in the mid-19th century, somebody wanting to exchange dollars for pounds would often have to wait the time required for a round-trip voyage to clear up the transaction. The telegraph shortened the time required, and modern telephone links have reduced transactions costs on foreign exchange to near zero for large transactions. Today's foreign exchange markets follow the sun around the globe with the help of communications satellites. West German marks, for example, can be traded between Europe and New York when the sun is over the Atlantic, between New York and San Francisco as the sun crosses America, between San Francisco and East Asia as the sun crosses the Pacific, and between East Asia and Europe as the sun returns to Europe. What the traders exchange are typically bank deposits denominated in different currencies. A New York bank selling U.S. dollars for British pounds is in effect buying the right to issue checks on a British bank, paying with a check on a New York bank, perhaps that bank itself. Verbal deals are quickly consummated by cable. The whole process of buying and selling different currencies proceeds at a hectic pace, with exchange rates changing at least every hour of business.

The foreign exchange market provides clearing services to many kinds of businesses and individuals. Ordinary tourists usually meet this marketplace in some airport, such as Juarez Airport in Mexico City, or Heathrow in London, at the exchange counter with the signboard announcing the current rates. Less familiar to most is the larger flow of billions each year in transactions involving internatinal trade in goods. At the center of the market process determining the value of any nation's currency is the set of currency transactions established by that nation's exports and imports of goods and services.

A nation's exports of goods and services cause foreign currencies to be sold in order to buy that nation's currency. If the United States sells a million dollars' worth of aircraft to a foreign buyer, it is likely, though not necessary, that somebody will end up trying to sell foreign currencies to get a million dollars. Let us say, as in most of the examples that follow, that the foreign country, here buying the aircraft, is the United Kingdom. If the British government or a private British firm pays by writing a check in pounds sterling, the U.S. firm receiving the sterling check must either be content to hold onto sterling bank balances or try to sell the sterling for dollars. Alternatively, if the U.S. firm will accept payment only in dollars, then it is the British buyer or his representative who must go searching for an opportunity to sell sterling to get the dollars on which the U.S. exporter insists. Either way, U.S. *exports of goods and services will create a supply of foreign currency* and a demand for U.S. dollars, to the extent that foreign buyers have their own currencies to offer and U.S. exporters prefer to end up holding U.S. dollars and not some other currency. Only if U.S. exporters are happy to hold onto pounds (or the United Kingdom importers somehow have large reserves of dollars to spend) can U.S. exports keep from generating a supply of pounds and a demand for dollars.

Importing goods and services correspondingly tends to cause the home currency to be sold in order to buy foreign currency. If the United States imports, say, a million dollars of British automobiles, then somebody is likely to want to sell a million dollars to get pounds. If the U.S. importer is allowed to pay in dollars, the British exporter of the automobiles faces the task of selling the million dollars to get pounds if he wants to end up holding his home currency. If the British exporter insists on being paid in pounds, it is the U.S. importer of the autos that must take a million dollars to the foreign exchange market in search of pounds. Either way, U.S. *imports of goods and services will create a demand for foreign currency* and a supply of the home currency, to the extent that U.S. importers have dollars to offer and foreign exporters prefer to end up holding their own currencies. Only if foreign exporters are happy to hold onto dollars (or the U.S. importers somehow have large reserves of foreign currencies to spend) can U.S. imports keep from generating a supply of dollars and a demand for foreign currency.

The traders entering the foreign exchange market in order to exchange currencies seldom transact directly with each other. Rather each trader deals with a bank, usually in his own country. The large banks accustomed to foreign exchange dealings then buy and sell currencies among themselves and with specialized foreign exchange brokers. It is in these interbank and bank-broker dealings that the foreign exchange rates are set, with traders simply being told by banks what the current rates are. It is because banks remain at the core of the foreign exchange market that exchange-rate quotations, such as those supplied by the Bankers Trust in New York and shown on the title page to Part III above, are released by major banks and not by exporters or importers. Thus the U.S. firm selling aircraft exports in exchange for payment in pounds would take the British importer's promise to repay and sell it to a U.S. bank, which sells this IOU in sterling to another bank wanting to buy sterling with dollars. The dollar checking accounts thus received by the U.S. bank compensate it for the dollars it paid to the U.S. aircraft exporter (along with small fees pocketed by the bank for helping the exporter get rid of his sterling). (In financial jargon, one could reexpress this pair of transactions as follows: The U.S. aircraft exporter "draws a bill on London" and "discounts" it with a U.S. bank, which "rediscounts" it, "repatriating" its proceeds through the foreign exchange market.)

Although foreign trade transactions bulk large in the foreign exchange market, they are not the only kind of transactions generating demand and supply for currencies. People can demand British pounds even without wanting to buy British goods and services. They may simply want to hold their assets in sterling, either to make an expected high rate of return or to hold sterling balances ready in case they should later want to buy British goods or services. People in the United States and Canada often also demand foreign currency in order to be able to send remittances and cash gifts to relatives in Italy or Mexico or some other country from which they emigrated.

Hedging

The fact that exchange rates can change makes people take different views of foreign currencies. Some people do not want to have to gamble on what exchange rates will hold in the future, and want to keep their assets in their home currency alone. Others, thinking they have a good idea what will happen to exchange rates, would be quite willing to gamble by holding a "foreign" currency, one different from the currency in which they will ultimately buy consumer goods and services. These two attitudes have been personified into the concepts of hedgers and speculators, as though individual persons were always one or the other, even though the same person can choose to behave like a hedger in some cases and like a speculator in others.

Hedging against an asset, here a currency, is the act of making sure that you have neither a net asset or a net liability position in that asset. We usually think of hedgers in international dealings as persons who have a home currency and insist on having an exact balance between their liabilities and assets in foreign currencies. In financial jargon, hedging means avoiding both kinds of "open" positions in a foreign currency—both "long" positions, or holding net assets in the foreign currency, and "short" positions, or owing more of the foreign currency than one holds. An American who has hedged his position in West German marks has assured that the future of the exchange rate between dollars and marks will not affect his net worth. Hedging is a perfectly normal kind of behavior, especially for people for whom international financial dealings are a sideline. Simply avoiding any net commitments in a foreign currency saves on the time and trouble of keeping abreast of fast-changing international currency conditions.

The foreign exchange market provides a useful service to hedgers by allowing hedgers of all nationalities to get rid of net asset or net liability positions in their respective foreign currencies. Suppose, for example, that you are managing the financial assets of an American pop group, and that the group has just received £100,000 in checking deposits in London as a result of selling its records in Britain. The group wants to hold onto the extra money in some form for a while, say for three months. But doing so exposes the group to an exchange-rate risk. The value of each pound sterling, which is now (say) $1.50/£, may drop or rise over the next three months, affecting the value in dollars that the group ends up with when selling the pounds in the future. Let us suppose that the group does not want to take on this risk and headache, and that it wants to assure itself right now of a fixed number of dollars. It can use the foreign exchange market, selling its £100,000 for $150,000, and investing those dollars at interest in the United States. Whether or not the group ends up making more money by getting out of sterling now is of limited relevance, since the group has decided that it does not want to have the value of its wealth depend on the future of the exchange rate between sterling and the dollar.

The foreign exchange market provides the same kind of hedging opportunity to people in all sorts of other situations involving foreign currencies. An American who will have to *pay* £100,000 three months from now need not wait that long to buy sterling at a future and uncertain exchange rate. He can hedge against this sterling liability by buying sterling now and holding enough money in Britain to be able to repay the £100,000 after three months. Similarly, somebody in Britain with dollars assets to get rid of can sell them at today's exchange rate and thus end any uncertainty about their worth in terms of pounds sterling. British residents with dollar debts to discharge in the near future can similarly buy dollars with pounds now and eliminate any uncertainty about how many pounds it will cost them to pay off their dollar debts. The same foreign exchange market that produces changing exchange rates gives hedgers a way of avoiding gambles on the future of exchange rates.

Speculation

The opposite of hedging is *speculation*, the act of taking a net asset position ("long" position) or a net liability position ("short" position) in some asset class, here a foreign currency. Speculating means committing oneself to an uncertain future value of one's net worth in terms of home currency. It can therefore be assumed that anybody who speculates is acting on the basis of something he or she expects about the future price of the foreign currency.

A rich imagery surrounds the term *speculator*. Speculators are usually portrayed as a class apart from the rest of humanity. These

Gnomes of Zurich, in the frequent newspaper imagery, are viewed as being very greedy—unlike the rest of us, of course. They are also viewed as exceptionally jittery and as adding an element of subversive chaos to the economic system. They come out only in the middle of storms: we don't hear about them unless the economy is veering out of control, and then it is their fault. Although speculation has indeed played such a sinister role in the past, it is an open empirical question whether it does so frequently. More to the present point, we must recognize that the only concrete way of defining speculation is the broad way just offered. Anybody is a speculator who is willing to take a net position in a foreign currency, whatever his motives or expectations about the future of the exchange rate.

The foreign exchange market provides the same bridge between currencies for speculators as for hedgers, since there is no credentials check that can sort out the two groups in the marketplace. The American pop group holding £100,000 in London has the option of speculating in sterling. It need not sell its sterling now, but can hold onto it in Britain for three months, earning interest and waiting to see how many dollars its pounds, including interest, are worth after three months. Whether a person willing to speculate in a foreign currency does so depends on home and foreign interest rates and also on his expectations about the future movement in the exchange rate. Suppose that the 90-day (three-month) interest rate is 3 percent in Britain and 2 percent in the United States. The group holding £100,000 could invest it in Britain at 3 percent and have £103,000 after the 90 days, or it could sell the £100,000 in the foreign exchange market at the exchange rate of $1.50/£, and invest this $150,000 at 2 percent, ending up with $150,000 × 1.02 = $153,000. Whether it is more profitable to end up with £103,000 or $153,000 clearly depends on what the exchange rate will be after 90 days. If the group feels certain that the pound sterling will not change in value over the 90 days, it will see merit in the idea of holding onto the sterling and earning 3 percent, bringing home £103,000 × $1.50/£ = $154,500, which is 1 percent better than having held the money in the United States and earning only $153,000. If sterling is expected to rise in value over the 90 days, all the more reason to hold the group's money in sterling. But if the value of sterling is expected to fall by more than 1 percent, then it is not a good idea to hold it. For example, if sterling were to drop 10 percent in value and be worth only $1.35 a pound after 90 days, the group would lose considerably by holding it. Keeping its money in sterling and in Britain would yield only £103,000 × $1.35/£ = $139,050 instead of the $153,000 that could be safely earned by converting sterling into dollars right away and earning 2 percent interest in the United States. So the profitability of speculating in a foreign currency depends on whether or not one expects the value of that currency to drop by as great a percentage as its interest rate exceeds the domestic interest rate. The existence of a foreign exchange market does not guarantee that speculation will be profitable. It only makes speculation feasible for those willing to take the chance.

It should be clear from examples like this one that anybody with wealth could be a speculator. Speculation need not be confined to an elite financial group, though having inside information is of some value on the average, just as it is in a stock market. Ordinary firms engaged in international trade can and do speculate. An exporting firm or an importing firm can speculate in the course of its ordinary international business, through what are known as *leads and lags* in trade payments. There is usually some leeway, often a few months' leeway, in when one gets paid for exports or pays for imports. If it is generally feared that the pound sterling will drop in value soon, U.S. exporters are likely to press for prompter payment from British customers, who are allowed to repay in sterling. (Alternatively, the exporter may simply refuse to accept delayed payment in sterling except at a much higher sterling price.) If the U.S. exports happen to be priced in dollars, then it is the British importer who has an incentive to pay in sterling to get dollars now, while each pound still buys more dollars. On the side of U.S. imports from Britain, lags in payment are likely to prevail if the pound is expected to drop in value. If the imports are priced in dollars, British exporters to the United States have some incentive to let the U.S. importers delay payment of the fixed number of dollars, which will probably buy more pounds if converted back into sterling later. If the U.S. imports are priced in pounds, it will be the U.S. importers who are suggesting delayed payment in order to have the chance to pay fewer dollars for the same pounds later. This kind of lead-and-lag behavior on the part of traders is tantamount to speculation: in each case somebody is deciding to hold or get rid of accounts receivable in a given currency on the basis of expectations about the future value of that currency.

THE FORWARD MARKET

For at least decades now, firms and banks heavily involved in the foreign exchange market have found it convenient to do their hedging and speculating in a separate market for future delivery. Each major currency can be bought or sold not only for "spot" delivery in the present (within two working days), but also "forward," for delivery at a future date. For example, on the title page to Part III, the following "spot" and "forward" prices for nondollar currencies were given by the Bankers Trust in New York:

	British pounds	Japanese yen	West German deutsche marks
Spot rate	$1.7160/ £	$0.003475/¥	$0.4141/DM
30-day forward rate	$1.7047/ £	$0.003474/¥	$0.4143/DM
90-day forward rate	$1.6825/ £	$0.003467/¥	$0.4149/DM
180-day forward rate	$1.6595/ £	$0.003463/¥	$0.4162/DM

There is thus a whole menu of exchange rates at which one can buy or sell a given currency. These forward markets, for delivery 30 or 90 or 180 days off, have come to be used more and more since the onset of fluctuating exchange rates among most major currencies in 1971. It is important to understand the basics of how the forward market works, what services it offers, and what difference it makes to government policy.

A contract to buy a currency forward is simply a written promise to sell some other currency for it at a preagreed rate of exchange. To buy £100,000 of 90-day forward sterling at the rate quoted above ($1.6825/ £), a dollar holder signs an agreement to deliver $168,250 in bank deposits and buy the £100,000 in 90 days' time. If this forward contract is signed on April 2, the exchange rate at which the exchange is consummated on July 1, 90 days later, is the preagreed rate, regardless of what the spot rate of exchange turns out to be on July 1. What makes the forward market so convenient is that it involves contracts for which one must today pledge only a margin of 10 percent of the contract as security, unlike a spot exchange in which one delivers the full amount now.

The forward market offers an alternative way to hedge or speculate. No matter what asset or liability position one has in a foreign currency, there is a way of adjusting it and moving into or out of each currency through the forward market. To see how the forward market can be an alternative route for hedgers and speculators, let us consider a few examples in conjunction with Figure 13.1. In Figure 13.1 each position represents a way of holding one's financial assets for the short term. Movements from one side to another represent transactions in the spot and forward exchange markets: people moving their assets from left to right are buying sterling and selling dollars, whereas those transferring from right to left are buying dollars with pounds. People moving upward in either country are lending, whereas those moving downward from forward to spot positions are either selling off interest-earning assets or actually borrowing at interest. The corresponding expressions in terms of exchange rates (r_s, r_f) and interest rates (i_a, i_b) show how the value of one's assets get multiplied by each move.

Example 1: A U.S. hedger gets out of sterling. The American pop group wanting to hedge against changes in the value of sterling could

FIGURE 13.1
Spot and forward asset positions in two currencies: The "lake" diagram

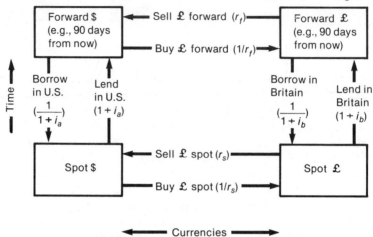

Currencies

i_a = 90-day interest rate in United States.
i_b = 90-day interest rate in Britain.
r_s = spot price of the pound ($/ £).
r_f = forward price of the pound ($/ £).

do so in the spot market, as in our example above, or in the forward market. Let us suppose again that the interest rates in the United States and Britain are $i_a = 2$ percent and $i_b = 3$ percent, respectively, and that the spot exchange rate is again $r_s = \$1.50/£$. We saw above that the group could hedge in the spot market by, in effect, traveling first leftward and then upward around the lake, buying dollars and lending them in the United States and converting £100,000 spot into $153,000 after 90 days ($153,000 = $r_s[1 + i_a]$). If there were no forward market, this would have been the only way the group could avoid having to convert sterling later at an unknown spot exchange rate. If the forward market exists, the group has another option, shown by Figure 13.1. It could lend its money in Britain at 3 percent, and arrange today to cover these sterling assets by selling sterling forward at r_f, traveling upward and then left through the forward market on top of the "lake." If today is April 2, it instructs the bank in London to hold its £100,000 at interest in either savings deposits or equally safe United Kingdom Treasury bills for 90 days. Also on April 2, it sells its sterling and its forthcoming interest (£103,000) at the April 2 forward rate of r_f, so that after 90 days, on July 1, the group just collects the known amount of dollars, paying the party buying its forward pounds with the £103,000 it has accumulated in London.

Whether or not hedging in the forward market is more profitable depends on the forward rate as well as the spot rate and the national interest rates. If the forward and spot rate were the same, with

$r_f = r_s = \$1.50/\,\pounds$, then hedging in the forward market is clearly better, since it lets the U.S. group earn the higher British interest rate without exchange risk. Yet if the pound is selling at a 2 percent "forward discount," or at a rate of $\$1.47/\,\pounds$, which is 2 percent below the spot rate, then it is better to sell sterling spot. If $r_f(1 + i_b) > r_s(1 + i_a)$, a U.S. hedger should sell sterling forward, but if the reverse is true, he should sell it spot. If the two expressions are equal, he is rightly indifferent between the two options. The important point remains that the forward market offers another way around the lake without exchange risk.

Example 2: A British hedger gets out of dollars. The forward market also offers an extra option to hedgers of the other nationality (or of any nationality wanting to cover a dollar position by getting into sterling). Suppose that the City of London has just received $\$1,000,000$ in San Francisco by selling used London double-decker buses to charm-hungry Californians (or by selling the last few pieces of the London Bridge to a wealthy Arizonan). If city officials want to cover themselves against future changes in the dollar-sterling exchange rate, they can sell their dollars either spot or forward. They could sell spot and just hold pounds in London for 90 days while deciding how to spend the proceeds. This route, rightward and then upward in Figure 13.1, nets them $\pounds686,667 = \$1,000,000\,(1/r_s)\,(1 + i_b)$, where r_s is again $\$1.50/\,\pounds$ and i_b is again 3 percent. Or they could invest the dollar proceeds from the sale in the United States, in savings accounts or U.S. Treasury bills, and sell all the dollars earned forward to get pounds. In this case they instruct the San Francisco bank to put the dollar deposits there in interest-earning assets as of today, April 2, and on the same day sell the dollars forward, buying forward pounds for delivery on July 1. After the 90 days are up, they pay dollars to the party selling them forward pounds by cashing in all of the dollars accumulated in San Francisco.

Again, the profitability of going the forward market route depends on how the percentage gap between the forward and spot exchange rates compares with the differential between the two countries' interest rates. If the forward rate equals the spot rate of $\$1.50/\,\pounds$, then the city officials would be making a mistake by buying forward cover. Doing so leaves them with only $\pounds680,000$ instead of that $\pounds686,667$ they could get by selling dollars in the spot market and earning the higher interest rate in London. Suppose, on the other hand, that sterling is selling at a 2 percent discount in the forward market, or at $\$1.47/\,\pounds$, 2 percent below the spot price of $\$1.50/\,\pounds$. Being able to buy sterling 2 percent cheaper in the forward market than in the spot market now outweighs the fact that interest rates are 1 percent higher in Britain. The city officials should lend their dollars at interest in the United States and also arrange to sell the dollars forward, buying forward pounds that cost only $\$1.47$ each. By thus traveling upward and across the top in Figure 13.1, they end up with £693,878 in this case. The rule for British hedgers is thus that they should buy pounds forward if $(1 + i_a)/r_f > (1 + i_b)/r_s$, and buy pounds spot if the reverse inequality holds. The forward market thus offers a British hedger an extra opportunity, one he will use if the forward price is right.

Example 3: An Englishman speculates against sterling. The forward market also offers an extra option to speculators, one that they tend to use heavily. Suppose that an Englishman with £100,000 is convinced that his sterling is likely to buy fewer dollars and goods in the future, and wants to abandon it for assets that are likely to have a higher sterling value. He could, of course, abandon his currency in the classic domestic way, by fleeing into such real assets as real estate and jewelry as a hedge against inflation. But let us say that his main suspicion is that the dollar and other foreign currencies will buy more pounds in the future, and that he wants to be holding dollars 90 days from now, when he will have the option of buying back pounds at what he expects to be a cheaper price of the pound. In terms of Figure 13.1, his immediate task is to get from spot pounds at the lower right to forward dollars at the upper left. If his pounds are not locked in by British exchange controls, he can take either route around the lake. First, he can sell pounds spot and lend his dollars in the United States, earning 2 percent interest. This gives him £100,000 ($1.50/ £) (1.02) = $153,000. Second, he can lend his money in Britain but contract now to sell pounds forward. In fact, he does not even need to have the £100,000 in hand right now. He can sell pounds in the forward market by just putting up 10 percent of the value as security and come up with the rest of the money anytime within the next 90 days, for example, by working for it at some high rate of pay or by selling some less liquid asset. If he is in fact playing with the sum of £100,000, the dollars he will end up with are £100,000 $(1.03)r_f$.

For the speculator as for the hedger, the profitability of using the forward market depends on how the forward exchange rate compares with the spot exchange rate and on the international differential in interest rates. If the forward rate and the spot rate are both $1.50/ £, he should lend in Britain and get out of sterling by contracting to sell sterling and buy dollars forward. Doing so nets him £100,000 (1.03) ($1.50/ £) = $154,500, 1 percent better than getting to forward dollars through the spot market and lending in the United States. The reader can work out that if forward sterling is at a 2 percent discount (at $1.47/ £), he should sell sterling in the spot market and hold his money at interest in the United States. For the English speculator wanting to end up with forward dollars, as for the U.S. hedger leaving sterling in Example 1, the key condition is whether $(1 + i_b)r_f$ is greater than $(1 + i_a)r_s$. If it is, the speculator should get forward dollars through the forward market. If the reverse inequality holds, he should get dollars in the spot market and lend in the United States.

What the speculator does with his dollars after 90 days cannot be determined from Figure 13.1. It all depends on the spot rate of exchange after 90 days, say on July 1. The more the pound sinks between April and July, the more our speculator has gained by abandoning it at the start of April. If, for example, he was able to sell his sterling forward at a 1 percent discount, at $1.485 on April 2, the £103,000 of money accumulated at interest in London will be automatically converted into $152,955 = £103,000 ($1.485/ £). If in the meantime the spot exchange value of sterling has sunk 10 percent, to $1.35/ £, he can turn around on July 1 and convert his $152,955 into £113,300 in the spot market, leaving himself better off (by about 10 percent) than if he had faithfully held money in Britain without speculating in foreign exchange. There's a catch, of course: if sterling fails to drop in value or even rises in value by July 1, he will have to pay more to get his money back home into sterling than the forward price at which he sold sterling back in April. (A July spot price of $1.50/ £ would leave him with only £101,970 after returning to sterling, and a rise in the spot price to $1.60 would leave him limping home with only £95,597 when he could have stayed patriotic all along and had £103,000.) To speculate is to gamble, and some speculators win while others lose.

Notice that all three examples led to the same key result: *The choice between using the spot and using the forward market depends on how the percentage premium or discount on forward exchange compares with the international interest-rate differential.* This general condition is crucial, regardless of whether one is a hedger or a speculator, and regardless of where one lives. This key result also suggests two corollaries:

1. The more the British interest rate exceeds the U.S. interest rate, the more people will be drawn to buy spot pounds, lend in Britain, and/or sell pounds forward.
2. A greater forward premium on sterling over its spot price also encourages people to buy pounds in the spot market, lend in Britain, and/or sell pounds forward.

Appendix G adds to these points by supplying an underlying formula governing the choice between spot and forward sales of a currency, and by showing how "arbitrageurs" can make profits in a way that reinforces the importance of this key comparison between forward premium or discount and the interest-rate gap.

Does the existence of the forward exchange market make any difference to the task of policymakers who are trying to regulate the spot value of a nation's currency? Appendix G argues that the forward market makes little policy difference. The forward market gives policymakers only some indirect clues about the magnitude of their currency-stabilizing task, and is of interest mainly to private individuals who want to know how to protect or maximize their own assets when different currencies are involved.

THE SPOT EXCHANGE RATE

The supply and demand for foreign exchange determine the foreign exchange rate within certain constraints imposed by the nature of the foreign exchange system under which the country operates. Assuming no foreign exchange controls, traders, banks, and speculators will trade in the market under any system.

The simplest system, though not necessarily the best, is the **flexible exchange standard** without intervention by governments or central bankers. The spot price of foreign exchange is determined by the demand and supply for foreign exchange, which are in turn determined by domestic and foreign prices of goods and services, domestic and foreign awareness of trading opportunities, international capital movements, the anticipations of speculators as to the future course of exchange rates, and so forth. The market clears itself through the price mechanism. Figure 13.2 shows how such a system could yield equilibrium exchange rates for the pound sterling and the West German mark at Points E. At these points the private demands and supplies are in line for each currency.

FIGURE 13.2
The spot exchange market, with and without official intervention

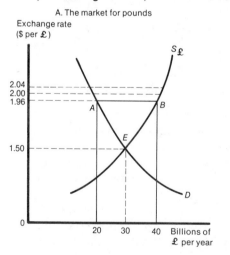

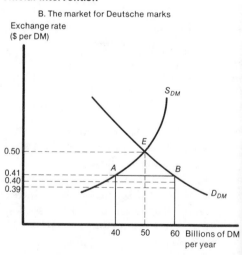

A. The market for pounds

B. The market for Deutsche marks

As Figure 13.2 is drawn, the demand and supply curves cross in the right direction for making the foreign exchange markets stable. If a higher price is temporarily quoted in an unregulated market, as at the $2/ £ exchange rate in Figure 13.2A, there will be an excess supply of this currency in pursuit of the dollar and the goods and assets that a dollar buys, and the price will tend to fall toward the equilibrium price. Conversely, if an exchange rate is temporarily below the equilibrium rate, as at the rate of 40 cents/DM in Figure 13.2B, there will tend to be an excess demand for this currency to buy the goods and assets whose prices are denominated in the currency, and its exchange rate will tend to rise to the equilibrium rate. This comforting case need not always hold. In Chapter 15 and again throughout Part IV we shall return to several arguments over the likelihood and the welfare meaning of exchange markets that have unstable equilibriums because demand and supply fail to intersect in the right way.

Under the **fixed exchange standard,** by contrast, officials strive to keep the exchange rate essentially fixed even if the rate they choose departs from the current equilibrium rate. Figure 13.2 shows how officials could keep the exchange rate essentially fixed. Their usual procedure under such a system is to declare a "band" of exchange rates within which the rate is allowed to vary. If the exchange rate hits the top or bottom of the band, the officials must intervene. In Figure 13.2A, sterling has weakened so that its equilibrium rate of $1.50/ £ is well below the officially declared "par value" of $2/ £. Officials have announced that they will support the pound at 2 percent below par, or $1.96, and the dollar at 2 percent above par, or $2.04. In Figure 13.2A, they are forced to make good on this pledge by buying up 20 billion pounds a year with their reserves of dollars, filling the gap AB. Only in this way can they bring the total demand for pounds, private plus official, up to the 40 billion being supplied per year by people wanting to unload pounds for dollars. If their purchases of pounds with dollars fall short, total demand cannot meet the supply and the price must fall below the official support point of $1.96. Needless to say, officials wanting to defend the fixed exchange rate may not have sufficient reserves of dollars to keep the price fixed indefinitely, a point to which we shall return several times.

Another case of official intervention in defense of a fixed exchange rate is shown in Figure 13.2B. Officials of some government or central bank, perhaps in West Germany itself, have declared that the par value of the West German mark shall be 40 cents in U.S. currency, and that the support points are 41 cents and 39 cents. As the demand and supply curves are drawn, they must intervene in the foreign exchange market and sell 20 billion DM a year to meet the strong demand at 41 cents. If they do not have enough DM reserves, or cannot tolerate buying enough dollars to plug the gap AB and keep the exchange rate down at 41 cents, they will have to give up and let the price rise.

The fixed-rate system has taken several forms. Before World War I, it was often maintained by the workings of the **gold standard**. When a currency fell in value, as sterling has fallen to $1.96 in Figure 13.2A, it fell in terms of other currencies with fixed official values in terms of gold. Even without official intervention, the gap AB would tend to become gold exports from Britain, as more and more individuals turned their sterling paper currency in for gold at the Bank of England at the official price and took it to the United States, where gold was being officially exchanged at par for money that now looked more valuable. Conversely, under the gold standard a gap like AB in Figure 13.2B would tend to become an inflow of gold into West Germany. More recently, between 1944 and 1971, the fixed-rate system took on the intercurrency form shown in Figure 13.2, with officials intervening in markets for paper currencies whenever their values deviated 1.25 percent from par values. It should also be noted that the fixed-rate system is analogous to any other system of official price-setting, such as the commodity-stabilization agreements discussed in Chapter 11 or the U.S. farm price support program, under which the government used to buy up surplus farm products to keep their price from falling in response to excess supply.

TYPES OF OFFICIAL INTERVENTION

When the monetary authorities intervene, there are the questions of, first, which set of authorities does so, and second, how. On the first score, for example, assume that there is an excess supply of country A's currency or an excess demand for country B's. To keep the A–B exchange rate from changing, the monetary authorities in B may intervene to buy up the A currency, supplying B currency to the market, or the A authorities may be required to sell off gold or B currency or to obtain B currency by one or another of various devices, such as swaps, loans, and selling B currency forward. Where officials in B buy up the excess supply of A's currency automatically, the total official reserves in the system are expanded, because B's official holdings of foreign exchange (here, deposits in A) are defined as official reserves. Where A draws on existing balances of B's currency, the total official reserves of the system are reduced (A's reserves are reduced, and B's are not increased), since A now holds less in foreign exchange reserves. Where A pays gold or a third country's currency to B, the total reserves in the system are unchanged.

Most of the implications of official intervention by the authorities in the foreign exchange market must be left for later discussion. Here we should provide the technical details, however, of three techniques: **forward operations**, currency **swaps**, and **Roosa bonds**.

A country's currency is under attack, let us say, and the country has to support its currency by selling off gold and foreign exchange. When these are used up, it may, if it chooses, sell forward exchange. In the middle 1960s, the British ran out of dollars. Instead of providing dollars to the market, they provided forward dollars. This had the effect of depressing the forward dollar and encouraging hedgers, speculators, and arbitrageurs (see Appendix G) to sell spot dollars and buy them forward. The arbitrageurs who were buying dollars forward and selling them spot for pounds propped the spot value of the pound.

Intervening in support of an exchange in the forward market rather than the spot market was proposed years ago by John Maynard Keynes and has been undertaken from time to time. Some economists have taken the view that this can be undertaken without difficulty, since maturing contracts can be swapped forward (see below). If this were so, a country could defend its currency forever with promises to deliver in the future—sometime.

The British, as indicated, tried this ploy in the 1960s and found that it did not work well. By the time Britain's forward sale of dollars amounted to several times its holdings of gold and dollars, the market refused to renew its old contracts and insisted on delivery. The devaluation which had been postponed from 1964 became inevitable in November 1967, and the pound was officially devalued to $2.40. The British officials had to honor their forward contracts by spending pre-agreed rates such as $2.67 to buy each pound that was now worth only $2.40 in international transactions. It was a hard way to make money, though no harder than the British officials' earlier purchases of spot pounds at such spot prices as $2.80, with each purchased pound destined to become worth only $2.40 after 1967.

Swaps are a means whereby two sets of monetary authorities can acquire claims on each other. Assume that the Bank of England seeks a short-term credit in dollars to meet pressures in the sterling market. Under its agreement with the Federal Reserve System, it would credit the Federal Reserve with, say, £100 million and would itself receive $175 million (if £1 = $1.75) credited to its account with the Federal Reserve Bank of New York. There is no net short-term capital movement, but the Bank of England is better placed to meet an excess demand for dollars. (Likewise the Federal Reserve could be seeking credit; the initial phase of the swap is the same.) Such swaps could be irreversible, that is, final transactions. In actuality, they have been almost entirely temporary transactions which are reversed after a fixed period of time under the terms of the original contract. Indeed, the term *swap* in the foreign exchange market means that a forward contract is involved. Thus the central bank swaps include a spot exchange of currencies with a contract to reverse the exchange at a specified future date.

Market swaps, either by individual traders or by central banks, are also common. The Italian authorities use swaps with Italian commercial banks as a means of domestic monetary control, or to limit the volume of dollars held overtly in official reserves. The Italian authorities will sell dollars to banks under repurchase agreements (that is, forward contract to buy dollars back at a fixed lira price). The spot and future rates are set so as to make the investment attractive to the Italian banks, with a forward rate on the dollar better than that generally available in the market. Since banks pay in spot lira under the swaps, local bank reserves are drawn down and lira credit is tightened. At the same time, the published foreign exchange reserves of Italy are reduced, as spot exchange is transferred to private holders against forward purchases.

The Federal Reserve System has constructed a network of swap or mutual credit agreements with foreign central banks. Any credits drawn under the agreements were limited in time, so that they were less useful to defend the foreign exchange rate than foreign exchange or gold owned outright would have been. However, like the forward contracts, with which they may have many similarities, they serve well as a device for meeting temporary pressure against the currency. It is because they are useful in the short run while more basic adjustment measures are getting under way that they are called perimeter rather than main defenses.

"Roosa" bonds are less a device to meet current pressure than one to relieve potential future strain. Where the excess supply of A's currency is met by B purchasing it, B has a demand claim on A. Such a claim, which may be used to purchase gold, may be funded into a long-term claim, denominated in A's currency. But it may be given additional attractiveness to B by a funding which provides a guarantee of its value in B's currency, against the possibility of a devaluation of A's currency. This device, named after former Undersecretary of the Treasury Robert V. Roosa, has been used extensively with foreign currency bonds issued to the authorities in Austria, Belgium, West Germany, Italy, and Switzerland. In effect, these bonds substituted future liabilities against current ones, much like the swaps or forward contracts.

THE EURODOLLAR MARKET

Thus far we have spoken as though the borderlines between national currencies matched the geographic borders of nations. We have talked of U.S. dollars as though this kind of money were always a liability of a resident of the United States, either a bank liable for a deposit or a government agency promising to redeem the national currency notes. This simplification must be used with increasing care. Ever since the late 1950s there has been an increasing tendency for non-U.S. banks to be willing to owe deposits denominated in U.S. dollars. This has given rise to the term **Eurodollar,** which means any liquid (money) dollar liability of a party outside the United States.

Eurodollars can be created as follows. Suppose that a bank in London acquires dollar deposits on a New York bank because of U.S. purchases of imports from Britain. If the London bank simply holds onto these deposits, no Eurodollars are created. But if it is willing to lend them to somebody else at interest, creating dollar deposit claims against itself, these claims are Eurodollars. They must be repaid with interest in dollars, of course, but as long as they are outstanding dollar deposit claims against a non-U.S. bank, they are Eurodollars. And as we shall see shortly, the London banks even have some limited capacity to create more Eurodollar claims against themselves than the amount of their own dollar deposits in New York.

A major factor which gave rise to the Eurodollar market was Regulation Q of the Federal Reserve System, which fixed the rates of interest paid on time deposits but did not apply to time deposits owned by foreign accounts. Competition among New York banks led returns on such deposits in 1958 and 1959 to rise one fourth of 1 percent above the Regulation Q ceilings. This in turn induced banks in London to bid for dollar deposits, which they in turn relent to New York. Moreover, some depositors, such as the official agencies of the Soviet Union, found it convenient to hold their dollar accounts in Europe, largely London, out of the jurisdiction of U.S. authorities. European lenders and borrowers in dollars also found it convenient to trade in dollars in London, rather than New York, because of the identity of the time zones, without the need to limit trading to the few hours a day when European and U.S. banks were open simultaneously.

Through the 1960s, the Eurodollar market grew rapidly. Currencies other than dollars were traded outside their domestic markets. The major location of the market is London. The depositors consist of European central banks, firms, and individuals and banks, firms, and individuals in the United States and in third countries outside Europe. In the 1970s, the practice of accepting deposits in U.S. dollars and other nonlocal currencies spread to banks in Singapore and Hong Kong. The link between a nation's international transactions and the use of its national currency in world finance has become progressively weaker.

The Euro-currency market poses a number of difficult questions for the international monetary system, which will be dealt with fully only in Chapter 22, but it may be useful to consider some of them here. In the first place, there is a considerable debate over whether the Eurodollar market creates dollars. Those who claim that it does not insist that dollars are created only in the United States. Behind every Eurodollar liability is a Eurodollar bank claim on the United States in dollars. When a European merchant borrows Eurodollars, he can only be paid by the transfer to him of the claim on the United States. The opposition, led by Milton Friedman, insists that Eurodollar banks create money, and primarily dollars, in the same way that ordinary commercial banks do, by making loans which are redeposited in the same banking system. If the first-generation banks (to use the Samuelson textbook phrase) lend to borrowers who spend dollars in the United States, there can be no money creation. But many of those who receive these dollars redeposit them in, say, London in a second-generation bank, which can relend. Initially the resolution of this dispute was found in the thought that very little was redeposited in the Euro-currency market, so that while that market created money, it did so on a modest scale, with modest gearing, like savings and loan associations in the United States. Later, however, it became evident that the dollars were often spent for local currencies in Europe, which meant that they were sold to central banks, which redeposited them in the Eurodollar market. This meant that the expansion rate was higher. In June 1971, however, major European central banks agreed to redeposit dollars in New York, which cut the connection. The Euro-currency market can create money, then, but not much.

Note here that total deposits of the Euro-currency market include interbank deposits, which on the usual definition are not money. Money is currency and demand deposits in the hands of spenders, not banks.

Another issue was whether the Euro-currency market should be regulated. In September 1968 the Federal Reserve Board required U.S. banks to maintain reserves against borrowings from the Euro-currency market in excess of the amounts outstanding on the previous May. This constituted a sort of reserve requirement. In 1970 the Export-Import Bank sold some debentures for dollars in London in an effort to mop up excess dollars in the market. This represented something like open-market operations. In 1966 a number of central banks, including the Swiss National Bank and the Federal Reserve Bank of New York, undertook to deposit more dollars in London at the year-end, to avert a squeeze when banks tried to improve their December 31 statements of condition. This came close to internationally coordinated open-market operations. Despite these rudimentary beginnings, however, the Euro-currency market has not been regulated on the whole, but has constituted a pool of funds available now for lending to

Italy when it suffers a credit squeeze, now to the Unied States in the "crunch" of August 1966. It is of great interest as a market falling outside the jurisdiction and responsibility of any one country, which has behaved flexibly and without undue strain—so far.

SUMMARY

A foreign exchange transaction is a trade of one national money for another at a negotiated exchange rate. The spot foreign exchange market, the market for immediate delivery, allows people either to hedge or to speculate. Hedging is the act of equating one's assets and liabilities in a foreign currency, so as to be immune to risk resulting from future changes in the value of the foreign currency. Speculating means taking a net asset position (a "long" position) or a net liability position (a "short" position) in a foreign currency, thereby gambling on its future exchange value. One can either hedge or speculate in the spot market for foreign exchange.

The forward market, for future delivery at an agreed price, offers an alternative route for both hedgers and speculators. Which route one chooses depends on the difference between the forward and the spot rates of exchange, as well as on interest rates in the two countries' lending markets. The higher a nation's interest rate is relative to that of the rest of the world, the more hedgers and speculators will be tempted to buy that country's currency in the spot market, lend in that country, and sell the country's currency forward.

The spot exchange rate is determined in ways which are affected by exchange-rate institutions. Under the freely flexible exchange-rate system without government intervention, changes in price clear the market. Under the fixed-rate system, officials buy and sell a currency so as to keep its exchange rate within an officially stipulated band. When the currency's value lies at the bottom of its official band, officials must buy it by selling other currencies or gold. When the currency's value presses against the top of its official price range, officials must sell it in exchange for gold or other currencies.

The international currency system is slightly complicated by the existence of Eurodollars and other Euro-currencies, or money liabilities of banks denominated in foreign currencies. The Eurodollar deposit liabilities of non-U.S. banks have grown since the late 1950s under a variety of influences. Although there is some debate over whether the Eurodollar system can create dollars and thus add to the world supply of dollars, the majority position is that it can to a slight extent. It remains unclear whether this slight net expansion of the world supply of dollar money raises the world supply of all money.

SUGGESTED READING

Two good alternative textbook views of the foreign exchange market are Leland B. Yeager, *International Monetary Relations*, 2d ed. (New York: Harper and Row, 1976), chap. 2; and Herbert G. Grubel, *International Economics* (Homewood, Ill.: Richard D. Irwin, 1977), chaps. 10 and 12.

Good descriptions of the internal workings of the foreign exchange market can be found in A. Holmes and F. H. Schott, *The New York Foreign Exchange Market*, 2d ed. (New York: Federal Reserve Bank of New York, 1965); and Robert Z. Aliber, *The International Market for Foreign Exchange* (New York: Praeger, 1969). On exchange risks, see B. A. Lietaer, *Financial Management of Foreign Exchange* (Cambridge, Mass.: MIT Press, 1971).

Many speculators lose. For the real-life tale of a loser who lost more money than he had by buying Mexican peso futures just before the sharp peso devaluations of 1976, see "No Mariachi Music, Please: Mr. X Isn't in a Fiesta Mood," *Wall Street Journal*, January 6, 1977, p. 1. If you would like a handy and readable guide to the forward market facilities Mr. X used, write to the International Money Market, Chicago Mercantile Exchange, for *Understanding Futures in Foreign Exchange* and related pamphlets. A technical guide is: D. R. Mandich (ed.), *Foreign Exchange Trading Techniques and Controls* (Washington D.C.: American Bankers Association, 1976).

Paul Erdman, *The Billion Dollar Sure Thing* (New York: Hutchison, 1973), is a tale of speculation gone awry, giving rich detail about foreign exchange markets. It was written in part while its author languished in a Swiss prison on financial charges.

QUESTIONS FOR REVIEW

1. How are hedging and speculation defined? Are you hedging or speculating if you agree to sell a thousand pounds forward and have no other assets or liabilities in sterling?

2. Describe two ways in which a Canadian who knows he will receive £10,000 in London 90 days from now can convert his funds into Canadian dollars 90 days from now. What determines which of these two routes is the cheaper way to move his money?

3. Which of the following is a Eurodollar: *(a)* a dollar deposit held in New York by a London bank, *(b)* a dollar deposit held against a London bank by a New York bank, or *(c)* a promise to repay dollars after 20 years, by a U.S. subsidiary company in France?

Answers:
1. Speculating, since you are "short" in sterling.
3. *b*.

14

The balance-of-payments account

The balance of payments of a country is a systematic record of all economic transactions between the residents of the reporting country and the residents of foreign countries during a given period of time. Such a record may be useful for a variety of reasons, large and small. The major purpose of keeping these records is to inform governmental authorities of the international position of the country and to aid them in reaching decisions on monetary and fiscal policy on the one hand and trade and payments questions on the other.

DEFINITION

The balance of payments of a country is "a systematic record of all economic transactions between the residents of the reporting country and the residents of foreign countries." This seems straightforward enough. But it also raises questions. For example, who is a resident? What is an economic transaction?

Tourists, diplomats, military personnel, temporary migratory workers, and branches of domestic companies are regarded as residents of the countries from which they come, rather than the country where they are. These decisions are arbitrary, but since the rest of the accounting is adjusted to them, that fact makes little difference. Some of these decisions which make sense from one way of looking at the balance of payments make little from another. Thus the Italian balance of payments, adjusted to fit national income categories, treats permanent and temporary migrants entirely differently, although there is

253

very little difference between them (that is, some workers who regard themselves as temporary *ex ante* turn out to be permanent *ex post*, and vice versa). The earnings of permanent workers are part of national income abroad, and all that enters into the balance of payments is their remittances to Italy as a "transfer." The earnings of temporary workers abroad, however, are sales of services which form part of Italian national income and go into the foreign accounts as exports; their local expenditures for room, board, and so on, are imports, and *their* remittances, as an internal Italian transaction, are excluded from the balance of payments. Whichever way it is done makes no difference for the total balance; but the national income approach in this case is the enemy of the foreign exchange budget approach, which would be interested in knowing directly how much is remitted from abroad by emigrants.

ECONOMIC TRANSACTIONS

An economic transaction is an exchange of value, typically an act in which there is transfer of title to an economic good, the rendering of an economic service, or the transfer of title to assets from one party to another. An international economic transaction evidently involves such transfer of title or rendering of service from residents of one country to residents of another country.

Normally an economic transaction will involve a payment and a receipt of money in exchange for the economic good, the service, or the asset. But it need not. In barter, goods are exchanged for goods, and in private compensation, assets against assets. Moreover, some goods are transferred to other ownership as a gift, without expectation of payment. In each case, there is an international economic transaction, and the necessity to make an entry in the balance of payments. But some entires are made where there is no international "transaction" in the sense of an international payment: the foreign subsidiary of an American corporation earns a profit in its foreign operations and reinvests it in the country where it operates, without paying a dividend to the parent company. There are those who insist that this should go into the balance of payments as a credit on current account, receipt of profits, and debit on capital account, new investment, even though no international payment takes place. The usual government practice, however, is to exclude the reinvested earnings of the foreign subsidiaries from both sides of the account. An artificial two-sided entry often arises in connection with the payment of transport costs on imports. Import values are officially recorded with transport and insurance costs included. If the goods were transported by U.S. carriers to the United States, their freight receipts must be reentered as a credit offsetting part of the import value, even though no international transaction took place.

BALANCE-OF-PAYMENTS ACCOUNTING

In theory, the balance of payments is kept in standard double-entry bookkeeping under which each international transaction undertaken by residents of a country results in a debit and a credit of equal size. An export is a credit for the movement of goods; the means of payment for that export would show up as a debit—the new claim on a foreign company, or bank, the purchase of a foreign security (capital outflow), the acquisition of gold, and so on. Conversely, imports (a debit) might be paid for out of an increase in liabilities to foreigners or by reduced claims on foreigners (both recorded as credits). In actuality, the Department of Commerce measures only one side of physical transactions and the net of the changes in assets and liabilities. Where one side of the transaction is caught by the accountants, say a CARE package sent abroad which results in an export but no balancing claim on foreigners, it is necessary to put in a contra item, in this case "donations" (a debit). It is not always possible to have sufficient knowledge of transactions to effect a complete record of international transactions. Some items can only be estimated. Others are carried out by individuals who, unlike bankers, brokers, security dealers, and large corporations, do not report regularly on their foreign operations. The result is that it is necessary, after summing total credits and total debits, to put in an item for "Errors and Omissions" in order to strike a balance between the two sides of the accounts. Where nonrecorded transactions are large and tend to be in one direction, the residual "Errors and Omissions" item may be sizable in comparison with other items in the accounts.

The nature of the resulting account can be seen more clearly with the help of the data and examples in Figure 14.1 through Figure 14.3. Note that each of the *credit* items can be thought of as an *outflow of value*, for which an offsetting inflow of value, or payment, is due this country. This will seem intuitively obvious for the first three credit items in Figure 14.1—exports of goods, sales of military goods to other countries, and exports of services. It may seem less obvious when it comes to the long- and short-term borrowing at the bottom of the credit column. Borrowing is indeed analogous to exporting goods and services. The borrower is selling the foreign lender an IOU, a promise to repay in a later year, much as the exporter is selling a good. The borrowing, like the exporting, is a way of receiving money inflows, since what is borrowed is money in the form of bank deposits that will soon be put to whatever spending use motivated the borrowing.

FIGURE 14.1

The U.S. balance-of-payments account for 1975 (billions of U.S. dollars)

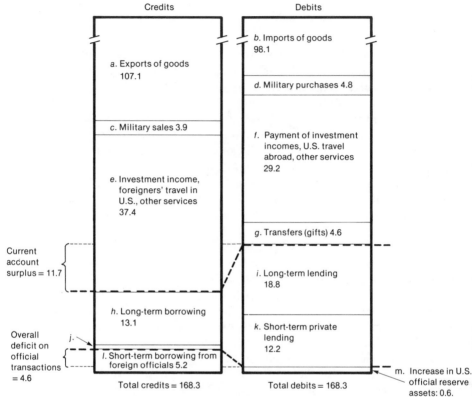

Notes: *h* includes $4.6 billion of net errors and omissions: *j* is short-term borrowing from private foreigners: $0.8 billion.

Source: U.S. Department of Commerce, Bureau of Economic Analysis, *Survey of Current Business*, December 1976, p. 33.

On the other side of the account, each *debit* item can be thought of as an *inflow of value*. Again, the items near the top of the account in Figure 14.1 fit this description easily. Imports of goods, purchases of military support services in West Germany, U.S. tourist expenditures in Mexico, and the like are clearly inflows of value for which residents of the United States must make a payment, probably in money. The entry for unilateral transfers, or gifts, as we have noted, is a fiction necessary to keep the double-entry accounting in balance. Gifts to foreign governments, and to relatives back in the old country, are inflows of value only in the artificial sense that they are inflows of goodwill, or gratitude, or whatever it was that the nation thought it was getting when making a unilateral transfer to foreigners. Like other

FIGURE 14.2
Examples of entries in the U.S. balance of payments

Credits	Debits
Current account	
a. Soybean sales to Japan.	b. Purchases of Arab oil, German
c. Sales of Phantom jets to Israel.	Volkswagens.
e. Interest earned on U.S. loans to	d. Purchases of Korean services for
Mexico; profits on U.S.-owned cop-	U.S. military bases in Korea.
per mines abroad; patent fees for	f. British Petroleum's profits on oil re-
IBM.	fineries in the United States, hotel
	bills of U.S. residents in Acapulco.
	g. U.S. aid grants to India, remittances
	from U.S. immigrants to their
	families abroad.
Capital account	
h. Inflows of Arab purchases of U.S.	i. Outflows of U.S. investments to
hotels, Japanese purchases of Iowa	Canadian mines, refineries in
farmland.	Singapore; new long-term loans to
j. Increase in private foreign holdings	Mexico.
of bank deposits in New York.	k. Increase in U.S. private deposits in
	Swiss banks.
Reserve items	
l. Increase in holdings of New York	m. Net increase in holdings of gold
bank deposits and U.S. Treasury	and bank deposits abroad by U.S.
bills by Bank of Japan and govern-	Treasury and Federal Reserve.
ment of Kuwait.	

debit items, they are to be matched by outpayment of the money or goods or services that are being given to foreigners. Lending, or "capital exports," is properly a debit item like imports of goods and services, since the nation is in effect importing IOUs, or promises to repay after this year. The increase in U.S. official reserve assets is also a debit item like imports, though this may not match one's intuition. Accumulating gold reserves in official vaults is analogous to importing a good even though the gold purchases are typically made possible by a net exporting of goods and services and IOUs. Increasing official foreign exchange reserves, like other forms of inflows of foreigners' IOUs, is an inflow of value and a debit item.

BALANCES WITHIN THE TOTAL

Although total credits must equal total debits by accounting definition, policy questions often call for an analysis of various net balances within the account. We shall distinguish four separate kinds of balances here—the merchandise balance, the current account balance, the liquidity balance (balance on regular transactions), and the overall

FIGURE 14.3
Canada's balance-of-payments account for 1975 (billions of
Canadian dollars)

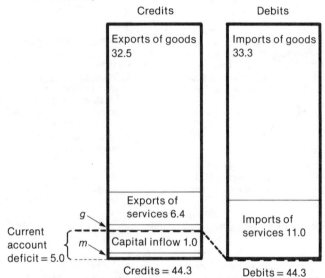

g = Net inflow of gifts (unilateral transfers) to Canada = 0.4.
m = Net reserve loss by Canadian monetary officials = 0.4.
Source: International Monetary Fund, *International Financial Statistics,*
December 1976.

balance (or the balance settled by official transactions, or the official
settlements balance). Each of these amounts to drawing a line through
the accounts, leaving some credit and debit categories "above the
line" and the rest "below the line." In each case, a surplus results if
the credits exceed the debits above the line, with an equal and opposite imbalance below the line. A deficit results if the credits fall short
of the debits above the line.

The merchandise balance

One balance that offers only limited policy insight but is readily
available each month is the net exports of goods, or merchandise,
alone. This balance is struck by measuring only these export and import flows above the line and finding their net balance. Separating
these flows of goods from flows of services is somewhat arbitrary. The
popularity of this balance stems from its availability on a monthly
basis. Customs officials can rapidly collect and report merchandise
trade data, whereas trade in services is measured only with difficulty,

and with a lag, by more complicated questionnaire procedures. Therefore the "trade balance" usually announced in the news media is generally just the merchandise balance. The United States has had merchandise-balance surpluses over most of the 20th century, as it has for 1975 in Figure 14.1. The period 1971–74, however, found U.S. imports greater than exports on merchandise account. Canada, by contrast, has often been a net importer of merchandise, as it was for the year 1975, shown in Figure 14.3.

The current account balance

One of the most important balances to strike within the accounts is the current account balance, shown for the United States and Canada in Figures 14.1 and 14.3, respectively. The current account balance puts above the line all credits and debits representing flows of goods, services, and gifts. It puts below the line all asset flows, both of private capital and of official reserves. The United States typically has had a current account surplus, with credits exceeding debits above the line, as in Figure 14.1 for 1975 (1974 and 1977 were exceptional years of U.S. current account deficit, however). Canada typically has current account deficits in peacetime, with its imports of goods and services exceeding its exports and its receipts of gifts, as shown for 1975 in Figure 14.3.

The meaning of the current account balance can be seen by comparing what is above the line with what is below it. The flows of goods, services, and gifts above the line represent flows of resources that are currently consumed, as a rule (some of the goods and services may in fact be durable assets and not all used up within the year). The capital and reserve flows below the line represent the changes in financial claims (and gold reserves) between us and foreigners. If there is a current account surplus, this means that through a net credit balance regarding goods, services, and gifts, this country is adding to its net foreign wealth. *A current account surplus, in other words, represents a net foreign investment.* A deficit on current account means that by importing more goods, services, and goodwill (on outward gifts), the nation is disinvesting abroad on becoming more of a net international debtor. The United States is usually in the position of a net foreign investor whereas Canada is usually in the position of the net foreign borrower (capital importer), as in 1975. (See Figures 14.1 and 14.3.)

A closer look at how the current account balance relates to the usual national income accounts gives added perspective on what a nation would have to do if it were to have a current account surplus. The closer look consists of noting that there is a key identity relating the national income accounts to the current account in the balance of payments:

$$Y - E = S - I_d = X - M = I_f, \qquad (14.1)$$

where

Y = The current value of this country's net national product,

E = The value of this country's spending—at home, for imports and for goodwill abroad (on outward gifts),

S = The value of this country's saving (increase in net worth),

I_d = The value of this country's domestic capital formation (plant and equipment, new houses, and so on),

$(X - M)$ = The current account balance (exports minus imports and gifts),

I_f = Net foreign investment, or the net increase in claims on foreigners and international reserve assets, such as gold.

All values here are expressed in current prices, and are not adjusted to correct for inflation. To see why the left-hand equality holds, let us subtract something identical from both sides of the expression $Y - E$:

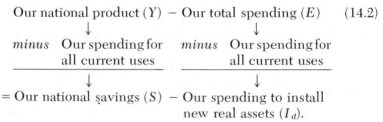

Thus $Y - E = S - I_d$, meaning that it takes a difference between what the nation produces and what it spends for all purposes to make its savings exceed its domestic real capital formation. The link with the balance of payments can be seen by subtracting something different from both parts of the expression $Y - E$:

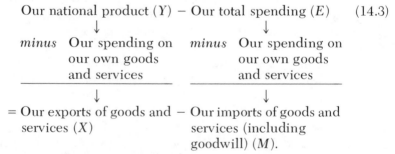

Thus $Y - E = X - M$, which we saw also represented our net foreign investment (I_f). It is easier to see that all these expressions should be the same thing as a nation's net foreign investment if one thinks of the analogy between a nation and a household. For a household, the difference between its income (Y) and its spending for all purposes (E)

naturally equals the value of its savings for the year minus the part of its savings that represents the purchase of home capital goods, such as a new house. Either of these expressions also represents the amount the household accumulates in net financial claims on the outside world (I_f).[1]

This identity will be useful when we come to look at the macroeconomic options for "improving" a nation's external accounts so that the nation has a current account surplus. It is clear that the current account surplus $(X - M)$ cannot be raised without at the same time managing to raise national product relative to national spending $(Y - E)$, and raising the difference between national saving and domestic investment $(S - I_d)$. If, for example, one were to hear a proposal that some policies would improve the current account of the balance of payments (for example, with higher tariffs against imports) without raising prices or affecting national output or spending, thus leaving $Y - E$ the same, one should be skeptical: the proposal could not have that set of effects without violating a fundamental accounting identity.

The liquidity balance

Since World War I, governments and central banks have become increasingly concerned about defending their fixed exchange rates against the onslaught of foreigners who might stampede to sell liquid claims in their currency in exchange for reserve assets in time of currency crisis. This concern over currency defense led to the view that a country should closely monitor the accumulation of liquid foreign claims against itself, lest these exceed its reserves and set the stage for a speculative attack on the country's currency and the reserves backing it up.

Worries about defending the dollar apparently led the U.S. Department of Commerce to focus on its liquidity balance, which is defined as follows:

$$\begin{matrix} \text{Liquidity balance} \\ \text{surplus} \end{matrix} = \begin{matrix} \text{Net accumulation of} \\ \text{official U.S. reserves} \end{matrix} + \begin{matrix} \text{Net decrease in liquid} \\ \text{U.S. liabilities to} \\ \text{private and official} \\ \text{foreigners,} \end{matrix}$$

or

$$\begin{matrix} \text{Liquidity balance} \\ \text{deficit} \end{matrix} = \begin{matrix} \text{Net decrease in} \\ \text{official U.S. reserves} \end{matrix} + \begin{matrix} \text{Net increase in liquid} \\ \text{U.S. liabilities to} \\ \text{private and official} \\ \text{foreigners.} \end{matrix}$$

---

[1] As for the equality $Y - E = X - M$ at the household level, this also follows. If Y and E are defined as sales and purchases of product (for example, the family's labor earnings are Y) with the outside world only, then $Y = X$ and $E = M$, and the equality holds.

The liquidity balance is being defined here by the flows falling below the line drawn through the balance-of-payments accounts when striking the liquidity balance. In Figure 14.1, the U.S. liquidity deficit was $5.4 billion for 1975, the net value of items $j + l - m$. It could also be defined as the net balance on all items above the line (items a through i and k in Figure 14.1), but that would be a more cumbersome way of reaching the same result. It is easier to focus only on reserves and liquid (or, roughly, short-term) liabilities, such as foreign bank deposits in New York, which are readily redeemable in exchange for reserves.

The purpose of the liquidity balance has been to focus on the danger that foreign claims on the country might mount to a point where the country would be unable to meet them if they were suddenly presented for payment. Concern is really with the stock position, that is, the balance of indebtedness discussed below, rather than the balance of payments, which is a flow concept.

Note the sharp asymmetry in the treatment of domestic and foreign short-term capital. This was justified by the Department of Commerce on the ground that the United States cannot be certain of being able to liquidate its claims on foreigners, whereas it must be in a position to make good if foreigners decide to liquidate their claims on the United States. U.S. short-term claims on the rest of the world were treated as unavailable; foreign claims on the United States were regarded as liable to be presented *in toto* at any instant in time.

The notion that the liquidity balance measures changes in the danger of being able to meet a nation's external obligations can be criticized. Perhaps one of the greatest threats in times of currency crisis or payments crisis comes from assets whose buildup is totally missed by the balance-of-payments account: the holding of liquid claims on this country by its own residents. If, for example, there were an attack on the dollar and/or a fear that the United States might soon have to restrict its payments to foreigners, U.S. residents might feel a strong incentive to sell their dollar bank deposits in exchange for assets in other countries and other currencies before the dollar is devalued or before the officials put restrictions on their ability to buy and invest abroad. There is no easy way to quantify the magnitude of this threat of the flight of domestic capital. It cannot be measured at all by the balance-of-payments account, which keeps no record of the growth of strictly domestic liquid claims.

There is also reason to question the "disloyalty" of foreign liquid claims on this country, especially if this country is a reserve center like the United States. It is possible to argue that some part of the accumulation of dollar claims in foreign hands was the result of the willingness of foreigners to hold dollars themselves rather than cash them in for goods and services. Claims against the United States may be so useful as liquid assets for use in international trade that many holders in other countries would just as soon hang on to them even during a crisis of confidence in the United States or its dollar. If so, the measured liquidity deficit might overstate the accumulation of threats against the dollar and the United States.

The overall balance (official settlements balance)

In the mid-1960s a special committee appointed by the U.S. Bureau of the Budget to review balance-of-payments statistics, under the chairmanship of Edward M. Bernstein, picked up this last criticism of the Commerce Department's liquidity balance, and proposed a new kind of overall balance. The Bernstein committee report urged removing the increase in private foreigners' liquid claims on the United States from the (below-the-line) measure of the U.S. deficit, on the argument that the growth of private liquid claims on the United States was less symptomatic of a deficit position for the United States than was any growth in foreign officials' liquid claims. The Department of Commerce accepted this argument and began to publish, alongside the liquidity balance, the overall balance (or official settlements balance, or balance on official transactions) as defined by the Bernstein report:

$$\text{Overall surplus} = \frac{\text{Net increase in official}}{\text{U.S. reserves}} + \frac{\text{Net decrease in liquid}}{\text{U.S. liabilities to}}_{\text{official foreigners,}}$$

or

$$\text{Overall deficit} = \frac{\text{Net decrease in official}}{\text{U.S. reserves}} + \frac{\text{Net increase in liquid}}{\text{U.S. liabilities to}}_{\text{official foreigners.}}$$

The overall balance, like the liquidity balance, is defined here by the flows falling below the line drawn through the account. The lower dashed line in Figure 14.1 demarcates the U.S. overall balance in 1975. In that year, the United States sustained an overall-balance deficit of $4.6 billion, since $5.2 billion was added to foreign official liquid claims on the United States, while U.S. official reserves grew by only $0.6 billion.

The motivation for the overall balance is the same as that for the liquidity balance: the search for a measure of the task facing officials wanting to defend the dollar and the United States against a financial attack. It is also subject to the same criticisms, since it cannot really measure the degree of threat of a crisis of confidence in either the country or the currency. It also seems to draw too sharp a distinction between private and official short-term capital movements. Finally, both the liquidity balance and the overall balance only get close to, but fail to match, another useful concept, which is the net balance of money flows between countries. Since money consists of bank deposit liabilities and reserve assets, a net balance of money flows should have placed below the line those international flows that are linked specifically to deposit liabilities of banks, which neither the liquidity nor the overall balance distinguishes.

BANKERS' DEFICITS

In the process of trying to agree on a best measure of the balance-of-payments deficits of the United States in the deficit years after 1958, economists came to notice and emphasize a basic point about the external payments position of a nation or a region or an institution that performs financial services by lending long-term and creating short-term deposit liabilities against itself: bankers are likely to run deficits in a growing economy. This is true of an ordinary bank within a national economy. As the economy grows, all items on the bank's balance sheet also grow—its reserves, its deposit liabilities, and its loans and investments. If its deposit liabilities remain a steady multiple of its reserves, as is normal, then each year its deposits grow by a faster absolute value than its reserves. If one strikes a balance-of-payments account for the bank itself, it turns out that the bank has overall deficits year after year. Yet few depositors view this as a symptom of growing crisis, even in a banking system lacking federal government deposit insurance.

What is true of an ordinary bank is also true in varying degrees of regions and nations that perform the banking function. New York City and London, as financial centers, probably have run payments deficits in times of growth (even without the budget deficits of the New York City government). Before 1914, Britain, as the financial center of a growing world economy, ran liquidity and overall deficits simply because its liquid liabilities, a multiple of its reserves, grew faster in absolute value than its reserves. Yet this fact was not publicized at the time. It may be that the absence of official measures of the balance-of-payments deficit before 1914 helped the world to keep a relaxed attitude about Britain's external position. There may be some truth in the 1965 statement by the British chancellor of the exchequer, James Callaghan (later prime minister), that Britain "had no balance-of-payments problems because we had no balance-of-payments statistics." To a large extent, the prevailing deficits of the United States after 1958 can be viewed in the same perspective. As the nation that lent long-term to the rest of the world, while allowing its liquid money liabilities to grow as well, the United States as world banker ran bankers' deficits. In each case it is not clear that the faster accumulation of liquid liabilities than of reserves is a sign of trouble. If there was a sign of trouble, it might have been more easily discerned by noting that between 1958 and the early 1970s the United States was losing gold and total reserves. Little in the way of concrete clues was added by noting the growth of liquid liabilities to foreigners, which could be interpreted as being as much a sign of foreign willingness to hold dollars as a sign of future unloading of dollars.

The line of argument has forced a retreat from the emphasis on liquidity and overall balances in the 1970s. The Department of Commerce now presents the balance-of-payments account in a more neutral way, advertising neither the liquidity balance nor the overall balance in its main tables. Although policymakers may still be mindful of their own calculations of liquidity and overall balances, the balance now most prominently displayed is the current account balance, which measures a nation's net foreign investment.

THE INTERNATIONAL INVESTMENT POSITION

The financial relationship of a nation to the rest of the world can be further illuminated by an accounting of its international investment position, or its "balance of international indebtedness," which measures a nation's foreign assets and liabilities at a point in time. Table 14.1 gives the international investment position of the· United States. This gives the stocks for which the capital account and reserve items on the lower half of the balance-of-payments account give the flows. The points just made about the payments position of a banker show up clearly in Table 14.1. The United States has had rising liquid (here, short-term) liabilities which have come to be a multiple of U.S. official reserves. Yet the United States has such extensive longer-term, less liquid, assets abroad that the nation is a heavy net creditor to the rest of the world overall. This is another way of discovering a point implicit in Figure 14.1 above: by running current account surpluses and having liquid liabilities grow faster than liquid assets, the United States is acting as a financial intermediary, lending long and borrowing short, with ever-positive net foreign investment.

NATIONS AND CURRENCIES

A final twist to the problem of interpreting summary balances in the balance-of-payments account was provided by the switch to a generalized floating of major exchange rates in 1971. Officials are now

TABLE 14.1
**International investment position for the United States at the end of selected years,
1897–1975 (billions of dollars)**

	1897	1914	1930	1939	1946	1960	1975
U.S. investments abroad	0.7	3.5	17.2	11.4	18.7	66.2	287.9
Private	0.7	3.5	17.2	11.4	13.5	49.3	246.1
Long-term	0.7	3.5	15.2	10.8	12.3	44.5	182.8
Direct	0.6	2.6	8.0	7.0	7.2	31.9	133.2
Portfolio	0.1	0.9	7.2	3.8	5.1	12.7	50.6
Short-term	—	—	2.0	0.6	1.3	4.8	62.3
U.S. government	0.0	—	—	—	5.2	16.9	41.8
Long-term	0.0	—	—	—	5.0	14.0	39.8
Short-term	0.0	—	—	—	0.2	2.9	2.0
U.S. official reserve assets*	0.6	1.5	4.3	17.8	20.7	19.4	16.2
Foreign investments in							
United States	3.4	7.2	8.4	9.6	15.9	40.9	210.5
Long-term	3.1	6.7	5.7	6.3	7.0	19.2	94.5
Direct	—	1.3	1.4	2.0	2.5	6.9	26.7
Portfolio	—	5.4	4.3	4.3	4.5	11.6	67.8
Short-term†	0.3	0.5	2.7	3.3	8.9	21.6	116.0
U.S. net creditor							
position (excl. reserves)....	−2.7	−3.7	8.8	1.8	2.8	25.3	77.4
Net long-term	−2.4	−3.2	9.5	4.5	10.3	39.3	129.1
Net short-term	−0.3	−0.5	− 0.7	− 2.7	− 7.4	−14.0	− 51.7

* U.S. official reserve assets consist of gold and foreign exchange reserves plus IMF credit tranches and special drawing rights.
† Includes U.S. government securities.
Sources: U.S. Bureau of the Census, *Historical Statistics of the United States: Colonial Times to 1970* (Washington, D.C.: Government Printing Office, 1976); and U.S. Bureau of Economic Analysis, *Survey of Current Business,* August 1976.

under less pressure to stabilize exchange rates, a change that has helped them de-emphasize the balance of payments. At the same time, the spread of the Eurodollar and other nonresident currencies around the globe has weakened the link between a nation's external transactions and the exchange value of its currency. These developments have turned attention away from the overall balance-of-payments surplus or deficit toward the foreign exchange markets. Although this is probably a healthy change, the balance-of-payments account still relates to the strength of a nation's currency. It is still true, if only roughly true, that such traditional concepts as the trade balance or the current account balance between a country and the rest of the world are prime determinants of the strength of that country's currency in foreign exchange markets. The study of what makes a national currency rise or fall in market value is still largely a study of how the trade and current balances respond to changing conditions.

SUMMARY

The balance of payments of a country is a systematic record of all economic transactions between the residents of the reporting country and the residents of all foreign countries. Certain problems must be settled in determining who is a resident and what is a transaction. But any consistent scheme of reporting is adequate for the purpose, so long as it is organized in such a way as to serve the uses to which it is put. The most important use of the balance of payments of most countries is to describe in a concise fashion the state of the international economic relationships of the country as a guide to monetary, fiscal, exchange, and other policies. The balance of payments was originally estimated to reveal the sources and uses of foreign exchange and then was thought of in terms of the contribution, positive or negative, of international transactions to domestic income determination. At the current time in the United States, interest is reverting to foreign exchange.

Although total credits must equal total debits in the balance of payments, it is often useful to draw lines through the accounts dividing some flows above the line from others below it. Doing so leaves a net surplus or deficit of credits above the dividing line. One such procedure is the measurement of the merchandise balance, the "trade balance" often cited in the press, which is the net export surplus of goods alone. The second, and most durable, balance within the accounts is the current account balance, which divides all flows of goods and services and gifts above the line from all capital and reserve flows below the line. The current account surplus equals the nation's net foreign investment (inclusive of reserve accumulation), which can also be shown to equal the gap between national product and national spending. Two other balances with the account focus on the problem of defending a nation's currency and its ability to repay obligations. One is the liquidity balance, the other the overall balance. Both compare reserve accumulation with the growth of liquid liabilities to foreigners.

There is a tendency for financial centers to run what look like deficits on the liquidity and overall balances while at the same time lending out enough on long term to raise their net foreign assets. These net foreign investments lead to a more positive international investment position, a rising net stock of foreign assets.

SUGGESTED READING

For an alternative textbook treatment, see Herbert B. Grubel, *International Economics* (Homewood, Ill.: Richard D. Irwin, 1977), chap. 13.

The balance-of-payments accounts of most nations are summarized in the IMF's *International Financial Statistics* and also in the *Balance of Payments*

Yearbook. More detailed accounts for the United States appear regularly in the *Survey of Current Business,* while those for Canada are in the *Canada Yearbook.*

Three studies of the meaning of the account and its various balances are: Review Committee for Balance of Payments Statistics, Burea of the Budget, *The Balance of Payments Statistics of the United States* (Washington, D.C.: Government Printing Office, 1965); Charles P. Kindleberger, "Balance-of-Payments Deficits and the International Market for Liquidity," *Princeton Essays in International Finance,* May 1965; and Donald S. Kemp, "Balance-of-Payments Concepts—What Do They Really Mean?" Federal Reserve Bank of St. Louis, *Review,* July 1975.

QUESTIONS FOR REVIEW

1. Which of the following transactions would contribute to a U.S. current account surplus on the balance of payments?

a. Boeing barters a $100,000 plane to Yugoslavia in exchange for $100,000 worth of hotel services on the Yugoslav coast.

b. The United States borrows $100,000 long term from Saudi Arabia to buy $100,000 of Saudi oil this year.

c. The United States sells a $100,000 jet to Libya for $100,000 in bank deposits.

d. The U.S. government makes a gift of $100,000 to the Israeli government, in the form of New York bank deposits, to pay for injuries caused by Libyan jet attacks.

e. The U.S. government sells $100,000 in long-term Roosa bonds to West Germany, getting bank deposits in West Germany and promising to repay in five years.

2. Which of the above transactions contributed to a U.S. deficit in the overall (official settlements) balance?

Answers:

1. *c.*

2. *d.*

15

The role of price in
international adjustment

A PREVIEW OF POLICY ISSUES

The world of international finance presents governments and central banks with a complex set of policy problems not encountered on the domestic front. The central policy problem is the task of deciding how a nation should regulate the exchange rates between its currency and those of other nations. It is this question of how exchange rates should work that has guided economists' exploration of how they actually work, just as the question of how trade policy should be run has guided the exploration of how trade actually works in Part I above. The rest of Part III's analysis of what happens when exchange rates and international payments flows are being adjusted has been shaped by the desire to resolve the adjustment policy issues of Part IV.

The policy debate over how exchange rates should be managed and how international payments should be adjusted has focused on these policy options of a country facing a payments deficit and reserve losses:

1. Financing—if the imbalance is known to be temporary, the nation can simply draw down its reserves for a while and maintain the same exchange rate.
2. The floating rate—the nation can let the exchange market take care of the exchange rate, by letting the value of its currency drop until exchange-market equilibrium is restored.
3. Exchange controls—the nation can keep the external value of its currency fixed by rationing the ability of its residents to acquire foreign exchange for spending abroad.

4. Adjusting the economy to the exchange rate (or "classical medicine")—deflating the domestic economy, lowering prices and incomes so that the supply and demand for foreign exchange will be pulled into equality at the same fixed exchange rate.
5. The adjustable peg (or the Bretton Woods system)—the nation can follow prescription 4 if small doses of domestic adjustment will suffice to defend the fixed exchange rate, or it can devalue its currency and peg it at a new official exchange rate if defending the old fixed rate required too much domestic adjustment.

This range of policy choices facing a country in a weak payments position, or the symmetrically opposite set of choices facing a country in a surplus position, can be resolved only after several questions about how international adjustment really works have been cleared up in this and the following chapters.

Most of the present chapter is organized around one of the questions about the actual effects of international adjustment: the question of what happens to the balance between demand and supply of foreign exchange if a country changes its exchange rate. A related issue, considered here as well, is how changing the exchange rate affects relative prices and relative incomes of different groups within the country.

THE SPECTER OF UNSTABLE EXCHANGE MARKETS

In most markets, one presumes that raising the price of the good or service or asset will tend to raise the quantity supplied relative to the quantity demanded. It is also common to presume that if the quantity supplied exceeds the quantity demanded, the price will tend to fall. Such presumptions amount to assuming that the market is stable, in the sense that any momentary displacement from equilibrium between demand and supply will act to restore equilibrium and make further price movements unnecessary until there is some change in underlying conditions of demand or supply or both.

Is the market for foreign exchange a stable one? If not, serious damage could result. Figure 15.1 sketches two ways in which exchange markets could yield an unstable result, each of which implies some social costs. Figure 15.1A shows a case of unstable equilibrium in the market for foreign currencies, here aggregated into one currency, the pound sterling. The equilibrium between demand and supply at Point A is unstable in the sense that a small displacement from the equilibrium price of $1.50 causes a cumulative movement away from equilibrium. A momentary market quote of $1.52 finds a greater quantity demanded than supplied. If an imbalance in this direction leads to a rise in price, then the rise will continue until a stable equi-

FIGURE 15.1
The possibility of unstable exchange markets, portrayed in two ways

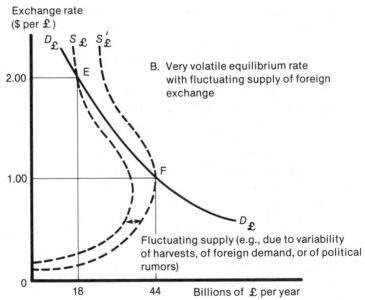

Exchange rate
($ per £)

A. An unstable equilibrium
   (point A)

Billions of £ per year

Exchange rate
($ per £)

B. Very volatile equilibrium rate
   with fluctuating supply of foreign
   exchange

Fluctuating supply (e.g., due to variability
of harvests, of foreign demand, or of political
rumors)

Billions of £ per year

librium is reached at $1.80 at Point B. Similarly, a momentary quote of
$1.48 sends the system spiraling down to $1.20 at Point C.

The sensitivity and unpredictability of movements from $1.50 in
Figure 15.1A is based on the backward slope and curvature of the
supply curve for foreign exchange. This slope and shape are not as
implausible as the analogy with ordinary markets might suggest. They
follow, first, from ordinary linearity in the demand and supply curves
for imports and exports, as an example will show below. Furthermore,
there are at least two economic reasons why such sensitivity could
occur. The first is that the trade balance could behave in a way which
magnifies exchange-rate movements like that from A to B. For example, if real quantities of exports and imports are unaffected by a rise in
the exchange rate above $1.50, raising the price of foreign exchange
could merely magnify an imbalance of demand over supply, as we
shall see. The other possible reason for such instability is that speculation might take any small rise in the exchange rate as a sign that further
increases are ahead. This kind of speculative behavior can be self-
fulfilling, driving the rate much higher, such as from a point just above
A all the way up to B in Figure 15.1A.

By itself, the instability of the equilibrium at Point A does not
suggest major damage, since such states are very temporary and would
quickly yield to stable equilibriums, such as those at Points B and C. If
this were all, one could retain the conclusion that the exchange market
is essentially stable. Yet the same possible shape of the supply curve
sets up a more serious kind of instability. If either the demand curve or
the supply curve fluctuates in its position, wide swings in the exchange rate could result. Such a possibility is shown in Figure 15.1B.
In this case, it is the supply curve that fluctuates, though demand-
curve movements could yield the same result. Given the way in which
the curves are sloped, it does not take much change in underlying
conditions (for example, crop failures or bumper crops in an agricultural export crop, or volatile foreign demand for the country's export
goods) to send the exchange rate oscillating between one equilibrium
at $2 and another at $1.

The welfare cost of such wide swings in the exchange rate can be
seen in any of several ways. Intuition suggests that wide swings in any
price complicate business planning, especially when the swings are
hard to forecast. Static welfare analysis agrees. In the context of
stabilizing commodity prices, Appendix F shows that avoiding wide
price swings in response to swings in supply or demand can bring the
world net savings. This point can apply to an exchange market as well
as a commodity market. Its identification of costs from wide price
swings is a more reliable point, though, than its prescription that officials can intervene by buying foreign exchange in some periods and

selling it in others to stabilize the price. If the equilibrium position is hard to predict accurately, officials may be very unlucky in trying to find some middling exchange rate (for example, between $1 and $2 here) at which they can stabilize the exchange market indefinitely without running out of reserves or accumulating cumbersome amounts of foreign exchange reserves.

A final clue to the social costliness of wide swings in the exchange rate, or any other asset price, can be drawn from the experience with Wall Street between 1927 and 1933. The stock market behaved in a way that can only be described as unstable. First speculators convinced themselves, on little evidence other than their own short-run behavior, that common stock prices on the New York Stock Exchange would soar indefinitely. They bid stock prices up far beyond what the trend in real business profits warranted, following the familiar pattern of being cumulatively reinforced by their own buying frenzy into believing that prices would keep rising. Once the bubble burst, in 1929, as it had to sooner or later, their pessimism became as cumulative and self-fulfilling as their previous optimism. And by the time the bottom was hit around 1933, there was no equilibrating mechanism left to bring stock values promptly back up to the level of, say, 1927 or 1929. The speculative excesses themselves had so beclouded all business moods that nobody could be tempted into believing that stocks or the real economy would recover soon.

It is essential to judge the likelihood that the foreign exchange market could yield this unstable and damaging result. Whether a nation's foreign exchange markets prove unstable depends on the real trade position of the nation and also on the decisions of all sorts of firms and individuals regarding what speculative positions to take. The issue is complex, especially because we lack an established model of the decision to speculate. There is one important guideline that can be offered, however: since trade in goods and services makes up the largest part of the transactions passing through the foreign exchange markets, if there is a source of stability peculiar to foreign exchange markets, it must lie in trade responses to exchange-rate changes. Speculators will have reason to believe that the exchange markets are stable *if* a rise in the cost of foreign exchange makes traders have a greater excess supply of it. If this condition holds, then a devaluation of a currency will be followed by the news that the devaluing country's trade balance is improving. Such news would help convince speculators to bet on a rise in the value of that currency. Conversely, if the trade balance reacts to a devaluation by worsening, yielding an even greater excess supply of the nation's currency, the speculators would have stronger reason to panic and rush to abandon the currency, accelerating its decline in the process. If we are to believe that an exchange market is likely to be stable, then we should be able to argue that devaluing improves the trade balance and thereby helps the nation's foreign exchange earnings (supply) catch up with its demand for foreign exchange.

LINKING THE FOREIGN EXCHANGE MARKET TO EXPORT AND IMPORT MARKETS

The first step toward resolving the question of whether foreign exchange markets are likely to be stable is to show how trade patterns affect the demand and supply of foreign exchange at each given exchange rate. To do so, we shall simplify by lumping all foreign countries into one, whose currency is the pound sterling. Using the United States as our example of a home country, we shall be assuming that exchange rates among all other currencies—the Canadian dollar, the British pound sterling, the West German mark, the Japanese yen, and others—are fixed. We shall also simplify by aggregating all exports into one good, such as the wheat of our trade examples in Part I, and all imports into one good, cloth. Capital movements and gifts shall be assumed to have a constant net balance of zero, and we shall refer to the net supply of foreign exchange arising from all flows of goods and services as simply the "trade balance."

Figure 15.2 and Table 15.1 show how the market for imports gives rise to the commercial demand for foreign exchange, how exports generate the supply of foreign exchange, and how changing the exchange rate affects all markets. To see the links, let us begin by focusing on the market for U.S. imports, here represented by the single commodity cloth. Figure 15.2A portrays this market, where the import demand curve is the net result of the undrawn domestic cloth demand and cloth supply curves. At the initial exchange rate of $1.50 = £1, the United States is importing 120 billion yards of cloth a year at the price of £1.00 or $1.50 a yard, at Point A. To make these purchases possible, £120 billion of sterling must be bought in foreign exchange markets by selling dollars, since this amount is the value (price × quantity) spent on imports.

The key to seeing how a change in the exchange rate would disturb this import market is to see that the demanders and suppliers in the import market are interested in different currencies. The demanders care about the dollar prices of imports, which they weigh against the dollar prices of other goods and services within the United States. The foreign suppliers of imports into the United States care about the prices they receive in terms of other currencies, here represented by the pound sterling. A change in the exchange rate has very different

FIGURE 15.2
Deriving the commercial demand and supply of foreign exchange from the import and export markets

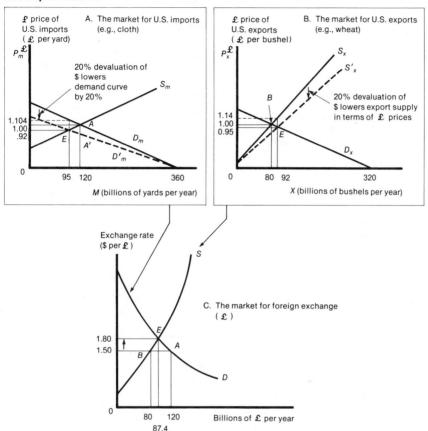

effects on these two groups. A 20 percent devaluation (or depreciation[1]) of the dollar, raising the price of the pound sterling from, say, $1.50 to $1.80, would make imports look more expensive in terms of dollars unless foreign suppliers were to drop the sterling prices of U.S. import goods and services by the full 20 percent. The foreign suppliers, on the other hand, would tend to see a lower pound price on their sales to the United States unless the dollar prices were raised by the full 20 percent.

---

[1] The term *devaluation* refers to an official act of lowering the pegged par value of the nation's currency in terms of other currencies and/or an international reserve asset, such as gold. *Depreciation* refers to a drop in the value of the nation's currency in exchange markets.

TABLE 15.1

Deriving the commercial demand and supply of foreign exchange from the import and export markets

	Before the 20 percent devaluation of the dollar (with £1 = $1.50)	After the 20 percent devaluation of the dollar (with £1 = $1.80)
Import market (Dollar price of cloth imports, or $P_m^\$$, in $ per yard)	($1.50)	($1.656)
Pound price of cloth imports, or $P_m^\pounds$, in £ per yard	£1.00 ×	£0.92 ×
Quantity of imports, M (billions of yard per year)	120 =	95 =
Demand for pounds (billions of £ per year)	120	87.4
Export market (Dollar price of wheat exports, or $P_x^\$$, in $ per yard)	($1.50)	($1.71)
Pound price of wheat exports, or $P_x^\pounds$, in £ per yard	£1.00 ×	£0.95 ×
Quantity of exports, X (billions of bushels per year)	80 =	92 =
Supply of pounds (billions of £ per year)	80	87.4
Excess demand for foreign exchange = trade balance deficit (billions of £ per year)	40	0

The way in which one portrays geometrically the effect of an exchange-rate change on import supply and demand depends on the currency in which prices are being graphed. One can plot either dollar prices or pound prices. If the diagram uses dollar prices, a change in the exchange rate changes the import supply curve of the foreign suppliers, because their attitudes toward any given pound price will look like a changing willingness to supply imports as a function of dollar prices. We shall use the other kind of diagram here. That is, we shall hereafter follow what happens to prices of imports (and exports) in the *foreign* currency, since we seek to link import and export markets with a market for the foreign currency. This convention makes no difference to the results, and one can confirm that all the results below come out the same as they would if dollar-price diagrams had been used throughout.

Figure 15.2A plots demand and supply behavior as relationships between pound prices and real quantities. Therefore, if the dollar is devalued by 20 percent, this must be portrayed as a change in the U.S. demand for imports, not a shift in the foreign supply of imports. Demanders are watching dollar prices, and so the devaluation makes them willing to go on buying each given amount of imports (cloth) only if the pound price is 20 percent lower, allowing the dollar price to look the same to them. Table 15.1 reinforces this point by showing both the dollar and the pound prices of cloth before and after the devaluation. Importers who had willingly bought 120 billion yards of foreign cloth at $1.50 (£1.00) a yard before the devaluation would go on doing so after it only if the dollar price remained at $1.50, or now only £0.833 (1.50/1.80), per yard after the devaluation (at Point A'). Yet this downward shift in the demand curve is not likely to leave us at a point like Point A'. In the typical cases, foreign suppliers will not put up with selling the same amounts at a pound price 20 percent lower. They will cut back somewhat on their exports to the United States, moving down their supply curve, and the new equilibrium at Point E is likely to involve lower imports and a compromise on price. The most likely price result finds the pound price somewhat lower and the dollar price somewhat higher, with neither changing by as much as 20 percent, as illustrated in Table 15.1.

By cutting both the quantity and the pound price of imports, the devaluation of the dollar has cut the value of foreign exchange demanded by persons wishing to import cloth into the United States, from 120 billion (= 120 billion yards times £1.00 per yard) down to £87.4 billion (= 95 billion yards times £0.92 per yard). This change in the demand for pounds is shown in Figure 15.2C as a shift from Point A to Point E in the foreign exchange market.

Similar reasoning lies behind the portrayal of how devaluation affects the export market, in Figure 15.2B. Since we are looking at pound prices, it is the behavior of U.S. export suppliers, such as wheat dealers, that seems to change when viewed in the foreign currency. U.S. grain dealers and other exporters would be willing to go on selling any given amount abroad, such as 80 billion bushels a year, as long as the dollar price looked the same. This means that they are willing to supply 80 billion bushels at a pound price that is 20 percent lower. Their willingness to do so will lead to some price competition and to an expansion of exports out to Point E, with a final pound price that is likely to be somewhat lower than the predevaluation price, as shown by the drop from 1.00 to 0.95 in Figure 15.2B. The movements from B to E in Figure 15.2B's view of the export market translate in Figure 15.2C into a movement from B to E in the foreign exchange market. As drawn here, it happens that the 20 percent devaluation was just sufficient to erase the deficit on the balance of goods and services. What amount of devaluation would do that in practice is an empirical question requiring careful estimation.

DOES DEVALUATION IMPROVE THE TRADE BALANCE?

It isn't obvious

In Figure 15.2 devaluing the dollar had the effect of closing the gap between the value of imports and the value of exports, and reducing the net excess demand for the foreign currency. It is not obvious that devaluation will have this effect. To see why the effects of devaluation on the balance of trade in goods and services (and gifts) are hard to resolve without further information, consider the likely directions of change in trade prices and quantities when a country devalues:

$$TB \text{ (the current account balance, measured in } \text{£/year)} = P_x^{£} \cdot X - P_m^{£} \cdot M$$

	£ price of exports	Quantity of exports		£ price of imports	Quantity of imports
	↓	↑	−	↓	↓
Effects of a devaluation of the dollar: =	No change or *down*	No change or *up*		No change or *down*	No change or *down*

As indicated in shorthand here, a dollar devaluation is likely to lower the pound price of exports if it has any net effect on this price. This is because, as shown in Figure 15.2B, U.S. exporters are to some extent willing to accept lower pound prices because the dollar prices still look higher. If there is any effect of this price twist on export quantities, the change would be upward, as foreign buyers take advantage of any lower pound prices of U.S. exports to buy more from the United States. It is already clear that the net effect of devaluation on export value is of uncertain sign, since pound prices probably drop and quantities exported probably rise. On the import side, any changes in either pound price or quantity are likely to be downward. The devaluation is likely to make dollar prices of imports look a bit higher, causing a drop in import quantities as buyers shift toward U.S. substitutes for imports. If this drop in demand has any effect on the pound price of imports, that effect is likely to be negative, as in Figure 15.2A. The sterling value of imports thus clearly drops, but if this value is to be subtracted from an export value that could rise or fall, it is still not clear whether the net trade balance rises or falls. We need to know more about the underlying elasticities of demand and supply in both the export and import markets.

Four important cases

Economists have derived a general formula for the net effect of a devaluation on the trade balance. Although we feel that this general formula is extremely valuable, it is also complicated and difficult to derive or memorize. The real-world likelihood of a "stabilizing" result, in which devaluing improves the trade balance as intended, is better judged by first looking at some important special cases, cases having varying degrees of realism. By studying these cases, one can grasp the logic behind a formula that may be hard to interpret by itself.

Case 1: Inelastic demands. Suppose that buyers' habits are rigidly fixed, so that they will not change the amounts they buy from any nation's suppliers despite changes in price. Examples might be the dependence of a non-tobacco-producing country on tobacco imports, or a similar addiction to tea or coffee or petroleum for fuels. In such cases of perfectly inelastic demand, devaluation of the country's currency backfires completely. This is shown in Figure 15.3. Given the

FIGURE 15.3
Devaluation and the trade balance—Case 1: Inelastic demands

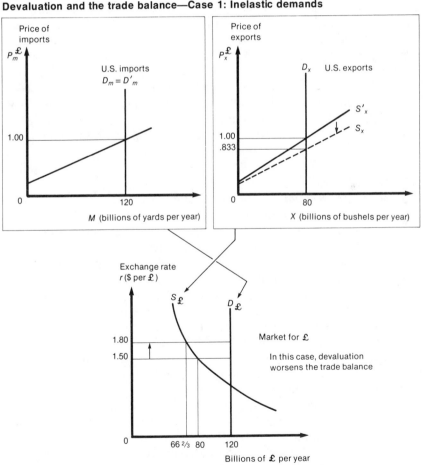

perfect inelasticity of import demand, no signals are sent to foreign suppliers by devaluing the dollar. Buyers go on buying the same amount of imports at the same pound price, paying a higher dollar price without cutting back their imports. No change in the foreign exchange value of imports results. On the export side, the devaluation leads suppliers to end up with the same competitive dollar price as before, but this price equals fewer pounds. U.S. exporters get fewer pounds for each bushel of wheat they export, yet foreigners do not respond to the lower price by buying any more wheat than they would otherwise. Thus the United States merely ends up earning less foreign exchange, and the deficiency of foreign exchange earnings becomes even more severe as a result of the ill-advised devaluation.

This is a strange and extreme result, though it is not impossible. It is strange because it implies that we make it harder for ourselves to buy foreign cloth with each bushel of wheat we export ($P_x^£/P_m^£$ drops), yet this impoverishing effect fails to get us to cut our spending on imports. The result looks even stranger upside down: Case 1 implies that a country could succeed in cutting its trade deficit and at the same time buy imports more cheaply (in terms of the export good) by cleverly *revaluing* its currency (for example, raising the purchasing power of the dollar from $1.50/ £ to $1.20/ £). If that were a common occurrence, governments would have discovered it long ago, and would have solved their trade deficits by happily raising the values of their currencies. Still, the perverse result in Case 1 is possible, and it can happen even without the complete inelasticities of demand assumed here. It is especially possible in the short run, before people have time to adjust the quantities they buy.

Case 2: A small country. The most relevant special case is the one in which a country's devaluation has no effect on the world prices, in foreign currencies, of its exports and imports, perhaps because the country's trade represents too small a share of world trade in each traded good or service to change the world price at which world demand and supply are equal. Many countries are likely to face such perfectly elastic foreign curves, at least in the long run. This is not likely to be true of the United States or Japan, whose exports of many goods take a large share of world trade in those goods, but it is closer to the realities of Canada's foreign trade. It is also likely that a majority of nations face such highly elastic foreign demand and supply curves.

The small country case is one in which devaluation is likely to have a strong tendency to improve the trade balance, lending stability to the foreign exchange market. This can be seen without any diagram or equation, just by noting the signs of the changes in export and import volumes. If the small country cannot change the foreign currency prices of either exports or imports, only the changes in volumes change the trade balance. We know that if the foreign currency price of U.S. wheat and other exports were fixed, devaluation would bring exporters higher dollar prices. They would respond by moving up their supply curve and exporting more at the same world price (a higher dollar price). On the import side, the maintenance of the same pound prices after a devaluation of the dollar means that importers end up facing higher dollar prices by the percentage of the devaluation. They would buy lower quantities in response to what look like higher prices to them. With export volumes rising and import volumes falling at fixed prices, the devaluation would unambiguously improve the balance of trade in goods, services, and gifts. Figure 15.4 illustrates this case, showing that a 20 percent devaluation improves the trade balance—in this case, so much as to shift it from deficit into surplus.

FIGURE 15.4
Devaluation and the trade balance—Case 2: A small country

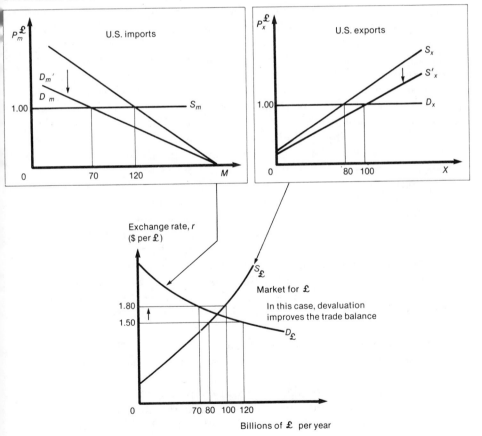

Case 3: Prices fixed in buyers' currencies. It is quite possible that both export and import markets are so structured as to keep devaluation from affecting the prices import buyers on both sides see in terms of their own currencies. This can be the result either of sellers' short-run pricing rules or of perfectly elastic long-run import demand curves.

A frequent real-world occurrence not easily represented with orthodox supply curves is that sellers in the short run try to shield buyers from fluctuations in cost conditions, by letting the cost changes alter only their profit margin and not the prices seen by their customers. Some exporters followed this short-run pricing rule during two recent exchange-rate adjustments. During the depreciation of the U.S. dollar after August 15, 1971, many U.S. exporters reportedly kept their foreign currency prices fixed, pocketing the full rise in the dollar value of these fixed foreign currency prices as the dollar sank. On the U.S. import side, foreign auto firms such as Volkswagen kept their prices fixed in U.S. dollars, apparently not wanting to disrupt the U.S. market and lose sales volume by having their prices jump when U.S. subcompacts were not rising in price very quickly. Volkswagen had to absorb the exchange-rate change by accepting fewer marks for the same dollar price on each car sold to the United States. It kept this up for several weeks, before raising its dollar prices to regain better prices in deutsche marks. Similar occurrences were noted when the British pound took a dive across the fall of 1976. British exporters of autos and electronic products pocketed the rise in pound prices implied by their maintenance of steady dollar prices on the goods they exported, at a time when each dollar earned bought more and more of the depreciating pounds. On Britain's import side, the opposite happened to profits because of the same pricing policy. Renault, the French auto giant, tried for a while to protect its sales volume in the British market by holding its pound prices fixed in the face of the pound's depreciation. This forced it to accept lower and lower prices in francs or dollars or other non-British currencies. After several weeks, Renault was accepting the equivalent of $3,175 in the British market on cars that would have been priced at $3,915 if they had been sold in France. After a while, it too, like Volkswagen in 1971, gave up and raised its foreign currency price (here sterling) in order to regain better franc prices and profit margins.

Whatever one may think of the profit and productivity consequences of this short-run pricing behavior, it does happen and it does clearly make a devaluation improve the devaluing country's trade balance. Although the foreign buyers of exports see a fixed foreign currency price and fixed sales volumes, the devaluing country saves foreign exchange on the importing side. In 1971, for example, the United States cut the foreign currency value of its given import volumes as long as companies like Volkswagen accepted lower foreign currency prices. In whichever currency one chooses to view this, it adds up to a trade-balance improvement for the devaluing country in the short run.

Over the longer run, the same result could obtain if prices were fixed in buyers' currencies by infinite demand elasticities. This variant on Case 3 is like the short-run pricing rule just considered, except that export volumes rise and import volumes fall. Export volumes rise because the U.S. exporters respond to what look like better dollar prices by exporting more, up to the point that keeps the pound price the same. Import volumes fall because the fixed dollar price imposed by the infinite elasticity of importers' demands offers foreign suppliers fewer pounds, causing them to cut back on their export quantities to the United States. With rising export volumes, fixed pound prices of exports, and declining import volumes and prices, this case again clearly improves the trade balance when a country devalues, as illustrated in Figure 15.5.

FIGURE 15.5
Devaluation and the trade balance—Case 3: Prices fixed in buyers' currencies

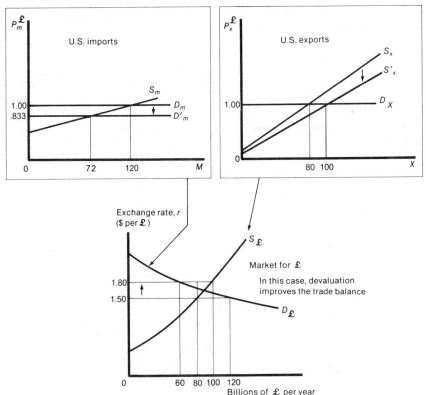

Case 4: Prices fixed in sellers' currencies. It can also be that prices end up by being unaffected by the devaluation when measured in the currencies of the exporters of the respective countries. This can result either from a short-run pricing policy by sellers or from a long-run infinite elasticity of supply curves. Either way, the assumed dependence of quantities on the positions of demand curves and the fixity of supply prices make this the most Keynesian-looking case.

Figure 15.6 illustrates this elastic-supply case with a set of numbers chosen to bring out the ambiguity of the results of devaluation. On the import side, it looks as though the devaluation brings a clear reduction in the demand for pounds, by cutting the volume of our imports without affecting their pound price. (The dollar value of U.S. imports might be raised or lowered, depending on whether the 20 percent rise in dollar price outweighs the reduction in import volume.) On the export

FIGURE 15.6
Devaluation and the trade balance—Case 4: Prices fixed in sellers' currencies

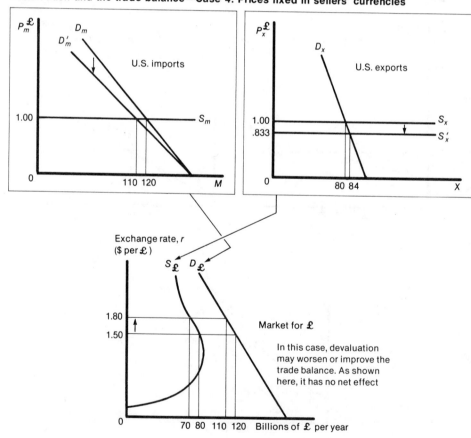

side, the dollar devaluation has opposite effects on pound prices and volumes. Maintaining the same dollar price of U.S. exports means a lower price in terms of sterling and other currencies, thus tending to cut down U.S. export earnings of foreign exchange. On the other hand, this same drop in the foreign currency price encourages foreigners to buy more U.S. exports, a fact tending to raise U.S. foreign exchange earnings. The net result depends on elasticities of demand. The more responsive export volumes are to the given change in the pound price of exports, the greater is the likely improvement in export earnings. The more elastic import demand is in response to the rising dollar price of imports, the more devaluation will cut down on the total demand for foreign exchange to buy imports. Thus in Case 4 the outcome depends on demand elasticities. Figure 15.6 brings this out by showing a set of numbers that falls right on the dividing line between balance-of-trade improvement and deterioration. In Figure 15.6, there is a zero net effect of the devaluation on net foreign exchange earnings (supply minus demand for pounds), which equal 40 billion pounds a year with or without the devaluation. Greater demand elasticities (flatter demand curves) would have brought an improvement, whereas lower ones would have brought a deterioration.

The pattern

By studying these four cases, we can spot a general pattern that might have been harder to see from general theoretical principles: *The more elastic import and export demand are, the more stable foreign exchange markets are likely to be.* It was in the cases of infinite demand elasticities that devaluation or depreciation of the nation's currency brought the largest shifts toward trade surpluses. This happened in the small country case (Case 2), in which the world price of exports was fixed by an infinitely elastic demand. It also happened in Case 3, in which infinite elasticity of demands on both sides kept prices fixed in buyers' currencies. By contrast, devaluation worsened the trade balance when demand elasticities were zero, in Case 1. In Case 4, too, we saw that the higher the demand elasticities the more the foreign exchange market tended to act in a stabilizing way, cutting the excess demand for foreign currencies when their prices rose.

Supply elasticities, on the other hand, had no clear direction of influence on the results. In Case 4, in which supply elasticities were infinite, devaluation could improve or worsen the trade balance, as it also could in the other cases whether supply elasticities were high or low. Apparently, the magnitudes of supply elasticities have ambiguous relevance for the likelihood of stable exchange markets, in which devaluation or depreciation improves the trade balance and cuts excess demand for foreign exchange.

The general formula, and the Marshall-Lerner condition

The crucial role of demand elasticities, and in fact all of the results given so far, can be deduced from a general algebraic formula for the effect of an exchange-rate change on the trade balance. Deriving this general formula is a tedious process. One differentiates the trade-balance identity

$$TB = V_x - V_m = P_x X - P_m M$$

and takes a couple of hours to put the result into elasticity form. The derivation is given in Appendix H. Here we shall only state the formula and note how it encompasses all the points made so far. The formula relates an elasticity of trade-balance response (E_{tb}) to demand and supply elasticities for imports and exports:

$$E_{tb} = \begin{matrix} \text{The elasticity of} \\ \text{the trade balance} \\ \text{with respect to} \\ \text{the exchange rate} \end{matrix} = \frac{dTB/V_m}{dr/r} = \frac{V_x}{V_m}\left[\frac{d_x + 1}{(d_x/s_x) - 1}\right] - \frac{s_m + 1}{(s_m/d_m) - 1},$$

where

TB = The trade balance, or the net surplus on current account, or the net excess supply of foreign exchange;

V_x, V_m = The values of exports and imports just before the devaluation or depreciation;

r = The exchange rate, or the price of foreign exchange;

d_x, d_m = The demand elasticities for exports and imports, defined as the (negative) percentage responses of export and import demand to percentage changes in export and import prices, respectively;

s_x, s_m = The supply elasticities for exports and imports, defined as the (positive) percentage responses of export and import supply to percentage changes in export and import prices, respectively.

All values and prices may be defined in either the home currency or the foreign currency, as long as the same currency is used throughout.

Policymakers and voters who are interested only in rough tendencies could perhaps afford to avoid use of this formula and rely on the patterns revealed by the special cases above. But economists wanting to provide specific quantitative measures of the effects of devaluation on the trade balance need to apply elasticity estimates to the general formula. Here we shall confine ourselves to noting, in Table 15.2, that

TABLE 15.2
Devaluation and the trade balance: Applying the general formula to special cases

	Assumed elasticities	Effect of devaluation on the trade balance
Case 1: Inelastic demands (Figure 15.3)	$d_m = d_x = 0$	Trade balance worsens: $E_{tb} = -V_x/V_m < 0$
Case 2: Small country (Figure 15.4)	$s_m = -d_x = \infty$	Trade balance improves: $E_{tb} = \dfrac{V_x}{V_m} s_x - d_m > 0$
Case 3: Prices fixed in buyers' currencies (Figure 15.5)	$d_m = d_x = -\infty$	Trade balance improves: $E_{tb} = \dfrac{V_x}{V_m} s_x + s_m + 1 > 0$
Case 4: Prices fixed in sellers' currencies (Figure 15.6)	$s_x = s_m = \infty$	It depends: $E_{tb} = \dfrac{V_x}{V_m} (-d_x - 1) - d_m \gtreqless 0.$

In Case 4, if trade was not initially in surplus, the Marshall-Lerner condition from Appendix H is sufficient for improvement: $|d_x + d_m| > 1$.

the formula does yield all the special-case results obtained above when the special elasticity assumptions are used.

The literature on this issue has derived a condition for stable exchange markets that has become known as the **Marshall-Lerner** condition. The Marshall-Lerner condition is that the absolute values of the two demand elasticities must exceed unity: $|d_x + d_m| > 1$. Appendix H shows that this condition is sufficient to guarantee the stable result that devaluation improves the trade balance *if* supplies are perfectly elastic (Case 4's assumption) and if the trade balance was not initially in surplus. More generally, when we cannot lean on these assumptions, the condition is a rougher guide to the likelihood of the stabilizing result, since it reminds us of the overall pattern that higher demand elasticities give more stable results. There is a tendency to argue that the Marshall-Lerner condition would be sufficient for devaluation to work as it should, though this follows only under Case 4's assumptions.

ELASTICITY PESSIMISM AND OPTIMISM

The estimation of trade elasticities is an area in which econometrics meets head-on with policy judgments. The willingness of policymakers to rely on exchange-rate and price adjustments to rectify payments imbalance, rather than intervene directly with exchange controls that ration the right to trade, depends on their faith in the demand elasticities, which in turn rests on econometric estimates. In the 1930s and 1940s, "elasticity pessimism" prevailed. It was generally feared that demand elasticities were so low (in absolute value) that devaluation would often worsen the trade balance. Although this belief was remarkably consistent with the general depression-bred doubts about the smoothness of any adjustment mechanisms that relied on price changes, it also rested on earlier econometric estimates that seemed to find low demand elasticities. Partly for this reason, the agreements about postwar international monetary institutions allowed many countries to resort to direct exchange controls instead of relying on changes in exchange rates and prices.

The elasticity pessimism of the 1930s and 1940s has given way to a guarded optimism in the 1960s and 1970s, one stressing that in most cases demand elasticities are probably high enough to make devaluation work as it should. This optimism has been based in part on estimates like those in Table 15.3, showing that in a bare majority of cases the Marshall-Lerner condition seemed to be met by import and export elasticities that summed below -1 in value (above 1 in absolute value). The estimates seemed especially comforting for the countries at the center of the world economy, such as the United States, Canada, Japan, and France, whose data were probably of higher reliability. The main holdout among major countries was Great Britain, whose demand elasticities seemed disturbingly low in some estimates, as in Table 15.3, though higher in others.

The reasons for the change in opinion are complex. The change may have been based in part on true changes in conditions. It may be that by the 1960s the greater share of modern manufactures in international trade, and the greater diffusion of trade across many countries, had raised price sensitivity above its levels in earlier times, when the greater share of possibly less elastic primary products brought smaller trade volume changes in response to wider price swings. Yet if changing conditions were the whole story, we would still be hard pressed to explain the shift to elasticity optimism, since the estimates from the late 1950s and 1960s, sampled in Table 15.3, are not high enough to lay pessimism to rest.

The drift toward optimism in regard to elasticity is based more on economists' increasing appreciation of some statistical biases that are likely to have made estimated elasticities understate the true elasticities, both in the early pessimistic studies and in those later ones sampled in Table 15.3. Led by a pathbreaking article by Guy Orcutt in 1950, economists have developed this list of reasons why the estimated elasticities are probably lower than the true ones:

1. By assuming that the responses of quantity to price were demand responses, the estimates failed to resolve a basic identification problem, namely, our inability to identify the shifting demand and

TABLE 15.3
Some trade-price-elasticity estimates

	Source and sample period					
	Houthakker-Magee (1951–1966)			Adams-Junz (1955–1963)		
Country	d_x	d_m	Sum	d_x	d_m	Sum
United States	−1.51	(−0.54)	−2.05	−1.41*	−0.41	−1.82
Canada	−0.59	−1.46	−2.05	−0.79*	−1.24	−2.03
United Kingdom	(−0.44)	(0.22)	−0.22			
Japan	(−0.80)	−0.72	−1.52	−0.83*	−0.77	−1.60
West Germany	(1.70)	(−0.24)	1.46	−1.18	(−0.41)	−1.59
Italy	(−0.03)	(−0.13)	−0.16			
Netherlands	(−0.82)	(0.23)	−0.59			
France	−2.27	(0.17)	−2.10	−1.41*	−1.49	−2.90
Belgium-Luxembourg	(0.42)	−1.02	−0.60			
South Africa	−2.41	(1.04)	−1.37			
Sweden	(0.67)	(−0.79)	−0.12			
Australia	(−0.17)	(0.83)	0.66			
Switzerland	−0.58	(−0.84)	−1.42			
Denmark	(−0.56)	−1.66	−2.22			
Norway	(0.20)	−0.78	−0.58			
Portugal	(−0.53)	(−0.07)	−0.06			

Notes: Estimates in parentheses are not statistically significant from zero at the 5 percent level of confidence.

Most estimates are same-year elasticities estimated from annual data. Exceptions are:

* Lagged one year behind the price variable.
† Lagged two years behind the price variable.

The estimates are regression coefficients from relative-price terms in log-log regressions involving income and other explanatory variables besides relative price. In each case the price variable is viewed as determined from the supply side.

d_x = Price elasticity of demand for exports.
d_m = Price elasticity of demand for imports.

Sources: Hendrik S. Houthakker and Stephen P. Magee, "Income and Price Elasticities in World Trade," *Review of Economics and Statistics,* May 1969; F. Gerard Adams and Helen B. Junz, "The Effect of the Business Cycle on Trade Flows of Industrial Countries," *Journal of Finance,* May 1971, pp. 267–68.

supply curves from data on prices, quantities, and a few other variables.

2. The estimates are based on an era in which price changes were smaller than they would be under devaluations, and demand may respond with lower elasticity to small price changes than to large.

3. The estimates of one-year elasticities are probably lower than the longer-run elasticities have been.

4. The use of highly aggregated data may give undue weight to goods with relatively low elasticities.

5. The data may reflect errors of measurement of quantity, price, and other variables, errors that are likely to bias the elasticity estimates toward zero.

FIGURE 15.7

Biased estimation of a demand elasticity due to failure to identify demand and supply shifts

The four observations:

Price	Quantity
7	18
8	20
6	24
5	22

This list cannot be discussed in full here.[2] The first item on the list needs elaboration, however, since the identification problem lies at the center of so many attempts to estimate structural relationships from readily available data.

It is not easy to identify the demand and supply curves when what we have to deal with are observations on price, quantity, and such third variables as income. Price is the result of both demand and supply. So is quantity. When both price and quantity change from one period to the next, it is not obvious whether demand has shifted, supply has shifted, or both. The estimates cited in Table 15.3 and in similar studies assume that price is determined from the supply side, with supply perfectly elastic (though shifting), so that quantity re-

---

[2] For a fuller treatment, see Guy H. Orcutt, "Measurement of Price Elasticities in International Trade," *Review of Economics and Statistics*, vol. 32, no. 2 (May 1950), pp. 117–32; and Edward E. Leamer and Robert M. Stern, *Quantitative International Economics* (Boston: Allyn & Bacon, 1970), chap. 2.

sponses can be conveniently interpreted as demand responses, yielding a demand curve. Unfortunately, convenient assumptions are not always valid.

The bias imparted by incorrectly assuming that prices are fixed by supply can be seen with the help of Figure 15.7, which shows how misuse of standard (least squares) statistical techniques can misestimate the slope and elasticity of the demand curve. The four price-quantity combinations are observed, and the estimator's task is to uncover the slope common to the two demand curves, D_1 and D_2. If there were a large number of observations and data on all variables that could correctly predict shifts in the demand and supply curves (for example, data on the weather, incomes, and fads), there would be little reason for ending up with biased estimates. But lacking all the requisite information, past studies have had to make the misleading assumptions already mentioned: they assumed that prices were independent variables on the supply side and that quantities were quantities demanded. Taking this tack, they found the best fits to the "demand" curve as the line through the data that yielded the least deviations (or squares of deviations) of *quantities* imported from the fitted curve. In Figure 15.7, this line having the least horizontal deviations is D'. Interpreted as a demand curve, it shows a low elasticity, lower than the true elasticities of the demand curves D_1 and D_2. This simplified example shows that when the true supply curves cannot be assumed to be flat, it is a serious mistake to assume that price is determined by supply and quantity by demand. Given the procedure used, this leads to underestimation of demand elasticities.

For the five reasons listed, economists have concluded that the true elasticities are likely to be quite a bit higher in absolute value than the estimates. This is the general consensus. It implies that as a rule there is indeed something stabilizing about the trade-balance response to changes in exchange rates. In most cases devaluation or depreciation of a currency is likely to improve the trade balance over a year's time. This in turn is likely to give speculators a more stabilizing signal than they would otherwise have received from the foreign exchange market, so that they too would gain faith in a currency as a result of its having dropped in value (other things equal!). Yet there is only a general tendency toward the stabilizing result. Exceptions can easily exist, and policy must be prepared for the possibility that they will.

DEVALUATION AND RELATIVE PRICES

A firm understanding of how devaluation works requires some exploration of just how or whether it changes relative prices. To know how devaluation affects national well-being, it helps to know whether it improves the nation's terms of trade. And to know whether devaluation really brings lasting improvement to the trade balance, it is necessary to ask how devaluation can change the ratio of domestic to foreign prices.

Devaluation and the terms of trade

To know whether devaluation ends up benefiting the devaluing country itself, it often helps to proceed in two steps, first examining whether the devaluation makes it easier for the country to buy imports with each unit of its exports, and then examining whether the devaluation allows the country more national production. We take the first step here, and leave the second for the next chapter.

Imported goods and services are part of the bundle that a nation consumes, and the relative cost of imports is thus part of the cost-of-living price index by which national product must be deflated in order to measure national purchasing power. Therefore, whatever makes imports costlier to purchase with units of (exported) national product makes the country worse off.

Whether devaluation actually worsens the ratio of export prices to import prices, or the "terms of trade" defined in Chapter 3, depends on the demand and supply elasticities for imports and exports. Experimenting with some of the cases above could lead you to the same result as is derived in Appendix H: *The more elastic are demands relative to supplies, the better the effect of devaluation on the terms of trade.* In terms of the four trade elasticities defined above,

Devaluation improves (P_x/P_m), the terms of trade, if $d_x d_m > s_x s_m$;

Devaluation has no effect on the terms of trade if $d_x d_m = s_x s_m$; and

Devaluation worsens (P_x/P_m), the terms of trade, if $d_x d_m < s_x s_m$.

The importance of this comparison of demand with supply elasticities can be seen by returning to Cases 2, 3, and 4 of the devaluation analysis earlier in this chapter. In Case 2, the small country case, foreign currency prices were fixed abroad and were unaffected by this country's devaluation (Figure 15.4). This meant that the terms of trade, P_x/P_m, could not change with devaluation. So the formula above also predicts, since the small country case is one in which $-d_x = s_m = \infty$, and the equality holds. In Case 3, with prices fixed in buyers' currencies, devaluation could not affect the foreign currency price of the country's exports, but lowered the foreign currency price of imports by the percentage of the devaluation (Figure 15.5). With imports thus cheaper to buy with each unit of exports, devaluation has improved the terms of trade. Again, the formula above would have predicted as much, since in Case 3, $d_x = d_m = -\infty$. Finally, if prices are fixed in sellers' currencies, as in Case 4 (Figure 15.6), the nation ends up accepting a lower foreign currency price on its exports while still paying the same foreign currency price for imports. This makes imports more expensive to buy with exports, worsening the terms of trade, as predicted by the formula, with $s_x = s_m = \infty$. In general, devaluation can affect the terms of trade of a large country in either direction, and is likely to have no effect on the terms of trade for a small country.

In the background: Nontraded goods and money

The material presented thus far in this chapter summarizes the usual analysis of the price effects of a devaluation. One could stop here in the knowledge that the usual analysis has been covered. One could also stop here in the knowledge that the analysis above is the best single device for analyzing the effects of a devaluation within a short run, say a year. Yet the more closely one looks into the effects of devaluation on relative prices within the national economy, the more one realizes that the analysis thus far has been based on certain assumptions about nontraded goods and about money, assumptions that are likely to break down over the longer run. Let us here uncover some problems that are usually swept under the rug by the analysis of the price effects of devaluation. These problems are not solved in the present chapter, and we shall return to them in Chapters 17 and 18.

In showing the range of possible responses of the trade balance to devaluation, we never explicitly introduced one case that is in the long run more realistic than it may at first appear. Now consider a "Case 5," in which both the domestic supply of exports and the domestic demand for imports are perfectly inelastic, as shown in Figure 15.8. In this case devaluation cannot affect the trade balance, since quantities are fixed by the vertical domestic curves and prices are fixed in foreign currency by the positions of the foreign curves, which do not shift.

One's first reaction to Case 5 is that it is an unrealistic special case because the export supply curve and the import demand curve are probably somewhat elastic and not vertical. But what makes them so? When we ponder this question, we begin to see some assumptions underlying our short-run analysis above. If we believe that export supply curves are usually upward-sloping (as in Figures 15.2 through 15.5), and if we believe that import demand curves are usually downward-sloping (as in Figures 15.2, 15.4, and 15.6), we must believe that changes in price shift resources between these trade-related sectors and others. Specifically, belief in elastic curves in the face of devaluation must be based on the belief that when a country devalues its currency, resources are attracted into both its export and import-

FIGURE 15.8
Devaluation and the trade balance again—Case 5: Inelastic home-country curves

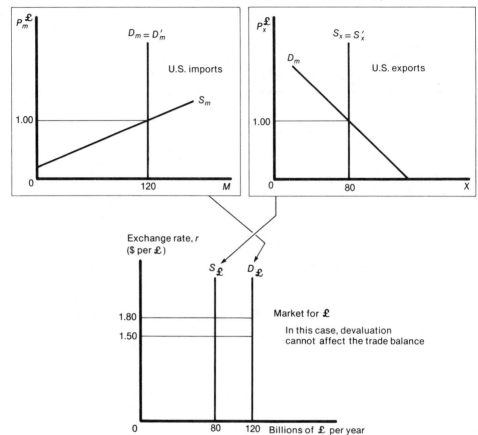

competing sectors in order to improve the trade balance. But where do the resources come from? What sectors of the economy are contracting and releasing resources if both the exporting and import-replacing sectors are expanding?

Implicitly the short-run analysis of a devaluation assumes that there is a sizable sector producing nontraded goods and services. Such a sector there surely is: such services as barbering and hairdressing, auto repair, and residential construction do not enter international trade. Human leisure time is another nontraded good, whether it is due to involuntary unemployment or to voluntary decisions not to work. When the national currency has just been devalued, labor and other resources are bid away from the non-traded-goods sector (including unemployment) toward the traded-good sectors, where prices are being bid up by the rising dollar prices of competing foreign goods. Meanwhile, domestic buyers are likely to cut back on their purchases of exportable goods and import-competing goods somewhat and to shift their demand toward the nontraded goods, whose prices have risen less.

For a time, perhaps for a year, this can happen. It also helps explain why both the export and import-competing sectors can expand after a devaluation, raising export volumes and cutting import volumes. Yet soon enough something has to give. By definition, the non-traded-goods sector cannot have net exports or net imports, the quantity demanded must equal quantity supplied for this sector. A tendency for the non-traded-goods sector to give up resources to other sectors and to attract demand must result in a rise in price in the non-traded-goods sector until quantity supplied comes back up to meet quantity demanded in this sector. This, however, means that after a while the non-traded-goods sector cannot achieve a net release of excess supply toward the traded-goods sectors. If the early rises in prices of traded goods in the wake of the devaluation lead to rises in the prices of nontraded goods, then relative prices between the sectors end up not changing much, and there is not likely to be much net shift of resources toward the traded-goods sectors. Perhaps after a while the export supply and import demand curves could end up looking practically vertical, as in Figure 15.8. Although the perfect verticality of Figure 15.8 is almost surely an overstatement, there is reason to believe that the trade balance shifts less in the long run than in the short run in response to a devaluation, in part because the non-traded-goods sector acts as more of a resource-releasing reservoir in the short run than later on.

The other element in the background beside nontraded goods is money. Thus far all of our price variables have been prices in units of national moneys, not the intercommodity price ratios (for example, bushels of wheat per yard of cloth) we were able to use in Part I, for which the "dollar" prices in Part II were just a proxy. Money is unavoidably involved in the devaluation analysis, because it is a national money that is being devalued and because the net trade balance is typically financed in part by a net flow of money. A complete model of devaluation will thus have to get into such issues as how the demand for holding money is affected by devaluation. This complication is taken up in Chapters 17 and 18.

The above analysis of devaluation, then, remains a good guide to its short-run impact, yet a correct analysis of the longer-run effects must be more complicated and is likely to point toward a dampened long-run effect of devaluation on the trade balance.

SUMMARY

If exchange markets are to be stable in the face of changes in the exchange rate, it is practically necessary that the commercial part of the market show stabilizing signs if speculators are to have a durable basis for believing in the stability of exchange rates. It is thus very important to know whether devaluation improves the trade balance as it should.

A detailed analysis of the general formula for the effects of devaluation and of some important special cases turned up the general pattern that the higher the demand elasticities for exports and imports were, the greater was the likelihood of an improvement in the trade balance following a devaluation. Since the cases yielding high demand elasticities, such as the small country case, seemed to have slightly greater applicability than did the special case in which perfectly inelastic demands made devaluation worsen the trade balance, it seems more likely that the result is in the stable and expected direction. What we know of econometric estimates of demand elasticities seems to reinforce this belief in the prevalence of stability. Yet there can easily be exceptions in which devaluation worsens the trade balance.

The analysis of this chapter is probably a fair representation of the short-run impact of devaluation, though it is based on implicit assumptions about the role of nontraded goods and money.

Devaluation will be likely to improve the terms of trade if the demand elasticities for imports and exports are high relative to the supply elasticities, and are likely to worsen the terms of trade if the reverse holds.

SUGGESTED READING

For alternative textbook treatments of devaluation, see Herbert G. Grubel, *International Economics* (Homewood, Ill.: Richard D. Irwin, 1977), chap. 14; Jaroslav Vanek, *International Trade: Theory and Economic Policy* (Homewood, Ill.: Richard D. Irwin, 1962), chap. 5; and Leland B. Yeager, *International Monetary Relations*, 2d ed. (New York: Harper and Row, 1976), chaps. 6 and 8.

QUESTIONS FOR REVIEW

1. People are very fixed in their habits. They buy the same physical volumes of imports no matter what the price. This is true of both U.S. importers and foreign importers. Under these conditions, will a 10 percent depreciation of the dollar improve the U.S. trade balance?

2. The prices of U.S. exports are fixed in dollars. The prices of U.S. imports are fixed in pounds (and in other foreign currencies). Will a 10 percent

depreciation of the dollar (for example, from \$1.50 to \$1.65 per pound) improve the U.S. trade balance?

3. Will the depreciation of the dollar in Question 2 improve or worsen the U.S. terms of trade (P_x/P_m)?

Answers:

1. No, it will worsen it. See Case 1 above.
2. It depends on whether the Marshall-Lerner condition holds. See Case 4.
3. The terms will worsen, since this case is one of infinite supply elasticities.

16

Income and international adjustment

Incomes, like prices, affect international trade and payments and exchange rates, and are affected by all of these. By sketching this mutual interaction between income and international adjustment, the present chapter puts in place another major analytic building block on which the policy conclusions of Part IV will rest.

SETTING PRICES ASIDE

Ever since the onset of the Keynesian revolution in the 1930s, one of the main difficulties in macroeconomics has been the forming of a satisfactory framework for predicting both changes in real incomes and changes in prices. A general consensus has formed, despite some lingering skirmishes, about the monetary and other forces that lie behind the aggregate demand side of the economy, raising and lowering both real incomes and price levels in tandem. But we lack a satisfactory supply side for standard macroeconomic models, which would allow us to determine income and price levels separately. Four solutions have been tried, each satisfactory for some purposes, but not for others:

1. One can make the extreme Keynesian assumption that prices do not matter to the internal processes of the economy, so that income and spending might just as well be measured in real (deflated) terms.

2. One can assume a Keynesian upward-sloping supply curve, relating real income and the price level, so that the effects of any upward shift in aggregate demand for what the nation produces are split between an increase in real income and a price increase.
3. One can assume a Phillips curve of the form relating levels of unemployment (and real income) to rates of price inflation.
4. One can assume a vertical supply curve, fixing real income (national product) at either "full employment" or "the natural rate of unemployment," from which it can be expanded only by supply improvements (productivity gains, population growth, capital accumulation, land improvement, and supply-raising institutional changes).

Much of the analysis of this chapter was first developed within the context of the first, the extreme Keynesian, assumption, which sets aside prices as either fixed or irrelevant and concentrates on processes relating real spending to real income. We shall follow that path for the first half of this chapter. If the Keynesian analysis of income and international adjustment were useful only under this assumption, we would find it embarrassing in today's inflation-ridden world and would be inclined to omit much of what follows. Fortunately, the same predictions follow, though with different magnitudes, under assumptions 2 and 4 as well as 1. In what follows, the level of national income, or Y, will be measured in current prices (not adjusted for inflation). In settings where unemployment is so great that one suspects that aggregate demand affects real income strongly and prices weakly, this analysis is to be used with the understanding that Y could stand for real national income as affected by demand-side forces. In settings of full employment and inflation, Y can be read as a measure of the price level of a real national income that cannot be changed by demand shifts. And in settings where both incomes and prices seem to be affected by demand changes, changes in Y are to be interpreted as changes in both real incomes and prices in response to demand changes. It is in this sense that we push prices to one side here—they can still be changed and are still relevant to international trade, but we shall consider their changes to be just a by-product of changes in income stemming from changes in demand.

TRADE DEPENDS ON INCOME

The volume of a nation's imports depends positively on the level of real national product. So say a host of empirical estimates for many countries, such as the estimates reported in Table 16.1. This positive relationship seems to have two explanations. One is that imports are

TABLE 16.1

Some estimates of the dependence of real imports on real national product

Country	(1) Income elasticity of import demand $(\Delta M/M)/(\Delta Y/Y)$	×	(2) Imports as a share of income (M/Y)	=	(3) Marginal propensity to import $(m = \Delta M/\Delta Y)$
United States	1.51		0.048		0.073
Canada.................	1.20		0.226		0.272
United Kingdom	1.66		0.189		0.314
Japan	1.23		0.094		0.115
West Germany	1.80		0.184		0.332
France	1.66		0.138		0.229
Sweden	1.42		0.222		0.315
Mexico	0.52		0.101		0.052
India	1.43		0.073		0.104

Notes and sources: (1) Estimated from log-log regressions on 1951–66 annual data by Hendrik S. Houthakker and Stephen P. Magee, "Income and Price Elasticities in World Trade," *Review of Economics and Statistics*, vol. 51, no. 2 (May 1969), tables 1 and 3, pp. 113 and 115. All income elasticities were statistically significant at the .001 level. (2) The ratio of the national accounts measure of imports to gross domestic product, for 1966, from IMF, *International Financial Statistics*, September 1973. (3) = (1) × (2).

often used as inputs into the production of the goods and services that constitute national product or, roughly speaking, national income. The other is that imports respond to the total real spending, or "absorption," in our economy. The more we spend on all goods and services, the more we tend to spend on the part of them that we buy from abroad. Although a nation's expenditures on goods and services are not the same thing as its national income from producing goods and services, the close statistical correlation between income and expenditure has allowed statistical studies to gloss over this distinction when estimating import functions.

The most important parameter of the dependence of imports on income is the *marginal propensity to import*, which is the ratio of a change in import volumes to the change in real (constant-price) national income causing the import change. The marginal propensity to import is represented geometrically by the slope of the import function in Figure 16.1. By linking extra income to extra imports, the marginal propensity to import shows the extent to which extra prosperity spills over into imports, worsening the balance of trade, rather than adding to the domestic multiplier process by becoming a further new demand for domestic goods and services. The marginal propensity to import, in other words, is a "leakage" from the expenditure stream. The estimates in Table 16.1 suggest that it is a more important "leakage"

FIGURE 16.1
Imports as a function of income

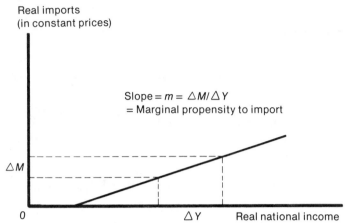

Real imports
(in constant prices)

Slope = m = $\triangle M / \triangle Y$
= Marginal propensity to import

$\triangle M$

0                          $\triangle Y$ Real national income

in those countries having high average ratios of imports to national product.

The dependence of exports on national income is more complex. It depends primarily on whether any changes in national income are the result of domestic demand changes, domestic supply changes, or changes in foreign demand for our exports. If domestic national income is raised by a surge in domestic aggregate demand which touches off an expansion of output and/or prices throughout the economy, then there is a good chance that the increase in national income will be accompanied by a drop in export volumes, as domestic buyers bid away resources that might otherwise have been exported. Although such a negative dependence of export volumes on national-income-as-determined-by-domestic-demand is plausible, the evidence for it is somewhat sparse, and most Keynesian models of an open economy assume that export volumes are independent of national income.

Two other outside forces can make export volumes seem to vary positively with national income. One is a supply-side expansion, or any cost cutting, whether due to productivity improvements or price-cutting institutional changes or any other supply-side shift. If national income is being expanded under such influences, this expansion will be accompanied by a rise in exports as the price reductions give the country a greater competitive advantage. Alternatively, the country could be experiencing a surge in foreign demand for its exports, allowing both exports and national income to expand. We shall consider just such a linkage when discussing foreign income repercussions below.

The usual Keynesian starting point, however, is to assume that the demand for exports is exogenous.

EQUILIBRIUM INCOME IN AN OPEN ECONOMY

The existence of exports and the dependence of imports on the level of national income add a slight complication to the Keynesian model of national income determination that is traditional in introductory courses in macroeconomics. The equilibrium level of national income is still the level matched by the level of spending on the nation's product that is desired for that level of national income. But now the aggregate demand for our national product is no longer the same thing as our national expenditures, as was the case in the simple closed-economy model of introductory courses. Recall from Chapter 14 that

$$Y \quad = \quad E \quad + \quad X \quad - \quad M, \qquad (16.1)$$

or

$$\frac{\text{National}}{\text{product}} = \frac{\text{National}}{\substack{\text{expenditures} \\ \text{(or ``absorption'')}}} + \text{Exports} - \text{Imports} .$$

In Chapter 14 these magnitudes referred to values in current prices. They can also double for real values (in constant prices) if each represents a domestic currency measure deflated by the same overall price index.

This equation can be interpreted either as an identity relating actual observed magnitudes or as an equilibrium condition relating desired magnitudes that depend on real income. Let us follow the latter interpretation here. Let the equation above be read as the following kind of equilibrium condition:

$$Y = \frac{\text{Aggregate demand for}}{\text{our national product}} = E(Y) + X - M(Y). \qquad (16.2)$$

Our desired expenditures depend on our national income, among many other things. This is most clearly true of our expenditures for consumption purposes. And since consumption depends on income, or $C = C(Y)$, so does total expenditure, which is the sum of consumption, domestic capital formation, or investment, and government purchases of goods and services $(E[Y] = C[Y] + I_d + G)$. Figure 16.2A illustrates the equilibrium level of national income, showing the matching between national income and aggregate demand at Point A. At levels of national income below 100, the aggregate demand would exceed the level of production, as shown by the fact that the AD curve is above the 45-degree line to the left of A. At any such lower levels of income,

FIGURE 16.2
Equilibrium national income in an open economy, shown in two equivalent ways

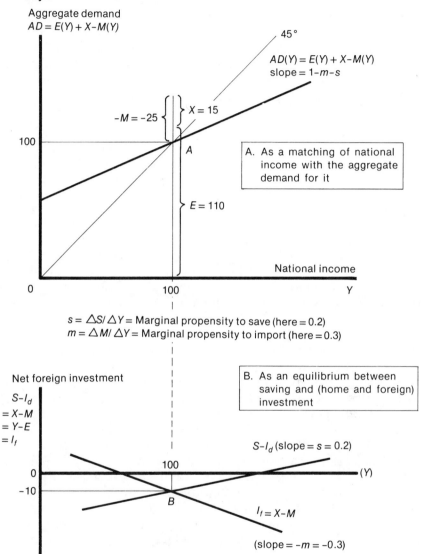

Aggregate demand
$AD = E(Y) + X - M(Y)$

45°

$AD(Y) = E(Y) + X - M(Y)$
slope $= 1 - m - s$

$X = 15$

$-M = -25$

100

A

A. As a matching of national income with the aggregate demand for it

$E = 110$

National income

0   100   Y

$s = \triangle S / \triangle Y =$ Marginal propensity to save (here $= 0.2$)
$m = \triangle M / \triangle Y =$ Marginal propensity to import (here $= 0.3$)

Net foreign investment

B. As an equilibrium between saving and (home and foreign) investment

$S - I_d$
$= X - M$
$= Y - E$
$= I_f$

$S - I_d$ (slope $= s = 0.2$)

100

0

-10

B

$I_f = X - M$

(slope $= -m = -0.3$)

the combination of home and foreign demand for what this nation is producing would be so great as to deplete the inventories of goods held by firms and the firms would have to respond by raising production and creating more jobs and incomes, moving the economy up toward A. Similarly, levels of income above 100 would yield insufficient demand, accumulating inventories, and cutbacks in production and jobs until the economy returned to equilibrium at Point A.

Figure 16.2A does not give a clear enough picture of how the nation's foreign trade and investment relate to the process of achieving equilibrium national income. To underline the role of the foreign sector, it is convenient to convert the equilibrium condition into a different form. This can be done with an algebraic step like one taken in Chapter 14, when we were discussing the current account of the balance of payments. The equilibrium condition given in Equation (16.2) above becomes an equilibrium between saving and investment once we have subtracted private and government expenditures for current use $(C + G)$ from both sides:

$$Y = AD = E + X - M$$
$$(Y - C - G) = \qquad (E - C - G) + (X - M)$$

or

$$S = \qquad I_d \qquad + \ ^{\cdot} I_f.$$

In other words, saving, which is the nation's net accumulation of assets, must match its domestic investment in new real assets (buildings, equipment, inventories) plus its net foreign investment, or its net buildup of claims on the rest of the world. In Chapter 14 this was an identity between actual saving and investment. Here it is interpreted as a condition necessary for an equilibrium level of national income, since both desired saving and desired imports (and therefore desired net foreign investment) depend on national income.

Figure 16.2B expresses this saving-investment equilibrium in a way highlighting the current account balance $(X - M, \text{ or } I_f)$. As drawn here, Figure 16.2B shows a country having a current account deficit, with more imports than exports of goods and services. This could serve as a schematic view of Canada's situation, since Canada typically has a net import balance on current account, financed partly by net capital inflows. The United States would typically have its version of Point B lying above the horizontal axis, representing a net export surplus and a positive net foreign investment. This only means, however, that the United States has a current account surplus. It may still have an overall deficit and a new outflow of liquid assets (as it did in 1975, as shown in Chapter 14).

THE FOREIGN TRADE MULTIPLIER

When national spending rises in an economy having enough unemployment to fit the Keynesian model, this extra spending sets off a multiplier process of expansion of national income, whether or not the country is involved in international trade. Yet the way in which it is involved in trade does affect the size of the national income multiplier. Suppose that the government raises its purchases of goods and services by ten and holds them at this higher level. The extra ten means an extra ten in income for whoever sells the extra goods and services to the government. The extent to which this initial income gain gets transmitted into further income gains depends on how the first gainers allocate their extra income. Let us assume, as we already have in Figure 16.2, that out of each extra dollar of income, people within this nation tend to save 20 cents, part of which is "saved" by the government as taxes on their extra income, and to spend the remaining 80 cents, 30 cents of it on imports of foreign goods and services. In Keynesian jargon, we would say that s, the marginal propensity to save (including the marginal tax rate) is 0.2, that the marginal propensity to consume domestic product is 0.5, and that the marginal propensity to import (m) is 0.3.

The first round of generating extra income produces an extra two in saving, an extra three in imports, and an extra five in spending on domestic goods and services. Of these only the five in domestic spending will be returned to the national economy as a further demand stimulus. Both the two saved and the three spent on imports represent "leakages" from the domestic expenditure stream. Whatever their indirect effects, they do not directly create new jobs or income in the national economy. Thus in the second round of income and expenditures, only five will be passed on and divided up into further domestic spending (2.5), saving (1), and imports (1.5). And for each succeeding round of expenditures, as for these first two, the share of extra income that becomes further expenditures is $(1 - m - s)$, or $(1 - 0.3 - 0.2) = 0.5$.

This multiplier process carries its own multiplier formula, as was the case in the simpler closed-economy models of introductory macroeconomics. The formula is easily derived from the fact that the final change in income equals the initial rise in government spending plus the extra demand for this nation's product that was stimulated by the rise in income itself:

$$\Delta Y = \Delta G + (1 - m - s)\Delta Y, \text{ so that} \tag{16.3}$$
$$\Delta Y (1 - 1 + m + s) = \Delta G, \text{ and} \tag{16.4}$$

The spending multiplier in an open economy, or the "foreign trade multiplier" $= \dfrac{\Delta Y}{\Delta G} = \dfrac{1}{m + s}.$ (16.5)

Thus, in our example the rise in government spending by 10 billion leads ultimately to twice as great an expansion of national income, since the multiplier equals $1/(0.3 + 0.2) = 2$. The value of this multiplier is the same, of course, whether the initial extra domestic spending was made by the government or resulted from a surge in consumption or a rise in private investment spending. Note also that the value of the "foreign trade multiplier" is smaller in an open economy than in a closed economy. Had m been zero, the multiplier would have been $1/s = 5$.

The results of the multiplier expansion in response to a rise in domestic spending can be reexpressed in a diagram like Figure 16.3.

FIGURE 16.3
The effect of a rise in government spending on foreign trade and national income

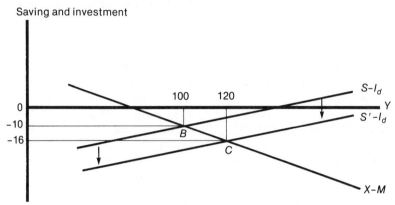

Here the initial rise in government spending is represented by a downward shift of the $S - I_d$ curve. The reason for this convention is that a rise in government spending by 10 is a change in government saving by -10, since government saving is the difference between government tax revenue and government spending. The rise in government spending by 10 produces the same final rise in national income by 20 here as in the discussion above. Note further that the multiplier of two works its effects not only on the final rise in income, but also on the final rise in imports. Imports rose by three, thanks to the very first round of new expenditures, but rose by twice as much, or $[m/(m + s)]\Delta Y = 6$ over all rounds of new expenditures, the amount of trade-balance worsening shown in Figure 16.3.

FOREIGN INCOME REPERCUSSIONS

In describing the marginal propensity to import as a leakage, we have argued as though whatever is spent on imports is permanently lost as a component of aggregate demand for our national product. This assumption works well enough for a small country, whose trade is negligible as an average or marginal share of world income. However, when a nation looms larger in the economies of its trading partners, this assumption underestimates the multiplier. The reason is that when the nation's extra spending leads to extra imports, these imports raise foreign incomes and create foreign jobs. This is true, of course, for either a small country or a large country. However, if a country is large, the expansion of foreign incomes encourages foreign purchases of the country's exports in amounts dictated by the foreign marginal propensities to import from that country. The extra demand for exports raises the country's income further, thus raising the value of the multiplier response to the initial domestic spending.

The existence of such foreign income repercussions helps account for the parallelism in business cycles that has been observed among the major industrial economies. Throughout the 20th century, when America has sneezed Europe and Japan have caught cold, and nowadays vice versa. This tendency was already evident in the business cycles in Europe and the United States in the mid-19th century, though the correlation between the European cycles and the U.S. cycles was far from perfect. The Great Depression of the 1930s also reverberated back and forth among countries, as each country's slump cut its imports (helped by the beggar-thy-neighbor import barriers that were partly a response to the slump itself) and thereby cut foreign exports and incomes. Correspondingly, the outbreak of the Korean War brought economic boom to West Germany, Italy, and Japan, as surging U.S. war spending raised their exports and incomes, leading to a further partial increase in their purchases from the United States. The same interdependence of incomes persists today, so that any drop in U.S. exports, whether due to a U.S. slump or to new U.S. barriers against imports, would end up cutting U.S. exports somewhat through the foreign income repercussions.

The foreign income repercussions can easily be incorporated into the multiplier formula. To see how, one should recognize that the income-determination model now has a separate equilibrium condition for the rest of the world as well as for this country. In equations, the saving-investment equilibriums for this country and the rest of the world are:

$$S(Y) - I_d = X(Y_f) - M(Y) \text{ and} \tag{16.6}$$
$$S_f(Y_f) - I_{d,f} = M(Y) - X(Y_f), \tag{16.7}$$

where the f subscripts refer to the rest of the world and imports and exports are consistently defined as seen from our country. To derive the multiplier formula, one lets our spending rise by the amount A and

differentiates the two equations with respect to national and rest-of-world incomes, solving for the effects on incomes. Omitting the intervening steps,[1] we arrive at the result:
result:

$$\text{The spending multiplier in an open economy with foreign income repercussions} = \frac{\Delta Y}{A} = \frac{1 + (m_f/s_f)}{s + m + (m_f s/s_f)} \qquad (16.8)$$

This formula reduces to the simpler multiplier formula of Equation (16.5) when the rest of the world does not raise its purchases of our exports in response to higher incomes (that is, when $m_f = 0$). The effect of recognizing foreign repercussions is to raise the value of the spending multiplier, in this formula as well as in common sense. To return to the example above, in which the nation had a marginal propensity to save of $s = 0.2$ and a marginal propensity to import of $m = 0.3$, adding the same values for the rest of the world ($s_f = 0.2$ and $m_f = 0.3$) would raise the value of the spending multiplier from its previous level of 2 to 3.125.

Although foreign income repercussions raise the impact of domestic spending on national income, they also dampen the adverse effect of extra domestic spending on the trade balance. This is because the extra exports caused by each round's rise in foreign incomes are greater than the subsequent addition to imports caused by these extra exports themselves.

DEVALUATION AND NATIONAL INCOME

Policy judgments on the wisdom of changing exchange rates depend in part on whether doing so seems likely to raise national income. At first it might seem to be obvious that devaluing the nation's currency does raise national income. After all, devaluing tends to raise the real volume of exports and to reduce the real volume of imports, thus giving extra jobs and income to our export and import-competing industries. Yet the effect of devaluation on national income is not quite this clear-cut. We must also remember that devaluation can worsen the terms of trade (P_X/P_m). It does so in some cases and not others, as we saw in Chapter 15. Cases in which the terms of trade do worsen with

---

[1] The two equations expressing income changes as functions of the shift in expenditures A are:

$$s\Delta Y - A = m_f \Delta Y_f - m \Delta Y \text{ and}$$
$$s_f \Delta Y_f = m \Delta Y - m_f \Delta Y_f.$$

Solving these for ΔY yields the formula in Equation (16.8).

devaluation are the Keynesian case in which prices are fixed in sellers' currencies (infinite supply elasticities) and the pessimistic case in which demands are inelastic. *If* the devaluation worsens the terms of trade, it can worsen the trade balance and national income as well. It can worsen the trade balance if the foreign currency price of exports sinks far enough relative to the price of imports to outweigh the trade-balance improvement implied by the rise in export volumes and the drop in import volumes.

National income can be lowered by the effects of any worsening of the terms of trade on perceived national well-being. If it costs more units of exports, and more of the effort and resources that go into making exportable goods, to buy imports after the devaluation, the devaluation will have made people feel poorer, possibly enough so to outweigh the extra incomes generated by higher export and import-competing sales. And when people feel poorer, they are likely to cut their spending, most of which is spending on domestic output. This contractionary effect of worsening terms of trade could prevail, making national income settle at a lower level.

Thus the effect of devaluation on national income depends on whether or not devaluation worsens the terms of trade. Appendix H shows that *devaluation can lower national income only if it worsens the terms of trade.* A sufficient condition for a rise in national income is that devaluation leaves the terms of trade the same or better.

Notice that if devaluation succeeds in initially improving the trade balance and national income, it ends up improving the trade balance less than it did initially. Figure 16.4 shows this, by showing the multiplier effect of a successful devaluation on national income. At first the trade balance improves from *A* up to *B*, an improvement of ten per

FIGURE 16.4
Devaluation and the trade balance with changes in income

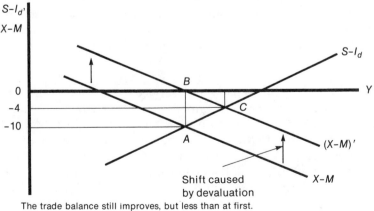

The trade balance still improves, but less than at first.

year. But this shifting of aggregate demand toward our national product sets up a multiplier process through which national income expands until we reach the new equilibrium income at Point C. The income expansion brings with it some extra imports, now that the nation can afford to buy more, leaving the trade-balance improvement smaller than the initial ten per year.

This macroeconomic reasoning might suggest that any devaluation is good for a country as long as it does not worsen the terms of trade. Yet this conclusion constitutes a misuse of the macroeconomic framework. Devaluation can be viewed in this way only as long as it moves the balance of payments toward equilibrium. As long as the devaluation is serving to remove a deficit, it is helping by getting the country out of the capital losses that would be felt if the central bank or the treasury used up its gold and foreign exchange reserves to hold up an artificial value of the nation's currency, only to realize when its reserves ran out that they were worth more of the national currency than it sold them for before they ran out. But if the nation overplays the devaluation idea and generates bigger balance-of-payments surpluses by devaluing, it is asking for a new kind of trouble. The surpluses will force its central bank or treasury to pile up foreign exchange reserves that in the long run will not be worth as much as their present artificial price. The possibility of official losses from buying up too much foreign currency at a disequilibrium price means that devaluation's chances of improving national income are good only as long as the devaluation is correcting a payments deficit.

DEVALUATION AND INCOME DISTRIBUTION

Thus far we have confined our discussion of the income effects of exchange-rate changes to effects on aggregate national income, without exploring the meaning of devaluation for individual groups within the nation. This is the usual approach. Yet to understand some of the shock waves set up by large devaluations, it is important to observe that devaluation affects different groups very differently in the short run.

Devaluation is likely to bring gains for groups that get their income by making and selling goods and services that enter international trade. For both exporters and import-competing groups, devaluation means a chance to compete more advantageously against their foreign counterparts. A drop in the value of the Canadian dollar, for example, would give Canadian wheat exporters a better chance to undercut U.S. wheat prices a bit in U.S. dollars while still receiving higher Canadian dollar prices that enable them to buy more in Canada. Import-competing groups would also be favored, since devaluation or depreciation tends to force Canadian buyers to pay more for the competing foreign product. To be sure, devaluation is also likely to mean that import-competing groups must also pay more for any traded goods and services that they wish to consume, but this cost-of-living effect is almost sure to be outweighed by their direct income gains.

Devaluation is almost certain to hurt somebody, however, even when it does not worsen the terms of trade. The group likely to be hurt is the group that receives its income by selling nontraded goods and services. Devaluation means only a higher cost of living for such groups as civil servants, teachers, construction workers, garage mechanics, and landlords. As sellers of goods and services not entering international trade, they experience no income gains from the devaluation until some of the extra purchasing power from the traded-sector groups trickles their way. Meanwhile they must pay more for importable and exportable goods and services.

The redistributive power of devaluation, and the limits on it, can be seen by studying national experiences after large sudden devaluations. One such dramatic experience was that of Argentina in the wake of its government's December 1958 decision to let the peso drop radically before pegging at a new par value. This decision to devalue was accompanied by other policy moves. The government temporarily tightened up on the money supply to help halt the inflation whose runaway rates had made the devaluation unavoidable. It also removed certain price controls, yet retained other price ceilings, most notably the ceiling on residential rents. Yet what happened across 1959 can nonetheless be interpreted as roughly the effect of devaluing the nation's currency more rapidly than the general rate of domestic price inflation.

Table 16.2 gives some clues about the effects of the December 1958 devaluation of the peso on the distribution of income within Argentina. The exchange rate itself nearly tripled, with most of the rise in the peso price of the dollar coming in the early months of 1959. All prices within the country also rose, fed by earlier expansion of the money supply and the devaluation itself. But some prices rose much more than others. Note that wholesale prices rose much faster on traded than on nontraded goods: the prices of rural products, especially the beef and wheat dominating Argentina's exports, and the prices of imports shot up faster than did the prices of other domestic products, many of which did not enter trade directly. This is a typical short-run effect of devaluation.

The rise in the relative prices of traded goods should have been accompanied by a shift in income distribution toward the groups tied most closely to producing traded goods. The data on Argentine incomes are sparse. We do know, however, that one group that suffered heavily was nonfarm labor. While farm workers' incomes did not ap-

TABLE 16.2
Price, wage, and income movements in the wake of a sharp devaluation:
Argentina, 1958–1960

	Change from 3d quarter to 3d quarter, 1958–1959	Change from 3d quarter to 3d quarter, 1959–1960
Change in the peso value of the U.S. dollar.............	+190.6%	− 2.4%
Change in peso wholesale prices		
All goods..	+147.7%	+ 4.6%
Rural products (mostly exportables)	+177.3%	+ 0.4%
Nonrural domestic products	+132.9%	+ 6.6%
Imported products	+207.7%	+ 3.5%
Change in peso cost-of-living index	+124.5%	+15.9%
Change in U.S. dollar price of Argentine exports........	+ 6.9%	+ 2.8%
Change in U.S. dollar price of Argentine imports	− 5.9%	+ 2.1%
Change in Argentina's terms of trade ($P_x^\$/P_m^\$$)	+ 13.2%	+ 0.7%
Change in yearly peso wage per worker in industry	+ 36.0%	+51.0%
Change in yearly real wage per worker in industry	− 39.4%	+30.3%
Change in real national income per member of working population	− 6.1%*	+ 8.7%†

* From year 1958 to year 1959.
† From year 1959 to year 1960.
Sources: Carlos F. Diaz-Alejandro, *Exchange-Rate Devaluation in a Semi-Industrialized Country* (Cambridge, Mass.: MIT Press, 1965), pp. 150 and 155; and Diaz-Alejandro, *Essays on the Economic History of the Argentine Republic* (New Haven: Yale University Press, 1970), pp. 408–29.

parently drop any more than national income per person in the labor force, workers in construction, commerce, and the general "industry" category mentioned in Table 16.2 saw their real incomes drop by a third or more within a year. This relatively severe decline seems to have been related in part to the fact that nonfarm labor was more tied to the production of nontraded goods and services than was rural land-ownership or farm labor, both of them tied to exports and favored by the quick devaluation. The decline in the real wages of nonfarmers should not be explained solely in these terms, since this labor group had some ties to import-competing production in and around Buenos Aires, and also because its misfortunes were probably also related to the temporary tightening of monetary policy that accompanied the devaluation. Yet with these qualifiers the decline of real wages in 1959 seems to illustrate the plight of sellers of nontraded goods and services when a nation devalues its currency sharply.

Notice that the effects of devaluation seem to have been confined to the year in which the devaluation was taking place. The 1959–60 record shows that relative prices were quite stable within Argentina. At the same time, real nonfarm wage rates recovered the ground they had lost across 1959, suggesting that the serious damage sustained by nonfarm workers was confined to the single year of the devaluation. This too seems typical of postdevaluation experiences. A recent study of a dozen devaluation episodes in developing countries found that after 12 months the prices of other goods and services within the economy had caught up with the prices of traded goods, leaving no further net effect on relative prices. In the long run, the relative prices of different goods and services are not likely to be altered much by a monetary event such as devaluation. Yet in the short run, relative prices and relative incomes are twisted by a devaluation.

SUMMARY

The fact that imports depend on income levels alters the effects of shifts in the aggregate demand for a nation's product. The higher a nation's marginal propensity to import (the share of extra income going into extra imports), the more any rise in aggregate demand spills over into a worsening trade balance. This leakage into imports, like the leakage into saving, cuts down the value of the multiplier and dampens the effect of extra spending on the final change in national income. It also means that any boom or slump in one nation's aggregate demand has repercussions on foreign incomes. If the rest of the world has a significant marginal propensity to import from this nation, then swings in the business cycle are likely to be internationally contagious, a conjecture easily supported by the experience of the 1930s.

Devaluation can raise or lower aggregate national income. Devaluation will raise national income as long as it does not worsen the terms of trade or generate prolonged balance-of-payments surpluses. Devaluation will also twist the distribution of income within the nation in favor of groups producing and selling traded goods and services (exports and import-competing goods and services) and against sellers of nontraded goods and services, such as teachers and construction workers. This effect of devaluation on relative incomes is likely to be temporary, however, and possibly confined to a single year.

SUGGESTED READING

The algebra of the foreign trade multipliers is laid out in Fritz Machlup, *International Trade and the National Income Multiplier* (Philadelphia: Blakiston, 1943), which uses a time-period analysis; and in appendix H to Charles P. Kindleberger, *International Economics*, 5th ed. (Homewood, Ill.: Richard D. Irwin, 1973). Algebraic treatments combining price and income effects are: Jaroslav Vanek, *International Trade: Theory and Economic Policy* (Homewood, Ill: Richard D. Irwin, 1962), chaps. 6–9; and Robert M. Stern, *The Balance of Payments* (Chicago: Aldine, 1973), chap. 7.

QUESTIONS FOR REVIEW

1. By how much will an extra $1 billion of government spending raise national income in a Keynesian underemployed economy having a marginal propensity to import of 0.2 and a marginal propensity to save of 0.1? Ignore foreign repercussions.

2. Extend the analysis of this chapter by calculating the net effect of the extra $1 billion in government spending on this country's imports.

3. Reanswer Question 1 with the same marginal propensities to save and import for the rest of the world as for this country.

Answers:
1. By $1/(m + s) = 1/(0.1 + 0.2) = \$3.33$ billion.
2. Imports will rise by the final change in y times m, or 3.33 (0.2) = \$0.67 billion.
3. Using the formula in Equation (16.8) yields a rise in y of \$6 billion.

17

Money in the adjustment process

As long as nations have their own currencies, trying to analyze international payments adjustment and exchange rates without looking at national money supplies is like the proverbial playing of *Hamlet* without the Prince. The overall surplus or deficit on the balance of payments is in fact a net flow of money between nations, usually tending to make the money supplies in each nation match the national demand for money. A change in exchange rates is a change in a price ratio between national moneys. To understand how international payments adjustment and exchange rates work, we must therefore understand how they relate to money supplies as well as to prices and incomes.

This chapter completes the basic tool kit of international macroeconomics by bringing the role of money into full view. This done, Part IV can combine the equipment of Part III with a few extra theoretical tools to derive the main policy conclusions of international finance. This chapter's survey of the role of money dwells at first on a world of fixed exchange rates, first noting the causal arrows that can often be drawn from the balance of payments to the money supply under fixed exchange rates, and then following the reverse causation from the money supply to international payments. Later in the chapter we return to changes in exchange rates as they relate to money.

FROM THE BALANCE OF PAYMENTS TO THE MONEY SUPPLY

A surplus in a nation's balance of payments represents a way in which the nation adds to its money stock, and a deficit is a way in which its money stock is depleted.

This generalization is broadly correct, though the implications of a payments surplus or deficit for the national money supply depend on how the surplus or deficit is measured, and on the nation's monetary institutions. For the purposes of this chapter we shall define the balance-of-payments surplus as the net increase in a nation's holdings of money assets abroad minus the net increase in the rest of the world's holdings of money claims against the nation (bank deposits, currency and the like).

In times past, money was the same thing as the international reserve asset. This was true for major countries before the late 19th century. Gold was the international reserve asset, and the domestic asset backing up paper money, and even a prime form of circulating money itself. This was especially true before the emergence of fractional-reserve banking across the 18th century. When banks stayed close to the cloakroom function of issuing banknotes that could all be fully redeemed in gold when the depositor wished to turn them in, gold was both money and reserves. Something similar held for many colonial economies before their independence. The colonizing country's currency circulated in the colony as its money supply, which was raised or lowered, depending on whether the country was in payments surplus or deficit. When money and reserves are the same thing, then there is a simple identity relating the balance-of-payments surplus to the national money supply.

When reserves and money are the same thing,

$$B = \Delta R = \Delta M , \qquad (17.1)$$

and the rate of growth of the money supply depends only on the balance of payments:

$$\frac{\Delta M}{M} = \frac{B}{M} , \qquad (17.2)$$

where B is the balance-of-payments surplus (net inflow of money from abroad), ΔR is the change in reserves, and ΔM is the change in the money supply. The balance-of-payments surplus thus measured both the extent to which this country's money supply was growing and the extent to which the rest of the world was losing money.

Today most countries' monetary institutions are more complicated than this. The money supply is no longer confined to an amount equaling the nation's monetary reserves, either domestic reserve assets or international reserve assets. Gold has long since been retired from private monetary circulation, though it is still an industrial and consumer good of rising value. A nation's international reserve assets are held largely by its central monetary authorities (central bank and treasury) and by its private banks, as part, but only part, of the backing for the nation's money supply. Most of modern money consists of demand deposits in banks backed up by only fractional reserves held by the banking system.

To simplify this more complex set of monetary institutions without changing any key results, we shall view the monetary officials and the private banks they oversee as one consolidated banking sector. We shall also assume that all foreign currency is held by this banking sector, that all money liabilities to foreigners are owed by it, and that the national money consists solely of bank demand deposits, ignoring currency in circulation. Under these assumptions, the national money supply (M) consists of the reserves held by the banking system (R) plus the domestic assets of the banking system (D), corresponding to the rest of its demand deposit liabilities.

When reserves and the money are not the same thing,

$$M = R + D , \tag{17.3}$$

and since $B = \Delta R$,

$$\Delta M = B + \Delta D , \tag{17.4}$$

so that the rate of growth of the money supply depends on the balance of payments but also on domestic credit:

$$\frac{\Delta M}{M} = \frac{B + \Delta D}{M} . \tag{17.5}$$

As long as the banking system does not alter its domestic assets (so that $\Delta D = 0$), the balance affects the money just as directly in this case as if there were no distinction to be made between reserves and money. If the money supply is initially 100, a balance-of-payments surplus of 10 per year raises the money supply by 10 percent a year.

Yet under contemporary institutions, the banking system can offset, or *"sterilize,"* the payments imbalance, that is, keep it from having any net effect on the national money supply. This sterilization can be performed by either the monetary officials or the private banks within the banking sector. Officials can do it by responding to any payments surplus by cutting the ability of private banks to lend (with such tight money policies as raising the reserve requirements of private banks). Private banks can do it, if they want to, by cutting their own lending to domestic borrowers by the amount of the payments surplus. Thus a payments surplus of ten per year can be kept from affecting the money supply if the banking system cuts its domestic credits by ten per year, making $B = -\Delta D$, so that $\Delta M = 0$. Correspondingly, the banking system could sterilize a deficit by expanding domestic credit enough to keep total money stock the same.

Thus a payments surplus or deficit affects the money supply only if the banking system does not sterilize the payments imbalance. There are clear limits to the ability of a banking system to shield its national money stock entirely from the balance of payments. If the country keeps running surpluses, and trying to offset this by cutting its domestic lending, after a while its reserves (for example, deposits in foreign banks) will become as high as the total domestic money supply, and further surpluses will necessarily raise the money supply (unless the banking system becomes a net borrower from the rest of the economy). On the other hand, if the country keeps running deficits, the banking system will soon run out of reserves. Although this is feasible if the country is willing to let its currency fluctuate in value without official support, it violates the fixed-exchange-rate system we are discussing at present. Thus the balance of payments is likely to affect the money supply sooner or later, but it might be much later in countries with small payments imbalances relative to their reserves and money supplies. We shall return in Chapter 19 to the extreme case in which there is such perfect international mobility of lending and money flows that it is impossible for central monetary authorities to sterilize international money flows even in the short run.

FROM THE MONEY SUPPLY TO THE BALANCE OF PAYMENTS

Hume's price-specie-flow mechanism

Economists have long noted ways in which changes in a nation's money supply end up causing outflows of money from the nation in the form of a balance-of-payments deficit. This tendency was given an early systematic formulation by the 18th-century British philosopher, historian, essayist, and economist David Hume. Hume found a simple way to ridicule the mercantilist obsession of his day, the obsession with accumulating as much specie (gold and silver) as possible by having a greater value of exports than imports. In shorthand, his argument ran as follows:

Payments surplus and gold inflow $\rightarrow$ M up $\rightarrow$ Prices (and perhaps income) up $\rightarrow$ Trade balance worsens $\rightarrow$ Surplus and gold inflow cease .

The first link in the argument was noncontroversial in Hume's own day, since money and reserves and specie were all the same thing then. The next step also seemed logical once he pointed it out. Like other observers since the 16th century or earlier, Hume felt that an increase in the supply of money would end up inflating price levels. This was a reasonable conclusion. He next argued that if our price levels were being bid up, our competitive position in international trade would be worsening. The higher prices of domestic products would make our exports less competitive in foreign markets and would also cause more of our buyers to prefer foreign goods, which have not risen in price. Hume therefore reached the policy conclusion that mercantilist attempts to generate larger trade and payments with import restrictions and export subsidies would backfire once the price-specie-flow mechanism sketched here transformed the surplus into higher prices and declining surpluses.

Hume envisioned the opposite adjustment process for countries that were initially thrown into deficit. They would lose specie reserves, contracting their money supply. This in turn would bid down their price levels and improve their ability to compete in international trade. The value of the trade balance would improve until payments equilibrium was again restored, ending the deficits that set the whole process in motion.

It should be noted that the step in Hume's logic running from domestic prices to the trade balance requires a condition of underlying stability. A general rise (decline) in all domestic prices has the same effects on whether buyers decide to buy this country's products or foreign products as would a revaluation (devaluation) of this country's currency. Both would tend to make this country's goods and services look more (less) expensive to buyers relative to foreign prices. The condition that must hold for general price rises to worsen the balance of payments, and for general price declines to improve it, is the same condition of trade-balance stability discussed in Chapter 15 and derived in Appendix H. If—and only if—this condition is met, Hume's argument is valid for the institutional setting in which money and reserves are the same thing.

Modern variations

Conditions have changed since Hume's day, forcing changes in theory. The most important change for present purposes has been the rise of banking systems which issue money on the basis of only fractional reserves. Roughly speaking, we can say that this evolution passed through two stages, the rise of fractional-reserve private banks and the rise of central banks overseeing the private banks. The end result, especially where central banks were given discretionary power over the reserve positions of private banks, was that the banking sector could sterilize the effects of payments imbalance, immunizing the money supply in the manner already described. To anticipate Chapter 21's sketch of international currency experience, we should add that this change had already taken place within the 1880–1914 heyday of the gold standard. In this period central banks offset many payments surpluses ($B = \Delta R > 0$) with contractions of domestic credit ($\Delta D < 0$), and offset many deficits with expansions of domestic credit, violating the so-called rules of the gold standard game requiring that they let the payments imbalance change the money supply in the direction called for by Hume's model.

Another important change was the rise in the importance of government bonds and other interest-earning assets. With each new war fought by national governments, government debt built up, and it was only partly retired after peace had returned. The efficiency of lending markets also improved. By the 20th century the decision to hold money was largely a decision to refrain from holding interest-earning bonds as well as from spending right away. Accordingly, Keynesian models of the demand for money came to stress more and more that the interest rate was a key determinant of money demand. Higher interest rates would make people more willing to give up the convenience of ready cash to hold less liquid interest-earning assets instead. Lower interest rates would raise the demand for cash. At the same time, Keynesian theories argued that changes in the banking system's willingness to supply money took the form of changes in their willingness to lend at interest (changing M and D together).

This gradual change in perspective set the stage for a new way of describing how the money supply could end up affecting the balance of payments. Keynesian descriptions of this link started with the premise that the money supply itself was indeed a magnitude that could be directly controlled by monetary policy. That is, they assumed sterilization, allowing the analysis to ignore the initial stage in Hume's argument that had pinned changes in the money supply to prior changes in the balance of payments. The Keynesian view also came to highlight two intermediate roles played by the rate of interest. Its portrayal of the effects of monetary expansion on the balance of payments is sketched in Figure 17.1.

The process begins with a change in the ability and willingness of banks to create money by lending out deposits. Let us follow the expansionary case shown in the upper half of Figure 17.1. The extra bank willingness to lend might typically be due to expansionary monetary policies of the central bank, such as lowering banks' reserve requirements, or lowering the discount rate at which banks borrow

FIGURE 17.1
The Keynesian view of how the money supply affects the balance of payments

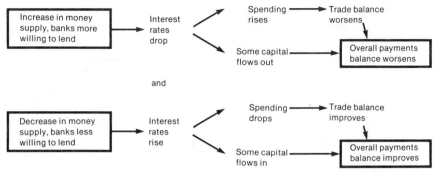

and

reserves from the central bank, or creating extra bank reserves by buying extra government bonds in the open market. The increased ability to lend will cause banks to offer lower interest rates to borrowers. More new loans are made, raising banks' domestic assets (D) and their money liabilities (M) at the same time. The borrowers use the borrowed funds to engage in new spending, on new houses, new plant and equipment, and new consumer durables. The extra spending becomes a multiplied expansion of spending and national income, probably accompanied by rising prices. The rise in incomes and prices in turn raises imports and worsens the trade balance. Meanwhile, the decline in domestic interest rates causes some holders of financial assets to seek out higher interest rates abroad. Their switch from lending at interest in this country to lending at interest abroad takes the form of a sale of bank deposits in this country in order to acquire interest-earning assets in other countries, and probably in other currencies. This lending outflow, or capital outflow, puts bank deposits in the hands of residents of other countries, so that part of the extra money supply ends up out of the country. Both the deterioration of the trade balance and the capital outflow contribute to a worsening of the overall payments balance. An expansion of the money supply thus unambiguously worsens the overall payments balance. Conversely, a contraction of the national money supply unambiguously improves the overall balance.

Monetarists subscribing to some form of the quantity theory of money would agree on the final result just described, though they would insist on portraying the intermediate steps differently. Since the quantity theory of money described a direct, and ultimately proportional, effect of the money supply on national income at current prices, monetarists tend to set aside interest rates when discussing the effects of money supply on the balance of payments. Another reason for their de-emphasis on the interest-rate link is the (correct) monetarist argument that raising the money supply often ends up raising interest rates rather than lowering them, once investors come to expect inflation and to ask for higher interest rates as protection against it. These doctrinal differences aside, monetarists and Keynesians agree that increasing the money supply worsens the overall balance of payments, with the monetarists arguing that the link from the money supply to spending is as direct as in Hume's first telling.

EXCHANGE RATES AND THE MONEY SUPPLY

Now that we have surveyed the relationships between the overall balance of payments and the national money supply, it is easier to grasp how exchange rates affect the money supply and how they are affected by it.

It is reasonable to suspect that devaluation (or depreciation) of a nation's currency raises the money supply, other things equal. If devaluation improves the overall balance, then it causes a net inflow, or stems a net outflow, of money. This follows by definition if we define the overall balance as exactly—and not just approximately, as with official definitions—equal to the net flow of money assets between the rest of the world and this country. One can therefore conclude that *the conditions under which devaluation causes a net inflow of money are identical to the conditions under which it improves the balance of payments.*

Although they should agree on this essential point, Keynesians and monetarists would insist on putting it in different ways. Keynesians tend to reason from the top of the balance-of-payments accounts on down, arguing that the key condition is the trade-balance stability discussed in Chapter 15 and derived in Appendix H. After adding a condition that the devaluation should also not cause such a large net outflow of capital as to outweigh the trade-balance improvement, they would arrive at a statement of what it takes for the devaluation to cause a net inflow of money. This Keynesian statement would be couched in terms of the elasticities and multipliers discussed in Chapters 15 and 16, and it would be backed up by econometric estimates of these parameters. Monetarists, whose view of the macroeconomy always centers on the money supply and money demand, would reach the same final point by working up from the bottom of the balance-of-payments accounts. They would tend to say that devaluation can improve the overall balance of payments only if it raises the money supply (relative to money demand), thereby causing a net inflow of money. A monetarist would thus say that the complicated elasticities formula for an improvement in the trade balance after devaluation was in fact a complicated way of expressing the conditions under which devaluation raised the national money supply to meet national money demand. It does not matter much which of these two views one takes, as long as one recognizes their equivalence.

The effect of a change in the national money supply on a flexible exchange rate is also something on which all economists would agree, despite lingering disputes over how to put the same point. *Raising the money supply unambiguously depreciates the national currency relative to other currencies when exchange rates are flexible.* Lowering the national money supply causes a rise in the value of a nation's currency when exchange rates are flexible. This should square with intuition, in view of the fact that raising (lowering) the supply of anything should typically lower (raise) its market price. In fact, the mechanisms through which the money supply are supposed to affect the exchange rate have already been described above, in our discussion of the causal chain leading from the money supply to the overall balance of payments. To see how a Keynesian would describe this linkage, one need only return to Figure 17.1 and replace the reference to the overall balance, on the right, with a reference to the value of the nation's currency in foreign exchange markets. A monetarist would shorten the same chain by merely leaving out the references to interest rates, again concluding that the money supply matters greatly to the equilibrium exchange rate.

Putting together the mutual links between the exchange rate and the money supply, we can see a potential problem with devaluing a nation's currency in order to improve the balance of payments and stem a reserve or money outflow. If devaluation (or depreciation) improves the balance of payments and causes a net money inflow, won't this expansion of the money supply in turn cause a worsening of the balance of payments and necessitate a further decline in the value of the nation's currency in foreign exchange markets, setting up the whole process once again? That is possible, and the monetary histories of many countries with depreciating currencies do show spirals of depreciation, money supply growth, and price inflation. We can see one way (but not the only way) to prevent this spiral when a country is devaluing by returning to an identity given earlier in this chapter. The rate of growth of the money supply depends on the balance of payments but also on domestic credit:

$$\frac{\Delta M}{M} = \frac{B + \Delta D}{M}. \tag{17.6}$$

If devaluation initially improves the balance of payments (raises B), monetary policy has an obvious way to keep this from raising the overall rate of growth of the money supply and causing price inflation. Monetary policy can sterilize, or offset, the rise in B by cutting the rate of growth of domestic credit ($\Delta D/M$). This suggests that a main way of making a devaluation "stick," in the sense of improving the balance of payments without necessitating further devaluations, is to accompany it with some tightening of domestic credit. Through a process of trial and error, many governments and central bankers have come to the same conclusion.

PURCHASING POWER PARITY

To explore further the relationship between money supplies and exchange rates, and to see more clearly the possible long-run combinations of currency depreciation and price inflation rates that are possible, we need to turn next to a long-standing hypothesis relating price levels and exchange rates.

It has often occurred to economists that goods that are substitutes for each other in international trade should have similar price movements in all countries when measured in the same currency. This should hold, at least, for a run long enough for market equilibrium to be restored after major shocks. Suppose that in December 1980 No. 2 soft red Chicago wheat costs $3 a bushel in Chicago. Its dollar price in London should not be much greater, given the cheapness of transporting wheat from Chicago to London. To simplify the example, let us say that it costs nothing at all to transport the wheat. It seems reasonable, then, that the dollar price of the same wheat in London should be $3 a bushel. If it were not, it would pay somebody to trade wheat between Chicago and London to profit from the price gap. Now if some major disruption temporarily forced the price of wheat in London up to $3.60, yet free trade was still possible, one would certainly expect that the two prices would soon be bid back into equality, presumably somewhere between $3.00 and $3.60 for both countries. In the case of wheat, which is a standardized commodity with a well-established market, one would expect the two price to be brought into line within a week.

For other commodities, price differences between countries are not so easily ironed out. Transport costs loom large for bulky items, and may provide a buffer between price movements in different countries if the good is not heavily traded. Goods that are strictly nontraded can have different price trends in different nations. Most manufactures are so heterogeneous that the product being produced and exported by one nation is only an imperfect substitute for the "competing" product in another country, again allowing their price trends to differ. Yet over a long period of time, or over a very short period of time during which wide price movements are expected and occur, one would expect similar price trends for the same traded good in all major trading countries, as long as the prices are measured in the same currency and are exclusive of tariffs and taxes.

This presumption that international trade does iron out differences in the price trends of traded goods has led to the **purchasing-power-parity hypothesis** linking national currency prices to exchange rates:

$$p_{US}^{\$} = r \cdot p_f^{\pounds}, \quad \text{or} \quad r = \frac{p_{US}^{\$}}{p_f^{\pounds}}. \tag{17.7}$$

Here the exchange rate r is again the price of the pound in dollars, and the price levels $P_{US}^{\$}$ and $P_f^{\pounds}$ are price levels in this country (say, the United States) and the rest of the world, respectively, each denominated in its own currency. The price variables have been interpreted and measured differently by different users of the hypothesis. Sometimes the prices are those of individual traded goods, such as wheat; sometimes they are price indexes covering all traded goods; and sometimes they are overall price indexes covering entire national economies (for example, wholesale price indexes, cost-of-living indexes, and national product deflators). When the prices represent individual traded goods, the hypothesis is unobjectionable and uncontroversial. Clearly, price trends measured in the same currency are indeed similar in different countries, especially for a commodity like wheat. When the price variables are export and import price indexes, their meaning is again clear. They are supposed to be given the same trends over time by trade arbitrage. One expects this to happen, even though the reliability of the available measures is compromised by the fact that different weights are given to different goods in each country's import and export price indexes. If the price indexes are overall national price levels, the hypothesis is no longer so closely related to trade competition itself, and must be intended as a statement about how exchange rates relate to the purchasing powers of national moneys over all goods and services.

Something like the purchasing-power-parity theory has existed throughout the modern history of international economics. The theory keeps resurfacing whenever exchange rates have come unfixed by wars or other events. Sometimes the hypothesis is used as a way of describing how a nation's general price level must change to reestablish some desired exchange rate, given the level and trend in foreign prices. At other times it is used to guess at what the equilibrium exchange rate will be, given recent trends in prices within and outside the country. Both of these interpretations crept into the British "bullionist-antibullionist" debate during and after the Napoleonic

Wars, when the issue was why Britain had been driven by the wars to dislodge the pound sterling from its fixed exchange rates and gold backing, and what could be done about it. The purchasing-power-parity hypothesis came into its own in the 1920s, when Gustav Cassel and others directed it at the issue of how much European countries would have to change either their official exchange rates or their domestic price levels, given that World War I had driven the exchange rates off their prewar par values and had brought varying percentages of price inflation to different countries. With the restoration of the fixed exchange rate during the early postwar era, the purchasing-power-parity hypothesis again faded from prominence, ostensibly because its defects had been demonstrated, but mainly because the issue it raised seemed less compelling as long as exchange rates were expected to stay fixed. After the resumption of widespread floating of exchange rates in 1971, the hypothesis was revived once again.

The purchasing-power-parity hypothesis has received mild, though mixed, empirical support. Its testing is complicated by the fact that each nation has several alternative price indexes, each of which often moves differently from the others, making the choice of a price index rather arbitrary. This difficulty arises largely from the existence of non-traded goods, for which it is wrong to expect any smooth equalization of same-currency prices across countries. Yet the hypothesis is *roughly* valid as a prediction about what happens to prices and exchange rates over a period of time sufficient for *large* price movements. When Germany experienced its more-than-trillionfold inflation of all prices and wages in 1923, both its external exchange rates on the dollar and its domestic price levels shot up at rates as equal as could be expected from so chaotic a process. The hypothesis also seems to do a fair job in matching rates of exchange-rate depreciation to differentials in inflation rates for the highly inflationary ABC countries—Argentina, Brazil, and Chile (as Table 16.2 partly attests for Argentina's 1958–60 experience). It was a rough guide, but only a rough one, to the mistake made by Britain in returning to the prewar gold parity for the pound sterling in 1925 despite greater inflation in Britain than in the United States and some other trading partners of Britain. The hypothesis has generally survived tests on changes across World War II and across the early 1970s, though one study by Bela Balassa found that it gave unbelievable results in a postwar comparison of developing countries, apparently because of biases imparted by the prices of nontraded goods. The hypothesis remains a fair guide, however, to the combinations of inflation and exchange-rate depreciation that can be expected to go together in a country whose price trend departs from that of the rest of the world.

MONEY, PRICES, AND EXCHANGE RATES IN THE LONG RUN

In recent years a monetarist revival on the international front, known as the "monetary approach to the balance of payments," has reinterpreted the conditions for long-run equilibrium in markets for money and goods. One contribution of this monetarist wave, but not the only one, has been to make explicit some long-run tendencies that fit both the facts and some recurring theories.

The reinterpretation of the long-run relationship between money supplies, prices, and exchange rates combines two traditional strands of theory: the purchasing-power-parity hypothesis and the quantity theory of money. The purchasing-power-parity argument as advanced in monetarist models is reexpressed as:

$$P = rP_f, \tag{17.8}$$

where P is now an overall price index (the GNP deflator) for this country, r is still the price of the foreign currency (the exchange rate), and P_f is the overall price index for the rest of the world, converted into a single foreign currency. The quantity theory of money says that the equilibrium between this nation's money supply (M) and money demand is usefully summarized in the equation

$$M = k P y , \tag{17.9}$$

where y is real national income and k is a coefficient defined by this equation. Monetarist argue that k is also a behavioral "constant" characteristic of how much money balances people tend to keep in order to support a given value of turnover of business ($P\ y$). Some monetarists argue that k is likely to be constant over the long run and that y is a full-employment income fixed by real forces but not by P or M. Keynesians tend to regard this equation as a not-so-revealing identity, arguing that k can vary a lot and that one cannot tell from the equation whether changing M will change P or y. Yet the equation helps frame the possible combinations of money growth, inflation, and exchange-rate drift even if the Keynesian criticisms are accepted.

Together the purchasing-power-parity hypothesis and the quantity theory of money imply a simple relationship among the variables introduced here:

$$M = k r P_f y . \tag{17.10}$$

To reflect on what this means about percentage changes, let us convert the equation into rate-of-change form. Whenever variables are related to one another in product form, as in Equation (17.9), their rates of change are related to one another in additive form. Thus

$$\overset{*}{M} = \overset{*}{k} + \overset{*}{r} + \overset{*}{P}_f + \overset{*}{y} , \qquad (17.11)$$

where the asterisks denote proportionate rates of change (percentages ÷ 100):

$$\overset{*}{M} = \Delta M/M, \quad \overset{*}{k} = \Delta k/k, \quad \overset{*}{r} = \Delta r/r, \quad \overset{*}{P}_f = \Delta P_f/P_f, \text{ and } \overset{*}{y} = \Delta y/y .$$

Over a period of time long enough to allow us to set aside subtle dynamics of expectations, real income effects of monetary changes, and effects on the international capital flows stemming from changes in interest rates, Equation (17.11) should hold. It carries several important implications about prices and exchange rates.

One implication stemming from the purchasing-power-parity hypothesis alone is that stabilizing a country's exchange rate is not the same thing as stabilizing its price level. Since $\overset{*}{P} = \overset{*}{r} + \overset{*}{P}_f$, any tendency toward inflation or deflation in the outside world ($\overset{*}{P}_f$ unequal to 0) faces this country with the task of choosing between stable prices ($\overset{*}{P} = 0$) with changing exchange rates and stable exchange rates ($\overset{*}{r} = 0$) with changing prices. This conflict, noted by Keynes in the 1920s, poses a dilemma for monetary authorities who feel that both stable exchange rates and stable domestic prices are high national priorities. This dilemma is acutely felt by West Germany and Switzerland today. Both countries want stable domestic price levels ($\overset{*}{P} = 0$) in a world beset with inflation ($\overset{*}{P}_f > 0$). To keep their prices nearly stable they have had to accept rising values of their national currencies ($\overset{*}{r} < 0$) in the 1970s, after trying to have both fixed exchange rates and stable prices across the 1960s, with declining success.

Equation (17.11) also maps out the rates of growth of the money supply that are consistent with either stable domestic prices or stable exchange rates. To stabilize the exchange rate ($\overset{*}{r} = 0$), one must have the money supply grow at a rate equal to ($\overset{*}{k} + \overset{*}{P}_f + \overset{*}{y}$). If k is truly a long-run constant, as some monetarists argue, the growth rate of the national money supply that is consistent with stable exchange rates equals the sum of the growth of real national income ($\overset{*}{y}$) and the foreign rate of inflation ($\overset{*}{P}_f$). To stabilize the domestic price level, so that $\overset{*}{P} = 0$, Equation (17.9) advises that the national money supply must grow at the same rate as real national product if k is constant. This is the monetarist's rule for a stable money growth consistent with stable prices.

The quantity theory of money summarized in Equation (17.9) can also be applied to the entire world economy as a closed system. In its rate-of-change form at the world level, this theory says that the growth rate of the world money supply will equal the world rate of inflation plus the growth rate of world product as long as k is constant. In symbols, this is $\overset{*}{M} = \overset{*}{P} + \overset{*}{y}$, where $\overset{*}{M}$ and $\overset{*}{P}$ are both converted into the same currency. Thus prices at the world level can be held stable in any one currency in the long run only if the growth of the world money supply, again measured in that currency, is held down to the rate of growth in world output. Though this condition allows positive growth in the world money supply, it has not been met in recent times.

Against this way of putting the long-run options run the various Keynesian objections against using such an aggregated and simplified monetary model. These objections assume greater weight when we focus attention on the shorter run that matters most to policymakers seeking results soon, such as before the next election. To grapple with these shorter-run policy problems, we shall employ somewhat more complicated models in Chapter 19.

SUMMARY

Since the overall surplus or deficit on the balance of payments is roughly a net flow of money or of the reserve that back up money, the balance of payments can clearly affect the national money supply. Contemporary institutions make it possible, within wide limits, for monetary officials to break this link by "sterilizing," or offsetting the balance-of-payment surpluses or deficits. Surpluses can be kept from adding to the national money supply by the banking system's offsetting contraction of domestic credit, and deficits can be offset by an expansion of domestic credit.

Changes in the money supply in turn affect the balance of payments. Both Hume's price-specie-flow mechanism and contemporary monetary analysis stress a direct positive effect of the money supply on spending and prices, which in turn worsens the balance of payments. Keynesians arrive at a similar final result by a different route. They stress that expanding the money supply lowers interest rates. The lower interest rates worsen the balance of payments, both by raising total spending—and with it, imports—and by causing an outflow of lending in search of higher interest rates abroad.

The exchange rate relates to the national money supply in the same way as does the balance of payments. A decline in the value of the nation's currency can affect the national money supply by stemming an outflow, or causing an inflow, of money, whereas a rise in the value of the nation's currency does the opposite, in the absence of sterilizing policies. Expanding the money supply depreciates the value of the nation's currency under a floating exchange rate as surely as, and in the same way as, it causes a shift toward payments deficit under a fixed rate.

The purchasing-power-parity hypothesis argues that a change in the exchange rate between two currencies has to follow, or be followed by, a change in the ratio of price levels in the two countries. This hypothesis is beset by some major problems of selecting the right index numbers for prices, but it has been shown to be roughly correct for either the long run or for a shorter run in which one country is experiencing hyperinflation.

Combining the purchasing-power-parity hypothesis with the quantity theory of money permits some conditional statements about how prices, exchange rates, and money supply growth must be linked in the long run, assuming equilibrium in markets for moneys and goods. The purchasing-power-parity hypothesis makes it clear that in an inflationary outside world an individual country cannot have both stable prices and stable exchange rates. This hypothesis plus the quantity theory of money roughly defines the long-run rate of growth in a national money supply that can be consistent with stable prices as well as the long-run rate of growth which is consistent with stable exchange rates.

SUGGESTED READING

An alternative textbook presentation is Richard E. Caves and Ronald W. Jones, *World Trade and Payments* (Boston: Little, Brown, 1973), chap. 16.

Tests of the purchasing-power-parity hypothesis can be found in Leland B. Yeager, "A Rehabilitation of Purchasing-Power-Parity," *Journal of Political Economy*, vol. 66, no. 6 (December 1958), pp. 516–30; Bela Balassa, "The Purchasing-Power-Parity Doctrine: A Reappraisal," *Journal of Political Economy*, vol. 72, no. 6 (December 1964), pp. 584–96; and Harry J. Gailliot, "Purchasing Power Parity as an Explanation of Long-term Changes in Exchange Rates," *Journal of Money, Credit, and Banking*, vol. 2 (August 1970), pp. 348–57.

Advanced contributions to, and debates over, the role of money in the adjustment process are found in a special 1976 issue of the *Scandinavian Journal of Economics* on flexible exchange rates and stabilization policy; Jacob Frenkel and Harry G. Johnson, *The Monetary Approach to the Balance of Payments* (London: Allen and Unwin, 1975); and Marina von Neumann

Whitman, "Global Monetarism and the Monetary Approach to the Balance of Payments," in *Brookings Papers in Economic Analysis*, (Washington: Brookings Institution, 1975), no. 3, pp. 491–555.

QUESTIONS FOR REVIEW

1. Return to the sketch of Hume's price-specie-flow mechanism for the surplus country. Would you conclude from Hume's model that price trends have to be the same in all countries (as the purchasing-power-parity hypothesis would predict for a fixed-exchange-rate system)? Explore this question under two different assumptions: (a) the initial surplus resulted from a drop in this country's aggregate demand, initially lowering its prices relative to those of the rest of the world; and (b) the initial surplus resulted because international demand shifted toward this country's goods and away from foreign goods, initially raising prices here and lowering them abroad.

2. Suppose that Brazil wants to stabilize the cost of foreign exchange (cruzeiros/dollar) in a world in which dollar prices are generally rising at 5 percent per year. What rate of inflation of domestic cruzeiro prices must it come down to, and what rate of money supply growth would yield this rate, if the quantity theory of money holds with constant k and Brazilian output is growing at 6 percent per annum?

Answer:
Inflation must drop to 5 percent, and the money supply growth must be held to 11 percent per year.

0-Day   Futures 9230   9242
0-Day   Futures 9227   9241
ina-Taiwan   (Dollar) 0   5
lombia   (Peso) .... .0275   .0275
nmark   (Krone) .... .1631   .1632
uad   (Sucre) .... .0385   .0385
nland   (Markka) 2   2
ance   (Franc) .... .2052   .2043
0-Day   Futures .... .20   0
0-Day   Futures 2
0-Day   Futures .... .2025   .2022

eece   (Drachma) .... .0280   .0280
ng Kong   (Dollar) .... .2139   .2142
la   (Rupee) .... .1170   .1165
onesia   .... .00259   .002590
n   (Rial) .... .01416   .
q   (   ) 3.44
ael   (Pound) .... .0951
ly   (   ) .... .00
an   (Ye   ) .... .003834   .
0-Day   Futures .... .0 845   .003 37
0-Day   Futures ....   1 .003839
0-Day   Futures .... .00   .00 362

anon   (Pound) .... .32 9   .32 31
laysia   (Dollar) .... .40 7   .4076
xico   (Peso) .... .04 1   .441
herlands   (Guilder) .... .40 8   .4078
w ealand   (Dollar) .... .9 2   .9825
  (Krone) .... .182   .1823
kistan   (Rupee) .... .1025   .1025
ru   (Sol) .... .0124   .0124
ilippines   (Peso) .... .13   .1355
tugal   (Escudo) .... .0 46   .0 46
di Arabia   (Riyal) .... .28 3   .28 3
gapore   (Dollar) .... .4109   .   0
th Africa   (Rand) 1.1522   1.1522

'Paper Gold,'
All Paper,
No Gold

Peso Falls Again
As Mexican Bank
Ends Its Support

Fund Effectively Devalued,
For the Third Time
Since August, to 3.5 Cents

AIRLINES PLAN END
TO USE OF DOLLAR
IN SETTING RATES

Major Companies Agree on
Shift Basis of Calculation
to I.M.F.'s 'Paper Gold'

STANDARDIZATION IS AIM

Reliance on Sterling Would
Also Halt—Governments'
Approval to Be Sought

End of Two-Tier Gold Market Offers U.S.
Political, Economic and Monetary Options

18

Policy options for payments adjustment: Overview

THE OPTIONS FOR ONE COUNTRY

With the help of the analysis in Part III, we can now turn to the task of bringing together what is known about the options facing nations and the world when it comes to ironing out imbalances in payments between nations, and imbalances between supply and demand for individual currencies.

Some headway toward policy judgments has already been made in Part III. In Chapter 15 we previewed five policy options facing a country trying to deal with its external balance on its own. These were put as five choices facing a country running a deficit at the current exchange rate, with opposite choices facing surplus countries. The choices, again, are:

1. Financing—if the imbalance is known to be temporary, the nation can simply draw down its reserves for a while and maintain the same exchange rate.
2. The floating rate—the nation can let the exchange market take care of the exchange rate, by letting the value of its currency drop until exchange-market equilibrium is restored.
3. Exchange controls—the nation can keep the external value of its currency fixed by rationing the ability of its residents to acquire foreign exchange for spending abroad.
4. Adjusting the economy to the exchange rate (or "classical medicine")—deflating the domestic economy, lowering prices and incomes so that the supply and demand for foreign exchange will be pulled into equality at the same fixed exchange rate.

5. The adjustable peg (or the Bretton Woods system)—the nation can follow prescription 4 if small doses of domestic adjustment will suffice to defend the fixed exchange rate, or it can devalue its currency and peg it at a new official exchange rate if defending the old fixed rate required too much domestic adjustment.

The task of choosing among these options was aided somewhat by Chapter 15's analysis of the effects of the exchange rate on the trade balance. There we argued that devaluing or depreciating a nation's currency is likely to improve the trade balance, though possible exceptions were carefully cataloged. This means that Options 2 and 5 are not yet to be ruled out, since the evidence suggests that the response of trade balances to exchange-rate changes is likely to be in the stabilizing direction. This at least sends speculators stabilizing signals, though it remains for Chapters 20 and 21 to discuss the likelihood that speculators will respond to such signals. Chapters 16 and 17 added further analytic material that will be mobilized in Chapters 19 and 21 in judging the macroeconomic workability of fixed and flexible exchange rates. Chapter 17's discussion of the role of money also added to our understanding of what it would take to adjust the domestic economy to the task of maintaining a fixed exchange rate.

This chapter educates adjustment policy choices further, by narrowing down the range of choices for a single nation and by confronting some problems of international policy coordination under the fixed-rate and adjustable-peg systems.

FINANCING TEMPORARY DISEQUILIBRIUMS

The first option, that of financing imbalances, is convenient and attractive for as long as it is possible. A nation running a payments deficit would be delighted to have the chance to go on financing it forever by just relaxing and having the rest of the world accept ever-growing amounts of its money liabilities (bank deposits). This is handy for the deficit country, which need not even pay interest on its accumulating money liabilities. What is more, in a world of rising commodity prices, the rest of the world is accepting this country's obligations and earning a negative real rate of return by having less purchasing power when it comes time to spend the same amount of currency reserves later on.

The reserve-accumulating surplus countries quickly lose patience with this form of implicit charity, especially if the deficit country is not in the favored position of a key-currency country, to be discussed shortly. Before too long, private parties in the surplus country will turn in the deposits in the deficit country, earned through trade and international capital transactions, to their central banks for conversion into domestic money. The central banks of the surplus countries will in turn demand that the monetary authorities of the deficit countries honor their domestic banks' liabilities by giving up foreign exchange or gold. After this continues for a while, the deficit country will be in danger of running out of internationally acceptable reserves. Even if the International Monetary Fund or some other international agency helps deficit countries finance their deficits, the ability of the international agency to extend this financial aid depends on how much reserve assets the surplus countries are willing to let the agency lend out. Thus financing cannot cover a permanent deficit in the balance of payments, and true payments adjustment must take place.

There is one set of circumstances, however, under which payments imbalances can be properly financed forever. This is the case in which the imbalances are clearly *temporary*, meaning that officials can finance a succession of deficits and surpluses indefinitely without being compelled to run out of reserves or to accumulate large amounts of unwanted reserves. In this case one can argue that financing temporary deficits and surpluses is better than letting the exchange rate float around, as in Option 2 above. This point is quite important for the debate over exchange-rate regimes, and it deserves an illustration.

Figure 18.1 gives an example of perfectly successful and socially desirable financing of temporary surpluses and deficits with a fixed exchange rate.[1] We have imagined here that the temporary fluctuations in the balance of payments and the foreign exchange market arise from something predictable, such as a seasonal pattern in foreign exchange receipts, with the dollar country exporting more and earning more foreign exchange in the autumn-winter harvest season than in the nonharvest spring-summer season. To help the example along, let us assume that it is costly for producers of the export crop to refrain from selling it in the harvest season and that something also prevents private speculators from stepping in and performing the equilibrating function being assigned to officials here. If the officials did not finance the temporary imbalances, the exchange rate would drop to $1.40 at Point B in the harvest season, when the nation had a lot of exports to sell, and it would rise to $1.60 in the off-season. In this there is a certain economic loss, since it would be better if the people who wanted extra foreign exchange to keep up imports in the off-season did not have to pay $1.60 for foreign exchange that is readily available for only $1.40 in the harvest season. The officials can recapture this eco-

---

[1] Those who have read Appendix F will recognize here another application of its treatment of the welfare economics of commodity price stabilization. The analogy is valid, and requires only that we substitute a foreign currency for the commodity whose price was being stabilized.

FIGURE 18.1
A successful financing of temporary deficits and surpluses at a stable exchange rate

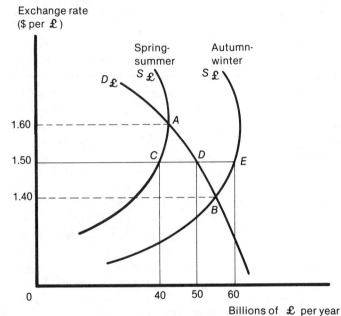

Autumn and winter: officials buy *DE* = £50 billion in foreign exchange.
Spring and summer: officials sell *CD* = £50 billion in foreign exchange.

nomic gain by stabilizing the price at $1.50. What makes their stabilization possible is that they have somehow picked the correct price ($1.50), the one at which they can sell exactly as much foreign exchange in one season as they buy in the other, exactly breaking even while stabilizing the price.

The official financing of spring-summer deficits with autumn-winter foreign exchange reserves brings a net social gain to the world. This gain arises from the fact that the officials gave a net supply of foreign exchange at $1.50 to people who would have been willing to pay $1.60 a pound in the spring-summer season, while also buying up at $1.50 the same amount of foreign exchange from people who would have been willing to sell it at $1.40. The net gain is measured as the sum of areas *ACD* and *BDE* (or about $1 billion a year). In this case financing was successful, and superior to letting the exchange rate find its own equilibrium in each season.

For the financing of temporary equilibriums to be the correct policy option for dealing with the balance of payments and exchange markets, some stringent conditions have to be met. First, it must be the case that private potential speculators do not see, or cannot take advantage of, the opportunity to buy foreign exchange in the fall and winter, invest it for a few months, and then sell it in the spring and summer. If private parties could do this, their own actions would bring the exchange rate close to $1.50 throughout the year, and there would be no need of official financing.

It is also crucial that the officials correctly predict the future demand and supply for foreign exchange at all likely exchange rates, and that they also predict what would be an equilibrium path for the exchange rate in the absence of their intervention. If they do not forecast correctly, their attempt to finance a deficit or a surplus at a fixed exchange rate can be very costly, because it involves them in unwanted net accumulation or depletion of their foreign exchange reserves.

To see some of the economic costs of trying to finance a "temporary" disequilibrium that turns out to be a *fundamental* disequilibrium, consider the attempt of her majesty's government and the Bank of England to prop up the sagging pound sterling at a value of $2.80 before they had to give up and devalue to $2.40 on November 18, 1967. The situation before and after that date is sketched in Figure 18.2. Throughout the period 1964–67, the official exchange rate of

FIGURE 18.2
An unsuccessful temporary financing of a fundamental disequilibrium

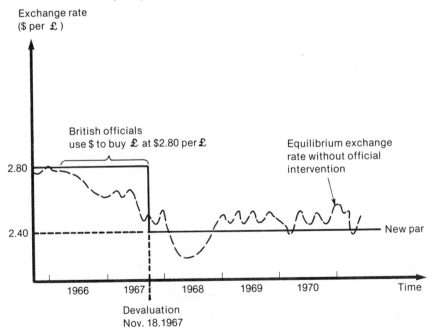

$2.80 was higher than the rate would have been without official intervention. If this had been only a temporary disequilibrium, as the officials dearly hoped, it would have soon been followed by a surge of demand for the pound, making the implicit equilibrium exchange rate rise above $2.80 and allowing the officials to switch from financing a deficit to financing a surplus by adding to their dollar holdings. The disequilibrium was not temporary. British officials found themselves buying up increasing amounts of pounds at the high price of $2.80, partly with dollars borrowed from the IMF and the Federal Reserve. When their reserves and their credit lines were exhausted, they had to give up and devalue to $2.40. As a result, they created a sudden shock to the international financial system. They also lost billions of pounds of taxpayers' money. The losses stemmed from their having tried to buy pounds dear, only to end up having to selling them cheap to recover the dollars they had sold earlier. They had to regain dollar reserves and repay the IMF and the Federal Reserve the borrowed dollars, by giving up pounds now worth only $2.40 each, versus the $2.80 paid for them by British officials. Buying dear and selling cheap is not the formula for profits.

The same misfortune has befallen officials whose currencies are bound to rise in value despite their vigorous attempts to hold down their values. For example, the Japanese government did not want the dollar value of the yen to rise in August 1971, even though President Nixon had openly invited speculation in favor of the yen by calling for its revaluation (rise in dollar value). Hoping to ride out a temporary surplus situation in order to keep Japan's export and import-competing goods competitive (to the advantage of powerful trading groups but to the disadvantage of Japanese consuming groups), Japanese officials bought up billions of dollars in a few months as a way of financing the "temporary" surplus. Dollars threatened to become the sole asset of the Bank of Japan if the trend did not stop. The Japanese officials soon gave up, and let the dollar value of the yen jump by more than 30 percent. This involved the Japanese officials in the same kind of currency losses as the British officials had sustained in 1967. The difference was that the Japanese officials were stuck holding *foreign* currency that was worth less than they had paid for it (the depreciating dollars), whereas the British had ended up holding less valuable domestic currency.

These experiences do not prove that it is futile to try to keep exchange rates fixed. What they prove is that when the existing official exchange rate is becoming a disequilibrium exchange rate for the long run, trying to ride out the storm with financing alone is costly. Something more has to be added. Fundamental disequilibrium calls for true adjustment, not just financing.

It is not easy for officials to judge what constitutes fundamental disequilibrium, any more than it is easy for them to forecast gross national product for the next five years. This problem has existed throughout the postwar attempt to allow countries to change their exchange rates only when disequilibrium is fundamental. The Articles of Agreement of the International Monetary Fund (IMF), signed at Bretton Woods, New Hampshire in 1944, permitted exchange-rate adjustment within limitations. These percentage limitations could be exceeded only in the case of fundamental disequilibrium. Yet nowhere in the Articles of Agreement is fundamental disequilibrium defined, nor have the deliberations of the IMF directors for over 30 years produced any further enlightenment on this issue. We are left with the knowledge that a fundamental disequilibrium is one that is too great and/or too enduring to be financed, but without a clear way of identifying one until after it has happened.

RESERVE-CENTER FINANCING

The opportunity to have the rest of the world gladly accept your bank deposits and hold them is more available to reserve-center countries such as the United States than to other countries. If the national currency is a key currency in international transactions, even in transactions not involving this nation, then the growth of the world economy is likely to lead to growth in the demand for this currency as a means of international payment. Throughout the postwar period, at least until the early 1970s, foreign demand for dollar bank balances grew and was only partly met by the growth of the Eurodollar market described in Chapter 13.

The growth of foreign demand for the dollar as a key currency gave the United States the opportunity to run "deficits without tears." Surplus-country critics, particularly in France, charged that the United States was helping itself to a free lunch by having the rest of the world hold the dollar bank deposits supplied by U.S. payments deficits. With the rest of the world willing to hold increasing amounts of its money liabilities, the United States could go on buying more foreign goods and services and firms than it earned through its own sales. The "deficits without tears" charge is broadly correct to the extent that it describes the effects of the deficits on the United States. Despite considerable official hand-wringing, the United States refrained from the kind of severe adjustment, such as deflation of the whole U.S. economy, that would have been necessary to eliminate the deficits in a context of fixed exchange rates without exchange controls. The United States was thus given extraordinary leeway to "finance" its deficits. On the other hand, the rest of the world did get something for its holding of dollar balances: it got the implicit services of the most widely recognized and accepted international money. By the 1970s, its private demands had become essentially satiated, and the United States could only accumulate dollar liabilities to those foreign governments, such as Japan, which were still trying to prop up the dollar to keep their currencies down and their goods competitive. The time had come when the United States, like other countries before it, had to contemplate options for adjustment instead of being able to continue financing deficits with growing money liabilities.

EXCHANGE CONTROLS

Among the options for true adjustment when financing is no longer possible, one can be indicted as socially inferior to the others. Oddly enough, it is widely practiced.

Many countries have responded to persistent disequilibriums in their external payments by defending the fixed exchange rate with elaborate government controls over the ability of their residents to buy foreign goods or services, to travel abroad, or to lend abroad.

Exchange controls are closely analogous to quantitative restrictions (quotas) on imports, already analyzed in Chapter 8 above. In fact, the analogy with import quotas fits very well, so well that the welfare economics of exchange controls is just the welfare economics of import quotas expanded to cover imports of IOUs (lending abroad) and tourist services as well as imports of ordinary commodities. In Chapter 8 and Appendix E we argue that the import quota is at least as bad as an import tariff on a one-dollar, one-vote welfare basis. So it is with exchange controls as well: they are at least as damaging as a uniform tax on all foreign transactions, and probably quite a bit worse.

To show the economic case against exchange controls, it is useful to start with an oversimplified view of exchange controls that is almost certain to underestimate the social losses coming from real-world controls. Figure 18.3 sketches the effects of a system of binding exchange controls that is about as well managed and benign as one can imagine. Figure 18.3 imagines that the U.S. government has become committed to maintaining a fixed exchange rate that officially values foreign currencies less, and the dollar more, than would a free-market equilibrium rate. This official rate is $1.30 for the pound sterling, with similar subequilibrium rates for other foreign currencies. The exchange-control laws require that exporters turn over all their claims on foreigners (which we shall equate with receipts in foreign currencies) to the U.S. government, which gives them $1.30 in domestic bank deposits for each pound sterling they have earned by selling abroad. At this exchange rate, exporters are earning, and turning in to the authorities,

FIGURE 18.3
Welfare losses from well-managed exchange controls

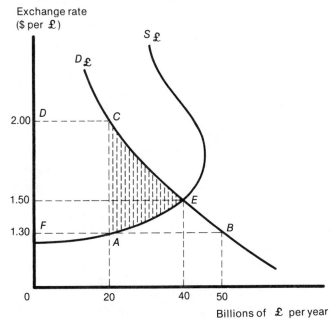

only £20 billion a year, well below the £50 billion a year that residents of the United States would want to buy in order to buy foreign goods, services, and assets. If the U.S. government feels committed to the $1.30 rate, yet is not willing to contract the whole U.S. economy enough to make the demand and supply for foreign exchange match at $1.30, then it must ration the right to buy foreign exchange.

Let us imagine that the U.S. officials ration foreign exchange in an efficient but seldom-tried way. Every two months they announce that it is time for another public auction-by-mail. On January 21 they announce that anybody wanting sterling (or any other foreign currency) for the March–April period must send in bids by February 15. A family wanting to be in England in April might send in a form pledging its willingness to pay up to $3 per pound for 200 pounds to spend in England, and its willingness to pay $2 per pound for 250 pounds. An importer of automobiles would also submit a schedule of amounts of foreign currencies he wished to buy at each exchange rate in order to buy cars abroad. Receiving all these bids, the government's computers would rank them by the prices willingly pledged, and add up the totals pledged at each price, thus revealing the demand curve $D_£$ in Figure 18.3. Estimating that it could allocate £20 billion per year, or

£.3¹/₃ billion for March–April, the government would announce on February 20 that the price of $2 per pound was the price making demand just match the available £20 billion per year. The family wanting to be in England for April would thus be able to get £250 by taking a check for $500 = £250 × $2/ £ to the local post office, along with the officially signed pledge form it had submitted before February 15. All who were willing to pay $2 or more for each pound would thus get the pounds they applied for, at the price of only $2 a pound, even if they had said that they were willing to pay more. Anybody not submitting bids with prices as high as $2 would be denied the right to buy abroad in March or April.

This system would give the government a large amount of revenues earned from the exchange-control auctions. Collecting $2.00/ £ × £20 billion = $40 billion per year while paying exporters only $1.30/ £ × £20 billion = $26 billion, the government would make a net profit of $14 billion each year, minus its negligible administrative costs. This government profit could be returned to the general public either as a cut in other kinds of taxes or as extra government spending. Area AFCD in Figure 18.3 represents these auction profits taken from importers but returned to the rest of society, and does not constitute a net gain or loss for society as a whole.

The foreign currency auction just described does impose a welfare loss on society as a whole, however. This loss is measured by the area ACE. To see why, remember the interpretation of demand and supply curves as marginal benefit and cost curves. When the exchange controls are in effect and only £20 billion is available each year, some mutually profitable bargains are being prohibited. At Point C the demand curve is telling us that somebody would be willing to pay up to $2 for an extra pound per year. At Point A the supply curve is telling us that somebody else, either a U.S. exporter or his customers, would be willing to give up an extra pound per year for as little as $1.30. Yet the exchange controls prevent these two groups from getting together to split the $0.70 of net gain in a marketplace for pounds. Thus the vertical distance AC = $0.70 shows the social loss from not being able to trade freely another pound per year. Similarly, each extra vertical gap between the demand curve and the supply curve out to Point E also adds to the measure of something lost because the exchange controls hamper private transactions. All these net losses add up to area ACE (or something like £7 billion a year).

Actual exchange-control regimes are likely to entail higher social costs than this hypothetical one. In practice, governments do not hold public foreign currency auctions. They allocate the right to buy foreign currency at the low official rate according to more complicated rules. To get the right to buy foreign currency, one must go through involved application procedures to show that the purpose of the foreign purchase qualifies it for a favored-treatment category. Importing inputs for factories that would otherwise have to remain idle and underutilized is a purpose that often qualifies for priority access to foreign exchange, over less crucial inputs, or imports of luxury consumer goods, or acquisition of private foreign bank deposits. Using exchange controls as a way of rationing according to some sort of officially appraised social merit can have its positive effects, of course. But in actual practice the existence of these controls is questionable, as is the basis for choosing exchange controls instead of more direct redistributive devices as a way of pursuing domestic social goals. And the clearest difference between actual exchange controls and our hypothetical one is that the actual controls involve much greater administrative costs to enforce the controls, private resource costs in trying to evade them or comply with them, and the social-psychological costs of the inevitable perceived injustices created by the controls or their evasion.

The costs of actual exchange controls are generally great enough to raise anew the question of what good purpose they were intended to serve. Since controls are one alternative to floating exchange rates, one might imagine that they reduce economic uncertainty by holding fixed the external value of the national currency. Yet they are unlikely to help reduce uncertainty if they leave individual firms and households in doubt as to whether or not they will be allowed to obtain foreign exchange at any price. Controls are likely to appeal mainly to government officials as a device for increasing their discretionary power over the allocation of resources. Controls undeniably have this effect. A charitable interpretation is that the extra power makes it easier for government officials to achieve social goals through comprehensive planning. A less charitable interpretation, consistent with the facts, is that officials see in exchange controls an opportunity for personal power and its lucrative exercise. In general, the costs of exchange controls seem so great that we shall drop this alternative from the list of policy options for true adjustment, and focus in what follows on the three-way choice among floating rates, fixed rates with classical medicine, and variations on the adjustable pegged exchange rate.

WHO SHOULD ADJUST?

Thus far we have talked only about policy options facing an individual country that has a payments imbalance. In choosing among policy systems, it is important to note that the fixed-rate system and the adjustable-peg system (or Bretton Woods system) both require not only that each country play by certain rules, but also that countries cooperate in removing major disequilibriums.

The need for international cooperation under fixed or fixed-but-adjustable exchange rates can be seen by first considering the case of a two-country world. Suppose that there are only two countries, North America and the rest of the world, and only two currencies, the dollar and the pound. If North America has a persistent deficit, and the rest of the world has a persistent surplus, who should adjust? It clearly matters, since adjustment bears costs. North America may demand that the rest of the world adjust, since North America already has unemployment and does not want to deflate its economy (or, let us say, to adjust its exchange rate) any further. The rest of the world may be suffering from what it considers excessive inflation already and may refuse to adjust, demanding that North Americans tighten their belts. We can easily suggest that they should both adjust, but it is unlikely that they can do so to the right extent if they are acting separately without consultation. The same problem exists if adjustments in officially pegged exchange rates are prescribed, as under the Bretton Woods system. If North America thinks that the dollar should be worth only half a pound, but the rest of the world thinks it should be pegged at two thirds of a pound, there is a serious international problem, because this two-country world has only one exchange rate. If the two countries try to set separate rates, they will create an unstable disequilibrium like that imagined in Appendix I. Choosing to let the exchange rate float to its market-equilibrium value is one way of resolving the dilemma *if* both countries agree on the float. If one country does not, it has a problem that can be solved only with the cooperation of the other country.

If there are more than two countries, the problem is the same. With n countries in the world, there can be at most $n - 1$ independent balance-of-payments or exchange-rate policies. This "$n - 1$ problem" is equivalent to a game of musical chairs. If the independent, non-cooperative balance-of-payments policies of the rest of the world add up to a payments deficit for West Germany, yet West Germany wants to pursue policies that will give it a surplus at existing official exchange rates, something has to give. If the rest of the world wants to establish new official exchange rates that make West Germany's currency worth more than West Germany wants, something again has to give. This dilemma is not merely hypothetical. As we shall note several times, much of the history of adjustment policies since the late 1950s revolves around the debate in which deficit countries insist that West Germany and other surplus countries inflate their economies to eliminate their surpluses, with West Germany and the other surplus countries refusing. Again, letting exchange rates float to the $n - 1$ market equilibriums that make a determinate solution can resolve the issue *if* all countries agree to float their currencies. The fewer the countries that agree to float, the more serious the problem, and the greater the need for international cooperation.

This problem was appreciated even during World War II, when plans were being made for the postwar Bretton Woods system of adjustable pegged exchange rates. In his proposal for an international clearing union, circulated before Bretton Woods, Lord Keynes proposed that interest be charged on balances at the clearing union, whether they were positive or negative. The point was to penalize surpluses as well as deficits in international payments and to provide surplus countries with an incentive to correct their imbalances parallel to that existing for deficit countries with their cost of deficit. During and after the war, other suggestions were put forward for placing all of the burden of adjustment on the surplus country, including some suggestions which would have required surplus countries to spend their credit balances within a specified period of time or have them written off. This would have meant that they would give away their export surplus.

In practice it has worked out that the adjustment burdens have fallen primarily on the deficit countries. It has been harder for them to sustain deficits that will exhaust their entire reserves and their entire credit lines than it has been for countries running the same surpluses (as a percentage of reserves) to go on accumulating reserves. As a result, the fixed-rate and adjustable-peg systems have had a general tendency to force deficit countries to deflate or devalue more than they have forced surplus countries to inflate or revalue. The main exception to this rule is the deficit-ridden reserve-center country, which can, as we noted earlier, let its liabilities abroad accumulate for a considerable length of time before those liabilities press against the limits of its ability to sustain deficits.

SUMMARY

An individual nation with a payments imbalance faces a five-way choice. It can finance the imbalance, float its exchange rate, impose exchange controls, adjust its economy to the fixed rate (with "classical medicine"—deflating to eliminate deficits and inflating to eliminate surpluses), or follow the rules of the adjustable-peg (Bretton Woods) system.

The option of financing deficits and surpluses by letting official reserves fall and rise can be defended as long as the imbalances are temporary and self-reversing. In this case it is not hard to show that the world experiences a welfare gain from stabilizing the exchange rates and letting official reserves vary. This approach assumes that private speculators could not perform the same stabilizing function, and that officials correctly foresee the sustainable long-run for the exchange rate. If these assumptions do not hold, then the case for financing deficits and surpluses with a fixed exchange rate breaks down.

The option of exchange controls is likely to involve large social costs even when that option is exercised with perfect hypothetical efficiency. In addition to the ordinary static welfare losses from prevented transactions, exchange controls are likely to involve large administrative costs and resource waste in the process of trying to evade the controls or of applying for foreign exchange licenses. These costs make exchange controls an apparently inferior alternative to the three remaining options: floating rates, fixed rates, and such compromises as the adjustable pegged rate.

Either the fixed-rate system or the adjustable-peg system requires some international cooperation because of the $n - 1$ problem: if there are n countries in the world, there can be only $n - 1$ independent payments-adjustment policies or $n - 1$ officially pegged exchange rates without an inconsistency between policies.

19

Internal and external balance with fixed exchange rates

The policy decision of whether to adopt fixed exchange rates, flexible rates, or compromises in between hinges partly on the macroeconomic issue of how easy or hard it is to stabilize the domestic economy under one or another exchange-rate regime. This chapter explores the economic theory of how a country could keep its domestic economy on an even keel while at the same time keeping its overall payments position in balance, under a fixed-exchange-rate system. Chapter 20 will look at the other side of the same macroeconomic issue, examining whether it seems easier or harder to stabilize the domestic economy under a system of changing exchange rates.

Part III has already introduced some of the economic mechanisms that link the state of the domestic economy with the balance of payments under fixed exchange rates. We saw in Chapter 16 that whatever raised national spending and national income was likely, other things equal, to worsen the balance of trade and payments by making this country tend to import more. Expansionary fiscal policies should do this, whether they take the form of higher government spending or of lower tax rates. So should expansions of the money supply. Chapter 17 added another link to the balance of payments, by briefly noting that higher interest rates would tend to attract capital inflows as lenders sought to earn the higher interest rates being offered in this country. The same interest rates that affect domestic activity thus also affect the balance of payments. The level of domestic economic activity and the balance of payments are thus clearly affected simultaneously by the same domestic fiscal and monetary policies. How then should a nation perform the juggling act of achieving both internal balance—the right compromise between full employment and price stability—and balance in its external payments position if it wants to keep the exchange rate fixed?

THE *IS–LM–FE* MODEL

To do justice to this macroeconomic policy issue, one must model the economy in a way that includes at least all the main variables through which policy affects internal and external balance. This requires a model at least as complex as the "*IS–LM*" model of intermediate macroeconomic theory, now modified to allow a direct view of the balance of payments.[1]

Assumptions

Although economists have tentatively settled on a particular family of macroeconomic models for analyzing the policy issue posed here, they have done so at the expense of making some simplifying assumptions with which they admit to being somewhat uncomfortable. These assumptions must be stated explicitly before we wade into the model and its provocative policy conclusions.

1.   Assume a *given aggregate supply curve*. The supply side of the macroeconomy continues to be an Achilles' heel of macroeconomic theory, even though a vast literature has been devoted to modeling it. This means that in what follows we must talk as though real national income or the price level or both are affected by aggregate demand shifts, ignoring shifts in supply. As in Chapter 16, we shall speak loosely about changes in Y, or national income, without specifying explicitly whether these are changes in real national income or just changes in the price level. As long as the underlying shifts are demand shifts and not supply shifts, we can do so in the knowledge that real national income and the price level are at least not moving in opposite directions.

2.   *Ignore changes in price expectations.* In an economy that has experienced price inflation and changes in exchange rates, perhaps one of the most important effects of any shift in aggregate demand is its likely effect on price expectations. If the demand for goods and services is expanded in a fully employed economy, raising the price level, people

---

[1] The basic *IS–LM* model is laid out clearly in such intermediate macroeconomic texts as J. Carl Poindexter, *Macroeconomics* (Hinsdale, Ill.: Dryden Press, 1976), chaps. 7–9; and Paul Wonnacott, *Macroeconomics* (Homewood, Ill.: Richard D. Irwin, 1974), chap. 5. Its extension to include the balance of payments is sketched in Poindexter, *Macroeconomics*, chap. 11, and in Herbert G. Grubel, *International Economics* (Homewood, Ill.: Richard D. Irwin, 1977), chap. 18.

will soon come to expect such inflation and begin to bargain accordingly. Both borrowers and lenders will tend to settle on higher nominal interest rates, knowing that inflation will make each dollar of loan repayment worth less in goods and services later on. Both buyers and sellers will also tend to settle on more rapidly rising levels of prices and wages, in the self-fulfilling belief that all other prices and wages will be going up as well. Economists have modeled these expectations effects in a variety of ways, but we still lack a simple consensus view of expectations that allows us to incorporate them into a textbook model.

3. As we shall explain more fully when introducing the *FE* curve, we assume that *international capital flows*, not stocks lent and borrowed, *depend on the level of the interest rate* at home and abroad. This is not fully satisfactory, since it is more likely that a given set of interest rates in this and other countries will cause an adjustment of stocks of lending or borrowing that will cease unless total wealth continues to grow.

4. We *ignore the accumulation of real capital,* even though the model includes net capital formation as a part of the aggregate demand for goods and services. Ignoring the buildup of residential structures, plant and equipment, and inventories has already been facilitated by the first assumption above, which suppresses any discussion of the effects of capital accumulation on aggregate supply. But it is necessary to add this assumption because the buildup of capital can act to depress the demand for new investment goods and services (for example, the existence of one railroad between Boston and New York depresses the demand for another one).

5. As we shall mention again when introducing the *LM* curve, we shall *assume "sterilization,"* in the language of Chapter 17, until we come to discuss perfect international capital mobility toward the end of the chapter. That is, we shall assume at first that the monetary authorities can shield the domestic money supply from the net international flow of money that a payments surplus or deficit constitutes, and we shall relax this assumption later.

These assumptions allow us to put together a model of short-run macroeconomic interactions that is useful and fits some facts, even though the assumptions are limiting. The model portrays an open economy with markets for foreign and domestic money, foreign and domestic bonds, and the sets of goods and services making up national product and foreign product.

The *FE* curve

The model begins with an identification of the conditions that are needed to keep the external balance of payments in equilibrium. We saw in Chapter 16 that whatever raised aggregate demand within our economy would tend to worsen the trade balance and the overall balance of payments. This followed from the fact that extra desire to spend tends to raise our price levels and/or real national income. That is, a rise in aggregate demand raises Y. This will tend to make us import more, either because we feel that we can afford to spend more on all goods and services, including those made abroad, or because home goods and services start to have higher prices relative to competing foreign goods and services. We further saw in Chapter 17 that higher interest rates tend to improve the balance of payments by inducing people to lend more in this country and less abroad, causing a net inflow of money (as the incoming lenders pay for interest-earning IOUs in the short run).

Thus the balance of payments depends on both the level of domestic economic activity and the level of the domestic interest rate. This means that we can graph the state of the balance of payments as a function of Y (the level of national income, as determined by aggregate demand for our national product) and i, the interest rate. Figure 19.1

FIGURE 19.1
How the external balance depends on national income and interest rates:
The FE curve

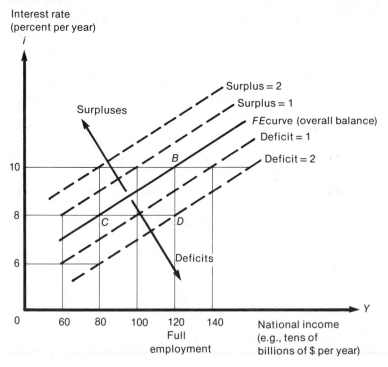

does this, by graphing isoquants for selected levels of the overall payments balance. One of these isoquants is the *FE* curve, which is the set of all combinations of income and interest-rate levels for which the overall payments balance is in equilibrium, that is, neither in surplus nor in deficit. The reason why the *FE* curve slopes up and to the right can be seen by comparing the overall balances at Points *C*, *D*, and *B*. At Point *C*, the diagram assumes, there is neither a surplus nor a deficit. If the economy could somehow have a full-employment level of national income of 120 without changing the interest rate, we would move from *C* to *D*. Yet at Point *D* this country has a payments deficit, because the higher income at Point *D* than at Point *C* means more imports (and perhaps less exports) in response to this country's higher ability to buy. To have payments balance at full employment we must have a higher interest rate while somehow keeping national income at 120. This desirable position is achieved only at Point *B*, where the higher interest rate serves to attract more capital from abroad and to offset any trade-balance deficit at full employment. Point *B*, then, represents the target for policy, the point at which the nation has achieved both internal balance (full employment without excessive inflation) and external balance. To know what policy combinations could get us there with fixed exchange rates, we need next to add the parts of the model that determine the interest rate and the level of income.

The *IS* curve

The economy will tend to gravitate toward an equilibrium in which aggregate demand for what this country produces just matches the country's current level of national production or, roughly, its national income. We saw in Chapter 16 that this equilibrium in the national product market can also be expressed as an equilibrium between desired saving and desired investment, or

$$\text{Desired } S = \text{Desired } (I_d + I_f) = \text{Desired } (I_d + X - M).$$

This $I = S$ equilibrium will now be portrayed a little differently from its representation in Chapter 16. There (in Figure 16.2 and the surrounding text) the $I = S$ equilibrium determined the level of national income. Yet now we must recognize that desired domestic investment, and possibly desired domestic saving, will depend on the rate of interest and not just on the level of national income. The higher the interest rate, the more some investment expenditures will be discouraged by the higher interest cost of borrowing funds with which to finance purchases of new homes, new plant and equipment, and extra inventories. A higher interest rate may also encourage more saving (less consumption) as households perceive the greater rate of return on postponing their consumption, and holding interest-earning assets instead. A higher interest rate thus cuts aggregate demand, or what comes to the same thing, it lowers desired investment relative to desired saving. This means that for each interest rate there is a different equilibrium level of national income consistent with the balancing of desired saving and investment.

Figure 19.2 shows this dependence of the equilibrium level of na-

FIGURE 19.2
Equilibrium in the national product market: The *IS* curve.

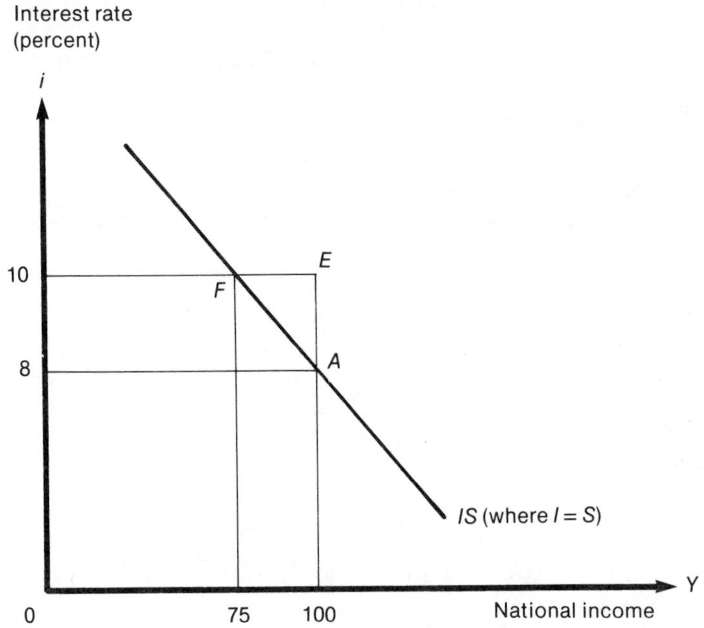

Interest rate
(percent)

Expansionary fiscal policy and rises in private spending desires shift *IS* to the *right*.
Contractionary fiscal policy and drops in private spending desires shift *IS* to the *left*.

tional income on the rate of interest. the *IS* curve is the set of combinations of income and interest-rate levels that yield equilibrium between desired saving and desired investment. To see why the *IS* curve is likely to have a negative slope, compare the three points shown in Figure 19.2. By assumption, Point *A* finds the economy in equilibrium between desired saving and investment. If the interest rate were somehow raised sharply to 10 percent, at Point *E*, 100 cannot continue to be the equilibrium level of national income. At the higher interest rate, fewer new homes will be desired, some business investment plans will be canceled, and some households are likely to want to save more and consume less. All of these effects of the higher interest rate add up to lower aggregate demand for national product than the 100 level. Firms trying to keep up this level of production will find inventories piling up on their hands, and will have to respond by cutting production, sending a multiple contraction through the economy until the economy settles at the lower equilibrium level of national income at Point *F*. Thus any equilibrium point having a higher interest rate than Point *A* must have a lower level of national income, as at Point *F*. Thus the *IS* curve must have a negative slope as long as both interest rates and national income matter to people's saving and investment decisions.

The position of the *IS* curve reflects saving and investment behavior. If this behavior should change, the *IS* curve will shift to the left or right. Any change toward desiring to spend more and save less for given income and interest rates shifts the *IS* curve to the right, making a higher level of national income consistent with each given interest rate. Conversely, any shift toward less spending and more saving will shift the *IS* curve to the left. In particular, expansionary fiscal policy—greater government spending and/or lower tax rates—will shift the *IS* curve to the right, whereas tighter fiscal policy will shift it to the left. This is because the expansionary fiscal policy is equivalent to a drop in the government's desired saving (tax revenue minus spending) at each level of income and interest rates. Fiscal policy thus affects national income, interest rates, and the balance of payments by shifting the *IS* curve.

The LM curve

When the rate of interest and the money supply are introduced into the discussion, as they were in Chapter 17, the determination of the level of national income and of the overall balance of payments depends on the state of financial markets as well as the state of the national product market. The money supply represents the supply side of one market, the market for money itself. The rate of interest represents the return to holding interest-earning assets, which we shall loosely call "bonds" as a shorthand for savings accounts, bills, bonds, and other interest-paying IOUs. We have already seen that both national income and the overall balance of payments depend on the rate of interest. We therefore need to look into the financial side of the economy, which affects both interest rates and national income.

One of the basic choices people and firms make is the asset choice—whether to hold their accumulated assets in the form of money itself, or interest-earning assets, or physical nonhuman assets (land, factories, and so on) or human assets (extra training, and the like). In our standard macromodel we shall follow the Keynesian tradition of simplifying this choice by assuming that income and interest rates are relevant only to the choice between holding money and holding interest-earning bonds. We can then describe influences on the demand for money alone, in the knowledge that whatever raises the demand for holding money lowers the demand for holding bonds (lending at interest), and vice versa.

The demand for money depends positively on the level of national income (price times real national income) and negatively on the interest rate. The greater the aggregate demand for goods and services, and the greater the value of national income, the higher the average stock of money people will want to have on hand to bridge gaps between receipts and expenditures. A higher rate of interest, on the other hand, is likely to lower the demand for money. With a higher interest rate, some people will decide to hold bonds and earn this interest rate while making do with lower money balances, which earn no interest.

Equilibrium in the money market can thus be described as equilibrium between the demand for money (or L, for liquidity) and the money supply M_s. In algebraic notation this equilibrium can be written as

$$L(\overset{+}{Y}, \overset{-}{i}) = M_s,$$

where the signs remind us that the demand for money is raised by higher Y but lowered by higher i. The supply side of this equation, M_s, is assumed for now to be totally under the control of the central bank's monetary policy. This is sometimes roughly correct, but sometimes farther from realistic. We shall consider a case in which this is not true later on.

For any given value of the money supply, equilibrium in the money market can be achieved by any of a whole set of combinations of income levels and interest rates. This can be seen by noting that the equilibrium condition above involves one equation and two variables, Y and i, thus leaving a whole range of possible equilibrium values for these variables. Another way to see the same range of possibilities is with the help of Figure 19.3. One equilibrium point for the money market is Point A. Its being on the LM curve signifies that the amount of cash people demand at $Y = 100$, and $i = 8$ percent just matches the existing money supply (the amount of which is not shown). The positive slope of the LM curve follows from what we have already said about the dependence of money demand on income and interest rates. If the level of national income were somehow raised, moving us from Point A to Point G, there would be an excess demand for cash. With the higher income level, people would want more currency and demand deposits on hand to cover their transactions need at the higher turnover rate of goods and services. In response, people would be less

FIGURE 19.3
Equilibrium in the money market: The *LM* curve.

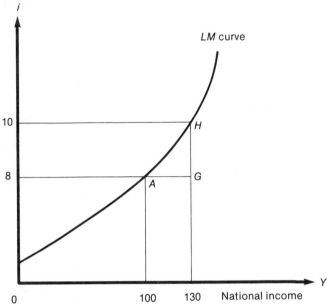

Expansionary monetary policy (increases in money supply) and declines
in private desire to hold money (that is, increases in desire to hold bonds)
shift the *LM* curve to the *right*.
    Contractionary monetary policy (decreases in money supply) and rises
in private desire to hold money (that is, declines in desire to hold bonds)
shift the *LM* curve to the *left*.

willing to lend at interest, and many would try to borrow more in order
to have more ready cash. This disequilibrium can be erased at the
higher income level only if people are enticed by a higher interest rate
to hold less money and hold more bonds. Point *H* shows a situation in
which equilibrium has been restored, by an interest rate just enough
higher to offset the effect of the higher income level on the demand for
money, making Point *H* as well as Point *A* an equilibrium situation as
far as the money market is concerned.

The whole *LM* curve can be shifted by changes in the money supply or money demand. If the central bank allows an increase in the
money supply available to residents of this country, the extra money
supply initially takes the form of extra bank lending. Having been
given extra freedom to create money liabilities against itself to be used
by the borrowers whose extra IOUs the banks now hold, the banking
sector raises the supply of money and the supply of lending. This

initially tends to bid down interest rates and to encourage real investment and the other kinds of demand for national product that depend
on the ease of borrowing. The process hereafter is as sketched in Chapter 17's description of how the money supply could affect the economy
and the balance of payments. In terms of the diagram of the *LM* curve,
this monetary expansion is represented by a rightward shift of the
curve.

The equilibrium levels of national income and the interest rate are
simultaneously determined by equilibrium in the national product
market and equilibrium in the money market. This overall equilibrium situation is shown in Figure 19.4. Given the initial *IS* and *LM*

FIGURE 19.4
Equilibrium national income and interest rate, determined by the
***IS* and *LM* curves**

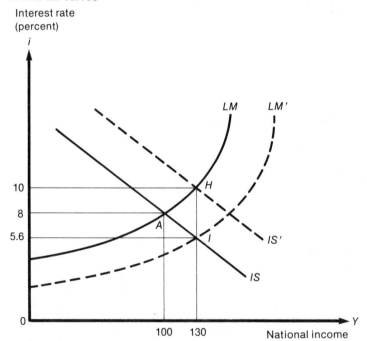

Expansionary fiscal policy, or other shift moving *IS* to the right, raises national
income and/or raises the interest rate (for example, from *A* to *H*).
    Expansionary monetary policy, or other shift moving the *LM* curve to the right,
raises national income and/or lowers the interest rate (for example, from *A* to *I*).

curves, only at Point *A* is there equilibrium in both the national product market and the money market. Any other point would show
symptoms of disequilibrium, such as unintended accumulation or depletion of inventories (being off the *IS* curve) or a scramble to get into

or out of money holding (out of or into bondholding—being off the *LM* curve).

A shift in either curve tends to affect both income and interest rates, though in special cases with vertical or horizontal curves, only one variable may change. Expansionary fiscal policy is almost certain to raise interest rates while raising national income, as shown by the shift from *A* to *H*. Interest rates are likely to rise because the government, in raising the gap between what it spends and the tax revenues it collects, must issue more interest-bearing bonds. This extra government borrowing competes with private borrowers for loanable funds, bidding up the rate of interest. (Another way of describing the same result is to repeat our reasoning about what has to happen to the interest rate to keep the demand for money unchanged at a higher level of national income.) An expansion of the money supply again has the effects described in Chapter 17: higher national income and initially lower interest rates. (Later, when people come to expect more inflation, the effect of expanding the money supply on the interest rate may be positive.)

TWO POLICIES AND TWO TARGETS

The fact that expansionary fiscal policies and expansionary monetary policies have very different effects on interest rates sets up an opportunity to combine fiscal and monetary policies in mixtures that suffice to solve the problem of maintaining both internal and external balance with fixed exchange rates.

To grasp the potentialities of fiscal-monetary mixes for an open economy, let us look first at the policy problem that loomed large in the thinking of U.S. officials and economic theorists in the early 1960s. This problem and their way of trying to solve it are portrayed in Figure 19.5. The United States had more unemployment than it wanted, whereas prices were generally stable. At the same time it had payments deficits. The policy target, represented by Point *B* in Figure 19.5, clearly lay up and to the right from the initial position represented by Point *A*. This posed a dilemma for monetary policy if it had to be used alone: expansionary monetary policy to create jobs would worsen the payments deficit, and tighter monetary policy to eliminate the payments deficit would depress the economy and add to the unemployment. Could fiscal policy handle the job alone? Only with the help of luck. Expansionary fiscal policy, aimed at raising national income, can either improve or worsen a deficit in the overall balance of payments. The reason its effects on the overall balance are ambiguous until we have detailed information is that fiscal policy has two opposing effects on the overall balance. By raising national income, it tends

FIGURE 19.5
Mixing fiscal and monetary policies to fight both unemployment and a payments deficit

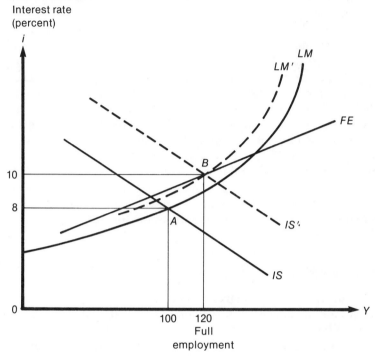

to worsen the trade and overall balances. Yet by raising the interest rate, it tends to attract a capital inflow that gives short-run balance-of-payments relief. If we were lucky enough to have the latter effect predominate, the unit impacts of fiscal policy on national income and the overall payments balance were not likely to be such as to make the same dosage of fiscal expansion solve both the internal and the external problems.

Theorists and U.S. policymakers together hit on the idea of mixing both fiscal and monetary policy so as to solve both problems simultaneously. In terms of Figure 19.5, the point they perceived was that the United States could mix expansionary fiscal policy with some sort of finely tuned monetary policy to approach both full employment and payments equilibrium. If policymakers knew that the curves lay as shown in Figure 19.5, they could combine a considerable expansion of fiscal policy with a slight tightening of monetary policy to move to the desired Point B. Interest rates would be raised enough to stop the payments deficit, yet on balance national income could expand enough to bring the country to full employment.

U.S. policy under Kennedy and at the start of the Johnson Administration approached this solution. Fiscal policy was stimulative, with investment-related tax cuts, the income and profits tax cut of 1964, and some increased government spending. Monetary policy was more mixed, reflecting the concern of the Federal Reserve over inflation and the payments deficit. At the same time, some effort was made to shield domestic investment from the effects of higher interest rates with a complicated "operation twist," which juggled government debt-management policies so as to raise short-term interest rates to attract foreign lending while holding down long-term interest rates to encourage domestic real investment. As of 1965, when Vietnam escalated and sent the economy into rising inflation and deeper deficits, the full-employment goal had at least been approached and the balance of payments had not deteriorated any further.

The idea of mixing fiscal and monetary policy can be expanded to cover other situations besides that faced by the United States in the early 1960s. As Robert Mundell has stressed, the more general point is that no matter where the target point is, there is in principle some combination of monetary and fiscal policies that will yield equilibrium at that point. What mixture should be applied depends on where the target is, and on whether we know the slopes of the IS, LM, and FE curves.

Figure 19.6 shows that *if* we know the slopes of the curves, it is easy to achieve internal and external balance with monetary and fiscal policies under fixed exchange rates. Our target point of both internal and external balance must lie in one of the four regions shown (or on the border between two of them, with the same kind of result). The policy mixtures required are clear in any case, as the reader can confirm.

THE ASSIGNMENT PROBLEM

Yet in practice policymakers cannot be sure where the curves lie, or how they are sloped. Government agencies do not produce regular estimates of the current positions of the IS, LM, and FE curves. What they do have are estimates of the current state of the balance of payments, the level of national income, and the rate of interest, plus good guesses as to the directions (but not the magnitudes) in which fiscal and monetary policies affect internal and external balance. It is possible to tell, for example, when the nation has a payments deficit and high unemployment. But this information does not tell us whether we are in Region I or Region II of Figure 19.6. Thus we cannot tell whether monetary policy should be expansionary or contractionary, though fiscal policy should clearly be expansionary to some unknown

FIGURE 19.6
Policy rules for internal and external balance with fixed exchange rates, when the positions of the curves are all known

Interest rate
(percent)

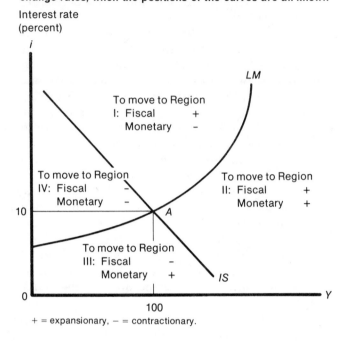

+ = expansionary, − = contractionary.

degree. What policy rules should be followed with such imperfect information?

Robert Mundell has devised a solution to this assignment problem. His *assignment rule* is to *assign monetary policy the task of pursuing external balance, and fiscal policy the task of pursuing internal balance.* This means the following prescriptions for specific imbalances:

Problem	Monetary policy	Fiscal policy
Unemployment and deficit	Contractionary	Expansionary
Unemployment and surplus	Expansionary	Expansionary
Inflation and deficit	Contractionary	Contractionary
Inflation and surplus	Expansionary	Contractionary

Each arm of policymaking could thus focus its attention on a single visible target, with the central bank watching and reacting to the latest balance-of-payments figures and the government watching the unemployment-inflation mixture.

If monetary and fiscal policy can be adjusted smoothly and continuously without long lags before their effects are visible, then the assignment rule can work quite well. In some cases it leads straight to the target. In others it may involve worsening one or the other problem temporarily, but will ultimately lead to the target point. Figure 19.7 shows a case in which the assignment rule could produce a somewhat roundabout path to the policy target. In this case, the *FE* curve is

FIGURE 19.7
A case in which the "assignment rule" yields a roundabout path to internal and external balance

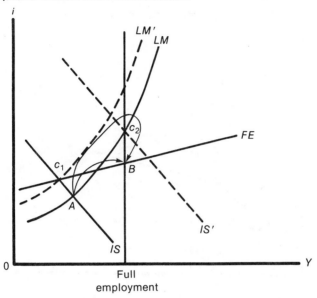

flatter than the *LM* curve and crosses it before the target of payments balance with full employment is reached at Point *B*. If both policies follow their assignment rules, we could start out by moving away from full employment. Monetary policy, seeing an initial deficit in the balance of payments at Point *A*, will be contractionary in order to raise interest rates and attract capital inflows. If monetary policy took effect first, we could move to Point c_1, achieving payments balance but at the expense of greater unemployment. Alternatively, if monetary policy did not react at first but fiscal policy pursued full employment by shifting to IS′, we could achieve full employment at c_2, but at the expense of breeding a large payments surplus. The possible paths are infinite in number, depending on the relative speeds of effectiveness of monetary and fiscal policies. Paths like those shown with arrows illustrate the kinds of possibilities. Yet if policies react and take effect smoothly and continuously without serious lags, the assignment rule still eventually gets us to Point *B*. It works even more smoothly in cases where we do not have to contend with crossing *LM* and *FE* curves, as in Figure 19.5.

Yet even the assignment rule poses potential problems if policies react discontinuously in response to imperfect information. Figure 19.8 shows a case in which an attempt to follow the assignment rule

FIGURE 19.8
A case in which the "assignment rule" yields explosive instability

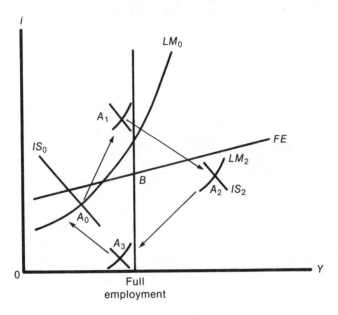

yields explosive instability. This case can be one in which the two branches of policy are poorly coordinated, due to a failure of the central bank and the government to consult each other. Or it can be a case in which the central bank and the government simply misjudge the magnitudes and timing with which incomes and interest rates respond to their own actions. Following the assignment rule at Point A_0, the central bank perceives a payments deficit and the government perceives unemployment. They respond with tighter monetary and easier fiscal policies. This combination propels the economy to Point A_1. The government finds that the unemployment has not gone away, partly because of the tighter monetary policy. The central bank finds that the payments deficit has been converted into a disturbingly large surplus now that the much higher interest rates (due to both tighter monetary and easier fiscal policies) have attracted so much capital from abroad. Each arm of policy resolves to try again. Fiscal policy expands slightly to get rid of the slight unemployment. Monetary policy is expansive to lower interest rates and eliminate the payments surplus. The combined expansions send the economy to Point A_2, where prices have risen too much and where a slight deficit has reappeared on the balance of payments. In response to this new disequilibrium, fiscal policy tightens up a lot and monetary policy tightens slightly, sending us to Point A_3. There the disequilibrium proves just as acute, and policy sets off on a new path just as far from Point B, the true policy target.

We do not know that the pessimism of Figure 19.8 is closer to the facts than the more optimistic views of Figures 19.5 and 19.7, in which the assignment rule brings us to the desired position. All that can be said is that this kind of explosive instability is a possibility. This possibility means that policymakers have a strong incentive to invest in getting better information on two fronts. They can use better information about one another's actions, in order to follow more coordinated policies. They also need to invest in research revealing the likely slopes of the curves. In particular, it would be very worthwhile to know whether expansionary fiscal policy improves or worsens the balance of payments, which amounts to knowing whether LM is steeper or flatter than FE. The better this information, the more effective the policy combination.

PERFECT CAPITAL MOBILITY

Across the 1960s the IS–LM–FE model came to be increasingly applied to a case that seemed to be more and more characteristic of major Western economies, the case of perfect capital mobility between nations. With the world economy expanding in a context of pegged (but adjustable) exchange rates, central bankers in several countries noticed a growing responsiveness of lending to interest-rate differentials between countries. Economists have extrapolated to the case in which these capital flows are so responsive that they eliminate any net change in the interest-rate differential. Any momentary tendency for interest rates to rise in this country while unchanged abroad would bring such a rush of lending from abroad as to bid the domestic interest rate down to its initial level. Conversely, any momentary drop in the domestic interest rate would cause such a large outflow of funds seeking better rates abroad as to be self-eliminating. This perfect capital mobility means that the domestic interest rate is given by foreign conditions, as when Canadians have complained that "Canadian interest rates are made in Washington."

To incorporate this case of perfect international capital mobility into the IS–LM–FE model, we must note that it implies a change in assumptions. Thus far we have assumed that the central bank can "sterilize" payments surpluses and deficits. That is, it can offset any effect payments surpluses and deficits would have on the money supply available to domestic residents by adjusting its own holdings of domestic assets (for example, government bonds), as noted in Chapter 17. This assumption must now be dropped. If perfect capital mobility is to affect interest rates in this country, this must mean that the flows caused by any momentary change in the domestic rate must be so large as to shift the domestic money supply. To assume perfect capital mobility is to assume that it is impossible to sterilize payments imbalances, with the result that the amount of money available to domestic residents is beyond the control of the central bank.

The policy importance of perfect capital mobility is shown in Figures 19.9 and 19.10. In both diagrams the *FE* curves is drawn horizon-

FIGURE 19.9
Monetary policy is impotent under fixed exchange rates with perfect capital mobility

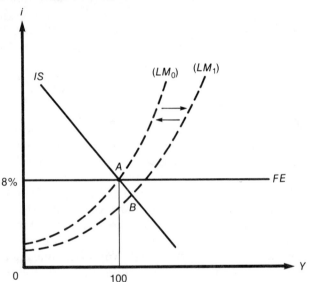

tally and as passing through the initial point, *A*. It is horizontal because, by assumption, the slightest change in the interest rate will cause an infinitely great capital flow. This means that changes in income cannot mean nearly as much to the balance of payments as equal percentage changes in the interest rate. The *FE* curve must pass through the initial point, *A*, for the same reason: if any deviation of the domestic interest rate from the equilibrium rate dictated by world financial markets causes a radical change in the domestic money supply that the central bank cannot control, then we must always be at that

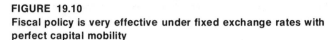

FIGURE 19.10
Fiscal policy is very effective under fixed exchange rates with perfect capital mobility

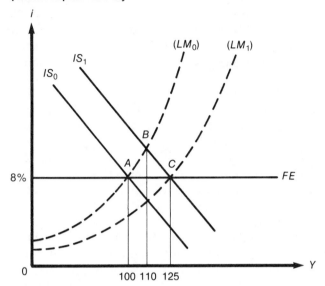

interest rate where these flows of money are zero, that is, on the *FE* curve.

Figure 19.9 shows why monetary policy cannot affect the level of national income under this extreme case of perfect capital mobility. An attempt to expand the domestic money supply could make money more available to those who want to borrow it, but could do this only for a moment. For this moment, the interest rate might be lower and national income raised, at Point *B*. But the lower interest rate causes a massive outflow of funds, as people scramble to lend in other countries at better interest rates. This outflow is so massive that the central bank cannot check the loss of money into foreign hands. As long as the outflow continues, people are turning money, in the form of bank deposits, over to foreigners who are borrowing at the going international interest rate. This outflow continues until the interest rate is bid back up to its initial level, at Point A, where the total money supply in the hands of domestic residents is also back to its initial level. Thus perfect capital mobility expanding the money supply by, say, $1 billion just causes $1 billion in money to flow abroad, leaving the domestic money supply and interest rate and national income unaffected. Attempts to cut the domestic money supply would also be ineffective.

The impotence of monetary policy under fixed exchange rates and international capital mobility is not just a theoretical possibility. Something like it has happened historically, as we shall note again in Chapter 21. Before World War I, national lending markets became increasingly integrated by internationally mobile capital, and interest rates converged. This growing capital mobility plus confidence in the fixity of exchange rates meant that by the first decade of this century many central banks experienced a great deal of difficulty controlling their own money supplies and specie reserves. Something similar began to plague monetary policy in many European countries as they moved toward greater international financial integration across the 1960s. Increasingly they found, as Canada had found earlier, that international financial conditions centering on New York exercised large sway over their own domestic money supplies despite attempts by each central bank to run its own monetary policy.

Fiscal policy, by contrast, has its effect on income enhanced by international capital mobility. Figure 19.10 shows why. An expansion in government spending (or a cut in the tax rate) shifts the IS curve to the right. For a brief initial period this is likely to raise the rate of interest, as shown in the move from Point A to Point B, simply because the government is borrowing more. This temporarily higher interest rate attracts large inflows of funds from abroad. The inflows are greater than the central bank can sterilize, and thus add to the domestic money supply, shifting the would-be LM curve farther to the right. The combination of the fiscal stimulus and the induced expansion in the money supply adds up to a considerable expansion in aggregate demand and national income. Fiscal policy thus has the effect of raising the money supply in this case, even though the government is assumed not to be printing any extra money.

Thus in a world of perfect capital mobility and fixed exchange rates, the policy prescriptions are clear. The net surplus or deficit on the balance of payments cannot be sterilized by monetary officials. In fact it takes care of itself. Internal balance can be maintained by fiscal policy. Monetary policy cannot help in this case.

QUALIFICATIONS

Though widely accepted among economists, the theoretical model used in this chapter is subject to some important qualifications. Most of its limitations are already clear in the set of initial assumptions listed earlier. The IS–LM–FE model's focus on aggregate demand rather than the supply side is a handicap. It means that the model does not contain any answers to the unemployment-inflation dilemma. The model must limit itself to prescriptions on how the right level of aggregate demand can be achieved, but offers no prescriptions on what to do if this best level gives too much unemployment and inflation at the same time. Ignoring price expectations is also handicapping, since it sets aside the point that expanding the money supply may end up raising interest rates rather than lowering them, once people come to experience and expect more inflation.

An additional important qualification relates to international interest payments. Thus far we have consistently talked about the tendency of higher interest rates in this country to attract capital from abroad. This point was crucial to the whole set of prescriptions about mixing fiscal and monetary policy, since the two kinds of policy differed in their effects only through interest-rate linkages. The reasoning above can be satisfactory for a short period of time. But within a year any capital flow starts producing a flow of interest payments in the opposite direction. We cannot attract lending from abroad without later paying interest on the newly borrowed funds. Either we pay out interest for a while and then repay the principal, or we pay out interest indefinitely while renewing the debt.

The reflow of interest payments clearly offsets much of the ability of policy to improve the balance of payments by attracting capital from abroad. Tightening the money supply, for example, can attract a capital inflow and thus improve the balance of payments in the way already described. But any given inflow leaves in its wake a net outflow of money, when it comes time to repay. Which is more important, the initial inflow or the subsequent outflow of a greater money value?[2] The answer depends on how present-minded or how farsighted policymakers choose to be. If they feel that the immediate short run is so pressing that they should discount the distant future heavily, then the problem about interest payments is assumed away, and the above analysis holds well enough. But the more farsighted policymakers become, and the more they care about the future relative to the present, the more serious the effect of the interest reflows seems. The same problem persists in the case of perfect capital mobility, since the larger the capital inflows triggered by a temporary rise in our interest rates, the greater the later interest outflows that contribute to renewed payments deficits.

SUMMARY

The IS–LM–FE model allows one to formulate policy combinations that make it possible in principle to achieve internal and external balance with fixed exchange rates. If policymakers know where these

---

[2] As long as the capital inflow attracted by a given rise in the interest rate does not grow rapidly forever, it is easy to see that the interest payments must overtake it eventually. Even if the capital inflow does grow rapidly, the same basic point in the text is valid, for reasons explored in Chapter 25.

curves lie, they can achieve any combination of internal aggregate demand and external payments balance, thanks to the fact that monetary and fiscal policies affect interest rates differently.

When policymakers cannot confidently estimate the positions of the curves, they can still follow a simpler "assignment rule" with fair chances of at least approaching the desired combination of internal and external balance. When policies are adjusted smoothly and take quick effect, internal and external balance can be reached by assigning the internal task to fiscal policy and the external task to monetary policy. This assignment rule can yield unstable results if policy changes discontinuously or if it takes effect with a long lag.

Perfect capital mobility between countries can effectively fix the nation's interest rate and take control of the money supply away from the central bank (under fixed exchange rates). Something like this situation came about when world financial markets were integrated increasingly under fixed exchange rates, first just before World War I and again across the 1960s. With perfect capital mobility and fixed exchange rates, an expansion of the domestic money supply just causes the same amount of money to migrate into foreign hands, leaving the level of national income unaffected. Fiscal policy, by contrast, has great effectiveness in this situation because it triggers an inflow of money.

The theorizing that has produced these conclusions rests on some shaky assumptions. In particular it is based on a very short-run analysis which ignores such delayed effects as changes in price expectations, international interest payments on induced capital flows, and capital accumulation itself. Yet the theory is a rough guide for the short run, and it suggests that policy targets can in principle be resolved under fixed exchange rates.

SUGGESTED READING FOR CHAPTERS 19 AND 20

Some of Robert Mundell's pioneering articles on internal and external balance and the implications of international capital mobility are reprinted in his *International Economics* (New York: Macmillan, 1968), chaps. 16 and 18.

The best advanced presentations of the *IS–LM–FE* model are found in Robert M. Stern, *The Balance of Payments* (Chicago: Aldine, 1973), chap. 10 and appendix; and Richard E. Caves and Grant L. Reuber, *Capital Transfers and Economic Policy: Canada, 1951–1962* (Cambridge, Mass.: Harvard University Press, 1971), appendix A. Caves and Reuber also estimate the effects discussed here, using Canadian data, though their empirically estimated model differs somewhat from the abstract model presented here and in their appendix.

20

Flexible exchange rates and internal balance

One obvious way out of the policy problem of reconciling the goals of internal and external balance is to let the exchange rate take care of external balance and to direct macroeconomic policies toward the problem of internal balance alone. This is an option worth considering as long as changes in the market-determined exchange rate really do restore equilibrium in the foreign exchange market, as seems likely on the basis of the analysis in Chapters 15 and 22. If we rely on a flexible exchange rate (or set of exchange rates), will it be easier or harder for macroeconomic policy to control the domestic economy with flexible exchange rates than with fixed rates?

FLEXIBLE EXCHANGE RATES IN THE *IS–LM–FE* MODEL

We can conveniently compare fixed and flexible exchange rates by using the same *IS–LM–FE* framework introduced in Chapter 19. Flexible exchange rates are easily represented in this framework. Exchange-rate flexibility means that the demand for foreign exchange matches its supply, so that there are no payments surpluses or deficits in the sense of disequilibrium flows of money between this country and the rest of the world. This means, in effect, that we are always on the *FE* curve when exchange rates are flexible. Other changes may shift the *FE* curve, by changing the combinations of income and interest rates that yield equilibrium in the foreign exchange market, but the economy always returns to a position on the *FE* curve.

MONETARY POLICY WITH FLEXIBLE EXCHANGE RATES

With flexible exchange rates monetary policy exerts a strong influence over national income, whether or not capital is highly mobile between countries. To see why, let us consider the case of a deliberate expansion of the domestic money supply, with the help of Figure 20.1.

FIGURE 20.1
The potency of monetary policy with flexible exchange rates

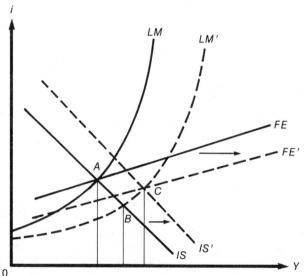

Expansionary monetary policy shifts *LM* to the right.
  FE is shifted to the right because our currency depreciates, improving the payments balance at each *i, Y* combination (assuming the stability conditions discussed in Chapter 15 and Appendix H).
  IS is shifted to the right by the depreciation, which shifts demand toward our national product.

An expansion of the money supply makes it easier to borrow, cutting the interest rate and raising spending. As we saw in Chapter 17, both the rise in spending and the drop in the interest rate should worsen the balance of payments in the short run. If the exchange rate were held fixed and the balance of payments were not allowed to affect the money supply, then the economy would just move from *A* to *B*. (If the payments deficit were not "sterilized" and were allowed to pull down the money supply as money left the country, then the economy would return to *A*.) With flexible exchange rates, however, the deficit cannot last. With demand for foreign currencies now greater than supply, our national currency depreciates in value (foreign currencies rise in value). If depreciation improves the trade balance, as we shall assume here, then the *IS* curve is shifted to the right. That is, for any given interest rate, the level of income that brings overall payments balance can be higher now that the depreciation of the exchange rate has made it easier for domestic firms to compete with foreign firms. At the same time, the depreciation shifts the *IS* curve to the right, because the new competitive advantage for domestic firms raises aggregate spending for what this country produces. This rise in aggregate demand due to depreciation augments the rise due to the extra money supply, expanding the economy all the way to Point *C*.

Thus monetary policy has greater unit effect over national income under flexible exchange rates than under fixed rates with sterilization, which in turn finds monetary policy more effective than without sterilization. Note that this conclusion holds whatever the degree of international capital mobility. Even if capital were perfectly mobile and the *FE* curve were flat, the effect of monetary policy would still be greater with flexible exchange rates. Expanding the money supply would still cause a depreciation, which would raise aggregate demand further (shifting *IS* to the right again). Perfect capital mobility could hold the interest rate fixed, but with flexible rates it does not frustrate monetary policy's attempts to control national income, as it does with fixed rates.

FISCAL POLICY WITH FLEXIBLE EXCHANGE RATES

How fiscal policy works with flexible exchange rates is a little more complicated, since fiscal policy could affect the exchange rates in either direction. Figure 20.2 shows the range of possible outcomes from expansionary fiscal policy when exchange rates can vary.

Figure 20.2A shows a case in which fiscal expansion would tend to worsen the balance of payments under fixed rates or to depreciate the national currency under flexible rates. This tendency is reflected in the fact that the *FE* curve is steeper than the *LM* curve. Starting from Point *A*, an increase in government spending or a cut in tax rates would cause a movement toward a point such as Point *B*. The economy would settle at Point *B* only if the exchange rate were fixed and payments imbalances were sterilized so as to keep the money supply (and the *LM* curve) under the firm control of the central bank. At Point *B* there is a payments deficit, since *B* is assumed to be below and to the left of the *FE* curve (that is, we assume that fiscal expansion has worsened the trade balance more than it has helped the capital account by attracting capital inflows with higher interest rates). If the exchange rate were still fixed but it were impossible for the central bank to sterilize the payments deficit, the outflow of money would cut the money supply and contract the economy to Point *C*, where the payments deficit has been eliminated by monetary contraction and higher interest rates.

FIGURE 20.2
The effects of fiscal policy with flexible exchange rates

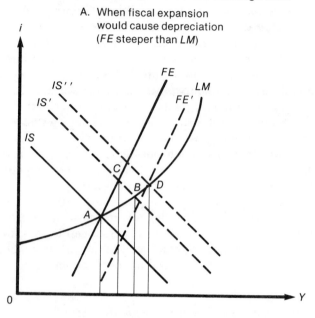

A. When fiscal expansion
   would cause depreciation
   (*FE* steeper than *LM*)

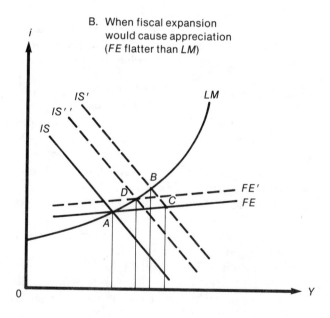

B. When fiscal expansion
   would cause appreciation
   (*FE* flatter than *LM*)

Exchange-rate flexibility brings an extra round of effects in Figure 20.2A. The incipient payments deficit at Point B quickly leads to depreciation of the exchange rate. With the country's currency now worth less, it becomes easier to sell exports and compete against imports. This means a rightward shift in the FE curve, improving the payments balance at each income-and-interest-rate combination (assuming the stability conditions described in Chapter 15 and Appendix H). The depreciation also shifts the IS curve rightward, from IS' to IS", to the extent that it shifts demand toward this country's product at the expense of foreign product. The FE and IS curves will shift rightward until a new equilibrium is reached, with both curves once again intersecting along the LM curve, at Point D. The result is that fiscal expansion (or contraction) has a stronger effect on national income with flexible exchange rates than with fixed rates, as long as the FE curve is steeper than the LM curve.

Figure 20.2B, by contrast, shows a case in which the FE curve is flatter than the LM curve and a fiscal expansion causes an initial payments surplus. Raising government spending or cutting tax rates would move the economy from Point A to Point B, where it would stay if the exchange rate were fixed, payments were sterilized, and no further shifts in IS or LM occurred. The situation at Point B is one of payments surplus (we are above and to the left of FE), apparently because the fiscal expansion has affected the balance of payments, mainly through its tendency to raise the interest rate and attract capital. If the exchange rate were fixed but the payments surplus were allowed to augment the national money supply (no sterilization), there would be a further expansion of the economy from B to C, where payments equilibrium would be restored at a higher money supply and higher national income.

In Figure 20.2B, as in Figure 20.2A, induced changes in the exchange rate bring an extra round of effects. The incipient surplus at B becomes an appreciation of the national currency in the flexible-rate case. The rise in the value of the national currency in foreign exchange markets tends to hamper the competitive ability of this country's export and import-competing sectors. This tends to eliminate the surplus and to shift the FE curve up and to the left (assuming the stability conditions of Chapter 15 and Appendix H). The loss of business to the domestic sectors involved in trade also means a drop in aggregate demand, shifting the IS curve to the left, from IS' to IS". The final equilibrium comes when the IS and FE curves intersect on the LM curve (at IS" and FE'), and there is no longer any tendency for the exchange rate to change. The dampening effect of the exchange-rate appreciation on domestic business offsets some of the expansionary impact of the initial fiscal expansion, making fiscal policy have less net effect with flexible rates than with fixed rates. (In the extreme case of perfect capital mobility and a perfectly flat FE curve, fiscal policy could have no effect at all with flexible rates, and Point D would be the same as Point A.)

Table 20.1 summarizes what we have learned from studying Fig-

TABLE 20.1
Rankings of exchange-rate systems by the unit impacts of monetary and fiscal policies on national income

Condition	Rank-ings	Effectiveness of monetary policy	Effectiveness of fiscal policy
FE steeper than LM (fiscal	1	Flexible	Flexible
expansion would cause	2	Fixed, sterilization	Fixed, sterilization
deficits or depreciation)	3	Fixed, no sterilization	Fixed, no sterilization
FE flatter than LM (fiscal ex-	1	Flexible	Fixed, no sterilization
pansion would cause sur-	2	Fixed, sterilization	Fixed, sterilization
pluses or appreciation)	3	Fixed, no sterilization	Flexible

ures 20.1 and 20.2, by ranking the alternative exchange-rate systems according to how powerful the effect of domestic policy is on national income. As we saw in Figure 20.1, monetary policy is unambiguously more powerful under flexible rates than under fixed rates. This seems plausible theoretically. It also accords with the impression one would get from a casual study of history. It has been in fixed-rate eras of highly mobile capital (for example, in the 1960s) that central banks have found the greatest difficulty in regulating their domestic money supplies and national incomes. By contrast, countries with runaway money supplies (for example, Germany during the hyperinflation of 1923) had little difficulty in getting the money supply expansions to send prices soaring under exchange rates that could only be flexible under the circumstances.

Table 20.1 also repeats the finding that the relative impact of fiscal policy under different exchange-rate regimes depends on the relative slopes of the FE and LM curves, that is, on whether fiscal expansion worsens or improves the payments position. In the former case, flexible rates make fiscal policy most effective and in the latter, they make it least effective. Which case is more realistic? In the short run the answer is unclear, even though it is more common to assume that fiscal expansion worsens the balance of payments, as it does with FE steeper. In the long run this case is indeed the more likely because of what we know about the overall effect of higher interest rates on the balance of payments. The higher interest rates caused by fiscal expansion and heavier government borrowing attract capital in the short run but oblige the nation to make greater net outpayments of interest to the rest of the world later on. Which of these two flows is more important depends on how heavily policymakers want to discount the future, as we noted toward the end of Chapter 19. If policymakers are about as myopic or as farsighted as private holders of bills, bonds, and savings deposits, then changing the rate of interest has something like a zero effect on the balance of payments when both the attracted capital flows and the interest reflows are given their present discounted values. This amounts to making the FE curve roughly vertical (insensitive to interest rates) in the context of our static IS–LM–FE model. This returns us to the steep FE-curve case, in which fiscal expansion clearly worsens the balance of payments because the higher incomes worsen the trade balance. And in this case, as we saw, fiscal policy is more effective with flexible exchange rates. If we accept the steep FE-curve case as more likely, then it turns out that with flexible rates *both* fiscal and monetary policies seem more effective in controlling national income.

IS NATIONAL INCOME MORE STABLE WITH FIXED OR WITH FLEXIBLE EXCHANGE RATES?

If monetary and fiscal policies could smoothly stabilize the domestic economy, then the question posed in this section would seem to have been answered by the discussion just completed. If, as just argued, monetary policy and fiscal policy are likely to be more effective under flexible exchange rates, then it might seem clear that flexible rates allow officials to keep the economy more stable. Yet monetary and fiscal policies work only very imperfectly. It is hard for officials to know how great or how prompt an effect a given policy action will have. Lacking this knowledge, they have difficulty in deciding just what policy actions they should take at any given moment. A current recession, for example, might or might not call for stimulative action. If the authorities expected the recession to reverse itself in the near future, they would not want to provide a stimulus to the economy that would start to raise aggregate demand only with a long lag, since the stimulus could then end up just heating up an inflation and making the economy less stable. Such are the knotty practical considerations of stabilization policy.

Given the difficulties of stabilization policy, it would help a lot if institutions could be designed in such a way as to make stabilization more automatic and less dependent on officials' fallible discretion. One such design would be a progressive tax structure that builds "automatic stabilizers" into aggregate demand by automatically siphoning off a large share of any extra income into extra taxes. International economists have been debating whether fixed or flexible exchange rates would be more likely to play the role of automatic stabilizer. Which exchange-rate regime would tend to cushion outside shocks to the economy, thereby lessening the size of the disequilibriums that policy has to contend with? The answer turns out to hinge critically on the kinds of shocks to which the economy is most liable.

Export demand shocks

A common source of major shocks to many economies is the variability of foreign demand for exports. This variability is particularly acute for countries specializing in exporting a narrow range of products the demand for which is highly sensitive to the business cycle in importing countries. This instability of export demand has plagued exporters of metals, such as Chile (copper), Malaysia (tin), and to a lesser extent, Canada. Although these countries could react to unpredictable shifts in export demand with offsetting macroeconomic policies stabilizing aggregate demand, the fact that discretionary stabilization policies are hard to design means, again, that it would help very much to have an exchange-rate system that obviated the necessity of correct discretionary policies.

Flexible exchange rates seem to perform better in the face of shifts in export demand.[1] To see why, suppose that foreign demand for Malaysian tin drops off sharply. There is no exchange-rate policy that can shield Malaysia from income losses when this happens, but some policies cushion the shock better than others. An intermediate degree of income loss occurs in the simplest case, in which Malaysia rides out the slump with a fixed exchange rate and monetary sterilization. In this case, the export sector suffers a loss of incomes and jobs in the usual Keynesian way and the multiplier process transmits this income loss through the economy. If Malaysia does not sterilize the new payments deficit, the loss of export revenues and the accompanying outflow of money will reduce the money supply, causing still further contraction of the economy. Clinging to the fixed exchange rate when sterilization is not practiced (or unfeasible) yields the worst outcome, the largest drop in income in the wake of a drop in export demand.

Flexible exchange rates offer an automatic partial cushioning against export demand shocks. When export revenues drop, the na-

---

[1] We shall not analyze here the more difficult case of import supply shocks. In addition to all the complications that beset the cases analyzed in the text, import supply shocks raise further uncertainties. Their effect on the money supply (without sterilization) depends on the elasticity of import demand, and their effect on domestic income and spending also depends on how important importable goods and services are as a share of national income. These complications make the effect of import shocks under any exchange-rate regime difficult to predict. This is unfortunate, given the importance of such import supply shocks as OPEC oil price increases.

tional currency starts to depreciate. This depreciation will generate some new demand for national product (assuming the stability conditions of Chapter 15 and Appendix H). Exporters will find that foreign demand for their product is buoyed up by the fact that their prices denominated in the depreciated home currency now look cheaper to foreign buyers. Import-competing industries will also tend to win a larger share of domestic markets now that the competing foreign goods look more expensive. These effects of the exchange-rate depreciation do not erase the effect of initial loss of export incomes, which is still being transmitted through the economy, but they do help to offset that effect with demand stimuli, helping to stabilize the economy automatically. Flexible exchange rates also make it easier to shield the domestic money supply from an external money drain, by bringing the net international flow of money back to equilibrium after any shock. (The case of unanticipated rises in export demand is symmetrical to the case of demand drop discussed here, with the threat being excessive inflation rather than excessive unemployment and real income loss).

International capital-flow shocks

Another external shock to which economies are subject is the unpredictable shifting of internationally mobile funds in response to such events as rumors about political changes or new restrictions on international asset holding. This kind of shock threatens to upset the domestic economy by causing a surge or plummeting of the money supply. A sudden capital inflow threatens to raise the money supply that can be lent, driving down interest rates and expanding spending, with inflation as a possible end result. A sudden capital outflow, conversely, threatens to drain off part of the money supply, triggering a recession.

To determine which exchange-rate system offers the most stability in the face of such capital-flow shocks, let us take the case of a sudden capital flight from the country. It is easy to see that the stablest exchange-rate system in this situation is that of a fixed exchange rate with sterilization of all payments imbalances. If the authorities can succeed in keeping the capital outflow, with its transfer of money into the hands of foreign borrowers, from affecting the domestic money supply, the shock will have no effect at all on the domestic economy. The central bank will just make up the loss of some money into foreign hands by lending more money to domestic residents. On the other hand, if the money outflow cannot be offset, the resulting contraction of the money supply will cut national income.

Flexible exchange rates yield an intermediate outcome in the face of capital-flow shocks. They clearly cushion the economy relative to the case of fixed exchange rates without sterilization, which allowed the capital outflow to bring an equal reduction in the money supply available to domestic residents. With flexible rates, the capital outflow is allowed to depreciate the nation's currency in the foreign exchange markets. This depreciation makes it easier for the nation's producers to compete with foreign producers, improving the trade balance and shifting the *IS* curve to the right. This stimulative effect is not possible with fixed exchange rates in the absence of sterilization. With flexible exchange rates, however, the net effect of the capital-flow shock on income depends on what happens to the money supply. With flexible rates, it should be easy for the central bank to offset the initial effect of the capital outflow on the money supply by an expansion of its domestic lending. If the central bank does sterilize the money outflow in this way, then the effect of the capital outflow is the stimulative effect just described, and the capital outflow actually adds an expansionary shock to the economy. If it does not sterilize the money outflow, then there are opposing effects: on the one hand, the depreciation of the currency stimulates the sectors of the economy involved in international trade; on the other, the money outflow cuts into the money supply and tends to contract the economy.

In the case of an economy subject to erratic capital movements, we thus get a variety of outcomes. Clearly the most stable exchange-rate policy, if it is possible, is to maintain a fixed exchange rate with sterilization. In this case, the capital flows have no effect on aggregate demand. The least stable case is likely to be that of fixed exchange rates without sterilization, in which capital outflows bring an equal contraction of the money supply. In between, and less certain, is the case of flexible exchange rates. In this case, the capital outflows could range between being less contractionary than fixed rates without sterilization and being somewhat stimulative.

Internal shocks

Instability in national income can also be threatened by erratic movements in domestic spending demand and monetary demand.[2] The disruption caused by such shocks again depends on the exchange-rate system. We have already dealt with the implications of

---

[2] Note that the cases of aggregate-supply shocks and money supply shocks are being ignored here (as in almost all of the literature on the macroeconomics of exchange-rate policy). Aggregate-supply shocks, such as labor strikes and harvest failures, make national production drop when prices rise. Letting such shocks depreciate the currency and cause a stimulus to demand for exports and import-competing goods and services would help offset the cut in real national income, but would add to inflation. The choice between exchange-rate systems would then depend on society's relative preferences about output stability and price stability. Money supply shocks are not discussed here because it is assumed that the central bank plays the role of a stabilizer of money growth whose task is to keep shocks from elsewhere from breeding erratic money growth.

these shocks when we discussed the effect of monetary and fiscal policies under flexible exchange rates. We found that monetary policy was more powerful with flexible exchange rates. It follows that erratic shifts in money demand, such as runs on banks or scrambles to unload money when inflation is feared, will be more powerful—that is, more disruptive—under flexible exchange rates. The analysis of fiscal policy also carries over as an analysis of the disruptiveness of any domestic spending shocks. Under the plausible assumption that expansions in domestic spending end up worsening the balance of payments (FE steeper than LM), domestic spending shocks seem more disruptive under flexible exchange rates for reasons described when we discussed fiscal policy.

Table 20.2 summarizes our results about the stability of national income in the face of exogenous shocks under different exchange-rate systems. Studying this table, one can see a rough general pattern: *As a rule, it is easier to stabilize the economy with flexible exchange rates if the shocks are external, but easier to stabilize with fixed exchange rates if the shocks are internal.* Flexible exchange rates offer some cushioning against foreign shifts, but tend to magnify the disruption from shifts of domestic origin.

TABLE 20.2
Rankings of exchange-rate systems by the unit impacts of various exogenous shocks on national income

| | *Rankings* | | |
	(1) Most disruptive— least stable	*(2)*	*(3)* Least disruptive— most stable
Effect of export demand shocks	Fixed, no sterilization	Fixed, sterilization	*Flexible*
Effect of international capital-flow shock	Fixed, no sterilization	*Flexible*	Fixed, sterilization
Effect of domestic spending shock With *FE* steeper than *LM*	*Flexible*	Fixed, sterilization	Fixed, no sterilization
With *FE* flatter than *LM*	Fixed, no sterilization	Fixed, sterilization	*Flexible*
Effect of domestic monetary shock	*Flexible*	Fixed, sterilization	Fixed, no sterilization

Compare to results in Table 20.1

Illustration: For "Effect of export demand shocks," the table says that such shocks are most disruptive to national income under fixed exchange rates without sterilization of payments imbalances and least disruptive (that is, the economy reacts most stably) under flexible exchange rates.

Whether a country that is worried about macroeconomic stabilization should choose fixed or flexible rates thus depends above all on the kinds of shocks it expects to experience in the future. Flexible rates would seem to recommend themselves to a country which must export metals such as copper or tin to industrial economies whose demands depend on the business cycle. The argument for flexible rates would be even stronger if the metal-exporting country were subject to strong shifts in international capital flows. To the extent that Canada, for example, fits such a description, it has at least a macroeconomic reason for preferring flexible exchange rates (which it chose in 1950–62 and again in the 1970s). On the other hand, countries subject to highly unstable domestic spending demand might be better off with fixed exchange rates. If, for example, fiscal policy is unstable because of recurrent attempts to buy election votes with spending binges that are reversed after the election, then the central bank (if it retains policy independence) should consider choosing fixed exchange rates on the ground that flexible rates would magnify the instability bred by erratic fiscal policy.

SUMMARY

The effects of monetary and fiscal policy under flexible exchange rates are complex, but can be fairly well understood with the help of the IS–LM–FE model. Monetary policy can affect national income more strongly with flexible exchange rates than with fixed rates. So can fiscal policy, under the plausible assumption that expansionary fiscal policy worsens the balance of payments (that is, that the FE curve is steeper than the LM curve). When this assumption is not applicable, fiscal policy is less potent under flexible rates.

The debate over whether it is easier to keep national income stable with fixed or with flexible exchange rates can be partially resolved with a rough rule of thumb: it is usually easier to stabilize with flexible rates if the economy is subject to external shocks, such as fluctuations in export demand or capital flows, and it is usually easier to stabilize with fixed rates in the face of internal shocks. This rule of thumb emerges from Table 20.2's more careful cataloging of some important cases.

It should be remembered that these conclusions rest on the assumptions of the IS–LM–FE model, which were listed in Chapter 19.

SUGGESTED READING

See the suggestions at the end of Chapter 19.

21

The debate over fixed and flexible exchange rates

The central policy debate in the international monetary arena continues to be that over the relative merits of fixed exchange rates, floating exchange rates, and compromises between them, as alternative ways to adjust nations' external payments positions. The experiences of the 1970s have brought converts to both the fixed-rate and the floating-rate camps. Some who had urged some variant on floating rates profess to be born again, and to have discovered new persuasive arguments for holding exchange rates fixed. At the same time, some previous defenders of fixed rates profess to have made their peace with the float. Yet expert opinion is still far from unanimous. A majority of monetary officials is still striving to restore greater fixity to exchange rates (though flexible rates have now attained greater popularity within the U.S. government). A bare majority of academic economists still seems to prefer flexible rates.

Though the debate continues, it is not completely unresolved. Both theoretical analysis and our understanding of actual experience have now built up to a point where it is possible to sketch rough answers to many of the questions raised in the debate over exchange-rate policy. We have already begun to sketch some of those answers. Chapter 18 argued that we can narrow the choice to fixed rates, floating rates, and compromises between them, since exchange controls have high costs and few advantages except to bureaucrats. Chapters 19 and 20 addressed the important issue of how easy it is to stabilize national economies under fixed and flexible exchange rates. In principle, Chapter 19 argued, one can design combinations of monetary and fiscal policy that achieve both internal and external balance under fixed exchange rates. Doing so may be difficult in practice, however. Chapter 20 argued that whether it is easier to stabilize under fixed rates than under flexible rates depends on the shocks to which the economy is subject. To repeat the broad pattern that emerged from more detailed analysis there, we found that flexible rates seem to cushion the economy better in the face of external shocks, whereas fixed rates offer better insurance against some of the damage of internal shocks. It remains for this chapter to pull together what is known about the remaining key issues in the exchange-rate debate: the issues of "price discipline," risk, and the possibility of destabilizing speculation.

THE ISSUE OF PRICE "DISCIPLINE"

One of the main arguments advanced in favor of fixed exchange rates has been that allowing floating rates would weaken official price discipline. The argument runs as follows:

1. The fixed-exchange-rate system puts more pressure on governments with international payments deficits than on governments with surpluses; it follows that allowing governments to switch to floating rates gives more new freedom to deficit countries than it gives to surplus countries.
2. Since classical medicine prescribes deflation for deficit countries and inflation for surplus countries, avoiding this medicine with floating rates permits policy to be more inflationary on the average.
3. This greater inflation with the float is a bad thing, since individual governments are biased toward excessive inflation if they are not disciplined by the need to defend a fixed exchange rate.

The first two parts to the price discipline argument seem roughly to fit the facts. The third requires a personal value judgment.

It does seem to be the case that the fixed-exchange-rate system constrains deficit countries more than surplus countries. Deficit countries must face an obvious limit to their ability to sustain deficits: they will soon run out of reserves and creditworthiness. Surplus countries, by contrast, face only more distant and manageable inconveniences from perennial surpluses. After a while, constantly accumulating foreign exchange and gold reserves becomes inconvenient. The central bank or treasury has to swallow these assets as private individuals turn them in for domestic currency. When the foreign reserve assets rise to some high levels, it becomes technically impossible for the officials to keep further payments surpluses from raising the money supply, because the officials no longer have any ability to cut their domestic lending once it has hit zero. (Theoretically, the officials could go on becoming gross and net debtors to the domestic economy, issuing official nonmoney IOUs to sop up domestic money, but monetary institutions are seldom set up for such pursuits by central banks.) Yet this constraint is quite distant. Countries can go on running surpluses for more years than they can go on running deficits that are the same percentage of initial reserves.

Experience seems to confirm this asymmetry. In the postwar period it has been possible for surplus countries, such as West Germany and Japan, to continue accumulating reserves for a considerable time without major inconvenience. It has been harder for deficit countries, such as Britain, to hold out so long. The main exception of a deficit country able to hold out is that of the United States. As we noted in Chapter 18, the United States was able to sustain deficits longer than were most countries because the reserve-currency status of the dollar made a growing world economy willing to accumulate dollars in large amounts for over a decade. The pre-1914 experience with fixed exchange rates looks much the same. Those countries for which classical medicine proved too much to take were deficit countries. The system of exchange rates fixed to gold was abandoned not by countries whose reserve inflows proved embarrassing but by countries which could not stem reserve outflows at fixed exchange rates. As we shall see later in this chapter, countries abandoning the gold standard before 1914 did so in response to rapid growth in their own money supplies, which caused their currencies to drop in value as soon as they unfixed their exchange rates. Countries running surpluses were in a comfortable position and saw no reason to let their exchange rates change. The main exception to this pattern, as in the postwar period, was that of the reserve-center country. Britain was able to run large balance-of-payments deficits before 1914 because a growing world economy was willing to accumulate greater sterling balances. With this exception, the asymmetry was clear: the fixed-exchange-rate system pressured deficit countries to deflate more than it pressured surplus countries to inflate.

Given this asymmetry in the burdens of adjusting to a set of fixed exchange rates in a changing world, it follows that allowing countries to begin floating their currencies will on balance release more inflationary policies. This conclusion is supported by the observation that world inflation of money supplies and prices seemed to pick up a bit after the generalized float of August 1971, in the first twelve months, though this occurrence can have other explanations as well.

Whether or not flexible exchange rates lead to *too much* inflation is an open question. Somebody who cares very much about full employment and is not much bothered about price inflation might prefer flexible rates because they enhance the ability of deficit countries to create jobs with expansionary policies. Somebody who fears inflation above all is more likely to favor fixed exchange rates for the same reason. The debate over fixed versus flexible exchange rates is thus partly a variant of the familiar debate over what mixture of unemployment and inflation is best. The price discipline argument thus makes some correct statements about how fixed-rate and flexible-rate systems differ in practice, and adds a value judgment in favor of fixed rates and greater price stability, a judgment one may or may not share.

THE RISK ARGUMENT

Another argument introduced into the exchange-rate debate by advocates of fixed rates is one stressing the role of risk in international trade and investment. People are generally risk-averse. We prefer less risk to more, as is evidenced by the fact that the insurance business is much bigger than the gambling business even where gambling is perfectly legal. It has been traditionally argued that flexible exchange rates increase risk. With the exchange rate free to change, traders and investors will feel less certain about its future. Fearing its changes, they will tend to be discouraged somewhat from socially profitable investments in developing foreign trade or production abroad. World product will be reduced. Hedging against exchange-rate risk by buying forward cover involves resource costs (work done by foreign exchange dealers). The fixed-rate system, it is argued, gives people rates they can count on and saves them worry and hedging costs.

This argument works against flexible exchange rates only in a much narrower range of cases than its proponents tend to think. It can hold if a nation's external payments are in a state of fundamental equilibrium, so that departures from that state are temporary and self-reversing. In such a case it makes good sense to keep the exchange rate fixed at its sustainable equilibrium level. Doing so cuts the risk of short-run fluctuations without involving any social costs. This is the same conclusion in favor of smoothing out temporary disequilibriums that we advanced in Chapter 18, though risk was not introduced there. On the other hand, if the disequilibriums are clearly temporary, one might expect private speculators to perceive this and to iron out the temporary swings even with a freely floating exchange rate.

As soon as one broadens one's view of the relevant risks, the risk argument ceases to damage the case for flexible exchange rates. The risk that people care most directly about is the overall risk of fluctuations in their real incomes, not just price or exchange-rate uncertainty. Fixed exchange rates may actually bring extra risks. A system of truly fixed rates imposes large adjustment costs on individual countries.

Deficit countries must put up with unemployment and deflation in order to adjust their entire economies to the exchange rate. Surplus countries, if they adjust, are burdened with unwanted inflation in the name of fixed rates.[1] For individuals and firms these adjustment costs can be viewed as a part of the risk cost imposed by a fixed-rate system that may in the near future call on a country to sacrifice its internal balance to defend the exchange rate. These adjustment costs of taking classical medicine are hard for firms and individuals to see. They may also seem inordinately great in a country which, like the United States, devotes only a small share of its economic activity to international trade and investment. The risk of having your government unexpectedly deflate or inflate the economy to maintain a fixed exchange rate in the face of outside shocks may seem costlier than the risk of changes in the exchange rate.

The adjustable-peg system has its own set of risks for the private investor or trader. It cuts the risk of nationwide deflation or inflation associated with a fully fixed rate, by letting occasional devaluations and revaluations do some of the adjusting. But these occasional devaluations and revaluations pose a new threat. Investors or traders now perceive that over a single weekend (a common time for official exchange-rate changes) they could lose or gain a very large percentage on any currency holdings. Fortunately this kind of risk comes only when general opinion perceives that a currency is "in trouble," but when it comes it can strike traders and investors as a large risk indeed.

Freely floating rates bring a different structure of risk. As compared with truly fixed rates, they allow generally greater stability of income in the face of external shocks but less stability in the face of internal shocks, as we saw in Chapter 20. As compared with the adjustable-pegged-rate system, they face traders and investors with the likelihood of more frequent but smaller rate changes.

An important difference between the risks of a truly fixed-rate system and the exchange risks of the float or adjustable peg is that the latter can be insured against. Traders or investors who want to avoid exchange-rate risk can hedge and buy forward cover for time periods up to a year or so, to insure that their assets and liabilities are in the currencies they want. It has been argued that this kind of cover is (a) expensive and (b) more in demand with changing than with fixed exchange rates. Argument (b) is correct, but (a) is hardly so. The resource cost of forward cover as an insurance service is trivial. The

---

[1] This argument implies pessimism about Chapter 19's policy formulas for achieving both internal and external balance with fixed exchange rates. Clearly, if both goals can be achieved easily, the fixed-rate system need not bring unwanted deflation or inflation. Yet as we argued in Chapter 19, there are many reasons to doubt the practical feasibility of rectifying both payments imbalance and internal imbalance with just monetary and fiscal policies, and without changing the exchange rate.

forward exchange market occupies the time of only several hundred specialists at most, plus very little capital cost. When people think of the cost of forward cover, they often think of a forward discount on the currency one wants to sell. Yet the same forward discount that looks unattractive to a seller looks good to a buyer, so that a forward discount or premium on a particular currency is neither a cost nor a benefit to the world as a whole. Only the use of real labor and capital resources in the forward market is a net cost, and this is a trivial sum. The greater use of forward markets for hedging when exchange rates are subject to change is probably an argument for, rather than against, flexible exchange rates. The existence of such facilities means that one can easily insure against exchange-rate risk, whereas it is much harder to insure against a sudden job loss or sudden inflation resulting from government attempts to defend a fixed exchange rate.

DESTABILIZING SPECULATION

Back in Chapter 15, we examined one kind of possible instability in foreign exchange markets in which the exchange rate can change. We looked at the conditions under which depreciating a nation's currency would yield the "stable" result of improving its trade balance. The tentative conclusion was that this result is likely to hold in a majority of cases, though nothing says that the trade balance must always respond in the stable way. This likelihood of a stable trade-balance response should send a stabilizing signal to speculators who are trying to bet on the future of the exchange rate.

Nonetheless, many officials and scholars have argued that speculative behavior can behave in a very destabilizing way when exchange rates are flexible, that they can disrupt foreign exchange markets by making swings in the exchange rate wider than these would be otherwise. The wider swings, in turn, are said to damage confidence in exchange rates and to give traders and investors a heightened fear of exchange-rate risk. Such destabilizing speculation is seen as an argument against both floating exchange rates and the adjustable-pegged-rate system, since if officials showed that they were fully committed to absolutely fixed rates speculators would not second-guess them and would themselves believe that rates will be stable.

The debate over destabilizing speculation often centers on diagrams like Figure 21.1. It is imagined that speculative behavior, here defined as the taking of open currency positions in response to expected movements in the exchange rate, affects the extent to which the actual exchange rate deviates from its long-run trend. In Figure 21.1A, speculation smooths out the fluctuations in the exchange rate. Speculators tend to sell the foreign currency (here the pound) when its

FIGURE 21.1
Hypothetical cases of stabilizing and destabilizing speculation in the foreign exchange market

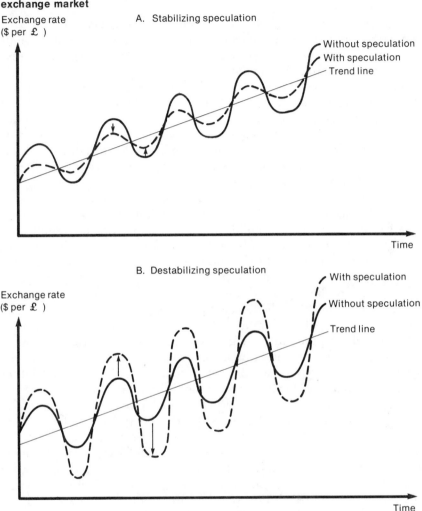

price is above trend and to buy it when it is below trend. Their actions have exactly the kind of stabilizing effect that officials are often told to achieve. In Figure 21.1B, by contrast, speculators tend to magnify swings in the exchange rate. This undesirable outcome could result if, for example, net speculative purchases of the foreign currency were in fixed positive proportion to the deviations of the nonspeculative equilibrium rate from the long-run trend. In this case speculators seem to expect rises in the exchange rate when its level is high and to expect drops when its level is low. They thus buy high and sell low, de-stabilizing the foreign exchange market and worsening the market's riskiness.

How likely is destabilizing speculation? An early argument by Milton Friedman led several economists into a theoretical debate. Friedman argued in 1953 that speculation must end up being stabilizing, because only stabilizing speculation is profitable. He pointed out that the stabilizing speculators in cases like Figure 21.1A end up making profits because they buy low and sell high over each cycle of exchange-rate movements. The destabilizing speculators in Figure 21.1B, by contrast, are clearly losing money by buying high and selling low over each cycle. Friedman argued that the destabilizing kind of behavior would tend to be self-eliminating because destabilizing speculators would go bankrupt if they kept it up.

Friedman's argument prompted a search for hypothetical cases in which destabilizing speculation was profitable. William Baumol offered some apparent hypothetical examples, and others argued over whether the speculators really ended up making money. The debate over hypothetical possibilities represents a diversion from the key empirical issue, however. Even if destabilizing speculators did lose money, as Friedman argued, they might still have wrought havoc in the markets in which they took their losses. To see how little the debate over speculators' profits educates our guesses about their possible destabilizing nature, imagine a 1927 debate over the possibility of destabilizing speculation in stocks on Wall Street. A theorist might have argued, as Friedman did later, that destabilizing speculation would be unprofitable and therefore self-eliminating, and might have concluded that speculation would keep stock prices near the long-run trend dictated by the long-run growth of real corporate profits. Others might have countered with hypothetical mathematical cases of destabilizing but profitable speculation. None of these contributions, however, could have resolved the key empirical question of whether speculation stands a good chance of being destabilizing in such unregulated markets. That question had to be answered by a study of actual experience. Such a study would have turned up many cases in which sharp changes in price expectations destabilized markets for stocks, tulip bulbs, real estate, and other assets. And subsequent events bore out the possibility: speculators between 1927 and mid-1929 took their own willingness to pay higher share prices as a sign that the stock market would go even higher, and then reversed their opinions and ruined themselves in the aggregate in the Great Crash. These destabilizing speculators lost money, of course, but that didn't prevent disaster.

The issue of the likelihood of destabilizing speculation under floating or pegged-but-adjustable exchange rates can thus be judged only empirically, by looking at actual exchange-rate experience.

INTERNATIONAL CURRENCY EXPERIENCE

A lot can be learned from the history of relations between national currencies since the establishment of a nearly worldwide gold standard over a century ago. This historical experience sheds light not only on the issue of destabilizing speculation but on the way in which payments adjustments worked under truly fixed exchange rates and the adjustable-peg system.

The gold standard era, 1870–1914

Ever since 1914 the prewar gold standard has been the object of considerable nostalgia. Both the interwar period and the postwar period saw concerted international efforts to reestablish fixed-exchange-rate systems, whose desirability was viewed as proved by the experience of the gold standard. Among scholars, too, the "success" of the gold standard has been widely accepted and research has focused on *why*, not whether, it worked so well.

The international gold standard emerged by 1870 with the help of historical accidents centering on Britain. Britain tied the pound sterling ever more closely to gold rather than silver from the late 17th century on, in part because Britain's official gold-silver value ratio was more favorable to gold than were the ratios of other countries, causing arbitrageurs to ship gold to Britain and silver from Britain. The link between the pound sterling and gold proved crucial. Britain's rise to primacy in industrialization and world trade in the 19th century enhanced the prestige of the metal tied to the currency of this leading country. As it also happened, Britain had the further advantage of not being invaded in wars, which further strengthened its image as the model of financial security and prudence. The prestige of gold was raised further by another lucky accident: the waves of gold discoveries in the middle (California, Australia) and at the end (the Klondike, South Africa) of the 19th century were small enough not to make gold too suddenly abundant to be a standard for international value. The silver mining expansion of the 1870s and 1880s, by contrast, yielded too much silver, causing its value to plummet. With the help of such accidents the gold standard, in which each national currency was fixed in gold content, remained intact from about 1870 until World War I.

In retrospect it is clear that the success of the gold standard is explained in part by the tranquility of the prewar era. The world economy simply was not subjected to shocks as severe as World Wars I and

II, the Great Depression of the 1930s, and the OPEC oil price jump of 1973–74. The gold standard looked successful in part because it was not put to a severe worldwide test.

The pre-1914 tranquillity even allowed some countries to have favorable experiences with flexible exchange rates. Several countries abandoned fixed exchange rates and gold convertibility in short-run crises. Britain itself did so during the Napoleonic Wars. Faced with heavy wartime financial needs, Britain suspended convertibility of the pound sterling into gold and let the pound drop as much as 30 percent in value by 1813, restoring official gold convertibility after the wars. Other countries were to repeat the same experience, as shown for selected countries in Figure 21.2. During the U.S. Civil War, the North found itself unable to maintain the gold value of the paper dollar, given the tremendous need to print dollars to finance the war effort. The newly issued greenback dollars had dropped in value by more than 60 percent as of 1864, before beginning a long, slow climb

FIGURE 21.2
Selected exchange rates, 1860–1913

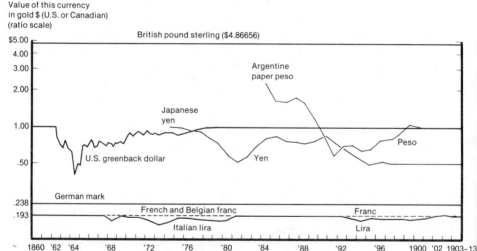

The data are annual averages of market exchange rates, except for the rates on the greenback dollar from 1862 through 1872, which are monthly averages for every third month.

The Argentine paper peso rates are the John H. Williams gold premiums cited in Alec G. Ford, *The Gold Standard, 1880–1914: Great Britain and Argentina* (Oxford: Clarendon, 1962), p. 139. The Italian series is from Istituto Centrale di Statistica, *Sommario di Statistiche Storiche Italiane, 1861–1955* (Rome, 1958), p. 166. The gold value of the paper Japanese yen was calculated using the mid-range New York dollar value of the metal-backed yen (Bank of Japan, Statistics Department, *Hundred-Year Statistics of the Japanese Economy* [Tokyo, 1966], p. 318) and the average price of silver in paper yen for the period 1877–1886 (Henry Rosovsky, "Japan's Transition to Modern Economic Growth, 1868–1885," in *Industrialization in Two Systems*, ed. Henry Rosovsky [New York: Wiley, 1966], pp. 129 and 136. The U.S. greenback dollar series is the W. C. Mitchell series cited in Don C. Barrett, *The Greenback and Resumption of Specie Payments, 1862–1879* (Cambridge, Mass.: Harvard University Press, 1931), pp. 96–98. The virtually fixed rates are available in the *Economist* for prewar years.

back to gold parity in 1879. Heavy short-run financial needs also drove other countries off gold parity. War was the proximate culprit in the cases of Russia, Austria-Hungary, and Italy.

The prewar experience with flexible exchange rates reveals some patterns borne out by most of 20th-century experience as well. Most countries abandoning fixed exchange rates did so in a context of growing payments deficits and reserve outflows. Note that in Figure 21.2 the end of fixed exchange rates was accompanied by a drop in the value of the national currency. This shows indirectly that the fixed-rate gold standard imposed strain mostly on countries which were in payments deficit situations, not on countries in surplus. Indeed, countries in surplus found it easy to continue accumulating reserves with a fixed exchange rate.

In general the prewar experiences with flexible exchange rates did not reveal any tendency toward destabilizing speculation. For the most part, the exchange-rate fluctuations were within the range to be experienced by Canada and other countries in the postwar era, and did not represent wide departures from the exchange rate one would have predicted, given the movements in price indexes. Two possible exceptions related to the U.S. greenback dollar and the Russian ruble. In 1864 the greenback dollar jumped 49 percent between April and July, even though the wholesale price index rose less than 15 percent, suggesting that speculation greatly accelerated the drop in the greenback, which then promptly rebounded. Similarly, in 1888 political rumors caused a dive in the thinly marketed Russian ruble. With the exception of these two possible cases of destabilizing speculation, it appears that flexible rates were quite stable in the prewar setting, given the political events that forced governments to try them out.

The method of payments adjustment under the prevailing fixed exchange rates puzzled Frank Taussig and his Harvard students after World War I. They found that international gold flows seemed to eliminate themselves very quickly, too quickly for their possible effects on national money supplies to change incomes, prices, and the balance of payments as Hume had imagined they would. The puzzle was heightened by a postwar finding of Arthur I. Bloomfield that central banks had done little to adjust their national economies to their exchange rates before 1914. Far from taking classical medicine, prewar central banks, like their successors in the interwar period, offset ("sterilized") external reserve flows in the majority of cases, shielding their national money supplies from the balance of payments. What, then, did keep the prewar balance of payments in line?

It must first be noted that most countries were able to run payments surpluses before 1914, raising their holdings of gold and foreign exchange. This removed the cost of adjustment to fixed exchange rates, since surplus countries were under little pressure to adjust. What made these widespread surpluses possible was, aside from the slow accumulation of newly mined gold in official vaults, the willingness and ability of Britain—and Germany to a lesser extent—to let the rest of the world hold growing amounts of its ready liabilities. Between 1900 and 1913, for example, Britain ran payments deficits that were at least as large in relation to official (Bank of England) gold reserves as the deficits that caused so much hand-wringing in the United States in the 1960s. It would in fact have been impossible for Britain to honor even a third of its liquid liabilities to foreigners in 1913 by paying out official gold reserves. The gold standard was thus helped along considerably by the ability of the key-currency country to give the rest of the world liquid IOUs whose buildup nobody minded—or even measured.

There were times, of course, in which Britain was called upon to halt outflows of gold reserves, which were more conspicuous than the unknown rise in its liquid liabilities. The Bank of England showed an impressive ability to halt gold outflows within a few months, faster than it could have if it had needed to contract the whole British economy to improve the balance of payments. It appears that monetary tightening by the Bank of England was capable of calling in large volumes of short-term capital from abroad, even when central banks in other countries raised their interest rates by the same percentage. This command over short-term capital seems to have been linked to the fact that London itself was the reserve center for the world's money markets. As the main short-term international lender (as well as borrower), London could contract the whole world's money supply in the short run if and when the Bank of England ordered private London banks to do so. In this way the prewar gold standard combined overall surplus for most countries with short-run defensive strength on the part of the main deficit country.

Interwar instability

If the gold standard era before 1914 has been viewed as the classic example of international monetary soundness, the interwar period has played the part of a nightmare, which postwar officials have been determined to avoid repeating. Payments balances and exchanges gyrated chaotically in response to two great shocks, World War I and the Great Depression. Figure 21.3 plots the exchange-rate history of the interwar period. The chaos was concentrated into two periods, the first few years after World War I (1919–23) and the currency crisis in the depths of the Great Depression (1931–34).

After World War I the European countries had to struggle with a

FIGURE 21.3
Selected exchange rates, 1913, 1919–1938

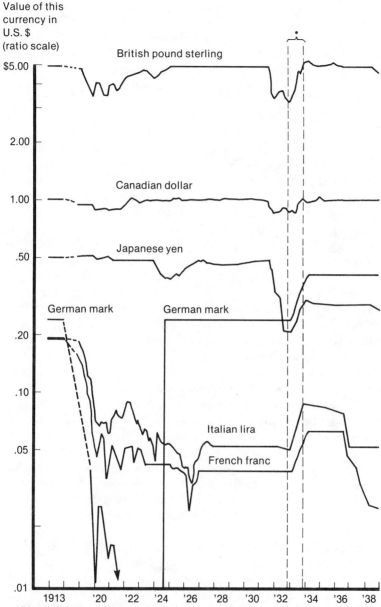

* March 1933–February 1934: the United States raises the price of gold from $20.67 per ounce to $35 per ounce.

Source: Monthly averages from U.S. Federal Reserve Board, Board of Governors, *Banking and Monetary Statistics* (Washington, D.C., 1943).

legacy of inflation and political instability. Their currencies had become inconvertible during the war, since their rates of inflation were much higher than that experienced in the United States, the new financial leader. In this setting Britain made the fateful decision to return to its prewar gold parity, achieving this rate by April 1925. Though the decision has been defended as a moral obligation and as a sound attempt to restore international confidence and Britain's role at the center of a reviving world economy, the hindsight consensus is that bringing the pound back up to $4.86656 was a serious mistake. It appears to have caused considerable unemployment and stagnation in traded-goods industries, as theory would predict.

France, Italy, and some other European countries chose a more inflationary route, for complicated political reasons. A succession of French revolving-door governments was unable to cut government spending or raise taxes to shut off large budgetary deficits that had to be financed largely by printing new money. Something similar happened in Italy, both before and immediately after the 1922 revolution that brought Mussolini to power. The ultimate in inflation, however, was experienced by Germany, where the money supply, prices, and the cost of foreign exchange all rose more than a trillionfold in 1922–23. Money became totally worthless, and by late 1923 not even a wheelbarrowful of paper money could buy a week's groceries. The mark had to be reissued in a new series equal to the prewar dollar value, with old marks forever unredeemable.

The early 1930s brought another breakdown of international currency relations. A financial community already stunned by the early postwar chaos and the Wall Street collapse became justifiably jittery about bank deposits and currencies as the depression spread. The failure of the reputable Creditanstalt in Austria caused a run on German banks and the mark, since Germany had lent heavily to Austria. The panic soon led to an attack on the pound sterling, which had been perennially weak and was now compromised by the fact that Britain had made heavy loans to the collapsing Germans. On September 19, 1931, Britain abandoned the gold standard it had championed, letting the pound sink to its equilibrium market value. Between early 1933 and early 1934, the United States followed suit and let the dollar drop in gold value, as FDR and his advisers manipulated the price of gold in an attempt to create jobs somehow.

What lessons does the interwar experience hold for postwar policymakers? During World War II expert opinion seemed to be that the interwar experience called for a compromise between fixed and flexible exchange rates, with emphasis on fixity. The Bretton Woods agreement of 1944 set up the International Monetary Fund and laid down a set of rules calling for countries to change their exchange rates only when fundamental disequilibrium made this unavoidable. This decision was paralleled by Ragnar Nurkse's book on *International Currency Experience*, written for the League of Nations in 1944. Nurske argued, with some qualifying disclaimers, that the interwar experience showed the instability of flexible exchange rates. Figure 21.3 adds some evidence to his premise: exchange rates did indeed move more sharply during the interwar era than at any other time before the 1970s.

Yet subsequent studies have shown that a closer look at the interwar experience reveals the opposite lesson: the interwar experience showed the futility of trying to keep exchange rates fixed in the face of severe shocks, and the necessity of turning to flexible rates to cushion some of the international shocks. At the same time, these studies have shown that even in the unstable interwar era, speculation tended to be stabilizing—it was domestic monetary and fiscal policy that was destabilizing.

This revisionist conclusion began to emerge from studies of Britain's fluctuating rates between 1919 and 1925. Both Robert Z. Aliber and S. C. Tsiang found that the pound sterling fluctuated in ways that are easily explained by the effects of differential inflation on the trade balance. Relative to the exchange-rate movements that would be predicted by the purchasing-power-parity theory of the equilibrium exchange rate (see Chapter 17), the actual movements stayed close to the long-run trend. The cases in which Figure 21.3 shows rapid drops in currency values were cases in which the runaway expansion of the national money supply made this inevitable under any exchange-rate regime. This is true of France up to 1926 and even more so, of course, of the German hyperinflation.

Closer looks at the currency instability of the early 1930s suggest the same conclusion. What made the pound sterling, the yen, and other currencies drop so rapidly in 1931–32 was the gaping disequilibrium built into the fixed-exchange-rate system by the depression (and for Japan, by the invasion of Manchuria). Once the fixed rates were abandoned, flexible rates merely recorded, rather than worsened, the varying health of national economies.

The Bretton Woods era, 1944–1971

In the more stable and faster growing postwar economy, international monetary institutions looked more successful.

The more tranquil postwar era brought a look of greater success to flexible exchange rates, to judge (as most have) from the Canadian experience of 1950–62. As shown in Figure 21.4, the annual average exchange rates between Canada and the United States showed little

FIGURE 21.4
Selected exchange rates, 1950–1977

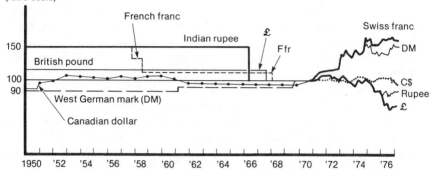

Index of the exchange
value of this currency,
in U.S. $ (Dec. 1970 = 100)
(ratio scale)

Sources: Year-end figures, 1950–69, and end-of-month figures, 1970–March 1977, from International Monetary Fund, *International Financial Statistics*, various issues, and the *Wall Street Journal* for 1976–77.

movement. By itself this does not prove that the Canadian experience was one in which speculation was stabilizing and flexible rates worked well. However, detailed studies of Canada's floating rate have borne out this inference. Statistical regressions have suggested that if the exchange rate on the Canadian dollar had any effect on capital movements, this effect was in the stabilizing direction. That is, a lower value of the Canadian dollar tended to cause greater net capital inflows into Canada, as though speculators expected the Canadian dollar to rise more when it was at low levels. Other studies have confirmed that the fluctuations in the exchange value of the Canadian dollar were no greater than one would have predicted by following movements in the relative U.S. and Canadian prices of traded goods. Given a stable economic environment, the Canadian flexible rate, like the fixed rates of the prewar gold standard, lived up to the claims of its advocates.

The postwar experience with adjustable pegged rates recorded only rare changes in exchange rates among major currencies, as Figure 21.4 suggests. Yet the adjustable-peg system revealed a new pattern in private speculation, one that has caused a great deal of official consternation. As the world economy grew, so did the volume of internationally mobile private funds. The new system of pegged-but-adjustable exchange rates spurred private speculators to attack currencies that were "in trouble." The adjustable-peg system gave private speculators an excellent one-way gamble. It was always clear from the context whether a currency was in danger of being devalued or revalued. In the case of a devaluation-suspect currency, such as the pound sterling, the astute private speculator knew that the currency could not rise significantly in value. He thus had little to lose by selling the currency short in the forward market. If the currency did not drop in value, he had lost nothing but his forward transactions fees and a slight gap between the forward rate and the spot rate. But if he was right and the currency was devalued, it might be devalued by a large percentage over a single weekend, bringing him a handsome return. In this situation, private speculators would gang up on a currency that was moving into a crisis phase. As one foreign exchange specialist in a leading U.S. bank put it, "In those days we could make money just by following the crowd."

This pattern of speculation under the adjustable-peg system meant serious difficulties for any government or central bank that was trying to cure a payments disequilibrium without adjusting the peg. A classic illustration of these difficulties was the attempt of Harold Wilson's Labour government to keep the pound worth $2.80 between 1964 and November 1967. When Wilson took office, he found that Britain's trade and payments balances were even worse than previous official figures had admitted. His government used numerous devices to make the pound worth $2.80: tighter exchange controls, soaring interest rates, selective tax hikes, promises to cut government spending, and massive loans from the IMF and the United States and other governments. Speculators who in increasing number doubted Britain's ability to shore up the pound were castigated by the chancellor of the Exchequer as "gnomes of Zurich." Yet in the end all of the belt tightening and all of the support loans worked no better than had the attempt to make the pound worth $4.86656 from 1925–31. On November 18, 1967, Britain devalued the pound by 14.3 percent, to $2.40. The gnomes had won handsomely. Those who had been selling sterling forward at prices like $2.67 just before the devaluation were able to buy the same sterling at about $2.40, pocketing the 27 cents difference. The British government and its taxpayers lost the same margin, by committing themselves to pay $2.67 for sterling that they had to concede was worth only $2.40 after November 18.

The existence of the one-way speculative gamble seems to make the adjustable peg of the Bretton Woods system look less sustainable than either purely fixed rates or purely flexible rates. If speculators believe that the government is willing to turn the entire economy inside out to defend the exchange rate, then they will not attack the exchange rate. Britain could have made speculators believe in $2.80 in the mid-1960s if it had shown its determination to slash the money supply and contract British incomes and jobs until $2.80 was truly an equilibrium rate. But as the speculators realized, few postwar governments are prepared to pay such national costs in the name of truly fixed exchange rates. Alternatively, the speculators might have been more cautious in betting against sterling if the exchange rate had been a floating equilibrium rate. With the float, speculators face a two-way gamble: the exchange rate could be higher or lower than they expect it to be, since the current spot rate is an equilibrium rate and not an artificial official disequilibrium rate.

Although the speculative attacks on an adjustable pegged rate are certainly unsettling to officials, it is not clear that they should be called "destabilizing." If the official defenses of the currency are primarily just ways of financing a deficit and not ways of raising the equilibrium value of the currency, then it could be said that the speculative attack is stabilizing in the sense that it hastens the transition to a new equilibrium rate. Whether it performs this stabilizing function is highly uncertain, however: officials may be induced to overreact to the speculative attack, and to overdevalue the pegged rate, necessitating another parity change later.

The postwar growth of the international economy led to a crisis involving the key currency of the system, the U.S. dollar. As the economy grew, and as Europe and Japan gained in competitive ability relative to that of U.S. firms, the U.S. payments position shifted into large deficits. In part those deficits represented the fact that a growing international economy wanted more dollar bank deposits in foreign hands to meet the monetary needs of international transactions. After a time, however, the deficits became a source of official concern in Europe and Japan. More and more dollars ended up in official hands. Something like this had happened before 1914, when other countries accumulated growing official reserves of sterling. In the postwar setting, however, few governments felt that they could be as relaxed about the gold backing of the U.S. dollar as the rest of the world had felt about the link between gold and Britain's sterling before 1914. U.S. gold reserves dwindled as France led the march to Fort Knox (actually, the basement of the New York Federal Reserve Bank), demanding gold for dollar claims. It became questionable whether the U.S. dollar was worth as much gold as the official gold price ($35 an ounce) implied.

In this situation, the United States clearly had the option of contracting the U.S. economy until foreigners were constrained to supply gold to the United States to pay for U.S. exports. Other alternatives were tight exchange controls and devaluing the dollar in terms of gold. Exchange controls were tried to a limited extent (in the form of the Interest Equalization Tax on lending abroad, the "Voluntary" Foreign Credit Restraint Program, and the like), but these controls ran counter to the official U.S. stance of encouraging free mobility of capital between countries. Devaluation of the dollar in terms of gold would have marked up the dollar value of U.S. gold reserves, but would not have stemmed the payments deficits and would have brought politically distasteful windfall gains to the Soviet Union and South Africa (the two major gold exporters).

Faced with these choices under the existing international rules, the United States opted for changing the rules. On March 17, 1968, a seven-country meeting hastily called by the United States announced the "two-tier" gold price system. The private price of gold in London, Zurich, and other markets was now free to fluctuate in response to supply and demand. The official price for transactions among the seven agreeing governments would still be $35 an ounce. As it turned out, the seven governments soon stopped dealing officially in gold at all at the $35 price. The gold-dollar price link had been severed, perhaps forever. Gold rose in value, no longer held down by official gold sales.

Though gold had been demonetized (or, if you prefer, the dollar had been stripped of its international gold value), the U.S. payments deficits continued, and had to be financed by increasing sales of U.S. foreign exchange reserves. Sooner or later the United States would have to adjust, either by taking classical medicine, or by imposing exchange controls, or by changing the international monetary rules and allowing the dollar to float in foreign exchange markets. Again the United States chose to change the rules, on August 15, 1971.

Floating rates after 1971

Figure 21.5 shows the course of exchange rates after President Nixon announced that the dollar would float on foreign exchange markets without official U.S. intervention. The resort to fluctuating exchange rates has become more widespread than it was even in the interwar period, though the range of percentage changes in individual exchange rates has perhaps not been so wide.

Despite the near universality of the float after 1971, one of the most noteworthy features of this recent experience has been the extent of official resistance to floating. The government of Japan has tried repeatedly to hold down the dollar value of the yen, apparently in order to give Japanese sellers of traded goods an extra competitive edge in international markets. In the process, Japanese official institutions have bought tremendous volumes of U.S. dollars that have nonetheless declined somewhat in yen value. The Japanese determination to resist the rise of the yen is a leading example of what has been called the "dirty float," a floating exchange rate involving considerable official intervention in one direction. Governments of the European Economic Community strove to prevent movements in exchange rates

FIGURE 21.5
Selected exchange rates, 1971–1977 (monthly)

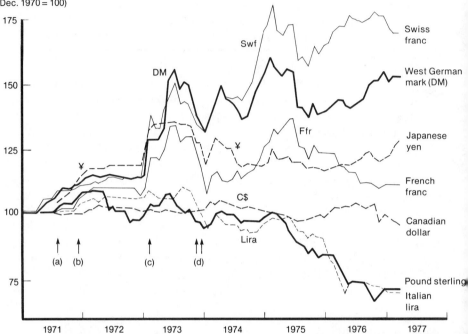

Index of exchange
value of this
currency, in U.S. $
(Dec. 1970 = 100)

Some noted events: *(a)* August 1971—Nixon announces dollar float; *(b)* December 1971—Smithsonian Accord tries to stabilize exchange rates; *(c)* February 1973—dollar weakens and is officially devalued relative to gold; *(d)* November–December 1973—OPEC oil price hike weakens European and Japanese currencies.

among their currencies, setting up "the snake" within "the tunnel" in December 1971. They agreed on maximum ranges of movement for the most appreciated versus the most depreciated member currency (the tunnel), and on maximum bands within which pairwise exchange rates could oscillate (the snake). This gesture at European unity, however, was short-lived. Britain, Italy, and France soon allowed their currencies to drop well below the tunnel, leaving little more than a fixed set of rates between the West German mark and the Benelux currencies. Meanwhile, France and Belgium have experimented with a system of "dual exchange rates," involving one official exchange rate for trade transactions and another for asset exchanges, in an attempt to insulate trade from capital-flow effects. The official desire for fixed rates has remained strong in Europe and Japan, but fixed rates have become increasingly hard to maintain, given the large international flows of private funds and the absence of strong U.S. support for fixed rates.

It is still difficult to tell whether the post-1971 experience shows the stability or the instability of flexible rates. A defender of flexible rates can argue for demonstrated stability by pointing to several facts. The initial movements of 1971–73 can be viewed as symptoms of the departure of the earlier fixed rates from equilibrium rates. The period also saw the OPEC price jump, which may have had complicated dynamic consequences. Studies have also tentatively shown that the observed exchange rates can be explained by the international disparities in the rates of growth of money supplies and productivity, without any necessary reference to destabilizing speculation. Although these results suggest stability in the functioning of flexible exchange rates, an advocate of fixed rates need not be impressed, especially if he views the disparities in money supply growth as a destabilizing force unleashed by the loss of the fixed-rate price discipline.

THE LIMITED CASE FOR FLEXIBLE EXCHANGE RATES

Experience to date does make a case for exchange-rate flexibility, but it is essential to avoid overstating that case. Flexible exchange rates do not cure cancer. They do not resolve the unemployment-inflation dilemma. Even their likely ability to regulate the balance of payments and cushion national economies is subject to qualifications. A review of the material since Chapter 15 will reveal frequent cases in which the conclusion helping to strengthen faith in flexible exchange rates has admitted exceptions. We found (in Chapter 15) that letting a currency depreciate tends to improve its trade balance, but may worsen it in some cases. Chapter 20 argued that flexible exchange rates tend to cushion an economy against some shocks, but not against others. And this chapter saw a rough tendency for speculation to be stabilizing under flexible exchange rates, but exceptions were suggested by the historical record. It must also be remembered that when fluctuations in the net demand for a currency are temporary and self-reversing, world welfare is raised if this cyclical element is prevented from causing cycles in the exchange rate.

Perhaps the argument in favor of flexible exchange rates that has done the most to persuade policymakers has been that monetary policy has greater control over the domestic economy with flexible rates than with fixed rates, as was shown in Chapter 20. In the last analysis, central banks have been unwilling to sacrifice this key monetary sovereignty to the vagaries of world demand and supply for money. As long as nations want control over their money supplies and national incomes to be national and not international, they are likely to find a strong case in favor of flexible exchange rates.

SUMMARY

Theory and experience have combined to resolve partially some of the key issues in the debate over fixed and flexible exchange rates. The argument that flexible exchange rates weaken officials' price discipline and allow more inflation is roughly correct. Whether one considers this an argument for or against fixed exchange rates depends on one's view of the unemployment-inflation dilemma. The argument that flexible exchange rates expose traders and investors to greater risks is at least questionable and probably wrong. The adjustments needed to defend fixed exchange rates against the shocks that face any system of exchange rates are likely to be costly and under fixed exchange rates individuals cannot hedge against those shocks in a well-defined market the way they can hedge against exchange risk in the forward market. The argument that flexible exchange rates breed destabilizing speculation is not persuasive on either theoretical or empirical grounds.

The success or failure of different exchange-rate regimes has depended historically on the severity of the shocks with which those systems have had to cope. The fixed-rate gold standard seemed extremely successful before 1914 largely because the world economy itself was more stable then than later. Many countries were able to keep their exchange rates fixed because they were lucky enough to be running surpluses at established exchange rates without having to generate those surpluses with any contractionary macroeconomic policies. The main deficit-running country, Britain, could control international reserve flows in the short run by controlling credit in London, but was never called upon to defend sterling against sustained attack. During the stable prewar era, even fluctuating-exchange-rate regimes showed stability (with two brief possible exceptions).

The interwar economy was chaotic enough to put any currency regime to a severe test. Fixed rates broke down, and governments which believed in fixed rates were forced into fluctuating exchange rates. Studies of the interwar period showed that in cases of relative macroeconomic stability flexible rates showed signs of stabilizing speculation. Those signs were less evident in economies whose money supplies had run away or whose previous fixed exchange rates were far from equilibrium.

Postwar experience has shown some difficulties with the adjustable-peg system set up in Bretton Woods in 1944. Under this system private speculators are given a strong incentive to attack reserve-losing currencies and force large devaluations. The role of the dollar as a reserve currency also became increasingly strained in the Bretton Woods era. Growing private foreign demand for dollars gave way to increasingly unwanted official accumulations that led to conversions of dollars into gold. Ultimately the United States was forced to bear large adjustment costs or to change the rules. The United States opted for new rules, breaking the gold-dollar link in 1968 and floating the dollar in 1971.

SUGGESTED READING

The issue of destabilizing speculation is well summarized in Robert M. Stern, *The Balance of Payments* (Chicago: Aldine, 1973), chap. 3. Important empirical contributions dealing with interwar speculation are Robert Z. Aliber, "Speculation in the Foreign Exchanges: The European Experience, 1919–1926," *Yale Economic Essays*, vol. 2, 1962, pp. 171–245; and S. C. Tsiang, "Fluctuating Exchange Rates in Countries with Relatively Stable Economies: Some European Experiences after World War I," International Monetary Fund, *Staff Papers*, vol. 7 (October 1959), pp. 244–73.

The best detailed survey of international currency experience can be found in Leland B. Yeager, *International Monetary Relations*, 2d ed. (New York: Harper and Row, 1976). The prewar gold standard is analyzed in more depth in Arthur I. Bloomfield, *Monetary Policy under the International Gold Standard, 1880–1914* (New York: Federal Reserve Bank of New York, 1959); and Peter H. Lindert, *Key Currencies and Gold, 1900–1913* (Princeton: Princeton University Press, 1969).

22

International monetary arrangements

THE ISSUES

The main issue of international monetary arrangements is in essence whether it is desirable to have international money. If there is to be an international money, there must be decisions as to how it is issued, in what amounts, and to whose benefit. A decision against any and all international money, with amounts of money to be determined solely by national monetary policy, implies fully flexible exchange rates. Between the two extremes lies a series of graded compromises. With one way of looking at it, the issue is what area by size, political characteristics, or economic behavior should have a single money, issued under a fixed set of rules by a single authority. In jargon, the question is, What is the **optimum currency area?** With another way of looking at the issue, the question can be put in terms of exchange-rate arrangements, with a variety of compromises possible between the fixed-rate system and the fully flexible rate. The most widely discussed of these compromises are the **wide band,** flexible within the limits, but prevented from going outside them; the **adjustable peg,** in which the par of exchange is altered from time to time as required by overvaluation or undervaluation; and the **crawling peg,** in which adjustment is minimal at any point in time but is continuous.

With flexible exchange rates, moreover, questions present themselves as to how much the monetary authorities should intervene in the determination of the rate exchange. Under **clean floating,** there is no intervention and the rate is left to the determination of the market.

By analogy, central bank intervention in the market to move the rate or prevent its moving has been pejoratively associated with **dirty floating.** Mixed systems are possible under which there is one international money, say, the dollar, the value of which is left to the determination of the market and the intervention of other authorities. This raises the issue of **symmetry,** or whether the rights and duties, the benefits and costs, of the international monetary arrangements are the same for all countries in the system.

INTERNATIONAL MONEY

If international money is adopted, it may be a commodity such as gold, a national currency such as the dollar or the pound sterling, or a specially created unit adopted by sovereign nations as a political act of will. As this is written, the world has all three, **gold,** the **dollar,** and **Special Drawing Rights,** or SDRs. None is functioning well, and there is little agreement as to how this functioning might be improved. Gold is sometimes traded as an official reserve asset, but more often as a commodity, with a fluctuating price in the free market. The dollar bulks large in the exchange reserves of major central banks of the world, so much so that these banks are anxious to reduce their holdings of dollars and to find substitutes. Since August 1971, moreover, the dollar has been inconvertible into gold by central banks, making *de jure* a condition which had taken effect with the adoption of the two-tier system in March 1968, but which the small central banks of Belgium, the Netherlands, and Switzerland ignored in the summer of 1971 to push the dollar off gold. The United States wants new and substantial issues of SDRs, without changing the volume of dollars in circulation; the European monetary authorities and the Japanese are interested in exploring the substitution of SDRs for the dollar but agree to no large issue until the question of the dollar overhang or redundancy is settled.

With any money, the questions are, Who issues it, in what amounts, and to whom? The commodity, gold, won out as money over clamshells, beads, tin, copper, and silver because its ore deposits were spread rather thinly in the world. Annual production has been roughly 40 million ounces, worth at $38 an ounce $1.5 billion. Much of this is needed in industry.[1] Much is also hoarded or bought in the free market for speculation. The price of gold is central to the question of liquidity.

---

[1] Even if gold should somehow lose its industrial usefulness, the Soviet Union at least will find a purpose it can serve. As Premier Khrushchev put it in a speech to the Paris Chamber of Commerce on March 24, 1960: "Gold we have, but we save it. Why? I don't really know. Lenin said the day would come when gold would serve to coat the walls and floors of public toilets. When the Communist society is built, we must certainly accomplish Lenin's wish."

Many economists want to raise the price of gold substantially, revalue gold holdings in central banks, and increase the value of current production. The increase in price from $35 to $38 agreed upon at the Smithsonian Institution in December 1971 had a purely technical reason, to offset the decline in the local-currency value of dollar reserves when the dollar was devalued. Some economists, such as Jacques Rueff, want to revalue gold and use the enlarged amount to replace the dollar as international money. Others are interested primarily in balancing the amounts of gold and dollars to escape from the clutches of **Gresham's law** (that excessively issued money drives scarce money into hoarding). At the depths of the Great Depression, in February 1934, the price of gold was raised from $20.67 an ounce to $35 an ounce. Subsequent inflation of prices and costs reduced the profitability of mining. The gold mining industry insists that a rise in the gold price would be *fair*, a word that does not belong in the economist's lexicon. The United States strongly resists an increase in the official price of gold (and France pushes for it, for Ruefflike reasons). The argument is bound up with two issues—whether the dollar should remain an international money, and how much liquidity is appropriate for the world.

The distribution of gold as international money is determined by who earns it by export surpluses. Gold producers run import surpluses, balanced by new gold production, which may properly be regarded as commodity exports. When gold leaves their shores it is monetary gold, available to the countries that provide goods in exchange.

The distribution of dollar reserves is determined partly by what countries earn them on current account and partly by what countries acquire them in **international financial intermediation,** through holding their interest rates temporarily above world levels and encouraging foreign investors to acquire their earning assets and local borrowers or asset sellers to seek liquidity abroad. With coordinated monetary policies, the distribution of dollars worldwide under a dollar standard would be determined by liquidity preferences and capital market imperfections. Any country where liquidity preference was high or where capital markets functioned badly would borrow or sell assets abroad in more than ordinary proportions.

Special Drawing Rights were introduced in 1968 as a supplement to gold and dollars. The concern of the United States was to add to its reserves so as to strengthen the dollar. In its view, SDRs were paper gold. Abroad the hope was that the availability of SDRs would make it possible to reduce reliance on the dollar. In July 1972, at a European Economic Community meeting of finance ministers, Anthony Barber called for the use of SDRs as international money instead of the dollar.

The volume and the distribution of SDRs have been determined by international agreement. At their issue, the SDR represents a claim on the world and a liability to the world. If the liability could be postponed to eternity, the SDR could be viewed as outside money, an asset which did not need to be repaid, a permanent addition to international money. If, on the other hand, it were necessary to keep open the possibility of repayment, the SDR would be inside money, a credit, rather than an eternal asset like gold. In the agreement, this issue was compromised. Each country was required to maintain at least 40 percent of its quota as a partial offset to its share of the liabilities, and no country could be forced to take more than three times its original quota, to prevent dumping the worthless claims on a few countries.

NATIONAL MONEY

We leave aside the issue of what constitutes the appropriate international money, who should issue it, in what amounts, and to whom in order to explore the opposite solution—reliance on national moneys alone, with each country adopting an independent monetary policy and flexible exchange rates between national moneys. The argument for this system rests on substantial benefits (or the avoidance of other costs) and low costs. In particular it is contended that a flexible-exchange-rate system obviates the need for countries to adjust monetary policies to the balance of payments, thus enabling them to gain an extra degree of freedom for domestic policies. It is also claimed that the costs in foreign trade and investment are minimal, since they can be maintained through the foreign exchange market, buttressed if need be by an expansion of forward dealings.

The second law of thermodynamics makes one doubt that an extra degree of freedom for domestic policies is available by adopting a technical solution to a problem. Economists know that perpetual motion is unlikely, and that there is no free lunch. And so on examination it proves to be with flexible exchange rates, although their more doctrinaire adherents will agree with reluctance. Any one country can gain an extra degree of freedom for monetary policy by adopting a floating exchange rate. Either the authorities intervene in the exchange market, or they do not. If they intervene, they can prevent destabilizing speculation from moving the rate to levels which add to the problems of domestic monetary management rather than ease them—a depreciated rate in a period of inflation or an appreciated rate during deflation. Control of the rate adds exchange policy to monetary and fiscal policy. With three policies, one can attack three targets (according to Jan Tinbergen's theory of economic policy): balance-of-payments equilibrium, price stability, and full employment. However, the weapon of exchange policy is not obtained out of thin air, but granted by the other countries with which the one country has trade and financial relations. If they too intervene, they may want to do so at cross-purposes. Just as in international money it is necessary to coordinate monetary policies, so in flexible exchange rates and intervention it is necessary, with more than one country floating and intervening, to coordinate exchange policies. Independence is either granted by other countries, or it is not obtained.

The purists among flexible-exchange-rate advocates (or the doctrinaire) push freely flexible rates without intervention. If speculation is stabilizing, this will work very well. If speculation is occasionally destabilizing, in the sense of moving the rate away from equilibrium rather than toward it, and threatening to produce irreversibilities in levels of prices, wages, costs, and the like, it seems inevitable that intervention will be resumed. Monetary authorities cannot lock the door and throw away the key.

Under flexible exchange rates, therefore, the choice is among all but the major financial centers managing their exchange rates independently, with passivity at the major centers; countries managing exchange rates cooperatively; or, less tolerable, leaving exchange rates free without intervention.

OPTIMUM CURRENCY AREA

Between a single world money (or the near equivalent), a permanently fixed set of exchange rates, and a world of separate nations with freely fluctuating exchange rates, how finely divided should the world be? Why stop at countries rather than groups of countries on the way to larger units, or why not go below countries to regions, states, cities, families, even people? If my balance of payments is in surplus, should I appreciate my rate of exchange on the world and be willing to work only for $1.10 dollars; or if I need work, should I depreciate my exchange and offer my services at 90-cent dollars? Between the world as a whole and the single individual, the issue may make more sense for countries, aggregations of countries above them, and regions within individual countries. The questions can be merged into one: What is the optimum currency area?

Robert Mundell was the first to pose the question, and he answered it in classical fashion by reference to factor mobility. A region is an area within which factors are mobile, whereas factors are not mobile between regions. Lacking factor mobility as a means of adjustment, one needs another degree of freedom such as exchange-rate variability provides. The region, in his view, should have a separate currency, a region which would sometimes be larger than a country, as in the

European Economic Community, but sometimes smaller than a country, as in the Maritime Provinces of Canada or Appalachia in the United States. Changing money is costly, to be sure, and in terms of convenience one should have as large a currency area as possible. But against this gain is the cost of having to endure unemployment as a means of balancing interregional accounts when the rate is fixed and emigration is limited.

A critic of Mundell, Ronald McKinnon, argues that factor mobility is not the essence of the optimum currency area. In his view, the need is for a closed economy, that is, an economy which has a large volume of internal transactions and a small volume of external ones, so that when exchange-rate changes occur, the impact of the change in foreign prices on the level of living of the community is not noticed. The need is for what has been called exchange illusion, after the analogy of money illusion, which disregards changes in prices arising from exchange-rate variation. An economy which is open in the sense that it trades widely with the outside world is unlikely to have exchange illusion. If its exchange rate is altered, various groups within the total are likely to alter wages, prices, costs, or income distribution so as to render the system homogeneous. Small open regions, cities, families, or individuals cannot kid themselves when they change their exchange rate.

The Mundell and McKinnon criteria for an optimum currency area point in somewhat different directions: Mundell to areas smaller than a country, or at least smaller than a big country such as Canada, and McKinnon to bigger units than a country, for example bigger than Canada, which trades to a great extent with the United States. Both criteria are economic. A very different criterion is political. In this view, the requirement of a currency area is coherent economic policies; the optimum currency area is a country. Regions lack the tools of economic policy in the fields of money, taxation, and governmental expenditure. Aggregations of sovereign countries may succeed in cooperating for a time in having their macroeconomic policies converge, but the fact of multiple sovereignty continually threatens the breakdown of coherence and a reversion to independence and divergence.

There can be little doubt that money and political sovereignty are intimately associated. Switzerland has three (or four) languages but one money. The attempt to extend the West German monetary reform of June 1948 to the three western sectors of Berlin led to the Berlin blockade and the split of Germany between what became the Federal Republic and the Democratic Republic, West and East Germany, respectively. Colonies and highly dependent independent political units may have currencies that are joined, but no single political unit has two moneys. Perhaps the best illustration, however, is the role of monetary unification in European integration. Most observers believe that monetary unification is impossible without merging central banks and coordinating macroeconomic policies in the fields of taxation, expenditure, capital markets, trade, foreign exchange, agriculture, and so on. This requires giving up most of national economic sovereignty. On one showing, the problem is to calculate what policies must be coordinated to achieve monetary unification. In another light, the issue is whether, given limits on the willingness of a number of countries to yield sovereignty, it is possible for Europe to achieve monetary integration.

EUROPE OF THE NINE AS AN OPTIMUM CURRENCY AREA

It seems evident that the crux of the issue for Europe is not the economic questions of whether Europe has factor mobility or is a closed economy. The crux is whether the countries, of Europe, and especially France, are prepared to merge their sovereignties in the fields of macroeconomic policy.

Europe of the Six—Belgium, France, Italy, Luxembourg, the Netherlands, and West Germany—made a start on a solution to the problem by appointing a committee under the direction of the prime minister of Luxembourg, Pierre Werner, to produce a report on "The Realization by Stages of Economic and Monetary Union in the Community." The Werner report, which appeared in the fall of 1970, called for adoption of the goal of monetary union or irreversible convertibility, the irrevocable fixing of parity rates, the complete liberation of capital movements within the Community, and if possible, the adoption of a single currency. Margins of fluctuations about parity were to be reduced in stages and ultimately eliminated. The balance of payments within the Community would ultimately be ignored, as within a single country, owing to the mobility of factors and "financial transfers by the public and private sectors" (meaning stabilizing capital movements and rediscounting by monetary authorities). It was recognized that responsibility would have to be transferred from the national to the Community level in some spheres, and that in other areas, policies would have to be coordinated. Especially would exchange, monetary, fiscal, and commercial policy have to be managed from a central place—for example, a committee of central bank governors, or even a new single central bank for the area.

The report laid out a series of stages for the realization of full monetary union in various functional areas. The first, to cover three years, called for consultation procedures, three surveys each year of economic policy, and Community directives to lay down guidelines in the monetary and fiscal field. The second stage, beginning in January

FIGURE 22.1
"The snake in the tunnel": Narrowing the range of fluctuation among European currencies while widening it with outside exchanges

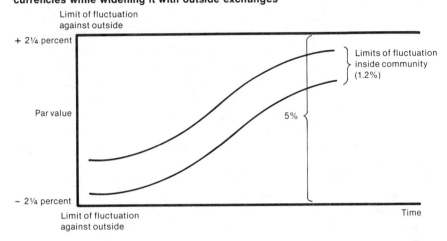

1974, called for tighter coordination of monetary and credit measures, but the details were left for future agreement. It was expected that complete monetary integration would be achieved by the end of the 1970s.

A number of technical issues interest economists. One turned on the width of exchange-rate variation, which was expected to widen between Europe and the rest of the world but progressively to narrow within the Community. As an example, the range of·fluctuation, as agreed later, could widen to 2.25 percent each side of par against the outside world, while the range of fluctuation was to decline from 0.75 actual (narrower than the 1.5 percent allowed by the IMF) to 0.6 and then to 0.45 before declining to zero. If all the currencies of the Community are equally strong or equally weak against the outside world, there is no problem; all can move together within the wider band permitted for fluctuations with the outside world. But if some currencies within the Community are strong and some weak vis-à-vis one another, and they move against one another by the limit, there is the question as to where the group finds itself in the band against the outside. The smaller band may move about within the wider band, giving rise to the expression "**The Snake in the Tunnel**," a sobriquet whose origin is illustrated in Figure 22.1.

THE COSTS AND BENEFITS OF A SINGLE MONEY

If we leave aside the technicalities and the modalities or means of achieving a single money, the question remains whether it is a good idea. As changes in tastes, production functions, technology, factor proportions, levels of income, and so forth occur, countries must adjust without independent monetary, fiscal, exchange, or commercial policies and must rely on coordinated action by others. The political loss in sovereignty is painful. The economic costs may be high. Is the game worth the candle? Are the benefits economic or political?

The argument for a larger currency area is largely the argument for money in general. Money serves as a medium of exchange, unit of account, store of value, and standard of deferred payment. The foreign exchange market can discharge the function of money as a medium of exchange. But if foreign exchange rates fluctuate, it is difficult without a stable unit of account to calculate costs and prices abroad. Foreign exchange cannot function properly as a store of value to bridge temporary gaps between the receipt of income from abroad and its expenditure, and there is no standard of deferred payment for the making of long-term contracts for lending or long-term purchase and sale of commodities. Money is a public good, which makes it possible to obviate barter. When no money is provided, foreign trade and investment are not eliminated but the functions of money must be discharged privately, at private cost, with the result that trade and investment must decline (in the long run).

The economic benefits of international money are substantial. The political benefits probably alter as the countries making up the currency area change. Europe wants a single currency in part because it wants to build a monetary rival to the dollar—a political purpose, though not necessarily an unworthy one. (Since the French are politically sensitive, one suggestion has been to call the single money the European Currency Unit, or ECU, which was also the name of an ancient French silver coin worth three pounds.) The political benefits of a world money, however, would be more questionable.

The political costs and benefits, moreover, are associated with the nature of the system adopted. There are strong economic reasons for believing that it is difficult to create a single world money or to reinstall gold as world money, which is different from the moneys used in at least one important country or area. Gold or SDRs, for example, would be less acceptable to international markets than national or monetary-union currencies like the pound sterling of 1913, the dollar of 1960, or possibly, the ECU of 1984. The reason is found in the fact that markets like to avoid excessive transactions, and in the idea, debated in classical monetary theory, that market acceptance rather than government fiat determines what is money. But much as the economist may deplore it, there are evidently overtones, positive and negative, to which national currency is adopted as world money. In particular, the dollar standard, so-called, evokes strong xenophobic reactions outside the United States, as well as jingoist feelings within.

COMPROMISE SOLUTIONS

In these circumstances, there has developed a certain measure of agreement among economists that the world should find a compromise between a world money, or a fixed-exchange-rate system, on the one hand and fully flexible exchange rates on the other. Three broad categories of compromise may be distinguished, all involving exchange-rate movement: the adjustable peg, which is basically the IMF system of changing rates whenever there is fundamental disequilibrium, but doing so for changes of more than 5 or 10 percent only with the agreement of the Fund; the crawling peg; which is changing the par of exchange but continuously by small amounts, perhaps as little as one half of 1 percent per month, which amounts (if all the changes are in the same direction) to only 6 percent a year; and the wider band, which in some versions provides for flexible movements 5 percent either side of par, or a total band of 10 percent.

The adjustable peg is generally believed to be discredited. For one thing, it is unclear what constitutes fundamental disequilibrium. For another, countries tend not to adjust the peg until the last minute, when speculators have been furnished a one-way option. Third, in a crisis there is never time to undertake the mutual consultations called for by the Articles of Agreement—and if there were, the rumors of such consultations would make the foreign exchange market intensely nervous and heighten short speculation. A few economists would like to introduce more frequent discrete changes, sped up in time so as to avoid the one-way option, but most regard the system as impractical.

The crawling peg and the band are both designed to discourage speculation. The crawling peg is intended to adjust the exchange rate slowly over time to correct for overvaluation and undervaluation. The changes through time are kept small to persuade speculators that adjustment is under way but that it doesn't pay to take positions for a rise or decline in the rate, because the change won't occur rapidly and the investor will do better to earn high rates of interest. The wide band, on the other hand, is intended to balance the one-way option by giving more room for the exchange rate to move against the speculator in case he guesses wrong. Although both compromises are addressed to containing speculation, they do so in different ways—the crawling peg focuses on long-run adjustment, whereas the wider band around a fixed parity permits some adjustment from movements of the exchange rate within the band but is not primarily dedicated to exchange-rate changes. But of course the two can be combined—a crawling peg with a wide band. It remains to be seen, however, if the question of whether to have the benefits (and costs) of international money can be compromised.

REGIONAL COMPROMISE

The suggestion is frequently made that compromise should run along regional rather than institutional lines. Let there be a dollar area, a European currency area, perhaps a yen area, and let the countries of the world choose up sides, joining one or another bloc. Within each bloc there should be fixed rates with narrow bands; between blocs, flexible exchange rates (whether freely flexible or guided, deponent generally sayeth not). This proposal fits into the monetary integration of the European Economic Community and emerges from somewhat larger "optimum currency areas"—but not so large that they cover the whole world. The benefits of specialization and exchange are kept by regions. Political independence is retained by the major power blocs.

Presumably within each bloc there would be a dominant power or powers and those that were followers. Political sovereignty would be gained for the former but more thoroughly lost for the latter. African trade would run to Europe, and Canadian and Latin-American trade to the United States, regardless of the Argentine and Uruguayan market for meat in Europe or the interest of the United States in African chrome.

SYMMETRY

With national moneys and flexible exchange rates which were guided by the intervention of the monetary authorities, the power of various countries to set their own exchange rates, in case they disagreed, would probably be proportional to their size as measured by some weighted average of national income and national capital market. If Canada wanted a depreciated exchange rate, for example, and the United States were determined to resist such an outcome, it seems clear that the United States could buy up Canadian dollars as fast as the Bank of Canada could issue them.

Under the gold standard, where all countries have pious faith in the rules of the gold standard game and are committed to follow them, no country has much more power than another. The other two forms of international money, however, are otherwise. Under, say, the dollar standard, power is distributed asymmetrically in the system. With something like the SDRs as international money and no tendency of markets to shift to a national money, power would be distributed in accordance with the weighted voting system.

If responsibility and power go together, an asymmetric distribution of power may not be altogether a bad thing for the international monetary system. Weighted voting often turns out to produce stalemates, as it has now done in the International Monetary Fund as well as the

Security Council of the United Nations. The United States started out in the IMF with a size of quota and a weighted vote that enabled it to veto any proposal which it did not approve. The United States had somewhat over 23 percent of the votes, and 85 percent of the votes were needed to carry a proposal. Later, with the enlargement of quotas and the General Arrangements to Borrow, the Europe of the Six acquired 20 percent of the votes, and a veto. The IMF could not act unless the EEC and the United States agreed.

Under the dollar system, or the sterling system before 1913, power with responsibility is not only tolerable; it may be desirable. Without leadership, little gets done. For the world monetary system to be stable, moreover, the world needs a stabilizer, some country or aggregation of countries not bound by vetoes or stalemate which will move in crises. The needs are to keep markets for distress goods open, fix a set of exchange rates which are not too far from equilibrium, maintain stable capital flows, and discount in a crisis. Britain performed these functions in the late 19th century up to 1913. The United States took over the task in the period from World War II to about 1968. The depression of 1929 was so wide, so deep, and so long because Britain couldn't and the United States wouldn't act as a stabilizer. The fallacy of composition reigned supreme as each country in turn tried to use its national sovereign powers to cut imports, restrict capital exports, and depreciate the exchange rate.

SEIGNIORAGE

Seigniorage is a technical term in monetary economics which means the profits from issuing money. The term comes, of course, from the right of the king, or "seigneur," to issue money (like another and different *droit du seigneur*), and it represents the difference between the cost of producing money and its value in exchange. With flexible exchange rates there is no international money and no seignorage. Under the gold standard, the international money is produced at cost and there is no seignorage. Under the dollar standard or with SDRs, international money is costless to produce. The question is whether there is seigniorage, and what to do with any seigniorage which exists under SDRs.

In the eyes of many, the United States has been exploiting the rest of the world through extracting seigniorage, issuing dollars which the rest of the world holds in exchange for goods and services on the one hand and securities and direct investments on the other. It was claimed by President de Gaulle of France, for example, that the dollar standard required France to finance U.S. intervention in the war in Vietnam.

On one showing, there is no seigniorage when the foreign holder of dollars is paid interest. Non-interest-bearing currency yields seigniorage, as do demand deposits. But time deposits which pay interest have a cost to the issuer of the liability, representing the present discounted value of the stream of income paid out to the holder.

This view is disputed. It is said in Europe, for example, that the deposits held in dollars are involuntary, in the sense that the European central banks would rather have gold or domestic assets or would rather see their bank statements reduced both by claims on the United States and by liabilities to domestic depositors. Under this circumstance, interest paid to a depositor is "like meals served to a kidnap victim, hardly an offset to the loss of liberty." The counter to this view is that the European countries that are experiencing a capital inflow do not have to hold the offsetting dollars. They could lower their interest rates and expand the money supply, which would partly repel the inflow of capital and partly assist in its real transfer in goods and services. European central banks acquire dollars because they have high **liquidity preference,** preferring liquidity to real assets. The difference between what the United States earns by lending long and what it pays out by borrowing short is its net return for financial intermediation and the European markets' payment for staying liquid with malfunctioning capital markets.

The beauty of the gold standard (if countries were willing to follow the "rules of the gold-standard game") is that, like the rule of free trade, it defuses this sort of highly political debate. The world finds itself in a transitional state, where it can no longer believe the claptrap that "gold is immutable, eternal, impartial," as President de Gaulle claimed, and is no longer willing to let a vestigial remnant of an ancient dogma dictate economic behavior. It has not yet achieved the state of grace, however, in which it can fashion new rules for optimum world money and count on all nations carrying them out under any and all circumstances.

SUMMARY

There are three types of international money—gold, a national currency such as the dollar, and created assets, such as Special Drawing Rights. A monetary system with no international money has flexible exchange rates. With any money, the questions are, Who issues it, how much, and to whom?

Flexible exchange rates, or the nonexistence of international money, are thought to add another policy instrument to a nation's armory. This they do, if at all, only by subtracting it from elsewhere in the system or by converting the need to consult on monetary policy to the need to consult on exchange policy. Like domestic money, international money has benefits as well as costs.

A searching question is, What is the optimum currency area within which there should be a single money? Two economic answers are given, one based on factor mobility, the other on exchange illusion. A political answer is that the optimum currency area is the one with sufficient macroeconomic powers to manage its affairs. It is an open question whether the European Economic Community will prove to be an effectively integrated currency area.

Various compromises between fixed and flexible rates include the adjustable peg, the crawling peg, and the wider band, plus a regional compromise.

In any national exchange standard, questions of symmetry arise, including that of seigniorage.

SUGGESTED READING

An excellent monograph on the question of interdependence or independence is Richard N. Cooper, *The Economics of Interdependence: Economic Policy in the Atlantic Community* (New York: McGraw-Hill, 1968).

The separate issues in international monetary arrangements are discussed in an enormous variety of articles, books, and monographs. Among the best collections are Robert A. Mundell and Alexander K. Swoboda (eds.), *Monetary Problems of the International Economy* (Chicago: University of Chicago Press, 1969); Lawrence Officer and Thomas Willett, *The International Monetary Systems: Problems and Proposals; The International Adjustment Mechanism*, Monetary Conference, Federal Reserve Bank of Boston, 1970; George N. Halm (ed.), *Approaches to Greater Flexibility of Exchange Rates: The Bürgenstock Papers*, arranged by C. Fred Bergsten and others (Princeton: Princeton University Press, 1970); and a special issue of the *Journal of International Economics*, September 1972.

The articles by Robert Mundell and Ronald McKinnon on the optimum currency area are in the *American Economic Review*, September 1961 and September 1963. McKinnon's article is reproduced in Richard N. Cooper (ed.), *International Finance: Selected Readings.*

For a useful study emphasizing the political aspects of monetary problems, see S. Strange, *Sterling and British Policy: A Political Study of an International Currency in Decline* (New York: Oxford University Press, 1971).

The text of the "Werner Report," that is, the *Report to the Council and the Commission on the Realization by Stages of Economic and Monetary Union*, is given in the *Supplement to Bulletin 11–1970* of the European Communities.

part V

Factor movements

0-Day Futures	....	.9230	.9242
0-Day Futures	....	.9227	.9241
na-Taiwan (Dollar)	....	.02...	...5
ombia (Peso)	....	.02.5	.0275
nmark (Krone)	....	.1631	.1632
uador (Sucre)	....	.0385	.0385
land (Markka)	....	.2...	..2
nce (Franc)	....	.2052	.2043
0-Day Futures	....	.2048	.2040
0-Day Futures	....	...	...
0-Day Futures	....	.2025	.2022
ece (Drachma)	....	.0280	.0280
ng Kong (Dollar)	....	.2139	.2142
ia (Rupee)	....	.1170	.1165
onesia (Rupiah)	....	.00259	.002590
n (Rial)	....	.01416	.01416
q (Dinar)	....	3.44	3.44
ael (Pound)	....	.0951	.0951
ly (Lira)	....	.001135	...35
an (Yen)	....	.003...	.003818
0-Day Futures	....	...5	.003827
0-Day Futures	....	.003...	.003839
0-Day Futures	....	...87	.003862
anon (Pound)	....	.3229	.3231
laysia (Dollar)	....	.4079	.4076
xico (Peso)	....	.0441	.0441
therlands (Guilder)	....	.40...	...
w Zealand (Dollar)	....	.9815	.9825
rway (Krone)	....	.18...	.18.3
kistan (Rupee)	....	...	.10.5
ru (Sol)	....	.0124	.0124
ilippines (Peso)	....	...5	.1.5
rtugal (Escudo)	....	.02...	.02...
di Arabia (Riyal)	....	.2833	.2833
gapore (Dollar)	....	.4109	.4110
th Africa (Rand)	....	1.1522	1.1522

Buy America

Many U.S. Investors Shun Firms That Have Major Stakes Abroad

European Monetary Woes, Spread of Protectionism, Lag in Economies Cited

Clampdown by Canadians on Investing By Aliens Alarms Multinational Firms

'Brain Drain' Gave U.S. $30 Billion, Report by U.N. Says

Figure Based on Immigration To U.S. of Skilled People From Developing Nations

23

The international movement of labor

LABOR MIGRATION

Most textbooks on international economics, and most courses, steer clear of the question of migration. This is probably only partly due to the pious classical assumption of factor immobility between countries; after all, international capital movements have been accommodated into the corpus of the subject. In part, migration may be thought to have been overwhelmed in importance by trade; the fact that Europe exported 60 million people overseas between 1851 and 1970 and that today approximately 4 million migrants in Europe are working outside their native countries, however, suggests that migration is not small. President Roosevelt once addressed the Daughters of the American Revolution, it will be remembered, as "fellow immigrants." The more likely reason is that the subject is thought to belong to sociology or demography rather than to economics. More recently, however, the reduction in transport costs has brought renewed interest in the economics of international migration and national migration policy. The latter may lie largely in the social field, but the economic questions are neither uninteresting nor unimportant.

THE INTERNATIONAL LABOR MARKET

There has always been a limited international market for labor. Workers commute to jobs across frontiers in Europe; between Windsor, Ontario, and Detroit, Michigan; and between Brownsville,

Texas, and Matamoros, Mexico. Casual workers journey from country to country in search of work, particularly moving northward with the harvest or in the construction season, whether they are Mexicans in North America or Italians, Greeks, and Spaniards in Europe. Government administrators in colonies, business executives managing foreign subsidiaries, planters, Peace Corps recruits, and, increasingly, professional and technical consultants spend varying amounts of time in economic roles outside the country of their permanent residence. And long-term or permanent migration is a familiar phenomenon, as masses of people have been driven abroad by one or another kind of trouble or have been attracted abroad by economic opportunity.

An international market for labor may be said, then, to exist. But classical economists were right to the extent that it is a most imperfect one. The return to common labor is not equalized around the world. And even within specialized noncompeting groups the equalization is far from complete. Indeed, equalization of wages does not take place within a country, except in broad terms and for some professional and technical classes; some labor economists make a lot (too much) of the fact that there is variability in wages for equal skills in the same town. Between continents, the returns to labor differ persistently, despite the fact that labor can move to a limited extent in overseas migration, and despite the tendency for international trade to bring about some equalization of factor prices, as discussed in Chapter 5.

In Europe, since about 1955, however, the international labor market has become more efficient. There is some increased movement across the borders of the developed countries in the Common Market, especially from the Netherlands to the Ruhr, from southeast France to southwest Germany, and from Belgium into the Netherlands and France. But the major change has been a northward movement, especially to Switzerland, Belgium, France, and West Germany, first by Italians and then by Greeks, Spaniards, Portuguese, Turks, and more recently, once they had overcome their ideological reluctance, Yugoslavs. Foreign workers comprised as much as 30 percent of the Swiss labor force before restrictions were imposed in the 1960s and early 1970s—a much higher percentage than in Belgium (10 percent), France (9 percent), and West Germany (4½ percent). But their importance is greater than these numbers, as the student of marginal analysis knows. As noted in Chapter 9, "Economic Integration," since the foreign worker is without strong ties to any one location away from his native heath, his mobility makes a vital contribution to the improvement of the European labor market at the margin. European wage rates have converged sensibly in the period since 1955, with emigration raising wages along the Mediterranean and immigration holding them down relatively in the north. Factor-price equalization, however, has not been achieved either for worldwide professional and technical labor or for common labor in Europe, much less for common labor between continents.

There is doubt that the factor-price equalization model is relevant for intercontinental migration. This migration, as we shall see also in the case of capital, follows well-worn grooves rather than spreading evenly over the world in response to economic signals. The design of many flows is political and related to noneconomic or quasi-economic considerations. Thus as subjects of the Queen, West Indians had the right to migrate to Britain, until that right was modified and virtually destroyed by the requirement that they line up a job in Britain before they arrive. Algerians and members of the French *Communauté* had strong cultural ties to France and legal discrimination in their favor from that country. The British emigrate largely to the English-speaking dominions or the United States. Even when cultural and political considerations are not initially present, moreover, migration is a positive feedback process which follows a learning pattern. The movement is initially small and slow, as the early migrants overcome inertia. Once the channel is opened up, however, institutions are built which make it possible to move large numbers.

THE PATTERNS OF LABOR MOVEMENT

Of particular interest among the world patterns of labor movement are the waves of immigration to the United States in the period up to 1914 that brought in large numbers of English, German, Scandinavian, Irish, Italian, and eastern European immigrants. Each wave had a pattern of cumulative growth. After small numbers of pioneer emigrants made a successful start, they sent for their relatives and friends, and the movement snowballed until the wave died down for one reason or another. Economic historians have debated whether the pull of opportunity was greater than the push of economic difficulty. In any case, however, it seems clear that these forces acted only against the background of a long-run migration cycle, which may or may not have had its origin in economic circumstances. In the burst of emigration from Ireland in the 1840s, the potato famine provided the push. Conversely, in the large-scale movement from Italy and eastern Europe, which had its beginnings in the collapse of the European wheat price in the early 1880s, the size of the annual flow was affected by conditions in the United States, slowing down as a consequence of the panic of 1907 and picking up with the subsequent revival.

Whether push or pull starts a movement, the history of the 19th century reveals a crystal-clear instance of forces in the home country stopping one. The rapid growth of the German economy in the 1850s cut off sharply (in 1854) the previously snowballing movement of distressed peasants and artisans to the United States. With continued growth in Germany, emigration died away. Incidentally, recent historical research makes clear that the flow of the late 1840s and early 1850s was by no means the ideological movement stemming from the unsuccessful Revolution of 1848 as some had believed. All but two or three hundred political refugees of the wave of German migration were seeking to improve their lot economically.

Brinley Thomas has detected a broad pattern in the Atlantic community in which long cycles connected with construction were counterposed in Europe and North America to produce rhythmic movements in migration. Large numbers of people were left stranded in rural occupations in Europe by the improvement in agricultural productivity in the first half of the 19th century and in the second half by the technological advance in transport, which made possible grain imports from the rich plains of North and South America, Australia, and the Ukraine. The industrial revolution created opportunities for work in European cities. In the upswing of the long construction cycle, the rural exodus was directed internally to the industrial cities. In depression, however, when it was necessary to pause and consolidate the domestic economic position, the rural reserve went abroad. One regulator of the movement that directed the Scandinavian, German, and British peasant now to the city and now to North America and (for the British) the Antipodes was the terms of trade. When the terms of trade favored Europe, economic opportunity at home was high in textiles, coal, and steel, and ultimately engineering trades and the chemical industry. In the slump, the terms of trade turned against Europe, and capital and labor went abroad.

This pattern is sketched in broad strokes, of course, and does not fit parts of the picture. In southern Italy, Hungary, Poland, and Russia, there was little industry to attract the rural surplus. For a long time it stayed put. When it moved, it headed almost entirely abroad. It has been said that the southern Italian was regarded as socially and culturally inferior by the inhabitants of the industrial cities of Milan or Turin and was more at home in New York or San Francisco—once, that is, the movement got under way. It is interesting, too, to note that upon their arrival in the United States the migrants found their way into limited occupations and limited places of residence. Much of this was largely accidental. It is claimed that the Irish settled in Boston in greater numbers than in New York because the transatlantic fare to the former port was five shillings cheaper. Communities of Germans in Milwaukee and St. Louis, Swedes in Minnesota, Norwegians in the Dakotas, Poles in Baltimore and Buffalo, and Polish and Russian Jews in New York emphasize that the migrants were seeking their own kind, in the beginning, to provide a transition to life in the new world. Construction attracted Irish and Italian labor; Germans and Scandinavians went in for mixed and grain farming; northern Italians took to truck gardening; and Polish, German, and Russian Jews went into the garment industry.

The imposition of immigration quotas by the United States in 1921 and 1924 is explained largely on social grounds. The cumulative flow of migrants from southern and eastern Europe, cut off by the war, showed signs of sharp revival. The check to cumulative emigration provided in Britain, Germany, and Scandinavia in the 19th century by industrial development and rising real incomes had never taken hold elsewhere, and the natural rate of increase had shown no signs of diminishing. Potential immigration was accordingly large. Its restriction posed grave social and economic problems for the affected areas, but its continuance would have done so for the United States and other receiving areas as they filled up.

Equally in Switzerland, the movement to restrict immigration had economic aspects (discussed below), but the basis was largely cultural and political. After a certain point, the Swiss felt their "Swissness" threatened by a large and indigestible lump of foreigners.

The growing consciousness of international differences in levels of living has led to significant streams of immigrants to Britain from the poorer portions of the Commonwealth, especially Malta, the Indian subcontinent, and the West Indies. This influx created economic and social problems which led in the 60s to a change from completely free immigration, by people in search of work, to immigration limited to workers already in possession of jobs.

THE EUROPEAN LABOR MARKET

Not every country in Europe welcomes foreign labor. In some, such as Britain, trade-union opposition keeps down readiness to import workers. In Scandinavia, there is a Common Market for Labor limited to Scandinavians, with the largest movement having been from Finland to Sweden, but all of the Scandinavian countries are reluctant to admit workers from the Mediterranean area, and justify this by saying that the southern laborer would find the northern climate dark and cold. As a member of the European Economic Community, the Netherlands has subscribed to the Rome Treaty providing for freedom of movement of labor within the Community; it is not, however, aggressive in recruiting labor in Italy. The other northern members of the EEC have not only welcomed the movement of labor within the Community, to the point of sending recruiting agencies abroad, but have extended the same generous provisions for national treatment (not most-favored nation) to Spain, Portugal, Greece, and Turkey. Until their labor shortages became so acute in the first half of the 1960s that foreigners with limited skills could not meet them, these countries depended on foreign labor for a significant contribution to growth, measured not by the proportion the foreigners constituted of total labor but by their contribution to holding wages down, and thereby profits up, at the margin.

Once inflation hit, costs rose, profits were squeezed, and the long upswing from the early 1950s to the mid-1960s in Europe was over. The pressure to hire more foreign workers was relieved, and the regular turnover of workers who had filled their contracts and were returning home with their accumulated "target" savings reduced the numbers of foreign workers in northern Europe. Again in the recession of the early 1970s, countries such as West Germany let old contracts of foreign labor run out without replacing the workers until the recession corrected itself. In one sense, this could be thought of as exporting unemployment; a more generous way of looking at it was that the country had exported its peak labor demand. But in any case, the position was very different from the 1930s, when the French forced the Poles and Italians in their count.y to return home by canceling their police permits, rounding them up, and shipping them out.

The return movement is due to more than just contracts running out, however. In depression, migrants generally tend to return to their native countries. Net migration in Britain was inward during the 1930s from all over the world, following the outward movement of the 1920s. Scientists who were attracted to the United States in the boom of the late 1960s returned on balance to Europe in 1970–72.

The returning foreign worker runs the risk of being disenchanted with life at home. Australia, which used to recruit in Britain the white immigrants it insisted on, now extends its search and finds that Mediterranean workers who have been to northern Europe and returned south make excellent prospects. The experience of higher standards of living and better working conditions abroad makes them intolerant of life at home. But then Australians assert that the immigrant from Britain does not become a real Australian until he has taken his first trip "home" to Britain.

One complex pattern of migration is found in Canada, where immigrants come from the United Kingdom and emigrants leave for the United States. Among the latter are young people who go to the United States for an education and decide to stay on, as many students from other countries would do if the student visa did not require them to leave the United States for at least two years. Recently education has been equated with investment in human capital, which has led to attempts to estimate whether Canada gains or loses on balance on capital account, that is, in terms of the education which it contributes to emigrants and gains from immigrants. Only about 10 percent of the immigrants entering Canada represent a net gain in numbers. But it was found that the gain in education is much higher than this, since trained Britons immigrate, and relatively young and less educated Canadians emigrate.

DOES EMIGRATION BENEFIT THE SENDING COUNTRY?

If we leave out convulsive population movements, an interesting question which has received some discussion from economists is whether emigration is a good thing. It has been argued against emigration that sending grown people abroad permanently is a form of capital export: the country of emigration raises them from birth; feeds, clothes, and educates them through an unproductive period; and then loses them as they begin to reach a productive stage. This loss of a productive worker is comparable to the export of productive capital, except that the exporting country does not in all cases get a return on the net marginal productivity of the labor, over and above the maintenance and replacement costs (subsistence).

If the workers were slaves, sent abroad to produce a higher return than at home, and if their net product above subsistence were returned to the capital-exporting country, the capital-exporting analogy would be appropriate, provided that the slaves were raised for the purpose of earning a return. As a rule, however, population growth is independent of the opportunities for emigration, at least in the short run; the choice is not between investing resources in productive workers for migration abroad or in more productive domestic lines. It is rather whether labor stays home in unemployment or underemployment or seeks a job abroad. The resources invested in raising the labor to working age can be regarded as sunk. It is then a question of whether a positive return on these resources is possible or, to put it otherwise, whether it is possible to relieve the pressure of the unemployed on the domestic labor market through emigration.

Broadly speaking, this is a general-equilibrium problem, and, as in all of them, the question is, Compared with what?—or, What would have been the likely course of events if the emigration had not taken place?

If, in fact, emigration means escape from the long-run check to population growth, it may be wasteful in terms of real income per head. The ideal policy would be not to allow emigration until the Malthusian barrier has been broken and family limitation is used to maintain per capita income.

Even with rapid population growth, large-scale emigration may add to disposable income for the remaining population and contribute foreign exchange to the balance of payments, if the rate of remittance home is high. Italy recovered rapidly from the depression of 1907 because the flow of remittances from the western hemisphere was so buoyant. Greece and, to a lesser extent, Turkey find their balances of payments today very much eased by emigrant remittances. It was necessary for Turkey to adopt appropriate policies. For a time, with a seriously overvalued exchange rate for the Turkish lira, Turkish workers in Europe would bring back goods—secondhand automobiles, television sets, or household appliances—rather than sending money, which would have accumulated foreign exchange for the economy. When a special and slightly undervalued rate was adopted and special interest rates were devised for emigrant deposits in Turkish lira, these remittances were transformed into foreign exchange of wider benefit for the total economy.

How long a worker will send remittances home depends on his personal circumstances and the length of time he has been away. Temporary workers remit heavily to their dependents, especially because they tend to be **target workers,** saving for a particular purpose. Permanent emigrants, including those who are temporary *ex ante* but become permanent *ex post,* cut remittances drastically when they marry abroad or are joined by an existing family initially left behind. They may send further moneys to parents and other relatives for a while, but these decline through time. Finally, as a generation passes, remittances dwindle to a trickle. Cultural change has altered the pattern as well as the time profile. In the 30 years before World War I, immigrants into the United States lived in ethnocentric groups in this country and moved only slowly to acquire the standard of living of the second- and third-generation families in the country as a whole. Today, the cultural hold of the immigrant group is virtually nonexistent, since members are so small, and the pressure is strong on the occasional immigrant, such as the Hungarian refugees, to adjust quickly to the American standard. Even if it were easy and convenient to remit to relatives abroad behind the iron curtain (which it is not), social pressures to be assimilated to the new level of consumption reduce the capacity.

But there are more elements in the calculation of the benefit of the emigrant to the country. The emigrant remits home. His relatives spend part of the money, and he or they save part. The part of the money spent leads to increases in imports, offsetting part of the foreign exchange gain. The savings belong to individuals, not to the state or to the country as a whole. They may gain; what about the country? This raises the question about the external effects of the remittances—

their impact on taxes, capital formation, factor prices, and factor combinations.

If there were no external effects of any kind, it could be argued that what a man did was entirely his business. If he earned more in one country or another, he consumed or saved more, and in either case the savings accrued to him. If all factors were paid their marginal product, changes in factor endowments brought about by migration have these impacts on taxes and other factor prices, but that's all. The concern that many people feel about the **brain drain** of talented professional youth leaving the less developed countries is overdone, according to this calculation. The main effects cancel out. If a scientist leaves Britain, he takes his production with him, but he also takes his income representing a claim on goods equal to his marginal product. Much of the analysis of migration, according to this way of looking at it, stresses the loss in output, but not the equal reduction in his claim on the output of others.

The external effects cannot be overlooked, however. Abundant and therefore cheap scientists and engineers, doctors, or even economists are an external benefit for other factors in the nation, and a scarcity of technical and professional personnel is a diseconomy. Above a certain minimum these effects are relatively unimportant. Thus the Netherlands and the Scandinavian countries, for example, export professional personnel because they cannot employ all their educated nationals at socially acceptable levels of remuneration. But larger countries can benefit from large numbers of scientists, to limit ourselves to one category, and small and poor countries may be dangerously close to the minimum needed as a fixed input critical to other activities. Emigration which pulls the numbers below these minimum levels is harmful to output in general.

These external effects are, for the most part, incalculable. This is especially true of the highest quality of scientist—the Fermis, Von Neumanns, Von Brauns—who change the course of scientific and technological history.

By no means is all emigration deleterious. A case can be made that when there is open or disguised unemployment, a distortion of factor prices, emigration helps to get rid of it. The point is limited to unskilled labor. If disguised unemployment means that the marginal product is zero or close to zero, this inhibits investment. Why install machinery when there is in effect free labor, or rather family labor which must be paid anyhow? When enough labor is drawn off so that marginal product rises to the wage, it pays to calculate the returns on investment. Emigration thus stimulates investment, technological advance, and growth. In these cases, as the experience of the Mediterranean countries shows, high emigration rates are accompanied by high rates of growth.

But it must not go too far. Below some optimum population, the economy has trouble supporting the variety of activities it needs, as Goldsmith's *Deserted Village* and the ghost towns of the West remind us.

DOES IMMIGRATION BENEFIT THE RECEIVING COUNTRY?

Whether immigration will benefit or hurt a country depends upon the country's resources of capital and land, relative to population, and the dynamic effects of the movements in question. Australia, Canada, Brazil, and similar large, underpopulated countries are interested in immigration of selected types of workers—the young, farmers, skilled factory workers, and so on—because their resources are large relative to labor supply and because the social overhead capital in countries of vast expanse typically produces increasing returns. Broadly the same investment in interurban roads, railroads, and harbors, for example, is required for a large population as for a small one, and a given population may be well below the optimum.

It is nonetheless likely that capital expenditure will be needed as a consequence of immigration, at least in the later stages. At the beginning, excess capacity exists in many lines of infrastructure, although in housing, where the indivisibilities inherent in a transport network should not exist, the increase in population without additional investment in housing often results in crowding in slums. The new immigrants in some countries, moreover, may get few public services. But this is less and less the case. Typically today, as immigration takes place, sooner or later the receiving country must provide housing, schools, hospitals, streets, and intraurban transport. One of the economic as opposed to cultural reasons for Switzerland's cutting down on immigration was that its social infrastructure was fully extended, thus limiting the potential gains from adding workers. A considerable volume of investment in Australia today is linked to immigration requirements.

The large-scale inward movement in Israel and West Germany cannot be said to have hurt these countries in the long run, despite the fact that they were well above the optimum population at the beginning of the movement in terms of social overhead capital. The reasons lie in the dynamic aspects of the movement. Israel's readiness to receive all Jewish refugees who were able to leave the countries where they constituted minorities contributed substantially to the spirit of dedication which evoked long hours of work and acceptance of low levels of consumption. These were extramarket phenomena which the economist has difficulty in explaining in terms of marginal productivity. In West Germany, the dynamism lay partly, but only partly, in the evocation of a national effort. In large measure it operated through short-run pressure on wages which held profits high and out of which a compulsive and even neurotic drive to work and invest by entrepreneurs rebuilt West German capital at a rapid rate.

But immigration does not always bring one's coreligionists or co-nationalists, and even when it does, as in the case of the Palestinian Arab refugees in the Sinai Peninsula and Jordan, there is no necessary dynamic result. (In these cases, the receiving countries discouraged efforts of the refugees to improve their economic conditions, since this might have implied an acceptance of the view that they were not entitled to return to their land in Israel.) The return of the European settlers from Algiers to France in the 1960s had an effect halfway between the stimulation of the East German refugees for West Germany and the deadening impact of the Jordanian Arabs.

Apart from external economies in social overhead capital and dynamic forces, immigration has effects on total output and on income distribution. It has been suggested by Abba Lerner that where diminishing returns exist, and where on that account marginal product is below average product, it might be possible for the receiving country to alter the market distribution of income after immigration in order to bribe existing workers to accept an inflow of labor. Immigration lowers the marginal product of labor, and hence wage rates, and raises the rent of unchanged factors, such as land and capital. Government, however, could pay new workers their marginal product, but old workers their old wages, using part of the increase in rent in the system to make up the difference between the new and old marginal product. Since the marginal product in the new country is higher than in the old, everyone benefits from this operation.

To a certain extent this happens automatically, at least in the short run. Immigrants form a noncompeting group which takes on the dirty jobs that no one in the rest of the economy wants, such as the Italians who move into farm, hotel, and other service jobs, plus some in heavy industry, and free the Swiss to transfer to skilled work and offices. The immigrants may be sought because native labor is not available for particular tasks which would be remunerative with cheaper labor available from abroad: the slaves needed to make cotton planting pay in the 1830s and 1840s kept down wage rates in cotton-farming areas. Similarly, the importation of Mexican and Puerto Rican truck-farm workers lowers wage rates at the margin. The pressure to halt immigration was primarily social but partly economic, the latter stemming from newly powerful trade unions. For example, Cesar Chavez of the United Farm Workers has opposed admitting more Mexican harvest workers into the United States, despite the strong ethnic ties of many UFW members to Mexico.

Or the immigration may be needed to keep down wages in general, as in West Germany. In part this may be the net effect of separate plants looking for workers, which ends up in the government establishing recruiting agencies overseas. Or it may be conscious. An authoritative writer on Latin America asserts that support for immigration into these countries comes from employer groups who are anxious to hold down wage rates and maintain rates of profit. As we have had occasion to observe in discussing tariff policy, one policy may recommend itself from an overall point of view, but another may be adopted for distributional reasons where the factor or group which benefits wields political power. In this instance, however, it seems likely, as in the support given for free trade by Manchester liberals in the 1840s and Detroit manufacturers in the 1950s, that the distributional argument and the total efficiency argument overlap. Although population is growing rapidly in many of these countries, such as Brazil and Venezuela, they have been underpopulated relative to resources and possesses a fairly efficient network of social capital.

Apart from its economic merits, however, the proposal is highly academic for social reasons. In the long run, the immigrants will want to be assimilated in the receiving country and to end discrimination against them in wages. Social and cultural conditions, including the color of their skins, will affect how rapidly this comes about. But the pressure will be ineluctable.

TECHNICAL ASSISTANCE

Current interest in the economic development of underdeveloped areas, with its emphasis on technical assistance, suggests that the international transmission of technology through personal visits is a new phenomenon. This is not so. Flemish weavers taught their secrets to the British woolen industry in the 13th and 14th centuries. Somewhat later Lombard merchants and bankers led the commercial revolution in London. After the industrial revolution, British engineers built the railroads of the Continent, and British textile workers and steelworkers communicated their skills to French, German, and Italian factories and mills. Up to about 1830 it was illegal in Great Britain to export machinery, for fear of competition; but master workers coming to the United States or going to Belgium, France, Germany, and Italy smuggled it out or reproduced it upon arrival from drawings.

There are, to be sure, differences in the extent and character of international diffusion of technical capacity now as compared, say, to the 19th century. International organizations, national governments, and international corporations provide new institutions for this transmission which are evidently more efficient than the single worker or engineer or the limited colony of workers. The result is that international travel and foreign residence of skilled personnel, professional and manual, have reached new heights each year since World War II. Crews of Texas oil drillers can be encountered anywhere; teams from Morrison-Knudson, Krupp, and similar construction enterprises are found from Afghanistan to Zanzibar; economists from Scandinavia and the British dominions—which produce impressive surpluses for export—are found advising central banks, planning boards, and treasuries in Asia, Latin America, and Africa. A special kind of technical assistance, not always of a very high technical caliber but certain to spread an awareness of modern economic life and of the capacity of man to improve it, is the Peace Corps of the United States and its smaller European and British equivalents.

The impacts are not always on the receiving country. In the Europe of the 19th century it was normal for sons of merchants to spend six months or a year working in one or more foreign countries to acquire languages, learn bookkeeping, and acquire a knowledge of markets. Today it is reported that the Italian Communists who went with the Fiat organization to Togliattigrad in the Soviet Union to build an automobile plant returned with a new understanding of economic and political issues in Italy, as well as those in the Soviet Union.

FREEDOM OF MOVEMENT AND SOCIAL INTEGRATION

Reduction in transport costs relative to income means that the populations of the world can mix with one another on an increasing scale. They become more aware of one another in other ways than travel—through motion pictures, magazines, radio, and television, including live overseas television by Telstar. But there is a significant difference between the interest of the outsider and the familiarity of the habitué who feels at home in what was once a strange environment. The social barriers against outsiders begin to be overcome when there have been so many trips that the traveler stops counting them. In some occupations persons have now stopped counting trips to Europe and Asia, as they once stopped counting trips between the East and West coasts, and before that trips from Washington to New York or Los Angeles to San Francisco.

Much of the world is still far from mobile. Some of it is in the stage of first trips. But increasingly people are beginning to feel at home over wider areas. The Harvard Business School graduate of the 1930s probably had strong preferences for work in a region of the United States—East, South, Middle West, Far West; the graduate of the 1950s was usually content to work anywhere in the United States. Today's graduate is willing to be hired for work (for an American company and at an American salary) anywhere in the world. The parenthesis in the last sentence indicates the room left to go. By the end of the century it seems inevitable that factor-price equalization will have taken care of the salary part, and social integration of the need to work with fellow nationals.

The trend is clearly in this direction, to extend freedom of movement, on a scale which leads to social integration, to more and more groups and classes in societies in more and more countries. The mobility poses problems for countries with few facilities which are or feel threatened by the loss of particularly intelligent, well-trained, and energetic individuals. Love of country (and difficulties in learning foreign languages) will retain some. Interest in the different and narrower differential returns will attract similar people from abroad. That the movement of peoples will become an increasingly important aspect of international economics, however, there can be no doubt.

SUMMARY

Labor moves across international boundaries in limited amounts, and generally in structured paths. Some movement is daily, seasonal, and institutionalized through companies and government bodies, and some is permanent. The pattern of migration in the 19th century tended to be synchronized with alternating long cycles in Europe and abroad. Waves of emigration from Britain, Ireland, Germany, and Scandinavia initially built up in cumulative fashion and then came to a halt as the difference in wage rates narrowed between Europe and the areas of settlement. From Italy and eastern Europe, however, the migration built up cumulatively until cut off by war and immigration quotas. Birthrates remained high, and there was no substantial domestic industry to assist in absorbing the rural surplus.

Large-scale European movements, mainly from the Mediterranean countries to Switzerland, Belgium, France, and West Germany, have helped to create a European labor market. Britain, the Netherlands, and the Common Market for Scandinavia stand largely aloof from this movement.

Emigration benefits the sending country through remittances, improvement in the terms of trade as a result of expanding production abroad, and relief for structural unemployment. In one sense, however, the raising and education of able-bodied workers constitutes a capital investment when it is not clear that overpopulated countries should export capital. Emigration may also attract the most vigorous elements in a society. Immigration is desirable for a country, provided that the process of social assimilation is not serious, if its population is below optimal. In addition, immigration may be undertaken for structural and distributional reasons. Immigration, however, may have dynamic effects in other circumstances which outweigh adverse economic considerations.

Technical assistance is provided partly by the written word, but most effectively through the international movement of people. Increased mobility is leading to wider intermingling on social and economic bases.

SUGGESTED READING

Brinley Thomas, *Migration and Economic Growth* (Cambridge: Cambridge University Press, 1954; revised and expanded, 1972), studies the experience of the Atlantic migration and contains a detailed bibliography. On migration in Europe and the creation of an international labor market, see Charles P. Kindleberger, *Europe's Postwar Growth: The Role of Labor Supply* (Cambridge, Mass.: Harvard University Press, 1967), especially chaps. 9 and 10.

Papers by A. Scott and H. Rieben discuss, respectively, "Transatlantic and North American International Migration" and the "Intra-European Migration of Labour and Migration of High-level Manpower from Europe to North America," in *North American and Western European Economic Policies*, proceedings of a conference held by the International Economic Association ed. C. P. Kindleberger and A. Shonfield (New York: St. Martin's Press, 1971). The former paper has a bibliography. See also Walter Adams (ed.), *The Brain Drain* (New York: Macmillan, 1968).

Harry Jerome, *Migration and Business Cycles* (New York: National Bureau of Economic Research, 1926), examines whether the push of depression is more significant than the pull of prosperity abroad. James E. Meade, *Trade and Welfare*, chap. 27, studies the effects of factor movements.

A stimulating essay on U.S. immigration policy is Elliott Abrams and Franklin S. Abrams, "Immigration Policy—Who Gets In and Why?" *Public Interest*, no. 38 (Winter 1975), pp. 3–29.

The welfare effects of the brain drain and some proposals for dealing with it have been ably discussed in recent writings by Jagdish N. Bhagwati: "Taxing the Brain Drain," *Challenge*, July–August 1976, pp. 34–38; *Taxing the Brain Drain: A Proposal* (Amsterdam: North Holland, 1976); and *The Brain Drain and Taxation: Theory and Empirical Evidence* (Amsterdam: North Holland, 1976).

24

Long-term portfolio capital

FORMS OF LONG-TERM CAPITAL

Long-term capital movements take place through instruments of longer than one-year maturity; short-term capital movements, through currency, demand deposits, bills of exchange, commercial paper, time deposits, and the like, up to a year. The distinction between portfolio capital and direct investment is that the latter carries with it control of a business; the former does not. Long-term capital is typically embodied in bonds and stocks, but can be in notes, convertible debenture bonds, term loans (made by banks), and the like. A significant distinction is between governments and private lenders, although this is occasionally muddied when private loans receive a government guarantee. Governments borrow as well as lend, of course, but if governments borrow from the private market, without a guarantee by another government, they must meet the market test, just like private borrowers.

Long-term capital flows can take place through the flotation of new securities, typically bonds, or by trading in outstanding securities. A considerable international flow of capital, for example, takes the form of purchases and sales of existing securities on the New York Stock Exchange. Foreigners trade substantially in the leading American stocks, just as American investors trade in Royal Dutch/Shell, Pechiney, Rhône-Poulenc, British Petroleum, Imperial Chemical Industries, and many more European and Japanese stocks. In what follows we will deal primarily, however, with the movement of capital through new bond issues.

The first part of the chapter deals with long-term lending among relatively developed countries. Thereafter we focus on some particular problems and points of view raised by foreign borrowing by developing countries.

NEW BOND ISSUES

The traditional form of long-term lending is the bond. For 100 years, up to 1914, the sterling bond dominated world financial markets. For the period from 1919 to 1930, the New York bond market assumed the role previously played by London. But this interlude was brief. Excessive lending, international disequilibrium, depression, the collapse of export markets, the notoriety given to certain questionable practices of bond promoters, all combined to turn the investor away from foreign bonds, except for those of Canada, which have never really been regarded as foreign. With few, but perhaps gradually increasing, exceptions, moreover, borrowers no longer liked fixed obligations in an uncertain world. The foreign bond fell on evil days.

After World War II, with the reestablishment of convertibility of European currencies, the New York bond market experienced a revival. European capital markets were compartmentalized. Those which had low rates of interest, such as the Swiss and the Dutch, limited issues to relatively small amounts. Others that could handle larger sums had high rates. The New York long-term market gradually overcame its antipathy to foreign issues and undertook new issues of bonds not only for Canada and Israel (the latter with a large element of charity about them), but also for European, Dominion, and Japanese borrowers. The net was smaller than the gross, since European investors, impressed with the breadth and liquidity of the New York market, bought dollar bonds issued by European borrowers, even though the rate of interest on New York issues was below that obtainable in Europe. So substantial was the expansion of the market that, given the weakness of the U.S. balance of payments, the Treasury authorities in July 1963 imposed a prohibitive tariff on new securities, the Interest Equalization Tax (IET). The market then moved to Europe, where Eurodollar bonds, that is, bonds denominated in dollars, were issued and bought, by borrowers and lenders, outside the United States. Although that market was smaller than the dollar bond market located in New York, with the strength of U.S. investors behind it, it remained at close to $1 billion of new issues a year, an amount well in excess of the foreign bond markets—both national and international—available in Europe.

The eclipse of the bond after 1928 or 1929 led to new forms of foreign lending. Some was private banking, some government lending at long term, some government banking. From 1930 to 1950 some private long-term lending by banks had been limited to advances against gilt-edged security, such as gold, or to loans made with governmental guarantees. In the 1950s there was renewed banking interest in medium-term financing of international trade, in part under the provisions of the little-used Edge Act of 1919 and in part with the help of an Export-Import Bank program of credits and guarantees. After the IET, European borrowers switched to long-term bank loans from the United States until the Gore amendment to the IET made the tax apply also to bank loans of more than one year. Governmental lending has been carried on partly through banking institutions such as the Export-Import Bank in the United States and, since 1946, partly through such international agencies as the International Bank for Reconstruction and Development (IBRD), the Inter-American Development Bank, the European Investment Bank, and the Asian Development Bank. Other governmental lending has taken place through specially created institutions such as the Lend-Lease Administration, the Economic Cooperation Administration, the Mutual Security Agency, the International Cooperation Agency, and the Agency for International Development, or has been arranged for particular purposes, such as ship disposal or disposal of surplus commodities.

We may restrict ourselves, therefore, to provate lending through the bond market and government lending in its many long-term forms. The flow of capital through bank loans can be neglected on the ground that it conforms largely to the principles of one or the other.

FOREIGN AND DOMESTIC INVESTMENT

Foreign investment is similar to domestic investment in that it increases income and employment in the process of capital formation and ultimately enlarges capacity for higher income after the capital has been formed. On the first score, loans lead to increased employment and income when the proceeds are spent on exports to obtain command over real resources either by the borrower himself or by the party who bought the foreign exchange from the borrower. On the second, foreign capital increases income through time in the same way that domestic investment does, although one needs to make a distinction between "national income" and "geographic product." If country A lends to country B, which adds to its productive capital, A's receipt of interest from B increases its national income received but not its net national product. Not all of B's increase in geographic product can increase its national income, since, under the terms of the loan, interest (which is part of geographic product) must be subtracted and paid to A. Hence such interest is counted in A's, not B's, national income.

The foreign lending alters factor proportions in the two countries from what they would have been without foreign investment. Foreign investment leaves domestic factor proportions unchanged and forestalls an increase in the capital labor ratio, which would have raised the marginal product of labor and lowered that of capital had the capital been invested domestically. One should accordingly expect labor to oppose foreign lending, in the same fashion that it has in the past approved of tariffs on labor-intensive imports. In recent years such concern has begun to be expressed by labor, but primarily in the direct investment field, where the connection between the foreign investment and local jobs can be clearly seen.

One old distinction made by Keynes turned on the location of the physical assets. The private investor runs risks whether he invests at home or abroad. If he makes a mistake in judgment and his investment proves worthless in the case of domestic investment, the physical assets at least are within the national boundaries, but if the unsuccessful investment is foreign, the physical assets accrue to foreigners. This distinction is an appropriate one if the risk the investor judges incorrectly is that of confiscation by government authority without adequate compensation. But the distinction cannot be made for economic risks. A worthless factory or railroad is worthless whether at home or abroad; and an asset with some salvage value can be sold for that value, again whether at home or abroad.

With perfect international capital markets, there would be one interest rate all over the world. But of course such perfect capital markets are far from achieved. There are risks of default and confiscation, which require a subjective risk premium, different for each country, before capital will flow from a safe home market to countries abroad. Moreover, most investors and borrowers are myopic in that their horizons are restricted to the home territory, both for investments and for loans. (This is not necessarily irrational, as there is a cost to obtaining information on investments and opportunities for loans abroad.)

Economists like to play with the idea that it would pay a country to limit the movement of capital abroad, if the unrestricted movement of capital lowered the interest rate abroad. The domestic price of capital under optimum lending should be equal to the marginal rate of return on foreign capital, not the average rate, if the two differed, as would be the case if the lending country were a price maker in the world capital market. The analogy with the optimum tariff is exact. Under an optimum tariff strategy it pays to limit exports and/or imports and, if the nation's trade has an impact on world prices, to equate relative prices at home to marginal rates of transformation abroad, not average rates. So with lending. There is even a small literature which combines the optimum tariff with the optimum level of foreign lending. This literature contributes to theoretical elegance more than to practical relevance.

Foreign bond markets tend, on the whole, to be competitive. Where there is private intervention organized by the bond buyers, as in Switzerland, its purpose is to provide the lenders with a wide choice of investment issues, rather than with the highest possible return. By limiting the size of foreign issues to SF 60 million (about $14 million) the oligopolistically organized market optimizes the spread of risk, not the rate of return.

THE INSTITUTIONAL PATTERN OF LENDING

The imperfection of the international capital market may have been diminishing prior to the IET, as a consequence of better communication and transport in the modern age, but it is still marked. Well-established attitudes of investors, practices of investment banking houses, governmental intervention, and controls have all contributed to confining capital movements to well-worn paths. To use a hydrologic analogy, the flow of capital is not like that of broad rivers which equalize levels over a vast area, but like that of irrigation canals and ditches which bring moisture to some areas and not to others, even though latter areas may be on a lower level and need it more. In these circumstances, the understanding of capital movements calls more for the techniques of the historian, who can explain where the channels of capital flow were dug, than the analysis of the economist, who merely describes the supply and demand for capital in separate markets without indicating how, and to what extent, they are connected.

From about 1825 to 1850, British foreign lending was largely to continental borrowers, with the largest amounts sought for railroads and the associated supplying industries. With the Revolution of 1848, however, British investors turned away from European loans to lending to the Empire, the United States, and gradually, the Middle East and Latin America. The emphasis continued on railroads, although the fact that colonial issues qualified as trustee investments, that is, as approved for investors requiring very safe securities, helped sell the bonds of colonial governments at rates approaching British government yields. The movement of capital to specific countries would follow a learning-process growth pattern: loans to Argentina, for example, started slowly in the 1880s and spurted from 1885 until the crash of Baring Brothers in 1890.

After getting its railroads started with British help, France turned to lending elsewhere on the Continent, largely for railroads and industrial banks, instead of developing capital issues for other French industries. French financiers and engineers contributed importantly to the development of Germany, Italy, Spain, and Austria. The high commissions received by French banking houses and the corruption of the press by foreign borrowers led to the flotation of numerous dubious issues. The czarist government, for example, managed to issue loans in Paris which it could not sell or refund in London or Berlin.

It is still an open question whether British and French foreign lending diverted capital abroad which could have been profitably employed at home. The city of London and the Paris bourse were widely accused at home of having slowed the growth of Britain and France prior to World War I by lending abroad for purposes of lower economic utility than that of loans refused at home.

In the interwar period, the demands of capital for reconstruction took London and Paris out of international lending, except for a continued flow of British loans to the Empire, then in process of becoming the Commonwealth. New York took over as the world's financial center and went in for an orgy of foreign bond issues, particularly those for Germany and Latin America. Big underwriting commissions led to abuses, including the high-pressure selling of bonds by investment banking subsidiaries of New York banks at times when these banks had private knowledge of the borrower's default. New York also took the place of London as the provider of investment capital to Canada, with U.S. insurance companies, which deny that they buy foreign bonds, ready to admit in the next breath that of course they buy Canadian.

The revival of the New York bond market in the late 1950s until it was hit over the head with the IET was largely for European borrowers, the Dominions, and Japan (apart from Israel and the International Bank for Reconstruction and Development). Most of the developing countries still needed to establish their creditworthiness. Mexico was one that did. The IET did not apply to Canada, to the less developed countries, or to Japan up to a limit of $100 million a year. Despite its exemption, however, Mexico chose to borrow in the Eurodollar bond market, at higher interest rates, in an effort to maintain its good credit standing in the New York market.

CAPITAL MOVEMENTS AND WELFARE

Factor-price equalization is an efficiency optimum and, with normal assumptions about distribution (for example, that a dollar for one is equal to a dollar for another), a welfare optimum. If freedom of capital movements helps to move in the direction of equalization of the return to capital worldwide, it helps move toward a welfare optimum.

But first we must face the question of whether freedom of capital movement does work toward equalization of capital returns. Where domestic capital goes abroad to evade taxes, it may move from jurisdictions where capital is scarce to those where it is abundant. Such movement does not promote welfare. Where capital moves from poor to rich countries, for lack of complementary factors, it may again be contrary to Pareto optimality. Where market returns do not reflect social return because of distortions, there is another reason for inhibiting freedom of movement. Still another reason would be destabilizing speculation, a wave of capital seeking refuge, say, in West Germany for fear of devaluation of the U.S. dollar, the British pound, or the Italian lira. The West German government adopted exchange controls in 1972 at the behest of the governors of the Bundesbank, and over the objection of Karl Schiller, the finance minister, who resigned. The possibilities that national interest rates may not reflect social values of abundance and scarcity and that private capital movements may not respond to market rates when they do are so pervasive that a number of economists believe that the presumption in favor of freedom of capital movement is very small indeed.

But thus far we have made only the negative case. The argument in favor of a national capital market in the United States is strong. Regions that have abundant savings can earn a higher return on them; regions with sizable capital needs can have them met more cheaply. Even if there were no net movement of savings, a single capital market would be useful, since there are economies of scale in joined capital markets. The wider number of borrowers and lenders provides the former with lower rates and the latter with greater liquidity, through trading on a broader market. This is why both California savers and borrowers move their operations to the New York capital market instead of just borrowing the net deficit—as is the case for net imports of goods.

When one region or country borrows and lends through different securities, again with no net capital movement, there is a gain in welfare through the reduction in risk from diversification. This was realized when it was proposed in Canada that the country mobilize its citizens' holdings of U.S. securities and exchange them for U.S. holdings of Canadian securities, including, to be sure, companies owned through direct investment. The reduction in the number of securities the Canadian investor could buy was recognized instantly as a loss in welfare.

The argument for controlling capital flows rests then on second-best grounds. If capital movements flow in directions contrary to welfare, that is, from capital-poor to capital-rich countries, without a gain in liquidity or diversification, it may be necessary to control them on second-best grounds because it is impossible to correct the underlying situation giving rise to the undesirable movement. However, the question of whether this is possible still presents itself.

THE FEASIBILITY OF CONTROLLING CAPITAL MOVEMENTS

When most investors and borrowers were myopic and scanned investment and borrowing opportunities limited largely to the domestic capital market and a few organized foreign securities, it was fairly easy to control international capital movements. Today, however, with much more mobility of persons and money, the question arises whether control of capital movements is technically possible. Much depends upon the discipline of a society. What might work well in a Scandinavian society accustomed to following governmental directives in an orderly fashion will not succeed in a Latin country emerging from foreign occupation in which civic virtue consisted of black-market operations. But there are technical as well as sociological aspects.

In July 1963, the U.S. government came to the conclusion that too much capital was flowing abroad through the foreign bond market for balance-of-payments comfort. It applied the IET to stop the flow, implicitly adhering to a partial-equilibrium view of the balance of payments. If $500 million of foreign lending were halted, the theory seemed to imply, the balance of payments would improve by $500 million.

The balance of payments, however, is a macroeconomic phenomenon, which means that microeconomic remedies work badly, if at all; and it responds to general-equilibrium, not partial-equilibrium, reasoning. In 1963, interest rates were low in the United States, high in Europe. There were many individuals, firms, and banks, moreover, that were interested in maximizing by lending in the dearer market and borrowing in the cheaper. When one form of borrowing was halted, others were set in motion.

The first response was an increase in long-term bank lending. This was halted through the Gore amendment, applying the IET to bank-term loans. Second, international firms found that they could earn more on Eurodollar deposits in Europe than they could on liquid funds in the United States. Time money started to move to Europe through firms. This was halted for 400 firms in January 1965 through the so-called Voluntary Credit Restraint Program. The number of firms was raised to 700, to 900. In January 1968 the program was made mandatory—the so-called Mandatory Credit Program (MCP). Then U.S. firms not permitted to send funds to Europe would go there and raise funds locally. If General Motors borrowed $100 million in Belgium to build a plant at Antwerp, this would raise interest rates in

Belgium, shift local borrowers from Brussels and Antwerp to the Eurodollar market in London, raise interest rates in London, and stimulate movements to London from Canada and from New York to Canada. Through the inefficient chain, some considerable amount of the moneys that General Motors was not allowed to bring to Belgium from New York got there from New York anyway, via the Canadian gap. Or an international firm would raise money in the Eurodollar market by selling convertible debenture bonds. These would pay higher returns than securities of the same company issued in the United States. Foreign holders of the American securities would sell them, repatriate the proceeds, and use them to buy the Eurodollar bonds. The foreign securities gap remained opened.

If two reservoirs are connected by a dozen pipes of some considerable size, cutting off a few pipes does not separate the levels of water. Foreign exchange control has never been efficient, even in the Nazi period in the 1930s, when violations carried the death penalty. In today's world, with hundreds of thousands of communications across national lines and with a commodity as fungible and easy to hide as money or securities, foreign exchange control is not likely to function effectively. To be sure of isolating the capital market of a country, one has to have censorship of mail, border searches of tourists, control of the credit terms of trade transactions, freezing not only of one's own nationals' dealings in foreign exchange but also of foreigners' dealings in national assets—actions which civilized countries abhor, except in wartime. A sloppy control is inequitable, as large companies can find their way through the labyrinth of regulation fairly easily.

We are left then with something of an impasse. Capital controls are difficult, unaesthetic, but possibly necessary if one cannot work out the first-best policies of serene coordination of national monetary and capital market policies. We shall return to this issue later. First, however, we have to address a few issues of foreign bond lending of particular relevance to the developing countries. Some of them have a counterpart in the lending country.

TIED LOANS

The incapacity of borrowing countries to transform gives rise to the necessity to borrow specifically for purchasing imports. The difficulties of lenders have led to the device of tying loans to the purchase of specific exports.

During the 1930s depression, loans were frequently made for the purpose of stimulating exports. For example, the Export-Import Bank in the United States, the Export Credit Guarantee Department in Britain, and similar organizations in other countries selling capital equipment found it necessary to provide governmental credit to continue to export machinery during the depression when the private international long-term market for capital collapsed. Here the purpose of the loan was to sell the exports. In some countries, such as Germany, moreover, there was never any thought of separating the finance from the sale of goods. But the problem posed by tied loans today is otherwise. Foreign loans or other forms of assistance are sought by the developing country. In order to prevent these loans from weakening the balance of payments of the United States, as the most notorious example, the loans are tied to expenditure in the United States.

Such tying of course violates the principle of Pareto optimality in which one should always purchase in the cheapest market. It would only happen by the rarest coincidence—at least in peacetime—that the cheapest market for the capital was also the cheapest market for the various imports to be bought with the proceeds of the loan. To the extent that tying is effective, it raises the cost of goods or reduces the value of the loan. The International Bank for Reconstruction and Development has estimated that the price level on which tied loans are spent is some 30 percent higher than the cheapest sources.

But tying is not always effective. Money is fungible, as we have indicated, and accountants over time achieve a certain low cunning. In partial equilibrium, with other things equal, a new loan which is tied will achieve its purpose. But other things have a habit of refusing to stay equal. Contemplate tied aid, for example. If military aid is available but economic aid is not, a country can switch its own resources from military to economic expenditure and, in effect, maintain the old level of military effort and expand the economic level. Or vice versa. It can shift a development project it was planning to undertake with the proceeds of exports to the lending country to a loan basis, and use the free exchange from exports for other purposes. Especially if it can transform its resources, a country can minimize the cost of tied loans (or tied aid) by using the loans (or aid) for inframarginal purposes, freeing up untied exchange for use at the margin.

In many countries, however, such capacity to transform is limited. Suppose that such a country is interested in a domestic investment. In this circumstance, tying loans to the foreign exchange content of an investment can present a considerable obstacle.

Let us assume that a country wants to undertake the construction of a railroad as part of a program of economic development. The total cost of the project amounts to $100 million. Of this total, $50 million, we may say, represents the foreign exchange value of materials and equipment which must be bought from abroad; the remaining $50 million constitutes cost to be incurred in local currency.

Under a system of tied loans, only $50 million could be borrowed in the United States, since the borrower must specify what U.S. goods are to be purchased with the loan. The United States may or may not be the cheapest place to buy the goods, but the loan is tied to U.S. goods. The remaining $50 million expended locally is likely to give rise to a foreign exchange requirement. Whether or not it will depends on how the local funds are obtained. If they are acquired through new savings or through taxation which reduces consumption, then the expenditure is not inflationary, that is it does not increase national money income or imports. If, on the other hand, as is frequently the case, some part or all of the local expenditure is financed through credit creation or deficit spending, the domestic expenditure will spill over into new imports. How large an increase in imports will occur depends on how much of the new spending goes for domestic resources and how much for imports, in the first instance and in successive rounds of spending. But there is no foreign exchange from the loan to finance these incremental imports. The exchange available was all used up on the first round of spending. Any increase from subsequent rounds of spending will have to be paid for out of reserves, or if these are inadequate, it will lead to depreciation or foreign exchange control.

THE PROJECT BASIS FOR LOANS

The International Bank for Reconstruction and Development started out to make what were essentially tied loans, although the officials of the bank denied that they could properly be called such. Loans were made on a project basis, that is, a borrowing country had to indicate the purpose for which the loan was sought, and this could not be so vague as "to fill the deficit in the budget." Moreover, the borrower was originally required to specify what new imports were needed for the project, and where these would be bought. If the bank approved the project and regarded the imports as reasonable, it was then prepared to lend the moneys needed to finance the imports.

This procedure, which the bank has now altered, was objectionable on two scores. It was "discriminatory," and it was likely to increase rather than mitigate the foreign exchange difficulties of the borrowing country. The discriminatory feature is found in the fact that the borrowing country was expected to spend in the countries whose currencies were lent. In a completely nondiscriminatory system, loans would be provided from the cheapest source—that is, the money market with the lowest interest rates—and the proceeds of those loans would be spent where the goods sought were cheapest. Dollars might be borrowed and spent in Britain, or, as during the 19th century, pounds might be borrowed and spent on the Continent. To lend only the currencies to be spent is to require the borrower either to borrow in a dearer market for loans or to buy in a dearer market for goods, unless the cheapest markets for goods and loans are the same. This objection was not perhaps important in practice up to 1950, because goods as well as loans were cheaper in the United States. But the principle of tying the currency of the loan to the currency of the projected import is discriminatory.

In the second place, a loan limited to the cost of imports needed for a project is insufficient to balance the international accounts except in the limiting case where all the local expenditure is raised in a deflationary fashion. Any inflationary financing of local expenditures of the project will raise income and imports and unbalance the international accounts. Purchasing power in general is neglected in favor of a limited amount of foreign purchasing power in particular. These loans and projects worsened rather than improved the borrowing country's balance of payments.

DEBT SERVICE RATIO

The increase in postwar borrowing by developing countries has recently excited interest that some countries may have borrowed too much and may be on the verge of default. The shorthand measure for the extent of a country's involvement is the ratio of its debt service— interest and amortization—to the current value of exports. This ratio on the average was under 5 percent on public debt for the developing countries after World War II until about 1955. Thereafter it rose to more than 10 percent in 1965. A number of countries defaulted in this period—Argentina, Brazil, Chile, Turkey, and so on. Others were rescued by international consortia. Still others, such as Indonesia and Ghana, which contracted debt for military operations and spectacular but impractical development projects, face very high debt service ratios and a strong possibility of the need to readjust external commitments.

The debt service ratio is hardly the neatest possible concept. As the ratios on the previous page indicate, interest should be related to the increase in exports and the decrease in imports. Equally important or more important are the capacity to transform resources from one sector to another, the productivity of new investment, and the marginal propensity to save out of increased income. Where a country maintains an overvalued exchange rate, with domestic inflation in excess of external depreciation, the outlook for its ability to maintain service on its debt is dim. The tendency to single out a particular ratio as critical in analysis is understandable, but the message of this chapter is that economists must keep an eye on a wide variety of aspects of international borrowing. Particularly critical points are that loans should be invested productively; that some considerable portion of the productivity should be skimmed off, part to pay debt service and part to save for new projects; that the economy must be able to reallocate resources from domestic to export and import-competing activities, to pay interest and principal on foreign debts; and that the economy must not be otherwise mismanaged. These are perhaps, rigorous conditions in today's world, but their fulfillment would make it possible to abandon a whole service of illogical views and expedients in the field of foreign lending, from tied loans to insistence on the lending of the interest on past loans.

SUMMARY

There are many forms of foreign capital movement, but the traditional one, which had virtually died out but is now coming back, is the foreign bond. Foreign investment is like domestic investment insofar as multiplier and growth effects on national income are concerned. There are differences in effects on factor proportions.

Capital flows internationally in deep channels dictated by institutional considerations as well as by differences in the marginal productivity of capital. Government control has been an important influence. Government has also developed into an important international lender, making stabilization loans and loans to finance particular projects or particular exports or imports.

Free movement of capital may not contribute to Pareto optimality if market prices diverge from private values, but the presumption of some economists that capital controls are generally justified flies in the face of external economies from joined capital markets, gains through diversification, and gains from moving capital from where it is abundant to where it is scarce. Foreign exchange control is difficult to apply except in highly disciplined countries.

There is general objection to tied loans, on the ground that they depart from the welfare-maximizing principle which calls for borrowing in the cheapest market for capital and buying in the cheapest market for goods. The project basis for loans is analytically unacceptable because of its tied feature, and in addition because borrowing countries typically need help in financing their general balance-of-payments deficits created by investment projects, not merely the projects' foreign exchange content.

The debt service ratio, which relates interest and amortization on outstanding foreign debt to the value of exports, is a crude measure of a country's capacity to borrow abroad, invest productively at home, and service its debt.

SUGGESTED READING

Texts

Murray C. Kemp, chaps. 11, 12, and 13. For a good account of 19th-century lending, with tables and references to the literature, see W. Woodruff, *Impact of Western Man* (New York: St. Martin's Press, 1966), chap. 4, including notes to tables and bibliography. See also Raymond F. Mikesell, *Public International Lending for Development* (New York: Random House, 1966) (paperback).

Treatises, etc.

For a modern rounded treatment, partly historical, partly descriptive, and partly analytic, see John H. Adler (ed.), *Captial Movements and Economic Development*, proceedings of a conference held by the International Economic Association (New York: St. Martin's Press, 1967). An international capital market among the developed countries is criticized in essays by Richard N. Cooper and Alexander Lamfalussy in *North American and Western European Economic Policies* ed. Charles P. Kindleberger and A. Shonfield (New York: St. Martin's Press, 1971), but held necessary by Richard N. Cooper and E. M. Truman in "An Analysis of the Role of International Capital Markets in Providing Funds to Developing Countries," *Weltwirtschaftliches Archiv* (June 1971) (in English).

For accounts of 19th-century lending by Britain, see Leland H. Jenks, *The Migration of British Capital to 1875* (New York: Knopf, 1927); Herbert Feis, *Europe: The World's Banker, 1870–1913* New Haven: Yale University Press, 1931) (paperback, Norton, 1966); C. K. Hobson, *The Export of Capital* (London: Constable, 1914); A. K. Cairncross, *Home and Foreign Investment, 1870–1913* (Cambridge: Cambridge University Press, 1953); and Rondo E. Cameron, *France and the Economic Development of Europe, 1800–1913* (Princeton: Princeton University Press, 1960).

On the pure theory, see Robert A. Mundell, "International Trade and Factor Mobility," in American Economic Association, *Readings in International Economics;* Ronald W. Jones, "International Capital Movements and the Theory of Tariffs and Trade," *Quarterly Journal of Economics*, February 1967; and Murray C. Kemp, "Foreign Investment and the National Advantage," in *Economic Record*, March 1961. An attempt to measure the welfare effects of U.S. capital controls is provided by Norman S. Fieleke, "The Welfare Effects of Controls over Capital Exports from the United States," *Essays on International Finance*, January 1971.

Points

The debt service ratio is analyzed in a series of books by D. Avramovic and others of the Economics Division of the International Bank for Reconstruction and Development, the latest of which is D. Avramovic et al., *Economic Growth and External Debt* (Baltimore: Johns Hopkins Press, 1964).

An excellent institutional discussion of the requirements of an integrated capital market is given in European Economic Community, *The Development of a European Capital Market* (Brussels, 1967).

25

The theory of
direct investment

Perhaps the most sensitive area in international economics today is direct investment. The United States and Britain try to restrain direct investment by companies domiciled within their borders, in order to limit the pressure on their balance of payments. Canada, European countries, and Japan seek to limit foreign investment within their borders lest their control over domestic resources be diluted by foreign ownership. Developing countries worry both that foreigners will invest in them and that they won't, fearing exploitation on the one hand and inadequate access to foreign capital and technology on the other. Prohibitions and restrictions are laid down against investment in certain lines of activity which are regarded as peculiarly vulnerable to foreign influence or as particularly wasteful—natural resources, banking, newspapers, retail trade, soft drinks. Conditions are laid down that there must be local participation, foreign exchange brought from abroad, training, components purchased locally, domestic research, exports, and so on. And still the trend toward internationalization of the firm continues.

This chapter explores the theory of direct investment, how it differs from the movement of portfolio capital, and its impacts on efficiency, welfare, and the balance of payments of home countries (investing) and host countries (in which the investment takes place). In the next chapter we will discuss policies toward direct investment from the host-country and cosmopolitan points of view. Students are reminded that the subject evokes strong emotions. They should be wary of any alleged objectivity on the part of the author, but should also be prepared to acknowledge any biases of their own.

DIRECT INVESTMENT AS CAPITAL MOVEMENT

It used to be thought that the major difference between portfolio and direct investment was that direct investment involved control, whereas portfolio investment did not. Control was a legal concept and rested on 100, 98, 51, or 48 percent ownership of the equity of a foreign corporation. Or control was thought of in decision-theory terms, which meant that the head office made decisions respecting foreign operations, within a clearly laid-out scheme, on such questions as choice of top personnel, new products, capital budgeting, research and development, and dividend policy. But direct investment was a capital movement combined with control and perhaps other elements, such as technology.

It was observed, however, that direct investment often did not involve a capital movement. A firm would undertake investment abroad with funds borrowed in the local country. It might provide the equity in foreign exchange, but if it were going into a joint venture, this equity investment might take the form of patents, machinery, technology, or other real considerations. Once the investment became profitable, moreover, it grew from local borrowing and reinvested profits. Direct investment represented not so much an international capital movement as capital formation undertaken abroad.

Other theories were not lacking. In one view direct investment was akin to gambling. A firm undertook a small investment abroad and tried to pyramid it into a large stake, much as gamblers leave their winnings on the table. It was noticed that 50 percent of profits on direct investment was reinvested on balance, so the rule of thumb developed that direct investment withdrew half of its earnings and pyramided the other half. Or direct investment was the last stage in a technological cycle, along lines touched on in Chapter 4. First comes domestic production, then exports, and when imitation abroad is about to take over, the company undertakes production abroad. This is akin to the "**defensive investment**" concept of Alexander Lamfalussy. Some investments, he asserted, with reference to domestic capital formation, are motivated not by the desire to make profits but in order to avoid losses. The marginal rate of return on such investments is equal to any other, measuring from the expected loss to the low profit. But the average is low. It is better to enter a market with a low expected profit than to get pushed out of it altogether. This theory is related to a business view: direct investment is undertaken where there are large and growing markets. It is markets, not profits, which guide it. Where markets exist, profits will be found in the long run.

MONOPOLISTIC COMPETITION

Although each of these explanations has a piece of the truth, none has the power and the generality of Stephen Hymer's MIT thesis on "The International Operations of National Firms." In Hymer's view, direct investment belongs to the theory of monopolistic competition rather than that of international capital movements. A local company has an advantage over a foreign company, other things being equal. It is expensive to operate at a distance, expensive in travel, communication, and especially in misunderstanding. To overcome the inherent native advantage of being on the ground, the firm entering from abroad must have some other advantage not shared with its local competitor. The advantage typically lies in technology or patents. It may inhere in special access to very large amounts of capital, amounts far larger than the ordinary national firm can command. The firm may have better access to markets in foreign countries merely by reason of its international status. Or, as in petroleum refining or metal processing, the firm may coordinate operations and invested capital requirements at various stages in a vertical production process and, because of heavy inventory costs and its knowledge of the requirements at each stage, it may be able to economize through synchronizing operations. It may merely have differentiated products built on advertising. Or it may have truly superior management. But some special advantage is necessary if the firm is going to be able to overcome the disadvantage of operating at a distance.

The firm must be able not only to make higher profits abroad than it could at home, but it must also be able to earn higher profits abroad than local firms can earn in their own markets. For all its imperfections, the international capital market would be expected to be able to transfer mere capital from one country to another better than could a firm whose major preoccupations lie in production and marketing.

The implications of this theory of direct investment are many. For one, direct investment will not occur in industries with pure competition. Few farmers operate overseas, nor do many retail distributors other than Sears, Roebuck, or many representatives of such industries as textiles, clothing, and leather. Second, a company is not interested in acquiring local partners in a joint venture, seeking to keep the good things for itself; at the same time, the local investors naturally resist the suggestion that they should buy the shares of the parent company: the return on the overall stock is diluted as compared with the profitability of the local situation, which they observe. Third, direct investment takes place in two directions in the same industry, which would not be the case if the movement were based on general levels of profit. This is in part a peculiar phenomenon of oligopolistic competition: each firm must do as the others do to prevent another firm from getting an unanticipated advantage. Thus with soap, Lever Brothers operates in the United States and Procter and Gamble in Britain; with oil, Shell in the United States and Exxon in its various markets; and similarly for Knorr and Heinz with soup, Agfa and Kodak with photographic supplies, and so on. When one automobile company builds a small and inefficient plant in Brazil, 15 more follow. Like the leader in a sailboat race, one must not let the second boat split tacks, but cover it to protect one's lead. This is "defensive investment" in which the return is not positive but the prevention of a possible loss.

The oligopolistic character of direct investment is easily misunderstood. To the local inefficient competitor, the difficulty is that the foreign invader competes too vigorously. As in the case of the chain stores in the 1920s and 1930s, the local monopolist decries the large firm from outside the district because it competes, although he accuses it of monopoly. And firms which teamed up with foreign firms, such as RCA briefly with Siemens of Germany in the computer field, or General Electric (later Honeywell) with Machines Bull of France, did so not to extend a monopoly but to gather strength to challenge the industry lead of International Business Machines. This increases international competition. The contrary example is furnished by the 1967 purchase from a Norwegian government by Alcan Aluminum Ltd. of Canada of a 50 percent interest in the Aardal Og Sunndal Verk, an aluminum smelter that had been "a source of price competition that had vexed the entire industry." Buying up a competitor tends to restrain trade. But one cannot judge whether any particular takeover or investment increases or reduces competition without examination of the particular facts.

Firms maximize profits within a horizon which extends in time and space. Horizons change. Prior to about 1950, the Campbell Soup Company had few if any foreign branches outside Canada, whereas the Heinz company had almost 57. The former was preoccupied with its domestic operations; the latter, finding domestic competition stiff, had expanded especially abroad. After 1950, however, the Campbell company put on a drive to expand overseas. In the same way the chemical and pharmaceutical industries in the United States had been so busy prior to World War II fending off foreign competition that they had not contemplated foreign operations. In the depression of 1954, after fulfilling the bulk of their planned postwar domestic investments, they lifted their eyes to the world horizon and started to invest abroad.

As indicated in Chapter 9, the Rome Treaty of 1957 perhaps stimulated U.S. foreign investment more through calling attention to existing profit opportunities than it did by creating new ones. Up to the beginnings of the Common Market, rapid and substained European growth had passed unnoticed over the horizon of many large firms that would have been capable of investing there. With the formation of the EEC, the horizon suddenly was enlarged to encompass Europe, and investment in Europe as a whole soared.

This theory of direct investment can be summarized with reference to a simple formula used in elementary economics for capitalizing a perpetual flow of income:

$$C = \frac{I}{r},$$

where C is the value of an asset or obligation, I is the stream of income it produces, and r is the market rate of interest or profit. Thus, the student will remember, a perpetual bond with a face value of $1,000 bearing a 4 percent coupon (an income of $40 per year, or I) will sell for $1,333 ($C$) when the market rate of interest (r) stands at 3 percent. Hymer's theory of direct investment states that foreigners can pay more for an earning asset, such as a business, in country A than residents of country A would, not because they are content with a lower r, but because they can earn a higher I. It will happen, to be sure, that international capital markets are less than perfect, and that differences in r contribute to the flow of capital. But the behavior of direct investment—the readiness of investors to borrow in the host country at the same r as residents face, its concentration in oligopolistic industries, its movement in two directions, and the insistence on complete ownership—indicates that it is I, nor r, that dominates.

This view of direct investment clashes head on with one expressed by Irving Brecher and S. S. Reisman. Things equal to the same thing, they said, are equal to each other. A firm located in Canada will try to maximize profits whether it is a Canadian or a foreign firm, say one whose head office is located in the United States. If both face the same conditions in Canada and abroad, both earn the same I and both capitalize it as the same r. The Canadian enterprise is thus worth the same capital value to Canadians and to citizens of the United States.

The analysis of this chapter, however, suggests that a larger international firm and a smaller Canadian firm will probably behave differently, owing to differences in the horizon within which they maximize. The Canadian firm expands within its borders, pays taxes only to the Canadian government, purchases components and equipment largely in Canada, recruits Canadians for unfilled positions, and so forth. The international firm faces a wider range of alternatives on many fronts. Typically its actions will be dictated by efficiency considerations, and its wider range of opportunity will result in greater efficiency. But it may not. The international firm may respond to its ownership-country citizenship against the dictates of efficiency, sending capital or profits home when they could usefully be invested in the host country or maintaining high-cost production in the home country in depression times in preference to low-cost production in the host country because of "patriotic" concern for employment in the country where its head office is located. Or it may, at the urging of the host-country government, or even without it, seek to be a good citizen of the host country, which in some cases may involve departure from the efficiency standard and from the short-run interest of the owner country.

BILATERAL MONOPOLY: DIRECT INVESTMENT IN RESOURCE INDUSTRIES IN DEVELOPING COUNTRIES

A particularly sensitive issue is the investment of large international companies in primary products—oil, copper, aluminum or bauxite, iron ore, and the like—in less developed countries. The true believers of the Left insist that the international companies "exploit" the developing countries in some sense, obtaining primary products cheaply and with great profits for themselves. Those at the other extreme maintain, on the contrary, that the international companies confer great benefits on the developing countries, providing them with capital, technology, markets, and so forth, that they would otherwise lack and furnishing a source of large gain through taxation. The difference in view arises because each critic compares the existing situation with a different alternative. To the Marxist, the alternative is the same oil wells, copper mines, refineries, ships, and so forth, but under local government ownership. To the staunch defender of the status quo, if the foreign direct investment were to be eliminated, the developing country territory would revert to desert or jungle.

The fact is that both company and host country have advantages to bring to the bargaining table. The company has an advantage to exploit: technology, preferred access to capital markets, efficient management, market outlets, and the like, and the host country has natural resources, the known or suspected existence of oil or minerals. This is a bilateral-monopoly situation, for which there is no determinate solution. Moreover, there is so much room between the minimum reserve price at which the country chooses to keep the company out and that at which the company chooses to stay out that the term *exploitation* confuses more than it clarifies.

Bargaining between the company and the country in this situation calls for the analysis of non-zero-sum game theory, akin to love and war, where the range of possible solutions runs from both happy (peace); to one happy, the other unhappy (victory); to both unhappy (devastating war). A more fruitful mode of analysis is to observe how the relative bargaining strengths of some hypothetical country and company change through time and as a consequence of policies. Initially, the advantage lies entirely on the side of the company. The underdeveloped country lacks markets, technology, capital, and management skills, which the company brings to the bargain. All the country has is the natural resource. Unless it can induce a great many companies to bid against one another for the concession, unrestricted by cartel divisions of territory, it has to take what is offered. If there is a gunboat in the harbor during the negotiations, its room for negotiation is still further restricted.

With the passage of time, however, the balance of bargaining strength shifts. The company is committed for a large investment. It may no longer have all the skills on its side, because native personnel has been technologically trained by the company, at the country's insistence, and government personnel has acquired economic sophistication about the industry. With proved reserves, the risks for new entrants are much reduced, which increases the readiness of competitors to enter. As the old agreement comes to an end, or if it can be abrogated, new terms much more favorable to the country replace the original arrangement. The companies make an attempt to "hold the line," as for a while was done in the petroleum industry with the 50–50 agreements under which the company and the local tax authorities divided profits plus royalties equally. But the bargaining position fails to come to rest. The country tends to enact new conditions: an overvalued exchange rate at which the company must buy local currency, for example, or a requirement that taxes be paid on the posted price rather than the sales price, which includes discount. New concessions provide for a 40–60 division, or a 25–75, and the old concessions must gradually be brought into line. The original bilateral bargain approaches the competitive solution. In the end the country may "exploit" the company by forcing it to accept less-than-normal profits, maintained just high enough to prevent it from withdrawing. And in many cases, of course, the countries go farther, and the companies do withdraw.

DIRECT INVESTMENT AND WELFARE

Where direct investment transfers capital, technology, and management from countries in which they are abundant to countries in which they are scarce, it is evident that efficiency has been increased and Pareto optimality approached. Whether world welfare has been increased depends on the observer's international social welfare function. Labor in the home country will be worse off, having to be combined with less capital, technology, and management, and hence receiving lower returns, and perhaps even experiencing unemployment. The gain for the investing country may include special benefits for capital and losses for labor which are regarded as unattractive; on the other hand, in the host country there are likely to be gains for labor and losses for capital, as well as the world cosmopolitan gain.

Apart from the static improvement through moving in the direction of equalizing factor prices internationally, there are also possibilities of dynamic gains: of training workers, or stimulating savings and capital formation through private and governmental increases in income.

There are also chances of blocking growth. The foreign firms may all be content to lose a little each year in defensive investment for the comfort of ensuring that no other company in the same field steals a march. All companies are of inefficient size. None can break out of the mold and start a process of growth. The seven refrigerator companies in the United States reproduce themselves in Canada, which has one tenth the population of the home country. In Latin America, there are too many, too small high-cost companies in the automobile field in Argentina, Brazil, and Chile.

The technology that the foreign firm brings to the host country may be suitable for the home country, with one set of factor proportions, but not for the host country with cheaper labor and more expensive capital. Nonetheless, it is often economical for the international company to adopt one technology worldwide rather than to adjust its technology and factor proportions from country to country to varying factor endowments and prices.

Research and development may be retained in the home office and confined largely to the needs of the home country, rather than each country having its own independent technology, competitive with those of other countries. The large economies of scale in standardization in manufactured goods confer a sizable advantage on the first in the field and may frustrate later superior innovations which cannot break through the stranglehold of the international corporation.

Although the international corporation is often accused of exploiting foreign labor through paying it too little (less than its marginal product?), through its superior purchasing power it may equally, or even more widely, contribute to dual markets in labor by overpaying its staff in terms of the conditions of the local labor market and by diverting bank credit, skilled workers, and growing firms from tasks needed for the domestic economy. In some oil countries it is said that many workers would rather wait in line for a high-paying job with the foreign firm than go to work immediately in the domestic economy, thus depriving the domestic sector of some of its potentially most energetic workers.

It is sometimes claimed that foreign firms distort efficient resource allocation by importing too much into the developing countries and exporting too little. This assumes either that the firms are not maximizing units or that the prices they face do not reflect social values. On the latter score, it is evident that where firms (occasionally) import components at high prices from tax-shelter subsidiaries in third jurisdictions, there is distortion from an efficient solution. Here the remedy is to eliminate tax evasion—as discussed in the next chapter. The suggestion that international firms restrict the exports of developing countries is one we deal with in the chapter that follows. It may now be noted, however, that to be valid, this suggestion presupposes that the international firm is not a miximizing entity.

THE INTERNATIONAL CORPORATION

It is an interesting question of economics whether markets or corporations are better devices for allocating resources among competing uses. The imperfections of markets have been discussed in Chapters 8 and 10. The possibility that international corporations may not maximize the efficient use of given resources has been touched upon in this chapter. But a case can be made that the development of the large international corporation in the 20th century will prove in the long run to be a more effective device for equalizing wages, rents, and interest rates throughout the world than trade conducted in competitive markets by small merchants. The analogy is with the national corporation, which in the United States after about 1890 helped to equalize wages, interest rates, and rents within the country's borders by borrowing in the cheapest market (New York) and investing where this was most productive in terms of cost and markets. The resultant movement of capital and shift in demand for labor were probably more effective in, say, raising wages in the South and lowering interest rates there than either trade by local companies or the limited direct movement of factors.

Today more and more companies are lifting their horizons from the national to the international scene, contemplating a wider geographic range of alternatives on where to borrow, build, sell, undertake research, or buy. The giant oil, chemical, automobile, tire, food-processing, and similar firms cover the world. Companies with subsidiaries in 40 or 50 countries are no longer rare, and those with 5 to 10 are common. To the extent that these companies coordinate the operations of firms in different markets with a view to achieving monopoly profits, and succeed in preventing new entry through imitation, it is not clear that they maximize welfare. To the extent that these companies buy in the cheapest market and sell in the dearest—with reference both to factors and goods—they provide an institutional network which may go farther than trade flows or the movement of labor or portfolio capital to equalize factor returns and improve welfare throughout the world.

It is not clear that international corporations do act in a nondiscriminatory way. Donald T. Brash observes that General Motors–Holden started out in Australia with a rule which said that purchases would be made in the United States unless the products concerned could be obtained 10 percent cheaper in Australia, and shifted over time to a criterion which said that products would be bought in Australia unless they were 10 percent cheaper elsewhere. Neither rule is justified. There is something to be said, to be sure, for rules of thumb which minimize the cost of decision making and do not require purchasing agents to get quotations from all over the world before they buy tacks. Costs of information are high, and some implicit rule for small amounts and differences as small as 10 percent may be justified on this account. If the General Motors regulations mean no more than this, they are understandable. If the discrimination is deliberate, however, and runs contrary to the rule of profit maximization when the facts are known, it suggests that corporations feel the need to have a citizenship, and that discrimination in favor of the country of citizenship can be the enemy of efficiency.

The international corporation is not truly international in another respect, despite the accusations of the Marxists. Each one has a home office and a home unit of account in which it keeps its liquid assets as well as calculates its maximization of profits. The truly cosmopolitan corporation which is prepared to move head office and liquid assets out of any country whose currency is weak has yet to arrive. Few have reached the position of even those U.S. corporations such as General Motors that have two offices, one for production (in Detroit) and one for finance (in New York). More and more corporations are organizing themselves worldwide with regional offices in Europe, Latin America, and the Far East. In the long run more companies may organize like the Arabian American Oil Company, with production in Saudi Arabia, marketing through its owning oil companies, and accounting in The Hague. It is a sign of the times, however, that the Saudi Arabian government wants the head office moved from New York to Dhahran.

That the large international corporation has not yet developed to its ultimate extent can be seen by looking at the balance sheet of any large American corporation which separates out earnings and assets and possibly sales in the United States and abroad. It will be seen that earnings are higher on foreign investment and on foreign sales than in the United States, whether for Otis Elevator, Du Pont, Gillette, Corn Products Refining, Standard Oil Company of New Jersey, or whatever. This trend would be much greater were it not for the existence of defensive investments in which the return is less than the average at home. The trend is partly a function of higher risks abroad than at home. But even if we had data on earnings per share and per dollar of sales in countries where the risks are little if any higher than in the United States, say for Canada, Australia, or the United Kingdom, the returns are still going to be higher abroad for the U.S. corporation (and higher in the United States for the foreign corporation with investments here) because the companies feel that they belong somewhere in particular and go afield only for a higher than ordinary return. When it earns an equal return (after risk) on every dollar and dollar equivalent invested everywhere in the world, the large corporation can be said to be truly international.

The truly international corporation would probably also behave differently from existing corporations, with their strong national base in recruitment, research and development, introduction of new products, reinvestment of earnings, and the like. The strongly nationalist company, for example, will hire its own nationals in all key jobs. The company which is trying to be a good citizen everywhere will hire local personnel. The truly international company will try to hire the best person for the job no matter what country that person comes from or what country he or she is going to. If there were such truly international corporations—and the trend is in this direction—it is evident that they would assist the pressure for factor-price equalization. Students may interest themselves in comparing the behavior of national corporations with foreign operations, multinational firms which try to act as good citizens everywhere, and truly international corporations which maximize profits worldwide on a variety of other dimensions: capital budgeting, exchange risk both for holding cash and for borrowing credit, research and development, new products, marketing, and the like.

DIRECT INVESTMENT AND THE BALANCE OF PAYMENTS

There is an apparent paradox that both home and host country are worried about the impact of direct investment on the balance of payments. The home country is worried that the initial investment supplies the home currency to world exchange markets; the host country puts it that once the investment has built up and becomes profitable, the annual drain on the balance of payments is likely to be serious.

The resolution of the apparent conflict, of course, is that the home country's worries are largely short run, the host country's long run.

In the home country

The Voluntary Credit Restraint Program of February 1965, replaced by the Mandatory Control Program of January 1968, was designed to limit the outflow of capital from the United States through direct investment and to increase remittance of dividends. Corporations were asked to produce a 5 percent improvement in the balance-of-payments impact of the enterprise, counting increases in goods exports and dividends repatriated plus reductions in funds transmitted abroad as "improvements." Attention was focused not on restraining direct investment but on limiting its impact on the balance of payments.

The initial naive notion was highly partial equilibrium in nature. It was thought, for example, that a reduction of $100 in direct investment would improve the balance of payments by $100 through reducing debits. It quickly became clear, however, that such a partial model was inappropriate. Other items in the balance of payments were affected by the change in direct investment. The task was to see what the total effect of a change in direct investment might be, counting repercussions and feedbacks throughout the system. The issue then became, What was the appropriate general model? If a given item of direct investment were reduced, what were the appropriate assumptions to make throughout the rest of the model as to the consequences that followed?

It was agreed, for example, that direct investment stimulates direct exports of equipment, especially where it takes place in developing countries without machinery industries of their own and also stimulates exports of components and inventories. A decline in direct investment would thus imply a decline in exports, at least in the first year. Direct investment also stimulated exports of other products in a company's line beyond that being manufactured abroad, since there was likely to be some excess marketing capacity along with that created for the new production. Here again was an offset loss to match part of the gain to the balance of payments from reduced investment. Other positive help to the balance of payments from direct investment consisted in rents and royalties from the use of the firm's technology, the flow of interest and dividends after operations were under way—although not all profits were remitted home. On the negative side were the displacement of exports by new production abroad, some imports of foreign output for the domestic market (such as components for the compact-car assemblies brought in by Ford, Chrysler, and General Motors), and, of course, the initial financial investment. The estimates for the various parameters were derived from balance-of-payments experience.

The most careful study for the United States was that undertaken by Gary Hufbauer and Michael Adler, which produced a series of different models, depending upon what one expected to happen in case a particular direct investment was not carried out. In the developing countries, for example, the alternative to a given direct investment might be that no other investment would be made in its place and that the market would continue to be supplied by exports from the United States (which had no foreign exchange content). In this case, direct investment produces serious losses in exports year after year and hurts the balance of payments. In Europe or Canada, on the other hand, a direct investment made at the right stage of the product cycle might be the alternative to a similar investment made by local enterprise. The exports displaced by the investment were lost in any event, so that the export loss was not an appropriate charge against direct investment. In this model, the balance-of-payments effects of direct investment are much less negative.

A similar study in Britain by W. B. Reddaway and his associates at the Cambridge Institute of Statistics came to the same conclusion: The impact of direct investment on the balance of payments on the home country depends upon what is assumed as the alternative, in case the investment is not made. A crucial assumption is what would happen to exports in the absence of the investment.

There is something to the view that the whole issue was blown up out of all proportion to its importance. A number of countries were concerned about direct investment, largely on noneconomic grounds. In the next chapter we conclude that this is fine so long as they recognize the economic consequences of intervention in the process. On the balance-of-payments question for the home country, the presumption is that the investor gets a fair return for his money, so that the present discounted value of the stream of net benefits is equal to or greater than the present value of the investment. If the country cannot afford to invest abroad, this suggests that the private rate of discount used by the investor in making his calculations is wrong, that is, too low, or that the investor has overestimated the value of I. There is something to this last possibility: direct investment can become a fad, just like any other activity of an economic, social, or cultural character. Firms can become confused by the fact that other firms are going abroad, and then rush abroad without seriously calculating the payoffs from so doing. The wave of direct investment abroad by American firms after about 1955 included some poor decisions which resulted in losses. In these cases, of course, the initial pressure on the balance of payments is not later offset by a flow of dividends.

The impact on the balance of payments of the host country

Direct investment can be regarded as negative for the balance of payments of both the investing and the host country if the one concentrates on the short run and the other on the long. And so the critics of investment do. Critics in the host country regard direct investment as "expensive." A small investment with little balance-of-payments impact in its early years will develop through reinvestment into a company with a sizable remittance of dividends abroad. Not infrequently, a comparison is made of the initial investment and the annual flow of dividends years later. In an early and notorious case, the Australian public became agitated in the early 1950s when it learned that one year's profits of General Motors–Holden Proprietary, Ltd., ran 14 percent of sales, 24 percent of funds employed, 39 percent of shareholders, equity, and 560 percent General Motors' original investment. Dividends paid from these profits amounted to 11 percent of funds employed, 18 percent of shareholders' equity, 260 percent of the original investment, and 8 percent of the Australian dollar export receipts for the year. All this occurred despite the fact that the company had priced the Holden car—occasionally held to be the forerunner of the Corvair—at a level which failed to clear the market. There was a six months' waiting list.

The General Motors–Holden case has been explained by one scholar as an example of the gambling-money thesis: direct investments grow at rapid rates because the companies plow back profits on the basis of some rule of thumb. The consequence is that the original investment pyramids rapidly and ultimately returns a stream of income which is large in relation to the original investment. Possibly. But this will only work if the product makes money, if, that is, the direct investor produces and sells a product the public wants. Not all direct investment can make profits to reinvest, and no direct investor will plow back profits unless the prospects for further profit are bright. Instead of being expensive, the direct investment may be regarded as efficient, in that it provided at limited cost an automobile the Australian public wanted very much.

On this score it is not legitimate to compare the subsequent rates of profits or dividends with the original investment. These are appropriately compared with total funds employed and with the foreign equity. Reinvestment each year must count as a separate and additional investment, so long as the investor had the option of taking his profits out. Reinvestment and pyramiding are not inevitable. In the last chapter we saw that investors don't have to lead the interest on past debts, nor do borrowers have to borrow it. Similarly, an initial direct investment does not always grow exponentially; such reinvestment as does take place is entitled to a return of its own.

One small point may be made about how Holden sales were financed. The introduction of a new product may produce a shift in demand to it. If total demand is unchanged, an increase in purchases of the Holden will involve decreases in purchases of other goods, which will cut back imports directly in part, and for the rest release resources which can be transferred into export-increasing or import-decreasing occupations. If, however, purchases of the Holden are all financed on credit—say installment loans—there will be an increase in total spending and an increased strain on total resources, leading to an import surplus. But the strain on the balance of payments should be blamed not so much on the direct investment as on the credit expansion.

A third point of considerable importance is that General Motors–Holden made its large profits behind substantial tariff protection. In July 1966, when the Japanese Toyota automobile managed to take over 7½ percent of the total market with imports into Australia, the Tariff Board raised the tariff from 35 to 45 percent ad valorem to ensure that the market was supplied by domestic manufactures instead of imports. The higher the tariff needed to maintain the marginal inefficient producer, the larger the profits of the inframarginal efficient producer. It is impossible to know what the General Motors–Holden profits were in the 1960s because the outcry in the 1950s was so great that General Motors bought up the minority stockholdings and transformed itself into a private company with a single owner under no obligation to publish its accounts. But to the extent that the Australian Tariff Board maintains high tariffs on imports, the General Motors–Holden profits are the result of Australian, not foreign company, action.

More fundamentally, when direct investment makes large profits, it is a sign that supply is very small in relation to demand and that new entry is called for to expand supply to the point where only normal profits are made. It would be desirable from the national point of view for a domestic producer to take advantage of the opportunity. But the high profits are there for the foreign investor because domestic enterprise is incapable of filling the vacuum. In the General Motors–Holden case, the high profits performed the function that they are supposed to under the capitalist system; the success of General Motors–Holden was followed by the establishment of Australian subsidiaries of other world automobile companies, such as Ford and Daimler-Benz, which would have restored profits to normal levels had it not been for the tariff. The high profits were needed as a signal of where output should be expanded. The monopoly power of the direct investor may preclude new entry. But where it is based on efficiency and skill, as in the General Motors case, imitation, not suppression, is called for.

It is of considerable interest that the rate of profits on U.S. direct investment in Australia went down sharply after 1960, when import controls were relaxed. Thus, of all the points made about the expensive character of direct investment and its impact on the balance of payments, it appears that the protection afforded to the foreigner through trade controls may be the most important. Monopolies and oligopolies make higher-than-normal profits. Tariffs and quotas protect monopoly positions. Governments which raise tariffs to give more monopoly protection have the capacity to reduce rates of profits on direct investment.

Note the possibility of a clash between the home and host country over the impact of direct investment on the balances of payments of the two. The home country may attempt to require the parent company to remit home profits earned abroad. The host country may impose foreign exchange control which prevents subsidiaries of foreign companies located within its borders (and hence squarely in its legal jurisdiction) from remitting dividends to parent companies. The conflict of interest is evident. We postpone its discussion, however, to the next chapter on policies toward direct investment.

SUMMARY

The foreign operations of domestic corporations, or direct investment, belong to the theory of monopolistic competition rather than to that of international capital movements. This theory explains better than any other the industries in which direct investment takes place, the crosscurrents, and the borrowing abroad.

Direct investment by developed countries in less developed countries cannot properly be regarded as exploitation without defining the terms. Typically the advantage in a bilateral-monopoly situation starts out all on the side of the investing company and gradually shifts to the host country.

The international corporation is likely in the future to become an important vehicle for equalizing the returns to factors of production and spreading technology internationally, as the national corporation has done domestically. Where the international corporation is faced by national jurisdictions with conflicting interests, it may slide between them, or it may be penalized by double penalties or conflicting commands. Harmonization of tax, antitrust, and balance-of-payments policies will help, especially if such policies put efficiency above citizenship as a criteria for corporate behavior.

The impact of direct investment on the balance of payments of the investing country is adverse in the short run, helpful in the long. The question as to what is the appropriate model for a balanced judgment remains open. Conversely the balance of payments of the host country is helped in the short run and may be hurt in the long. This is especially the case if profits on direct investment are helped by loose credit policies and high tariffs.

SUGGESTED READING

Texts

Charles P. Kindleberger, *American Business Abroad* (New Haven: Yale University Press, 1969).

Treatises, etc.

The Harvard Business School has a substantial program of research and publication under way on the international corporation. See especially Raymond Vernon, *Sovereignty at Bay* (New York: Basic Books, 1971). A useful collection of essays on various functional aspects of the subject is Charles P. Kindleberger (ed.), *The International Corporation* (Cambridge, Mass.: MIT Press, 1970).

Among the periodical literature, see H. W. Singer, "The Distribution of Gains between Investing and Borrowing Countries," in American Economic Association, *Readings in International Economics;* and Edith T. Penrose, "Foreign Investment and the Growth of the Firm," *Economic Journal,* June 1956, and "Profit Sharing between Producing Countries and Oil Companies in the Middle East," *Economic Journal,* June 1959.

The major monographs on the balance of payments are Gary C. Hufbauer and F. Michael Adler, *Overseas Manufacturing Investment and the Balance of Payments,* Tax Policy Research Study No. 1 (Washington, D.C.: U.S. Treasury Department, 1968); and W. B. Reddaway, J. O. N. Perkins, S. J. Potter, and C. T. Taylor, *Effects of U.K. Direct Investment Overseas* (Cambridge: Cambridge University Press, 1967).

Peter H. Lindert, "The Payments Impact of Foreign Investment Controls," *Journal of Finance,* December 1971 and December 1976, shows how the effect of capital flows may be good or bad for the balance, depending on policymakers' time preference.

The concept of defensive investment mentioned in this chapter is from Alexander Lamfalussy, *Investment and Growth in Mature Economics* (Oxford: Basil Blackwell & Mott, 1961).

The view that national firms and international firms behave identically is set out in I. Brecher and S. S. Reisman, *Canadian-American Economic Relations* (Ottawa: The Government Printer, 1957), chap. 7.

26

Policies toward
direct investment

In dealing with policies toward direct investment in the host country, the home country, and the world as a whole, greatest attention is
given to the first in this chapter. Host-country discontent with foreign
control of local enterprise is an important factor in policies of direct
investment. Some attention is paid to the labor case against foreign
investment in the United States, as represented by the Burke-Hartke
bill, which would change the basis of taxation of direct investment in
an effort to prevent the "export of jobs." The desirability of some
international regulation of the multinational corporation is also explored, with a view to alleviating the politicoeconomic problems
raised by direct investment.

No attention is given to the balance-of-payments questions raised in
the previous chapter. Interference with direct investment to improve
the balance of payments is clearly a second-best policy. The best attack is through macroeconomic tools.

INSTINCTIVE REACTIONS

It is only a slight exaggeration to suggest that the normal individual
has certain instincts which come into play in discussing foreign investment, irrational instincts which the study of economics is perhaps
designed to eradicate. Social man tends to some considerable degree
to be a peasant with a territorial instinct which leads him to object to
foreign ownership of national natural resources; a Populist, which
makes him suspicious of banks; a mercantilist, which makes him favor

exports over imports; a xenophobe, which leads him to fear those from outside the tribe; a monopolist who reacts strongly against competition; and an infant, to the extent that he wants to eat his cake and have it too. It is overstating the case to suggest that these instincts are at the basis of three quarters of the objections to foreign investment, but the proportion cannot be much below two thirds, or five eighths, or three fifths.

The peasant instinct appears more clearly in the reaction to foreign ownership of our land, or natural resources. The thought is that Nature or God gave the land to "us" and intended us to have it. It is all right, perhaps, for foreigners to build factories within our borders, but it goes contrary to nature to have them own our mines, forests, waterfalls, petroleum reserves, farms, or grazing land. To an economist, this is an example of the fallacy of misplaced concreteness. Natural resources, like man-made plant and equipment, are capital assets. If the asset is worth more to a foreigner than to a citizen of the country, it adds to natural wealth and income for the citizen to sell the natural resources to the foreigner and use the financial capital gained from the sale in lines of greater productivity. There is no difference between "natural" and man-made capital in this regard. Some natural resources, such as farmland and forests, are replaceable. These are exactly like man-made capital. Where natural resources are not replaceable, as in the case of mines, the capital values can be maintained through depletion allowances which are invested in exploration and discovery of new natural resources, or maintained as other kinds of productive capital, earning an equivalent income.

One sound economic reason might militate against the sale of a natural resource or any other asset to a foreigner. This is that while the foreigner may earn a higher return today on, say, the petroleum deposits, the day may come when the local resident can earn a still higher profit. The time profiles of the streams of income look like those shown in Figure 26.1, with I_f the return on the petroleum deposits in foreign ownership and I_h the return in local hands. In a world of perfect markets and perfect knowledge, the foreigner would not be able to outbid the local resident for the asset at period T, assuming that the amount by which I_h exceeded I_f after $T + 3$ was sufficient to pay interest on the shaded area by which I_h had initially been below I_f. But without perfect knowledge or perfect markets, or with a high degree of uncertainty attaching to the long-run shape of I_h, the foreigner may outbid the local investor. This is the infant-industry argument for restricting foreign investment, and of course it is a second-best argument. First best is to improve the perfection of knowledge and markets; second best is to save the asset from the clutches of the foreigner until the local resident can develop its full earning power. As in the

FIGURE 26.1

Possible time profiles of income earned on an investment in natural resources by foreign and home investors

Income earned on natural resource

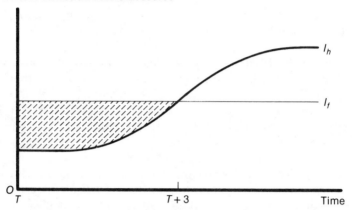

case of tariffs, the infant-industry argument can be a valid basis for interference with the market in the absence of optimal intervention. (Of course, if I_h is always below I_f, then allowing foreign ownership is optimal.)

We may recognize another argument against foreign ownership of, say, land—the national defense argument. A country might be nervous having all its oil wells, or all its coal mines, or strategic defense areas along its borders, in foreign ownership. The national defense argument, like the infant-industry argument, can be a valid basis for interference with the international market for assets within a country's borders. One can say more: Like the valid arguments for a tariff, **noneconomic and second-best arguments are the only potentially valid arguments for having the host country restrict foreign investment.**

Norway and Sweden limit foreign ownership of natural resources. Canada, Australia, and West Germany object to foreign ownership of banks. In the West German case, the basis is simple concern that the local monopoly might be adversely affected by competition. Like most industries that asset a transcendental reason for restricting imports of competitive goods, so local industry, including banking, is likely to produce high-minded rationalizations for limiting foreign bankers. It is sometimes hinted that foreign banks can serve an industrial espionage function, learning the financial strengths and especially the weaknesses of domestic industry and feeding the information to foreign competitors. But the main objection to foreign banks is the instinct of Populism, which has such a strong hold in the South and West of the United States. Fear of Wall Street and its malign schemes is endemic among farmers, small merchants, and Populists. That Populism merges into simple xenophobia or dislike of foreigners was indicated when the Canadian government decided against the First National City Bank's application to buy the Mercantile Bank on the ground that it was opposed to foreign ownership of banks, only to discover that the Mercantile Bank was already foreign owned—by Dutch interests. As in Australia, where British-owned banks are tolerated but American attempts to acquire ownership of banks are resisted, it may be less the fact of foreign ownership than the nationality of it.

FOREIGN ENTERPRISE AND EXPORTS

The restrictive business practice of parent companies' forbidding subsidiaries to export except as directed from the home country arises primarily in manufactures, since direct investment in primary production is generally for the explicit purpose of exporting; in fact, the complaint often expressed in this regard is that the foreign company is too ready to export, rather than to process goods within the national borders. Several points can be made relative to this essentially mercantilist criticism, which rests on the notion that exports are good, whereas import-competing industry is somehow not so worthy.

First, where the company is rational, it will export from the cheapest source. If a company does not export from a given country, there is a presumption, though perhaps not a very powerful one, that the subsidiary is high cost.

Second, where the country in question resists foreign investment and some resident enterprise enters into agreement to employ foreign technology, the resident enterprise is likely to obtain the patent or copyright only for the home market. It is thus unable to export patented products without permission. This is not meant to condone the restrictive practice, but rather to recognize that in awarding rights, the patent system avowedly monopolizes markets for the sake of encouraging invention.

Third, even if the investing enterprise maximizes profits by producing in the cheapest source, it is not disposed to invite surprises by encouraging all its subsidiaries to compete with one another in all markets. The supplying of third markets tends to be directed from the head office to avert surprise, in particular "dumping" or low-profit sales by one branch at the expense of another.

Fourth, the record of foreign enterprises in exporting manufactures from investments in developed countries is a good one. In Britain, for example, there is no complaint.

Fifth and last, the initial complaints in Canada over the poor export record of U.S. companies investing in manufacturing north of the border was based upon a tyro's error in economic reasoning. Most of the investments were in tariff factories, import-competing industry which was able to survive only because of high tariffs. An import-competing industry has a comparative disadvantage. To export, a company needs a comparative advantage. If it has a comparative disadvantage, it cannot have a comparative advantage. Therefore, it cannot export.

It is true, however, that occasionally an import-competing industry which needs a tariff to get started achieves low costs through economies of scale, learning by doing, and the like, and converts a comparative disadvantage into an advantage. This is the infant-industry argument, which, as an example of the second best, is valid. In the usual case, however, the criticism of foreign industry for its failure to export is made without recognition of the conditions necessary to give it validity. It is usually based on instinctual mercantilism.

FOREIGN CONTROL

To a considerable degree host countries object primarily to having foreigners control their enterprises. This nationalist sentiment is understandable and normal, but it is noneconomic. The economist has no basis for objecting if a country chooses to exclude foreign enterprise on the ground that it wants to preserve its national identity, or worries about being overwhelmed by goods made to foreign designs and specifications. Nationalism can be regarded as a public good, like national parks, paid for not by taxation but through forgoing opportunities for increases in national income. All the economist can rightly do is ask the decision makers to recognize that nationalism has a cost, and that they should be prepared to decide how much they want at what cost.

What is unacceptable is to want to have your cake and eat it too. The Watkins and Gray reports in Canada are surely within proper bounds when they urge the limitation of new foreign investment. Where they give rise to doubts is in their implications that policies of restriction are at the same time the ones that will maximize Canadian national income.

There is one possibility that the Watkins and Gray analysis is correct. This is the **optimum restriction** argument, exactly comparable to the optimum tariff line of reasoning. If a country restricts foreign investment, it might get it cheaper, given up nothing in the way of economic gains from foreign investment and achieving a measure of freedom from foreign control. Some observers claim that Japanese policy has been an adroit one of this kind. But the optimum tariff increases the welfare of a country only on the assumption of no retaliation. The non-zero-sum game of restricting foreign investment may readily evoke retaliatory measures. In this case it loses. And it seems unlikely that a country like Canada, with so few of the assets that the Japanese brought to their policy of restriction—cheap labor, a high marginal rate of savings, effective capacity for imitation and innovation—could gain from optimum restriction even without retaliation. Foreign enterprise on the whole is not that anxious to invest in Canada and, if restricted, will go away rather than beg to be let in on less favorable terms.

The choice for Canada and for countries like France is thus whether or not to leep out or keep down the foreigners, at some cost to national income but a gain for cultural independence. It is not without interest that the same issue is being faced within Canada by the French Canadians and within France by the Bretons. It is not an easy choice.

MARKET FAILURE

A strong case can be made for restricting foreign investment when markets function badly. When markets are evidently not working, it is a mistake to follow their dictates. In 1898, after the Spanish-American War, American carpetbaggers (like those of the North in the South in 1865, after the Civil War) went into Cuba and bought up much of the good sugar land. With the dislocation of war, it was not clear what such lands were worth. The prices at which they were sold did not represent the values that would have been achieved by orderly markets. It was a mistake for the newly independent Cuba to permit such purchases, and especially for the United States not to restrain its citizens. In Germany after World War II, a moratorium on new foreign investment was imposed in the three Western zones, largely at the insistence of the United States, until monetary reform and a reparations settlement had been achieved and market prices came closer to representing economic scarcities.

A less dramatic market failure of the same sort occurred in Brazil in the mid-1960s. A short, sharp deflation was produced by a Brazilian government attempt to adopt the recommendations of the International Monetary Fund. Stock market values were hard hit by the loss of liquidity. American and other foreign firms bought up Brazilian shares. To the Brazilians it looked like a plot to deprive them of the ownership of their enterprise. A strong second-best argument against permitting markets to operate when they are in a pathological state would have condoned orders by the Brazilian government forbidding the transfer of shares to foreigners in liquidity panics.

RESTRICTING NONESSENTIALS

Foreign investments are often thought to bring products that are not wanted—cosmetics, breakfast foods, soft drinks, or commodities such as ink—which local manufacturers can make (at least after a fashion). Steel, machinery, export products would be welcome; breakfast foods should stay home.

This is an excellent example of implicit market failure. What the critics are saying is that private values represented by market prices do not reflect social values, with the result that even if a foreigner could make a large profit in producing, say, Coca-Cola, which the market wants (as evidenced by profits available), the market is wrong, and its indications must be ignored. Consumer sovereignty is rejected.

This again is a second-best argument, and within its assumptions it is entirely valid. If the market is wrong, don't follow the market. It is unlikely, however, that the market is wrong for all "nonessentials" produced by foreigners, and right on everything produced at home. If a foreigner can make a profit producing ink, for example, this suggests that locally produced ink is a poor product or is wastefully made, so that a gain in resources is available to the community by shifting out of existing ways of making ink into different ones. If this were to mean unemployment for the labor currently engaged in ink production that was not offset by increased employment in the foreign plants, there is another second-best argument that factor prices do not reflect factor scarcities. Again the argument is valid within its assumptions, and asssuming that it is impossible to tackle the problem with first-best methods.

MITIGATING THE EFFECTS OF FOREIGN INVESTMENT

The agonizing character of national decisions over these issues is illustrated by the on-again, off-again quality of many decisions regarding foreign investment. Even before J.-J. Servan-Schreiber published *The American Challenge* in 1968, the French government changed its mind three times in five years, veering between encouragement and restriction. Many other countries (with and without changes of governments) confiscate foreign enterprise one year and pass new legislation to attract it the next. In the case of Peru, the nationalization of the International Petroleum Company's property, with a tangled legal history, and of some farm properties of the W. R. Grace Company, along with indigenous holdings, as part of land reform was accompanied in a matter of days by an advertisement in the *New York Times* welcoming foreign investment.

When they are not restricting foreign investment altogether, a number of countries have tried to develop solutions which would gain them more or most of the benefits of foreign investment—capital, technology, management, access to markets, training, and the like—without incurring the costs of loss of national control. In particular, countries have tried insisting on joint ventures; being selective as to the types of enterprises they will admit; limiting takeovers as contrasted with new enterprises; excluding foreigners in whole or part from the local capital market; entering into contracts separately for management, technology, and patents, and borrowing through portfolio securities; and forming "cartels" with neighboring countries to limit tax concessions granted to foreigners. It may be useful to say a word on each.

JOINT VENTURES

The insistence by many countries that they will welcome foreign enterprises in joint ventures with their own nationals, but not by themselves, seems, offhand, to be designed to provide training effects to domestic capitalists, at some cost in reducing total capital formation by excluding the import from abroad of the capital furnished locally. The insistence of joint ventures is often vaguer in purpose. In Canada, for example, there is talk of the desirability of a "Canadian presence" in ownership, direction, management, and upper staff to ensure that "Canadian interests" will be taken care of. Some simpleminded observers fear that foreign enterprise will dominate government circles; a more sophisticated view is that wholly and jointly owned foreign enterprises reduce the vitality of local politics by subtracting the political influence of a large share of Canadian business, as the foreigners stand aside rather than mix in.

The enterprises themselves appear to detest joint ventures, not, so far as one can tell from what they say (if this can be believed), because of the "national presence," but because of the built-in conflict of inter- est. The local shareowners may want dividends, whereas the foreigners may want capital gains. Or the time may come when the enterprise needs more capital and the local capitalists are unable to provide their pro rata share.

In a rational world, of course, any owner would be willing to sell off any proportion of his ownership of an enterprise "if the price were right." The view of many firms that they are willing to enter into joint ventures where the local partner contributes something "in kind," but not money, is irrational, since with an adequate pricing system any contribution in kind can be valued in money. But the market for direct investments is not a perfect market, as our oligopoly theory asserts. Joint ventures in Japan are usually welcomed by investors because the culture is so strange to Western ways that Caucasians need an indigenous partner to interpret market and government to them. In Latin countries with peculiar systems of negotiating over corporate income taxes, the local partner makes a contribution in serving as a cultural filter between foreigner and tax authorities.

But partners frequently fall out. The general record of joint ventures is that one ultimately has to buy out the other. An oil company wants its profits in producing areas. Its marketing partner is unhappy unless profits are made in marketing. In this regard, of course, every taxing authority is a joint partner of all firms, including those that appear to be 100 percent owned. To redistribute profits nationally so as to minimize taxes is certain to get the company into trouble with this particular partner.

SELECTIVITY

Selectivity is choosing among industries in permitting foreign investment, with limitations for nonessentials, banks, newspapers, natural resource industries, and the like. It may be an optimum restriction strategy or a second-best policy in a world of market failure. It is likely to be played badly, from instinct rather than careful economic reasoning, in which case it will lose national income.

LIMITING TAKEOVERS

There is a strong argument for encouraging new enterprises and prohibiting the purchase of existing firms. It rests on opposition to monopoly. In an industry of six firms in a country, a takeover keeps the number at six; a new entry moves it to seven, and perhaps nearer "workable competition."

The argument, as we have said, is strong. But the policy is recommended as well in cases where it is weak, where there is already plenty of competition, and where a country instinctively feels that buying out an old firm is somehow very different from building a new one. The thought verges on the fallacy of misplaced concreteness.

Assume that in an industry with 20 firms there is one which makes no profit because its technology is old, its management moribund. The plant and equipment will be worth more to a foreign firm than to the existing owners. If the assets are sold to a foreigner through a takeover, some of the difference will be shared with the old owners. They are better off. The foreigner is better off for having bought the assets below their value to him. There is net gain all around. A policy of requiring the foreigner to build a new plant and the existing owner to scrap his plant is clearly wasteful.

EXCLUDING FOREIGNERS FROM THE LOCAL CAPITAL MARKET

It was noted in the previous chapter that foreign enterprise can adversely affect local markets for labor and capital by dominating them, drawing off skilled workers and young managers, or siphoning off savings which might otherwise be invested in nascent indigenous firms. Because of training effects, the host country typically requires foreign firms to hire certain percentages of its labor at all levels of skill on the local market. It may be desirable in the capital market, however, to deny foreign enterprise access to local banks and investment bankers.

The restriction has a balance-of-payments aspect. The foreign exchange authorities are suspicious of firms that enter a country without bringing in foreign exchange, tendering technology or management or similar investment in kind as their share of the equity and expecting to raise the funds for bricks and mortar in the local market. With growth and reinvestment, the ultimate strain on a country's foreign exchange earnings may be substantial on a trivial investment in foreign exchange. This, however, is an inadequate way of analyzing the problem, since the postponement of repatriation of profits at all stages has been the equivalent of an investment in foreign exchange.

Where capital markets function poorly, however, there is a second-best argument for requiring foreign investors to bring money, and to furnish none locally. It must be used gingerly, however, because if the screw is tightened too hard, the investor may be driven off. The matter is one for bargaining, not doctrine.

TAKING THE PACKAGE APART

The success of the Japanese in resisting foreign investment while hiring technology and borrowing capital to the extent that they were needed has led a number of observers to urge "taking the foreign investment package apart"—buying technology, management, and capital separately, as required, rather than acquiring them gift-wrapped in a foreign enterprise. The notion is a useful one to analyze. It is strongly possible, however, that it lends itself much better to the Japanese, with their skill in imitating foreign technology and adapting it to their requirements, than it would to the ordinary run of developing or even developed countries.

The basis for foreign investment is that the corporation can earn more on its management, technology, capacity to coordinate operations in different vertical stages, and the like, than it can by selling its skills separately. It earns, that is, a rent, rather than an ordinary return on marginal product. Sometimes it is a close decision whether to sell the technology under a royalty contract or to invest oneself. In these cases, strong insistence of the host country in favor of a royalty arrangement may tip the balance. But as a rule the decision is not close. Technology leased abroad is quickly dispersed; one keeps control of it best by using it oneself in a direct investment.

Creating new products through hiring research firms is said to be expensive. This is possible. Advice is also expensive. It may be possible to improve local management permanently under contracts with Peat-Marwick, Booz-Allen, or McKinsey for a short period, rather than to pay for management through infinity by permitting direct investment. In this case, the local management must be quick learners.

Surely it is desirable for the host country to explore the potential for taking the package apart and buying only those parts of it that are needed, in the right quantities. The opportunities for doing so are probably limited so long as the host country is relatively undeveloped.

DISINVESTMENT AND DISAPPEARING INVESTMENT

Albert Hirschman has made the point that portfolio investment is superior to direct investment in that it can be repatriated in small increments, bond by bond, whereas the repatriation of direct investment is all or nothing, and convulsive. He would provide for government policies of disinvestment, the host country undertaking bit by bit over time to pay off the capital investment. P. N. Rosenstein-Rodan wants to provide in initial investment contracts that after a certain period of time the ownership reverts to the country, at a price agreed upon in advance.

There is much to think about in these proposals, but they suffer from the same weakness as long-term commodity contracts—the inability to find the right price long in advance. Suppose that company A invests in mining in country X in the year T, with a provision in the contract that at $T + 15$ the property will revert from company A to country X, or the company it designates, at a price of $1 million. For the next 14 years, but especially the last 4 or 5, company A is trying to make sure that it does not have more than $1 million of assets in its investment, and country X is trying to make sure that the amount does not go below $1 million. How best to employ the assets so as to maximize the present discounted value of the firm—the efficient solution—is lost to sight. What is implied by long-term future arrangements is revealed by the action of the government of Venezuela in 1971 in imposing conservators for certain oil companies whose concessions run out in 1984, on the ground that the companies' interest was to leave as little as possible of plant and equipment or oil in the ground, whereas Venezuela wanted to inherit going concerns. The price in this case was zero, but the principle is the same: to agree on a price long in advance is to distort incentives. It might be possible to agree in advance that the company would remain a going concern and to agree on a technique for appraising its value. But even this is likely to be fraught with controversy.

THE BURKE-HARTKE BILL

If the world and the United States gain from foreign investment, as was suggested in the last chapter, it is by no means clear that American labor gains. In fact, the case can be made that direct investment is the export of jobs, and that plants going abroad to serve the foreign market better or to produce components or finished goods for the United States are "runaway plants," like the firms in the garment industry in the first quarter of the century that ran to nonunion towns as the needle trades were organized into unions. In the late 1960s and early 1970s, the AFL-CIO altered its traditional benevolent attitude toward world trade and investment and called for a change in taxes on international income, supervision of foreign investments, U.S. government regulation of U.S.-based international firms, "fair labor" standards worldwide, and as a stopgap measure pending the adoption of these policies, regulation of the flow of imports into the United States. In due course, the labor movement got behind the Burke-Hartke bill, which was unsuccessfully introduced into Congress in 1972. This bill proposed to "close tax loopholes" which favored foreign investment and in particular to shift from the principle of "crediting" income taxes paid abroad against corporate income taxes due in the United States to the practice of deducting such taxes from income, and imposing taxes on foreign income when it is earned, rather than when it is repatriated to the United States.

The significance of these provisions can be illustrated by a simple example. Suppose that a U.S. firm with a subsidiary in Canada earns $100 there, pays a tax of $50 in Canada, and repatriates $50 to the United States. Its income for U.S. tax purposes would be $100. Assuming that the U.S. corporate tax rate were the same as the Canadian, its tax liability would be $50, but the payment made to Canada would count as a tax credit, and it would pay nothing in the United States. Shifting from crediting foreign taxes to deducting them as an expense would mean that income for U.S. tax purposes would be $50 ($100 less $50 of taxes paid in Canada). At a 50 percent rate, the U.S. tax on this amount would be $25. Total taxes on the $100 would thus be $75.

A change from taxing on the basis of repatriated profits to taxing on profits when earned is best illustrated by an example in which tax rates abroad are lower than those in the United States. Assume that the $100 of profits was earned abroad in a jurisdiction with a corporate tax rate of 25 percent and that the $75 remaining after foreign corporate taxes were paid was reinvested abroad. No U.S. tax liability would accrue. In a sense, the U.S. government would be granting the corporation an interest-free loan of the U.S. tax liability ($25 with the tax credit, or $37.50, with foreign taxes a deduction rather than a credit) until the funds were ultimately repatriated, which might be never. The Eisenhower Administration proposed a shift from repatriated profits to earned profits in the legislation which ultimately resulted in the Revenue Act of 1962. It was rejected by Congress after the vigorous protests of business. The argument for taxing earnings is equity with U.S. taxpayers. The argument against is that the double taxation, or the higher rate of taxation of the United States, distorts competition against the local companies. It is also insisted that until the funds are repatriated, the parent company has nothing to pay with.

It is impossible in this space to discuss adequately the efficiency, equity, and administrative features of the two systems of taxation. A case of sorts can be made for or against almost any principle. To change from the tax credit to deducting foreign taxes where tax rates are roughly equivalent is to submit foreign investment to double taxation, as against domestic investment. On the other hand, to apply taxation on the basis of repatriated profits rather than earnings where taxes abroad are lower than U.S. rates is to subsidize foreign investment at the expense of domestic investment. **Tax neutrality** would appear to call for the tax credit and taxation on earnings rather than remittances. But the AFL–CIO, in supporting the Burke-Hartke bill, is perhaps not concerned with tax neutrality. Protection for domestic industry is admittedly discriminatory. The optimal policy would seem to be to maintain full employment in the United States by macroeconomic means and to allow capital to be invested where it can earn the highest return in the world, without reference to taxes (or assuming that rates of income tax are harmonized). This is a Pareto optimal solution under certain conditions. Since it would reduce its labor's monopoly position, it would be too much to expect labor to embrace it.

GOVERNMENT GUARANTEES AND INSURANCE

A corollary of the case for tax neutrality is that the United States may have made a mistake in the postwar period in seeking to stimulate foreign investment by insurance and guarantees against expropriation in the developing countries. The theory was that foreign economic development could be assisted by private investment, which would relieve the government of the necessity of making loans directly. To

the extent that private investment was inhibited by fear of expropriation, there was a case to be made for insuring the investor against
political, but not economic, risks. The difficulty has been that this has
injected the U.S. government into investment disputes which are
doubtless better settled without its intervention.

The home country is a partner in any foreign investment to the
extent that it earns a tax on the profits and permits losses to be written
off against other corporate taxes due. This may be enough. Where the
investor is sophisticated and the host country is learning gradually that
it cannot have it both ways—nationalizing old properties without
compensation and expecting to continue to get new capital, technology, and management assistance from abroad—it is sufficient to leave
the complex issues of foreign investment to the private market on the
one hand and the host country on the other. The home country's
intrusion—through the application, say, of the Hickenlooper amendment, which requires cutting off foreign assistance to countries which
nationalize U.S.-owned property—is frequently counterproductive.

A FORUM FOR RESOLVING CONFLICTS OVER DIRECT INVESTMENT

Much of the difficulty over direct investment is political. A corporation with assets in two jurisdictions may well be a vehicle for the
intrusion of one sovereign power into the jurisdiction of another. The
United States tell corporations in its midst not to allow their foreign
subsidiaries, located in the jurisdictions of other governments, to trade
with the enemy, to provide sophisticated equipment which would
assist a country to become a nuclear power, or to act in restraint of
trade. It urges those corporations to bring home profits, and the like.
Thus such corporations may be subject to both double taxation and
conflicting directives. A useful device might be a forum to discuss
such issues.

If a corporation of this kind is sometimes subject to double taxation,
it frequently threads its way between tax systems, or systems of regulation, so as to escape any or all of the controls governments have
found it useful to impose. It may divert profits from one jurisdiction to
another by charging arbitrary "transfer prices" on materials or components. It may establish financial subsidiaries in the Bahamas, Panama,
Liechtenstein, or Luxembourg to escape financial regulation. In due
course, with national regulations on such issues as pollution not
everywhere uniform, corporations may evade the restraint of the best
regulation by establishing themselves where regulation is weak or
nonexistent.

It has been claimed that the rise of the national corporation in the United States weakened the power of the states, counties, and cities and required a corresponding rise in the power of the national government and of national unions. Today the rise of the international corporation has produced a corresponding loss of sovereignty on the part of nation-states, calling for the beginnings of international regulation in the fields of taxation, trading-with-the-enemy acts, and antitrust and financial regulations. The process is necessarily conducted case by case, rather than by writing a code with rules and exceptions. The developing countries would undoubtedly be suspicious of rules agreed upon by the developed countries, and though invited, they should not be pressured into joining. If developing countries were to choose to do so, they could stand aside, as in the trade field from GATT, and even organize on their own, as in UNCTAD.

The rise of neomercantilism in the world in the past few years may be a reflection of the weakening of sovereign states in a world of mobility of capital, skilled labor, and corporate management. As the world gets smaller, it becomes more and more necessary to harmonize tax rates, economic policies, and attitudes toward forces like the multinational corporation, which implies a loss of national sovereignty. One reaction is to try to suppress the mobility and the international forces. Another is to seek to contain them with international institutions.

SUMMARY

Host-country restrictions on foreign investment are generally motivated by the instinctive feelings of the peasant, the Populist, the mercantilist, the xenophobe, the monopolist, and those who want to have their cake and eat it too. The only valid arguments for restricting direct investment in the host country are noneconomic or second best. When markets fail to work, it makes little sense to accept the dictates of the market.

Many countries concerned about direct investment seek to restrain it by requiring joint ventures, selectively refusing certain types of investment, refusing permission for takeovers of existing companies, or limiting access to the local capital market. They may also seek to get the benefits of foreign investment without foreign control by hiring capital, technology, management, and so forth, separately. Agreements among potential host countries to limit tax concessions are useful but difficult to achieve. To restrict investments to a particular period of years poses the problem of determining in advance what the investment will be worth in future, or at a minimum agreeing to procedures for establishing such values.

The opposition to direct investment in the United States seems to be largely in the interest of a single factor—labor. This opposition poses a complex issue of keeping the tax system neutral. Early postwar attempts to stimulate investment in developing countries may now be ready for the scrap heap.

In the long run, it is desirable to develop a body of international regulations to prevent companies from sliding between national regulatory and tax systems and to guard them against double jeopardy, with two jurisdictions taxing a given profit or pulling a corporation in diverging directions.

SUGGESTED READING

Texts

V. Salera, *Multinational Business* (Boston: Houghton Mifflin, 1969).

Treatises, etc.

The issues faced by host countries are raised for the most part in the monographic literature, for example: Donald T. Brash, *United States Investment in Australian Manufacturing Industry* (Cambridge, Mass.: Harvard University Press, 1966); John H. Dunning, *American Investment in British Manufacturing Industry* (London: Allen and Unwin, 1958); Helen Hughes and You Poh Seng, *Foreign Investment and Industrialization in Singapore* (Canberra: Australian National University, 1969); M. Kidron, *Foreign Investment in India* (London: Oxford University Press, 1965); A. E. Safarian, *Foreign Ownership of Canadian Industry* (Toronto: McGraw-Hill of Canada, 1966; and A. Stonehill, *Foreign Ownership in Norwegian Enterprises* (Oslo: Central Bureau of Statistics, 1965).

Policy-oriented statements are found especially in the so-called Watkins report in Canada: "Foreign Ownership and the Structure of Canadian Industry," *Report of the Task Force on the Structure of Canadian Industry*, prepared for the Privy Council (Ottawa: Queen's Printer, January 1968); and the so-called Gray report: *Foreign Direct Investment in Canada*, published by the government of Canada, Ottawa, 1972.

Points

Worth reading for its political points, if not its economic analysis, is Jean-Jacques Servan-Schreiber, *The American Challenge* (New York: Atheneum, 1968). A Marxist view is set forth by Harry Magdoff in *The Age of Imperialism* (New York: Modern Reader Paperbacks, 1969) (paperback).

The Hirschman proposal for disinvestment is found in his *How to Divest in Latin America and Why;* Princeton, 1969. The Rosenstein-Rodan proposal is published in Inter-American Development Bank, *Multinational Investment in the Economic Development and Integration of Latin America* (Bogota, Colombia: Round Table, April 1968).

Lawrence B. Krause and Kenneth W. Dam, *Federal Tax Treatment of Foreign Income* (Washington, D.C.: Brookings Institution, 1964) explores the complex tax issues. Marina v. N. Whitman's thesis explores guarantees and insurance in *Government Risk-Sharing in Foreign Investment* (Princeton: Princeton University Press, 1965).

A strong statement of the AFL–CIO objections to foreign investment by American companies is contained in vol. 1 of *Papers Submitted to the Commission on International Trade and Investment Policy,* in Nathaniel Goldfinger's "A Labor View of Foreign Investment and Trade Issues."

appendixes

appendix A*

Factor supply, technology, and production possibilities

DERIVATION OF THE TRANSFORMATION CURVE FROM THE PRODUCTION FUNCTION AND FACTOR SUPPLIES

A **production function** is a statement of the relationships between physical quantities of inputs of factors and the physical output of a given commodity. Geometrically it can be shown by plotting the various combinations of two factors needed to produce given amounts of the commodity in question. In Figure A.1A, T–T is an **isoquant** representing a given quantity of a single commodity, cloth. T'–T' is a higher isoquant, that is, a greater amount of cloth, such as 200 yards, in comparison with the 100 yards represented by T–T. At a given point, such as W, production is in equilibrium if the ratio of marginal physical products of labor and land is equal to the ratio of the prices of the two factors. A line tangent to an isoquant represents the relative price of land and labor. Given the production point, W, one can deduce the relative price of the factors, equal to the slope S–S, or given the quantity to be produced, T–T, and the price of the factors, S–S, one can find the least cost combination, W. OR is an expansion path for the relative price S–S (to which S'–S' is parallel). By adding inputs of land and capital, with the relative prices equal to the slope of S–S, one proceeds to higher isoquants by the path OR. If there are constant returns to scale, the expansion path at constant factor price will be a straight line. This simplest form of production function is called **linear homogeneous**. The isoquant T–T in Figure A.1A shows that labor can fairly

---

* Appendix to Chapter 2.

FIGURE A.1A
Production function for cloth

FIGURE A.1B
Production functions with fixed factor proportions

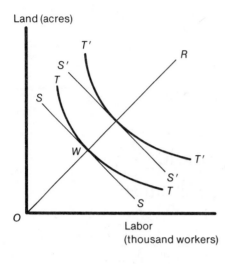

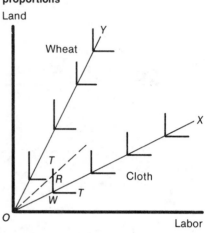

easily be substituted physically for land in the production of cloth, and vice versa.

The foregoing is by way of review. In Figure A.1B we show two production functions, for wheat and cloth, in which factor proportions are rigidly fixed but different in each commodity. The expansion paths, OX for cloth and OY for wheat, are straight lines for any positive set of factor prices. Any different set of factor proportions, such as OR instead of OW on the isoquant T–T, will reduce the marginal physical product of one factor (in this case land) to zero. Its price will also fall to zero.

In Figure A.1B cloth is unambiguously labor intensive and wheat unambiguously land intensive. At any positive relative price of land and labor, cloth will use more labor relative to land than wheat.

In Figure A.2 we construct a so-called **Edgeworth-Bowley box diagram,** in which the dimensions of the box represent the amounts of land and labor in a country, which we shall call Britain. These factor supplies are assumed to be homogeneous in character and fixed in amount. The production function for cloth is drawn with its origin in the lower left-hand corner of the box at O, and with its isoquants, T–T, T'–T', and so on, moving out and up to the right. Its expansion path is OX. If all the labor in Britain (OR) were used to make cloth, only RX of land would be required, and $O'X$ of land would be left unemployed. At X, the marginal physical product of land would be zero.

The production function for wheat is drawn reversed and upside down, with its origin at O' and extending downward and to the left. Its

FIGURE A.2
Edgeworth-Bowley box diagram with fixed factor proportions

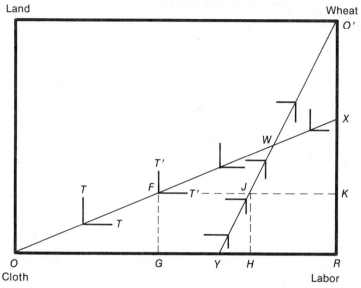

expansion path is *OY*. At *Y*, all the land would be employed, and *YR* of labor, but *OY* of labor would be unemployed. *OX* and *O'Y* intersect at *W*, which is the only production point in the box diagram where there can be full employment and positive prices for both factors. At any other point on either expansion path, say *F* on *OX*, land and labor will be able to produce at *J* on the expansion path for wheat; *OG* of labor will be engaged in cloth, and *HR* in wheat. *RK* of land will be employed in cloth, and *O'K''* in wheat. But *GH* of labor will be unemployed.

The curve *OWO'*, as in Figure A.2, is in effect a transformation curve, showing the various combinations of wheat and cloth which can be produced in Britain, given the factor endowments of the country. The only point providing full employment of the two factors and positive factor prices is *W*. *OWO'* does not look like a transformation curve, because it is given in terms of physical units of land and labor, rather than physical units of production. If we remap the *OWO'* curve in Figure A.2 from factor space into commodity space in terms of units of wheat and cloth and turn it right side up, it appears to be a normal production-possibility curve, though kinked at *W*, as in Figure A.3.

If cloth and wheat were produced with fixed factor coefficients, and these were identical, the two expansion paths would coincide, as in A.4A, and the transformation curve becomes a straight line, as in A.4B. But this means that land and labor are always used in the same combi-

FIGURE A.3
Transformation curve derived from Edgeworth-Bowley box diagram with fixed factor proportions

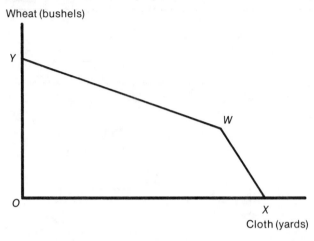

nation so that they might well be regarded as a single factor. This is equivalent to the labor theory of value and its resultant straight-line transformation curve. A similar straight-line transformation curve would be produced by constant costs and identical production functions in the two commodities. It is vital to distinguish between **constant costs** and **constant opportunity costs.** The straight-line transformation curve represents constant opportunity costs. If the production functions for the two commodities differ, the transformation curve will exhibit curvature even though there are constant returns to scale in each commodity taken separately.

FIGURE A.4A
Constant opportunity costs: Identical fixed factor proportions

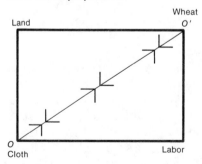

FIGURE A.4B
Transformation curve derived from Figure A.4A

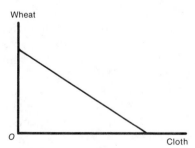

When the law of variable proportions holds and there is the possibility of substitution between factors in the production of a commodity, there is no unique expansion path. Instead, a separate expansion path can be drawn for any given set of factor prices, or we can draw in the isoquants for both commodities and trace out a locus of points of tangency between them. This locus represents the efficiency path, or the maximum combinations of production of the two goods which can be produced with the existing factor supply. It is shown in Figure A.5A. Suppose that production were to take place at W, away from the

FIGURE A.5A
Maximum efficiency locus under variable factor proportions

FIGURE A.5B
Transformation curve derived from Figure A.5A

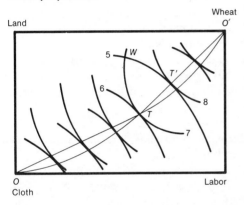

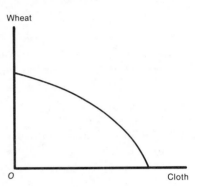

efficiency locus. W is on cloth isoquant 7, and on wheat isoquant 5. But there is a point T, also on cloth isoquant 7, which is on a higher isoquant (6) of wheat. It would therefore be possible to produce more wheat without giving up any cloth. Or there is a point T' on wheat isoquant 5 which is on cloth isoquant 8. It would be equally possible to produce more cloth and the same amount of wheat. Any point off the locus of tangencies of isoquants of the two production functions is therefore inefficient, insofar as it would be possible to get more output of one commodity without losing any of the other, by moving to the locus.

The efficiency locus is the exact analogue of the "contract curve" in exchange theory. Here the dimensions of the box are given by fixed supplies of commodities; a point off the contract curve represents initial endowments of two individuals, with utility maps measured from origins in the two corners; and the two individuals can improve their utility by moving from the initial endowment point to the contract curve.

When the Edgeworth-Bowley box is used for production, it shows not only the efficient combinations of outputs but also factor combinations and factor prices. Unlike the transformation curve (A.5B), it cannot show the relative price of wheat and cloth. If we assume that production is at T, however, the factor proportions in cloth are represented by the slope of OT, and the factor proportions in wheat by $O'T$. It will be obvious that the indicated allocation employs all the land and all the labor. The relative price of land and labor with these outputs is represented by the slope of the tangency to the maximum efficiency locus at T.

VARIABLE FACTOR SUPPLIES

To use the Edgeworth-Bowley box approach in its usual form, one must assume that the national factor supplies are fixed. This is somewhat unrealistic, since the total size of the labor force, the stock of accumulated nonhuman capital, and even the supply of improved land do respond to the rewards being offered to such factors in the marketplace.

Fortunately, the geometry can be altered to allow for a response of each factor to its rate of return. Jaroslav Vanek has demonstrated that it is possible to distinguish between two kinds of production-possibility curves, one showing the technical transformation schedules between two goods, which does not allow for reactions of the factors to changes in factor prices, and an economic one, which takes such reactions into account. The economically possible curve lies within the technically feasible curve, except at one or more points where they coincide, since the technical possibilities frontier is an envelope curve of various feasible curves.

SUGGESTED READING

The literature on comparative advantage and factor supply is enormous, and the student is referred to Richard E. Caves, *Trade and Economic Structure* (Cambridge, Mass.: Harvard University Press, 1960), chaps. 3, 4, and 5, for a review and bibliography. Two of the outstanding articles, R. Robinson, "Factor Proportions and Comparative Advantage," *Quarterly Journal of Economics*, May 1956, and T. M. Rybczynski, "Factor Endowment and Relative Commodity Prices," *Economica*, November 1955, are gathered in the 1967 American Economics Association, *Readings in International Economics*, part 1.

The geometry of adding variable factor supplies to the model is sketched in Jaroslav Vanek, "An Afterthought on the 'Real Cost–Opportunity Cost Dispute' and Some Aspects of General Equilibrium under Conditions of Variable Factor Supplies," *Review of Economic Studies*, June 1959.

The algebraic version of the basic two-by-two-by-two model common to most of Chapters 2 through 5 and Appendixes A through C has been elegantly condensed into a workable rate-of-change form in Ronald W. Jones, "The Structure of Simple General-Equilibrium Models," *Journal of Political Economy*, vol. 73, no. 6 (December 1965), pp. 557–72. Vanek's portrayal of trade and production under variable factor supplies can be incorporated into the Jones model by making the rates of change in factor supplies depend partially on rates of return.

appendix B

Deriving the offer curve: Another way of modelling trade demand and supply

The supply and demand curves introduced in Chapters 2 and 3 have several advantages. They are familiar, and they offer the easiest way of seeing how to quantify the welfare effects of trade on producer and consumer groups in each country. They are also easily extended to the task of analyzing trade effects in many different goods, each taken one at a time. Yet much of the theoretical literature uses another geometric device that gives some of the same information: the *offer curve,* showing how the export and import quantities a nation chooses will vary with the international terms of trade. The frequent use of the offer curve in the more advanced literature means that anyone seeking to master that literature needs to know how the curve is derived and used. This appendix gives the geometric derivation of the offer curve. Appendix D shows how it has been used in discussing optimal tariff policy.

James E. Meade has set out a neat geometric device that builds the offer curve out of the production-possibility curve and the consumption indifference map. The beauty of the technique rests partly in its bridging this gap, but also in that it enables one to demonstrate, neatly and simply, the impact of trade on production, consumption, the gains from trade, and so on. Although many students may be terrified at the prospect of learning still another geometric technique, the braver are encouraged to plunge ahead and acquire another analytic tool.

The first step is to draw the production block and consumption indifference curve for country A without trade, in the usual way. This is done in Figure B.1. Following Meade's notation, the horizontal axis

FIGURE B.1
The derivation of the trade indifference map from the consumption indifference map

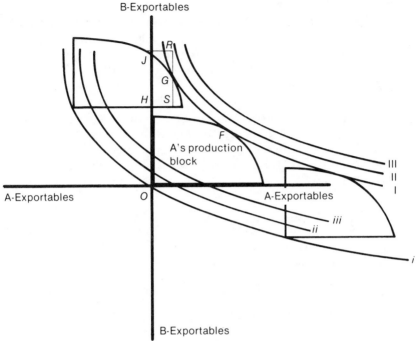

measures A's exportables, which are B's importables; the vertical axis, B's exportables.

Now, holding it level and upright, slide the A production block up and down the no-trade consumption indifference curve, keeping it tangent to the same consumption indifference curve, I. The origin of the block, O, will trace out a trade indifference curve, i. At every point on this curve, A will be indifferent whether it trades or not. It can remain at O and produce and consume at F. Or it can move along the curve to the point where the origin of its production-possibility block is at T. It will then produce at G, and trade HT of A-exportables for HO of B-exportables. The reason that it is indifferent between O and T is that it can produce at either F or G along its production-possibility schedule (transformation along the schedule is assumed to be cost-less); and G is on the same consumption indifference curve as F. At G, of course, it consumes $GS + HO$ of B-exportables and only SH of A-exportables.

Note that the trade indifference curve has a different shape than the consumption indifference curve. This is because production has shifted as well as the proportions of goods consumed. If J in the upper left-hand position of the A-block corresponds to F in the no-trade position, it is clear that in shifting from O to T, production of A-exportables has increased by RJ, and production of B-exportables has decreased by RG. A trade indifference curve is flatter, to take account of these production changes. When production is fixed and no movement of resources is possible, the trade indifference curve will parallel the consumption indifference curve.

There is a trade indifference curve corresponding to every consumption indifference curve, and hence a trade indifference map. A country is better off, the higher the trade indifference curve it is able to reach. Along any single curve, it is indifferent between one position and another. But in Figure B.1 country A is better off the higher the trade indifference curve it can reach (moving from southwest to northeast).

A's offer curve will now be constructed. It represents the locus of a series of tangencies of various price lines to the trade indifference map of successively higher indifference curves. This is shown in Figure B.2. The initial slope of the offer curve through the origin represents

FIGURE B.2
The derivation of the offer curve for country A from its trade indifference map

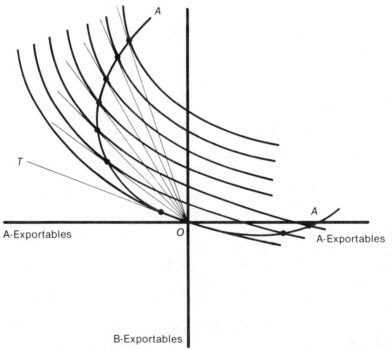

the price which would prevail without trade. As higher and higher prices for *A*-exportables are offered in terms of *B*-exportables, *A* will be enabled to move to higher and higher trade indifference curves and will be disposed to offer, as the figure is drawn, first more and more *A*-goods for larger quantities of *B*-exportables, and then less. Note that if the price for *B*-goods gets higher than *OT*, *A* will export *B*-exportables in exchange for *A*-goods. The offer curve moves into the southeast quadrant, but only for very high prices for *B*-exportables (whose name is then misleading because they are imported by *B*).

Country *B*'s offer curve can similarly be traced out from a series of trade indifference curves imposed on the same set of coordinates but developed from sliding *B*'s production-possibility block along its consumption indifference curves in the southwest quadrant. Figure B.3 shows the *A* and *B* offer curves intersecting at the balanced trade position where the terms of trade line, *OT*, is tangent to trade indifference curves of *A* and *B* and go to the origin. There are other tangencies of trade indifference curves, and a contract curve, *K–K*, may be drawn along them. This contract curve, like that of the Edgeworth-Bowley

FIGURE B.3
The contract curve and trade equilibrium

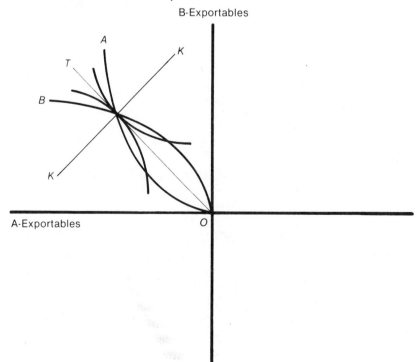

FIGURE B.4
Production and consumption under trading

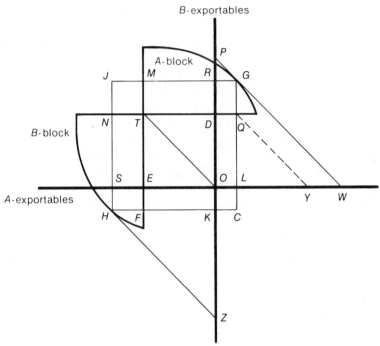

box in Figure A.5A when it is used in exchange and not as an efficiency locus in production, represents different distributions of welfare between A and B. A is better off the farther the point of trade is toward the northeast; and B the nearer it is to the southwest. Only at the intersection of OA and OB, however, do the terms of trade balance A's exports and B's imports under free trade.

These three figures neatly show the relationship of the offer curve to consumption indifference curves and to production. The technique can be used in its simple manifestation, however, to show the gains from trade. This is done by leaving the A and B production-possibility blocks at the trading position, as in Figure B.4. Trade and consumption indifference curves and the offer curves are omitted to eliminate clutter.

In Figure B.4, production is measured from the intersection of the origins, T, of the production blocks. In A, production consists of QG of B-exportables and GM of A-exportables. B produces NH of B-exportables and FH of A-exportables. These outputs can readily be added to give production of GJ of A-exportables in the two countries, and JH of B-exportables.

Consumption is measured from the original coordinates, intersecting at O. A consumes only GR of A-exportables, but GL of B-exportables; in its turn, B consumes only SH of its G-good, and KH of the A-exportable. This made possibly by trade, in which A exchanges DT of the A-good against TE of the B-good, at the terms of trade, OT.

This is a free-trade position, without transport costs. Thus the terms of trade are equal to the internal prices (WG and ZH are parallel to OT and to each other). National income in A is WO expressed in A-exportables, or PO expressed in B's good, whether we take income produced or income consumed. These are the same because trade is balanced. Income produced directly in A-goods is YO, which is the same as GM or QT (YQ is drawn parallel to OT). That part of income produced which originally consisted of B-goods, GQ, is the equivalent, at the price WG, of WY.

For income consumed, GR of A-exportables is equal to LO, and GL of B-exportables, at the price WG, is the equivalent in A-exportables of WL. $WL + LO = WO$. Similar exercises can be carried through for national income in A measured in B-goods and for income produced and consumed in B in either good.

The gains from trade are more elusive and present an index-number problem. We can measure A's gain in terms of either prices before trade or prices after trade. In Figure B.5 a and b are the before-trade

FIGURE B.5
The gains from trade measured in terms of A-exportables

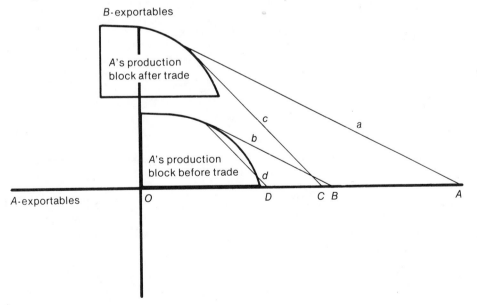

terms of trade drawn to the A production block after and before trade, respectively. On the other hand, c and d represent the posttrade prices drawn to the same block positions; a, b, c, and d intersect the horizontal axis at A, B, C, and D. The gains from trade in A, expressed in A-exportables, may then be regarded as AB, using the terms of trade before trade, or CD, representing them in after-trade prices. But one should not make the mistake of measuring the gains from trade as the change from the national income in the no-trade position at no-trade prices (BO) to national income with trade at the with-trade price (CO). In that event, the gain from trade would be negative, or a loss (BC).

It is true that the gains from trade will be larger, the larger the change in prices before trade and after. The larger the price change, the higher the consumption indifference curve and the higher the trade indifference curve the country can reach. But measurement of the distance between indifference curves requires a scale, and this can be one commodity or the other, but only at a consistent set of prices.

SUGGESTED READING

This appendix is based on James C. Meade, *A Geometry of International Trade*, chaps. 1–4.

appendix C*

Factor-price equalization

FACTOR-PRICE EQUALIZATION

There are at least three geometric ways to demonstrate the factor-price equalization theorem. The first, taking off from the Edgeworth-Bowley box, which was explained in Appendix A, is illustrated in Figure C.1. There we construct Edgeworth-Bowley boxes for each of two countries, the United States and Britain, with widely different factor proportions but identical production functions, which differ as between the two commodities, wheat and cloth. The two boxes have a common origin in cloth at O. The different factor proportions result in two separate origins for wheat, Y in the United States and Y' for Britain. Before trade, the two countries are assumed to be producing and consuming at S and T, respectively, determined separately with the help of demand conditions. The land/labor ratio is higher in wheat than in cloth, in both the United States and Britain. (The diagonals are not drawn in, to simplify the diagram, but OS is steeper than OT in cloth, and SY than TY' in wheat.) With more land employed in both commodities in the United States than in Britain, land will be relatively less expensive, compared to labor. Conversely, with a higher labor/land ratio in both commodities, Britain will have a lower return to labor than will the United States.

When trade becomes possible, it is assumed that prices are fully equalized in the two countries because of the absence of transport costs and other barriers to trade. With identical production functions

---
* Appendix to Chapter 5.

FIGURE C.1
Factor-price equalization after trade

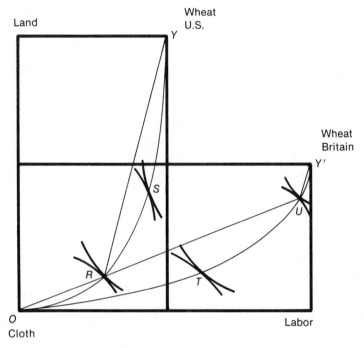

showing constant returns, and something of each good produced in each country, at equal prices, the returns to factors must be identical if the factor proportions in the production of each commodity are identical between countries—if, that is, trade results in production at such points as R and U. At R and U, the equality of factor proportions is demonstrated by the fact that R lies on the straight line OU (there are identical factor proportions in the production of cloth in both countries) and that YR and $Y'U$ are parallel.

There are a variety of reasons why two such points as R and U may not exist. After trade, one or both countries may be completely specialized, Britain producing cloth at Y' or the United States producing wheat at O. Demand conditions may be so sharply different in the two countries that trade results in shifting production in the United States from S toward Y rather than toward O, so that it would export the labor-intensive good despite its abundance of land. Or land and labor may so substitute for one another in the production of either cloth or wheat that wheat is labor intensive in Britain and land intensive in the United States. This possibility can be illustrated on this diagram but is more conveniently set out in the other two methods.

The second method of illustrating factor-price equalization is one
worked out by Abba P. Lerner. It is shown with the aid of single
isoquants representing the production functions of the two commodities, as in Figure C.2. The trick is to pick isoquants for the two

FIGURE C.2
**Factor-price equalization illustrated with production
functions**

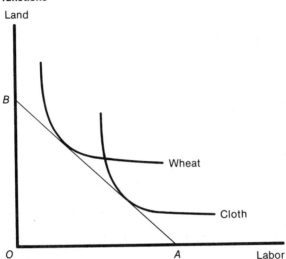

commodities which represent their relative prices, or the quantities in
which they are exchanged, after trade is established. Thus the
isoquants may represent, say, 3 yards of cloth and 2 bushels of wheat,
or 30 yards of cloth and 20 bushels, or 300 and 200. Since the production functions are linear homogeneous, the shape of successive
isoquants representing larger quantities is always the same (and the
expansion path represented by larger and larger outputs at given factor
prices is a straight line). Since the units chosen reflect goods prices
which are the same in the two countries after trade (assuming no
transport costs and perfect competition), Figure C.2 applies to the
United States and Britain alike. And as the figure is drawn, there can
be only one factor-price ratio, the line of tangency to the two isoquants,
A–B. This then is factor-price equalization.

But notice what happens if the isoquants cross more than once, as in
Figure C.3. This situation implies that there is a wide range of factor
substitution possible in at least one of the commodities which permits
the same goods price, but differing factor prices, to prevail in the two
countries. In Figure C.3, the production function for wheat is the same

FIGURE C.3
**Failure of factor prices to equalize because of factor intensity
reversal**

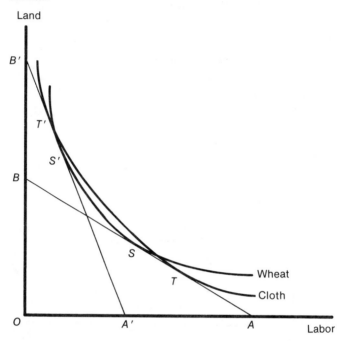

as in Figure C.2, but there is much more room for factor substitution in
cloth. In these circumstances, Britain, with a high labor/land ratio, may
produce cloth with the factor proportions represented by the ray from
the origin (not drawn) O–T, and wheat with the proportions O–S,
yielding a factor price A–B. In this country cloth is relatively labor
intensive. But in the United States, land is substituted for labor in
producing cloth, and with production at S' and T', cloth is land intensive, wheat labor intensive. Factor prices will differ, and one cannot tell from factor endowments which country will export which
commodity.

The third method of illustrating factor-price equalization is at the
same time the most complex and the most helpful, since it puts factor
proportions, goods prices, and factor prices all on the same diagram.
Figure C.4 shows the relations between land/labor ratios and the ratio
of wage rates to land rents in the upper half of the diagram, and the
relationship between the wage/rental ratio and relative goods prices in
the lower half. The central horizontal line is the wage/rent ratio, or the
wage rate, which rises as it moves to the right. In the upper half of the

FIGURE C.4
Factor-price equalization with factor proportions, goods prices, and factor prices

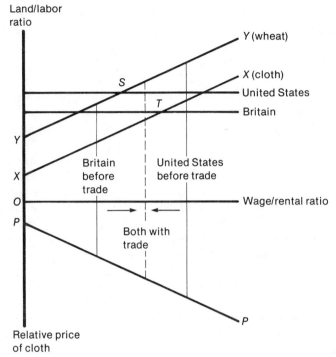

diagram, land/labor ratios for cloth and wheat are shown rising as wages increase: the higher the wage relative to rents, the more incentive there is for firms to substitute land for labor. Note that cloth is unambiguously more labor intensive, that is, less land intensive, at every wage rate, since the X–X schedule for cloth lies everywhere below the Y–Y schedule for wheat.

The relation between goods prices and factor prices is shown in the bottom part of the diagram. Here relative goods prices are measured in reverse order, that is, downward. The higher the wage, the higher the relative price of cloth, that is, the higher the P–P line, measured negatively from O. This relationship is obvious enough after the student has become used to handling rising prices upside down: as wages rise, the price of the labor-intensive commodity rises, and cloth is labor intensive at every land/labor ratio portrayed in the diagram.

British and U.S. factor proportions are given by horizontal lines in the upper half of the diagram which show that the United States is relatively land intensive, and Britain, labor intensive. Before trade, production and factor rewards in the separate countries are determined by demand conditions, but as portrayed, the vertical lines for Britain and the United States before trade show that the relative price of cloth and the wage/rental ratio are lower in Britain than in the United States. Conversely, of course, the price of wheat and the rental rate for land are relatively higher in Britain. When trade is opened up, goods prices have to move together, and the two countries' wage/rental ratios become identical, which means factor-price equalization.

The separate conditions necessary for factor-price equalization can be illustrated by varying this diagram, but we shall content ourselves with word pictures except for factor-intensity reversals. Linear homogeneity of production functions is required to have the land/labor ratios for the separate commodities appear as straight lines, as shown. Perfect competition and the absence of transport costs are required to have identical goods prices after trade on the P–P line. The importance of having incomplete specialization is a little more difficult to make clear, but if the price line after trade were to move to the left of S, where the United States is fully specialized in wheat, or to the right of T, where Britain is fully specialized in cloth, goods-price change no longer imply factor-proportion change, and factor proportions would no longer be uniquely related to factor prices.

The condition that demands must not be too skewed is to ensure that after trade is opened up the price of cloth in Britain rises, rather than have the country so addicted to cloth that it tries to buy more of it from the United States. Trade should make the price of the goods that are produced intensively by the abundant factor rise, not fall.

The condition about factor reversals is illustrated in Figure C.5. In Britain wheat is land intensive relative to cloth, but in the United States, with a much higher land/labor ratio, land is so plentiful that it is copiously substituted for labor in making cloth. This is not very realistic, perhaps, but it might be more confusing to shift the commodities. Notice that as the wage rate rises, the price of cloth rises relative to wheat until the land/labor curves cross. When cloth is more land intensive than wheat, the relative price of cloth declines as wages rise. In these circumstances, it is possible to get goods-price equalization without factor-price equalization. After trade, each country exports the labor-intensive good, and trade raises wages in both countries.

We should supplement these geometric proofs by noting that the factor-price equalization theorem can also be proved within a system of equations that also derives the Stolper-Samuelson theorem and a few other key results. An ingenious article by Ronald W. Jones has shown that several results that were separately and laboriously deduced in the trade-theory literature all fall out of a single, simple

FIGURE C.5
Failure of factor prices to equalize because of factor intensity reversal

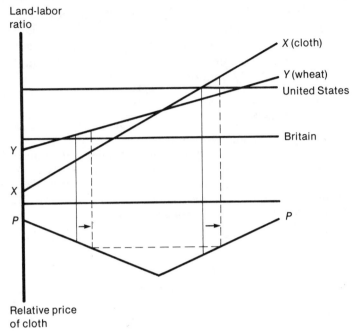

general-equilibrium model.[1] Before Jones's article, the task of converting the geometry of the Heckscher-Ohlin model into a neat set of equations had seemed intractable, since there was no easy way to derive the equations for the production-possibility curves of each country, even when the factor endowments and production functions for each sector were known. Jones skirted this problem by converting the system into its rate-of-change equivalent. Thus the unknown formula for the production-possibility curve relating one sector's output to the other sector's output was replaced with an approximately linear system of equations linking rates of change in each sector's output to exogenous rates of change in technology, factor supplies, and demand or price conditions. As a by-product, the same set of equations also showed how factor prices were also determined by the same exogenous variables. Thus one could derive the Stolper-Samuelson and factor-price equalization theorems (showing the factor-price response

[1] Ronald W. Jones, "The Structure of Simple General Equilibrium Models," *Journal of Political Economy*, vol. 73, no. 6 (December 1965), pp. 557–72. The model is reexpressed in various appendixes of R. E. Caves and Ronald W. Jones, *World Trade and Payments* (Boston: Little, Brown, 1973).

to price changes and to free trade between countries with different factor endowments), as well as the Rybczynski theorem, which states that added supplies of one factor will raise output in one sector and lower output in the other. Extensions of the Jones model to cover three factors and two commodities show that trade may not equalize factor prices in such cases. For international commodity price equality to equalize factor prices between nations, there cannot be more factors than output sectors in the model.

SUGGESTED READING

Three alternative approaches to the classic factor-price equalization theorem are: (1) Paul Samuelson, "International Trade and the Equalization of Factor Prices," *Economic Journal*, June 1948 and June 1949; (2) Abba P. Lerner, "Factor Prices and International Trade," *Economica*, February 1952; and (3) Harry G. Johnson, "Factor Endowments, International Trade, and Factor Prices," *Manchester School*, September 1957.

appendix D

The nationally
optimal tariff

It is not difficult to derive a basic formula for the tariff level that is nationally optimal for a country that can affect the foreign-supply price of imports without fear of retaliation, as in the first part of Chapter 7. This appendix does so using both the demand-supply framework of Part II and the offer-curve framework of Appendix B, showing that similar simple formulas emerge from both. An analogous formula is derived for the optimal export duty, both for a nation and for an international cartel.

We saw in the demand-supply framework in Chapter 7 that a small increase in an import tariff brings an area of gain and an area of loss to the nation. Figure D.1 compares these two areas for a tiny increase in the tariff above its initial absolute level, which is the fraction t times the initial foreign price level, P. The extra gains come from being able to lower the foreign price on continuing imports, gaining the level of imports M times the foreign price drop dP/dt. The extra losses come from losing the extra imports (dM/dt) that were worth tP more per unit to consumers than the price (P) at which foreigners were willing to sell them to us.

The optimal tariff rate is that which just makes the extra losses and extra gains from changing the tariff equal each other. That is, the optimal tariff rate t^* is the one for which

$$\frac{\text{Extra}}{\text{gains}} - \frac{\text{Extra}}{\text{losses}} = M \frac{dP}{dt} - t^*P \frac{dM}{dt} = 0 ,$$

511

FIGURE D.1
The gains and losses from a slight increase in the tariff, in a demand-supply framework

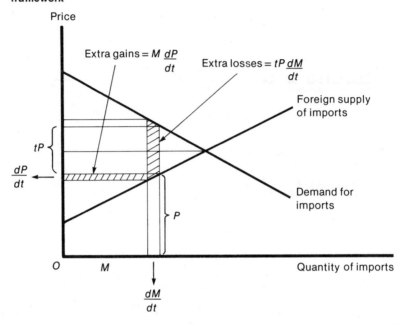

so that

$$t^* = \frac{dP/dt}{dM/dt}\frac{M}{P}.$$

Since the foreign supply elasticity is defined as $s_m = \dfrac{dM}{dP}\dfrac{P}{M}$ along the foreign supply curve, the formula for the optimal tariff is simply $t^* = 1/s_m$, as stated in Chapter 7. If the world price is fixed beyond our control, so that $s_m = \infty$, then the optimal tariff rate is zero. The more inelastic the foreign supply, the higher the optimal tariff rate.[1]

---

[1] Figure D.1 makes it easy to show that the nationally optimal tariff is lower than the tariff rate that would maximize the government's tariff revenue, even when the foreign supply curve slopes upward. The optimal tariff in Figure D.1 was one that equated the "extra gains" area with the "extra losses" area. But at this tariff rate a slight increase in the tariff still brings a net increase in government tariff revenue. By raising the tariff rate slightly, the government collects more duty on the remaining imports, M, while losing the "extra losses" area on the discouraged imports. However, its gain in revenue on M is not just the "extra gains" area already introduced, but this plus the thin unlabeled rectangle above the tP gap, which takes the form of a higher price to consumers importing M. A slight increase in the tariff would still raise revenue even when it brings no further net welfare gains to the nation. It follows that the revenue-maximizing tariff rate is higher than the optimal tariff rate. Thus a country would be charging too high a rate if it tried to find its nationally optimal tariff rate by finding out what rate seemed to maximize tariff revenues.

Oddly enough, the level of the optimal tariff depends only on the foreign supply elasticity, and not at all on our own demand elasticity of imports. The same cannot be said, however, about the gains given us by the optimal tariff rate. These do depend on the elasticity of our own import demand curve. For example, with a perfectly vertical import demand curve we get no gains from the tariff as an extreme result. The optimal tariff rate (or any other) simply taxes consumers, with an equal advantage accruing to government plus domestic producers.

One can derive the optimal rate of *export* duty in the same way. Just replace all terms referring to imports with terms referring to exports, and redraw Figure D.1 so that the extra gain at the expense of foreign buyers of our exports comes at the top of the tariff gap instead of at the bottom. It turns out, symmetrically, that the optimal export duty equals the absolute value of $1/d_x$, or the reciprocal of the foreign demand elasticity for our exports.

The formula for the optimal export duty can also be used as the optimal rate of markup of an international cartel. Since both the international cartel maximizing joint profits from exports and the single nation optimally taxing its exports are monopolistic profit-maximizers, it stands to reason that the formula linking optimal markup to foreign demand elasticity should hold in both cases. So the optimal markup for an international exporting cartel is $t^* = \left| 1/d_c \right|$, or the absolute value of the reciprocal of the world demand elasticity for the cartel's exports.

We can extend the formula to show how the optimal export markup for cartel members depends on the other elasticities and the market share discussed in Chapter 10's treatment of cartels like OPEC. The formula given in Chapter 10 can be derived easily here. We can link the elasticity of demand for the cartel's exports to world demand for the product, the supply of perfect substitutes from other countries, and the cartel's share of the world market by beginning with a simple identity:

$$\frac{\text{Cartel}}{\text{exports}} = \frac{\text{World}}{\text{exports}} - \frac{\text{Other}}{\substack{\text{countries'} \\ \text{exports}}},$$

or

$$X_c = X - X_o .$$

Differentiating with respect to the cartel price yields

$$dX_c/dP = dX/dP - dX_o/dP .$$

This can be reexpressed in ways that arrive at an identity involving elasticities:

$$\frac{dX_c/dP}{X} = \frac{dX/dP}{X} - \frac{dX_o/dP}{X}$$

$$\frac{dX_c}{dP}\frac{P}{X_c}\frac{X_c}{X} = \frac{dX}{dP}\frac{P}{X}\frac{X}{X} - \frac{dX_o}{dP}\frac{P}{X_o}\frac{X_o}{X}.$$

The cartel's share of the world market is defined as $c = X_c/X = 1 - (X_o/X)$. The elasticity of demand for the cartel's exports is defined as $d_c = (dX_c/dP)(P/X_c)$; the elasticity of world export demand for the product is $d = (dX/dP)(P/X)$; and the elasticity of noncartel countries' competing export supply of the product is $s_o = (dX_o/dP)(P/X_o)$. Substituting these definitions into the equation above yields

$$d_c \cdot c = d - s_o(1 - c),$$

so that

$$d_c = \frac{d - s_o(1 - c)}{c}.$$

Now since the optimal markup rate is $t^* = |1/d_c|$, this optimal cartel markup rate is

$$t^* = \frac{c}{|d - s_o(1 - c)|}.$$

As noted in Chapter 10, the optimal markup as a share of the (markup-including) price paid by buying countries is greater, the greater the cartel's market share (c), or the lower the absolute value of the world demand elasticity for exports of the product (d), or the lower the elasticity of noncartel countries' export supply (s_o). (For a generalization of this formula to cover cases in which the export supplied by noncartel countries is an imperfect substitute for the cartel's export product, see Carl van Duyne, "Commodity Cartels and the Theory of Derived Demand," *Kyklos*, 28 (1975), 3, pp. 597–611.)

The nationally optimal tariff on imports (or exports) can also be portrayed using the offer-curve framework of Appendix B, though this framework is less convenient for showing the *formula* for the optimal tariff. A trade-taxing country can use the tariff to move its own offer curve until it reaches the point on the foreign offer curve which maximizes the country's well-being. Figure D.2 shows this optimal tariff for a wheat-exporting country. Our country, the wheat exporter, has pushed its offer curve to the right by making the price of imported cloth in units of wheat higher within the country than the price received by our foreign cloth suppliers. At Point T domestic consumers must pay for cloth at the domestic price ratio SR/RT, giving up SR in wheat for RT in cloth. The foreign suppliers receive only OR in wheat for their RT of cloth. The government has intervened to collect tariff revenue at the tariff rate SO/RT.

FIGURE D.2
An optimal tariff, portrayed with offer curves

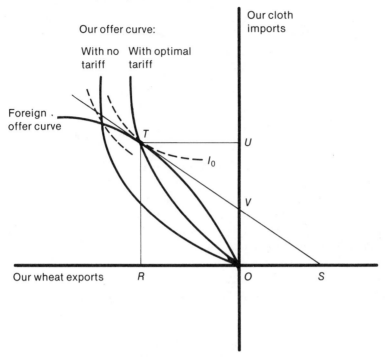

Figure D.2 shows that this particular tariff rate happens to be optimal, since at Point T the foreign offer curve is tangent to I_0, the best indifference curve we can reach through trade. The optimal tariff is positive because the foreign offer curve is not infinitely elastic. If it were infinitely elastic, in the form of a fixed world price line coming out of the origin, our optimal tariff would be zero, since no other tariff can put us on as high an indifference curve as we can reach on our free-trade, no-tariff offer curve. The same principle emerges here as in the demand-supply framework: the more elastic the foreign trading curve, the lower is our optimal tariff.

Deriving the formula for the optimal tariff rate is a little more complicated with offer curves than with demand and supply curves. The elasticity of the foreign offer curve is conventionally defined differently from a foreign supply curve, and defined in a way that is hard to identify in the offer-curve diagram itself. Any country's offer curve elasticity is conventionally defined as the ratio of the percentage response of its import demand to a percentage change in the relative price of its imports:

$$\text{Offer-curve elasticity } (e) = \frac{-(\% \text{ change in } M)}{[\% \text{ change in } (X/M)]}$$

Since the change in the price ratio X/M is not easy to spot on an offer-curve diagram like Figure D.2, let us convert this definition into a more usable equivalent:

$$e = \frac{-(\% \text{ change in } M)}{(\% \text{ change in } X) - (\% \text{ change in } M)}$$

$$= \frac{-1}{\dfrac{(\% \text{ change in } X)}{(\% \text{ change in } M)} - 1} = \frac{1}{1 - \left(\text{Slope } \dfrac{\partial X}{\partial M}\right)(M/X)}$$

This last expression can be translated into a relationship among line segments in Figure D.2. We now take the foreigners' point of view, since it is their offer curve we are trying to interpret. The foreigners export cloth and import wheat. Thus the slope of their cloth exports with respect to their wheat imports at Point T is the ratio RT/RS, and the world price of their wheat imports (M/X) is RT/OR. Therefore the elasticity of their offer curve becomes

$$e = \frac{1}{1 - \dfrac{RT}{SR}\dfrac{OR}{RT}} = \frac{1}{1 - \dfrac{OR}{SR}} = \frac{SR}{SR - OR} = \frac{SR}{SO}.$$

(Some authors derive an equivalent ratio on the cloth axis: $e = UO/VO$.)

We can now see the close link between the optimal tariff rate at Point T and the elasticity of the foreign offer curve:

$$t^* = SO/OR = \frac{SO}{SR - SO} = \frac{1}{\dfrac{SR}{SO} - 1},$$

or

$$t^* = \frac{1}{e - 1}.$$

This expression seems to differ slightly from the formula relating to the foreign supply elasticity for our imports, derived above. But the difference is only definitional. The elasticity of the foreign offer curve is defined as the elasticity of the foreigners' wheat imports with respect to the world price of cloth, not the elasticity of their cloth exports (supply of our cloth imports) with respect to the same price. Since the ratio of the foreigners' cloth exports to their wheat imports is just the world price of wheat, the offer-curve elasticity ([% change in wheat]/[% change in cloth/wheat]) is equal to one plus their elasticity of supply of our import, cloth. So the expression above is equivalent to the reciprocal of the foreigners' supply elasticity of our import good, as in the demand-supply framework.

One word of caution in interpreting the optimal tariff formula relating to the foreign offer curve: the tariff rate equals the formula $1/(e - 1)$ for *any* tariff rate, not just the optimal one. To know that the rate is optimal, as at Point T, you must also know that the foreign offer curve is tangent to our indifference curve.

appendix E

The monopoly effect
of a quota

A significant difference between a tariff and a quota is that the conversion of a tariff into a quota that admits exactly the same volume of imports may convert a potential into an actual monopoly and reduce welfare even further. Figures E.1 and E.2 give a demonstration.

Figure E.1 returns us to the case of a tariff on a product for which our nation faces a fixed world price, P_0. By raising the domestic price to P_1, the tariff cuts imports to M_1 and causes deadweight welfare loses b and d, just as in Chapter 6. Figure E.1 brings out the point that this is the result of the tariff even if there is only one domestic producer. Though the tariff gives the producer some extra economic rents, represented by area a, it still leaves him a price taker, since any attempt on his part to charge a higher price than P_1 would leave buyers the option of shifting all of their demand to imports. Facing this flat demand curve, he does not charge more than P_1, and society loses only b and d from the tariff.

The quota shown in Figure E.2 is equivalent to the tariff in the sense that it also allows imports of M_1. But it plays into the hands of the sole domestic producer better than the tariff does. It leaves him with an upward-sloping demand curve for his product, by sharply limiting the ability of buyers to avoid him by buying abroad. Realizing this, the domestic producer will (slowly and discreetly) let his price drift up to the higher price that restricts his output back to where marginal costs

FIGURE E.1
With a nonprohibitive tariff, the sole domestic producer still lacks market power

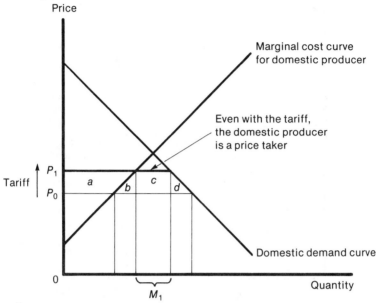

and marginal revenues match. That higher price is P_2, and the more restricted domestic production level is S_2. The quota thus makes domestic output lower, and domestic price even higher, than the equivalent tariff does.

When a domestic monopoly is created by a quota, the nation as a whole loses *both* the deadweight loss from the reduction of imports and an extra social waste from the monopoly. In Figure E.2 the reduction of imports costs society areas b and d, and the new monopoly power costs the shaded area. All of these areas represent a lost opportunity to let consumers buy something that cost the nation less to obtain than the extra purchases were worth to consumers. By holding production back at S_2 and imports at M_1, the quota plus monopoly keeps consumers from enjoying purchases that they value at P_2 or near that even though the marginal costs of obtaining the extra units are as low as the marginal cost curve or the world price, whichever is less.

The quota is also worse than the equivalent tariff when it is administered in a way that makes otherwise competitive foreigners act like a group monopoly when selling to us. Chapter 8 noted that this seems to have been the result of the U.S. attempt to put a quantitative limit on imports of textiles and other goods while not technically administering

FIGURE E.2
With an equivalent quota, the sole domestic producer becomes a monopolist

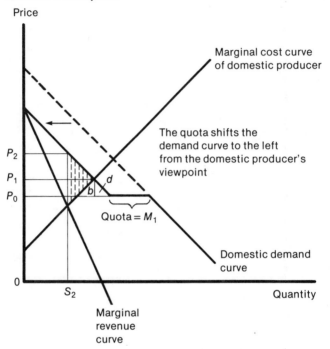

Price

Marginal cost curve of domestic producer

The quota shifts the demand curve to the left from the domestic producer's viewpoint

P_2

P_1

P_0

b d

Quota $= M_1$

Domestic demand curve

0

S_2

Quantity

Marginal revenue curve

the quotas itself. Figure E.3 shows how much more this procedure might cost an importing nation. If the government of the importing country administers an import quota of M_1, it will get the goods at the world price and somehow allocate the price-markup gains, areas c and e, among domestic residents. (As Figure E.3 is drawn here, the world price is the low level P_2 because the foreign supply curve is assumed to be upward-sloping. If the importing country faced a fixed world price, then the goods would arrive at the price P_1.) But if the quota is enforced by the foreigners, say, by their agreeing on fixed shares of this country's import market, no authority intervenes between them and buyers. Faced with this limited but prearranged import demand, they as exporters charge the highest price the traffic will bear with M_1 of imports, or the high price P_1. The importing country loses not only the triangle $b + d$ but also the price-markup rectangles c and e. These latter losses are the additional cost of having foreign exporters collude to limit this country's imports instead of having a regular official import quota.

FIGURE E.3
The extra cost of a quota enforced by foreign suppliers

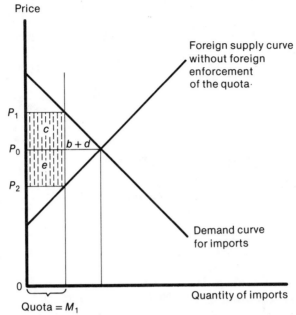

SUGGESTED READING

Jagdish Bhagwati generalizes the possibilities of monopoly among domestic producers, quota holders, and foreign exporters in "On the Equivalence of Tariffs and Quotas," in *Trade, Growth, and the Balance of Payments,* essays in honor of Gottfried Haberler, ed. Robert E. Baldwin (Chicago: Rand McNally, 1965).

appendix F

The welfare effects of stabilizing commodity prices

Successful commodity price stabilization seems to bring a clear net gain to the world as a whole, yet has more complicated effects on the separate well-being of exporting and importing countries, as argued in Chapter 11. This appendix derives these basic results, using a simplified demand-supply model.

To analyze the effects of price stabilization, we begin by simplifying the portrayal of the shocks to which world trade is subject. Let one of the two trade curves, either import demand or export supply, occupy two parallel positions in two time periods while the other trade curve stays unaltered. A demand-side variability is thus represented by two parallel demand curves, one for the period of stronger import demand (for example, an importing-country boom) and the other for the period of weaker import demand. A supply-side variability is shown by fixing the position of the import demand curve and varying the position of the competitive supply curve between two parallel positions—say, one for good-weather years and one for bad-weather years. Assume at first that the demand curves all slope downward and that the supply curves all slope upward.

If officials stabilize the price, it is assumed that they do so by correctly seeing that the trend in the good's real price is in fact zero. They stabilize by buying exactly the same amount in excess supply periods as they sell in excess supply periods, and at the same stabilized price. Their costs of maintaining the buffer stock are assumed to be zero, so that the officials make neither profits nor losses.

The well-being of a country is proxied by its net producer surplus or consumer surplus on exports or imports, respectively. For an exporting country, the net producer surplus on exports is simply the horizontal difference between producer and consumer surplus in a demand and supply diagram for the exportable good. For an importing country, similarly, the net consumer surplus on imports is obtained by subtracting the producer surplus from the consumer surplus on importables. The key element of well-being left out of these measures is just how much psychic benefit exporters and importers derive from the stability of either price or their own producer and consumer surpluses. Our procedure here is to describe how the degree of instability in these surpluses is affected by price stabilization, and to leave open the question of how much average welfare one would willingly give up to achieve a given reduction in the instability of that welfare from period to period.

Figures F.1 and F.2 and Table F.1 summarize the varied effects of commodity price stabilization. To grasp the results, let us look first at

FIGURE F.1
The effects of price stabilization in the face of demand-side disturbances

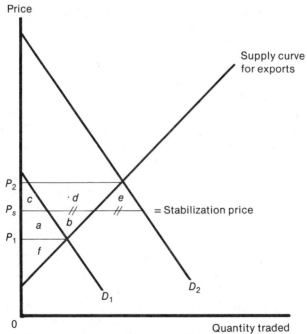

Note: This Figure is patterned after the analysis in Benton F. Massell, "Price Stabilization and Welfare," *Quarterly Journal of Economics*, May 1969. Massell's analysis has been extended by C. P. Brown, *Primary Commodity Control* (Kuala Lumpur: Oxford University Press, 1975).

FIGURE F.2
The effects of price stabilization in the face of supply-side disturbances

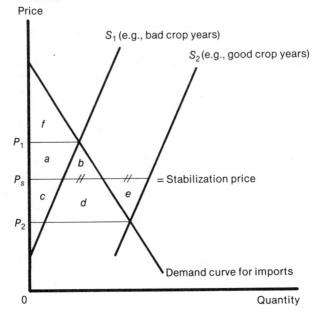

Price

S_1 (e.g., bad crop years)

S_2 (e.g., good crop years)

P_1

f

a b

P_s //   //   = Stabilization price

c d e

P_2

Demand curve for imports

0   Quantity

Figure F.1, which portrays a simple case of demand-side instability, such as might be experienced by the world market for metals like tin, whose demand fluctuates with business cycles in the industrial countries. Figure F.1 condenses this instability into two parallel demand curves, D_1 for the low-demand troughs and D_2 for the high-demand peaks. It is assumed that officials stabilize the price of the product by buying exactly the same amount of the product in Period 1 as they sell in Period 2. This amount is represented by the two crosshatched line segments below areas d and e in Figure F.1. As a result of the officials' actions, the equilibrium price equals p_s in both periods instead of settling at the higher p_2 in the second period and the lower p_1 in the first.

The price stabilization appears to be a mixed blessing for the exporting countries. It makes their producer surplus on exports $a + b + f$ for both periods instead of f alone in Period 1 and $a + b + c + d + f$ in Period 2. This means that exporters get a more stable flow of gains across periods, which is good. Yet keeping the price at p_s has lowered their total gains over both periods, by the amount $c + d - a - b$. It has done this by keeping the exporters from pursuing the better price p_2 with the greater sales that their upward-sloping supply curve shows

TABLE F.1
The welfare effects of price stabilization: Results of the simple two-period analysis

Group we care about	Source of disturbance	Effect of price stabilization on producer or consumer surplus over two periods	Effect of price stabilization on "risk" (that is, variance in consumer or producer surplus over two periods)
Demanders (importing countries)	Demand side	Higher welfare (gain $c + d + e - a$ in Figure F.1)	More risk
	Supply side	Lower welfare (lose $c + d - a - b$ in Figure F.2)	Less risk
Suppliers (exporting countries)	Demand side	Lower welfare (lose $c + d - a - b$ in Figure F.1)	Less risk
	Supply side	Higher welfare (gain $c + d + e - a$ in Figure F.2)	More risk
Both together ("the world")	Demand side	Higher welfare (gain $b + e$ in Figure F.1)	No difference
	Supply side	Higher welfare (gain $b + e$ in Figure F.2)	No difference

Note: As stated in the text, the separate effects on demanders and suppliers are sensitive to assumptions about the slopes of the curves. The results above are based on the case of parallel shifts in straight lines, with downward-sloping demand and upward-sloping supply.

they would have willingly made at the higher price. By preventing the exporters from shifting their sales toward the higher-price periods, it has denied them some overall gains. Note, however, that this mixed blessing is fragile. If the supply curve were vertical in the short run, as it might be for perishable crops, then the net welfare effect on exporters would be zero ($c + d - a - b = 0$) and price stabilization would simply stabilize their gains across periods, which is only to the good. One could also show that if the two demand curves are not parallel, the mixed blessing can again fail to hold. (Consider the case in which demand fluctuates between the D_1 curve and the perfectly elastic curve at p_s: here exporters again gain unambiguously from stabilization.)

Keeping price steady in the face of the demand-side fluctuations in Figure F.1 is also a mixed blessing for importing countries. If the market had not been stabilized, the consumer surplus of the importing countries would have included the areas c and a when the price was down at p_1 and none of the lettered areas when the price was up at p_2. By contrast, keeping the price at p_s keeps the importing countries from picking up area a as part of the bargain in the first period, yet gives them areas $c + d + e$ by holding down the price in the second period, when their demand is stronger. Their gains end up greater for the two periods, by the amount $c + d + e - a$. Yet with the price fixed at p_s their gains are also more variable across the two periods.

For the world the price stabilization is a clear net gain, rather than the mixed blessing facing either side of the market. The world consumer plus producer surplus on international trade is raised by the areas $b + e$, as can be seen by adding together the net effects mentioned above. The logic behind this net gain is given in Chapter 11: the officials are acting like a merchant or arbitrageur who improves the match-up between net buyers who value a good highly and net sellers who will produce and sell it for less. They do so by matching buyers and sellers across time rather than across space.

Figure F.2 pursues the opposite case of supply-side instability in parallel fashion, and Table F.1 summarizes the full set of results for the simple two-period analysis. There is a pattern to the results: the distribution of overall gains depends on whether instability comes from the demand side or the supply side; any group of countries helped to higher average gains by the price stabilization is also exposed to wider fluctuations in those gains across periods; and the world always gains as a whole.

appendix G

The forward exchange market

The theory of what governs forward exchange rates and what these rates mean for policy has been developed more rigorously than was shown in Chapter 13's overview of foreign exchange markets. This appendix extends the forward market analysis, picking up on several points that were developed only partially in Chapter 13.

THE COVERED INTEREST DIFFERENTIAL

Chapter 13's examples of spot and forward options for hedgers and speculators turned up a remarkably consistent pattern: no matter how one wanted to move from one currency to another, the choice between using the forward market and using the spot market always depended on whether

$$(1 + i_b)r_f > (1 + i_a)r_s, \qquad (G.1)$$

or

$$(1 + i_b)r_f - (1 + i_a)r_s > 0, \qquad (G.2)$$

where i_a and i_b are the U.S. and British interest rates and r_f and r_s are the forward and spot prices of the pound, respectively. When this inequality held, people had an incentive to move their assets, in effect, counterclockwise around the "lake" in Figure 13.1, buying sterling in the spot market and/or selling it in the forward market. When the reverse inequality held, people seemed to move in the opposite direction, or clockwise, buying pounds forward and/or selling them spot.

Observers of the foreign exchange markets have converted this formula into the measurable concept of the covered interest differential, which summarizes the net incentive to move money counterclockwise around the "lake" in Figure 13.1. The expression in Equation (G.2) above is equal to the covered interest differential per spot pound invested. Its counterpart per dollar invested is found by dividing through Equation (G.2) by the spot exchange rate:

$$CD = (1 + i_b)r_f/r_s - (1 + i_a). \tag{G.3}$$

This formula can be interpreted more easily after it has been rearranged:

$$CD = \frac{r_f}{r_s} + \frac{i_b r_f}{r_s} - 1 - i_a = \left(\frac{r_f}{r_s} - 1 \right) - i_a + \frac{i_b r_f}{r_s} \tag{G.4}$$

$$= F - i_a + i_b + i_b F, \tag{G.5}$$

where $F = (r_f - r_s)/r_s$ is the premium or discount on the forward pound relative to the spot pound. Now the last term in Equation (G.5) is a product of two small fractions, F and i_b, and can be viewed as approximately equal to zero for purposes of rough calculation. Therefore the covered interest differential is about equal to the regular interest-rate differential plus the net premium on the forward pound:

$$CD = (i_b - i_a) + F. \tag{G.6}$$

Financial reporters refer to a positive value of CD as a covered differential "in favor of London." This is an appropriate label, since a positive value of CD would give people incentives to buy pounds in the spot market, invest them in London, and sell pounds forward. For example, in the case of the British hedger who wanted to get out of dollars in Chapter 13 (Example 2), when $i_b = 3$ percent, $i_a = 2$ percent, and $F = 0$, CD was $+1$ percent, and the British hedger would rightly have chosen to buy pounds spot and invest them in Britain rather than to buy them forward. (Yet if F were -2 percent, CD would $= -1$ percent, and he would have been well advised to buy forward pounds and not spot pounds.) Conversely, a negative value of CD is a covered differential "against London," and there will be an incentive to sell pounds spot and invest them in the United States instead of in London.

INTEREST ARBITRAGE

The covered differential is such a handy guide to the profitable transfer of money across currencies that banks have developed the art of interest arbitrage in order to cash in on the differential. **Arbitrage** is the simultaneous buying and selling of an asset in two markets in order to profit from the price difference between the markets. **Interest arbitrage** is buying a country's currency spot and selling it forward, while making a net profit off the combination of higher interest rates in that country and of any forward premium on its currency. Interest arbitrage is essentially riskless, though it does tie up some assets for a while. One way of engaging in arbitrage is in fact the ultimate in hedging: one can start with dollars today and end up with a guaranteed greater amount of dollars today, by going all the way around the "lake."

To see how arbitrage works, let us again suppose that British and U.S. interest rates are $i_b = 3$ percent and $i_a = 2$ percent, respectively, and that both the spot and forward exchange rates are $1.50/£, so that there is neither a premium nor a discount on forward sterling ($F = 0$). Seeing that this means $CD = +1$ percent, a New York arbitrageur gets on the telephones and sets up a counterclockwise journey around the "lake." He contracts to sell, say, $100,000 in the spot market, buying £66,667. He informs his London correspondent bank of the purchase and instructs that bank to place the proceeds in British Treasury bills that will mature in 90 days. This means that after 90 days he will have £68,667 = £66,667 × 1.03 to dispose of. Not waiting for that to happen, he contracts to sell the £68,667 in the forward market, receiving $103,000 deliverable after 90 days. He could leave the matter there, knowing that his phone trip in and out of Britain will give $103,000 90 days from now instead of the $102,000 he would have gotten by lending his money within the United States. Or if he has excellent credit standing, he can celebrate his winnings by borrowing against the $103,000 in the United States at 2 percent, giving himself $100,980 = $103,000/(1.02), or about 1 percent more than he had before he got on the telephones. So that's $980 in arbitrage gains minus the cost of the telephone or telegraph communications, any transactions fees, and a few minutes' time. The operation is also riskless as long as nobody defaults on a contract. (The reader can confirm that if forward sterling were at a 2 percent discount ($F = -2$ percent and $r_f = 1.47), the New York arbitrageur would lend in the United States, buy forward sterling, borrow or sell bills in Britain, and sell pounds spot, making a net arbitrage profit of about 1 percent.)

INTEREST PARITY

John Maynard Keynes argued that the opportunities to make arbitrage profits would be self-eliminating if the forward exchange rate were caused to adjust so that the covered interest differential returned to zero. In this way if a positive covered differential made arbitrageurs buy spot pounds and sell forward pounds, there would be a tendency for the forward rate to drop into a discount relative to the spot rate.

This tendency would continue until CD was so close to zero as not to be worth exploiting. **Interest parity** would be the result, in the sense that the gaps between interest rates would be matched by the forward discount on the pound. Keynes's argument is certainly correct as a description of a general tendency, and there is also some validity to his assumption that the forward rate would adjust to make CD approach zero, since the forward exchange market is thinner (of lower sales volume) than are national lending markets or the spot market for foreign exchange. Yet we do observe covered differentials half a percentage point or more from zero, and this observation calls for a closer look at what determines the equilibrium forward rate.

EQUILIBRIUM IN THE FORWARD MARKET

The net demand for forward pounds has to be zero, since every forward pound demanded by somebody offering to sell dollars forward must be matched by a pound being supplied by somebody in search of forward dollars. The equilibrium forward rate is thus the one that makes the net demand for forward pounds equal to zero.

Figure G.1 shows a forward market for pounds. Here the exchange rate is defined relative to the spot rate, so that a forward premium of zero means that the forward rate equals the spot rate of, say, $1.50/£: a 1 percent discount on the forward pound means that it is selling at $1.485; and so forth. The horizontal axes show net purchases and net sales of pounds. Equilibrium occurs when there are neither net sales nor net purchases of forward pounds.

If there were only hedgers and arbitrageurs in the forward market, its equilibrium forward rate would be easy to predict and easy to interpret. Hedgers and arbitrageurs react to the covered differential. If interest rates were higher in Britain by 1 percent and there were no premium or discount on forward sterling, hedgers and arbitrageurs would rush to sell sterling forward, because they would be lending their money in Britain to take advantage of the higher interest rate. Their tendency to stampede into lending in Britain and to sell the proceeds in the forward market would not be infinite, however. Hedgers and arbitrageurs can devote only so much money and time to taking advantage of covered differentials, and so a zero premium on the forward pound would cause them to try to be net sellers of forward pounds in the amount OB. But if they were really the only group in the forward market, they could not be net sellers. Their scramble to sell sterling forward would bid its forward rate down into a discount relative to the spot value of the pound. This tendency would continue until the forward rate moved into a 1 percent discount that offset the 1 percent higher interest rate in Britain, bringing hedgers and arbit-

FIGURE G.1
Equilibrium in the forward market, with hedgers, arbitrageurs, and speculators

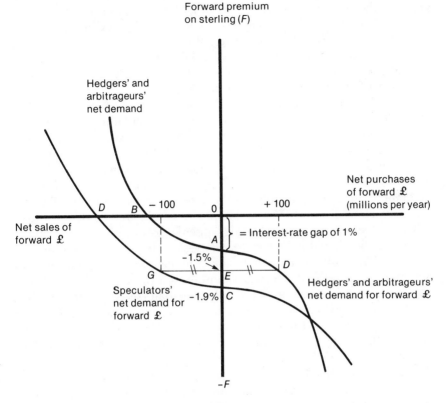

Forward premium
on sterling (F)

Hedgers' and
arbitrageurs'
net demand

Net purchases
of forward £
(millions per year)

− 100   0   + 100

Net sales of
forward £

= Interest-rate gap of 1%

−1.5%

Hedgers' and arbitrageurs'
net demand for forward £

Speculators'
net demand for   −1.9%
forward £

−F

Forward discount

rageurs into equilibrium at Point A. If we felt that the forward market were patronized only by hedgers and arbitrageurs, we should expect to find the forward discount on sterling always matching the gap by which interest rates were higher in Britain.

But suppose that there are speculators willing to play in the forward market. This is certainly a warranted supposition. After all, a speculator in the forward market only has to pledge and tie up a value of money worth 10 percent of his forward contracts outstanding. This is an easier game to play than spot speculation, so it is a fair guess that speculators have some preference for acting on their expectations in the forward market for foreign exchange rather than the spot market. Speculators' expectations about the future of the spot rate are what shape their demand for forward exchange. The more they are betting that sterling will take a dive in value, the more the forward rate would have to sink into discount to keep speculators in balance. This follows from the way in which a speculator uses the forward market. If he expects the value of sterling to sink, he will contract to sell it forward if the forward rate is above what he thinks sterling will be by then in the spot market. That way, he can buy up sterling that he thinks should be getting cheaper, just before it is time to deliver the forward sterling he agreed to sell, and then resell it at the higher contracted forward rate, making a profit.

Different speculators will have different views of how far sterling will fall, or whether it will fall at all. The speculators' net demand curve in Figure G.1 summarizes their different expectations. If the forward rate were equal to the spot rate (F = 0), there might be some who would be willing to buy sterling forward in the belief that after 90 days they would be able to resell it at a higher spot price. But the diagram assumes that at Point D these speculators are in an effective minority, since at Point D speculators as a whole are heavy net sellers of forward sterling. In other words, speculators on the average expect sterling to fall in value. What they expect on the average is shown at Point C. The forward rate that would make speculators neither net buyers nor net sellers of forward pounds is a discount of 1.9 percent below the spot rate. If there were only speculators in the market, this is what the forward rate would tend to be. At any higher forward rate, speculators would be net sellers of sterling because they would expect, on the average, a 1.9 percent decline in the spot price, so that they could unload their forward sterling at higher prices and rebuy it at what they expect to be lower later spot prices. At forward rates deeper into discount than 1.9 percent, speculators would be net buyers of forward sterling, since they would not expect it to drop so drastically in spot value. If there were only speculators in the forward market, the forward rate would settle at a discount of 1.9 percent, which can be interpreted as the average expectation of gamblers, much like the average "point spread" being quoted for a pro football game by oddsmakers in Las Vegas.

The real-world forward market has both hedgers-arbitrageurs and speculators in it. The first group's demand for forward sterling, as we have seen, depends on the width of the interest-rate gap, whereas the demand of speculators depends on their expectations regarding the future of the spot rate. Equilibrium in the forward market is a tug-of-war between these two groups. As Figure G.1 is drawn, speculators expect the spot value of sterling to fall faster than the interest-rate gap in favor of Britain (−1.9 percent versus −1.0 percent). The forward market can be in balance only if the forward rate settles at that percentage of discount at which what the hedgers and arbitrageurs are buying matches what the speculators are selling in the forward market.

This equilibrium has to be at Point E, with a discount of, say, 1.5 percent on forward sterling, where the £100 million being sold by speculators (GE) is just matched by the £100 million being bought by hedgers and arbitrageurs (ED) taking advantage of the covered differential in favor of lending in the United States and buying the cheap forward sterling.

This view of equilibrium in the forward market reveals how we can interpret a real-world situation in which we observe that the forward discount does *not* just match the interest-rate gap between countries. What we can observe in the newspapers are interest rates and forward rates, essentially equilibrium rates, like the forward discount of 1.5 percent at Point E. Yet these tell us something about forward speculators' average rate of expected change in the spot price. As a rule of thumb:

If the forward rate on the pound is at greater discount that the interest-rate gap, as in Figure G.1 with $CD < 0$, we can conclude that speculators expect spot sterling to drop below its current forward rate within the 90 days.

If the forward rate on the pound is above the interest-parity point (for example, Point A in Figure G.1), speculators must expect the spot rate to be above its current forward rate 90 days from now.

Thus one can tell from the sign of the covered differential alone whether speculators expect the spot rate to end up above or below its current forward rate. This is only a rough rule of thumb, however, since there are transactions costs that could keep the covered differential (CD) different from zero even if speculators are not particularly active. The sign and magnitude of the covered differential can nonetheless be used by officials as a rough measure of the speculative tide they are dealing with in trying to decide when and whether to stabilize the exchange rate. Unfortunately, speculators can read the same signal: when they see that officials have not intervened enough to erase a wide covered differential against a country whose currency is under attack, it is at least possible that they will become even more excited into speculating against that currency, possibly destabilizing the exchange markets.

HOW DOES THE FORWARD MARKET AFFECT SPOT BEHAVIOR?

We have seen that the behavior of hedgers, arbitrageurs, and speculators links the forward rate and the spot rate. Yet as a rough generalization, it is fair to say that the response of the spot exchange rate to any outside event is at least in the same direction, if not of the same magnitude, with or without the existence of a forward market.

A rise in the British interest rate, for example, would tend to raise the spot value of the pound sterling with or without a forward market. The higher interest rate attracts more funds to Britain and into sterling through the spot market, even if the existence of a forward market tends to make arbitrageurs first rush into spot sterling and then stop the rush once the forward rate has dropped enough to reclose the covered differential.

A shift in speculators' expectations against sterling will depress the spot rate without a forward market, since speculators can use either market. Even if bearish speculators bid against sterling only in the forward market, where they need commit only 10 percent of their contracts in the short run, this will have the effect of depressing the spot rate as well. The forward speculators' added pressure to depress the forward rate further into discount will make arbitrageurs scramble to do their lending in the United States and buy the cheap pounds forward. But arbitrageurs' attempts to get the U.S. dollars to lend in the United States will find them bidding down the spot price of the pound (bidding up the spot price of the dollar) as well. Thus even purely forward speculation against the pound would depress its spot value.

Official intervention to prop up the pound would also tend to raise its spot value, even if the officials bought sterling only in the forward market. Heavy forward purchases of sterling would raise the forward rate toward premium, causing arbitrageurs to want to lend in Britain and sell their sterling forward. Their attempt to lend more in Britain would cause them to buy more pounds in the spot market, again bidding up the spot pound. Thus the officials can intervene in either the spot or the forward market with similar results.

SUGGESTED READING

The major work on the subject of forward exchange is Paul Einzig's *A Dynamic Theory of Forward Exchange* (London: Macmillan, 1961). Einzig is highly critical of the view expressed here that the addition of a forward market does not greatly alter the way the spot foreign exchange market performs. An alternative theory of forward rates is contained in Egon Sohmen, *Flexible Exchange Rates,* rev. ed. (Chicago: University of Chicago Press, 1969).

Two empirical studies of the forward market are Fred R. Glahe, *An Empirical Study of the Foreign Exchange Market: Test of a Theory* (Princeton: Princeton University Press, 1967); and Jonathon Kesselman, "The Role of Speculation in Forward Rate Determination: The Canadian Flexible Dollar," *Canadian Journal of Economics,* May 1971.

Forward rates are incorporated into a model of portfolio choice and macroeconomic policy by Jay H. Levin, *Forward Exchange and Internal-External Equilibrium* (University of Michigan, Graduate School of Business Administration, 1970).

QUESTIONS FOR REVIEW

1. You are willing to engage in interest arbitrage, and you have $100,000 in bank deposits to play with in New York. Under each of the following sets of interest rates and exchange rates, calculate the covered differential in favor of London (CD), and decide whether it is more profitable to lend in London and sell pounds forward or to lend in the United States, avoiding pounds altogether:

	Interest rate in London (i_b)	Interest rate in New York (i_a)	Spot price of £ (r_s)	Forward price of £ (r_f)	Forward premium (F)
(a)	3%	2%	$1.50	$1.50	0%
(b)	3	2	1.50	1.47	−2
(c)	4	3	1.50	1.485	−1

2. You are given the following market information: the Toronto interest rate is 4 percent for 90 days; the U.S. 90-day interest rate is 2 percent; and the Canadian dollar sells for exactly one U.S. dollar in the spot market and for 99 U.S. cents in the forward market (1 percent discount from spot rate). What can you infer about forward speculators' view of the likely value of the Canadian dollar in spot markets 90 days from now?

Answers:
1. (a) CD is 1 percent, buy sterling spot, lend in London, sell sterling forward. (b) CD is −1 percent, lend in the United States. (c) CD is 0—you are indifferent.
2. Interest rates are 2 percent higher in Toronto, yet the Canadian dollar is at a forward discount of only 1 percent. Speculators must be buying forward Canadian dollars from arbitrageurs, and must be expecting the Canadian spot dollar to be worth at least 99 U.S. cents after 90 days, and maybe worth more.

appendix H

Devaluation, the trade balance, and the terms of trade

This appendix derives Chapter 15's key formulas for the effects of exchange-rate devaluation (or depreciation) on the trade balance (net surplus on current account), on the terms of trade (P_x/P_m), and on national income.

FOREIGN EXCHANGE ELASTICITIES[1]

To derive the elasticity of the trade balance with respect to the exchange rate, one must begin by linking the change in the exchange rate to elasticities of the demand for and supply of foreign exchange within the exchange market itself. To do so, we begin by differentiating the trade balance. The trade balance defined in foreign currency is:

$$TB_{£} = S_{£} - D_{£} = V_x - V_m = P_x^{£}X - P_m^{£}M , \qquad (H.1)$$

where $S_{£} = V_x$ is the supply of foreign exchange on current account, or the value of exports, and $D_{£} = V_m$ is the demand for foreign exchange on current account, or the value of imports. Differentiating yields:

$$dTB_{£} = dS_{£} - dD_{£}, \qquad (H.2)$$

---

[1] Our derivation of effects on the trade balance and the terms of trade follows that given in Jaroslav Vanek, *International Trade: Theory and Economic Policy* (Homewood, Ill.: Richard D. Irwin, 1962), chap. 5.

536

or

$$dTB_{\pounds}/V_m = dS_{\pounds}/V_m - dD_{\pounds}/V_m \,. \tag{H.3}$$

Let us define

$E_{tb} = \dfrac{dTB_{\pounds}/V_m}{dr/r} =$ The elasticity of the trade balance with respect to r, the exchange rate (or price of the foreign currency, in \$/$\pounds$);

$E_s = \dfrac{dS_{\pounds}/S_{\pounds}}{dr/r} =$ The elasticity of the supply of foreign exchange, or value of exports, with respect to the exchange rate r ;

$E_d = \dfrac{dD_{\pounds}/D_{\pounds}}{dr/r} =$ The elasticity of demand for foreign exchange, or the value of imports, with respect to the exchange rate r :

Then if we divide both sides of (H.3) by the proportion of change in the exchange rate (dr/r), we get:

$$E_{tb} = \frac{V_x}{V_m} E_s - E_d \,. \tag{H.4}$$

Deriving the formula for the effect of the exchange rate on the balance of trade amounts to deriving a formula relating E_{tb} to the underlying elasticities of demand and supply for exports and imports.

GOODS ELASTICITIES AND THE FOREIGN EXCHANGE ELASTICITIES

The foreign exchange supply (or demand) is linked to the export (or import) market by the fact that it is defined as the product of a trade price and a traded quantity. We therefore need to derive expressions giving the elasticities of these trade prices and quantities with respect to the exchange rate. Let us do so on the export side. There the supply, which depends on a dollar price $(P_x^\$ = P_x^{\pounds}/r)$, must be equated with demand, which depends on a pound price. We start with the equilibrium condition in the export market, differentiate it, and keep rearranging terms until the equation takes a form relating elasticities to the change in export prices:

$$X = S_x(P_x^{\pounds}r) = D_x(P_x^{\pounds}) \tag{H.5}$$

$$dX = \frac{\partial S_x}{\partial P_x^\$} (r\, dP_x^{\pounds} + P_x^{\pounds}dr) = \frac{\partial D_x}{\partial P_x^{\pounds}} dP_x^{\pounds} \tag{H.6}$$

$$dX/X = \frac{\partial S_x}{\partial P_x^\$} \frac{1}{S_x} (r\, dP_x^{\pounds} + P_x^{\pounds}dr) = \frac{\partial D_x}{\partial P_x^{\pounds}} \frac{1}{D_x} dP_x^{\pounds} \tag{H.7}$$

Multiplying within both sides by $P_x^\$ / r = P_x^\pounds$ and dividing by dr/r yields

$$\frac{dX/X}{dr/r} = \left[\frac{\partial S_x}{\partial P_x^\$} \frac{P_x^\$}{S_x}\right]\left(\frac{dP_x^\pounds/P_x^\pounds}{dr/r} + 1\right) = \left[\frac{\partial D_x}{\partial P_x^\pounds} \frac{P_x^\pounds}{D_x}\right]\frac{dP_x^\pounds/P_x^\pounds}{dr/r}. \quad (H.8)$$

The expressions in brackets on the left and right are the elasticities of export supply (s_x) and demand (d_x), respectively, so that

$$\frac{dX/X}{dr/r} = s_x\left(\frac{dP_x^\pounds/P_x^\pounds}{dr/r} + 1\right) = d_x\frac{dP_x^\pounds/P_x^\pounds}{dr/r}, \quad (H.9)$$

and the percentage response of the pound price of exports to the exchange rate is

$$\frac{dP_x^\pounds/P_x^\pounds}{dr/r} = \frac{s_x}{d_x - s_x}. \quad (H.10)$$

This has to be negative or zero, since d_x is negative or zero and s_x is positive or zero. (The response of the dollar price of exports to the exchange rate equals this same expression plus one.)

Recalling that the supply of foreign exchange equals the price times the quantity of exports, or the value of exports, we can use the fact that any percentage change in this supply of foreign exchange equals the percentage price change plus the percentage quantity change:

$$E_s = \frac{dX/X}{dr/r} + \frac{dP_x^\pounds/P_x^\pounds}{dr/r}. \quad (H.11)$$

From (H.9) and (H.10), we get the relationship between the elasticity of supply of foreign exchange and the elasticities of demand and supply of exports:

$$E_s = \frac{d_x s_x}{d_x - s_x} + \frac{s_x}{d_x - s_x} = \frac{d_x + 1}{(d_x/s_x) - 1}, \quad (H.12)$$

which can be of any sign.

Going through all the same steps on the import side yields expressions for the responses of the pound price of imports, the quantity of imports, and the demand for foreign exchange with respect to the exchange rate:

$$\frac{dP_m^\pounds/P_m^\pounds}{dr/r} = \frac{d_m}{s_m - d_m} \quad (\leq 0); \quad (H.13)$$

$$\frac{dM/M}{dr/r} = \frac{s_m d_m}{s_m - d_m} \quad (\leq 0); \quad (H.14)$$

and

$$E_d = \frac{s_m + 1}{(s_m/d_m) - 1} \quad (\leq 0). \quad (H.15)$$

THE GENERAL TRADE BALANCE FORMULA AND THE
MARSHALL-LERNER CONDITION

We have now gathered all the materials we need to give the general formula for the elasticity of response of the trade balance to the exchange rate. From (H.4), (H.12), and (H.15), the formula is:

The elasticity of
the trade balance
with respect to
$$\text{the exchange rate} = E_{tb} = \frac{V_x}{V_m} \frac{d_x + 1}{(d_x/s_x) - 1} - \frac{s_m + 1}{(s_m/d_m) - 1}, \quad \text{(H.16)}$$

as reported in Chapter 15.

The literature has tended to focus less on this general formula than on the expression it equals when one makes the Keynesian assumption of infinite supply elasticities on both sides ($s_x = s_m = \infty$):

$$E_{tb} = \frac{V_x}{V_m}(-d_x - 1) - d_m. \quad \text{(H.17)}$$

Devaluation will improve the trade balance if the right-hand expression is positive. As long as the trade balance was not positive before devaluation ($V_x/V_m \le 1$), then a sufficient condition for trade-balance improvement is the famous Marshall-Lerner condition that the absolute values of the elasticities should add up to more than one:

$$|d_x + d_m| > 1. \quad \text{(H.18)}$$

The Marshall-Lerner condition was sufficient for improvement in our Keynesian Case 4 in Chapter 15, and also in a couple of other special cases.

DEVALUATION AND THE TERMS OF TRADE

Whether or not devaluation improves or worsens a country's terms of trade, or the ratio of its export prices to import prices expressed in the same currency, depends on demand and supply elasticities, as noted in Chapter 15. This dependence follows from the formulas for the effects of devaluation on export and import prices, given in (H.10) and (H.13) above:

The elasticity of
the terms of trade
with respect to
$$\text{the exchange rate} = \frac{dP_x^£/P_x^£ - dP_m^£/P_m^£}{dr/r} = \frac{s_m}{d_x - s_x} - \frac{d_m}{s_m - d_m} \quad \text{(H.19)}$$

$$= \frac{s_x s_m - d_x d_m}{(d_x - s_x)(s_m - d_m)}.$$

Since the denominator must be negative, the terms can improve with a devaluation only if the numerator is also negative. This leads us to the general result stated in Chapter 15:

Devaluation improves the terms of trade if $d_x d_m > s_x s_m$;

It leaves the terms the same if $a_x d_m = s_x s_m$;

It worsens the terms of trade if $d_x d_m < s_x s_m$.

DEVALUATION AND REAL NATIONAL INCOME

Chapter 16 raises the question of how devaluation really affects national income, in the context of models in which devaluation has both price and income effects. Here we derive the key result that the condition for devaluation's improving national income is very close to the condition for its improving the trade balance.

We must begin by distinguishing two concepts of national income. One is real national income, which is the current-price value of national income divided by the prices of the goods this nation produces. In symbols, this real national income is $y = Y/P_x^\$$, where the dollar price of exports will here double as the price of the single good our economy produces. The other concept is the real purchasing power of our national income, or the amount of the things this nation wishes to buy that it can have by producing the national income. The real purchasing power of our national product is:

$$y_p = \frac{Y}{(1-a)P_x^\$ + aP_m^\$} = \frac{y}{(1-a) + (a/T)}, \qquad (H.20)$$

where

a = the share of our total expenditures that we spend on imports and

$T = P_x^\$/P_m^\$$ is the terms-of-trade price ratio.

Each concept has its own use. Ordinary real national income, y, is tied to the number of jobs existing in the national economy. The purchasing power of national income, or y_p, is closer to being a measure of national well-being and is also the sort of perceived aggregate purchasing power to which spending decisions are likely to be tied.

The immediate question is whether devaluation will raise either of these concepts of national income. Let us first ask what the conditions are under which devaluation will raise y. A careful derivation of the result requires a cumbersome model, including separate equilibrium conditions for the export market, the import market, and the market for national product, and the model might even justifiably include markets for national currencies and bonds. We shall avoid such a model and confine ourselves here to a sketch of how the effects of devaluation on y relate to its effects on the trade balance and the terms of trade. To simplify, we ignore wealth effects, interest-rate effects, and foreign income repercussions, and we standardize all physical units so that all prices initially equal unity ($1 = r = T = P_x^\$ = P_m^\$$).

With the variables for total expenditures (E), exports (X), and imports all measured in real, deflated units, the equilibrium condition for the national product market is:

$$y = E(y_p) + X(T) - M(T, y_p)/T. \tag{H.21}$$

Differentiating with respect to the exchange rate yields

$$\frac{dy}{dr} = (1 - s)\left(\frac{dy}{dr} - a\,\frac{dT}{dr}\right) + \frac{dX}{dr} - \frac{\partial M}{dr} + M\,\frac{dT}{dr} - m\left(\frac{dy}{dr} - a\,\frac{dT}{dr}\right), \tag{H.22}$$

where s is the marginal propensity to save, m is the marginal propensity to import, and $\dfrac{\partial M}{\partial r}$ is the partial derivative of imports with respect to the exchange rate via the price effects alone (and not income effects). By rearranging terms, we can express the effect of the exchange rate on national income as a function of its effects on the trade balance and the terms of trade:

$$\frac{dy}{dr}(s + m) = \underbrace{\frac{dX}{dr} - \frac{\partial M}{\partial r} + M\,\frac{dT}{dr}}_{\partial TB/\partial r} + (-1 + s + m)\,\frac{dT}{dr} \tag{H.23}$$

$$\frac{dy}{dr} = \frac{\partial TB/\partial r + (s + m - 1)\,dT/dr}{s + m} \tag{H.24}$$

The net effect of a devaluation on national income thus depends on the results, already derived, giving the effects of devaluation on the trade balance and the terms of trade via demand and supply elasticities. It should be noted that the formula in Equation (H.22) is based on a little sleight of hand, since we have not let the change in income affect the terms of trade in any explicit way. Yet this is unlikely to bias the results, since there is no clear direction of effect of a generalized multiplier process on the country's terms of trade. In the important special cases we have been considering (small country case, price fixed in sellers' currencies, and so on), there is little or no feedback from domestic demand to the terms of trade.

Knowing the effect of devaluation on real national income also allows us to give a formula for its effect on the purchasing power of that income:

$$\frac{dy_p}{dr} = \frac{dy}{dr} - a\,\frac{dT}{dr} = \frac{\partial TB/\partial r - a\,dT/dr}{s + m}. \tag{H.25}$$

It is clear from this formula that the conditions under which devaluation improves the purchasing power of national income $(dy_p/dr > 0)$ are closely linked to the conditions under which it improves the trade balance through its relative-price effects $(\partial TB/\partial r > 0)$. Indeed, if the terms of trade remain the same, as they do in the "small-country" case, then devaluation will improve national income if and only if it improves the trade balance. The Keynesian case in which prices are fixed in sellers' currencies (Case 4 in Chapter 15) is one in which the terms of trade turn against the country by the full percentage of the devaluation, so that this impoverishment through an adverse turn in the terms makes national income rise less, and the trade balance ends up improving more, than it would have if the terms of trade had stayed the same. The case in which prices are fixed in buyers' currencies (Case 3 in Chapter 15) is the one in which the terms of trade improve by the full percentage of the devaluation. Here national income is raised further and the trade balance eroded by the extra purchasing power that this improvement in the terms of trade brings. It still turns out that the balance of trade ends up improved in this case. Thus as a general rule of thumb the conditions under which devaluation improves the trade balance are roughly sufficient for devaluation to improve national income.

It should be noted that the present conclusions differ a bit from the conclusions usually reported on this issue. It is frequently said that when one takes account of the income stimulus coming from devaluation, the extra imports created by this extra income can turn a trade balance that looked stable under the elasticity formula into a deteriorating balance. This usual conclusion is based on a model which assumes that domestic spending on either imports or all goods and services is a function of national income.[2] It is almost surely more accurate to postulate that domestic spending is a function of the real purchasing power of national income—of y_p, not y. When this change is made, the present conclusions follow.

---

[2] For the algebra of the usual model, see Robert M. Stern, *The Balance of Payments* (Chicago: Aldine, 1973), Chap. 7.

appendix I

High finance, or, the international beer-drinking puzzle

At several points in Chapters 13, 15, and 18 we touched briefly on the issue of the welfare aspects of disequilibrium exchange rates. Here is a puzzle to ponder on that subject.

In a certain town lying on the border between Mexico and the United States, a peculiar currency situation exists. In Mexico, a U.S. dollar is worth only 90 centavos of Mexican money, while in the United States the value of a Mexican peso (= 100 centavos) is only 90 cents of U.S. money.

One day, a cowhand strolls into a Mexican cantina and orders a ten-centavo beer. He pays for it with a Mexican peso, receiving in exchange a U.S. dollar, worth 90 centavos in Mexico. After drinking his beer, he strolls over the border to a saloon in the United States, and orders a ten-cent beer. He pays for this with the just-received dollar, receiving a Mexican peso (worth 90 U.S. cents in the United States) in exchange. He keeps on repeating the process, drinking beer happily all day. He ends up just as rich as he started—with a peso.

The question: Who really paid for the beer?

(In addition to explaining who really paid for the beer, discuss the foreign exchange aspects of this situation. What conditions are necessary for such a situation to persist for a long time, and what might bring it to a stop? What are the effects of this situation on the domestic economies of the United States and Mexico?)

The source of this puzzle is E. Krasner and J. Newman, *Mathematics and the Imagination* (1940), p. 162. Sorry, they didn't include the answer, and we leave that to you.

543

index

Index